TREK IT YOURSELF
IN
NORTHERN THAILAND

MAP OVERVIEW of NORTHERN THAILAND

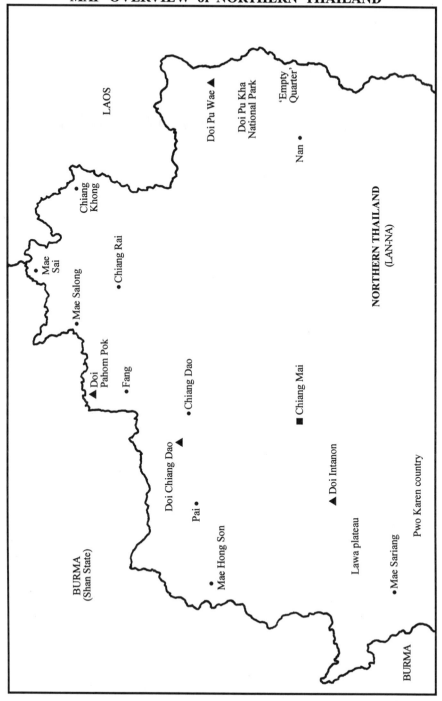

LAOS

Doi Pu Wae ▲

Doi Pu Kha
National Park

'Empty
Quarter'

Nan •

NORTHERN THAILAND
(LAN-NA)

• Chiang
Khong

• Chiang Rai

Mae
Sai •

• Mae Salong

▲ Doi
Pahom Pok

• Fang

• Chiang Dao

■ Chiang Mai

Doi Chiang Dao ▲

Pai •

▲ Doi Intanon

Lawa plateau

Pwo Karen country

• Mae Hong Son

• Mae Sariang

BURMA
(Shan State)

BURMA

About the author

Christian Goodden, 1949 vintage, grew up in the English county of Suffolk. After completing a modern languages degree at the University of East Anglia (Norwich), he went on to do research at Gonville & Caius College, Cambridge, where he was awarded a Ph.D. in 1977 for a thesis on Austrian literature and thought at the turn of the century. In the following eleven years Dr Goodden lectured in English and translation at the Universities of Cologne, Trier and Basel, publishing at the same time a variety of articles on German and English culture in journals and newspapers. In 1988 he returned to Britain to work as a freelance translator, editor and proofreader, specializing in art, art history, photography and travel. At the same time he started travelling in South-East Asia. A keen photographer and travel writer, he currently divides his time between England and northern Thailand. The author of three books about Thailand, he is currently researching the material for a fourth travel book, a follow-up do-it-yourself trekking guide. He has one daughter.

Also by Christian Goodden

Three Pagodas: A Journey down the Thai-Burmese Border

*Around Lan-Na: A Guide to Thailand's Northern Border Region
from Chiang Mai to Nan*

DEDICATION

For my father, Antony Clive Goodden, with whom I walked out in the Suffolk countryside even as a small boy, and who still enjoys stretching his legs even in his eighties.

TREK IT YOURSELF

IN

NORTHERN THAILAND

TWENTY-FIVE SOLO JUNGLE TREKS
ON FOOT & BY MOTORCYCLE

CHRISTIAN GOODDEN

JUNGLE BOOKS

"BY TRAVELLERS FOR TRAVELLERS"

First published in 2000 by
JUNGLE BOOKS (HALESWORTH)
England

e-mail: junglebooks@compuserve.com

ISBN 0-9527383-2-5

Printed in Thailand

Front cover photo: Lawa girl Bua in traditional costume
at the village of Ho Gao (Trek 23)
Back cover photo: Doug and Tanya at jungle campsite
near Khun Nam Pua Waterfall (Trek 12)

CONTENTS

LIST OF TREKS

Part 1

Treks 1-4: North of Chiang Mai in Chiang Mai & Chiang Rai provinces

1 & 2 based on Mae Salong; 3 & 4 based on Fang & Chiang Dao

Part 2

Treks 5-17: In Nan province, east of Chiang Mai, based on Nan town

(2a) Treks 5-8: East of Nan town near Thai-Lao border

5-7: three treks launched from Mae Sa Nan village
8: launched from Sa Wang

(2b) Treks 9-15: North-east of Nan town in Doi Pu Kha National Park

9-10: two treks launched from the Park HQ
11-14: four treks involving Maniploek village
14-15: two ascents of Mount Pu Wae

LIST OF MAPS

The Maps are located all together in the Map Section (pages 360-408)

ACKNOWLEDGEMENTS

' Trek It Yourself in Northern Thailand' would never have come into being without the extensive selfless assistance of Nittaya 'Daeng' Tananchai, who helped implement almost all the treks contained in it. Warmest thanks are due also to Doug 'Birddawg' Boynton of Taipei, Taiwan, and of Virginia, the USA, who – initially on the lookout for birdwatching sites – ultimately came along on 15 of the 25 expeditions, aiding their progress and leavening the effort of completing them with his inimitable gross-out drollery. These two have been my invaluable research assistants and companions in hardship – so to speak my left-hand woman and my right-hand man. My daughter, Tanya, too, deserves acknowledgement. In accompanying us trio on some four of the more taxing hikes, she proved that even seven-year-olds can handle and enjoy jungle treks. The research for this guide was conducted over a number of years, and too many people – notably unofficial hill-tribe guides, forestry staff, headmen, teachers and villagers – have helped me in the detailed execution of its component outings to be able to acknowledge them all individually. My sincere gratitude, therefore, is expressed to them collectively.

However, I would like to single out for especial thanks the following for showing particular helpfulness, kindness and hospitality: Malee and Som of Ban Tam, Chiang Dao; Mrs Amporn 'Porn' Kanluang of Sa Wa; Mr Sangwian and Mrs Sommart Utama of Tung Kwang, near Mae Charim; Hmong man Somboon Saelao of Huai Yuak; U.S. missionaries Scott and Annette McManigle of Mae Pae Luang; and Lawa headman Moen Sericharoon of Ho Gao village.

The unsung heroes of the treks in this book are the many (mostly hill-tribe) guides, hired on the spot, who not only guided, but portered heavy loads for long hours in trying conditions, sometimes hacked a way where there was none, occasionally even acted as 'human ladders', prepared campsites, fetched water, gathered wood and lit fires. I am perpetually in awe of their strength, solicitude, persistence and tolerance. Perhaps the photos of them are at least some kind of monument to their sterling efforts. Of five guides in particular I could not have asked more: Lua brothers Nit (or Taan) and Kham Akara of Mae Sa Nan; the Lua duo Pae and Yod of Maniploek 2; and Karen boy Loe Mo Po or Pongsak ('Mr Nice Guy') of Mae Sa Koet and Kiu Kamin.

Friendly greetings and thanks are also expressed to Soeren Skibsted of Denmark for his generous assistance supplying technical information, sketch maps, and also colour slides; to René Reinert of Nan and Switzerland for his help researching Trek 16 and cross-checking some route details; and to 'Yai', 'Toon' and everybody else at *Doi Pu Kha Guest House*, Nan, for their amicable support. Last, but by no means least, I must once again handsomely thank my best friend Richard Gibbens for his heroic, painstaking and most professional efforts in the darkroom printing up all the black-and-white photographs in this book.

PREFACE

This book describes 25 do-it-yourself treks in the mountainous jungle and forests of northern Thailand which independent travellers aspiring to adventure, but discontented with the expensive farce of most organized trekking, can do on their own. The majority of the treks are undertaken on foot, but a sizeable minority are best carried out by motorbike. Many are optimally executed by a combination of the two modes of transport, and a few could be implemented by jeep or even mountain bicycle. By 'do-it-yourself' and 'on their own' I mean that travellers can mount the expeditions solo, on their own initiative, without applying to a trekking agency, and without taking part in a fee-paid organized trek accompanied by other trekker-strangers. But I do not mean that trekkers go unguided or wander singly into the jungle. While some of the trips can indeed be done completely solo, i.e. you undertake them simply with one or two friends, most involve being guided by local hill-tribe men or youths hired on the spot in villages at or near the beginning of the treks proper.

There are nominally 25 treks in the book. In reality, however, *Trek It Yourself* contains closer to perhaps 100 treks. This is because almost every one of the nominal treks, described in its standard form (usually as I have done it), can be modified to produce 3 or 4 variations. The treks can be truncated or made easier for the less ambitious, extended or made more difficult for gluttons for punishment, can be combined to form supertreks, can be rescheduled, done backwards, or made in places to follow alternative routes or to take in detours. Generally speaking, things are flexible. I have indicated these possible variations in the respective trek chapters.

It is not easy to say exactly what proportion of the expeditions are foot treks and what motorcycle trips. But about 13 of them are straight foot hikes (cannot be done wholly or in part on a motorbike), some 5 are ambiguous, i.e. can be either biked or walked or can be in large part biked, and ca 7 are straight biking trips, where it would not be appropriate or sensible to walk the route because the distance is too great or the way is used by vehicles.

All the hikes go to places and along routes that are wholly unfrequented by organized trekking parties from the agencies (which typically operate out of Chiang Mai, Chiang Rai, Mae Hong Son and Pai) and largely untrekked by anyone else. The expeditions in this book are exactly the 'non-touristic' treks to 'new unvisited' areas that the trekking agency hype cynically advertises and promises, but fails to deliver. The greatest extent to which just one or two of the trips are trekked is that they are walked by the occasional group of Thai people or are ridden by a small trickle of independent Western ('*farang*') bikers. Thus the mountains of Doi Chiang Dao (Trek 4) and Doi Pu Wae (Treks 14 & 15) are sometimes climbed by parties of Thais, and the routes from Hin Taek to Hua Mae Kham (Trek 2) and from Mae Hong Son via Wat Chan to Samoeng and Chiang Mai (Treks 24 & 25) are occasionally biked by *farang* riding offroad on enduro machines. Also, many of the routes are sometimes walked wholly or in part ordinarily by local hill-tribe people. But you won't anywhere in these pages encounter gaggles of agency 'trekkies', or at least I hope not. Most of the expeditions are too severe for them, or the circumstances unsuitable. At the other end of the scale, some of the routes described here are hardly ever or never trekked by anyone at all, e.g. the ways to Huai Dua (Trek 6), through the 'Empty Quarter' from Mae Sa Nan to Sa Wang (Trek 7), and down Huai Pla Jaad Waterfall (Trek 8).

Overview of the treks
The 25 outings in *Trek It Yourself* all take place in northern Thailand in basically four areas: (1) north of Chiang Mai in Chiang Mai and Chiang Rai provinces (Treks 1-4); (2) east of Chiang Mai over by the Lao (Laotian) border in Nan province (Treks 5-17); (3) west of Chiang Mai near the Burmese border in Mae Hong Son province south-east and north-east of Mae Sariang town (Treks 18-23); and (4) north-west of Chiang Mai in Mae Hong Son and Chiang Mai provinces south-east of Mae Hong Son town (Treks 24-25). It is evident that more than half the treks in the book are in Nan province. That is no accident. Nan, which is surely Thailand's least-known province and best-kept secret, still abounds with jungle and – in spite of this, amazingly – has virtually no organized trekking. To provide a more detailed overview of the book's treks and scope, I now give a loose breakdown of the expeditions area by area and sub-area by sub-area.

(1) North of Chiang Mai
Treks 1 and 2 are based on the mountaintop KMT Chinese 'town' of Mae Salong and make their way, the first on foot and the second by motorcycle, over a couple of ridges, on separate but intertwined and partially overlapping routes to Ban Hin Taek, opium warlord Khun Sa's former HQ. From here Trek 2 rides to out-on-a-limb Hua Mae Kham, a multi-ethnic village on the Thai-Burmese border. Trek 3, much of which can be biked, but which can also make a walking trip, climbs Thailand's second-highest mountain, Doi Pahom Pok, which lies remotely just a stone's throw from the country's border with Burma. Trek 4, a foot trek only, climbs spectacular Doi Chiang Dao, Thailand's third-highest mountain. Readers will probably ultimately base all of the first four treks on Chiang Mai, but in Treks 3 and 4 they will use respectively the towns of Fang and Chiang Dao as their local jumping-off points.

(2) In Nan province
In the thirteen treks numbered 5-17, travellers will undoubtedly use as their ultimate base the town of Nan with its guest houses, shops, restaurants and pair of motorbike rental places (small machines only).

(2a) East of Nan town in the Lao border area
The first four of the 'Nan' trips (Treks 5-8) take place east of Nan in an area of mountainous jungle and forest close to the border with Laos – an area I like to call the 'Empty Quarter' owing to its remoteness and because it is uninhabited. Treks 5-7 all start from the Lua (Htin) village of Mae Sa Nan, which is a kind of gateway to the Empty Quarter. Trek 7 is an extended adventure through the heart of the Empty Quarter, while Trek 8, which is the most difficult expedition in this book, is another protracted 'Rambo' adventure, going to and then climbing down the inaccessible multi-stepped Huai Pla Jaad Waterfall.

(2b) North-east of Nan town in the main northerly part of Doi Pu Kha National Park
The venue of the next clutch of Nan treks (9-15) is north-east of Nan town in the upper or northern part of Doi Pu Kha National Park. The expeditions either take place in or pass through this heartland of Nan's famous National Park. Treks 9 and 10, both of which are foot hikes capable of being launched from the Park's at-altitude Headquarters with its range of amenities, cut off respectively a smaller and a bigger corner of the Park heartland. There is scope in the latter (Trek 10) for using a motorbike, although it is not possible to ride the whole route. Treks 11-14, the first of which (11) is an extended motorbike outing, while the latter three (12-14) are straight foot hikes, all involve the double Lua and Hmong village of Maniploek, where trekkers can camp at a forestry station. Trek 12 strikes from Maniploek in a north-south direction through the very heart of the main northerly part of Doi Pu Kha National Park, past pretty jungle-bound Khun Nam Pua Waterfall, to the village of Nam Pua Pattana 2, ultimately issuing near the Park HQ. Trek 13 proceeds north from Maniploek to the River Nan, optionally takes in Huai Khon Waterfall, issues near Huai Sai Kao on the 1081 road, and leaves room for a stay at the Tai Lue village of Huai Khon. Trek 14 climbs imposing Doi Pu Wae, starting from the Lua part of Maniploek village (Maniploek 2) and approaching the peak from the south-west. It is the first of two ascents of the celebrated mountain, the second being the subject of Trek 15, which approaches from the north-east, starting from the villages of Dan (on the 1081 road) and (Lua) Huai Poot.

(2c) West of Nan town in Mrabri country
The locale of the last of the Nan treks (16 and 17) is respectively NW and SW of Nan town in the low mountains of Mrabri country, the habitat of the famous, rare and elusive 'pi tong luang' people or 'Spirits of the Yellow Leaves'. Trek 16, a long foot trek that used to be and may just still be bikable, cuts through from the 1091 road to the 1082 and 1148 roads, taking in the villages of Pi Nuea, Santisuk and Sob Khun. Trek 17, likewise an extended foot hike, but which can definitely be ridden by skilled offroad bikers, cuts through from the 101 highway to the 1091 road, passing through a string of Khmu, Lua, Hmong and Yao hill-tribe villages, including Huai Yuak.

(3) Treks from Mae Sariang town in Mae Hong Son and Chiang Mai provinces
The six treks numbered 18-23 take place over in the western part of Lan-Na or northern Thailand, towards the Burmese border. They are best based on the small pleasant town of Mae Sariang, with its guest houses, restaurants and shops, but not – as far as I am aware – motorbike rental places. With the exception of the first (18), they are all motorcycle treks. The outings are made south-east and north-east of Mae Sariang in the mountainous plateau country of respectively the colourful Pwo Karen and the ancient Lawa hill-peoples. All the 'Mae Sariang' trips are in Mae Hong Son province, except for the last (23), which crosses over into Chiang Mai province.

(3a) South-east of Mae Sariang in Pwo Karen country
Trek 18, a walking expedition, starts from the village of Mae Waen, passes Mae Rit Waterfall, and then in a large loop movement takes in a number of Pwo Karen villages, including Kong Pae, Ton Ngiu, Huai Hia and Mae Pae, before returning to Mae Waen. Trek 19, envisaged as a biking trip, describes a similar loop, passing some of the same villages, but starts at Huai Goong on the 108 highway and ends on the same highway at km-stone 65 (but ultimately beginning at and returning to Mae Sariang). In both these treks readers can or must stay overnight in settlements of the alluring, prettified, much-beringed and tricked-out Pwo Karen.

(3b) North-east of Mae Sariang in Lawa country
Treks 20-23 are four motorcycle expeditions up on the remote and extensive Ob Luang plateau – the plateau of the Lawa people. The rides, mostly on rough dirt and only for experienced bikers, form a complex that pivots on the elevated village of La Ang and centres on the La Ang/Chang Mor axis, an obscure and lonely trail. The way I have ordered this complex of treks is only nominal. They can be reordered, combined and permuted at will, making a variety of overall trips. Thus, as I have structured and presented the clutch of outings, Trek 20 proceeds east from Mae Sariang to Kong Loi, then climbs up north via Lao Li to Chang Mor, and winds up in La Ang. Trek 21 likewise starts in Mae Sariang and heads east, but after only 13 or so kms leaves the 108 road to cut up through difficult terrain via the villages of Pa Pae and Huai Haak Mai Tai to Chang Mor, where it joins Trek 20, leaving the option of continuing to La Ang or of descending to Kong Loi. Treks 22 and 23 provide onward journeys for Trek 21 (and possibly 22) and escape routes from far-flung La Ang. Thus Trek 22 goes west down from La Ang via Du Lo Boe and Mae La Oop off the plateau to Mae La Noi and the 108 Mae Sariang/Mae Hong Son road, from where it is possible to return to Mae Sariang or proceed to Mae Hong Son. Trek 23 strikes east from La Ang to Ho Gao and other villages, crosses into Chiang Mai province, and comes down off the Lawa plateau to Mae Chaem, from where bikers can cross Doi Intanon National Park, making a small detour to visit the summit of Doi Intanon itself (Thailand's highest mountain), and proceed via Chom Tong all the way to Chiang Mai. When combined, as they must be (you must always exit from La

Ang), these treks form long loop or linear rides of hundreds of kms on stony dirt. Accordingly, they envisage overnight stops at intermediate Lawa villages such as Ho Gao and Mae La Oop.

(4) Trekking the 'Old Elephant Trail' between Mae Hong Son and Chiang Mai
The last two treks in the book (24 and 25) basically follow the route of the so-called 'Old Elephant Trail' from Mae Hong Son via Ban Wat Chan to Chiang Mai or vice versa. It is so named because, before the southerly 108 and northerly 1095 roads were built from Chiang Mai to Mae Hong Son via respectively Mae Sariang and Pai, this was the way that people used to go from the Lannatai capital to remote Mae Hong Son and back, especially noblemen, administrators, tax-collectors and tradesmen, often on elephants. Further, corralled elephants were brought from the Mae Hong Son area to Chiang Mai along the trail, and elephants were used on it for ferrying goods to and fro. Trek 24 describes the first part of the trail from Mae Hong Son via Mae Sa Koet, Huai Hi, Huai Tong and other villages (all Karen) to Wat Chan with its famous pagoda, while Trek 25 provides an account of the second part from Wat Chan via numerous Karen, Hmong and other villages to Samoeng and Chiang Mai. Trek 24 can be either walked or ridden (very difficult on a bike), while Trek 25 is only sensibly ridden. People do ride the Old Elephant Trail the whole way (said to be the longest dirt trail in Thailand) – a small trickle of expert *farang* bikers on suitable machines make it during the dry (winter) season, often involving the town of Pai in their trip, which can be accessed from Wat Chan and which, conversely, feeds to midpoint Wat Chan. If Trek 24, from Mae Hong Son to Wat Chan, is wholly or largely walked, it is the longest hike in this book, up to 90 kms long. Readers walking Trek 24 must exit by public transport from Wat Chan to Pai, unless they can get a lift to Samoeng. People trekking the Old Elephant Trail in the direction that I have described (from W to E) will use Mae Hong Son – with its plethora of guest houses, restaurants, shops and motorbike rental places – as their ultimate base, unless they do the journey 'backwards' (from E to W), in which case cosmopolitan metropolitan Chiang Mai will be their starting point.

In *Trek It Yourself* I have not explained how to reach the four main areas indicated above, or how to arrive at the primary bases from which the individual treks are ultimately launched. Thus there is no data on accessing Chiang Mai, Nan, Mae Sariang and Mae Hong Son. I must assume that readers can manage their journeys to these places by either bus or plane or motorbike themselves. If they can handle the treks below, they will not need telling how to get to the overall areas and base towns. Or, to put it more bluntly, if you cannot organize that, you will never manage the actual treks. On the other hand, once we are in the base towns, I provide (I trust) precise information about how to access the villages or spots at the start of the treks proper. Thus, assuming we are in, say, Nan, I detail how to reach e.g. Mae Sa Nan or Maniploek. This brings me to the structure both of the book and of the individual trek chapters.

Structure of book and of individual trek chapters

I have structured the book in three or four main sections. First comes this introductory section, in which this preface, with its hints and tips below, forms an important integral part of the whole. The preamble section also contains an index to the treks and to the maps. Second comes the textual section with the treks themselves, one after the other, thick and fast. Then comes the section with the maps, 50 of them, all placed together. And at the end comes a small final section with a glossary and a list of, I hope, useful words and phrases. There is also a photo section with 24 pages of colour pictures and 12 pages of black-and-white shots (some 80 individual images altogether). Hopefully these photographs will give readers an impression of some of the places visited in the treks, the features seen, the people and hill tribes encountered, and the atmosphere of the hiking and camping, perhaps motivating the reader to go and have a look or explore. In one sense the photos are crucial. Many of them show almost all the guides that I have used on the treks, and are an aid for you in your efforts to locate them, if you want to use guides or the same guides.

Readers might think it odd that I have lumped all the maps together in their own section, instead of integrating them into the text at the places where they pertain to the text, i.e. put a map of Mae Sa Nan next to the place in the trek text where Mae Sa Nan is mentioned. And that is what I originally intended to do. But I soon ran into difficulties. For I found that very often one and the same map applied to a number of places spread over several treks, or, conversely, reference was made in various places and treks to one and the same map. Clearly it would have been wasteful and inappropriate to keep reincluding the same map. So the solution seemed to be to incorporate the map where it was first relevant, putting, e.g., the map of Mae Sa Nan at the first place where Mae Sa Nan was mentioned or visited. But this would have meant that in subsequent treks, when Mae Sa Nan was again mentioned because other later treks started from there, the reader would have had to go hunting back through the book for the place where Mae Sa Nan was first mentioned and the map given. Too often the maps would have been dissociated from their context, and scattered and lost in the pages. So in the end it seemed better first to sequentially order and number the maps and then to put them all in one consolidated, easily locatable place, in their own section. Then readers, instead of searching through the book, could simply turn to the map section and quickly locate the map by its number, perhaps bookmarking the relevant maps in advance for even easier reference while following the text. To some extent the same applies to the photos.

In the individual trek chapters, I have structured the material as follows. First comes a set of parameters, which give an at-a-glance summary of the trek in question, allowing readers to decide whether it is right for them or not. Indications are given as to whether it is a foot or biking expedition or both; how long both the core part of the trip and the overall trip (including, where appropriate, accessing and exiting times

20

relative to the base town) might be expected to last; how long the hike is distancewise; how difficult the trek is for walkers or riders; whether guides are needed and, if they are, the names of the guides I used; whether a tent is required; and the maps which apply to the trek. The outline parameters are followed by an overview of the expedition, painting a picture of it, mentioning its main features and attractions, and fleshing out the itinerary by saying where trekkers go on which day and where the nights are spent. In a zooming-in process of description that becomes progressively more specific, the introduction is followed by considerations relating to strategy, to how the trek can be variously and best tackled, to how it can be modified, and to hiring guides. Information is given about accessing the core part of the trek from the base town (whether by motorcycle, by public transport, by hitch-hiking, or by a combination of the latter two), about accommodation and food first in the base town and then in the village or place from where the core trek is launched, and about preparing for the trek. Sometimes, where appropriate, I have included a thumbnail sketch of the base towns and jumping-off points as well as other places en route (e.g. of Mae Sariang, Mae Salong, Hin Taek, Mae Sa Nan and Maniploek Forestry Station). Also at this midpoint of the text I have sometimes included brief background information about the (hill-tribe) people encountered in the trek. Thus the book contains thumbnail sketches of the KMT Chinese, Lua (Htin), Hmong, Yao, Tai Lue, Pwo Karen, Lawa, and Mrabri or 'Yellow Leaf' people. The descriptive and organizational part of each trek is followed by a practical section, which I have called 'trekking route detail'. Based on notes in my trekking diaries, it gives a blow-by-blow, on-the-ground account of the hike, whether on foot or motorcycle, logging times, distances and km-readings. After the practical account of the core part of the trek, information is given, where appropriate, about exiting the trek and returning to the base town or wherever.

Difficulty of treks & other problems
In the trek chapters I have tried to grade the expeditions in terms of difficulty and from the standpoint of both walkers and, where appropriate, bikers. My assessments relate to a person of average fitness and riding ability. Actually, they are based on how I found the treks to be, a no-longer-very-young (!) person with precisely the above-mentioned average fitness and riding skills. The author is no hard man or dirt-biking freak. The trips range from easy to very difficult, from an extended stroll to a waterfall lasting a couple of hours to a fairly extreme 'Rambo' adventure through the jungle stretching over 3 days. In the book there is something for everyone. At the same time, however, there is nothing for the faint-hearted or for those not prepared for hands-on action, or unwilling to get dirty and sweaty, or shy of getting their feet wet. A degree of self-motivation, perseverance and flexibility is presupposed, as well as a preparedness to 'get stuck in', to get the treks up and running on the basis of the ideas presented. Can you sleep on the floor of a classroom in a village school, or in a squalid room with a

hill-tribe headman? Can you put a tent up in the dark, wash in a muddy stream, or do a bodywash at a tap in the middle of a Lua village, gawped at by a score of villagers? Can you wander into a village and, cold, start hunting out a guide? Can you cook scrappy food in a smoke-blackened pot over a little wood fire? Can you go the extra mile when you are tired, fed up, and parched in the throat, your iodene-tinctured water having run out? On the other hand, there is nothing unviable even in the more demanding treks. Proof of this is the fact that some of them have been done by my infant daughter (seven years old at the time). She, for example, climbed Doi Pu Wae from Ban Dan and Huai Poot (Trek 15), walked from Maniploek 2 via Khang Ho and Khun Nam Pua Waterfall to Nam Pua Pattana 2 (Trek 12), and hiked from Maniploek 1 via Pong Tom and the River Nan to Huai Sai Kao (Trek 13). Children *can* handle jungle trekking and are even in some respects more resilient than adults – more resistant to heat and sweating, able to sleep anywhere, light on their feet, and with a capacity to find fun in everything.

My main worry with this do-it-yourself trekking book concerns the problem of language and communication. I am afraid that readers will have trouble negotiating with guides, villagers, headmen, forestry office staff, and the drivers of public-transport pick-ups. I can imagine you muttering: "It's alright for you (me), you can speak a bit of Thai and/or travel around with people who can. But what about us? How can we organize guides, explain what we want?" To this I can only say the following. You *will* manage, somehow. On the basis of ten years of observation of *farang* travellers and trekkers moving around Thailand, I am constantly amazed at how, with little or no knowledge of the language, they get what they want and get to the places they want. I think I underestimate the independent traveller's resourcefulness. From time to time I have myself, with minimal Thai, successfully trekked both on my own and with *farang* friends, the latter speaking no Thai. Sign language, a few words of the language picked up here and there, a phrase book, and a local Thai teacher with some very broken English can get you a long way. So make use of the conventional phrase books and, if you can, my little list of useful words and phrases at the end of this book. Acquire a smattering of Thai, as many travellers do, which will help you disproportionately. In any case, it should be easier for you to implement the treks than it was for me because the groundwork has already been done, the routes discovered, and guides identified, and you can follow in footsteps already made, using the book's information, route detail, maps, photos, hints and tips. All the guides that I have used and who are featured in this book are expecting you to come, are anticipating that you will want to repeat the treks, have expressed a willingness to redo the treks and guide other people, and appreciate that there might be language difficulties. Various village headmen and forestry officials or workers have been primed, have expressly said to me that it is OK for you to stop by, and are positively expecting, even hoping, that you will pay a visit. Looking on the gloomy side, if you do not feel up to hiring guides or can get no sense out of them, you can still do the treks that require no guides. And if things go completely wrong, you can always cop out and return to base – you will still have had a nice trip out. A good idea is to trek with friends in a group of 2-4 people (not much more as the party then threatens to become unwieldy). There is solidarity in numbers, and when problems of language or with guides and headmen do arise, you can laugh them off together, spread the load, take the heat off yourself, in a way that a solitary traveller or a pair of trekkers cannot so easily do. Feel better now? Go for it!

Another potential problem concerns the way everything changes in Thailand, just as it does in other fast-developing and also tropical countries. Paths become overgrown and unrecognizable, and 4WD tracks are reclaimed by the jungle or are upgraded to dirt roads. Dirt roads are paved, and paved roads break up into dirt. New ways are cut to isolated villages, and villages are moved, especially out of National Parks or Wildlife Sanctuaries. Guest houses and restaurants come and go. Night markets are moved, and prices go up. Thus, every time I trek the stretch from Pi Nuea to Santisuk (Trek 16), its status changes. The village of Charaeng Luang in Trek 10 is earmarked for relocation. When I retrekked the Mae Salong to Hin Taek route recently (Trek 1), I found that sections had altered to the extent that I could hardly recognize them, wondered if I had taken a wrong turn, and even got lost on one of my own treks armed with my own notes! And even as I write, I have learned that the village of Pong Tom in Trek 13 has been moved somewhat. The upshot of all this is that readers will have to take such developments in their stride. But it is only an inexperienced and unintelligent traveller who expects things never to change and who reckons on the details in his guide book being set in stone. It is a penalty of writing guide books that the information and maps do slowly go out of date. By way of compensation, I have tried to choose and write up treks and routes that seem unlikely to change because, for example, they are in National Parks or other conservation areas.

Getting around: motorbikes & biking, public transport & hitch-hiking
Some of the treks in this book are straight motorcycle treks, and others can be walked or biked, while yet others are basically foot treks, but could profitably be partly ridden. To do them, a motorbike is needed. Bikes can be hired in Chiang Mai, where there is an oversupply of them, meaning that rental prices are very competitive, and also in Nan and Mae Hong Son. Most of the machines for hire are 100-cc Honda Dream 'stepthru' (clutchless, semi-automatic) town bikes with their shopping basket on the front, or they are a similar machine made by Yamaha. Bigger bikes, such as 200-cc offroad machines and the 400-cc Honda AX, are also available, but are significantly more expensive and perhaps too costly for longer-term rent. In my opinion, for all sorts of reasons it is worth avoiding the nervous susceptible 125-cc Honda MTX. When hiring, remember to bargain the price down, especially if you are hiring for more than a day or two. You should be able to get a decent Honda Dream in Chiang Mai for about 150

baht per day (1999 prices) and in Nan or Mae Hong Son for 150-180 baht per day. Rental bikes in northern Thailand are no longer as good or as dutifully maintained as they used to be, so pick your machine carefully. It may be worth spending a bit more to get a fairly new machine than to cheesepare and pick up an old bargain-basement job. That way, you might well save yourself money in the end, as well as time, repair-hassle and general aggravation. In Chiang Mai there are many bike hire shops along the Moon Muang and Kotchasan Roads (each side of the moat), in Nan there are two on the central Sumondheveraj Road, and in Mae Hong Son there are several on the town's central drag.

I recommend you hire a Honda Dream, unless you are an affluent dirt-riding aficionado who can justify the expense of and get the value out of a bigger, better, offroad machine. Initially many people laugh disparagingly at the Dreams, as I once did. But it is not for nothing that they are widely used, selling in their millions. They are light, easy to ride, economical, air-cooled, reliable and surprisingly strong and powerful workhorses that can get to and be taken anywhere, even to near the top of Doi Pahom Pok on forestry trails. In first gear they are virtually unstoppable. Many times I have ridden a little Dream, e.g. over the mountains through Nan's Doi Pu Kha National park, laden with two people, two backpacks, a tent, cameras and water, as well as a load of clobber (food, sleeping bags, flipflops) in the front basket. One backpack (the bigger one) can go between the rider's legs in the space between the seat and the steering column, while the passenger can wear the other pack, carrying any tent on his or her lap, between rider and passenger.

When hiring a bike, check it over thoroughly and test-ride it. Look especially to see that there is plenty of tread on the tyres, that all the lights work (headlight, brake and indicator lights), that the horn sounds, that the brakes work efficiently, that the wheels spin freely, and that the odometer (milometer, tripmeter) is functioning, i.e. that the cable connecting it to the front wheel has not been disconnected or cut – a favourite wheeze of the hirers, who like to keep the mileage on the clock low. Especially if you are hiring for several days, don't be afraid to ask to have things changed (a new back tyre) or repaired (brake light inoperative) or to complain. Ensure that the steering column lock on the ignition switch works, and ask for some additional means of locking the bike (chain and padlock or similar). Routinely use these locks.

A hire bike can not only be used for doing the motorcycle treks, but is an ideal means for accessing and exiting many of the foot treks. It is also a useful way of getting around the base towns, exploring the area around them, of setting up treks in advance, and of going from trek to trek. If you cannot or do not want to use a motorbike, or if a bike is unsuitable for a particular trek, you will have to resort to public transport and/or hitch-hiking. Buses are cheap and frequent in Thailand, but it is not so much these that you will use to access or exit a trek as those ubiquitous public-transport pick-ups called *silor* (= 'four-wheeler') or *songtaew* (= 'two-

24

bencher'). Usually departing from a market, they go everywhere, including to outlying villages, although progress with them can be slow. Where these pick-ups do not go to a village or other starting point of a trek, travellers will have to resort to hitch-hiking. Once outside the base towns, trekkers might prefer to do that anyway. Thumbing a lift is easy in Thailand and generally quick, although sometimes rather terrifying or downright dangerous (speeding, impatient, risk-taking drivers – get out at the first available opportunity if you find yourself in this situation). I have resorted to hitch-hiking many times and successfully. Some Thais, on seeing *farang* at the roadside, can hardly resist stopping to pick them up – it's *sanuk* or fun. You can meet some friendly, helpful, interesting and useful locals this way. Many drivers will transport you free, especially affluent Thais and people in official trucks (forestry, highways, military and educational personnel). Others will be glad if you help with the cost of petrol (offer to pay anyway). A few (mostly hill-tribe people) will look upon you as a way of making money. Don't allow yourself to be ripped off, and negotiate a fare before hopping aboard. Your position is weak if you start haggling after you have arrived at your destination. In the matter of equitable fares, a rule of thumb is to pay 1 baht per km. Some of the treks in this book could perhaps be done by mountain bicycle, and it is often the case that wherever a motorbike can go, a jeep can go too. However, not being a cyclist or a jeep-driver, I have little to say about these options. Mountain bicyclists would need sturdy machines and a lot of stamina and persistence. Most of the bikable treks are long, in the mountains, and on poor, often stony, steep and rutted surfaces, occasionally deep in bulldust.

Security, dangers & risks
These considerations are largely a personal affair, a matter for the judgement of the individual trekker or of common sense, and again I do not want to be drawn into a lengthy discussion of them. Let me preface my brief observations by saying that in 11 years of travelling and trekking in Thailand, nothing seriously untoward has ever happened to myself or to any of my companions, and we have frequently been in places that would be considered by many people to be hazardous, either because of malaria or owing to the skirmishing of military factions not so far away. The worst that has happened to us is that we have taken the odd tumble on a motorbike, or have slipped or fallen into a hole while walking. You do occasionally hear of travellers coming unstuck, but this is often because they break the basic rules of travelling and trekking, or are naïve, imprudent or foolhardy. I always feel safe with and from the hill-tribe guides I have hired, no matter how wild or skulking they look. I trust them implicitly, and it is actually they who are guarding me from trekking perils. By far and away the most dangerous thing for travellers in Thailand is its mindless and undisciplined traffic. You are much more likely to be mangled in a long-distance bus, or tossed from the back of a crashing pick-up, than, say, attacked and robbed by bandits in the jungle or in the border areas. Trekkers often wonder what

25

they should do with their valuables when out on an expedition (passport, traveller's cheques, flight tickets, credit cards, cash). In my opinion you should never leave these in a guest house, not even in a GH/hotel safe, but should take them with you, kept in a stout money-belt securely fastened around your waist or secreted elsewhere.

In my estimation, the greatest hazards for trekkers, especially foot trekkers in the jungle, are snakes and malaria, in that order. It takes some time to succumb to malaria, but little time to succumb to a snake bite, and a snake bite is no laughing matter if you are two days out from the nearest village and even further from the nearest hospital. In such a calamitous or potentially disastrous situation, hill-tribe guides, with their sharp eyes and profound knowledge of the ways of the jungle, could save your life, a good reason to take a couple along with you. Tread carefully on trails, watching where you put your foot – even better, let the guides or someone else go first! I have had some alarmingly close shaves with snakes, but in ten years of trekking in sometimes dangerously malaria-infested areas both down the Lao and Burmese borders, I have never caught malaria, although I have come across many – mostly local hill-tribe – people who have. Malarial mosquitoes only bite at dusk and after dark, therefore during that time wear a long-sleeved shirt and long trousers, be aware of exposed patches of skin, liberally apply mosquito repellent, and ideally spend as much time as possible in your tent or mosquito net. It seems that many of the malaria prophylactics no longer work because the malaria mosquitoes have become resistant to them. But, anyway, I have long since given up using them because I am against filling up my body with chemicals. The only sure way not to get malaria is not to get bitten, and the only sure way of preventing yourself from getting bitten is to be where the mosquitoes cannot get – in a net or tent.

It is unwise to go into the mountains, forest or jungle on your own, either on foot or by bike, unless you know what you are doing and can speak some Thai. For reasons of security and self-help, it is sensible to go in a group of two or three or more, unless you are with a guide. If something happens to you (an accident, or your bike breaks down, or you run out of petrol), one or two of the others can get assistance, and when the going gets tough (you get lost, or you find yourself walking in the dark), a group of people can help and comfort each other.

Food, drinks & water
These considerations become more problematic the further you go away from towns and villages into the mountains and jungle. I will deal with water first because it follows on from the health hazards just mentioned. There is a distinct risk of getting sick from bad water. At the start of a trek, for the first day, you can survive on good bottled water bought from a shop in a town or in a regular Thai village (but not usually in a hill-tribe village – the people have no use or money for bottled water). Fill up your water bottle with such clean water. When it runs out, you will have to rely on

stream or spring water. Before you drink this, you should either boil it in a pot for 7-10 minutes, or filter it, or treat it with water-purifying tablets or chemicals. Whatever you do, do not draw your unpurified water from a river (e.g. the Rivers Nan or Wa), if you can help it, because there is a likelihood of contamination upstream. Take it from a side stream or spring running into the river. This is what the guides do, drinking the water without further ado! Water that is to be filtered should be taken from a spot where the stream or trickle is both running and clear. If you cannot purify your water with a filter, treat it with iodene tablets or droplets or with chlorine pills. Filters and tablets are great for obtaining good water during the day, while you are actually walking. Boiling is appropriate at a forestry station or at a campsite in the evening. Almost the first thing I do when I arrive at an overnight campsite (after washing) is get a fire going and boil water. Then you can not only make a welcome mug of tea or coffee, but can replenish your water bottle, and have a supply of good water ready for cooking supper, drinking or cleaning your teeth. A good trick is, when you eat supper and while the fire is still hot, or last thing before you go to bed, to boil up water for the next day's trekking – it has time to cool down overnight in your water bottle.

My trekking companions and I find that, as we trek in northern Thailand in the jungle or forest or mountains, where it often very hot and humid, we progressively lose our appetite for food, but increasingly develop a raging thirst. Eating a skimpy breakfast of cake or bread and coffee, snatching a light lunch or perhaps a tuna or peanut butter sandwich, and consuming a soupy supper, we have a perpetual desire for water, fruit juices and salty liquids. There is a sense in which we starve ourselves of food for two or three days, 'pigging out' in a restaurant when we get back to Nan town or wherever, and largely survive on liquids – numerous cups of tea and coffee. But with this we come on to food and drink.

Most hill-tribe villages, which are typically the jumping-off points for the core treks, do not have regular shops where you can buy provisions for trekking. Most do have a couple of shops, but these are not shops as you or I understand them, but rudimentary stores selling what the villagers want or need or can afford: tins of sardines in tomato sauce, washing powder, sweeties and saccharine drinks for the children, often packets of 'Ma-maa' instant noodles, shampoo and so on. So you must do all your shopping for provisions back in the base towns, in the supermarkets, and bring them with you for the treks. Sometimes the headman or villagers in a start-of-trek place will be happy to provide sticky rice or eggs, and often you can buy greens for a couple of baht from the vegetable garden of a villager or of the village school. I have described how to cook, eat and get by at a forestry station in an ad hoc manner in the relevant trekking chapters.

The following is a list of some of the food items that I may buy when getting supplies for a trek: packets of the ubiquitous above-mentioned 'Ma-maa' instant noodles (how often have my companions and I eaten these damned but convenient reconstituted noodles!); packets of macaroni soup;

27

packets of spaghetti; small tins of bolognaise sauce; stock cubes to improve packet noodles and soups; tins of tuna or sardines or of tuna salad; bread, if you get tired of rice (any guides you have with you will have sticky rice, either raw or cooked); a jar of peanut butter; sachets of coffee mix; tea; little briquettes of fruit juice; honey bananas; raisins, chocolate bars as comforters and a source of energy; bars of peanut brittle; fig rolls or similar, perhaps for breakfast; and a small jar of mayonnaise to dress cucumbers, tomatoes and shallots bought in local village markets (a small jar or tube of mustard also makes a nice way of pepping up things like plain tuna).

Equipment

Here too is a checklist of non-edible things to take along when trekking solo in the jungle or mountains, which is based on my experience of many years of such hiking. A consideration of paramount importance is to take as little with you as you possibly can, keeping the weight to a minimum – everything has to be hauled in the heat often up steep inclines. In the way of clothing, I take and wear a cotton shirt, a light baggy pair of cotton trousers, a pair of lightweight trekking boots (not leather – when they get wet, they never dry out and go mouldy), socks, my safari jacket (its many pockets are useful for stowing notebook, pen, compass, knife, purse etc.), and a sun hat. I pack as spare clothing a second shirt, pair of cotton trousers and pair of socks, changing into these (after first washing myself) as soon as I arrive at an overnight stop, and washing through the first dirty set of clothing to dry and be ready for the end of the next day. In this way there is always something clean to change into. The alternation might seem pedantic, but on the one hand it is nice and psychologically satisfying to get into clean clothes, and on the other jungle trekking is a filthy business which requires constant clean clothes – take and wear your oldest, least valued attire, as the guides and hill-tribe people do. A pair of lightweight cotton pyjamas is also a good idea, doubling up as a clean dry second set of clothes to change into. And a Burmese- or Karen-style *longyi* (sarong) can be useful for changing into in the evening when your trousers are filthy or wet, is also handy as a sheet for sleeping on, and, further, is invaluable for women wanting to wash Thai-style in a river with guides looking on. I used to carry flip-flops, but now find these dead weight, wearing my boots all the time.

Other essential or useful items include: a lightweight tent with good ventilation (more below); or, in place of a tent, a large square plastic sheet which can form a canopy to sleep under when attached overhead to trees by its four corners (if you opt for this solution, you will then also need a big mosquito net); string and possibly screw-in hooks for hanging your net where there are no obvious nails or similar (e.g. in a room in a forestry office or in a headman's house); a lightweight sleeping bag; a sleeping mat (there are now high-tech, lightweight, self-inflating mats on the market that pack down to a minimal volume – smaller than a small sleeping bag); water bottle; small traveller water filter or iodene/chlorine tablets/droplets; an aluminium pot with a lid and handle for boiling water in and cooking food in; a plastic or steel coffee mug; a spoon, tin opener, cigarette lighter and pocket knife; a torch or flashlight (a vital piece of equipment – it is pitch black in the jungle or in your tent after dark); candles; maps and a compass (the latter is essential for orientation in the hills and helpful in towns too – throughout this book I have given positions that are best understood with a compass); your camera plus films and spare batteries; a towel (when folded up, it can also double as a pillow); toilet paper and your toilet bag; vitamin pills; antiseptic cream for cuts and bites; 'Disento' diarrhoea tablets (from any Thai pharmacy), prickly heat powder; and sachets of washing powder. An item that I find really useful, but which is not obvious, is 3 or 4 expanders (in US speak: 'bungee cords'), which can be bought for 10 baht each at any motorbike or bicycle shop or motorcycle rental place. They can be used for tying stuff into the basket of a hired Honda Dream, for attaching a tent to the back of a motorbike seat or to the top of a backpack, and for making a washing line in a guest-house room or outside a tent in the jungle.

Accommodation & tents
There was a time when I and my companions used always to stay during treks in villagers' houses, in schools and forestry buildings, carrying and sleeping in a mosquito net. But in those days we went less often into the jungle, and when we did, we simply borrowed a tent from a guest house or friends. But then we went more often to places where there were no buildings, and I bought my own lightweight trekker's tent. I came to appreciate its virtues, not offered by accommodation in a headman's house or wherever. A tent offers freedom, privacy, independence, a quiet night, a clean place in which to sleep and stow your belongings, protection against mosquitoes and bugs, and a refuge from the bored, talkative, boozy, loud headmen, teachers and soldiers that you can encounter in out-of-the-way hill-tribe or border villages. So then a tent became my preferred accommodation option when trekking away from towns, either on foot or by motorbike, and now I take one everywhere with me, using it almost always.

It is not easy to buy a tent in Thailand, especially a state-of-the-art high-tech tent, but you can undoubtedly obtain one in Bangkok and in Chiang Mai either in camping shops or perhaps in the big department stores. If I remember correctly, there are some outdoor-activity shops on Chiang Mai's Mani Noparat Road, and I once saw a couple of tents in a shop in Nan. You might be able to hire a tent from a trekking agency or from places like the headquarters of Nan's Doi Pu Kha National Park. But the best thing is to bring your own from home. And the most important considerations to bear in mind when choosing a tent to bring along are that it is lightweight, packs up small, has a strong waterproof floor that is an integral part of the inner tent, and has the best possible ventilation.

A tent that is designed for mountaineering, for cold conditions, and to withstand storms is exactly wrong for jungle trekking. You want a tent that will dissipate heat and moisture as effectively as possible, that will keep all the creepy-crawlies out, that will isolate you from the dampness of the jungle floor, and that will protect you from heavy nighttime dews. The biggest problem is heat and humidity. Until things cool down in the night, it can be unbearably steamy in a tent in the jungle. Hence the importance of ventilation. A suitable tent is one with a flysheet against the dew or even against a sudden deluge; with an inner tent that is highly breathable; with plenty of space between inner and outer tents so that there is a good flow of air; with an inner tent that has a double door with two layers of material, one of which is just netting that can let plenty of air in and out, while keeping mosquitoes out; with, optimally, two entrances, one at each side (tunnel tent), so that when both are open (net doors assumed) you get a welcome cross-draught.

An ideal tent is one whose inner part is a netlike construction that can be separated from the outer tent or flysheet and erected on its own. The virtue of this is that, apart from offering good ventilation, the inner can be erected on its own, e.g. on the floor inside a forestry or health or school building, thus doubling as a mosquito net. A simple but effective solution, if you have no tent, is that outlined earlier: sleep on a groundsheet in a net under a 3 x 3-metre plastic sheet or 'tarpaulin' strung overhead from trees, branches or sticks. This not only keeps you airy and cool, but dry from dew, although you have no privacy. Other avenues to explore are hammocks with mosquito nets. You can buy mosquito nets of all sizes cheaply in any Thai town or market for ca 100-200 baht.

Before you get into nature, there are often many accommodation possibilities that are perhaps preferable to staying cramped in a tent, for example in rooms in forestry stations, village schools and health centres, or in rooms in village headmen's houses. Of course, in the base towns (Chiang Mai, Mae Salong, Fang, Chiang Dao, Nan, Mae Sariang and Mae Hong Son) there are guest houses and hotels aplenty, and accommodation is easy. But, as said, outlying places have possibilities too. Paradoxically, the smaller and remoter a settlement, the easier it is to stay in it in some building. You might find it problematic overnighting in intermediate-sized places such as small-town Pua or big-village Huai Khon, but securing a lodging in, say, Mae Sa Nan or Maniploek or Sa Wang is usually easy-peasy. This is because everyone there can appreciate that at nightfall you or any passer-by needs floorspace, and they are all geared up for putting visitors up, in fact there is a tradition that they do so.

In hill-tribe villages you can almost always stay with the headman, indeed it is almost his duty to put you up or find somewhere in his village for you to bed down. Forestry offices, which fortunately and by definition are located in far-flung places, are generally amenable to accommodating genuine travellers and manifest trekkers, and often have a special guest room for the purpose. Schools and teachers are also frequently willing and able to help, the teachers often happy to do so because a passing foreigner represents a distraction and fun in their isolated humdrum work teaching (hill-tribe) village children. But remember that border schools are mostly unmanned at weekends, when the teachers go to either their homes or the nearest town, and in the holidays, which begin at the end of March. Likewise, health centres, roadbuilders' camps and adult education centres in outlying areas are also mostly sympathetic to a visitor's needs. And it is usually possible, if you can find no alternative and have no tent, to put up at a monastery-temple (*wat*), assuming there is one. In general, Thai and hill-tribe people can be very helpful and enjoy making contact. In the trekking chapters I have discussed in an ad hoc manner the accommodation possibilities in a town, village, forestry station, natural place or whatever, suggesting spots where you could erect a tent, or buildings in which you could stay, and generally giving tips and describing local strategies.

Guides

The necessity, advisability or non-necessity of hiring and taking guides on a self-organized trek is discussed instance by instance in each trekking chapter. You do not always need them, and sometimes it is better to dispense with them. They can be one extra problem to have to manage. But in general I recommend taking one or more guides, even if you do not need them actually to find the way. They can act as porters, making things less strenuous and more enjoyable for you, provide companionship and security, can interface with other (often to you dubious-looking) people met on the trail, can help if you have an accident, and with their incomparable junglecraft can facilitate the trekking and camping in a million and one ways. I like to take guides with me just to observe them operating in their forest, mountain or jungle element, which is fascinating and instructive. When you hire guides, you are also directly benefiting them, putting money into their pockets and helping the economy of mostly very poor people. You are not imposing on them because they would go out into the forest anyway, hunting and gathering. For them, guiding is a bonus as they will hunt and gather during the trek, now getting paid for doing so.

The guides are not official, trained or officially sanctioned guides, but just (mostly hill-tribe) men and youths hired on the spot in villages. A fair fee to pay them (in 2000) would be about 200 baht per guide per day, for which they carry your backpack (not absurdly heavy – they have to shoulder their own things as well). This is rather more than they would earn working in their own fields, or labouring for the forestry authorities or on a building site in a town, or guiding in, say, Doi Pu Kha National Park for the park authorities. If you pay more than 300 baht a day, you are being ripped off, and in disbursing so much you make life difficult and expensive for trekkers coming after you. Remember to pay your guides pro rata for any time they spend getting back to their home villages, especially if the trek is not a loop hike, but an A-to-B trip where you abandon the guides at B. You should also foot any travel and food expenses they incur on their way home (*silor* fares, noodle soups), anything that they would not otherwise have had to fork out for. I like to tip my guides extra, especially if they have been helpful and have worked hard. They get a pleasant surprise at the end, leave the trek and you with a good feeling, and will be more inclined to repeat the performance for someone else. Do not settle up with your guides in advance, but only after the trek. In the various trekking chapters, where guides are necessary or advisable, I have given the names of people who I have used, all of whom have expressed a readiness to guide other trekkers (you), and who are expecting you to come and ask. Armed with their names and with my photos of them in the photo section, you should be able to locate them in their villages. Just wade in, searching around and looking at people's faces, or show the photos to villagers, asking for the guides. The guides may be unwilling to guide for some reason (they want to go to their fields, may have to visit someone in another village, or may not be there), but they or their relatives will be able to suggest someone else. Otherwise the headman will be able to collar people for you. In general it is not difficult to get guides – they are keep to earn the money.

Miscellaneous considerations
Make sure that you have enough money with you not just to pay for the trek and for the duration of the trek, but for time after the trek. As I know to my cost, treks can sometimes take longer that expected, or you decide you want to stay longer out in the field than you originally planned (something interesting crops up), or you get back to the base town on a Friday evening to find the banks closed until the following Monday, or you arrive back from a trek to find that the banks are closed the next day because it is a public holiday, of which there are many in Thailand. Don't get caught out with no money. Change that extra traveller's cheque – it is embarrassing having to try to borrow from your guest house or live on credit there, it is time-wasting having to wait through a weekend until the banks open again, and the whole thing just cramps your style. In Chiang Mai, of course, there is no problem because the town has many exchange booths, separate from the banks, that are open everyday, moreover until late in the evening. But in e.g. Mae Sariang, Nan and Mae Hong Son change facilities are in the banks and keep banking hours.

Finally, a couple of things occur to me that relate to the actual trekking itself. Remember that hiking in the tropics in steamy heat of up to 30°C or more is at least twice as exhausting as hiking, say, in the Alps or in England's Lake District – four or five hours is enough in one day. I like to end my day's jungle trekking at 3 or 4 in the afternoon. This gives adequate time to strike camp, get cleaned up and start cooking before night falls between 6 and 6.30pm. Sometimes a fork in a path can leave you puzzling. If in doubt, follow what looks like the main or bigger way. Small side ways often end up in crop fields. Sometimes dividing paths rejoin a bit further along. Do not mistake, as I have done, tracks made by cattle and buffaloes for paths – they end nowhere, with you getting lost. And if you are in real doubt as to which way to go, or if you get properly lost, you can always backtrack and return to where you started from. You will not have lost much and can always start out again, having got better instructions. If you have a tent and food with you, and if there is water nearby, there is no

32

problem anyway, even if it is getting dark. You can strike camp, make a reconnaissance, and set off again when you have found the right way. But long before all that happens, some hill-tribe people will probably have come past you, whom you can ask.

Disclaimer
Independent trekkers, both on foot and on bikes, who choose to use this book and its maps to undertake wholly or in part the treks described in it do so entirely at their own risk. The author cannot be held liable for anything that may happen to them and hereby explicitly disclaims all responsibility. At the same time he enters and draws trekkers' attention to the warning at the end of this preface and on the book's imprint page (verso of title page).

Transliteration
In the matter of the transliteration of Thai, Karen and other words and names in the book, a spelling has generally been adopted which best allows an English-speaker to reproduce the sound of the original word and may also be helpful to speakers of German and other languages. Thus, for example, I have transliterated the Thai for *lao kao* as 'lao kao' rather than as 'lou kou' or 'low kow', and I have dropped many confusing and seemingly redundant "h's", especially after 'p' and 't', where they might lead readers to pronounce 'f' or the English 'th', hence 'pratat' instead of 'phrathat' and 'Pu Wae' instead of 'Phu Wae'. The exception to this is sometimes with words where an inserted 'h' will not affect the pronounciation (e.g. 'khon' in Huai Khon or in 'khon muang') and in well-established transliterated words, such as 'Mekhong' whisky, where it would be churlish to render them otherwise. At the risk of ambiguity and confusion, because the word has many meanings (see the glossary at the end of the book), I have opted for 'Lao' as the adjectival form of 'Laos' in preference to 'Laotian' (which comes circuitously from the French), hence the Thai-*Lao* border. This is both more correct, consistent with the Thai and Lao languages, and in keeping with a practice that is becoming increasingly established.

C. G.
Suffolk, England
Spring 2000

WARNING

In the past some border areas in Thailand have been dangerous or potentially dangerous. This applies especially to the Thai-Burmese border region. Most of the treks in this book are in territory away from that region. Trek 3, which climbs Doi Pahom Pok, although it seemed safe enough when the author undertook it, nevertheless takes one close to Burma and a stretch of border near Doi Ang Karng, Nor Lae and Doi Larng which is peopled by a volatile mixture of Burma Army troops and militiamen from various warlord factions and narcotics-trafficking groups. Be circumspect. Hin Taek and Hua Mae Kham (Treks 1 & 2) are or have been until recently dubious semi-restricted places adjoining sensitive drug-producing and trafficking areas. Act prudently. Both flitting out of Thailand and flitting into Burma (or Laos), which can be done easily enough either unintentionally or by design, are illegal. Trekkers who cross into the Shan State could be playing with their lives. Thailand's western border with Burma is a troubled area, which securitywise can change from year to year. What was safe last year might not be so this, and vice versa. By contrast, the Kingdom's eastern border with Laos has mostly been quiet for some years now, although there may be a minimal residual danger from criminals and insurgent guerrillas in the jungles of the 'Empty Quarter' region between Sob Mang and Nam Duang. Similarly, although they are open now, Nam Duang and Sa Wang were until recently restricted (no-go) places. These days, however, the problem here, if there is one, is not with factional militiamen or cross-border banditry, but of being beyond help's reach in some difficult and very isolated terrain. Anyone intending to poke about in northern Thailand's remoter corners, mountainous forests and jungle should either travel with a hill-tribe guide, or speak Thai and/or take along a Thai companion, or first ascertain from locals if it is safe to proceed.

THE TREKS

Part 1

Treks 1-4: North of Chiang Mai in Chiang Mai & Chiang Rai provinces

1-2: two treks launched from Mae Salong
3-4: two mountain-climbing treks based respectively on Fang & Chiang Dao

Trek 1

Mae Salong – Saam Soong – Mo Long – Ma Hin Gong – Pa – Hin Taek

Parameters

trekking mode: on foot
trek time: ca 5 hours (excluding eating and sightseeing stops)
accessing time: none from Mae Salong, 1 day from Chiang Mai
exiting time: none if you stay in Hin Taek; ca 2 hours if you return
                  to Mae Salong by road & public transport
degree of difficulty: easy
guide(s):   not necessary
tent: not required
map(s):   see 1 & 2

Overview & strategy

This easy but surprisingly tiring little trek, which proceeds basically north from the mountaintop KMT outpost of Mae Salong to opium warlord Khun Sa's former headquarters of Hin Taek (also known officially as Toed Thai), is a good hike for travellers to cut their teeth on. It is not so long, nor should the way be difficult to find. No camping or staying in peoples' houses is required en route, and food and accommodation is available at each end. The trek crosses a couple of low ridges, taking in some Loimi-Akha settlements. It can be shortened a little by missing out the village of Ma Hin Gong. When I first trekked this route in 1994 with Nittaya Tananchai, it took us 4½ hours, bypassing Ma Hin Gong. When I retrekked it in 1999 with Doug Boynton, rechecking trail details, it took us about 5 hrs, but including Ma Hin Gong. If the hike has a disadvantage, it is that some of it is walked on a new (little-used) dirt road and that the descent from Ma Hin Gong off the mountains and down into the Mae Kham valley and Hin Taek is drawn-out and perhaps a trifle tedious.

The trek can be managed in two ways. Either you can walk to Hin Taek, have a late lunch there, and return straightway to Mae Salong by road, taking a public-transport *songtaew* via Saam Yaek and the H1130 (see Map 1), which would mean that the hike is completed in one day. Or you can walk to Hin Taek and stay the night there in a guest house, the next day either returning to Mae Salong by road as above, or going on to somewhere else, such as Hua Mae Kham (see Trek 2), or Pasang and Mae Sai. A further possibility would be to make a round trip from Mae Salong combining the first part of Trek 1 and the second part of Trek 2, which would never go to Hin Taek. Thus you could walk from Mae Salong to Saam Soong, and then back to Mae Salong via Mae Toe. I have not done this inviting loop, but the way is very clear, and it could certainly be hiked in less than a day.

Accessing the trek
The start of the trek is accessed directly from the centre of Mae Salong. Mae Salong itself can be accessed from Chiang Mai in one day either by bus or by your own transport (motorbike or jeep). By the former, take a bus from Chiang Mai's northern Chang Puak bus station via Fang to Taton. Change at Taton (cross the bridge and bear right) onto a *songtaew* for Kiu Satai (about 25 baht), and at Kiu Satai change onto another *songtaew* for Mae Salong (about another 25 baht). By motorcycle or jeep, head north out of Chiang Mai on Route 107, pass Chiang Dao, and proceed to Fang. From Fang, continue north now on the H1089 to Taton and after a further 31 kms to the junction at Kiu Satai. Here turn left onto the H1234 and follow the road another 13 kms across the mountains to Mae Salong. Allow about 6 hours of riding/driving for the trip. Mae Salong is also easily reached from Mae Sai, Mae Chan and Chiang Rai.

Accommodation & food in Mae Salong
As is immediately apparent, this small town is quite developed, and staying as well as eating here presents no problem. Half a dozen relatively expensive 'resorts', which cater primarily for affluent Thai tourists, are unlikely to be used by do-it-yourself trekkers. Most foreign travellers stay in one of the two surviving guest houses in Mae Salong, which, centrally located, lie opposite one another near a volleyball pitch and the early morning market. *Sin Sae* (= scholar) (also written 'Shin Sane') *Guest House* is the town's original hotel and serves adequate food. Easygoing *Akha Guest House* has spacious teak-floored rooms upstairs for 100 baht each, but serves no food. My preference is for the latter because it is run by amusing Akha people and is a kind of meeting point for the local Akha, making it a good place for observing them. There is a problem with motorbike theft in town, so if you arrive by bike ask the owners of *Sin Sae* and *Akha GH* to show you where you can leave your machine overnight.

Similarly, the resorts have upmarket restaurants serving 'authentic Yunnanese food', at a price, although you can eat very adequately at one of the many roadside eating places and noodle soup shops. A 'must' is the humble noodle place on the right (south) side of the main street, in the middle of the steep downgrade, which serves a generous and delicious bowlful of Chinese noodle soup for just 20 baht. There are shops and a small supermarket in Mae Salong where you can buy water and other provisions for the trek.

Thumbnail sketch of Mae Salong

Mae Salong, or 'Santikiri' as it has been dubbed by Thai officialdom (= 'Hill of Peace' or 'Peaceful Mountain'), is a well-known KMT (Kuomintang) or Chinese Nationalist refugee settlement. One of a score of such outposts in Thailand, it is the biggest KMT settlement in the Kingdom and, outside Taiwan, the largest Chinese Nationalist enclave in the world. Nestling in the lee of Mount or 'Doi' Mae Salong and snaking out along a ridge at an altitude of some 4000 ft, this thriving town has burgeoned out the former headquarters of Gen. Duan's KMT 5th Army. The town and the HQ date back to 1961, when Duan led his 3500-strong 5th Army, together with numerous civilian followers, out of Burma into Thailand, settling just inside the border on Doi Mae Salong. Prior to 1961, they had been pushed in 1949 out of the Chinese province of Yunnan by Mao's communists and made their way down to the Thai border. Gen. Duan, who died in 1980, is buried just above the town in a fine marble tomb, which can be visited.

Given this provenance, Mae Salong, not surprisingly, has a distinctly Yunnanese-Chinese atmosphere and look to it. Until about 1975, the mountainsides all around the town used to be covered with opium poppy fields, after which time they were turned over to the cultivation of temperate fruits and tea. Much of the fruit grown is preserved, and you can see, taste and buy the candied cherries, apricots and prunes etc. in the flourishing market at the back of Mae Salong, which has become a regular stopping place for tourists doing the rounds in Thailand's far north. Mae Salong's China tea, the cultivation of which forms an important part of the town's economy, has acquired a reputation throughout the country and can likewise be bought in the market. With its scenic location, many facilities and pleasant Yunnanese ambience, Mae Salong remains, despite its development, a nice place to 'hang out' for a few days, although it is perhaps worth avoiding at New Year and Chinese New Year, when it is crowded with visitors, and accommodation is hard to find. I have written at length about this Nationalist outpost and about the KMT in my book *Around Lan-Na*, to which the reader is referred for a more detailed account.

Preparing for the trek

No special preparations are required. Eat a good breakfast in Mae Salong and buy some snack food to consume on the way and tide you over until Hin Taek, where you can take a late lunch. Fill up your water bottle with bottled water from the little supermarket. Try to set off by 9am at the latest.

*

TREK 1: MAE SALONG – HIN TAEK

Trekking route details

Time log

Start/0 hrs   Step out of the entrance of *Akha GH* and turn left (from *Sin Sae Hotel* cross the road and go past the front of *Akha GH*). Drop down the steep little hill and bear left as you join the village main street. Continue on down for about 100 m to the bottom of hill and at the 4-way junction take the second turning left (north) (the first brings you back up to the volleyball pitch and GHs, while straight on is the continuation of the main street). A path runs behind a big new house to join a small cement road. Follow it through outlying Chinese and Akha houses and past an L-shaped kindergarten with a flagpole. Just before the cement road ends, cut left through some houses to pick up a contour path visible on the hillside.

Follow the contour path, which is joined from the left by a higher path. The path, more a pony trail, skirts hillside fields and winds down to:

45 mins   a stream with a wooden bridge. The bridge, covered with a tin roof and complete with seats, makes a pleasant resting point.

Just one minute after the first stream and bridge come a second stream and bridge, the bridge likewise tin-roofed. Here we were passed by people on motorbikes and were amazed that the locals ride down this footpath! From the two bridges, climb up to join a:

55 mins   rough dirt 'road', negotiable by bikes and 4WD vehicles. Right (our way) goes to Saam Soong and Hin Taek, while left goes to the Akha village of Mae Toe (Ter) and ultimately back to Mae Salong. You can see Mae Toe lying WSW (250° on the compass) in the distance in an elevated position among trees. It would be possible to abort the trek here and return to Mae Salong via Mae Toe (see Map 2), making a pleasant round trip, capable of being done in a day. I have no times for this option because I have not trekked it yet. Go right, as said, and continue up to:

1¼ hrs   **Saam Soong**, a Loimi-Akha village, split by the dirt road, with the bulk of the village and its dusty central compound lying to the left (west) of the road. On a first visit to Saam Soong in 1994, we were welcomed by children running out to greet us with a sunny but inexplicable "Bye bye". Their mothers sat in groups on house platforms in immaculate full costume doing appliqué work, and everyone was very friendly. In 1999, on a second visit, we were greeted with the same unaccountable "Bye bye", but we could see no costumes, and the villagers were indifferent to us. In fact some old people sought to scrounge money, pointing to our money belts. Living just an hour's walk from Mae Salong and its tourist-frequented market, where many Akha women sell tribal souvenirs, the Akha of Saam Soong are quite used to *farang* and to trying to get money out of them. In the village, look for the traditional towering Akha village swing. Three types or sub-groups of Akha live in Thailand: the Loimi-Akha, the Ulo-Akha, and the Pami-Akha. They can be distinguished in terms of the women's headdress. You can tell that the Akha of Saam Soong are Loimi by the trapezoidal plate of repoussé silver projecting upwards at the back of the women's headdress.[1]

After a 15-minute pause, leave Saam Soong, exiting by a path at the far northern end of the village (or go back to the dirt road). The path passes through trees before rejoining the dirt road, which here more resembles a 4WD track. At the junction go left (north). The track comes out on top of the first ridge. Here, in an exchange of vistas, you leave behind the view back towards Mae Salong and its giant – but from this distance miniaturized – pagoda, and enjoy a new prospect north across the Mae Kham valley to the temple and pagodas of Wat Doi Tung gleaming miles away on the horizon. The track proceeds through woods to:

1¾ hrs   a junction. Right goes to the mixed Loimi-Akha and Lahu village of Saem Ma, while straight (our route) proceeds to Mo Long, the track now turning into more of a regular dirt road.

2¼ hrs   Pass a village sign and a way left down to a river.

2 hrs 20 mins Arrive at **Mo Long**, a large and relatively developed Loimi-Akha village, strung out on a spur and easily accessible to vehicles using a new gravel and dirt road coming up 5.3 kms from the eastern end of Hin Taek. Make a short snack-lunch stop somewhere in the main street, before setting off again.

2¾ hrs   The exit to the village is marked by a fork. Right, the continuation of the gravel road, proceeds through rather bleak countryside directly to Hin Taek. Left, our way, descends on an orange track through bushes to a river. On your right side, the gravel road shadows your progress for a while before disappearing from view, while on your left you see a small valley with stepped paddy fields.

3 hrs   Cross the river and, bearing left, pick up a path which climbs up through bamboos. Now a little valley with paddy fields appears on the right.

3¼ hrs   At a fork go left, aiming for the village of Ma Hin Gong on the skyline. Coming along here in 1999, Doug and I made the mistake of going right and ended up getting lost and losing time (!), with the result that my time indications might be slightly inaccurate from here on, although I have tried to compensate for the error.

Aiming for an orange path across the valley, descend gently down the northern flank of the hillside to a stream, cross the stream, and climb up the orange path, proceeding roughly NNW or 320°.

3 hrs 35 mins At the top of a field, by a corner of woodland extending down from above, the orange path divides. Right, the main way, running below bamboos, is a short cut which takes you directly to the Ma Hin Gong to Hin Taek road, missing out Ma Hin Gong. Left, our way, is a path contouring above fields which leads to Ma Hin Gong. Near the village, go left or right, as you please, to enter:

---

[1] For an account of the Akha people and their culture, see Paul and Elaine Lewis' *Peoples of the Golden Triangle*, Jim Goodman's *Meet the Akhas*, or my *Around Lan-Na* (Chapter 8).

3¾ hrs   Loimi-Akha **Ma Hin Gong** and hit a dirt road. Left goes 4 kms to the mixed Akha, Lahu, Lisu and KMT village of Huai Hop, while right, our way, exits Ma Hin Gong in the direction of Hin Taek. Short rest. Descend to a cement section of road.

4 hrs 5 mins Ten or 15 minutes out from Ma Hin Gong, the short cut mentioned earlier joins our way from the right on a bend of the cement section. Hoof it down the dirt road until the uninteresting:

4 hrs 25 mins Lahu village of **Pa**, offroad left. At the fork, go right and downhill.

4 hrs 45 mins Arrive at a bridge and T-junction. Go right immediately to cross a second bridge (over the Mae Kham river) and arrive at another T-junction and the main street of Hin Taek, which you have approached from a south-western angle, hitting Hin Taek's main drag at its western end. Left goes to distant Hua Mae Kham, while right proceeds some 500 m to:

5 hrs   the centre of **Hin Taek**. Reward yourself with a chilled soft drink from the big store in the middle of the main drag (left side), and then tuck into a decent but belated stir-fry lunch and a large beer at *Ting Ting* restaurant towards the eastern end of the main street!

Thumbnail sketch of Hin Taek

Hin Taek or, as it is officially known, 'Toed Thai' (= cherish Thailand) is a relatively large, multi-ethnic village with a dubious recent history. Home mainly to Shan, KMT, Wa and Thai people, and also to some Akha, Lahu, Lisu and Hmong tribals, it was the headquarters between 1975 and 1982 of the "Golden Triangle's" pre-eminent narcotics warlord, Khun Sa. Here, even though the village lies well inside Thailand, several miles away from Burma's border, the Burmese Shan Khun Sa stationed his private trafficking army, the Shan United Army (SUA), until they were expelled by the Thai Army in January 1982 after a fierce three-day battle. The 'Poppy King' had operated with impunity out of Hin Taek, funnelling vast amounts of Golden Triangle drugs through Hin Taek, because he had basked in the patronage of various high-ranking Thai Army and police officers and because his SUA (the forerunner of his MTA) had even been considered by Bangkok to be a useful plank in the country's anti-communist strategy. But in the end Hin Taek became so notorious as a heroin-producing hub and the warlord and his private militia such an embarrassment for the Thai authorities that he and the SUA had to go. When the Boucaud brothers visited Hin Taek in 1978, they found a thousand SUA soldiers and their families, barracks, sandbagged bunkers, trenches, fortifications, hilltop posts, barbed wire rolls, radio aerials, and a sports ground. Khun Sa himself lived in a villa in a secluded basin a few hundred metres north of where today Hin Taek's market lies. You can still see and visit the warlord's old quarters by striking north along a track behind the market, keeping the hilltop *wat* on your left (west) side. There are no longer any opium refineries and heroin factories in town, but the Mae Kham valley and hence Hin Taek are still a major conduit for drugs passing from Burma into Thailand and on out into the wider world. For an account of Khun Sa, of his role in Golden Triangle narco-politics, and of his recent exit from the Golden Triangle stage, see my *Around Lan-Na* (Chapter 9) and also my *Three Pagodas* (Chapter 3).

As recently as the early 1990s, Hin Taek still retained something of the rough wild-west atmosphere of previous decades. When I first went there at that time, there was nowhere to stay in town and almost nowhere to eat, and in the market people eyed me suspiciously. Friends in Mae Salong advised not to stay after dark because of Hin Taek's lawlessness, and indeed the town was patrolled by heavily armed BPP men. How things have changed in a short time! You can easily eat and stay, the town is connected up to the outside world by a tarred road, share-taxi *silor* shuttle between Hin Taek and Pasang down in the valley on Highway 110, and there are general stores, modest petrol stations and even a karaoke place. Considerable development is in progress, and the Hin Taek area has been earmarked by the local authorities as a future tourist destination. Apparently, even Khun Sa's old compound is to be done up and made into a tourist attraction! With all this transformation, Hin Taek is no longer so very interesting, although the market is still worth a visit. Lots of Ulo-Akha people (the women wear a distinctive pointed or conical headdress) stop by from outlying villages, and you can see for sale Burmese and Chinese goods, including Burmese cheroots at the incredibly low price of 20 baht for 50.

Food and accommodation in Hin Taek
As you walk along the main street from west to east, you will pass a string of noodle soup shops and small restaurants. *Ting Ting* restaurant, which is located towards the eastern end and which is run by the headman's wife, serves, as said, quite nice chow and has a menu in English. In recent years Hin Taek has had two guest houses, again located at the eastern end of town, and situated close to each other. They are similar – a little compound of three or four bungalows – and at 200+ baht a night (no discounts) are rather overpriced for humble Hin Taek, which is perhaps why they are little used. They keep changing their names. One, which belongs to the headman and is near *Ting Ting*, used to be called *Hin Taek Lodge* and now (still?) goes by the name of *Rim Taan* (= stream edge) *Guest House*. Slightly east of this establishment is the preferable *Surawong Guest House*, which in 1999 seemed to be called *Gred Petch GH*.

Exiting the trek
To build a second part onto the Mae Salong-Hin Taek trek, even if you do not have your own transport, consider going west from Hin Taek to the border village of Hua Mae Kham. There is little sense in walking this route, which is a road (partly tarred and partly dirt) with a fair amount of traffic. Take one of the *songtaew* that ply the 32-km-long Hin Taek to Hua Mae Kham stretch, or try hitch-hiking. A description of this stretch and extension can be found in Trek 2.

TREK 1: MAE SALONG – HIN TAEK

To return from Hin Taek to Mae Salong by road and public transport, flag down and get into one of the many *songtaew* going east up Hin Taek's main street, which are leaving town for Saam Yaek and Pasang. The roundabout 25-km return trip to Mae Salong is done in two stages. You travel first (fare 20 baht in 1999) via the villages of Huai Poeng (mixed Shan, KMT & Wa), Ja Kham Noi (Akha), Ton Muang (Akha) and Mae Sa Laep Bon (Akha) to Saam Yaek (Akha), a distance of 13 kms. 'Saam Yaek' in Thai means 'three ways', and this last touristy little village is situated on a key junction. From Saam Yaek the *songtaew* you have been travelling in will probably continue to Pasang, descending to the lowlands on the H1130 road, in which case you will have to get out and catch a *songtaew* coming up from Pasang and going to Mae Salong. Wait on the corner by the police station. In the second stage (fare again 20 baht in 1999) you travel 12 kms west on the H1130 uphill via Klang (KMT) to Mae Salong. Allow about 40 minutes for each of the two stages. If you find yourself waiting a long time either at Hin Taek or at Saam Yaek, consider hitch-hiking back to Mae Salong.

Trek 2

Mae Salong – Mae Toe – Saam Soong – Mo Long – Hin Taek – Hua Mae Kham

Parameters

trekking mode: by motorcycle (possibly mountain bike)
ride time: 2½ - 3 hrs (excluding eating & sightseeing stops)
accessing time: none from Mae Salong, 1 day from Chiang Mai
exiting time: same as outbound time, returning either same way or via Saam Yaek
degree of difficulty: for average riders in places moderately difficult; for experienced bikers should present few problems; for skilled dirt riders a nice trip out
guide(s):   not applicable
tent: not required
map(s):   see 1, 2 & 3

Overview, strategy & background information

This motorcycle trek is in two stages. The first stage (Map 2) proceeds basically north from the mountaintop Chinese KMT town of Mae Salong to the village of Hin Taek (also known officially as Toed Thai), which not long ago used to be the headquarters of the notorious Burmese Shan opium warlord Khun Sa. The second stage (Map 3) strikes west from Hin Taek 32 kms to Hua Mae Kham, a multi-ethnic village lying on the Thai-Burmese border.

The first stage, which is a direct cross-country route from Mae Salong to Hin Taek used by few vehicles, is (at the time of writing) quite rough in places, with the worst section coming after Mae Toe. If you find that your biking skills are not up to the job, do not despair. You can return to Mae Salong, set off again, and reach Hin Taek by a 25-km alternative indirect route, which goes by road via Saam Yaek (see Map 1 and Trek 1). At Hin Taek you can rejoin the trek, heading for Hua Mae Kham, for which your skills should be adequate. The second stage is on a mixture of paved and dirt road. In 1999 the road had been asphalted as far as the turn-off for Na To, about half way between Hin Taek and Hua Mae Kham, after which the surface consisted of prepared gravel and then dirt and bulldust. This second stage is a relatively flat road which should present few or no difficulties even to only moderately skilled riders. The unpaved section from the Na To turn-off to Hua Mae Kham will undoubtedly be asphalted sooner or later, Thailand's economic circumstances permitting, which will make things easier for less skilled riders and perhaps less interesting for more skilled bikers. But in that case the latter can go offroad, exploring the dirt side trails in the 'wild-west' 'adventure-playground' hinterland to the north-west and west of Hin Taek.

A glance at a regular topographical map of northern Thailand shows that the goal of the trek, Hua Mae Kham, is a truly out-on-a-limb place, located at the end of a horn of Siamese land that sticks out into Burma. The village, like Hin Taek and the area west of Hin Taek, lies in country that has only recently been opened up to outsiders. It is territory that used to be controlled variously by warlord Khun Sa and KMT as well as Wa drug refiners and traffickers, improperly secured by the Thai authorities. Hin Taek no longer has heroin factories, and the area is now under Thai control, but nevertheless Hua Mae Kham abuts a sensitive and notorious drugs-producing area just across the border in Burma, and the road (our route in reverse) down the Mae Kham valley from that border village to Hin Taek and the outside world remains a major drugs-trafficking conduit. This makes for trekking with a frisson of excitement, but also means that common sense is distinctly the order of the day both at Hua Mae Kham and on the back roads and trails locally. It also means that trekkers are liable to be stopped and searched for drugs on this route by the police or army, as has happened to me.

From Map 2 it can be seen that the first stage of the trek, from Mae Salong to Hin Taek, intertwines with and partly duplicates (from Saam Soong to Mo Long) the route of Trek 1. I discovered this way in 1999, when checking the details of Trek 1 with my US friend Doug Boynton. After we had rewalked the foot trek, we came back with bikes to try out the motorcycle route. As only moderately skilled bikers, riding Honda Dream townbikes, we needed about 1 hour to go from Mae Salong to Hin Taek. Unfortunately, I cannot tell you the precise distance between these two places, because on both our hire bikes the odometer cable had been cut by the owners at the rental shops in Chiang Mai (a common scam), but it must be between 15 and 20 kms. The second stage to Hua Mae Kham I have ridden more than once with Nittaya Tananchai, likewise on a Honda Dream (two up), and each time the journey has taken about 1½ to 2 hours. Dirt road freaks will be able to blast through the two stages much more speedily, and when the road to Hua Mae Kham is paved right through, the time needed for the second stage will be shortened for everyone. If you ride not directly via Mae Toe, but indirectly via Saam Yaek, it is 12 kms from Mae Salong to Saam Yaek, 13 kms from Saam Yaek to Hin Taek, and 32 kms from Hin Taek to Hua Mae Kham, 57 kms in all. Allow about 2½ hours for the whole trek using the alternative roundabout road route via Saam Yaek, the same as for the whole trek using the short dirt route via Mae Toe.

45

As with many of the motorbike treks in this book, it might be possible to ride all or most of the two-stage route on a bicycle, although your mount would have to be a sturdy mountain bike and you yourself would have to be strong and persistent, wheeling the bike on steep up- or downgrades or over stony or rutted passages. Not being a mountain cyclist, I cannot say how long the stages of this (or any other) trek might be, but the amount of time needed would obviously lie between that needed to ride them and that needed to walk them, probably approximating more to the former. Nor need foot trekkers without their own transport miss out on the fun of visiting Hua Mae Kham. Public-transport *silor* go frequently from Mae Salong to Saam Yaek, and from Saam Yaek to Hin Taek (see Trek 1), but also fairly regularly, about hourly, from Hin Taek to Hua Mae Kham.

After Hua Mae Kham bikers will have to return to Hin Taek, from where (after possibly staying in Hin Taek) they can either go back to Mae Salong the same way via Mae Toe, or go back to Mae Salong via Saam Yaek, or go down to Pasang via Saam Yaek, or continue north to Mae Sai up the new border road via Huai Poeng, Sa Ma Ki and Doi Tung.

Accessing the trek, accommodation & food in Mae Salong, thumb-nail sketch of Mae Salong: see Trek 1

Preparing for the trek
No special preparations are required, but take some water in case you break down and have to wait or have to walk to get help from the nearest village. If you think you might try to stay in Hua Mae Kham, perhaps buy a few items of food in either Mae Salong or Hin Taek.

*

Route detail Mae Salong – Hin Taek via Mae Toe
From *Akha GH* and *Sin Sae GH* turn north, going under the house arch across the road, continue a short distance to the end of the road, and turn left at the T-junction by the volleyball pitch. Proceed a short way up towards a resort and turn right into a brick-surfaced road. Pass a phone box on your right and turn left onto a dirt road that passes a couple of water tanks (left). This is the way to the village of Mae Toe, and it runs below the giant pagoda dominating Mae Salong on the mountain immediately up behind the town.

A flattish dirt road, rutted in places, runs 3 or 4 kms round the mountainside and through some woods to a junction. Right goes to the offroad Akha village of **Mae Toe** (Ter), while straight on (our route) continues a short distance to another junction. Here, straight ahead proceeds 3 kms to the village of Mae Cham Luang, while right, our route, swings north and north-east in the direction of Hin Taek. Now comes the worst section of the route. With the Akha houses of Mae Toe high up right in the trees, the road, stony and in very poor condition, winds steeply down to a valley floor. Follow the road along the valley floor, by some fields, and through two fords. Now the 4WD track winds up, is joined from the right by the footpath from Mae Salong, and reaches the Akha village of **Saam Soong** (details: Trek 1).

TREK 2: MAE SALONG – HUA MAE KHAM

From Saam Soong continue on a pleasant elevated interconnecting trail, down through some woods to a junction. Right goes to some kind of forestry or agricultural station and to the village of Saem Ma, while straight on (our route) continues downhill and along a spur to the drawn-out Akha village of **Mo Long**. At the bottom end of the village, where the walking track forks off left, continue on the gravel road, bearing right. The road, punctuated by some long steep rutted sections, descends another 5 kms through rather bleak country and past a *wat* and pagoda (right), to hit a T-junction on the eastern outskirts of **Hin Taek**. Turn left and proceed a short distance, past two guest houses and *Ting Ting* restaurant (all left), to the centre of Hin Taek. Shops, noodle places and fuel stops line the main street, while the market lies a couple of hundred metres right (north) of the main drag.

Thumbnail sketch of Hin Taek, food & accommodation in Hin Taek:
see Trek 1

Route detail Hin Taek – Hua Mae Kham (Map 3)

From Hin Taek we proceed on the second stage of our motorcycle trek to Hua Mae Kham (now see Map 3). If the first stage was less amenable to being cycled by mountain bike, the second is much more so. Surprisingly, the flattish purposeful road from warlord Khun Sa's old stamping ground north-west to the far-flung border village turns out to be a relatively busy one, and you soon see why. Many villages, all growing and developing, line the route, and more lie offroad. Noticeable in 1998 were the numerous houses in these villages either being built new or undergoing renovation, a sign of the growing affluence of the area and of a Taiwanese gratuity recently paid to many local KMT and Wa residents. Most of the villages have ethnically mixed populations containing variously and in varying proportions KMT Chinese, Wa, Shan, Akha, Hmong, Lisu and Lahu.

The second stage starts at the western end of Hin Taek's main street at the turn-off left by a bridge for the villages of Pa and Ma Hin Gong (junction = km 0). You do not take this turn-off, but follow the main road, passing a checkpoint, a bridge and a turn-off right for Mae Mo and also the Akha village of Paya Prai Lao Ma (+ 14 kms to latter). Paya Prai, incidentally, which is an Ulo-Akha place, was where the Akha first settled when they migrated into Siam a hundred years ago. Intermittently, the Kham river shadows the road on the left side. You pass the villages of Sam Tao (Wa), Muang Song (especially Shan) and Ja Tor (especially Lahu). A turning right leads to Ka Yaeng (Akha) and its church. Saen Muang Goh follows and then **Lao Liu** (especially KMT), where a side road goes left to Huai Yuak and Ba So. A short distance further is the turning left (km 13) for Na To (+1.8 kms). This is where in 1998 the paved road gave over to gravel.

A couple of kms beyond the Na To turning, you come to a reservoir left and Mae Kham Noi (km 15), where a side road goes off right to Paya Prai Lao Jor (apparently KMT) and extensive tea plantations, before linking up with Paya Prai Lao Ma, completing a side loop. Continuing north-west, and passing a bridge, a settlement and a forestry place (right), you arrive at the village of **Pang Mahan** (km 19.2), peopled by KMT, Lisu, Akha and Lahu. At the fork, bear left, keeping the health centre to your right (a place to stay in an emergency). Crossing a bridge, you come to a checkpoint and barrier, and then the White Hmong village of **Kao Lang** (km 23). It is to Kao Lang that the drugs first come after they have crossed the border from the refineries opposite Hua Mae Kham in Burma, before they continue their journey down to Mae Chan and Chiang Rai (for some brief background information on the Hmong people, see Trek 16 under 'Santisuk'). You pass next an Akha settlement (left side) and cross a bridge, to arrive at Mae Kham Mai (Lisu), the last village before your destination. Ignoring several side turnings, proceed to a junction (km 29). Either way leads to Hua Mae Kham, but right proceeds 3 kms to the Hmong part, while left goes 3 kms to the main Lisu and Akha part. Go left, pass a checkpoint and Lahu settlement, ignore a turning left for a monastery, and arrive at **Hua Mae Kham** (km 32). In recent years the entrance to this mountainside border village has been a dreadful mess of deep bulldust. Leave your bike at the bottom (locked) if you cannot negotiate it (coming down is even worse than going up).

Hua Mae Kham

A big multi-ethnic place spread out on a mountainside, Hua Mae Kham lies, as its name suggests, at the source of the River Kham, which runs from here, on Thailand's western border with Burma, right across northern Lan-Na to flow into the Mae Khong, near Chiang Saen, on the country's eastern frontier with Laos. Cascading down the east-facing side of the border ridge, the village is broadly divided up horizontally into four bands, each one inhabited by one of Hua Mae Kham's different tribal groups: Lisu live in the upper band, Hmong in the middle band over to the right (north-eastern) side, Akha in the lower band, and Lahu at the lowest level by the checkpoint. In 1998 the village had several shops, but no electricity. At the top of the steep access, there is a kindergarten, and rather higher than that, in the middle band, a place which calls itself *Dok Buatong Guest House* (right side of road). It has a 'restaurant' – just a couple of tables on a balcony – where a Chinese lady has twice cooked for me a feeble overpriced fried rice. Apparently you can stay here in 'bungalows' for 50 baht per person per night, although it might be better to befriend a Lisu family and stay with them, which should not be difficult, or even pitch a tent somewhere. The Chinese lodging is named after the *dok buatong* or Mexican sunflowers that cover the whole mountainside in November, said to be a grander sight even than the *buatong* fields at Mae Surin near the town of Mae Hong Son.

In the vicinity of Hua Mae Kham there are two waterfalls, to which you can walk. It is also possible to walk an hour up to the border. This should only be done guided by a villager. Collar a Lisu man and pay him 50 or 100 baht. On top of the ridge are Thai Army, Burma Army and Red Wa positions, and from the border crest you can look over Burma and poppy fields. Chinese-operated Wa heroin refineries and drugs production plants lie close by. Formerly owned by Khun Sa and his Mong Tai Army (MTA), they are now in the hands of the Chinese-Wa brothers Wei Siao-gang and Wei Siao-long, the two of them the new opium kings of the 'Golden Triangle', and churn out hundred of kgs of heroin each year. Most recently, reportedly, these factories have appreciably switched to producing speed, ecstasy and other 'designer' drugs, for which there is an enormous market not just in Thailand.

48

TREK 2: MAE SALONG – HUA MAE KHAM

When Hua Mae Kham's access road from Hin Taek is paved right through, this scenically located border village can be expected to develop – how long is it before the first resort arrives? – and so there will never be a better time to enjoy the outpost unspoilt than now.

Exiting the trek

Whether or not you try to stay overnight in Hua Mae Kham, you will have to return to Hin Taek, as there is no other exit, from where (after possibly staying in Hin Taek – accommodation details under Trek 1) you have four exiting options. You can either return to Mae Salong by the way you came, via Mae Toe; or return to Mae Salong via Saam Yaek (see Map 1); or go down to Pasang via Saam Yaek and on to Chiang Rai or Mae Sai; or continue north to Mae Sai up a new border road via Huai Poeng, Sa Ma Ki and Doi Tung. Using back roads up the border, it is 54 kms from Hin Taek to Mae Sai, Thailand's northernmost town, a trip that has only recently become possible, first with the construction of the new border security road from Doi Tung to Mae Sai, and then with the completion in 1997 of a crucial link way between Huai Mor and Sa Ma Ki. It would be advisable to set out on this last option fresh in the morning, after staying overnight in Hin Taek. I have described this new northbound border trip in my book *Around Lan-Na*.

Trek 3

Climbing Doi Pahom Pok

Fang – Huai Pa Sang – Pu Muen – forestry HQ – Doi Pahom Pok – Huai Ma Yom – Huai Bon – Fang

Parameters

trekking mode:	combination of motorcycle and foot trekking; or all foot trekking
trek time:	2 days/1 night (combining m/c and foot trekking); 4 days/3 nights (basically trekking on foot)
trek distance:	67 kms of motorcyclable roads and trails from Fang to Fang, plus ca 3 hours of walking during actual scaling of summit; ca 52 kms (32.5 miles) of foot trekking from Huai Pa Sang to Huai Bon plus ca 3 hours scaling summit
accessing time:	none from Fang, ½ day from Chiang Mai
exiting time:	none from Fang (round-trip trek); 1 day from summit for bikers; 2 days from summit for walkers
degree of difficulty:	by m/c: for experienced bikers moderately difficult in places; on foot: easy, including summit climb
guide(s):	advisable, but not essential
guide name(s):	Joy (see photo)
tent:	required
map(s):	see 4, 5 & 6

Overview & strategy

This attractive, satisfying and relatively straightforward trek climbs Doi Pahom Pok, at 2260 m or 7415 ft Thailand's second-highest mountain. If the Kingdom's highest mountain, Doi Intanon, is discounted because a highway runs to its summit, because large numbers of Thai trippers and foreign tourists visit it daily by vehicle, and because the summit itself is the site of a Thai military installation, Pahom Pok is actually the country's highest peak worth climbing. The expedition takes the trekker into a remote, essentially unvisited, scenic area very close to the Burmese border, and involves camping on the very top of Mount Pahom Pok, with the possibility of enjoying spectacular sunset and sunrise views over Burma.

TREK 3: CLIMBING DOI PAHOM POK

Doi Pahom Pok lies in Mae Nam Fang National Park, and it is from the district town of Fang that the mountain is climbed. There are two ways to approach the peak (see Maps 4 & 6). You can either go north from Fang to the village of Huai Pa Sang and then west via Pu Muen village to a forestry headquarters, from where you can launch your 'assault' on the summit. Or you can head west from Fang and then strike north via the villages of Huai Bon and Huai Ma Yom to the same forestry HQ, from where you can likewise scale the mountain. However, the obvious and most appealing thing to do is to use one of these ways as the outward journey and the other as the return journey, making the trek into a loop. However, which way round should the loop be tackled? For one very good reason it is better to go via Huai Pa Sang and Pu Muen, and to return via Huai Bon. This is that it is in Pu Muen that you can hire a guide to lead you to the top of Pahom Pok, whereas you may well be unable to find a guide in Huai Bon or Huai Ma Yom. But a reason to start the loop via Huai Bon and Huai Ma Yom is that of the two ways of accessing the mountain this is the easier, and that motorcycling trekkers with less confidence in their biking skills might prefer to use this easier access, even returning the same way via Huai Bon, than to flounder around on the other more difficult one, with its dire ascent (in 1998) up to Pu Muen.

If we make the loop, then, in an anticlockwise direction, proceeding first to Pu Muen, we find that the distances pan out as follows. The whole loop from Fang to Fang is some 67 kms long, which excludes the ascent on foot of the actual summit itself (add perhaps another 4 kms or 1½ hours, and the same for the descent). Broken down, this results in 11 kms from Fang to Huai Pa Sang, 11.5 kms from Huai Pa Sang to Pu Muen, 5.5 kms from Pu Muen to the forestry HQ, 11 kms from the HQ to an outlying forestry station at the foot of the summit of Pahom Pok, from where the climb up to the top is made, 11 kms back from the station to the HQ, 12.5 kms from the HQ to Huai Bon, and another 4 or 5 kms from Huai Bon back to Fang centre.

With an overall distance of some 67 kms, excluding the summit climb, this long loop trek is clearly best done making use of a motorcycle, assuming that trekkers can handle the rough country trails and occasional problematic passages to be encountered on it (such as Nittaya Tananchai and I found when we trekked this route in 1998). Another compelling reason to bike the trek is that motorcyclable trails go to within a few kms or ca 90 minutes' walk of the summit. Because these bikable backwoods trails exist, it might seem a bit pointless not to travel them on a bike. And this is how we trekked Pahom Pok in 1998, mostly by bike and 'knocking off' the actual summit on foot; and it is from this point of view that the Pahom Pok trek is described here. Undertaken in this mode, mostly on two wheels and partly on foot, the expedition lasts two days. On the morning of the first day you ride from Fang to Pu Muen, hire a guide, and ride with him to the forestry HQ, where you can have lunch (or in Pu Muen). From the HQ you ride with the guide in the afternoon to the outlying forestry station at the foot of the summit of Pahom Pok, leave your bikes at the station, and climb up to the summit, camping on top overnight. On the morning of the second day you climb back down to the bikes and ride back to the HQ, having lunch there, and in the afternoon ride back to Fang via Huai Bon.

Some travellers may be content to avail themselves of motorcycles for this trek, but not wish merely to 'blast through' it mostly on two wheels in under two days. They may be happy to speedily access and exit it by bike, not wanting to invest too much time in the trip overall, but wish to increase the central walking component, spending more time on the real 'meat' of the trek, climbing Doi Pahom Pok. Such trekkers can do so by leaving their bikes at the midpoint forestry HQ and walking from there to the mountain and back, on top of scaling the summit itself. This second compromise option would add some 22 kms to the distance walked and lengthen the overall trek by perhaps a day and a night.

But it would also be entirely possible to walk not just the central part of the trek, whether shorter or longer, but almost the whole of it, which is why this trekking chapter is headed up by the icon of the hiker as well as that of the biker. Thus purist foot trekkers could walk all the way from Huai Pa Sang to Huai Bon. Taking public transport from Fang up the main road to Huai Pa Sang, they could hike up via Pu Muen to the forestry HQ on the first day, spend a night there, walk on the second day to Pahom Pok, climbing it, spend a second night on the summit, walk back on the third day to the forestry HQ, spend a third night there, and walk down on the fourth day to Huai Bon, from where they could hitch-hike or get a public-transport *songtaew* back to Fang. The distance walked would amount to 52 kms (32.5 miles), excluding the summit climb – say 60 kms in total (37.5 miles). It may well be possible to walk from Pu Muen directly to Pahom Pok on footpaths. Ask in the village.

If this trek can be managed on a motorbike (we even did it two-up on a Honda Dream townbike), then it must surely be negotiable by bicycle, albeit on a sturdy mountain bike. Some awful sections on the way up to Pu Muen would necessitate pushing the bike, but the pleasant riding elsewhere on contour trails through woods and open alpine country would compensate for this. Again, as for motorbikes, if the way up via Pu Muen should prove too difficult for bicycling, the other way via Huai Bon would make easier access.

Strictly speaking, a guide is not really necessary for this trek, neither to show the way nor to porter baggage. Aided by the maps accompanying this chapter and by the route detail below, trekkers should have little difficulty finding their way to the summit of Pahom Pok. And if they use bikes as far as the outlying forestry station, trekkers have only a short distance, about 1½ hours up to the mountaintop, to carry their backpacks and tents. Nevertheless, it is advisable to take a guide, who can smooth the way, for example at the forestry posts, ensure you do not lose the way, provide a measure of security in this isolated border terrain, and, when you reach the summit, fetch water from lower down. In 1998 we hired as our guide in Pu

TREK 3: CLIMBING DOI PAHOM POK

Muen a roguish likeable character named Joy (see photo), who lives in the village. He could take you up Pahom Pok (or elsewhere), and if unavailable, would find a replacement guide. Expect to pay him about 200 baht for a full day and 100 baht for half a day.

Accessing the trek

Because this is a round-trip trek, starting and ending in Fang, there is, strictly speaking, no accessing and exiting of the trek, assuming you have already made your way to Fang. The route to Doi Pahom Pok and the way back down from the mountain are all part of the trek. To access Fang and the start of the trek from Chiang Mai, proceed 150 kms north from Chiang Mai up Route 107 by motorbike or bus. Buses for Fang leave regularly from Chiang Mai's northern Chang Puak bus station on the Chang Puak Road. On a motorbike or in a jeep allow 3 to 4 hours to get via Chiang Dao up to Fang. If you are coming to Fang south from Mae Salong by motorcycle or jeep, allow two hours for the journey, travelling on the H1234 and H1089 roads via Taton and Mae Ai.

Fang & Doi Pahom Pok: background information

Fang is a small town lying, as said, 150 kms north of Chiang Mai. Founded, according to old chronicles, in AD 1274 by King Meng Rai of Chiang Saen, it was destroyed in 1717 by the Burmese and lay deserted for some 160 years until 1880, when it was resettled. Late 19th-century travellers, explorers and surveyors passing through Fang were amazed to find a walled moated 'city' in a state of advanced dereliction, overgrown with jungle and littered with thousands of fallen and broken Buddha figures. The same travellers remarked on the numbers of tribals beginning to cross the border west of Fang, migrating from Burma to the Pahom Pok area, a migration that continued especially in the first half of the 20th century.

One of these travellers, the Irish surveyor James McCarthy, who in 1890 came to Fang and climbed Doi Pahom Pok, says of the peak, whose name he translates as 'Cover-Blanket Mountain': 'This magnificent mountain stands on the north-west, and as its position was fixed by the Indian triangulator, I made a mental resolution to start my [triangulation and surveying] work from this peak.' At the time the tribals in the Pahom Pok area were mainly Lahu (or Musoe), tribals 'who in the last ten years have been clearing and settling hillsides that no human being ever approached before'. McCarthy engages local Lahu to guide him and help him, and, setting off from Fang with a party of ten men and one elephant, proceeds north-west towards the mountain, coming upon extensive clearings that the Lahu have made in the cover, mounting a hillside among oaks, ascending 200 ft very steeply from a stream, and stopping for the night at an elevated Lahu village (Pu Muen or Huai Ma Yom?). Here he makes many interesting contemporary observations on the Lahu. Some of them, for example, carry crossbows and antiquated 'Brown Bess'-type guns dating back to the time of George III. Of Pahom Pok itself, McCarthy says that wild tea grows all over it, which the Lahu use, although do not cultivate. Taking some men from the Lahu village, he then climbs to the summit of the mountain. 'Pahom Pok was not difficult, and on 24 February I reached the top, [finding] to the west a perpendicular scarp.' He gets the men to clear any mountaintop trees, except for some signal-trees, which are necessary for his triangulation, and spends three or four days on the summit engaged in this work and also waiting for haze to lift. 'The morning of the 27th was gloriously fine, and the remarkable peak of Chieng Dao stood out well.' Basing his calculations on Pahom Pok and also on Chiang Dao, whose positions are already known, he begins his surveying work, making triangulations, checking latitude and azimuth, measuring base lines, and making chain and compass traverses. From the summit of Pahom Pok, McCarthy went on to make the first survey of the north of Siam, proceeding via Chiang Saen and Chiang Khong right across into present-day Laos, to Luang Prabang and Chiang Kwang.

Accommodation & food in Fang
These days Fang is an unprepossessing place with a long wide main street lined on each side by characterless squat buildings. There is little reason to come here except to use the town as a base for exploring the Doi Ang Karng area, for visiting the Palaung people at Suan Cha, and for climbing Pahom Pok. Almost the most interesting thing to do in Fang is to watch the local tribals come to buy and sell in the market. Just as the town is not rich in appeal, so it is not blessed with an abundance of decent places to stay and to eat. A reasonable lodging is the *Ueng Kham (UK) Hotel*. More of a guest house than a hotel, this place, pronounced 'oe-ang' and 'come' (as in English), is situated at the north end of town. At the top of the main drag, the road turns right and then left, before heading off to Mae Ai. In the middle of this kink, a *soi* or side road goes off left, and the "UK" lies just a short distance up it on the left. A number of new and less new rooms surround a parking compound. They are spacious, pleasant, clean, with fan and hot shower, and with some pleasing attention to detail: coat-hangers, flip-flops for the shower, toilet paper, and rattan furniture outside the door. In 1998 the superior rooms were 180 baht and the ordinary ones 140 baht. Another possibility is the nearby *Wiang Kaew Hotel*, and a further option might be the more pricey and upmarket *Chok Tani Hotel* on the main street.

Foodwise, an attractive restaurant is the *Non Tri* (pronounced 'tree'), which, as you go up the main street from S to N, is situated midway, on the left (W) side, set back from the road, and slightly obscure at the end of a short entrance drive. It lies broadly opposite the bus station and market. At *Non Tri* you can sit inside or out, the menu and service are OK, and large cold beers are 50 baht. Fang's night foodmarket (along parts of the main street) is relatively feeble, but if you want a cheap meal without lingering over drinks, *Sawan* (= heaven) dishes up good chow. The open-air stall is located on the W side of the main drag, almost backing onto Fang Telecoms Office and looking diagonally across to the night fruitmarket and a petrol station.

TREK 3: CLIMBING DOI PAHOM POK

Preparing for the trek

No special preparations are required, but think about what food you will need for how long, have some good water in reserve for staying on the summit, and take a tent.

*

Trekking route detail (outbound): Fang – Huai Pa Sang – Pu Muen – forestry HQ (F1) – outlying forestry station (F2) – Doi Pahom Pok

From the centre of Fang go north up the H1089 about 11 kms (10.9 from *UK Hotel*) in the direction of Mae Ai and Taton, and in the village of **Huai Pa Sang** turn left (west) onto an orange dirt road, which starts almost opposite a barber's shop (see Map 4). If you are travelling without your own transport, take a bus or, better, a *songtaew* from Fang and ask for Ban Huai Pa Sang, perhaps indicating that you are going to Doi Pahom Pok. From this rather inconspicuous turn-off (= km 0) proceed along the dirt side road to a puzzling fork (km 1.6), at which you go left. You pass through lychee orchards until the way begins to climb, deteriorating alarmingly. A very bad rutted track climbs in places steeply up. In 1998 it was so bad that we almost gave up, fearing that the disaster might go on for a long time or even get worse. Fortunately we did not, or we might never have climbed Pahom Pok. Persevere and, if you are riding two-up on a hired Honda Dream, be prepared for the pillion passenger to have walk up in places, while the rider scrambles the bike up the bad sections. At a fork you can go either left or right – the two ways meet up again. I seem to recall that the way right is easier. You pass through some trees, rejoin the other way, and come to a turning left, marked by a seat. Continue straight on, past a *sala* or waiting hut and a turning (both right), and through some forest. Now the track levels out suddenly to emerge at another *sala* and the bottom end of the mixed Red and Black Lahu village of **Pu Muen** (km 11.6), which enjoys fine views.

Pu Muen is the place to find one or more guides if you decide you need them. After Pu Muen there are no further villages, just the forestry HQ, and so there is nowhere else to hire a guide, although the forestry HQ might be able to provide one. Pu Muen is also a place to have some lunch. Eat either some cold things, or get someone to boil water for you to make Ma-maa instant noodle soup. You can eat at the forestry HQ, too. Arriving in Pu Muen, we applied to the school (up right), where some helpful BPP teachers immediately sorted everything out for us. They brought boiling water and bowls for us to make packet soup, and sent a boy to get a guide from the village. Within minutes Joy appeared, a rather wild-looking Chinese-Wa man with a moustache, chintuft beard and beret, who declared himself ready to set off with us at once and guide us up Pahom Pok. When you arrive in Pu Muen, and if you want a guide, ask for Joy in the village or at the school and show people the photo of Joy in this book. If Joy does not want to go with you, he will find someone else.

Our plan had been to hire two guides, the two of them sharing the weight of our two backpacks and tent. But Joy would have none of this idea. If he could earn double pay, he would carry everything himself. He needed the money for some special purpose connected with his daughter's studies in Chiang Mai. We laughed at his suggestion, but later he did indeed haul the two backpacks, the tent, his own bag and belongings, and a water container to the top of Pahom Pok. We paid this doughty, heavily-laden, Wa Sherpa 500 baht for the trip, about twice what he would have earned if we had taken a second guide along. On the strength of the anticipated pay, he bought 20 Burmese cheroots for 10 baht – a smoke was scarcely ever far from his lips – and we set off.

The route goes next to the forestry HQ. In front of the school three ways seem to continue past Pu Muen. In fact two of them merely lead into the village, which lies to the left. For the HQ and Pahom Pok take the uppermost of these three ways, the one immediately below the school. Joy had collected his motorbike, a battered old trails machine, from his house (he lives in Pu Muen), and we continued on a flattish, elevated track through open country and light woods towards the HQ. Not far out of Pu Muen there is a division of the way, marked by a checkpoint (km 13.3). At this junction go left and continue, bearing left at another little junction, across three log bridges to a third junction (km 16.5). The way right is the route to Pahom Pok, but for the moment we continue left (straight) just 500 m to the forestry HQ (km 17.0).

The **forestry Headquarters**, 17 kms out from Huai Pa Sang and the H1089 road, is a complex of buildings in a pleasant setting with a small lake. Various people live and work here (let us call it F1), and we found everyone to be very friendly. They said that *farang* trekkers passing through are welcome to stay at the HQ or put up a tent. If you have walked to F1 from Huai Pa Sang, you will need to camp here overnight anyway. Actually, everything is so attractive and laid-back at this forestry complex that a tempting idea would be simply to hang out at F1, regardless of whether you go to Pahom Pok, making little exploratory walks in the vicinity, one of which might be to the mountain. There is a kitchen at the HQ. If you are on foot, use it for boiling safe drinking water, for making tea or coffee, and for preparing any hot meals. Later, after climbing Pahom Pok, we used it on our way back down for making an instant noodle soup. If you are a dirt bike rider interested not in climbing Doi Pahom Pok, but in making a pleasant one-day loop ride from Fang, you could break your trip for lunch at F1 and then continue back to Fang via Huai Bon (see Map 6 and route detail below). If you are a walking enthusiast who has come this far by bike, but who is interested in extending the trek's walking component as outlined earlier, consider leaving your bike at F1 and walking from there. You could either set off after lunch on this first day, walk the next 11 kms to the outlying forestry station (let us call it F2), and camp there overnight, before climbing Pahom Pok the next day; or you could camp at F1 and walk the next morning to F2, climbing the mountain in the afternoon. We rode the next section to F2, leaving at F1 everything that did not seem essential for the trek up the mountain and a night tenting on its summit.

From the forestry HQ (F1 = km 0 again) we first backtrack (see Map 5) 500 m to the junction passed earlier (km 0.5). Turn left, and you come immediately to a barrier across the trail. If the barrier is down and you cannot get your vehicle under it or round it, there is a key to the lock at F1 (or Joy will have the key with him). The barrier is to frustrate illegal logging, not you. A rough flattish forestry trail runs around the back of the Pahom Pok ridge on its west-facing flank. In this remote isolated territory, a magnificent panoramic view opens up. Due west, across the valley, is Burma, with its unfolding and receding succession of mountain ridges. To your left (approximately south-west) you can see the corkscrew road that runs up from Nong Pai to Nor Lae and Doi Ang Karng. Snaking along the border ridge across the valley, and running from left to right relative to you as you look out, is the new border security road (blocked and closed in early 1999) that runs from Doi

TREK 3: CLIMBING DOI PAHOM POK

Ang Karng up to Doi Larng. At a junction go right (straight), not left. After 30 minutes of rugged contouring, the track fetches up on a knoll near the outlying forestry station or F2 (km 11.1). F2, which is a collection of grass-roofed huts for a big mixed Lahu and Lisu family engaged in local reforestation, lies to the right (north) of the track. If you are on a bike, get it in among the huts and lock it. You could pitch a tent on the knoll if you wanted. If you stand on the knoll, Doi Pahom Pok is the round-topped lump with rock formations above the trees that lies northeast of F2 and of the track we have just come in on.

Leaving our bikes with the Lahu-Lisu family, we set off on foot from F2 for Pahom Pok at 2.30pm (having started from Fang on the morning of that same day). Joy shouldered the two backpacks, tied together, our tent, his bag and his water container, and cut such an impressively macho look that we dubbed him 'Rambo', a nickname he liked, repeating it as 'Lambo' through his cheroot-stuck lips. If you walk 100 m away from the knoll and F2, back down the incoming trail, you can find the beginning of the footpath for Doi Pahom Pok heading north-east from a cement post (left side of trail). The path climbs steeply up through some great cloud-forest cover. The trees are covered with moss and dangling air roots, and horizontal lianas interconnect the trees like washing lines. When we were resting at length under an avocado tree, Rambo Joy said that Burma Army soldiers sometimes left their border camps, 7 kms away, to come walking around here on the flank of Pahom Pok – a reason perhaps to take a guide. They came hunting, and Joy pointed to evidence at the foot of the avocado tree that monkeys had recently visited the treetop. He also indicated the tracks of some kind of antelope creature, and said that long-tailed peacocks lived locally. As you climb up the side of the peak of Pahom Pok, you keep getting marvellous glimpses through the vegetation of the west-facing 'perpendicular scarp' that McCarthy talked about.

Swinging east-south-east, the path climbs up to a T-junction on a col, which we reached at ca 4pm or 1½ hrs out from F2. The way left goes, according to Joy, to the town of Muang Saat (Hsat) in Burma, while right is our way. After just a short distance, you branch rightish again, climbing now up the east side of Pahom Pok. The path emerges onto the exposed top of the Pahom Pok ridge and almost immediately, at 4.15pm, we are at the summit (1¾ hrs from F2, going gently).

Summit of Doi Pahom Pok

A sign on the summit says that the mountain is 2260 m high, or 7415 ft. Many maps give its altitude as 2285 m (7497 ft). Whichever, Doi Pahom Pok is Thailand's second-highest mountain. It is difficult to believe this, in view of how easy and effortless it is to climb. Another surprising thing is that, while a regular ant trail runs up Doi Intanon and while plenty of people climb Doi Chiang Dao, scarcely anybody, apparently, scales Pahom Pok. We found few traces of fires and almost no litter on the summit. The reason for this may be that, unlike Doi Chiang Dao, which is conspicuous, looks good, and is fairly accessible, Doi Pahom Pok is obscure and rather unimpressive (at least from the E side), is not easily accessed, and until recently was in the hands of various warlords and their private armies. Nevertheless, you can tell that you are high up by that certain starkness of the light and colours that you get on mountain peaks, the coolness of the air, the fact that all around you look down on everything, and the fact that you stand above that brown film of bad air that carpets the lowlands.

The summit is not pointed but domed, just as it appears from afar. Immediately to the west do indeed lie those celebrated precipitous cliffs. You can walk about on the top, and there are flat places in among the pervasive white-flowered bushes where you can pitch a tent. From the summit you can see considerable distances in all directions. To the west, of course, lies Burma. From Pahom Pok the eye travels across a valley with a quilt of forested low hills to an intermediate ridge with the white gash of a road running from south to north along its crest. The ridge is the Thai-Burmese border, and the road is the new border security road linking Doi Ang Karng with Doi Larng. At the time of writing this isolated road was closed and dangerous. No one should attempt to travel along it until it is released for public use by the military. I have given an account of this exciting 66-km-long dirt trail in my book *Around Lan-Na*. Beyond the intervening ridge lie the high ridges of the Burmese hinterland. Note the apparent absence of villages. Looking south (190°), you can see Fang. The lake you can see is a reservoir at Nong Pai. Doi Ang Karng and the village of Ban Khum lie at 230° on the ridge behind the one with the border road on it. At 250°, relatively close at hand, is F2, from where you start walking. At 70° lies Doi Larng, a flat pyramid with a white top. The town of Mae Ai lies in the direction of 130-140°.

The strange wooden platform-like structures dotted about on the summit ridge are for catching butterflies. People come up and sit on the structures trying to net the butterflies of a particular rare and valuable species. This species breeds on Pahom Pok around February and March, and collectors will pay, so Joy explained, between 100,000 and 200,000 baht for a perfect male and female pair of the lepidoptera. Our guide seemed unenthusiastic about the butterfly-catching pursuit and showed zero respect for the platforms that people had built when he started destroying one to get a pile of seasoned firewood for an evening fire later. Joy had assured us in Pu Muen that there was no problem with water on or near the summit, and, after we had put up our tent, we went with him in search of the two streams which lay 'about 20 minutes away'. We wanted a wash and also some water for brewing up tea and coffee. After hacking our way 20 minutes through the undergrowth, we came first to the one stream and then to the other, but both were dried up! While Joy went even further down the mountain, continuing the search for water, we climbed back up, arriving even more tired and dirty than when we had first arrived – a completely futile round trip of 40 minutes. Presently, when we had got a fire going and the light was failing, Joy arrived bearing enough water in the container – actually an old plastic canister for engine oil – to make drinks and noodle soup, but not enough to have a wash. I mention this story to forewarn you.

When we were standing around having supper by the fire, Joy, one of the most memorable trekking guides I have ever hired, talked copiously about this and that, while smoking up his cheroots. Three bald-headed eagles, so he knew, visited Doi Pahom Pok. The summit of the mountain was a commanding height, like Doi Larng, that had been occupied by and fought over by various forces, including Khun Sa, the Wa and the Burmese. This explained the numerous defensive trenches and protective tunnels that could be found all over the summit. The trenches are a hazard, as I found out to my cost. Taking a step back from the fire in the dark with a cup of hot coffee in my hand, I dropped straight into one of these overgrown trenches, to a depth of five feet, cutting and scalding myself. Incidentally, another hazard both on Pahom Pok and during the climb up are the swarms of bees and other biting insects – we all got bee stings. As a result of the fighting for Pahom Pok, 'Lambo' continued, hundreds of dead soldiers were lying around the summit. And below the cliff, in the forest, lay the remains of a Burmese helicopter that had crashed into the cliff. Of himself, this obliging chatterbox with typically Wa, black-brown skin said that he had been born in China of a Chinese father, who now lived in Xing Shoon or Mai Nong Bua, and a Wa mother, and had come down from Yunnan and the Wa State to the Thai border with the KMT (5th Army), which he had joined at the age of 10. Then he had served with the UWSA or 'Red Wa', moving all over the local area, before settling in the Lahu village of Pu Muen. He was 58 (in 1998), so he claimed, and had a daughter aged 33. He had a Lahu wife in Pu Muen and a Thai wife near Fang. And so the anecdote went on until we had had enough and went to the tent. Joy grew so excited and voluble that it seemed as if he must have taken some kind of stimulant. I thought it would be cold on the top of Pahom Pok during the night, but this was not the case, with a warm wind blowing up from the valley to the west, causing the tent walls to flap.

Route detail (homebound): Doi Pahom Pok summit – F2 – forestry HQ (F1) – Huai Ma Yom – Huai Bon – Fang
Our guide Joy said that it would be possible to trek (with him) some three days and two nights from Doi Pahom Pok to Doi Larng, passing no villages on the way – a tantalizing prospect, but one that would have to wait for a future trek. With the bikes waiting down at F2, we had leave Pahom Pok by the way we had come up. Retracing our steps, we took exactly an hour to get back down to the reforestation huts, and from there it was another 30 minutes riding back to F1, where we cooked up an early lunch, paid off Joy, and took our leave of him.

If you managed to bike up from Huai Pa Sang to Pu Muen, you will have had no problem scooting round to F2, and will have no trouble returning to Fang via Huai Bon (see Map 6). The way from F1 to Huai Bon and Fang (which, seen in reverse, is an alternative way of accessing Doi Pahom Pok) is all down hill on a dirt road in a much better state than the route up to Pu Muen. Owned by the forestry authorities down to Huai Ma Yom, the road off the mountain is not a public 'highway' and so is both little used and not abused by the public. It took us about one hour to bike from the forestry HQ down to Fang.

Leave the forestry HQ (km 0) by heading south-east past the pond and on out past a checkpoint/barrier and a sign. On a fair winding dirt surface you descend evenly through pleasant woods, go through a 'crossroads' (km 2.5), and eventually arrive at a barrier by a turning right (km 7.8) to Huai Bon cave monastery. The barrier (firmly locked when we passed it, but you can get round or under it on a bike), which is an anti-logging device, no doubt also marks the end of the jurisdiction of the forestry authorities and maybe signals the exit/entrance to Mae Nam Fang National Park. Not for beyond the barrier and turning lies the Lahu Nyi village of **Huai Ma Yom** (km 8.9), which is situated to the left side of the road. Entering hot, more open country back in the lowlands, you come next to a junction (km 11.5) by a reservoir (left). At the junction, which is also marked by six water tanks on the right side of the road, the way left goes to some orchards and houses. If you look back across the reservoir, you can see Pu Muen village high up. Just a short distance further comes the regular rural Thai village of **Huai Bon** (km 12.7), which is marked by various turnings left and right. Go straight a few hundred metres until you hit Fang bypass at a crossroads (km 13.3). If you have no further business in Fang, you can go left here for Mae Ai, Taton and Mae Salong, and right for Chiang Dao and Chiang Mai. To return to Fang, go straight through the crossroads and on some 4 kms (see Map 6), past two temples and various turnings right and left, to *UK Hotel* (km 17.2) and Fang town centre (ca km 17.5).

Exiting the trek

Exiting Doi Pahom Pok itself is part (the second part) of the loop trek Fang to Fang, and has just been described. From Fang you could exit the overall trek by proceeding north to Mae Salong (see Treks 1 & 2), or heading south 150 kms down the H107 road to Chiang Mai, perhaps stopping en route at the town of Chiang Dao, from where, after notching up Thailand's second-highest mountain, Doi Pahom Pok, you could 'knock off' the country's third-highest peak, impressive Doi Chiang Dao.

Trek 4

Climbing Doi Chiang Dao

Parameters

trekking mode:	on foot
trek time:	2 days/1 night; 6½ hrs of climbing on ascent, ca 4 hrs of climbing on descent
accessing time:	2 hours from Chiang Mai; 2 hours from Fang; ½ hr by motorcycle from Chiang Dao town; none from guest house in Tam village
exiting time:	1 day from summit of mountain; none from end of trek at guest house in Tam village; ½ hr from end of trek in Tam village to Chiang Dao town & 2 hours to Chiang Mai or Fang
degree of difficulty:	physically: tiring, but not difficult finding route: room for confusion
guide(s):	not essential
guide name(s):	Som
tent:	needed, or borrow from Som a plastic sheet to sleep under
map(s):	see 7

Overview

This meaty energetic trek climbs Doi Chiang Dao, at 2180 m (7150 ft) Thailand's third-highest mountain. Also known as 'Doi Luang' ('Great Mountain'), it is eclipsed heightwise in the country only by Doi Intanon and Doi Pahom Pok. In other respects, however, Mount Chiang Dao (*doi* = mountain), which lies in Chiang Dao Wildlife Sanctuary, may justifiably claim to be the Kingdom's or at least northern Thailand's premier peak. Where Doi Intanon and Doi Pahom Pok are rather unprepossessing domes topping off a larger lump, Chiang Dao mountain is a spectacular monolith rearing apparently sheer from the River Ping valley floor. It is that looming grey block, its summit frequently shrouded in cloud, which, when you motor north from Chiang Mai on Route 107, catches your eye just to the left (W) of the road beside Chiang Dao town. As you drive past, marvelling at the famous landmark, you ask yourself: Can it really be possible to climb up and stand on the top of that formidable, steep-sided sugarloaf? That was a question I often used to ask myself before, in March 1997, accompanied by Nittaya Tananchai and guided by Thai man Som, I first trekked up this monarch of a mountain, which you can scale too.

There are three ways to climb Doi Chiang Dao: an easy way, a steep way, and a normal way. For a reasonably fit *farang* or Westerner, the normal and steep ways both take two days and one night, while the easy way would take possibly three days and two nights. We went up the normal way and came down the steep way, making a loop, all of which took two days and one night, with the night spent just below the summit. The mountain is best climbed from the village of Tam, which lies a few kms west of Chiang Dao town at the foot of the peak, and it is from Ban Tam (*ban* = village, *tam* = cave) that the steep and normal ways start. There is a guest house in Tam village, which can be used as a base and starting point for the climb (more about accommodation below). Chiang Dao town on the main road could also be used as a jumping-off point for the trek, and it would make sense to stay there if you intended to go the roundabout easy way. I have not climbed Doi Chiang Dao taking the easy way and starting from Chiang Dao town, and so I cannot comment on this option. But that is not to neglect overmuch because the easy route joins the normal route about halfway up the ascent, after which they follow the same trail. The route detail below describes the trek done from the GH in Tam and, as said, going up the normal way and descending by the steep way.

Accessing the trek

Most travellers will no doubt access the trek from Chiang Mai. To do so, proceed by motorbike, jeep or bus 70 kms north from Chiang Mai up Route 107 to Chiang Dao. Buses for Chiang Dao leave regularly from Chiang Mai's northern Chang Puak bus station. If you do not have your own transport, and hence use the bus, take a *tuk-tuk* in Chiang Mai to the bus station, which lies about halfway up the Chang Puak Road, on the right, and board the first bus for Chiang Dao. With two- or four-wheeled transport of your own, allow about 1½ hrs to get up to Chiang Dao. The route passes through the chaotic little town of **Mae Rim** (km 15), the busy trading place of **Mae Ma Lai** (km 35), which marks the key turn-off west for Pai and distant Mae Hong Son, and the small town of **Mae Taeng**. Then it twists and turns through lychee orchards and wooded mountain country beside the River Ping, before emerging at Chiang Dao and its namesake mountain. Some trekkers might come from Fang to the north, perhaps having first climbed Doi Pahom Pok or 'done' the Mae Salong to Hin Taek trek. If you are coming to Chiang Dao from Fang by motorcycle, jeep or bus, allow a couple of hours for the drawn-out 80-km journey, which simply follows the H107 road south in the direction of Chiang Mai.

Once in Chiang Dao, you will need to turn off the H107 and head west on a small country road to Tam village and the guest house. The entrance to this side road lies at the top end of the town's main street, on the left side, diagonally opposite a restaurant and small petrol station. A sign at the junction points to 'Chiang Dao Cave'. Ban Tam lies about 5 kms up this road, and the GH can be found just beyond it at km 6.5 (see Map 7, diagram 1). If you have your own transport, the journey to the GH will take about 10 minutes. If you have come by bus, you will need to change in Chiang Dao onto one of the public-transport *silor (songtaew)* that serve the outlying villages. They used to gather at the northern end of the main street on the western side, not far from the turn-off. A few baht will get you at least as far as Tam village or Chiang Dao Cave, from where it is a short walk to the GH. Otherwise consider hitch-hiking or even walking – the distance is not great, and the way agreeable. The road heads straight towards Chiang Dao mountain, proceeding through a wood of tall trees and Tam village, which is named after the celebrated local cave system that burrows into the base of Doi Chiang Dao. Go past the cave complex, situated on the left (km 5.2), ignore a right turn for a monastery and a second right turn leading to another monastery and also Muang Khong, and proceed past a bizarre-looking Hindu meditation building (left) until you reach the GH (km 6.5), situated right, set back from the road. Beyond the GH the road continues a short distance until another *wat*, where there is another cave.

Accommodation & food
For many years there was no accommodation in Chiang Dao properly suited to traveller-trekkers' needs. You had to stay either in an old downmarket wooden hotel in the main street, or in a new upmarket hotel opposite the restaurant and fuel station already mentioned. But in 1997, while researching this trek, we discovered a pleasant new place to stay at Chiang Dao, albeit not in the town itself, but just west of Tam village, as indicated. It is the place that we are heading for, from where you can climb Doi Chiang Dao, and used to have the rather cumbersome name of *Malee's Nature Lovers' Bungalows*. This congenial, 'drugs-free', eco-conscious lodging, situated 6.5 kms from Chiang Dao on the far side of Ban Tam, could well have been rechristened meanwhile, so now readers should be prepared to spy out 'Malee's House', 'Malee's Bungalows' or some other similar title (the place is named after Malee, the lady owner). This GH is not only a convenient place from which to trek up Doi Chiang Dao, but is a pleasant base from which to make walks in the local wildlife sanctuary among the foothills of the mountain, do some birdwatching, or make motorcycle forays into the wider vicinity (for example, to the KMT village of Nong Ook, to the Karen village of Muang Khong, or to the far-flung Shan village of Wiang Haeng and the KMT outpost of Piang Luang). The GH has developed something of a reputation for birding. Not only does the wildlife sanctuary boast a wealth of birds, but birders have left at the GH their logs and details of the routes they have walked.

Nestling at the foot of Doi Chiang Dao, *Malee's House*, as I shall call it for convenience's sake, enjoys wonderful views of the mountain, especially in the early morning and towards nightfall. The accommodation, consisting of the main house and half a dozen bungalows, is set in an attractive garden with many shrubs and flowers. All the bungalows have their own bathroom and toilet, and guests can use the owner's hot shower by the house. The rooms are rather spartan, but clean. Nominally the bungalows are a relatively pricey 250+ baht per night, although, staying two or more nights, you should be able to bargain this down somewhat. There is a limited, slightly overpriced menu, and supper used to be served at the inclusive price of 60 baht. The owners do not mind if guests eat out in Chiang Dao or bring food back to the house. Judging by other people's bills in the room books, visitors can typically reckon here with a bill of up to 1000 baht or more, so this is not a place for haggling shoestring backpackers. Indeed, the owners are consciously setting higher prices in a bid to discourage penny-pinching travellers and to target those on a middle budget.

The new guest house was set up and is owned and run by Malee and her brother Som, both aged about 40. The round-faced, Chinese-looking pair hail from Bangkok, and they left the metropolis because they were tired of its pollution and wanted to lead a quieter greener life. Which is not to say that the house is devoid of modern technological conveniences – at Malee's you can watch BBC and CNN programmes via a satellite dish. Somewhere in the background is a German man Charlie, apparently Malee's former husband. While Som has some command of English, the breezy self-assured Malee speaks good English. Having been married to a German, she not only understands barbecues, but can knock up a fine *Kartoffelsalat*. Both brother and sister are pleasant and obliging, but, in keeping with Bangkok Chinese, they have an eye for business. If for some reason you need a sympathetic interpreter to accompany you on some mission, Malee is a person to speak to. Som guides people up Doi Chiang Dao and can be booked for other local walking or birding expeditions.

Chiang Dao & Doi Chiang Dao: background information
Two late 19th-century European travellers, the Irish surveyor James McCarthy and the British fact-finder Holt Hallett, have some interesting things to say about Chiang Dao town, its inhabitants, its mountain and cave. Arriving in 1890, McCarthy says: 'The road [from Chiang Mai] was not particularly interesting until we reached Chiang Dao, an irregularly shaped village, surrounded by a rickety palisade. The peak of Chiang Dao stands boldly up 7160 feet above sea level. This is a very imposing limestone rock, springing almost perpendicular to a height of 6000 feet above the plain. It is visible from Chiang Mai... In the matter of superstition, the inhabitants of Chiang Dao are unfortunate beyond most of their fellow countrymen. They themselves accept the current belief in evil spirits, and they are regarded by their neighbours as associated with spirits in such a manner as to be dangerous. They are known as *pi pawb* or "spirit people", and even their own headman, a minor prince from Chiang Mai, when obliged to hold official intercourse with them, recites a prayer to charm away the malevolence of the spirits.'

McCarthy was treading in the footsteps of Hallett, who passed through six years earlier, in 1884, during his 'thousand-mile journey by elephant in the Shan States'. Hallett writes: '...we continued through the rice plain for a couple of miles, and then, passing through the southern gate of the palisaded city of Kiang Dow [Chiang Dao], entered the city.' 'The city of Kiang Dow, which is barely a quarter of a mile square, is situated 37 miles from Zimmé [Chiang Mai] and is 1254 feet above sea level. The whole province contains only 250 houses, 75 of which are in the enclosure. The city is said to have been resettled in 1809 by seven householders from Ban Meh Lim [Mae Rim]... and was destroyed by Chao Paya Kolon, a Burmese Shan chief, in 1869 or 1870. On his retiring, it is said to have been at once reoccupied.'

Of Doi Chiang Dao Hallett says: 'It rises like the rock of Gibraltar straight up from the plain to five times the height of that rock, and can be seen on a clear day from the neighbourhood of Chiang Mai, 36 miles distant, looming up over the hills... Its crest towered up apparently to more than a mile above the plain, and we guessed its altitude to be 8000 feet above the sea.' He reports that 'a lake – Ang Sa Lome – is said to exist on the summit of Loi Kiang Dow [Doi Chiang Dao]' and that in this 'precipitous mountain... a monarch amongst the hills... is the entrance to the Dewahs' country [tae wa = fabulous spirit deities, angels], where the great genius Chow Pee Luang Kam Doang [Chao Pi Luang Kham Duang] resides, who is the guardian spirit of the Chiang Mai states.' The entrance to the Dewahs' country, Hallett narrates (and I paraphrase), is apparently a cave that exits in Doi Kat Pi, a spur of Doi Chiang Dao. Proceeding through the cave [manifestly Chiang Dao Cave] for several hundred yards, you come to a stream, beyond which is a gold image. No one without superabundant merit will get past the stream. 'A month's journey through the cave brings you to the Dewahs' country and the city of the Yaks, which is ruled over by Chow Pee Luang Kam Doang. There you have but to wish to obtain all you can desire...'

These days it is not the small district town of Chiang Dao, strung out along the main 107 road, that is of interest to the traveller, but its cave and, of course, its famous mountain. The cave is, actually, just one of several in the region. Most of them are attached to *wat* (monastery-temples), or, rather, there are a number of caves, around which temples and pagodas have been built. Chiang Dao Cave, the principal cave (at Tam village), merits a brief visit, perhaps as you make your way from town to *Malee's House*. The cave system extends many kms into the base of Doi Chiang Dao and is said to be largely unexplored. An interesting but little-known thing about this cave, in addition to the legend that Hallett recounts, is its connection with a Lawa treasure hoard. Thailand's ancient Lawa people (see my *Three Pagodas* for an account of the tribe), an aboriginal group who now live mostly north-east of Mae Sariang (they predate the Tai), have a legend that there used to be a book, complete with maps, telling where all the Lawa treasure is buried – buried presumably to hide it from either the Mon or the arriving conquering Tai or the invading Burmese. A Siamese king had then got hold of this inventory and hidden it. Unfortunately, he had then died, and the book had been lost for generations. Lawa rumour has it, however, that this book was found again not long ago in Chiang Dao cave...

Trekking strategy

To return to the three ways up Doi Chiang Dao mentioned earlier, we can say of them, more specifically, that the easy way approaches the mountain from the west, the steep from the east, and the normal from the north-west. The easy way is perhaps worth avoiding in that it adds an unnecessary third day to the trek (with all the extra logistical problems of more food and water) and also adds a thousand baht to the cost – this is what local *silor* drivers apparently charge to take you 30 kms via Mae Na (on the H107 south of Chiang Dao) to the out-of-the-way westerly starting point for the easy route. The steep way starts very near *Malee's House* in Tam village, but is a relentlessly steep climb lasting 5-7 hours, probably nearer 7. No actual climbing on rock faces or with ropes is involved, but you would need to be very tough and persistent to scale Doi Luang via this desperate route. The easterly steep route is the way to come down after you have ascended the mountain by the normal route. The normal route is a varied, steadily ascending way, lasting two days: the first day to climb to an overnight stop near the summit and perhaps also to reach the summit; the second day perhaps to reach the summit and then to descend via the steep route. Going the normal way, it took us (of average fitness) about 5 hours' walking to reach the overnight camp, plus one extra hour to get to the summit and another ½ hour to get back down to the tent site (altogether 6½ hours). Starting relatively late, we managed all this by nightfall. On the second shorter day it took us about 4 hours to get precipitously down to Tam. These indications include plentiful stopping times – the load is heavy and the heat intense. Camping is either in a tent in a clearing, or under a plastic sheet among some trees.

Concerning a guide or guides, you can trek up Doi Chiang Dao either with or without a guide. Obviously, we had to take a guide in order first to discover the route. But you, armed with what we discovered in the form of the route detail, diagrams and other information in this chapter, should be able to manage things on your own – at your own risk, of course. Or you may wish to take a guide or guides anyway, for company's sake. Som from *Malee's House* is prepared to guide trekkers to the summit and does so during the dry season on average about four times a month. He can find other guides locally if more are needed or if he is unavailable. In 1997 he charged us 500 baht for two people for the two days, i.e. 250 baht each for the trip and asks 200 baht per person for parties of five or so. This price excludes portering of baggage (you will have to carry your backpacks yourself unless you hire extra guides at an extra charge), but includes some food and is a very fair deal. Would you do two days of exhausting climbing and guiding work for £10? On top of his own baggage, Som will also help carry a small part of your load (the food, a plastic sheet, machete etc.). In addition, he will arrange at the Chiang Dao Wildlife Sanctuary HQ a pass for you to enter and trek in the sanctuary.

TREK 4: CLIMBING DOI CHIANG DAO

The option of you doing the trek without a guide I have cleared with Som and Malee. If you take this option, it is not as if you in conjunction with me are cheating Som of income. He and Malee have nothing against people doing the trek without their guidance. In fact, they prefer it that way. Som is tired of repeating the trek, is not so young any more, and the pair are really more interested in concentrating on running the guest house, which is anyway more lucrative. The Bangkok duo quickly saw that more people coming to trek 'Doi Luang' off their own bat would mean more guests at the house. If you climb the mountain on your own, get Som to arrange the pass for you with the Wildlife HQ, or organize it yourself the evening before you set off. The HQ is not far from *Malee's House*. Should you for some reason be refused entry to the sanctuary at the checkpoint, you can always get round the problem by doing the trek backwards, which avoids the checkpoint at the beginning – there is no control on the route starting at Tam. But that will mean grinding up the steep way! Of course, if you do the trek backwards – up the steep way and down the normal way – you will somehow have to read the notes backwards. A critical consideration when doing the trek on your own, unguided, is finding the place (1½-2 hrs on foot from the GH) where the path proper starts. There is room for confusion here. Unless you hitch a ride in a truck (as we did), with Som explaining to the driver exactly where you want to get off and start walking, consider paying Som to walk with you (he could even ride his motorbike while you walk) to the place where the summit path leaves the truck track.

A good time to climb Doi Chiang Dao is in February or March. It may be hot during the middle of the day, and in March there may be bush fires, but in these months it is not so cold for camping on the top – about 15° C in the night, according to Som. Early February is perhaps an ideal time because it is neither too hot nor too cold. The penalty for climbing towards the end of the dry season is that the air is hazy and the views imperfect for photography. On the two days we climbed, we saw not a single other walker. But it need not be like that. Doi Chiang Dao, because of its renown and eye-catching format, is a fairly popular climb with Thais. If you want to miss gaggles of slow-moving, chattering, partying, song-singing Siamese, avoid trekking the mountain at weekends and especially during Thai public holidays (above all over the Christmas/New Year period). As with all the treks in this book, it is not really advisable for one person to attempt Doi Chiang Dao on his or her own – you might get lost or have an accident. A little-known (hush-hush) fact is that there are numerous illegal poppy fields near the mountain's summit. Anything to do with narcotics is ticklish, so handle the situation cautiously and intelligently.

The single biggest problem with the Doi Chiang Dao trek is that there is not a drop of water *en route*. This means that, on top of your normal baggage (clothes, sleeping bag, tent, camera, food etc.), you have to carry enough water for two days of drinking, making tea and coffee, cooking and washing. You will need a minimum of 4 and a maximum of 6 litres, which will add the same number of kgs to the weight of your pack. Of all the treks in this book you will never be more heavily laden than when out on this expedition. When packing up, pare down your possessions to a minimum and contemplate not washing until you get back to the GH except to flannel your hands and face before going to sleep and after getting up. The trek is a fine exercise in rationing water over two days and a lesson in appreciating just what a precious commodity water can be!

Preparing for the trek
Get Som to organize permission/a pass to enter the wildlife sanctuary. If he is not guiding you to the summit, settle with him whether you want him to accompany you as far as the sanctuary checkpoint or as far as the place where the summit path starts out from the dirt road. Take a tent, and, if you do not have one, borrow Som's lightweight plastic tarpaulin. Buy between 4 and 6 litres of bottled water each in Tam village or at the GH, and discuss with Som the food question or what food to take in addition to what he provides. We particularly rejoiced in some Hershey bars and other high-energy chocolate, toffee and peanut sweeties we had brought along, bought out of the fridges in the stores along Chiang Dao's main street. If you are relying guideless on the notes below, remember to take your compass.

*

Trekking route detail (outbound): Guest house – wildlife sanctuary checkpoint – campsite below summit – summit of Doi Chiang Dao
From the back of *Malee's House*, go across some open ground to the beginning of the road for Muang Khong, or walk round from the front to the same via the Hindu meditation building and the 'main' road (see Map 7, diagram 1). The first 100 m of the Muang Khong side road are paved with cement. Almost immediately there is a junction. Straight on goes to Tam Paak Piang temple and cave, while left (our route) proceeds on rough dirt in the direction of Muang Khong. At this junction you could wait for a lift in a passing truck to take you to the start of the summit path, or you could start walking. We waited for a lift, and after more than an hour finally got one. If you walk this first part of the trek, past the sanctuary checkpoint, along the Muang Khong dirt road, to the start of the footpath, you will add an estimated 1½-2 hours of walking to the first day's trekking – a lot because the way to the summit will now involve at least 8 hrs of walking with fully laden backpacks. It makes sense to hitch-hike, or to start walking and hop into any passing truck. A problem is that most of the vehicles passing the junction go only as far as the sanctuary HQ and checkpoint, whereas what you need is a truck going either all or most of the way to Muang Khong, of which there are perhaps two or three a day. Enlist Som's help, if he not going with you, to get you started on the right foot. We got a lift in a pick-up truck, driven by Lisu people, that was going to Na Lao Mai, a Lisu village beyond the start of the summit path, but not as far as Muang Khong. We paid the driver 30 baht each. In the following record of our trek up Doi Chiang Dao by the normal way, the time log is cumulative for each day since starting out.

68

Time log	Ascent
Start/0 hrs	Set off in the back of the pick-up we had stopped at the start of the dirt road to Muang Khong, near *Malee's House* and Wat Tam Paak Piang. Truck bumps and splashes through half a dozen fords to wildlife sanctuary/*anuraak* checkpoint (estimated time thus far on foot: 30 mins).

Continue along dirt track through lovely jungle, skirting precipitous north side of Doi Chiang Dao, past a tooth outcrop on the right side.

Get off truck after about 40 minutes on a corner of the second paved section, on a flat piece of road, in a clearing (estimated time on foot since guest house: 1½ - 2 hours). We say goodbye to the dirt road now and start on the summit path. It is critical that you establish that you have alighted from any truck at the right place and that you have found the start of the right path. Double-check with the driver or anyone passing. If Som has walked or ridden with you to show you the beginning of the path, but goes no further, he will leave you here.

Set out on foot on a path going left (south) towards the mountain. Follow contour path, climbing slowly, with a view right to the Lisu village of Na Lao Mai on the other side of the valley.

Climb towards two pinnacles and go between them. After an hour's trekking since the dirt road:

1¾ hrs	Lunch near this little col. Surrounded by white-flowering trees, we eat the best meal of the trek: toasted bacon, tomato and cheese sandwiches that Som had brought! Break into precious water supply. 30-minute lunch stop.
2¼ hrs	Set off again down into a basin with numerous little forest fires. Pass through a mini karstic fairyland of grottos, pinnacles and roots, to reach after 45 mins since lunch a camping place (3 hrs), which is used by Thai people as the goal of their first day's trekking! Som tells us that Thai people trek at about half the speed of *farang*.
	Proceed out of the fairyland into an arena with three mountains towering right (= Saam Pinong or 'Three Peaks').
3¼ hrs	After 15 mins: cave visible in cliff at approximately 40°. Direction: heading broadly E now.

10 mins later our path is joined from the right by the path coming up the 'easy way' from its starting point 5 kms down in the valley. From this junction onwards, the 'easy' and 'normal' routes combine to form a single way to the summit (approaching from the west side of the mountain). Just to the left of the junction, in the direction of the cave in the cliff, is a camping spot which people trekking up the easy route use as their first overnight stop!

Head up scenic valley, lined on each side by mountains.

3¾ hrs	20 mins out from the junction, a trail of toilet paper beside the path leads to another camping place, just a clearing in the scrub.

Route goes E, veering left. Som promises us that we will see our destination peak in about an hour. The countryside takes on a more alpine look, with cooler air, although curiously all the ridges and peaks on every side are topped by palm trees silhouetted against the bright sky.

4¼ hrs   Half an hour later: another camping place – a nice one, flat and with fire sites.

4½ hrs   15 mins further, at 210°, in a crook in the ridge, in the lee of an outcrop: a poppy field. There are others nearby, higher up. They are invisible from lower down, even from an equivalent height, but emerge as you look down on them – more and more of them, cleverly tucked from view. We are surprised to find so many opium poppies on famous Doi Chiang Dao and relatively near to civilization. At the time of our trek, the poppies are broadly ready, many secreting opium resin from their pods. They do not all become ready together, but are staggered (as now) still green, some in flower, and some with pods and their telltale triple incisions. The fields belong to the Lisu of Na Lao. We wonder aloud that the authorities must know that these poppies are here, but do not destroy them, and learn that the wildlife sanctuary officials are in cahoots with the Lisu. They tell the anti-narcotics authorities that there is nothing up here and receive a kickback.

At the head of the valley, facing cliffs, veer left.

4¾ hrs   Another quarter hour later: view S – various poppy fields visible.

After veering left, path continues up steeply, before bearing right into cool primaeval jungle. Among the moss-covered trees, air roots and parasitic plants, this is a possible overnight camping place, from which the summit can be climbed. Som advised us against camping on the top of Doi Chiang Dao itself, as the summit is exposed and can be very windy. There is no wood on the summit, either, for making a fire to cook food or boil water. However, you could conceivably sleep up there to watch the sunrise if you had a serious sleeping bag.

5¾ hrs   Proceed down from and out of jungle copse to emerge at clearing, overnight camping place and crucial dividing of the ways (see Map 7, diagram 2).

Orientation from campsite clearing:
30°:   Summit of Doi Chiang Dao now plainly visible – a big rounded lump, like the back of a tortoise, glowing in the teatime sun!
50°:   Path going to summit
140°:   Path going off right, steep uphill to big camping place, then steep downhill to Tam village (is our way off Doi Chiang Dao or, in reverse, the steep way up the mountain)
290°:   Path by which we have come

Hiding our backpacks in the trees by the clearing, we set off for the summit late afternoon. Route approaches summit from east side. Just below top: wild roses and primrose-type flowers.

6¾ hrs   One hr after arrival at overnight camp and about 6½ hrs of trekking since getting out of the Lisu truck: reach summit of Doi Chiang Dao.

TREK 4: CLIMBING DOI CHIANG DAO

Summit of Doi Chiang Dao

The top of Doi Chiang Dao, at 2180 m (7150 ft) Thailand's third-highest mountain, is a mixture of tufted grass, limestone rock and low scrub. Much more so than on the summit of Doi Pahom Pok, you really get the impression here of being elevated, actually on a mountain top, on top of the world. The summit is exposed, falls away on all sides, and enjoys magnificent views down valleys and of neighbouring peaks.

Orientation:
250°:   Saam Pinong (Three Peaks), impressive
290°:   Pyramid Mountain
         All these peaks seem higher than Doi Luang – an illusion?
150°:   Yellow flag on ridge crest, which drops almost sheer
         down to Chiang Dao Cave and Tam village
300°:   Big poppy field (in 1997)
South: Three big, bright green poppy fields (in 1997)

It is evident from the summit and also from the trek up that Doi Chiang Dao is not the monolithic lump apparent from the H107 road as you approach Chiang Dao town going north from Chiang Mai, but is a complex of dispersed peaks, rather like an upturned molar tooth. We spent half an hour on the summit drinking in the view while the sun lowered, casting long shadows in a soft light, and then hurried down 30 minutes from the summit back to the campsite before nightfall. Assuming you return on the second day to Ban Tam via the steep route, there is time before setting off for another visit to the summit.

If you have a tent, pitch it somewhere in the clearing. If not, and you or Som has brought along his 3 x 3-m plastic awning, hoist the makeshift canopy over one of the sleeping places among the trees by the clearing, tying the corners to branches or propping them up with long sticks, as appropriate. In the trees, you will see two or three sites where generations of trekkers have bedded down for the night. Each one has a fire or hearth at its centre, around which on three or four sides people stretch out on level patches. Clear out any rubbish and old bedding left by previous walkers, and from around the clearing cut some swatches of elephant grass to lie on. Cover the grasses with plastic sheeting, and later lie on this around the hearth area in a sleeping bag. Get a fire going for tea, cooking, illumination, creature comfort, warding off animals... How much water have you got left for day two?

At the beginning of March, sleeping on that occasion not in a tent but under Som's tarpaulin, we had a pleasant, if long, not too cold night around a flickering fire, just below the summit. Sleeping wild like this so high up is a fun experience in itself. There were no other campers, but animals made noises in the surrounding undergrowth.

Route detail (homebound): Campsite – Tam village – guest house

As indicated earlier, there is time to visit or make a repeat visit to the summit on the morning of Day 2 of the trek, providing that you get up there early and that you leave Doi Chiang Dao by the quick steep route.

Time log	Descent
Start/0 hrs	After breakfasting and packing up camp, set off along the path leaving the clearing to the 'right', as you look at Doi Chiang Dao (see Map 7, diagram 2). Almost at once, making a small detour from the path, fork left and proceed 2 mins to Lisu poppy fields. A nice feature of these fields is that they are backgrounded by Doi Luang summit, making an impressive sight and photo. Our guide Som once saw a king cobra by these poppy fields!
	After 15 mins set off again, either backtracking to the path or breaking through the trees to pick up the path a bit further along.
20 mins	A camping place. Fork right into woods (follow the litter!), and climb steeply uphill a short distance to reach:
40 mins	Crest of ridge. Right goes uphill to a big camping site and lots of rubbish. Left, our route, descends steeply and continuously through shady jungle, past a custard apple tree, whose fruit is scattered all over the ground, and banana palms.
1¾ hrs	Emerge into sunny clearing, then into a second clearing, and pass through a jungle wilderness of bizarrely weather-sculpted limestone rocks 6-12 ft high.
2 hrs	About halfway down.
2¼ hrs	In a bamboo forest we find a resting place with benches and a table. It is for slowcoach Thai tourists coming up. A welcome breeze causes the massive *mai huak* bamboos to strain and creak like the rigging of an old galleon.
3 hrs	30-minute lunch stop at some wayside bamboo seating.
3½ hrs	With almost no water left, set off again. It is difficult not to run-walk down through the bamboos and woods.
3¾ hrs	First view of valley floor and houses in middle distance.
	Little path joins from left. On left: rusty wildlife sanctuary sign on post. (NB: if you are doing the trek in reverse, coming up this steep way, go left at this sign, taking the main path.)
	Enter orchards and flatter terrain.
4 hrs	Deserted tin-roof shack. Voluptuous scent of blossom on orchard grapefruit trees.
	Path develops into truck track.
	First house left.
	Another house left, numbered 234/5.
4 hrs 5 mins	Track hits main street of Tam village at T-junction. Go left to walk back to *Malee's House*. Between the junction and a metal-railed concrete bridge 100 m away, there is a shop selling noodle soup and most welcome icy soft drinks.

TREK 4: CLIMBING DOI CHIANG DAO

(For anyone doing this trek in reverse, you can identify the turn-off from Ban Tam's main street by locating the concrete bridge with its metal railings and nearby dam system, proceeding 100 m away from Chiang Dao Cave complex in the direction of Chiang Dao, and turning right into a side alley situated between a chalet-style house left and three houses right, the house on the corner being numbered 198/5.)

4½ hrs   Walk along road past cave complex 1.5 kms back to *Malee's* – and a barbecue with potato salad??!!

Exiting the trek

To exit the trek from the GH, ride or hitch-hike or walk the 6.5 kms past Chiang Dao Cave and through Tam village back to Chiang Dao. At a T-junction you hit the main H107 road. Left (north) goes a couple of hours or 80 kms to Fang, from where you could climb Thailand's second-highest mountain, Doi Pahom Pok (see Trek 3), and right (south) proceeds through the centre of Chiang Dao 70 kms or 1½ hrs by bus and bike to Chiang Mai.

Part 2a

Treks 5-8: In Nan province, east of Nan town
near the Thai-Lao border
ultimately based on Nan town

5-7: three treks launched from Mae Sa Nan village
8: launched from Sa Wang

Trek 5

Mae Sa Nan – Mae Sa Nan waterfall – River Wa – 'Sandy Cove' campsite – Nam Nae – Mae Sa Nan

Parameters

trekking mode:	on foot
core trek time:	1½ days/1 night; ca 6¼ hrs of jungle trekking
accessing time:	from Nan town to Mae Sa Nan village 2 hrs by motorcycle or half a day by a combination of public transport and hitch-hiking
exiting time:	from Mae Sa Nan to Nan town 2 hrs by motorcycle or half a day by a combination of hitch-hiking and public transport
overall trek time:	from Nan to Nan 2-3 days
degree of difficulty:	a bit tricky in places, a mini Rambo trek!
guide(s):	helpful but not essential
guide name(s):	Wan & Yook (see photo section)
tent:	required
map(s):	see 8 & 9

Overview & strategy

Here is a juicy little introduction to genuine jungle trekking that will soon have you marvelling, but also perspiring and cursing – a first taste of the real thing. Heading up 13 treks in undiscovered Nan province and 3 treks from the Lua (Htin) village of Mae Sa Nan, it clips the western edge of a wilderness area of remote mountains and jungle that I like to call the 'Empty Quarter', on account of the fact that it is uninhabited, almost all of its villages having been moved out. The Empty Quarter forms part of Nan province's Doi Pu Kha National Park, specifically the south-eastern section that lies east of Nan town and abutting the Lao border. The trek (see Map 9, diagram 2) goes from the forestry station at Mae Sa Nan south-west down the Sa Nan river to Mae Sa Nan waterfall and on to where the Sa Nan river flows into the River Wa. From the confluence it strikes north to clamber along the western bank of the Wa river to a campsite in a sandy cove, where a night is spent by the river. On Day 2 the route continues north a short distance until the Nam Nae (Nae stream), where it strikes west and south, following the Nam Nae upstream, to return to Mae Sa Nan village and the forestry office.

TREK IT YOURSELF IN NORTHERN THAILAND

The trek, therefore, forms a loop. In December 1998, when I went round it with Nittaya Tananchai and Doug Boynton, we took about 5 hrs to get from the starting point at the forestry station to the overnight campsite, and a further 1½ hrs to get from the campsite back to Mae Sa Nan, making some 6½ hrs altogether, which includes stops for resting and lunch. On Day 1, starting from the forestry place at around 9am, we reached the campsite at 2pm. In view of this early arrival, and of the fact that the loop can be done in ca 6½ hrs, it would be possible to do the trek within one day, not bothering to spend a night camping by the River Wa (instead, returning late afternoon, you would have stay in Mae Sa Nan). This option might appeal to people not interested in camping out in the jungle or to solo trekkers unaccompanied by guides who are nervous about tenting in the jungle on their own, but who can nevertheless relish an adventurous daytime 'walk'.

For the less ambitious, the trek can be truncated or modified in other ways, too. Thus you could walk from Mae Sa Nan village to the waterfall and return the same way to the village, a ca 2-hr round trip that could even be done as part of a day outing from Nan town (assuming you have a hire motorbike). Or you could push on from the waterfall to the confluence of the Sa Nan and Wa rivers and likewise retrace your steps to Mae Sa Nan village, either merely stopping for a picnic at the confluence, or even tenting overnight there (see route detail below for outbound timings). A very soft option would be to start out on the trek, but going the other way round. Thus you could walk an easy hour from Mae Sa Nan village down the Nae stream to the River Wa, turn right (S), and continue 10 mins down the W bank of the Wa to 'Sandy Cove', where you could either have a picnic lunch, returning to the village the same day (as part of a day outing by motorbike from Nan), or camp overnight, the next day likewise returning to Mae Sa Nan.

Going down one river (the Mae Sa Nan), up the bank of another (the Wa), and up a third (the Nam Nae), this is basically a flat trek, involving no mountain climbing. However, with the route following the Sa Nan down a steep-sided valley full of boulders and ledges, and following the Wa similarly up a V-shaped valley, the trip does involve quite a lot of clambering over rocks. As anyone will know who has negotiated jungle streams and rivers, this can be much more arduous, filthy and annoying work than you might at first suppose. The rocks are often slimy and lethally slippery, and all kinds of roots, branches and thorns along the way conspire to snag and frustrate you. You will certainly get your feet and boots wet on this trek, as will become apparent almost at the outset. The most difficult part of the trip is perhaps between Mae Sa Nan waterfall and the Wa river, the next most difficult is along the Wa, and the easiest is from the Wa up the Nam Nae back to Mae Sa Nan. So, if you can manage the first part, the rest should be a piece of cake for you. But I do not want to exaggerate the severity. If we, average folks, can do it, so can you. It is a short adventure with a small 'Rambo' element in it. Because it is not long, is not so difficult, and does not venture so far from civilization, it makes a good jungle trek for travellers new to this kind of thing to cut their teeth on.

TREK 5: MAE SA NAN – NAM NAE

It is not essential to take a guide or guides with you on this trek. Because the route follows three rivers, you can hardly get lost. Sometimes, especially in the central section, going along the bank of the River Wa, you may lose the path. But it is only a matter of hunting around before you find it again. The direction is clear: keep going up the river. Occasionally in this central section the path surprises you by suddenly climbing high up overhead. Be prepared for that – it is usually to avoid a small cliff that falls straight into the river. Nowhere in the central part does the path cross to the other (eastern) side of the River Wa. Of course, with no guides, and having to carry your backpack yourself as well as find the way, your trekking times could be slower than indicated above. But you have got all day on Day 1 to get to the campsite. The advantages of taking one or more guides, besides the fact that they can porter your luggage and lead the way, is that they can help you if some mishap occurs, can prepare the campsite and make a fire, and can provide you with a feeling of security as you sleep in the jungle night-time darkness, surrounded by wild animals and hunters. It is also interesting to watch how these local jungle-attuned tribals operate out in the wild, how they fish, hunt, cook, eat and sleep, to observe their junglecraft.

In Mae Sa Nan we hired two guides between three of us, making a party of five. We had intended to engage Nit and Kham, two Lua guides we had hired in the village twice before, but they were unavailable, so we took on two others, who were collared for us by Nit. One was the 17-year-old boy Yook, Nit's son-in-law. The other was 33-year-old Wan, a man with a square Karen-type face and outline beard, who, it transpired, ten days before we engaged him, had caught malaria while out hunting in the Empty Quarter – a salutary reminder of the malaria danger lurking in the jungle and of the need to take precautions against it after dark. Both Wan and Yook said that they were prepared to guide other trekkers coming after us, i.e. you! We paid them 200 baht per day each, with them carrying our backpacks, which for a short 1½ days worked out at 300 baht per guide, or 600 altogether for the trip (a measly £10 in 1999, borne by the three of us).

Accessing the trek (Map 8)

Undoubtedly travellers will tackle Trek 5, as well as the two others starting from Mae Sa Nan (Treks 6 & 7), using Nan town and its guest houses as their main base. To get from Nan town to Mae Sa Nan, the forward base or jumping-off point for the three treks, will take a couple of hours if you have your own transport, and up to half a day or longer if you do not. The village lies 58 kms away from Nan in an out-of-the-way area reached by little-used backwoods roads. With your own hire bike or jeep, in Nan town centre cross the bridge over the River Nan and almost immediately turn left into the H1169 road (see Map 8). This leads out through several suburban villages, in places along the east bank of the Nan river, of which there are some nice glimpses, to a small ridge. The road crosses the ridge, passing through the village of Kiu Muang on the top, before descending to a crossroads, marked by a checkpoint and small fuel station. Here you have two options. Go straight across if you want to press straight on for Mae Sa Nan. A shortcut road takes you through more rural villages to the H1257, where at a T-junction you go left for Mae Sa Nan. Otherwise, at the crossroads turn right. You enter a cluster of villages which are the site of *ampoe* Santisuk or Santisuk district. Down here, after a school situated on the right side, but before a hospital on the left, there is a popular noodle soup shop, where many drivers break their journey. Why not stop, too, and have an early lunch? The last time we rode this way it took us 50 mins to get from Nan to the noodle place, riding two up on a Honda Dream. Continue a short distance beyond the noodle shop and turn left at the junction (34 kms out from Nan) on the outskirts of Si Boon Ruang village. Now head roughly north through the three outlying villages of Don Klang (or Don Glua), Pong (where the first way joins from the left at a junction), and Si Na Man. The H1257 road climbs up to bring you into marvellous upland scenery. As if on a roller coaster, you dip and dive, and twist and turn through giant trees, before plunging steeply down to the Hmong village of Don Prai Wan in a valley, and then climbing just as steeply up to the turn-off for Mae Sa Nan (right side of road, near km marker-stone 23, i.e. 23 kms out from the Si Boon Ruang junction, and 57 from Nan). Now leave the 1257 tarred road and plunge 1.3 kms down the dirt access road to Mae Sa Nan village (see Map 9, diagram 1). The last time we rode from the Santisuk noodle place to Mae Sa Nan, it took us another 50 mins to add to the 50 taken to get to Santisuk.

Getting to Mae Sa Nan without your own motorbike or jeep is more problematic and time-consuming, because there is no public transport that will take you all the way. So you will have to mix public transport and hitch-hiking. But it is entirely possible – I did it once (it took about 3 hrs), and on the occasion when we came to do the trek under discussion our friend Doug, using a *silor* and hitch-hiking while we travelled by bike, arrived in Mae Sa Nan before we did! From the site of the evening market in the centre of Nan (quasi opposite the *Dheveraj Hotel*), take a blue public-transport *silor* to Santisuk (ca 25 baht per person) and get off as far down the main street as possible – the driver will probably put you down by the noodle soup stall just mentioned. From here hitch-hike or walk the short distance to the Si Boon Ruang junction, and turn left to hitch-hike up the H1257 road to Mae Sa Nan (see Map 8). It is too far (24 kms) to walk from this junction to Mae Sa Nan, so you will have to get a lift. With luck you can team up with a driver eating his lunch at the noodle soup place. At the turn-off for Mae Sa Nan (right side of road, near km marker-stone 23) abandon your lift and walk 1.3 kms down the dirt access road to Mae Sa Nan, lying in a valley.

Accommodation & food
Assuming you undertake this trek as we did it, following the route detail below and not modifying anything, things will pan out like this: you make your way from Nan to Mae Sa Nan on the day before the trek, arriving in

the afternoon to give you time to look around the village, find somewhere to stay, and possibly engage a guide or guides; you stay overnight in Mae Sa Nan; you set off the next day and camp by the River Wa at 'Sandy Cove'; and you return to Mae Sa Nan the following morning, after which you return to Nan. That would mean that the overall trek lasts the best part of three days and two nights, including accessing and exiting time.

In Mae Sa Nan you have various accommodation possibilities. The village is well represented in terms of government agencies together with all their respective buildings, implying rich possibilities for an overnight stay. For example, there is a big new health centre (where you could undoubtedly put up in a room), a school, and an extensive forestry station. If you can get no sense out of the health officials, teachers or forestry workers, you could simply pitch a tent on the grass by the weaving project, or apply to the headman (*pu yai baan*), who is called Wat, or enlist the help of our Lua guiding friend Nit (see photo section), whose house lies close to the weaving project. But easily the best thing to do is go to the forestry complex, which can be found at the south-western end of Mae Sa Nan, beyond the school, up on a hill. This forestry station, where we have stayed several times, is possibly the most extensive and luxurious to be found anywhere in northern Thailand. Its numerous buildings, set off in model gardens, include a show office, a guest suite for visiting officials, offices, kitchen, eating-out balcony, bedroom block, workers' quarters, nurseries and sheds. Trekkers are welcome to stay here, and can do so free of charge. They are so welcome that in December 1998, when we last came to the forestry, researching Trek 5, a woman gardener lamented: "We're longing for *farang* to come, but none have come since your last visit, a year ago."

At the forestry HQ you can either pitch a tent, or stay in one of the buildings. In the winter of 1998, we put up our tents in an idyllic spot in the model gardens right in among the flowering plants, bushes and trees. It was on the manicured grass at the very top of the forestry station hill, roughly behind the cookhouse and the boss' quarters. Up here, there are grand views in both directions, north and south, although in the morning your tent can be dripping from a heavy overnight dew. Regarding staying in the buildings (where you should use a mosquito net), it is hit and miss what kind of room you will be offered. If the boss or deputy boss is present (the former is often away in Chiang Mai), you can find yourself allocated the VIP suite, but if you are given a room by one of the junior officials, you can end up in a scruffy workers' shack. Staying once in the guest suite, better than any guest house, we were flabbergasted to find wickerwork furniture, mattresses and bedding, a drinks cabinet, and in the bathroom a full complement of gleaming enamelware, complete with towels, toilet paper, toothbrushes and even toothpaste. If you stay on the grass in your tent, you will find that the officials unlock this bathroom and allow you to use it.

Concerning food, there are no restaurants or noodle soup places in Mae Sa Nan (this is a poor Lua village), and it is not even possible to buy food at a shop, although you might be able to pick up some packets of instant noodles. There are some half dozen shops in the village, but they are mostly hidden away inside people's houses, and sell virtually nothing, in 1999 not even soft drinks ("Nobody buys them or can afford to buy them"), and so you must bring all your own food with you to Mae Sa Nan. Stock up in the supermarkets of Nan with everything you will need for a night in the village and for the trek. At the forestry complex you may find that the workers offer you some of their food – they eat their breakfast and supper on the balcony by the cookhouse. You can reciprocate by offering them some of what you have brought. You will find that they throw open the kitchen and its facilities for your use, and here you can boil water in a kettle on a gas ring, make noodle soup and coffee, borrow bowls, cups and cutlery, and wash up. Don't wait for anyone to organize you here – just get stuck in yourself.

Mae Sa Nan
Mae Sa Nan (the 'Nan' is pronounced 'naan' or 'nahn'), which is also graced with the official Thai name of Rat Pattana, is a village inhabited by Lua people (or 'Htin' people, as they are also sometimes, inappropriately, called), about whom more will be said in a moment. The village is quite a dispersed place, lying at the bottom of a hot little valley and surrounded by the low Doi Khun Mae Sa Nan mountains. It takes its name from the small Sa Nan river (*mae* = river) that runs down the valley, and which we walk down on our trek. The village houses and main street likewise follow the valley, on a north-east/south-west axis. About 150 dwellings – a mixture of primitive and somewhat developed – house 500 people, who first enjoyed the benefits of electricity as late as December 1997. If you can find them, there are, as said, half a dozen poorly provisioned shops dotted around Mae Sa Nan. A couple lie near the entrance, and a third, which has petrol and sometimes whisky, belongs to headman Wat. The Lua inhabitants of this obscure settlement have always struck us as handsome and friendly, if astonished. They look like Wa folk, some of the men sporting chintuft beards, even full beards. These are ex-CPT (Communist Party of Thailand) people, having surrendered to the Thai authorities as late as 1984, and former headman Som is a witness to the fighting between the CPT's People's Liberation Army of Thailand (PLAT) and the Thai military: he has a wooden leg. Impoverished, the people of Mae Sa Nan do a lot of hunting and fishing in the rich jungle and rivers east of their village. Twenty elephants used to live locally, and hunters here have said that across the 'Empty Quarter', on the Lao side of the border mountains, tigers still roam.

An interesting feature of the village is a ruined temple and pagoda, evidently Burmese (the locals refer to it as a *wat maan* or Burmese temple), which lies on a knoll behind the big new health centre. The Burmese ruin is one of a pair in the locality, for there is another one in the nearby Lua village of Huai Loi. Some mystery attaches to the age of the ruins and to how two Burmese *wat* and *chedi* should come to be positioned here, in such an obscure easterly part of Thailand, so far away from westerly Burma. It is possible that the ruins date back to the time of the Burmese occupation of northern Thailand (ca 1558-1800), or the original temples and pagodas could have been built towards the end of the occupation, when the Burmese were campaigning against territory not far east of Nan in Laos. But the ruins might date back only to the late 19th and early 20th centuries, when Burmese merchants, involved in the timber trade in northern Thailand, and especially in Nan, became rich and, wishing to make merit, erected temples all over. What looks like a well beside the ruined foundations of the Mae Sa Nan temple is in fact the base of a pagoda, its top missing. The top was destroyed and the 'well' dug when a *farang* once came by, excavating and raiding.

The Lua people: brief background information

I have provided an in-depth account of the Lua people, their history and culture in my book *Around Lan-Na* (1999) and so I do not propose to repeat it in full here, which would in any case be inappropriate in a trekking guide, except to give just some outline information so that trekkers have an idea of who they are encountering when they come to Mae Sa Nan and truck with Lua guides. I provide a thumbnail sketch also because more than half the treks in this book are among the Lua and with Lua guides.

The Lua are possibly the most obscure, neglected, underresearched and poorly understood of all Thailand's highland peoples. Unlike, say, the colourfully attired Akha or 'exotic' 'long-neck' Padaung tribe, they figure hardly at all in the consciousness of tourists and do not exactly loom large in the minds of ethnologists, Thai officialdom, state and foreign welfare organizers, and missionaries. There are several reasons for this. One is that the Lua do not wear any eye-catching traditional costume. In fact, they wear no tribal costume at all, and in this sense are indistinguishable from local lowlanders or *khon muang*. It is not known, and the Lua themselves do not know, if they ever wore a tribal costume and, if they did, what it looked like. In the old days the men used to wear loincloths, but then so did many other people. Occasionally you see old Lua women wearing hand-woven tube skirts and bolero jackets with horizontal banding and lozenge designs, but to my mind this costume has simply been borrowed from local Tai Lue people.

Another reason for the obscurity of the Lua is that in Thailand they are only to be found in one out-of-the-way pocket, which is the north-eastern corner of Nan province. Here they live in the mountains of Doi Pu Kha National Park and on the west-facing flank of the Thai-Lao border ridge. In Laos more Lua live in Sayaburi province (opposite Nan province) on the east-facing flank of the same border ridge. A third reason is that the Lua are a conservative and profoundly enigmatic people who reveal little of themselves and are hard to get to know. This is in keeping with their behaviour and demeanour. Typically when you enter one of their villages, especially a more isolated one, you find that they tend not to approach you and greet you, but keep their distance, peeping and staring at you from behind a tree, a window, or a half-closed door. What can they be afraid of? With the Lua you sometimes get the impression that they are in a world of their own. As for their outward appearance, they often look despondent, seemingly suffering from low self-esteem. It is as if they not only know that they are at the bottom of Thailand's social pile and feel inferior especially relative to the Thais, but also know that they are an ancient people who have fallen on hard times, who are in decline, an entropic people who perhaps dimly intimate that once, long ago, they had a grander past – an idea which has some foundation, as we shall see.

The Lua in Thailand probably crossed from Laos in the late 19th and early 20th centuries as a result of unrest in Laos. However, whether they originated in the territory of present-day Laos or in that of Thailand (or, indeed in that of both) is unclear. Compelling arguments suggest that the Lua might be indigenous to Thailand (or to Thailand and beyond), for they once belonged arguably to a widespread civilized aboriginal folk (an *Urvolk*) that included today's Wa and Lawa peoples and which lived all over 'Thailand' (or in Thailand and the wider area). This aboriginal folk was then split into three some thousand years ago by Tai people migrating southward from China, who came to settle in and dominate 'Thailand'. They pushed the three sundered parts of the *Urvolk* out into marginal mountainous areas, where each went into decline. Thus one part was squeezed north to the meagre terrain of today's Wa State in Burma, where it became the Wa, another was forced into the mountainous hinterland west of Chiang Mai, where it became the Lawa, and the third was pushed east into the mountains of the Nan area, where it became the Lua. On this reading the Lua would, indeed, be an ancient people that have declined from a once much more glorious position.

And ethnologically, linguistically and physically the Lua are related to the Wa and the Lawa. Within the Austro-Asiatic or Austronesian family of peoples, they belong to the Mon-Khmer branch, which also includes the Wa, the Lawa, the Khmu, Mrabri, Mon and other peoples. Like these other Mon-Khmer tribes, they are short stocky mountain peasant people with the strikingly dark skin pigmentation that is characteristic of Wa-related tribes, and angular facial features and a hairiness that is quite uncharacteristic of smooth-skinned Mongoloid, Sinitic or Siamese peoples such as the Tai, Chinese, Hmong, Yao and Akha.

There is no real or satisfactory ethnonym for the Lua. Apparently, they have no name for themselves, and the name 'Htin', which is often applied to them, and which has crept into the guide books, is a Thai invention, which the Lua find derogatory and do not use. In the absence of a proper ethnonym, 'Lua' is the best name for them – they use this name themselves to refer to themselves vis-à-vis the outside world, and it is a name that the Thais also traditionally use to refer to the Lua, Wa and Lawa. The Lua in Thailand number perhaps 25-30,000 people, accounting for some 4-5% of the country's hill-tribe populace, making the Lua one of its least numerous groups. They have their own language (no written form), and all Lua also speak Thai in the form of the northern Thai dialect. The Lua, as said, wear no tribal costume. They are renowned hunters and are famous for the utensils – baskets and cylindrical sticky rice boxes – which they weave out of bamboo and which feature dark geometrical patterning. The Lua are champion tipplers of home-distilled *lao kao* or rice whisky, as anyone will find out who stays in one of their villages.

Disregarding the Mrabri, the Lua are undoubtedly the poorest of Thailand's minority groups. Most live in grinding poverty. They do not have enough fields to support their growing numbers foodwise, and the soil is poor and overused. A typical meal for them is sticky rice, chilli dip or powder, perhaps a dried fish, and some boiled or raw vegetable. They have received comparatively little in the way of hill-tribe welfare programs, royal projects, and aid from state or foreign organizations, although this picture is at last changing with the advent of health centres and weaving projects in some villages. As said, this is because of their obscurity as a group, the remoteness of their location, their low profile, and their reserve and modesty. But it is also because they are not recent 'exotic' immigrants, but are poor mountain farmers who, from the point of view of Nan people and officials, have always been there and who have traditionally been looked down upon. Another reason is that most of the Lua of Nan, finding themselves neglected by the state and having nothing to lose, sided with the CPT during the insurgency, incurring the wrath of the authorities. During the communist insurgency in the 1960s, 70s and 80s in Thailand, and in the wake of the 1975 communist takeover in Laos, the lives of all Lua were seriously disrupted, further exacerbating their plight.

The Lua are animists, not Buddhists, and both Buddhist monks and Christian missionaries have had minimal impact on them. They live in fairly sturdy houses constructed of wood and bamboo, and raised on stilts. Lua society is village-based. The village is for Lua people the highest social unit, and they have no tribal consciousness, just as there are no Lua leaders with power over a group of villages or an area. In fact the Lua are hardly a tribe at all, but a number of more less autonomous villages. Lua villages and society are characterized by fragmentation and heterogeneity, a fission that is reflected in their language, where dialectal differences exist even between neighbouring villages.

Preparing for the trek
As always, ensure that you start with your water bottle full of fresh water. Either decant into your water bottle good water from plastic bottles you have brought from Nan, or at the forestry office boil up some good water, preferably doing so the night before you start, so that the water has time to cool down overnight.

*

Trekking route detail (outbound): Mae Sa Nan – waterfall – River Wa – 'Sandy Cove' campsite

Time log

Start/0 hrs	Set off from forestry complex, proceeding downhill in a south-westerly direction. After about 400 m you come to a small stream. Cross it, bearing left (the way right goes to Don Prai Wan), and continue another 800 m or so to arrive at the bottom of a steep hill. (If you have come this far on a motorcycle, perhaps because you are going only as far as the waterfall or the River Wa, intending to return the same way, you will have to park your machine here – often you will see other bikes parked nearby in the bushes.)
¼ hr	Go straight up the brown track of this hill, avoiding a fork right.
20 mins	You come to the Mae Sa Nan river (actually just a stream here). Cross and recross it, following the path. It is hopeless trying to keep your boots dry by taking them off and walking barefoot through the water. There are too many crossings and they will get wet anyway. So just splash right through. Continue to follow path down the valley through grasses and bamboos.
½ hr	Pick up the river again, already slightly larger and beginning now to flow through rocks. Henceforth river and path are intertwined. Find a way through, passing a big boulder midstream and a drinking spring in the form of a bamboo conduit (left). If there is no school, children from Mae Sa Nan village can often be found paddling and crabbing down here.
	At a bend in the river keep to left side of valley, making use of a kind of rock ledge.
¾ hr	You come to a small fall and a bigger fall, which is **Mae Sa Nan waterfall**. Go past it on the right side, taking care. A log has been put in place to allow you to clamber across a small cliff face, and there are roots to hold on to. The fall is best viewed from lower down.
	The next stretch, a 50-minute clamber downstream and downvalley to the River Wa, is the most taxing section of the trek, with a couple of distinctly tricky places. The guides will help you if you have brought some along. Take it easy. If you don't feel like Rambo yet, you will now! I find it difficult to describe the stretch because every time I come down here the vegetation and path have changed. Find a way through to arrive, hot and sweaty, at the confluence of the Sa Nan river and the:
1 hr 35 mins	**River Wa**, flowing from left to right (roughly north to south). To the right, the Wa flows off through a defile, while left it presents a typical profile of the Wa river – altogether my favourite river in northern Thailand. Look at the far bank: you are right in the jungle here! On the left (north) side of the confluence, there is a sandy place with bushes, where you could pitch a tent if you wanted to stop here, go no further, and backtrack to Mae Sa Nan.

1¾ hrs   After a 10-minute rest (if you started out at 9am, it will be about 11 now), set off left (north) along the left (west) bank of the River Wa, which for the first few bends is rocky, after which is flatter and sandier. It is another 3 hrs to the 'Sandy Cove' campsite (or another 3¼ hrs to the Nam Nae).

Initially the path climbs up from the river, contours, and then descends to hug the water's edge. Along here, on some banks of red-brown mud, I found swarms of primrose yellow butterflies alighting to lick minerals. Continue thus for nearly an hour until a shelter, where you could make a:

2 hrs 35 mins Lunch stop, lasting 35 mins.

3 hrs 10 mins Set off again after lunch.

3½ hrs   Across the river is **Huai Din Kuen** (= earth-moving stream). Here, on the far bank, the Din Kuen stream flows into the Wa. Just a trickle in the dry season, this can be a raging torrent in the rainy season, tossing russet boulders and earth (which is how it gets its name) down to the confluence. In early 1996 the confluence was an open expanse of such boulders, but in early 1999 the bare avalanche had become completely overgrown with bushes and vegetation, making Din Kuen almost unrecognizable – proof of how the scenery can quickly and dramatically change in tropical climes.

ca 3¾ hrs   A few minutes later, diagonally opposite Din Kuen (on our side of the Wa), a path climbs steeply up left. In fact it crosses a ridge and leads 1¼ hrs to Mae Sa Nan village. It would be possible here to abort the trek and return directly to Mae Sa Nan, making a shorter loop. This path and Din Kuen is where the route of this trek (5) intersects with that of the trek from Mae Sa Nan to Sa Wang (Trek 7), for during the first leg of the latter 'Empty Quarter' expedition the way comes down this path to the Wa, crosses the Wa to Din Kuen, and heads off up the Huai Din Kuen towards the Nam Miang, the Nam Mao, and Sa Wang.

All along here, on the far bank of the Wa, there is super jungle.

We walk on a more regular path now beside a more tranquil Wa. Pass through cool woods. The path climbs up away from the river, and goes down and up.

4 hrs 20 mins I come now to the only critical, weak and confusing spot in the route detail of this trek. Our guides, having led us away from the Wa (perhaps to circumvent a precipitous headland), had to correct the deviation by bringing us back to the river. They did this by striking right from the main path and descending 10 mins down a dried-up streambed to the Wa. If you cannot find the exact streambed, cut through right and make your way back down to the river. (If you continue along the main path, so the guides told us, you will come to the Nam Nae.)

4 ½ hrs   Back down by the River Wa, rapids can be heard nearby. Continue upstream along the river bank. Before the rapids, you climb for a short distance across a precipitous piece of valleyside to arrive at the rapids on a bend in the river and a cove with a sandy 'beach', which I have dubbed:

4¾ hrs   **'Sandy Cove'**, where you can camp overnight. If you set off from the forestry office in Mae Sa Nan at about 9am, it should now be, assuming all has gone to plan, about 2pm, time to relax, and have a swim-wash in the river. In many respects Sandy Cove campsite could hardly be bettered. The river purls over the rapids with a rushing sound, and the cove is ringed around by a wall of tumbling jungle. At the northern end, there is a little promontory which makes a nice viewing point. The soft sand of the raised sloping 'beach', which the guides levelled for us in a couple of places and cleared of plants so we could pitch our tents, is comfortable to sleep on, conforming to the body like a waterbed. Dry driftwood lies around for making a fire. But the site has a downside. The fine pink-brown sand gets everywhere, into your tent, sleeping bag, shoes and food, making everything filthy. And we had trouble getting a frog out of our tent!

Trekking route detail (homebound): 'Sandy Cove' campsite – Nam Nae – Mae Sa Nan

Time log

Start/0 hrs   The guides had said that there was a difficult passage just after the campsite, but when we climbed past the little promontory, we found nothing much worse than a scramble on a steep slope through thorn bushes, after which, almost immediately, we arrived at:

10 mins   **Nam Nae** or, rather, the confluence of the Nae stream and the River Wa. Although it was still well before 9am, we found here quite a gathering of Lua people from Mae Sa Nan, including a man who was landing several sacks of grain from a bamboo raft, which he had punted up- or downriver from a field somewhere. We chatted to them a bit, which may have distorted my timings.
Go left (broadly north-west) up the Nam Nae. We passed many more Lua coming down to the Wa.

40 mins   A drinking spring (left).

1 hr 5 mins   About an hour after leaving the campsite, swing south, leaving the Nam Nae to pick up a cart track, which ascends gradually and continues to Mae Sa Nan.

1 hr 15 mins   Reach first houses, headman's house, phone booth, little wooden bridge and main street of Mae Sa Nan village. Go left.

1 hr 25 mins   Arrive back at forestry complex. If you set off from 'Sandy Cove' at 8.30am, you should be back here by 10.

Exiting the trek

When you exit this trek or any of the treks from Mae Sa Nan, you will probably want to return to Nan town to get cleaned up and properly fed, and so exiting is the same as accessing, except in reverse. Climb from the village 1.3 kms back up to the 'main' road, turn left, and either ride or hitch-hike through Don Prai Wan down the H1257 road in the direction of Santisuk (see Map 8). If you are riding, cut right in the village of Pong through to the crossroads, go straight across, and follow the H1169 back to Nan. The 58-km trip should take you less than 2 hrs. If you are hitch-hiking – be prepared for a wait at the beginning – turn right either in Pong or, depending on what your lift is doing, at the latest at the junction in Si Boon Ruang. Then make your way respectively to the crossroads near Santisuk and the fuel station (see Map 8). From here either hitch-hike or take a public-transport *silor* along the H1169 road to Nan. Allow between 3 hours and half a day for the trip.

Trek 6

Mae Sa Nan – Nam Nae – Huai Dua – Mae Sa Nan

Parameters

trekking mode: on foot

core trek time: 1½ days/1 night; ca 6 hrs of jungle trekking (3 hrs out and 3 hrs back)

accessing time: from Nan town to Mae Sa Nan village 2 hrs by motorcycle or half a day by a combination of public transport and hitch-hiking

exiting time: from Mae Sa Nan to Nan town 2 hrs by motorcycle or half a day by a combination of hitch-hiking and public transport

overall trek time: from Nan to Nan, including access and exiting times, 2-3 days

degree of difficulty: moderately difficult, a semi-Rambo trek!

guide(s): helpful, but not essential

guide name(s): Nit & Kham, or Wan & Yook (see photo section)

tent: required

map(s): see 8 & 9

Overview & strategy

This modest but beautiful and rather tough little trek, the second to start from the Lua village of Mae Sa Nan, leads not to a mountain summit or waterfall or village, but to the Dua stream, specifically to the place where the Huai Dua flows into the River Wa. Like Trek 5, it takes the trekker into the western edge of that remote uninhabited area of mountainous jungle east of Nan town and adjacent to the Lao border which I like to term the 'Empty Quarter'. Because the trip visits not a feature but just a spot in nature, the fun of this trek is mainly in the actual trekking and also in camping out in the jungle.

Like Trek 5, this is a flat, not a hilly, expedition, following the courses of rivers and streams (see Map 9, diagram 2). From Mae Sa Nan, the trek strikes broadly north-east to hit the Nam Nae (Nae river or stream), goes east down the Nae to where the Nae flows into the River Wa, and goes north along the west bank of the Wa to where the Huai Dua flows into the Wa on the opposite east bank of the Wa. Unlike Trek 5, it does not form a loop – the way back is the same as the way out. It would be possible to extend or truncate the trek. You could extend it by crossing the River Wa and exploring up the rocky jungle-bound Dua stream, perhaps doing so from your campsite at the Wa/Dua confluence. I have not done this and so cannot comment on it, but, to judge by the view up the Dua from the confluence, it must certainly be an adventure. Such an extension would perhaps add another day and a second night to the outing. You could truncate the trek by going only as far as the confluence of the Nae and the Wa. This soft option might appeal to less ambitious sould who want to make an easy hourlong stroll from Mae Sa Nan down to the River Wa (plus an hour back), but who do not want to camp out in the jungle or get themselves filthy from scrambling. It could be done as part of a day trip out by motorbike from Nan to Mae Sa Nan, perhaps incorporating a picnic by the Wa at the Wa/Nae confluence or at nearby 'Sandy Cove' (see Trek 5).

I did this trek in late March 1997 with Nittaya Tananchai. It took us 3 hrs to reach Huai Dua from Mae Sa Nan (one hr down to the Wa, and two along the Wa to Huai Dua), and about the same amount of time back. Our strategy was as follows. We went from Nan to Mae Sa Nan in the afternoon of Day 1; stayed overnight at the forestry complex in Mae Sa Nan; went from the village to Huai Dua on the morning of Day 2; lazed in the afternoon of Day 2 and spent the second night camping at Huai Dua; and on Day 3 trekked back to Mae Sa Nan in the morning, returning to Nan in the afternoon. This is doing things in a leisurely way, and it would be possible to do the trek in two days or even in one. You could bike from Nan to Mae Sa Nan by mid-morning, take an early lunch in the village and/or look for guides, go to Huai Dua in the afternoon, camp overnight there, and return to Mae Sa Nan and Nan the next day. Or, making an early start and travelling light (no tent or backpacks), you might be able to squeeze everything into one day, skipping along the Wa to arrive at lunchtime at Huai Dua, and skipping back to Mae Sa Nan village by teatime, to ride back to Nan by early evening (if you run out of time, you could stay overnight in Mae Sa Nan).

The slow part of the trek is along the Wa river bank from the Nae stream to Huai Dua. The reason for this is that progressively you are obliged to clamber over rocks. In one place, just before the goal of Huai Dua, there is a short alarming stretch, where you have to edge your way on bamboo poles across a cliff face high above the Wa. When people in Mae Sa Nan learned that we were intending to go to Huai Dua, they all remarked 'quite difficult' and 'you have to walk along the side of a cliff'. We were inclined not to believe them, but for a brief moment it is true. Accordingly, although the trek is short, it requires some persistence. This, combined with the fact that the scrambling is through jungle, merits Trek 6 the grading of moderately difficult and semi-'Rambo' in style. Incidentally, nowhere does the path cross to the other side of the Wa, but sometimes it unexpectedly climbs high up from the water's edge to avoid an obstacle. Be prepared for that, and if you find no way forward, consider going up and around.

It would be possible to do this trek without guides. The way is clear, and the distance is not great. If you went alone (never completely alone, but as an unguided group of two or three), you would undoubtedly have a real unalloyed jungle experience, although you would need strong nerves. You would be very much on your own because Huai Dua is a lonely spot which even the local Lua do not much frequent. Factors counting against going unguided are all the usual ones: you would have no one to carry your backpack and tent in the sultry heat, no one to help you over giant slabs of rock or past the tricky places, no one to prepare a tenting spot for you (slashing down vegetation, cutting palm fronds for underbedding), no one to gather wood and make a fire, no one to help in the case of an emergency or accident, and no one to provide security. You would also miss out on the interesting company that local guides make, as well as on the thing that I enjoy most in these situations – observing their junglecraft. On this trek we took along Lua guiding friends Nit and Kham (see photo section, and see Trek 7 under Nam Miang for a thumbnail sketch of this duo), whom we also hired to accompany us on Trek 7 to Sa Wang, but you could also engage Wan and Yook of Trek 5. All four live in Mae Sa Nan. We paid Nit and Kham 300 baht each for the trip (about 1½ days' work for them), which included their carrying all our baggage except cameras and water bottles. If this seems like not much money for a lot of hard work, remember that by local standards it is a fair wage and that from the perspective of Lua boys it is pay for an easy trip out, during which they can do a spot of fishing and shooting – a hunting expedition they would make anyway!

Accessing the trek, accommodation & food, background information on Mae Sa Nan & the Lua people, and preparing for the trek: see Trek 5.

*

Trekking route detail: Mae Sa Nan – Nam Nae / River Wa – Huai Dua

Time log

Start/0 hrs   In the north-eastern part of Mae Sa Nan village go east, away from the main street, over a wooden bridge, past a phone box, past the headman's house (on a bend, right), and follow the track out past some outlying houses, heading approximately NE.

Where the track enters an open area, which is the valley of the Nam Nae, go right (E), either climbing a little hill or following the Nae downstream. It does not matter which – the two ways meet. We followed the Nam Nae.

Cross and recross the river, and bear right, continuing to follow the Nae downstream. In the small river we found some Lua girls fishing for frogs and water beetles. When we asked them why they wanted the black beetles, they replied that they would curry them!

Both the track and the river swing south.

Follow the cart track.

35 mins   Right: a drinking spring.

Shortly before a tin-roofed hut, branch left onto a path which goes down to the River Nae again.

Keeping the hut on your right, cross the river and climb over a small hill. (If at this juncture you get lost, it does not matter. Follow the Nae somehow until it flows into the Wa river and turn left. All we are doing is cutting off a corner.)

For some time the path slices through bamboos, crossing an open piece of hillside, which is a field for growing crops.

Press on until you hear the rushing sound of the River Wa.

1 hr   River Wa, flowing left to right (approximately north-east to south-west). Time for a 5-minute rest beside this superlative jungle river. There is great swimming all along this stretch of the Wa, swimming in pure jungle surroundings – what more could you want?

Proceed left, upstream, along the west bank of the Wa.

In two or three spots we found Lua men sawing up *mai tien* trees into planks for house-building, the red-brown wood giving off a lovely savoury smell.

Clamber along rocks, past two rapids. Both sides of the Wa are steep and lushly covered with trees and vegetation. If you lose the path, in some places indistinct, you will find it again by trial and error. If you go the wrong way, you will immediately come to a bit where you can go no further. Mostly there is only one route along this steep narrow river bank. Sometimes, unexpectedly, the path climbs high up.

High up, negotiate bamboo bridges acting as ledges across gaps.

A couple of sandbank 'coves', which could be used as campsites.

The further you go, the more climbing there is. If you are losing heart because of the strenuous rock clambering, take comfort from the fact that the mountain now visible in the middle distance, at the 'head' of the river, is the goal.

Pass a rocky headland.

2 hrs 35 mins Rapids and a little bamboo shelter. Time for another rest.

The sting in the tail: just before the end of the trek comes the most difficult and (for non-mountaineers) slightly alarming section. For a short distance the path climbs high up (perhaps 50 m), and you edge your way along a rock and earth ledge, with the hillside beneath your feet plunging almost vertically into the river. But don't worry, and don't look down. With your camera swinging round your neck and insects bothering your face and arms, there are roots you can hold on to for dear life.

3 hrs   Almost immediately the path descends to a flat area opposite the mini-confluence where on the far eastern bank of the Wa the Huai Dua flows into the Wa – the goal of the trek. The flat area is suitable, but not perfect, for camping. It is imperfect both because of swarms of aggressive flies, diminutive jungle bees and mosquitoes, and because it is not easy to get to the water's edge just here. If you find the tent site inadequate, consider backtracking a bit, or wade across the Wa to the mouth of the Dua (about waist-deep, slippery rounded stones, keep away from the rapid) and go right on the opposite bank to an open flat area, marked by a small hut, which offers an alternative tenting site.

Setting off from Mae Sa Nan at 9am, we arrived at Huai Dua at midday. In late March it was very hot and humid down on the Wa river bank. After the exertions of the trek, especially of the final 'hairy' bit, the sweat was pouring off our faces. We had lunch and then all dozed until 4pm in the shade of overhanging trees. We tucked into bread and tinned tuna salad, as well as packet soup boiled over a wood fire. With interest we watched our guides set about getting their lunch. They had brought nothing except the wherewithal to acquire their food and a lump of cooked sticky rice, wrapped in muslin. They followed a familiar pattern practised many times. The domestic Kham got a fire going and fashioned fat bamboo tubes for boiling river water in. Nit cut two long thin bamboo poles, got out a fishing net, and trawled the river for fish. He soon had three or four. On his way back to camp, he gathered up some greens, roots and herbs growing wild. Adding a stock cube solicited from us, the two guides boiled all these ingredients up in the bamboo tubes, fashioned bowls and spoons out of banana leaves, and then ate the Wa fish soup, supplemented with rice – a tasty meal provided free by the jungle.

After our nap, we explored the immediate vicinity and went for a swim-cum-wash. A hundred metres upstream, around a corner, we found a one-man raft moored by the river bank. On a half-dried mudflat myriads of fabulous butterflies had alighted to suck minerals. Some were of outsize dimensions, with iridescent green wings and turquoise patches; others were similarly large, but in black and white. Yet other smaller butterflies were coloured cochineal red, deep violet, or ochre. This stretch of the Wa is an isolated lonesome spot. In two days we saw no one outside our party of four. People did not go to Huai Dua, Nit explained, except occasionally to hunt. It is a tract of jungle you can have all to yourself. As indicated earlier, it is possible to push on up the Dua streambed to a waterfall and hunting area, which would extend the trek by another three hours (six there and back, i.e. by another day), but, looking up this dark, sinister, dank, jungle-enclosed ravine, we had little appetite on this occasion. It seemed like an all-out Rambo adventure.

Washing in the Wa, we got bitten many times by the killer midget bees, and, swimming in the deep emerald pool by the Dua confluence, I could not banish from my mind the spectre of water snakes. My unease was justified because, no sooner had I finished my swim, than we saw a five-foot snake enter the water just upstream by our camp, swim diagonally across to the far side, and look for a place to slither up the bank, after which it disappeared in a sunny clearing. We reported the snake to the guides, who immediately got excited. Nit grabbed his stovepipe hunting gun, took the one-man raft, and went after it, punting to the sunlit clearing, where for a while he searched around for the serpent. Alas, he did not find it, and it was fish stew again for the Lua boys for supper.

Kham again showed his caring touch when it became time to put up the tent and bed down. With his machete he levelled the ground and then fetched ferns and banana leaves for us to lie on. Bedtime is early and the nights are long in places like Huai Dua. Because of the swarms of deadly malarial mosquitoes, you cannot easily sit out under the stars, and so we soon turned in to nip surreptitiously at a 'flattie' of Regency (Thai brandy), which is a nice comforter to take along on treks like these. The two Lua boys slept all night around the fire, uncovered and unprotected.

Trekking route detail (homebound): Huai Dua – Nam Nae – Mae Sa Nan

On the return journey, simply backtrack along the outbound route. Follow the path for about 1½ hrs back down the River Wa (the bad bit does not seem quite so alarming a second time, does it?) and turn right onto the little short-cut path by a large boulder, where you can hear the rushing sound of the Wa. It does not matter if you miss the turning – you will continue to the confluence of the Wa and the Nam Nae, where you should go right and follow the Nae upstream in a broadly north-westerly direction (as in the latter part of Trek 5), linking up with the short cut.

From the large boulder or the Wa/Nae confluence, it is about an hour back to Mae Sa Nan.

Pass the drinking spring on the left side.

Swing south, leaving the Nam Nae to pick up a cart track, which ascends gradually and continues to Mae Sa Nan.

Reach first houses, headman's house on corner, phone booth, little wooden bridge and main street of Mae Sa Nan village. Go left to arrive back at village centre and, beyond it, the forestry complex.

Exiting the trek: see Trek 5.

Trek 7

Through the 'Empty Quarter'

Mae Sa Nan – River Wa / Huai Din Kuen – Huai Miang – Nam Mao – Kiu Lom ('Windy Col') – Sa Wang

Parameters

trekking mode:	on foot
core trek time:	3 days/2 nights
accessing time:	from Nan town to Mae Sa Nan village half a day by a combination of public transport and hitch-hiking
exiting time:	from Sa Wang to Nan via Nam Duang, Nam Poon and Mae Charim a minimum of half a day hitch-hiking
overall trek time:	from Nan to Nan, including access and exiting times, 4-5 days
degree of difficulty:	difficult, a full-scale Rambo trek!
guide(s):	impossible without guides
guide name(s):	Nit & Kham (see photo section)
tent:	required
map(s):	see 8, 9, 10, 11 & 12

Overview

This substantial jungle trek runs on a north-west/south-east axis from the Lua (Htin) village of Mae Sa Nan to the Lua village of Sa Wang. It passes clean through the heart of a remote area that I like to call the 'Empty Quarter'. This is an area of magnificent mountainous jungle – forming a south-eastern portion of Nan's Doi Pu Kha National Park – which lies east of Nan town and adjacent to the Lao border. The quarter is empty because no one lives in it any more, all the villages that once existed there having been moved out in a twin bid to create and preserve this part of the National Park and also to neutralize the Lua and Hmong CPT guerrillas who operated in the area both during Thailand's communist insurgency and even after it was over. The trek is a long exhausting 'Rambo' expedition, not to be underestimated. The core part of it is 3 days of walking and scrambling, to which can be added the best part of a day at each end for accessing and exiting from and to Nan. The trek involves climbing over four ridges in

94

succession, at the same time crossing three rivers (the River Wa, the Huai Miang and the Nam Mao), which lie in the valleys between these ridges. It can be seen that the trip is not a pleasant flat stroll down valleys or along ridge crests, but means repeatedly plunging down and up – a dispiriting business. Even the fleet-of-foot local Lua (some of whom, travelling light, can do the stretch in 10 hrs!) curse this route as 'all up and down', avoiding it wherever possible, which they can now easily do by taking the very circuitous road route via Si Boon Ruang, Mae Charim, Nam Poon and Nam Duang.

The existence of this alternative road route means that the direct cross-country way linking Mae Sa Nan and Sa Wang is now little used, either by Mae Sa Nan Lua going to Sa Wang or by Sa Wang Lua coming to Mae Sa Nan. The upshot of this is that the path, which until recently used to be a regular one, is growing over and in some places has already disappeared, as my party found when we trekked it. This is especially true in the central section, where the guides sometimes had to slash a way through (by contrast the end sections, near Mae Sa Nan and Sa Wang, are well-trodden by people out hunting or getting wood). As the years go by, this situation will worsen, the path becoming ever more overgrown and indistinct, and ultimately it might prove impossible to find anyone willing to guide trekkers along it.

I did this trek at the end of January 1996 in the company of Nittaya Tananchai and guided by two Lua friends from Mae Sa Nan, Nit and Kham. I believe that at that time I was the first *farang* traveller to trek through here, and I may still be (has anyone else meanwhile done it?). A sign of this, and also of the scope of the expedition, was that when we emerged at Sa Wang, we provoked considerable amazement among the Lua inhabitants there, as well as among some Thai soldiers and officials stationed in Sa Wang and Nam Duang. This jungle trek remained my most ambitious one until the subsequent Huai Pla Jaad trip (Trek 8) and then the 'Elephant Trail' trip (Trek 24). In my book *Around Lan-Na* I have given a written-up, anecdotal account of the 'Empty Quarter' trek, to which the reader is referred for more background and incidental information. The best time to do this trek is late January or early February – at that time it is not too cold at night. On no account attempt to do it in the rainy season. Even if you could get across the River Wa, the other rivers would be raging torrents, your blood would be sucked dry by leeches, and you would be eaten alive by malarial mosquitoes.

Strategy & accessing the trek

Undoubtedly you will start this trek from Nan town, likewise ending it there. If you execute it as we did (not necessarily the best way), things will pan out as follows. On Day 1 of the overall trek, you go from Nan to Mae Sa Nan. For details of how to access Mae Sa Nan (as well as information on food and accommodation in the village, on the village itself, and on the Lua people) see under Trek 5. Given that you will end up in Sa Wang, far away from Mae Sa Nan, and that you will exit the trek at Sa Wang by heading back to Nan town, there is no point in going to Mae Sa Nan by motorcycle. If you do so, you will have to return after about 4 days to Mae Sa Nan to retrieve it, which is a long and awkward journey by road, involving a series of hops by *silor* and hitch-hiked lifts. So you will have to access Mae Sa Nan by public transport and hitch-hiking. An ideal arrangement would be to have some third party who could deliver you to Mae Sa Nan, pick you and the guides up from Sa Wang or Nam Duang, and deliver you to Nan, while the guides were transported back to Mae Sa Nan. This problem of motorbikes stranded at the start and guides stranded at the goal is a perennial one afflicting all longer non-loop treks, and there is rarely any easy solution to it.

Arriving in Mae Sa Nan by mid-afternoon, you familiarize yourself with the village, find somewhere to stay, and organize guides. Ideally, and this is what I try to do ahead of all longer treks, you should make a preparatory visit by motorbike to Mae Sa Nan to sound out and book guides in advance. Stay overnight in Mae Sa Nan, and bright and early on Day 2 start the trek, climbing over the first ridge, crossing the River Wa, and crossing the second ridge, to arrive at the Huai Miang (Miang stream), where you camp overnight in the jungle. Starting from Mae Sa Nan at 9.15am (too late), we arrived at Huai Miang at 3.30pm. On Day 3 you climb over the third ridge, reach the Nam Mao (Mao river), where you have lunch, cross it, and climb a long way up the fourth ridge, the biggest one, to reach Kiu Lom or 'Windy Col', where you spend a second night tenting out. Starting at 8.45am, we reached Windy Col campsite at 6.45pm in darkness, a mismanagement of time and of the second day's trekking that needs rectifying (see below). On Day 4 of the overall outing (third day trekking) you continue to the summit of the great fourth ridge, then gradually descend to Sa Wang. Starting from Windy Col at 9am, we arrived in Sa Wang at 12.45pm. With the afternoon unaccounted for, you have several options. You could either relax in Sa Wang, spend a fourth night there, and exit to Nan on Day 5; or you could walk or hitch-hike from Sa Wang to nearby Nam Duang, where you could likewise spend another night, exiting to Nan the next day; or you could try to exit to Nan during the rest of Day 4, which could be accomplished if you were pretty lucky with lifts. From Nam Duang to Nan is 87 kms, and from remote Sa Wang it is getting on for 100 kms. After Nam Duang you pass through Nam Poon, Na Sia, Mae Charim and Na Bua, and you reach Nan by going past Wat Pratat Chae Haeng (see Map 12). There are more details on exiting the trek below.

On the second day of trekking (from Huai Miang to Windy Col) we both utterly exhausted ourselves by going too far too fast in one day, and ended up trekking in the jungle in pitch darkness, a foolish and risky thing to do, irrespective of the difficulty of putting up a tent and hunting for water in the dark. A better management both of time and of this part of the trek would be to stop on the second day of trekking at Nam Mao at lunchtime and spend the afternoon as well as a night there. Nam Mao marks the midpoint of the trek and is very beautiful. It is much more suitable for camping overnight than either Huai Miang or Windy Col, the two places at which we did camp. Huai Miang is cramped, gloomy and damp, although otherwise alright as a campsite. But Windy Col is not really a suitable place to camp. There is almost no water there, it is indeed windy, and it is already too near Sa Wang. If you camped at Nam Mao, you could spend the third day of trekking climbing over the great fourth ridge in its entirety in a leisurely way, which would mean that you could cut out staying at Windy Col altogether and that you would arrive in Sa Wang not, somewhat unsatisfactorily, in the middle of the day, but, more satisfactorily, late afternoon. Then you could spend a night in Sa Wang relaxing at the end of the trek, and exit to Nan the next day.

The overall trek could be better organized too. I say this at the risk of annoying readers, who will now think that they are being presented with inferior route details and will ask: Why not give us the better way of doing the trek at the outset? But it is difficult to see the best way of doing a trek before you have done it, easy to see the best strategy in retrospect, and I doubt if I will ever do this trek again, in any form. Thus, if I *were* ever to repeat the 'Empty Quarter' trip, I would do the whole thing in reverse, from Sa Wang to Mae Sa Nan. Further, I would first pick up the guides from Mae Sa Nan and take them to Sa Wang. This would have three distinct advantages. First, in going broadly from south to north, you are not marching all day into the sun. Rather the sun is behind you, illuminating the landscape in front of you (nicer to look at and better for photography). Second, at the finish of the expedition the guides would end up in their home village, not in some other village from where they must then find their way home. And third, from the trekker's point of view it is easier to exit from Mae Sa Nan than from out-on-a-limb Sa Wang and Nam Duang.

If desired, the Empty Quarter trek could be truncated or even extended. Modest trekkers could confine themselves to the very first part of the trek, climbing over the first ridge on the doorstep of Mae Sa Nan, and going as far as the River Wa (about 1¼ hrs, and the same back). They could stop for a picnic or a swim there perhaps as part of a day trip out by hire motorcycle from Nan. Trekkers with a crazy appetite for even more adventure than is already on offer could make side trips from the main route to take in Huai Pla Jaad waterfall (the subject of Trek 8) and/or Pu Fa mountain, both of which detours would add at least an extra day to the overall trek.

Trekkers should on no account attempt this expedition on their own. One or more guides is essential (note that these guides, like all the guides in this book, are not official, trained, registered guides, but – far better – just local men hired on the spot to guide unofficially). Without guidance you will almost certainly get lost. As said, the trail has been obliterated in places. That was in 1996. By now it will be even less clear. There is a danger of straying into Laos. The Empty Quarter used until very recently to be territory in which guerrillas roamed and hid out: residual pockets of Lua CPT insurgents and of royalist, anti-Patet Lao Hmong rebels loyal to Vang

Pao. The Lua communist rebels of Sa Wang only laid down their arms as late as 1990. At New Year 1995/96 a group of 50 of the former gave themselves up to the authorities at Sob Mang, not far from Mae Sa Nan, and in early January 1996 Nam Duang was once more closed to outsiders because fighting had flared up locally yet again between the Vang Pao Hmong and the Lao Army (we missed the skirmishing by days). All would seem to be quiet now on both counts, probably definitively, and in 1998 Nam Duang, which in the past had been completely forbidden to outsiders, and which was then sometimes restricted and sometimes derestricted, was thrown open to outsiders, apparently for good. Even if you are unlikely to encounter insurgents (whose sentiments are in any case not directed against the likes of you and me), you may very well come across dubious individuals or even criminals, who like to hang out in remote jungle. Local guides can act as a buffer or interface between you and such people. In 1996, during our Empty Quarter trek, we ran into a gang of no less than 35 men on a thieving raid in these depths of the National Park!

As our guides we hired Nit (also known as Taan) and his brother Kham (pronounced 'come', as in English), surname Akara. They are good people to take. They are both ex-CPT guerrillas who know the Empty Quarter like the backs of their hands. Both have trekked from Mae Sa Nan to Sa Wang many times. Kham used to live in Sa Wang, before moving not long ago to Mae Sa Nan. More than that, prior to living in Sa Wang, he used to live until 1993 in the heart of the quarter at the now defunct village of Nam Mao Mork, near the Nam Mao and close to the midpoint of our trail. In 1996 we paid Nit and Kham a total of 1250 baht for the trek (i.e. 625 baht each). This was a concessionary rate, and they made it clear that they would only be prepared to guide other people for at least 1000 baht per person per journey, so arduous is the trek. This price includes the guides carrying the backpacks and food, but not water bottles or cameras. It is not far off what you would expect to pay anyway, multiplied out by the normal fee of 200 baht per day. Thus 3 days at 200 baht/day = 600 baht, to which you can add the expense of a fourth day that they will need to get back to Mae Sa Nan (= 800), plus their travel expenses, say 100 baht (= 900), plus a tip of another 100 (= a total of 1000 baht). All guides will expect to be paid for any time they need to get back to their homes, whether walking back the way they came, or taking transport with you, and they will expect you to pay any bus or *silor* fares, even noodle soups eaten at the roadside. But that is only fair – why should they pay for expenses they would not otherwise have incurred?

Preparing for the trek
Make sure, as usual, that you start off with full flasks of good or boiled water. Because you cannot possibly carry sufficient good water for the whole journey, you must have with you the means of making good water, either a pot for boiling up and purifying stream water over a fire and/or a water filter. Carefully plan your food requirements. You will need food for an evening in Mae Sa Nan on the eve of the trek, food for 3 meals a day for

3 days during the trek, and food in Sa Wang or until you get to Nam Duang, where there are simple shops with soft drinks and snacks, and in 1998 even a noodle soup stall. A final warning: do not undertake this trek unless you are fit, have stamina, and can persevere in trying circumstances.

*

Trekking route detail
Day 1 (of core trek): Mae Sa Nan – River Wa/Huai Din Kuen – Huai Miang (Maps 9 & 10)

Time log

Start/0 hrs	Set off at 8am if you can, when the going is nice and cool. By the time everyone is gathered and ready, it may well already be 9am – don't leave after 9.30. Opposite the village school and behind a pond-reservoir, climb up a path, past a cement tank, directly into the early morning sun. Ascending steadily, and soaking up dew from wayside bamboos and plants on your arms and clothes, you soon gain the height of the H1257 road west of Mae Sa Nan across the valley. Taking a last look back at the village nestling down in its hollow, say goodbye to Mae Sa Nan and to 'civilization' for at least 3 days, and continue through rustling bamboos.
30 mins	Come to a stream. Time for a first little rest.
45 mins	Reach top of first ridge, dotted with *mai yang* trees, after which a steep descent begins into the valley of the River Wa. Still near the top, fork left and pass a hut to enter a series of bamboo tunnels, lethally carpeted with dead leaves, which will soon have you shouting out and sliding down on your bottom. The tunnels lead into a forest of muscled *mai hai* trees, about 60 ft high, from out of which the murmur of the Wa is now audible.
1¼ hrs	At the bottom of the descent, a right turn by a tree brings you to the beautiful River Wa. Diagonally opposite lies Huai Din Kuen or, rather, the confluence of this 'earth-moving stream' and the Wa. In early 1996 the mouth of the Din Kuen stream was a bare avalanche of brown-red boulders and stones, but in late 1998 it had become unrecognizably overgrown with plants and bushes. Incidentally, this spot, where the path comes down to the Wa opposite Din Kuen, is where the route of this trek intersects that of Trek 5, which, coming from the right, proceeds along the west bank of the Wa from the Mae Sa Nan river to the Nam Nae river (Map 9).

Now a tricky and complicated operation. You must cross the River Wa, which when we forded it was a full 50 yards wide at this point. As you inspect the water, shallow for the most part, crossing looks easy enough, but there are deeper places, the current is quite strong, and the bottom is covered with slimy rounded stones. It is hard not to fall over, imperilling backpacks and especially any cameras. Give them to the more practised and sure-footed guides, who will wade across holding the backpacks above their heads and with cameras slung around their necks. Don't be too proud to hold onto the hands of the guides, who will lead you across. For tall *farang* trekkers the turquoise water may swirl around their waists, but for the short Lua guides it can lap around their chests, leading to an amusing if tense 20-minute interlude. With wet trousers, underwear and boots, you arrive on the east bank of the Wa at Huai Din Kuen. Welcome to the Empty Quarter!

1 hr 35 mins   Set off again, heading due south up the Din Kuen stream, along the left bank, negotiating the stones and vegetation.

1 hr 55 mins   After 20 mins turn right to leave the streambed and climb up an embankment. Now begins the ascent of Doi (Mount) Din Kuen and the second ridge. The path, heading broadly south-east, toils steeply up, passing the occasional clearing and resting point. The rock-hard, fist-sized, turdlike objects sometimes littering the way are *muai*, the inedible fruit of a parasitic plant. Amidst the jungle vegetation, tree trunks rise up like fluted cathedral pillars, telling you that you really are in the jungle.

2 ¾ hrs   Climbing up a little stream, you reach a drinking point (for the guides), which is a place to snatch a quick 20-minute lunch (we arrived here at midday).

3 hrs 5 mins   Press on to emerge above the stream at a place affording splendid views back towards the paved road behind Mae Sa Nan as well as towards the gash of the new dirt side-road to Huai Loi, not far north of Mae Sa Nan.
The climb levels out into a traverse around the north side of Din Kuen mountain. Continue until a stream, and climb up the stream through bamboos to arrive on top.

3 ¾ hrs   Top of second ridge and a pass. Is the graffito, etched into the bark of a tree, of a man and a woman standing up copulating still there? In their eternal bark-bound activity they enjoy a good view: a clear and final prospect of the gash of the Huai Loi road.
Leave the mountaintop by the left side. The path continues in a south-easterly direction (ca 120°), past an orange-flowering tree, to reach 30 mins later:

4¼ hrs   a kind of camping place, which, when we passed by, had a deer trap, set by Hmong people. I dallied here half an hour photographing with a macro lens jungle blooms and fruits we had all collected along the way. Avoid handling the clusters of purple flowers you see – they give you a nasty rash. Nit produced some two-inch-long ladybird-type insects, which make a bad smell. The distraction with the photography means that my timings are now slightly distorted (i.e. you should arrive at Huai Miang rather sooner than we did).
The 'camp' marks a turning point in the trek. Now the north-westerly Mae Sa Nan vista is replaced by a new view of mountains and ridges unfolding to the SE. At the same time the trekking direction changes to S. Due E (90°) lies Doi Pu Fa (1750 m), a significant mountain, close to the Lao border, which Lua and Hmong tribesmen sometimes climb when hunting. The brown patch ahead, across the valley, is the next immediate goal of the trek, while, to reach Sa Wang, you have to climb over the high ridge on the horizon – still some way to go!

4¾ hrs   Leave the camping place.

5 hrs   15 mins later reach another camping place, complete with fire site, and also a big tree with more graffiti cut into its bark: 'Mathao 24-1-96' and 'Don', as well as further fornication images.

At a tree trunk and division of the way, fork left to begin a steep descent down the far side of the second ridge to the Huai Miang.

5 hrs 35 mins Another tree graffito: of a nude female torso.

6 hrs   An old CPT base by a dried-up stream in a clearing in dark forest. The forest is interspersed with incredible, seemingly muscle-bound trees, ripples of wood coiling snakelike around them.

Follow the parched stream downwards, bearing left, to arrive at:

6¼ hrs   Huai Miang or the Miang stream.

Huai Miang

If you are expecting, as we were, a regular broad open river with proper banks set in sunny jungle and enough water for swimming in (rather like the Wa), you will be disappointed with the Miang, which, incidentally, takes its name from a wild tea bush (*miang*), whose leaves are used to make a tea-leaf mixture (also called *miang*), which hill-tribe people like to chew, rather as we chew gum. For the Huai Miang is little more than a stream, full of brown boulders, in a V-shaped cleft in deep jungle. Somewhere downstream it flows into the River Wa. Being so enclosed and jungle-bound, it is gloomy, damp and claustrophobic. This, together with the fact that there is hardly anywhere level or free of undergrowth for pitching a tent, makes the spot rather unsuitable for camping. And yet this is where you must make your first overnight stop, just as we had to. If you arrive at Huai Miang at about 3.30pm after some 6 hrs of trekking (as we did), it is too late and too far to go on. A much better and nicer place to camp is at Nam Mao, but it lies at least another 4 hrs away on the far side of the next and third ridge. If you think you can handle 10 hrs of up-and-down trekking in one day (but pity the poor guides humping the backpacks), you could proceed to Nam Mao (perhaps even spending a whole day and two nights there – a joyous prospect), but to manage this you would have had to set off from Mae Sa Nan at about 7am and would need to arrive at Huai Miang earlier than 2pm, to get to Nam Mao before dark. So, unable or unwilling to go further, buckle down to the inevitable and strike camp as best you can.

Actually, reconnoitring reveals a number of camping places in among the trees. Some are old PLAT guerrilla encampments and others lairs where poachers have spent the night. Just downstream from the patch we chose to camp on (beside a tiny side creek), on a bend in the Miang, stood the remains of no fewer than 10 freebooters' makeshift huts. Our own cramped tenting spot we soon discovered, upon clearing the undergrowth, to be a former PLAT camp. In the weeds and leaves we found an old rusting enamelled Chinese washing-up bowl. "The communist guerrillas used to sleep in hammocks between these trees", Nit explained. "We had rations and lived off nature. Under this dense canopy there was little chance of detection."

TREK IT YOURSELF IN NORTHERN THAILAND

When we did this trek, stopping overnight at the Miang, we found that the best campsite, about 100 m upstream from us and on a broad ledge above the river, was occupied by a gang of no less than 35 poachers. They were all men, mostly from Prachinburi. Some were in fake army uniforms, others were unshaven and seemed dubious. At best they looked like a motley happy-go-lucky crew, and at worst a bunch of suspicious ne'er-do-wells, who could with impunity attack us in the night and steal our things or worse, such was their overwhelming superiority in numbers compared to us in this isolated god-forsaken place. We grew alarmed and voiced our concern to Nit and Kham about the advisability of camping so near to the illegal intruders. But they shrugged off the threat, reassuring us that "we have come across such parties before; we trust them; sometimes 50 or 60 of them camp down here". Later, after we had erected our tent and washed in the river, we paid the poachers a visit up on their ledge, and reeled at the spectacle: fires were burning, plants and trees had been cleared away, washing was drying, personal belongings were strewn around, people were chatting and cooking or just sleeping, and various devices had been fashioned out of wood for the purposes of grilling food, holding water containers, or sleeping on. At the sight of a *farang* face, they all fell into an uneasy silence. I mention this encounter to forewarn you in case you unexpectedly stumble upon such people in the middle of nowhere.

The men all had sacks with them, which contained their few personal belongings but mainly 'jungle things we are collecting'. We quizzed our guides about these 'jungle things', who explained that the poachers were looking for a particular rare type of tree. The white wood of this tree had veins of brown wood, which was very valuable. It was used for making incense, perfume, and traditional Chinese-style medicines. Good quality brown wood could fetch 10,000 baht or more per kilo, and on one expedition a party could gather wood worth perhaps 100,000 baht, a formidable sum. Parties typically entered this area near Mae Sa Nan and exited just before (but not at) Nam Duang. In this way they avoided the forestry officials at the Lua village and both the Thai Army and the forestry officials at Nam Duang. In a word, the Prachinburi men were stealing things from Doi Pu Kha National Park, at the same time systematically destroying a particular type of tree in it. It annoyed us that no one apparently attempted to do anything about these organized raiding parties, which was odd because the parties were large, noisy and conspicuous, and to the Lua at least were well-known. The forestry authorities do a valuable job in many respects (reforestation), but in others their efforts seem disappointing. What for the show offices, model gardens and lavish installations up and down the border if the forestry department could not send rangers into its own area of jurisdiction to round up, arrest and exclude poachers, which would not be a difficult task? After hearing our guides' account of the Prachinburi crew, we took to referring to them as the 'incense raiders'. The following day we saw a lot more of them, because they were going the same way as us. After we had skipped past them, puffing under the weight of their sacks, on the steep upgrades, they then overtook us when we stopped for a rest or a snack.

TREK 7: MAE SA NAN – SA WANG

A pause at Huai Miang is perhaps a good place to comment also on the two guides Nit and Kham, and on their way of operating when out trekking in the jungle. In 1999 Nit was aged 36, Kham 32. Both speak Thai, but no English. As indicated, they are both ex-CPT guerrillas, Nit having joined the communists when he was 10 years old. They are thin wiry men, and short by *farang* standards. They have wives and children. Nit has a small moustache and every half hour smokes a rollie made with home-grown tobacco. When he is not looking after his fields and lychee orchard, he is out hunting or fishing. In 1996, during the rainy season, he went down to Bangkok to work as a labourer on a building site, a source of income during the inclement season that has now dried up in the wake of the Asian economic crash. In Mae Sa Nan, Nit's house is situated opposite the new health centre and to the left of the weaving centre, set back, but it can be a problem finding him there to hire. Often he is in his field or out hunting. Nit has an eye for business and routinely overquotes when asked how much he would charge for guiding a certain trek. Nor is he easy to beat down, which must be done remorselessly. When out trekking, he and his brother are like a husband-and-wife team, each with his own skills and tasks. Nit is the hunter-fisherman, forging ahead, grumpy; Kham lights the fires, cooks and prepares camp, domesticated, intelligent and humorous. The 'special' outfits they wear when out hunting or trekking are amusing: filthy tattered shirts and trousers, and those ubiquitous, yellow-coloured, rubber shoes (worn without socks) so popular with hill-tribe men, which are called in dialect *rongtao kaopote* or 'sweetcorn shoes'. Actually, these 'corn shoes' are worth investigating as trekking footwear. You cannot ruin them by splashing through rivers and mud, they dry out in a matter of minutes, and they grip on slimy rocks almost like no other shoes or boots. And they cost only 60 baht a pair in the market or in a shoe shop.

To watch Nit and Kham from behind as they head up a trekking column, you can see little of them except their lower legs. They carry the backpacks, on top of which they load their own bags and food, almost obscuring their heads, and to the bottom of which they sling the tents, which hang down to their knees. It is incredible how these slight Lua men, like almost all the tribal guides I have hired, can carry such loads for long hours up and down steep hillsides in torrid heat. Nit likes to race ahead, while Kham proceeds at a more measured pace. Kham and the rest of us are forever catching Nit up, at intervals finding him sitting in the shade of a tree, rolling a cigarette or indulging in *miang*. He keeps the slimy, green-coloured, tea-leaf mixture, which is bitter and tannic dry when you chew it, making the saliva come, in a plastic bag, and when it is time for another chew, remarks in Thai: "Time again for my chicken shit."

Here at Huai Miang, while we set about erecting our tent, an awkward process interrupted by a brown snake slithering past, the two guides fell to their routine customary upon arriving somewhere. Domestic Kham lit a fire, while hunter Nit went off with his gun and fishing net. Within minutes Nit had returned with a pair of freshwater crabs, which Kham roasted, cooking rattan, too. From the muddy spring close to our tent, they drew water, which they boiled up in fat sections of bamboo to make 'Ma-maa' instant noodle soup. They folded up banana and *tong ching* leaves, deftly fashioning bowls and spoons, and we all began feasting ravenously on the Ma-maa, supplementing it with tinned tuna in masman curry sauce, sticky rice, raisins and coffee. Into their instant noodles the two guides chopped fiendish 'mouse shit' chilli peppers. Not content with that, they then started casually chewing the little devils. Asked how they could bear to eat such hot things, they replied: "We get a headache if we don't eat chilli every day."

Night comes early and quickly when you are on a jungle trek, as you will find, and in the gloomy vegetation-obscured ravine of Huai Miang, it is already quite dark by 6.30pm, making for a long 12-hour night. You can spin out the cooking and eating process for an hour or two, sitting round a fire and taking the very greatest care not to get bitten by malarial mosquitoes, but after that there is nothing else to do except crawl into your tent and try to sleep until dawn. While you snooze on the bumpy rooty floor of the jungle inside your little canvas house, away from the mosquitoes and innumerable creepy-crawly things outside, you will be horrified to see the guides sleeping unprotected on leaves around the fire. If you poke your head out through the flysheet, the darkness is total except for the faint glow of the guides' fire and the darting neon trails of fireflies. Back inside you doze off lulled by the jungle's night-time orchestra: along the Miang a hundred fat frogs incessantly croak 'waak-waak' in a syncopated rhythm, from the trees and bushes crickets peep and trill, and from out of nowhere some insect makes an ear-splitting searing sound like an electric drill going into masonry.

Day 2: Huai Miang – Nam Mao – Kiu Lom ('Windy Col') (see Map 10)

The task of Day 2 is to climb from Huai Miang over the third ridge to Nam Mao, cross the Mao river, and ascend to halfway up the fourth ridge, stopping for the night at Kiu Lom (= Windy Col). Describing the second leg of this trek, I find myself giving details of an unsatisfactory day's march (we arrived at 'Windy Col' too late and in the dark). I provide the details of things as they unfolded for us in the hope that you will be able to improve on or avoid our efforts. You could do this either by starting earlier from Huai Miang (we left at 8.45am), and/or by spending less time for lunch at Nam Mao (we spent a full 2 hrs there), or by spending a night at Nam Mao and going the whole way from Nam Mao to Sa Wang on the third day of trekking (an appealing option outlined earlier).

Time log

Start/0 hrs   If you are intending to press on to Windy Col on Day 2 (not camping at Nam Mao), see if you can get away from Huai Miang before 8am. After breakfasting and packing up (our guides ate banana pod stewed in river water for their breakfast!), cross the little Miang river to pick up the path again, continuing on the far bank.

The path proceeds east and then immediately south, climbing uphill very steeply indeed, causing the sweat to run freely.

Stop to cool off by a massive *mai yang* tree (*Dipterocarpus alatus*), its trunk about 6 ft in diameter. You will come across many *yang* trees on this trek. Like giant telegraph poles, they rise straight up to a great height and have no branches or leaves anywhere up their trunks, these coming only at the very top. Many of them have old tapping slits or pockets hacked into them. When tapped, the trees bleed a resin, and during the CPT insurgency, the guerrillas in the Empty Quarter used to burn the resin in lamps.

Continue to climb.

¾ hr   Now heading east again, pass a Hmong resting hut. Take a short rest to gather strength for the steep climb to the top of the ridge. From the hut: a long view SSW (210°) to Doi Palang Ngu (= tooth mountain) in the distance. The Palang Ngu ridge marks the boundary of Mae Charim district. Before the ridge, but beyond a patch of red earth, lies the Wa river.

1½ hrs   Came to a place where a Hmong man died of fever in 1995. He is buried where he died, and a hutlike construction has been built to mark the spot.

On the top of a knoll the direction changes to due south.

Bearing right, continue along and up a connecting spur to reach at long last, after nearly 2 hrs of unbroken climbing:

1¾ hrs   the top of the third ridge. View north-east (60°) to Doi Pu Fa.

From the top, climb down mountain on the left side. When we passed by here, there was no path, and the south-easterly descent from the third ridge was a scramble which, without a guide, would cause you to get hopelessly lost.

As you descend: views ahead across a valley towards the great fourth ridge (ESE), which remains to be crossed before Sa Wang. Somewhere halfway up it is Windy Col and today's goal and campsite. The singular trees you see around here, with a knobbled section midway up their trunks reminiscent of the knurling on a pineapple, are *kor* palms.

After more than an hour of breasting your way down through elephant grass and bushes, you emerge onto:

2 hrs 55 mins a headland directly overlooking the valley. Graffito carved into a tree: 'Yia, I love you – 25.1.96'.

From the headland, a Rambo climb now begins down the second lower half of the ridge, busting and slithering through sheer jungle. The heat increases, you become wet with sweat, your clothes and body are scratched by thorns and lacerated by bamboos, you find yourself bleeding, and you almost give up caring, just wanting to get to the bottom and the river. On the positive side: every conceivable type of bamboo, palm and fern presents itself; you traverse lovely patches of wild galangal, exuding a liquorice smell; and you pass through a copse of wild durian trees (their fruits inedible) as well as a grove of rattan (edible). Particularly impressive is a great *sai* or

105

banyan tree (*Ficus bengalensis*), its branches and multiple stems intertwined like a number of elephant trunks curling round one another and shooting off at right angles both vertically and horizontally.[1] It looks for all the world as if it is growing upside down. Its strangeness is tinged with beauty, for lining its branches are rows of wild orchids.

Bearing left at the bottom of the mountainside, you clamber down a dried-up streambed, finally to emerge at:

4¼ hrs   Nam Mao.

Nam Mao

We arrived at Nam Mao or the Mao river at 1pm, yet this was supposed to have been, in Nit and Kham's original scheme of things, our destination for the previous day! But unless one was almost superhuman, how could one have added the exhausting 4-hr Ramboesque climb across the third ridge to the journey of Day 1? We stopped for 2 hrs at Nam Mao, washing, lunching and resting, with the result that we did not set off for Windy Col until 3 o'clock – too late. If you want to get to the Windy Col campsite before nightfall, you should have arrived at Nam Mao before 1pm and you should spend not more than one hour there over lunch. Otherwise consider spending the second night camping at Nam Mao and proceeding on Day 3 via Windy Col (not camping there) across the fourth ridge all the way to Sa Wang. It is another 4 hrs or so to Windy Col.

Nam Mao is an idyllic spot and would make the best campsite of the Empty Quarter trek. Even as I write this, I hanker after lolling in its jungle remoteness for a day or two. Unlike the Miang, the Mao is a regular fast-flowing river about ten metres wide. Like the Miang, it flows through a steep-sided ravine, the sides of which are clad in luxuriant vegetation. However, being wider that the Miang and more open to sunlight, the Mao is less dingy and spooky than the latter. Its riverbed is strewn with pink-brown boulders, and, when we were there, the air was a-flutter with dozens of butterflies – small blues, large blacks, and medium-sized ochres. Until about 1993 the people of Sa Wang used to live near here in the village of Nam Mao Mork, until they were relocated. Guide Kham, coming from Sa Wang, must once have lived near here too, in which case our arrival at Nam Mao was for him something of a homecoming.

Following the guides' usual practice, Nit went off hunting while Kham made a fire and boiled water in bamboo tubes. We thought that the wily Nit would be gone some time, but, astonishingly, within 5 minutes he was back with 4 nine-inch-long silvery fishes. These they popped into the tubes along

---

[1] The *sai* or banyan is a species of fig tree. A parasitic growth, it is known as the strangler fig tree. One of its seeds lodges in the trunk of a host tree. As the seedling grows, it drops air roots to the ground, which then root and develop into secondary trunks. Forming a new multiple-trunked tree, the parasitic fig strangles the host, until in the end the host dies and disappears, leaving only the fig tree. The banyan can become enormous and hugely ramifying, a complex of those weird characteristic elements branching out horizontally, vertically upwards, and, as if upside down, vertically downwards.

with some wild galangal and lemongrass, plugged the open ends with leaves, cooked the fish for a few minutes, and poured the stew out to eat. Sticky rice they likewise cooked in bamboo tubes. It has to be said that after the morning's exertions their meal on the hoof tasted delicious. After lunch and while we were washing and resting, Nit went off again, trawling the river with a small net and a bamboo stick. Miraculously, he returned within 20 minutes with another 13 fish, coloured silver, black and pink. These he wrapped in banana leaves to eat for supper and possibly at Sa Wang.

0 hrs	I set the 'clock' back to zero because of the complication in scheduling at and after Nam Mao. The Mao river marks the beginning of the climb over the great fourth and last ridge of the trek, a climb which, in the guides' words, takes some 6 hrs.
	Crossing the Mao by a bend in the river and some rapids, you climb up steeply from the river bank and valley floor to pick up a path. Here, as at other junctures, the impossibility of trekking without a guide was again borne in on us. You would not know in which direction to proceed, let alone be able to hit off the path.
	Heading approximately south, continue to gain height, in places climbing almost vertically. You make your way through dense cover and a series of 'tunnels', forcing you to stumble on, head and back bent – an exasperating business.
50 mins	End of the matted vegetation and tunnels. On a tree, another graffito: 'Y.I.A. 27/1/95'.
1¼ hrs	Completion of first stage of ascent. Trekking is now more on the level, gaining height gradually.
1½ hrs	A way off right in some woods goes to the legendary Huai Pla Jaad waterfall (see Trek 8).
1¾ hrs	Reach a new elevated position with a view south across intervening low ground to a preliminary ridge and behind it to a higher ridge on the horizon. The preliminary ridge (all part of the big fourth ridge) is Hill 306, CPT N° 6 Area (Mae Sa Nan N° 3 Area), while a dip on the horizon ridge is the pass over which you go on Day 3 to reach Sa Wang. Left, east, affords a view of the Lao border ridge. It is the source of the Nam Mao and also the location of Pa Pae, a cliff so called because of wild goats living there.
	Passing through elevated woods, you enjoy next some fine contour walking with views both ways. (When we trekked along here, the sun was already low in the sky, and, with a long way still to go until Windy Col, we kept looking anxiously and ever more frequently at our watches. We were growing so weary from the heat and the climbing that we kept stopping for a little rest or a drink at shorter and shorter intervals and for ever longer times, to the despair of Nit and Kham. In this dispirited state we began to make the final push to the campsite. Not much further we were so tired that we could hardly put one foot in front of the other, and, although it was impossible to camp where we were, it seemed we would never make it to Windy Col that night – a mini crisis. But after a longer rest, during which we consumed a whole packet of high-energy honey bananas, we were

<table>
<tbody>
<tr><td></td><td>able to go on, stumbling through the vegetation and arriving at the campsite in darkness.)</td></tr>
<tr><td>2½ hrs</td><td>Enter a banana grove to hit upon a former CPT encampment, Camp 306. Poking about here briefly, we came across an old military cooking range languishing in the undergrowth.</td></tr>
<tr><td>3 hrs 20 mins</td><td>Arrive at the top of the preliminary ridge (Hill 306). A contour walk brings you to:</td></tr>
<tr><td>3¾ hrs</td><td>Kiu Lom or 'Windy Col'.</td></tr>
</tbody>
</table>

Kiu Lom ('Windy Col')

Kiu Lom, which means 'Windy Col', is the location of this trek's second campsite, where, with two days of trekking now behind you, you spend the second night out under canvas. The campsite is among trees in a col, and used to be a place where PLAT guerrillas stayed during Thailand's communist insurgency. True to its name, this is, indeed, a windy spot – when we were there, a strong wind blew all night through the col, buffeting our tent, making us feel cold, and hampering cooking over a fire as well erecting the tent. The elevation of the site, more than halfway up the big fourth ridge, added to the coolness, which otherwise would have been welcome. Disregarding the wind and cold, the main problem with Kiu Lom campsite is its lack of water. There is no water actually by the tents, and what water there is in the vicinity, just a feeble trickle running into and out of a murky pool among some rocks, lies 10 minutes away (and another ten back) down a precipitous slimy 50-metre incline. An errand to fetch water in an open billycan is so awkward that you spill half the contents, dirtying yourself in the process. But I am sure that on another occasion and under different circumstances Kiu Lom could be a very pleasant campsite. Our guides told us that a Hmong village, Kiu Nam, used to be situated near Windy Col, until it was relocated by the authorities. Evidently, the remains of its school can still be seen. The resettled Kiu Nam now lies between Sa Wang and Nam Duang.

When we stayed at Windy Col, we were too tired and dispirited to attempt getting down to the spring in the dark, and, anyway, Nit dissuaded us from going, instead bringing some water up for us in our billycan and also in a leaking plastic bag! In the beam of our torch we saw immediately that this water was both dirty and quite insufficient for our needs. The situation was so pathetic that it began to seem funny. Half the precious murky liquid we took to prepare a macaroni soup supper, and the rest we filtered for drinking. But there was no water for washing, and so later we had to get into our sleeping bags covered in the dirt and sweat from the day's trek. Few words were exchanged that evening, and everybody bedded down as soon as they had eaten. The two Lua guides again slept in the open, either side of a fire. Their feet were bare, but otherwise they had put on all their clothes against the cold, including balaclava helmets.

Day 3: Kiu Lom ('Windy Col') – Sa Wang (see Map 10)

0 hrs   From Kiu Lom to Sa Wang is about 3¾ hrs of hiking. If you are starting the third day of the trek at Windy Col, you have just a morning's march ahead of you, and a pleasant one at that. If you spent the second night camping down at Nam Mao, you will probably stop for lunch at Kiu Lom, already having a ca 3½-hr climb behind you, and will have an afternoon march of about 4 hrs in front of you.

The path to Sa Wang leaves from behind Windy Col campsite and winds SE up through trees onto the side of the topmost part of the great fourth ridge, which the local Hmong call 'Sakio'. It seems to be composed not of laterite, but of granite, for the rocks sparkle with diamantine quartz crystals.

½ hr   Just 30 mins out from Kiu Lom, you are already on the top of the ridge, and the big climb is over. There is no startling view from the crest because it is covered in cloud forest, identifiable by the fact that all the trees have moss on them.

Traverse round to the east side of the mountain on which you are standing, and begin the long descent.

1 hr   ESE (70°): view of Sa Wang distant in the valley.

From a headland you can enjoy (if you started from Kiu Lom) fabulous early morning views E and NE across a valley to the mist-covered mountains of Laos. In the valley lies the Duang river, which gives its name to the Hmong village of Nam Duang, just beyond Sa Wang. The border already begins on the other side of the valley. Our guides pointed out to us a brown patch on the far side, close to which the border runs. Pu Fa mountain now lies due N.

Continue on down through banana palms, along a slowly descending spur.

At a fork, right proceeds straight to Nam Duang, while left heads for Sa Wang. Go left.

You might think the trek is almost over, but there are still two or three hills to climb. We imagined that the path must surely skirt round the sides of these, but, no, it crosses over each in turn, as if the Lua idea of walking is to go from summit to summit.

Heading steadily E now

3½ hrs   First palpably near glimpse of Sa Wang down in the valley, its huts and roofs individually distinguishable.

3¾ hrs   You emerge from some tall grasses to arrive, joy of joys, at Sa Wang. If you look back, the elongated crest of the great fourth ridge is plainly visible, and you, doughty trekker, have just crossed it, as well as three other ridges beyond it. (In case anyone should ever attempt this trek going 'backwards', the beginning of the path leads away from the top end of Sa Wang village at a compass bearing of 280° or approximately west.)

Sa Wang (see Map 11)

Sa Wang is a remote Lua (Htin) village, whose inhabitants include, curiously, three Khmu families. A small place, consisting of some 50 dwellings, it lies almost 100 kms (by road) from Nan town and just a stone's throw from Laos. This gives it an out-on-a-limb, end-of-the-road feel, and indeed beyond the outpost there is nothing except a small waterfall (Huai Ja Lue waterfall, 2 kms to the north) and the jungles of the Empty Quarter. Set on a hillside tumbling down to the River Duang on the valley floor, Sa Wang is a new village, founded in 1993. The villagers are all ex-CPT people, who used to live (guide Kham included) in the Empty Quarter at Nam Mao Mork, a place not far from Nam Mao, where we lunched on Day 2 of this trek. They surrendered to the Thai authorities in 1990 and in 1993 were relocated to Sa Wang, partly so that they would no longer be within the National Park, but also so that they would have better access to the outside world.

When I first visited the village in early 1995 (researching this trek), it had the distinct feel of a refugee place, which in a sense it was. The huts, all new, were shabby, makeshift, impoverished affairs, woven bamboo boxes on stilts, uniformly topped off with corrugated tin roofs. There was still no vehicle access at that time, and reaching Sa Wang meant a long hour's hike from Nam Duang through the forest and along a mountain saddle. But in 1996 a poor 7-km-long dirt track was pushed through from Nam Duang, allowing access to trucks and connecting the village with the outside world. The state of this access track was unchanged in 1999. Meanwhile a school and forestry office have sprung up, a weaving project plus a couple of little shops have appeared, and the villagers have started to rebuild their huts as sturdier wooden houses. Once they have got used to *farang* visitors in their midst, the people of Sa Wang are very friendly. The village headman or *pu yai baan* is Som Yot. Now that Sa Wang has a forestry station (near the school at the southern entrance to the village), there is an obvious and satisfactory place to stay.

Exiting the trek (see Maps 11 & 12)

Once you have arrived at Sa Wang, you will have to decide how you propose to exit the trek and establish with your guides whether they intend to return to Mae Sa Nan by road (in which case they will accompany you about as far as Mae Charim) or on foot, returning the same way via Nam Mao and Huai Miang, an option they might well take up. Whatever their intention, you should now pay them off, remembering also to recompense them for the time they need to reach home (probably a day) and any transport fares or food money. In our case, the guides returned to Mae Sa Nan by road.

If you plan to stay in Sa Wang, either because you want to spend an afternoon there, or because it is already early evening, just put your tent up

110

anywhere or go to the forestry station (*pamai*) and, after asking, pitch camp on the lawn right by the flagpole (as we have done)! Do not worry about the guides – they will have friends in Sa Wang, with whom they can stay.

Now you must make your way to Nam Duang. Decide if you are going to walk or hitch-hike. If you hoof the 7 kms, it will take you about 1½ hrs. If you want to get a lift and you see vehicles in Sa Wang, try to ascertain when they will be leaving, where they are going, whether you can ride with them, and how much they might charge (beware: Hmong drivers may try to rip you off). A lift to Nam Duang should only be a few baht, and a ride all the way to Nan would be good value at 100 baht per person. Most trucks leave Sa Wang and also Nam Duang either early morning or late afternoon. Look for a forestry or other official vehicle if possible – your ride will then probably be free. Halfway between Sa Wang and Nam Duang is the Hmong village of Kiu Nam, which is another recently established place that has been moved out of the Empty Quarter.

Nam Duang
It may be that you are obliged to spend a night in Nam Duang, either because you have walked or hitch-hiked there and for the moment can get no further, or because you have been caught out by nightfall waiting there for an onward lift. But that is no problem. In fact, in some ways Nam Duang is a better place than Sa Wang to overnight in – it is bigger and has more facilities. Also, there are more lifts going out of Nam Duang. Go and stay (as we have done) at the well-equipped and welcoming forestry complex on the hill above the village; or just pitch your tent in any suitable discreet corner; or search out a friendly educated Hmong man we once met, called Noo, who said that we or any *farang* could stay in his house. Noo lives near the centre of the village, just off the main street, on the northern side, on an elevated piece of ground. Apply to him if you have any problems or needs. Some Hmong have been to the US and similar places, as a result of which they have a smattering of English and are foreigner-friendly. Undoubtedly there are a few such in Nam Duang. (For some brief background information on the Hmong people, such as inhabit Nam Duang and also Kiu Nam, see Trek 16 under 'Santisuk'.)

The place to wait for lifts out of Nam Duang is at the waiting hut at the bottom of the village, near the junction for Sa Wang. People also wait at the noodle soup stall, which likewise lies near the bottom junction. Again, if the driver offering you a lift is a Hmong, fix a fare before you climb aboard.

Nam Duang is a big, spread-out, White Hmong place, with shops, petrol, and, as said, a noodle soup stand. The authorities (army, BPP, forestry, health, welfare organizations etc.) have piled in here, so there is a certain amount of toing and froing. Located a mile or two from the Thai-Lao border, the village is apparently about 10 years old and consists of some 70-80 houses or more than 100, if an offshoot of Kiu Nam is included, which is tucked away behind the school. Nam Duang has always struck me as depressed, some of its houses being little more than hovels and many of its inhabitants being impoverished and afflicted. You can see mules in use here, and some local Hmong still wear traditional costume. Posters around the settlement proclaim 'The 19 Rules' (to be loyal to the King, to serve the country, to support democracy, and so on), a sign that this is a village undergoing pacification and Thaiization. Forestry men whispered to us that near Nam Duang more specimens of the rare *chompu pu kha* tree had been found, of that celebrated 'unique' tree that stands by the side of the Bo Glua-Pua road in the middle of Doi Pu Kha National Park.

Nam Duang is a place of some notoriety and until 1998, when it was thrown open – apparently for good – to visits by outsiders, was for years a closed or restricted village. The reason for this is that it was a seat of resistance to the Patet Lao, the communist Lao authorities who seized power in 1975, abolishing the monarchy, sparking a kind of civil war, persecuting the Hmong, and causing the displacement of huge numbers of Hmong and other people. The Hmong, royalists loyal to the charismatic semi-mythical leader Gen. Vang Pao of the former Royal Lao Army, combatted the Patet Lao, both seeking revenge for defeats suffered at their hands and continuing to pursue Vang Pao's dream of an independent Hmong district. They conducted their warfare, sabotage and subversion from Nam Duang, leading to sporadic clashes between the Hmong there (backed by Hmong sympathizers in the US) and Lao forces dug in just across the border, with the two sides trading fire, bombarding each other, and even making use, reportedly, of chemical weapons.

When skirmishing was underway, access to Nam Duang was barred, meaning that *farang* travellers coming from Nan could not get past the checkpoint in Nam Poon, but when things were quiet again, the restriction was sometimes relaxed, enabling outsiders to get to the Hmong village. Thus over New Year 1992/93 there was fighting at Nam Duang, the distant heavy crump of Lao artillery shells exploding there being plainly audible from Nam Poon, and I and other travellers were rejected at the checkpoint at Nam Poon. But I have not heard of any skirmishing at Nam Duang recently, nor of visitors being turned back. It could even be that the area is soon opened up to the extent that a cross-border road is built at the village.

Nam Duang – Nan town (see Map 12)
From Nam Duang hitch-hike a lift with any vehicle. Most traffic will probably go as far as Mae Charim, the local district 'town', or even to Nan. When we exited this trek from the Hmong village, we had the good fortune to get a single ride right to the door of our guest house in a lorry that had been delivering building materials to Nam Duang school. The way from Nam Duang to the first next place, Nam Poon (Nam Pun), is a 19-km stretch of endless, lonely, stony dirt on a military road winding through the mountains that was only completed as recently as 1994. At the edge of Nam Poon, by the large concrete bridge spanning the Poon river, you pick up an

asphalt road (the H1168), the first since above Mae Sa Nan. On the far side of the assimilated Lua village of Nam Poon, you pass the checkpoint that used implacably to thwart travellers coming from Nan.

Proceeding west along the patchy rural H1168 road, you now pass through more assimilated Lua villages, including Nam Lan, Nam Nae, Nam Pang and Nam Wa, before hitting, just south of Na Sia, a T-junction (44 kms out from Nam Duang). Incidentally, the huge concrete bridge at the village of Nam Wa spans our old friend the River Wa, broader and more leisurely at this point. At the T-junction left is the beginning of the H1243 road south to Haad Rai and Nam Muap, while right continues along the H1168 to Mae Charim. Go right and pass through the villages of Na Sia, Huai So and Tung Kwang to reach after a further 5 kms the little town of Mae Charim (km 49). Now continue a further 6 kms through four more villages to Na Bua and another junction, marked by a checkpoint (km 55). Here, right heads north up the H1225 road via Tong and other backwoods villages to Si Boon Ruang, Santisuk and Mae Sa Nan (the way the guides will take for Mae Sa Nan), while left (straight on) takes you on the H1168 another 32 kms over a low ridge via Chae Haeng temple-monastery to Nan town (87 kms from Nam Duang, 94 from Sa Wang).

Trek 8

Sa Wang – Kiu Lom ('Windy Col') – Huai Pla Jaad waterfall – Nam Mao Mork – River Wa – Tong

Parameters

trekking mode:	on foot
core trek time:	3 days/2 nights
accessing time:	from Nan town to Sa Wang village one day by a combination of public transport and hitch-hiking
exiting time:	from Tong to Nan between ½ and 1 day by a combination of hitch-hiking and public transport
overall trek time:	from Nan to Nan, including access and exiting times, 4-5 days and 3-4 nights
degree of difficulty:	very difficult, Rambo extreme!
guide(s):	impossible without guides
guide name(s):	Niran, Nguan & Sutat (see photo section)
tent:	required
map(s):	see 12, 11 & 13

Overview

This trek starts in the out-on-a-limb Lua (Htin) village of Sa Wang and heads approximately in a south-east/north-west direction via the legendary and spectacular Huai Pla Jaad waterfall to the backwoods Thai village of Tong. The core part of the expedition, which you will undoubtedly do using Nan town as your overall base, takes 3 days and 2 nights, to which can be added a further day and a night at each end for accessing and exiting, making some 5 days and 4 nights in all. Involving trekking and scrambling a straight 8 hrs a day for 3 days in succession, this is a tough and exhausting expedition, which cuts through the bottom south-eastern part of Nan's Doi Pu Kha National Park, an area of remote uninhabited jungle and mountains that I like to call the 'Empty Quarter'.

On Day 1 you walk from Sa Wang via Kiu Lom ('Windy Col') to the top of Nam Tok Huai Pla Jaad or 'Jaad Fish Stream Waterfall' (*nam tok* = waterfall, *huai* = stream, *pla* = fish), in the process repeating the final leg of Trek 7 (but in reverse) and rescaling the great fourth and last ridge of that trek. You spend a first night camping at the top of the waterfall. On Day 2 you spend all day climbing down the waterfall and Pla Jaad stream, tenting the second night at the foot of the fall, where the Huai Pla Jaad runs into the Nam Mao Mork. On Day 3 you cross the Mao Mork river, hike to the River Wa, cross that, climb steeply out of the Wa river valley, and hoof it a fair distance to Tong village.

The above overview makes everything seem much easier than it is. In fact, **this is the most ambitious and difficult trek in this book**, and out of 50 or so treks that I have now done in Thailand it is the most severe, warranting the grading 'Rambo extreme'. Don't even think of attempting this little foray unless you are an adventurer prepared to trash yourself, your clothing and equipment. The problem is a double one. First, when near 'Windy Col' you leave the main trail (which is the Sa Wang/Mae Sa Nan path taken in Trek 7), there is no real path down to the top of the waterfall, which means busting your way through the undergrowth and down creeks. But second, and much more drastically, there is absolutely no path down the side of the Huai Pla Jaad waterfall. You have to climb down the waterfall itself, which in places is very difficult (so problematic that a rope would be helpful) – my guides had to find a way as we went along, and occasionally, coming to great slimy rock faces, it seemed as if there was no way of descending at all and we could get no further. I did this trek in late January 1998 with Nittaya Tananchai and accompanied by 3 Lua guides from Sa Wang (see below). At the time it seemed that none of them, or perhaps just one of them, knew the way beyond the waterfall and the Nam Mao Mork, and certainly none of them knew the way from the River Wa to Tong or had ever been to Tong. On Day 3 and in Tong and beyond the village, we found ourselves leading the way and researching things as we went along. But now the details of the trek are etched forever on the minds of the 3 guides!

The Huai Pla Jaad stream and waterfall (the latter seems also to be known as Pu Fa waterfall) are named after the *jaad* fish which swim in the stream, in the pools of the fall, and at the bottom of the fall. The waterfall is undoubtedly 'the big one', the largest fall in the Empty Quarter and one of the largest in Thailand. Here, deep in remote inaccessible jungle, the small Pla Jaad river tips a considerable height down some dozen cascades into the Mao Mork river. It is difficult to say exactly how many chutes there are because some come in groups of two or three. Perhaps there are 8 main falls, some comprising a couple of steps. There may be more cascades, which we have not seen, above the first campsite at the 'top' of the fall. Nor is the overall fall a continuous succession of cascades. Between each main component fall, you have to walk a bit, more on the level, to the next one. It is rather like a series of huge steps. The Lua occasionally go to the Huai Pla Jaad to catch the *jaad* fish and also to get sugar palm growing wild in the surrounding jungle. But in 1997, according to our Lua guiding friends Nit and Kham of Mae Sa Nan, no trekking party, either *farang* or Thai, had ever been to the fall, let alone climb all the way down or up it, and it had only ever been properly seen and photographed by helicopter. One local Lua man did create a stir hereabouts recently by taking a few shots of the fall for an official in Mae Charim district office, for which the official, but not the hill-tribe man, was rewarded with 20,000 baht by a Thai princess visiting the area for 'discovering' the 'new' fall! His fading photos are still proudly on display in the *ampoe*. Being so spectacular, as well as inaccessible and difficult, Huai Pla Jaad waterfall has acquired a mystique and legendary quality in Nan province and beyond. All that was until our party negotiated the fall in, as said, 1998. After leaving Tong village (bringing the guides back to Sa Wang, where we had also left our motorbike), we were obliged to spend a night in Mae Charim. Here, when local people and officials discovered that we had just trekked the fall, we caused a local sensation and were feted as heroes. Everyone was dumbfounded, and we were pressed for information about and begged for photos of Huai Pla Jaad. So, until we hear to the contrary, I and our party humbly claim to be the first *farang* and group to 'do' this waterfall. Who said that there was nothing left to discover in Thailand, no more adventure to be had?!

Strategy
When we came to research and set up this trek, trying to find out where best to start it from, how long it would last, and a suitable route, we ran into a barrage of contradictory information and endless debating. No other trek, out of all the treks I have done in Thailand, has generated at the preparation stage so much discussion and confusion. For one thing, in Sa Wang, which looked like the best starting point, no one, nor any of our guides, knew, as indicated, what happened beyond the Huai Pla Jaad, during the last third of the trek! But you, enviable readers, are spared and can profit from our troubles and frustration. So we started from Sa Wang. With this trek, as with all longer treks, it is a good idea to try to set it up in advance, in this case by riding out on a hire motorcycle from Nan to Sa Wang and talking to and hiring guides. It is worth going to Sa Wang for the trip alone. If you turn up 'cold' at the starting point of a trek, you run the risk of making a wasted visit (if you cannot find guides) or of spending a lot of time at the start, whereas, if you arrive 'warm', you know what is afoot, can better prepare, spend less time at the start, and probably shorten the overall trekking time.

Your first decision, when you come to do the trek, is to decide whether you want to go to Sa Wang by motorbike(s) hired in Nan or by public transport and hitch-hiking. Biking (our option) is quicker and more convenient, but the disadvantage is that you have to return to isolated Sa Wang afterwards to collect the machines, and that for 3 days or so during the trek the machines are lying idle and costing money. Travelling to Sa Wang by public transport and/or hitch-hiking is a relatively complicated procedure, for which you should allow a whole day before the trek. The actual practicalities of accessing Sa Wang are set out below. Spend the night before starting the trek in Sa Wang (but not in the village before it, Nam Duang – you don't have the time on Day 1 of the trek to get from Nam Duang to Sa Wang). Stay at the forestry station, which is near the school and situated at the entrance to the village, pitching your tent (ask permission) on the lawn right by the flagpole (as we did), or just camp anywhere in the village, perhaps down by the river in the valley (the Duang river). Familiarize yourself with Sa Wang and organize guides if you have not already done so. People in the village are very friendly. Do the trek, hiking (our times) 7¾ hrs on Day 1, 8¼ on Day 2, and 7¾ hrs on Day 3. You will arrive in the village Tong late afternoon on Day 3. The modalities of exiting the trek are set out after the route details.

If you follow the information in this chapter, you will trek from Sa Wang to Tong, as we did. But things do not have to be like this. In retrospect, and wiser after the event, I can now see a way of improving the route, how the trek should have been done! It would be better to trek the other way round, from Tong to Sa Wang. The reason for this is that it would be easier to climb up the waterfall than to come down it. But a problem with starting in Tong is that, this being a regular rural Thai village, you would be unlikely to find guides there willing to take you and your backpacks to Sa Wang, even if they knew the way. However, you could get round the problem, further improving the strategy of the trek, by going to Sa Wang first (a solution suggested by our guides themselves), perhaps leaving your hire bike there, and coming with the Lua guides round to Tong, from where you could start the trek with them, you and they then ending up in Sa Wang, which is their home village and where you have perhaps left your transport.

The trek can be modified in several ways, and indeed there are other treks you could do, starting at Sa Wang. You could trek 8 hrs to the top of Huai Pla Jaad waterfall, camp a night there, and return the same way. This option might appeal if you do not fancy the terrifying scramble down the fall. You would still get a good 2-day jungle adventure, but you would need a guide. Or, starting at the Tong end, you could trek either as far as the River Wa, camping there, or to Nam Mao Mork and the foot of Huai Pla Jaad waterfall, where you could likewise camp, subsequently returning to Tong. This would also leave you with a good 2-day adventure. For these latter two options you might be able to manage without a guide, reading my notes backwards and/or tagging along with local people. Other trips that could be made from Sa Wang include (1) trekking 3 days and 2 nights through the Empty Quarter to Mae Sa Nan, which is Trek 7 backwards; (2) trekking up the Laos border via Doi Pu Fa ca 4 days and 3 nights to Sob Mang or Huai Loi, which I have not done, but which looks exciting; and (3) walking 2 kms beyond Sa Wang to Huai Ja Lue waterfall, which is a stroll for modest travellers who are perhaps out on a day trip by motorbike from Nan.

We took three guides on this trek for the two of us. The guides themselves suggested that three of them should go, a generous number of which we were sceptical at first, thinking that they were trying to make money out of us, but which in the end proved quite justified. Two, as they said, were for carrying the backpacks and a third for carrying the food for all five of us, or, as we put it, two were for portering and the third was for being eaten by the remaining four of us, a quip that met only with a puzzled look. We took (all from Sa Wang village – see photo section) Niran, in 1998 aged 39, a thin wiry-haired character, the most outgoing of the three, who we came to call 'The Scout'; 'Pretty Boy' Nguan, aged 27; and Sutat, aged 26, a smallish, serious, even gloomy, man with dark brown skin, a moustache and a chintuft beard, who always had his head down as if ashamed of something, and who was once reputedly the headman of Sa Wang. We paid them 200 baht each per day for 3 days, and tipped them an extra 100 baht each (3 x 200 = 600 x 3 = 1800 + 3 x 100 = 2100 baht), also paying their travel fares from Tong to Sa Wang and meals and drinks in Mae Charim, the whole cost being an amazing bargain, considering how very hard and selflessly they worked for us, as will soon become apparent.

Accessing the trek (see Maps 12 & 11)
It is nearly 100 kms from Nan town to far-flung Sa Wang, so allow half a day to get there if you are on hire bikes, and a whole day if you are going by public transport and/or hitch-hiking. If you are doing the latter, take an early morning blue *silor* from the market quasi opposite the *Dheveraj Hotel* in the centre of Nan (actually this is Nan's evening market) and for about 25 baht ride to Mae Charim or even further if you can manage it. From Mae Charim take the same or another *silor* to Nam Poon or Nam Duang or even Sa Wang (as far as you can get). There is a regular, if infrequent, *silor* service to at least Nam Duang, we have been told, and it should cost about 40+ baht per person from Mae Charim. Otherwise hitch-hike, following the route described below for motorcyclists.

Leave Nan by crossing the bridge over the River Nan, ignore the first turning left, and continue out of town, over the rice fields, 2 kms to Chae Haeng monastery-temple. Turn left (north) in front of the temple and proceed along the H1168 road through some outlying villages, over a low ridge, about 32 kms to the village of Na Bua, just before which there is a junction, marked by a checkpoint. Incidentally, it is only a few years ago that travellers used to be stopped at this CP and quizzed by soldiers about where they were going, being made to enter their particulars in a duty book. At the junction, the road left goes past 5 villages to Tong, the goal of our trek. But we go right (straight on), still on the H1168, through Na Bua and 4 other rural villages 6 kms to Mae Charim, a small district 'town'. There are shops and various eating places here. Buy some bottled water if you have not already done so. Continue beyond Mae Charim through 3 more villages 5 kms to another junction, also marked by a checkpoint. Straight on (right) is the H1243 road for Haad Rai and other places, while left, our route, proceeds, still on the H1168, over a shoulder to Nam Wa, an assimilated Lua village beside and named after the River Wa. Crossing the river, wide and shallow at this point, on a long cement bridge, continue a long way, amidst increasingly attractive mountain scenery, through the villages (mostly assimilated Lua) of Nam Pra Thai, Nam Pang, Nam Nae and Nam Lan, to Nam Poon (Nam Pun). In Nam Pang ignore a turning right over a big new bridge, and continue straight (east). At the top of the hill, just before Nam Poon, there is yet another checkpoint on the right side of the road. If for some reason there is trouble in Nam Duang, which is the next village, and Nam Duang (and in consequence Sa Wang) is closed off to outsiders, which has happened many times in the past and could happen again in the future (see Trek 7, under Nam Duang, for details), you will be intercepted at this CP and either prevented from continuing or quizzed as to your business. In 1998 the checkpoint became benign, and hotspot Nam Duang as well as Sa Wang were thrown open to visitors, seemingly for good. You need not worry about getting into trouble – the army will always bar your way if you face potential danger.

From Nam Poon proceed now across a bridge to pick up a new military road (completed only in 1994), which for 19 bone-shaking kms takes you on twisting stony dirt through lonely mountains to the White Hmong village of Nam Duang. Not far out from Nam Poon , by a bridge and river, there is a place called 'Doi Pu Kha National Park Conservation Office' – somewhere to stay in an emergency. If you are offered a ride by a Hmong driver, avoid the danger of being ripped off by negotiating a reasonable fare before you climb aboard. Hmong people like to try it on. Wait for another lift if you are asked for more than 20 or 30 baht per person from Nam Poon to Nam Duang or Sa Wang. At the bottom end of Nam Duang (see Map 11), go right at the junction and proceed along a very poor (in 1998) dirt track the last 7 kms to end-of-the-road Sa Wang. If you can get no lift beyong Nam Duang, which is likely, or if as a biker you find the way too difficult (the worst part is right at the beginning), consider walking this last stretch – about 1½ hrs fully laden! – leaving your vehicle, if appropriate, somewhere sensible, such as at Nam Duang's forestry complex. Halfway to Sa Wang you pass the Hmong village of Kiu Nam.

Nam Duang & Sa Wang, and preparing for the trek

For practical and background information about these two remote villages near the border with Laos, see the latter part of Trek 7. There is no food in Sa Wang, so you will have to take your own. In Nam Duang there is fuel, some simple shops with cold beers and soft drinks, and (in 1998) even a noodle soup place. Both villages have forestry offices, at which you can stay, either inside in a room or outside in your tent. Ensure when you start this trek that you have plenty of drinking water with you. There is no water before Kiu Lom ('Windy Col'), which is situated some 4 or 5 hrs away on the far side of the first ridge to be crossed (a mere 1700 m high).

The Lua & Hmong peoples

For background information on the Lua (Htin) people, such as inhabit Sa Wang, see Trek 5. For a thumbnail sketch of the Hmong people, such as live in Nam Duang and Kiu Nam, see Trek 16 under 'Santisuk'.

*

119

Trekking route detail (Map 13)
Day 1: Sa Wang – Kiu Lom – Huai Pla Jaad (top end of w/f)

Time log

Start/0 hrs	Set off on a path that leads away from the top end of Sa Wang village on a compass bearing of 280°. (We started at 9am.) Follow path through bamboos up a spur, heading ca 300°. Keep to main path, which rises continuously. It is the same path which you follow at the end of Trek 7, when you climb – coming this way – over the great fourth and last ridge of that expedition.
ca ½ hr	At a fork, go right towards a high ridge.
	Looking right, you can see down below the track that leads to Huai Ja Lue w/f, 2 kms from Sa Wang. Views also of Lao border ridge. Continue on bearing of ca 330° along a twisty bit of the path, indistinct for us because of fallen leaves.
	Contour along left side of spur, with view left of the Sa Wang to Nam Duang 'road', then along right side.
1 hr 10 mins	Rest in a copse.
	Up and down, and then up through airy woods.
1 hr 50 mins	Rest on a spine.
	Hike steep up through jungle and banana palms.
2 ¾ hrs	130°: view back of Sa Wang.
2 hrs 50 mins	Stop for another rest on a second spine. Grand view NE into Laos.
3½ hrs	Finally reach top of ridge, called the 'Saang Si' ridge and including 'Hill 1700', so named because it is 1700 m (5577 ft) high. Same ridge is also called, apparently, by local Hmong, 'Sakio'.
	Contour round a shoulder of the ridge in dark cover.
3¾ hrs	Lunch stop in dried-up streambed amid dense jungle. While we tucked into bread and tinned tuna salad, our guides ate black sticky rice, chilli dip and leaves! (We arrived here at 12.45, spent 45 mins on lunch, and set off again at 1.30pm.)
4½ hrs	Set off again, reaching 10 mins later:
4 hrs 40 mins	Kiu Lom or 'Windy Col'. (On Trek 7, going from Mae Sa Nan to Sa Wang, this is the site of Camp 2, where the second night is spent. We tented here in 1996. Two years later, in 1998, it looked overgrown.)
5 hrs	Reach the top of a small knoll. Great forested views all round. Near here our guides gathered a length of some root, which, they said, had an effect like paracetamol.
5¼ hrs	Leave main path by going left (west) on a secondary trail down a spur in the direction of the Huai Pla Jaad and Nam Mao Mork.
5¾ hrs	Up through jungle to a wooded knoll with the remains of a sleeping hut.
	NW down spur.
6 hrs	View north of Doi Pu Fa
	Hop from knoll to knoll, now heading approximately N.

TREK 8: SA WANG – HUAI PLA JAAD – TONG

6 hrs 40 mins Proceed down into a small valley, before making a last hop from one knoll to another, to begin the descent to the Huai Pla Jaad.
Rest.
Make a 'Rambo' descent, the guides hacking a way with machetes. Lots of twirly things to admire, while other growths snag around your ankles and neck, barbed plants latch on to your clothes, entangling and tearing them, and bamboo leaves lacerate your arms. With the sweat dripping off your nose and off your glasses (if you are a spectacles-wearer), and with bees and insects stinging and bothering you, you:

7 hrs 10 mins Come to a dried-up streambed with red rocks. Pick your way down the stream bed until it ends by joining:

7 hrs 40 mins the **Huai Pla Jaad** at a pool. The pool marks the top end of Huai Pla Jaad waterfall. Both the stream and the fall flow here from E to W.

It is not so easy to camp at this first campsite. The sides of the pool are mostly rocky and steep. Our guides pitched camp on a spot somewhat above the pool, making a large mat for sitting on out of spiny, dark green, 6-ft-long fronds, and getting a fire going. We put up our tent nearby on an awful sloping patch. While we washed in the stream, also washing through our clothes and hanging them out to dry on branches, the boys caught fish from the pool. On the fire we boiled stream water in a pot to make coffee and instant noodles for supper. For their food, the Lua boys boiled up their fish in a bamboo tube and grilled some jungle frogs they had caught. In these beautiful, rank, wild, remote-as-hell surroundings, I reflected that I am probably the first *farang* ever to set eyes on this top end of Huai Pla Jaad waterfall. I don't know whether the chute where water falls into the pool is the uppermost cascade of Huai Pla Jaad waterfall. There may be more chutes above it – we were too tired to go poking around up there. Technically, so the guides told us, this chute by the pool and Camp 1 is not the first step of Huai Pla Jaad waterfall – the real first step comes lower down in the form of a double cascade.

Day 2: Descent of Huai Pla Jaad waterfall from top end at Camp 1 to bottom end at Camp 2 by Nam Mao Mork

Day 2 is the day of the gruelling and filthy climb down the waterfall. Take it nice 'n' easy! It is difficult and rather dangerous. The rocks are wet or slimy and hence hard to grip on to. In some places they are vertical. There is no path. The way down is just wherever you can find a way down. Nor can many of the obstacles be avoided. The sides of the gulley down which the Huai Pla Jaad flows are for the most part too steep and rocky. So, often you simply clamber down the face of the fall, or pick your way from foothold to foothold beside an actual chute. Without the sterling help of our guides, we would never have got down here. Sometimes in the latter half of the descent, where there really seemed no way forward, and where things had become just too fraught, we felt like giving up and returning to the top, except that this would have been almost as difficult and that, with the day advanced, there was no longer enough time to get back up. So we were compelled against our will to continue. After a breakfast of coffee and peanut butter sandwiches, we set off at 9.30am. The guides had been out hunting before breakfast and had caught a jungle fowl and two squirrels. After roasting them on the fire, they ate half of this game, keeping the rest for lunch.

Time log

Start/0 hrs   From the campsite clamber down the bed of the Pla Jaad stream, negotiating numerous difficult passages. We found ourselves abseiling down 20-ft blocks of moss-covered rock using lengths of air root cut by the guides. In one place we were lowered down a vertical drop by one guide, stepping onto the shoulders or head of a second guide, to be rescued by the third as we jumped off the second. It is quite some way – about 3 hrs – until the falls proper begin.

3 hrs   Arrive at the first real fall, a twisting double one, the first of 7 main falls in the overall Huai Pla Jaad waterfall complex (by my calculation).

In a pool, one of our guides, Pretty Boy Nguan, went fishing by swimming in the icy cold water and feeling under rocks with his hands. When he caught a fish, he gripped the flapping thing in his teeth, while continuing to search for another, only throwing the fish right out of the pool to the other guides when he had two or three.

3½ hrs   Near the first main fall we had lunch (1pm). The guides also found and raided a bee hive, cutting into the host tree with their machetes. Food was the rest of the squirrels and jungle fowl (very tough), boiled fish and wild honey, complete with grubs, supplemented with our rations.

4¼ hrs   After lunch, set off again (1.45pm).

4 hrs 25 mins   Move into more open country and come to the top of the second main fall, which is the biggest of all the component chutes and cascades. In my diary I wrote that it was a vertical 100-m drop, but in retrospect this estimation must be exaggerated, the product of momentary euphoria. Maybe it was 50 m, or perhaps I meant 100 ft. It took us 25 mins to climb down it.

4 hrs 50 mins   Reach bottom of this biggest single fall (2.20pm).

In my notebook I have no further timings for another 2½ hrs and only the sketchiest information. The chutes were coming thick and fast, seemingly indistinguishable, and my endeavours to record them were overtaken by the excited and anguished effort of picking our way down them. So I cannot reconstruct the pattern, except to say that after 7¼ hrs (at 4.45pm) we had just spent 50 mins negotiating a triple fall, which was followed by a 25-m cascade, itself part of a further triple fall. Beyond that I note another fall tumbling into a pool at the confluence of the Huai Pla Jaad and Nam Mao Mork. My photos tell a different story, but here again I don't think I systematically snapped all the falls, perhaps only the most photogenic – we were pressed for time and often the light was all wrong. It is hard to combine such adventuring with quality photography. To adequately capture every stage of the Pla Jaad fall would itself take a couple of days. My photo record speaks of seven main constituent falls: (1) the already-mentioned twisting double fall at the top end; (2) the big fall, which is like a curtain tumbling almost vertically over rock strata into a pool, and which is mimicked to one side by a slighter fall; (3) an elegant chute which, close to trees to one side, swooshes down like a child's slide into a pool; (4) a staggered triple fall tumbling into a pool; (5) a straight chute falling elevator-like into a pool, which in 1998 had a huge tree trunk sticking up out of it; (6) a complicated double- or triple-step fall; and a final extended multi-stepped fall flowing into a big pool at the bottom at the confluence. Even if I have not missed any steps out, this still makes seven main component falls with at least 12 or 13 individual cascades overall.

8 hrs 20 mins Reach the big pool (5.50pm) at the confluence of the Pla Jaad stream and the **Nam Mao Mork** at the bottom of Huai Pla Jaad waterfall. The Nam Mao Mork (= Misty River) flows here roughly N to S.

In the middle of the confluence, by the big pool, there is an island, on which you can camp. It is a decent and a fun site to tent on. At Camp 2 you spend a second night regaled with the constant sound of rushing water. If you can find your way here, starting from Tong, still a day's march away, you could have a great time camping on the island, swimming in the pool, doing a spot of fishing, exploring up and down the Nam Mao Mork, and poking around up Huai Pla Jaad waterfall. Again, I was too bushed to make notes about Camp 2, but I remember that the Lua boys netted dozens of fish in the Mao Mork river, and also hunted another squirrel and jungle fowl. This was the trek, too, when the guides kept alluding to me as 'the master', 'the boss' and 'the leader'!

Day 3: Bottom end of Huai Pla Jaad waterfall / Nam Mao Mork – River Wa – Tong

On our expedition, no one – not even one of the guides – knew the way forward from the confluence of the 'Jaad Fish Stream' and 'Misty River' to the village of Tong. We did not even know whether to strike north up the Nam Mao Mork or south downstream. But we had some good luck. After a while we ran into two local men, who sketched out a rough route. We set off late on Day 3 (at 10am) – the guides could not be kept from their favourite activity: hunting, preparing and cooking game, to be eaten on the spot and taken on the trek.

Time log

Start/0 hrs Go north (right, upstream) up the Nam Mao Mork, crossing the river. Proceed along the far (western) bank, past one camping spot to a second, which in 1998 had the remains of some structures.

25 mins By a tree with a charred hollow interior, opposite a jungle ravine, go left up an indistinct path.
You climb very steeply up, heading broadly NW.

50 mins 150°: views back to one part of Huai Pla Jaad waterfall.

1 hr Top of ridge, and time for a 15-min rest. Somewhere hereabouts there is, according to our informants, an old helipad, dating back to the days of the CPT insurgency.

123

1¼ hrs   Set off again, proceeding in a westerly direction downhill and then along.

1½ hrs   Come to a dried-up streambed with a scarp down one side.

1 hr 40 mins Leave streambed to right, picking up a path that proceeds down through bamboos.

1¾ hrs   Rejoin Nam Mao Mork, which is now flowing from SE to NW. In effect we have cut off a great bend of the Nam Mao Mork. Here we ran into the two men who drafted a map for us, the first people we had seen outside our party for 2½ days.

Walk downstream along northern bank of Nam Mao Mork. The path goes up high and then down, cutting off a spur of the river, which is quite big now.

2 hrs 20 mins Opposite on left bank: fabulous wall of jungle.

2¾ hrs   Reach confluence of Nam Mao Mork and **River Wa**, the Wa flowing from NE to SW. Walk ca 150 m along east bank of River Wa and then:

2 hrs 50 mins cross Wa river. At the end of January (in 1998) it was 75 m wide, and the water was crotch-deep.

3 hrs   Quick stop for snack lunch on far (western) bank (1pm).

3 hrs 20 mins Set off again. Proceed ca 200 m along river bank upstream. Here, to our annoyance, we found a raft which could have been used to ferry everyone across the Wa without getting wet!

Turn left away from the river and proceed for about 10 mins, before turning left again to begin a killer ascent out of the Wa river valley.

Skirt round left (western) flank of ridge.

4 hrs 35 mins Resting place on spine, with views back to Hill 1700 on the great Saang Si ridge near Sa Wang.

Path levels out and passes as if through olive groves.

5¼ hrs   Top of ridge and end of ascent.

Now the long slow descent to Tong village begins. The way is well-trodden and clear.

6¼ hrs   Resting place in jungle.

Groves of banana palms.

6 hrs 40 mins Reach the Nam Muap or Muap river, really more of a stream. Cross and recross it.

6 ¾ hrs   By a crossing, fork left.

Fork left again.

7 hrs   Orange orchards.

Path joins from right.

Path turns into a bullock cart track. People ride down here on motor-bikes. You could too, were you to visit the Huai Pla Jaad from Tong.

Path divides to rejoin.

A big long lake appears on left side.

March up and over a shoulder of hill, and follow the main track to:

7¾ hrs   **Tong** village, which we reached, exhausted, at 5.45pm, just before dark! The paved H1225 road lies on the far side of the village.

TREK 8: SA WANG – HUAI PLA JAAD – TONG

Exiting the trek (see Map 12)
If, having hiked 8 hrs from the Huai Pla Jaad across two ridges, you wearily
arrive at the village of Tong towards nightfall, as we did, you will be faced
with a problem of how to exit this trek, as we were. Probably you will want
to get back to Nan, and the guides will need to return to Sa Wang. But both
destinations are some distance away and not easy to reach, even during the
daytime. At dusk any public transport leaving or passing Tong will have
long since gone. So, unless you are prepared to pay someone handsomely to
drive you onwards, to will have to resign yourself to spending a night
locally or perhaps to hitch-hiking as far as, say, Mae Charim, where you
will also get caught out by the night and be forced to stay. The Lua guides
compound the problem. We found that, faced with a regular and unfamiliar
Thai village, they went all goofy and retiring, and were no help at all,
leaving us to try to engineer some solution. No longer in the jungle, they
were suddenly like fish out of water. Further, while you as *farang* might be
able to find villagers willing to take you in, the guides will hardly, from a
Thai family's perspective, constitute welcome guests – wild-looking, filthy,
sweaty, hill-tribe men carrying stove-pipe hunting guns and bamboo tubes
full of fish!

After you have drunk your fill of cold drinks from the little stores of
Tong (how good a beer tastes after 3 or 4 days of arduous trekking in the
heat!), consider opting for one of the following exiting strategies. (1) Try to
stay in Tong, perhaps putting up your tent at the edge of the village or by
the lake. Or get yourself taken in by a villager or by the headman and give
your tent to the guides. Don't worry too much about the guides; they can
certainly look after themselves. Rustle up food in Tong. The next day hitch-
hike or take a *silor* to the junction near Na Bua village and on to Nan (see
below). Undoubtedly, early the next morning, trucks, both private and
public, will be going in that direction, probably all the way to Nan. (2)
Station yourself on the 'main' road by the entrance to Tong and try to hitch-
hike – or just walk – south to a Doi Pu Kha National Park office. I cannot
remember the exact distance to this office, but it is not so far. You pass the
village of Na Maan and then find the branch office on your left, above the
road. The staff are friendly here and you will be welcome to stay, guides
included. 'Mini macho man' Suwit, as I like to call him (for reasons that
will be obvious if you meet him), has a smattering of English. From the
office, people even trek, reportedly, to the bottom of Huai Pla Jaad and to
Pu Fa mountain. The next day get a lift on to the Na Bua junction and Nan
– Suwit or his colleagues will help you on your way.

(3) Hitch-hike or pay a Tong villager to drive you to Mae Charim. This
small district 'town' does not lie on your way to Nan (see Map 12), and it
only makes sense to go there if you are returning to Sa Wang, as the guides
will be doing or you must do if you have left your motorcycle in Sa Wang.
But a virtue of going to Mae Charim is that there is more going on there,
there are more facilities, and you are better placed for travelling the next

125

day to either Sa Wang or Nan. Plenty of public as well as private and official transport starts from here. And this is the exit option we took, but chiefly because we had to retrieve our bike from Sa Wang and also wanted to see the guides safely home. Allowing ourselves to be overcharged, we paid the son of Tong's headman 200 baht to take the five of us in his pick-up to Mae Charim, which was all the more a rip-off because it transpired he was going there anyway to a meeting. At the entrance to Tong village, you go left (south) down the H1225 road, past Na Maan and the National Park branch office (left), through four further rural villages (Ko, Fai, Bon and Na Kit), to a T-junction, marked by a checkpoint. Here, right takes you on the H1168 road 32 kms over a low ridge, past Wat Pratat Chae Haeng to Nan town (see Map 12), while left takes you through five villages (Na Bua, Kwaeng, Nong Daeng, Don Prai Wan and Na Ka) 6 kms, likewise on the H1168, to Mae Charim.

At the end of our Huai Pla Jaad trek we had a ball in **Mae Charim**. Everyone said we (or anyone) could camp at the district office (east side of road), which we did, pitching our tent on a lawn directly in the *ampoe* grounds, while the guides bedded down on tables and benches in a meeting hall. It was amusing watching the dark dirty Lua boys, complete with their guns, march into these bureaucratic surroundings. We got water for washing with in plastic buckets from some houses at the back of the compound. There are places to eat and drink in Mae Charim, even after dark. We treated ourselves and the guides to beers and a double supper in a little restaurant operating out of the police station compound (further south down the main street, also on the east side)! Our party caused such a diversion for the policeman owner and his cronies that on top of our double meal of fried rice and gravy noodles (*raat naa*) we were given free pork crackling, frog curry and *lao dong ya* (rice whisky in which herbs, barks and roots have been steeped)! It was in Mae Charim that, when word got out that we had explored the whole length of legendary Huai Pla Jaad waterfall, we caused a furore among local officials and people, being pumped for information and begged for photos, as well as being feted as pioneering heroes.

That evening in Mae Charim we ran into development officials from Sa Wang, who said we could get a lift in their lorry to Sa Wang early the next morning, which is how we and the guides got back there. The route is as described earlier in this chapter under 'Accessing'. A rather radical way of avoiding the above-mentioned imperfect ways of exiting the trek would be to camp the third night not at Tong or at the National Park office or in Mae Charim, but back at the River Wa. Then on the fourth day you would reach Tong by lunchtime, which would give you half a day to make an orderly exit.

Part 2b

**Treks 9-15: In Nan province, north-east of Nan town
in the main northerly part of Doi Pu Kha National Park
ultimately based on Nan town**

**9-10: two treks launched from the Park HQ
11-14: four treks launched from or involving Maniploek village
14-15: two ascents of Mount Pu Wae**

Trek 9

Doi Pu Kha National Park HQ – Pang Kob – Pa Kham – Sa Wa

Parameters

trekking mode:	on foot
core trek time:	2 half days/1 night
accessing time:	from Nan town to the Park HQ via Pua allow about half a day using public transport and 2-3 hrs using your own hire motorcycle or jeep
exiting time:	from Sa Wa to Nan via the Park HQ and Pua allow at least half a day
overall trek time:	from Nan to Nan, including access and exiting times, 2-3 days and 1-2 nights
degree of difficulty:	easy
guide(s):	perhaps possible without guide
guide name(s):	Wan
tent:	required
map(s):	see 14 & 15

Overview

This modest 2-day/1-night trek takes you into the main northerly part of Nan province's Doi Pu Kha National Park. Starting from the Park headquarters, it cuts in a north-easterly direction through a corner of this heartland of the Park, a corner which is bounded to the south by the H1256 road and to the east by the H1081. The trek takes in the fast-disappearing Hmong settlement of Pang Kob and the traditional Lua (Htin) village of Pa Kham, exiting in the upper part of Sa Wa village, which lies some way up that fabulous secluded valley running north from Bo Glua close to the Thai-Lao border. Passing more through alpine mountain terrain than through jungle, this is a relatively comfortable hike, made all the more pleasant by the fact that, starting high up in the Doi Pu Kha massif at the Park HQ and ending down in a valley at Sa Wa, it is largely downhill. Because of this, and because the distance is comparatively short, the trek is suitable for travellers new to this kind of thing, who want to try out do-it-yourself jungle trekking. They will be further aided by the fact that the trek is easily accessed and exited, public transport going to the Park HQ and from Sa Wa, and by the fact that, starting from the HQ, they can draw on all the HQ's facilities. But this should not deter more ambitious trekkers. The expedition remains a little peach of an outing – varied, interesting and satisfying. For one thing the route in places follows parts of the old salt caravan trail trodden for centuries by people and pack animals (including elephants) going from Bo Glua to Pua and on to Nan. I did this trek in mid-February 1997 with Lannathai Nittaya Tananchai, US couple Peter Alcorn and Kelley Martin, and one Lua guide, making a party of five.

Strategy & accommodation
You will probably undertake this trek from Nan town, basing yourself on one of the guest houses there. From Nan via Pua to the National Park headquarters (and vice versa) is about 90 kms. Reaching the HQ and also returning to Nan after the trek is best done by motorcycle (you can hire Honda Dreams in Nan for about 150 baht per day). The ride to the HQ is a splendid trip, worth doing in its own right, and a bike gets you much more speedily to the start of the trek and also away from its end, possibly saving you one or more nights at the HQ. But the accessing and exiting can also easily be done by public transport. On Day 1 you travel from Nan to the Park HQ (details below), ideally arriving for an early lunch there. Assuming you have come by bike, you leave your machine locked at the HQ (it is quite safe to do so). If you feel you need a guide, you arrange to hire one with the friendly Park officials. After lunch you set off guided or unguided and hike 3 hrs to Pang Kob, where you spend the night (Map 15). On the morning of Day 2 you trek 3¼ hrs down from Pang Kob via Pa Kham to upper Sa Wa, crossing the Wa river just before Sa Wa. Total walking time, therefore, is just over 6 hrs. From Sa Wa you either hitch-hike or take a public-transport *silor* south down the valley to the small town of Bo Glua (Map 14), from where – after a quick late lunch, and a brief inspection of the salt well and its adjoining salt-extraction sheds – you hitch-hike or take public transport back to the Park HQ. Arriving there mid-afternoon, you should still have time to get back to Nan both by motorcycle (a couple of hrs) and by public transport or by a combination of hitch-hiking and *silor* (longer). But if, without your own transport, you run out of time, you can easily stay at the Park HQ.

The **Park HQ**, which travellers like to visit and stay at during an excursion from Nan, combining their visit with a trip through Doi Pu Kha National Park and with a stop in Bo Glua, is an organized and well-run complex of buildings. Lying some 30 kms east of Pua and about 22 kms west of Bo Glua, it is situated up a driveway just off the H1256 Pua/Bo Glua road on the north side. At the HQ, there are maps and 3-D models of the park, you can get a coffee and buy souvenirs, people are on hand to advise, you can take a stroll or launch a longer trek, you can hire a guide, and you can stay overnight in National Park accommodation. The boss is called Wittaya, and a girl called Wacharaporn (nickname 'Pla') is knowledgeable about the area, while a local Lua boy, called Chaloem, speaks reasonable self-taught English. Accommodation is at two places: at the HQ itself, and at a place called **Laan Du Dao** (= 'star-gazing place' or 'star viewpoint'), which is sited 5 kms east of the HQ (in the direction of Bo Glua), by the road on the south side (Map 14). At the HQ you can stay in a private room or bungalow with use of hot shower for about 200 baht a night, including food, or you can pitch a tent behind the HQ buildings either free or for a nominal sum. At Laan Du Dao, which is an annexe of the Park HQ, you camp in a tent, either pitching your own or hiring a Park one. Be warned, sleeping under canvas up here, either at the HQ or at Laan Du Dao, can be shiveringly cold in the night – make sure you have a decent sleeping bag or adequate blankets. The 'star-gazing place', which enjoys a fine view south into the mountains of the southern part of the National Park, also has a couple of little shops, selling snacks, drinks and fried rice, as well as other facilities. Doi Pu Kha National Park, its HQ and Laan Du Dao are popular not just with *farang* travellers, but also with Thai trippers. If you want a peaceful visit and trek, it is worth avoiding the HQ and Laan Du Dao at weekends and quite especially during Thai public holidays, such as at New Year and Chinese New Year. Another slight disadvantage of the HQ is that, if you start a trek from it, hiring a Park guide, you are in danger of being fussily overorganized by officials.

The trek can be modified as follows. It would be possible to arrive from Nan at the Park HQ late afternoon on Day 1, stay overnight at the HQ or at Laan Du Dao, and on Day 2 do all the walking (about 7 hrs, including a lunch stop) in one day, returning to the HQ late afternoon, after which you could either spend a second night at the HQ or attempt to get back to Nan (feasible if you have your own transport). The route could be varied, too. From Pang Kob you could proceed not to Pa Kham and Sa Wa, but to the double Lua village of Go Guang, trekking out at the H1256 road about 8 kms above (west) of Bo Glua (see Map 14). Similarly, after Pang Kob, you could trek not to Pa Kham and Sa Wa, but to Nong Nan, issuing at the H1081 road between Sa Wa and Bo Glua (north of Bo Glua).

For obvious reasons (we were opening up the trek), we hired a guide, a taciturn Lua man called Wan ('one', as in English), from the Park HQ, paying him 150 baht a day. This fee, the standard Park charge at the time, was in 1997. Three years on, you might like to pay 200 baht per day. I reckon you should be able to do this trek without a guide (no comeback, please), and our guide did not know the way after Pang Kob anyway. On the other hand a guide makes you feel securer and can also facilitate with things such as camping and negotiating lifts. I have no photo of Wan, but any guide from the HQ will do. Friendly Chaloem would make good company. Consider setting up the trek and a guide in advance, perhaps during a preliminary trip out by motorbike from Nan.

Accessing the trek (see Map 14)
If you are planning to follow our schedule, beginning the trek from the Park HQ after an early lunch, you will need to make a reasonably early start from Nan, no matter whether you are biking up into the Park or using public

transport. With transport of your own, take the main H1080 road north from Nan to the small market town of Pua, on the way passing Ta Wang Pa, which lies 16 kms before Pua. The 60-km journey should take you about an hour. In the centre of Pua you need to turn right at the crossroads, negotiating the exasperating new elongated reservation in the centre of the highway. If you have not already tanked up at the Shell station on the run-in to Pua, do so now at the fuel place near the beginning of this road going right (approximately SW), which is the H1081. Almost immediately, after just 200 m, turn left into the H1256 National Park road. Going downhill, you should find a temple on your left. Now comes the second half of the access way to the Park HQ, which will take you about another hour. You head out through some outlying rural Thai villages, before beginning the great climb up into the Doi Pu Kha massif, a spectacular, scenic and joyous ride. Various side tracks lead off the H1256 to offroad villages, but the main features of the route are the village of Na Lae, the 3 big signs indicating the entrance to the National Park, a paved side road (marked by a board with the names in Thai of 5 villages) going north, a viewpoint on the left side, and then the turning left for the Park HQ.

If you are accessing the trek without your own transport, take one of the hourly local red buses from Nan to Pua, getting off in the centre of Pua by the crossroads (the buses go further north). The journey should take about an hour. Cross the highway with its central reservation, and look for the place where the *silor* (public-transport pick-ups) bound for Bo Glua congregate. This has always been in front of the market. You should aim to get to Pua by 10am at the latest. The *silor* move quite slowly, stopping frequently, and the last regular vehicle leaves Pua at about 11am, after which these *songtaew* ('two benches') leave when enough people have gathered. Take the first available vehicle (fare about 25 baht to the Park HQ), or, if you are a party of several people, consider chartering one (price about 400 baht). After an hour or so (details as in preceding paragraph) alight by the driveway to the Park HQ and walk 100 m up to it.

The Lua & Hmong peoples
For background information on the Lua (Htin) people, such as inhabit Pa Kham, see Trek 5. For a thumbnail sketch of the Hmong people, such as live at Pang Kob, see Trek 16 under 'Santisuk'.

*

Trekking route detail (Map 15)
Day 1: Doi Pu Kha National Park HQ – Pang Kob
Starting from Nan at 9am, we reached the Park HQ, riding Honda Dreams, at 11am. After taking some lunch and fixing up a guide, we began the trek at 12.30pm.

Time log

Start/0 hrs	Set off from the back of the HQ, proceeding in a northerly and north-easterly direction.
¼ hr	Almost immediately you come to the Hmong village of Lao Sua (or possibly Lao Leng). Keeping right, walk uphill towards a ridge. The conical mountain left is Pu Huat.
	A path left goes to a reforestation area.
	At the end of the village, fork right onto a path.
	Contour through a copse.
	Streambed.
	At a fork, go left by a seat and up. The path is well-trodden because, before the H1256 road through the National Park was built, this was the old walking track from Bo Glua to Pua, which the salt caravans also used.
50 mins	A clearing. The half-bald mountain immediately right, overlooking the Park HQ, is Pa Tu Pa (1939 m/6362 ft). Owing to a long cliff, the path you are on is the only one going this way.
1 hr	Reach crest of ridge. The pile of leaves you pass is an animist offering to the path spirit, and everybody in our party was required to pluck and add a leaf to the pile.
	Pass one of the 'ancient' 'fishtail' palms that grow here and there in the National Park. You see many more of them from the H1256 road as you go from Laan Du Dao to Bo Glua (for background info on these prehistoric-looking growths, see below under 'Exiting the trek'. Walk along the pleasantly shady lee side of the ridge.
	View left of Sa Khun village in valley. If you get lost or cannot find Pang Kob, you could head for this settlement (as an alternative to returning to the HQ).
1½ hrs	Stream in glade. Turn left. (My notes are unclear to me at this point. I mention '120°', but I cannot remember whether this is a direction bearing or refers to a tree, probably the latter. The tree, on the right side, has a notice on it saying "Pua Spirit", and is a parasitic 'upside down' vine growth, where separate saplings have intergrown to form one tree. If you see it, you are on the right path.)
2¼ hrs	At a 'crossroads' by a big tree, go straight across. Tree can be walked through, having a huge hole in its middle.
2¾ hrs	Path joins from left. It goes to Sa Khun and Ta Noi.
	Panoramic views in the open:
	330° tooth mountain Khun Nam Pua, part of the Pu Wae ridge
	60° Thai-Lao border ridge
	30° dirt track to Pu Wae (so our guide said – I don't believe this)
3 hrs	Arrive at Pang Kob.

Spilled down an east-facing hillside, **Pang Kob** is a White Hmong place. Consisting of only some ten houses, it is hardly a village any more, just a settlement. Most of its inhabitants have moved out (been relocated), although a few, mostly old people, remain. These days Pang Kob is more a place where Hmong come from elsewhere to keep and graze their animals, and there are goats everywhere. Frankly, it is a hole, although, when we had got used to it, we had a pleasant enough stay here. We put our tents up on the only flat area we could find: the dried-up mud of a pond. Guide Wan slept "in the jungle" in a hammock, which he slung between two trees on the southern edge of Pang Kob. After we had pitched camp, an old lady said we could stay in her house. Water for washing and making hot drinks can be found at the bottom end of the settlement, pouring from a pipe. We brewed up coffee and instant 'Ma-maa' noodles in the house of a man with two wives. By these wives he had had eight children, four of whom had died, two from malaria (be warned!). He told us that the Lua Prai village of Go Guang was accessible from Pang Kob. Situated 1½ hrs' walking away, it was a double village, with a big and a small part. You can see one part of Go Guang from the H1256 road, about 8 kms up from Bo Glua. It is that group of houses scenically perched (NW of the road) on top of a ridge. In Pang Kob the wind blew all evening, and we spent a cold night on the hard baked mud of our pond campsite.

Day 2: Pang Kob – Pa Kham – River Wa – upper Sa Wa

We started from Pang Kob at 9.15am and soon found out that our guide, Wan, had never been to Sa Wa, and did not know the way after Pang Kob! We reached upper Sa Wa at 12.30pm after 3¼ hrs of trekking – all downhill.

Time log

Start/0 hrs	Leave village at the bottom end by the track passing the washing place. Immediately you come to a fork. Right goes to Go Guang, left (our route) to Sa Wa and also Nong Nan. View of Lao border ridge. Proceed downhill through attractive alpine terrain, regaled with the tintinabulation of cowbells.
5 mins	Come to a triple fork. Right goes downhill towards Nong Nan. Left goes to – I don't know where. Take the middle uppish way for Sa Wa. The path contours, with a valley to your right. Head N, NE and E down a spine, the valley remaining on your right side.
¾ hr	At a 'crossroads' go straight across. Another path joins from right. Follow main path down through some mini defiles. Join another main path coming from the left. Go right to reach village of:
1 hr	**Pa Kham.**

This very traditional Lua Prai village, which at the time of our visit still had no vehicular access or electricity, is reputed not to welcome outsiders, and we had been advised by some people to give it a wide berth. But everyone seemed friendly enough, and when we put the settlement's alleged inhospitality to a man, he laughed, saying that anyone was welcome not just to visit Pa Kham, but also to stay there. Why, a Japanese girl had just spent a year there, researching the Lua, and the villagers had helped build her house! In the village there is an adult education centre, manned in the evening by a teacher from Sa Wa, where you could perhaps stay overnight if you felt so inclined. Note the dark Mon-Khmer/Austronesian pigmentation of the inhabitants' faces and skins, and notice too the housing style – Lua dwellings are built not straight onto the ground in the Hmong fashion, but above ground on stilts. The first big dwelling you come to on entering Pa Kham houses six families. Visible due N on a hillside is another Lua village, Nam Choon (on the route of Trek 10).

1¼ hrs	Set off again after 15 mins' rest, leaving Pa Kham immediately right (relative to your point of entry).
	Proceed straight on to a bridge and village sign (for people coming up to Pa Kham from down in the valley).
	Bearing right, walk uphill and over, then go left along a spine.
1 hr 55 mins	View of H1081 road down on valley floor.
	Fork right.
2 hrs	Sign for people coming up in the opposite direction: 'Pa Kham left, Huai Lua right'.
	Path joins from left .
2 hrs 25 mins	Stile.
2 hrs 35 mins	Steep descent to River Wa.
	Cross the river, go right and splash your way 20 mins along to a dam and 'swimming pool' by a cliff left.
	Now either head for the big bridge visible in the distance down by the road by recrossing the river, or go up left on a path to come to the back of:
3 hrs 15 mins	**Sa Wa** (upper part of this double village).
	Make your way through the village to the H1081 road, go right to arrive at the big bridge over the Wa river and a roadside store with drinks.

Exiting the trek (see Map 14)

To return from upper Sa Wa to the National Park HQ – which you will have to do if you have left your motorcycle there – and to Pua and Nan, proceed first south down the H1081 road to Bo Glua. Take the first *silor* passing the bridge (fare about 10 baht) or just hitch-hike. Getting a lift in backwaters such as these is easy-peasy. The 8-km journey passes through lower Sa Wa (the main part of the village) and some 4 villages on and off the road, before coming to a junction, marked by a police box and a 'restaurant' (both left). You can eat in this restaurant, but there is a better place in the centre of Bo Glua. Turn right, leaving the H1081 to enter the H1256, and go down the hill. After 200 m there is a second junction. A waiting hut on this junction is a good place to look out for a lift back up to the Park HQ, either taking public transport or hitch-hiking. The road left off this second junction drops down into the main street of Bo Glua, which has many shops and some eating places, as well as a celebrated salt well and some salt-extracting works.

Bo Glua & its salt-production

Also known as Bo Luang (= big well), Bo Glua (pronounced 'bor' or 'baw' 'gleua' and meaning 'salt well') is an attractive, sleepy, isolated little place, nestling on the valley floor of the southward-flowing River Mang. Populated by *khon muang* or local northern Thai people from Nan province, it has burgeoned in the last few years. Where until recently it was just a few huts engaged in salt-production, now it has a hospital, a school, district buildings, a health centre, a library, and, as said, shops and 'restaurants'. The change began with the advent both of electricity about 1990 and of roads linking the village to the outside world. The H1081 road in from the south reached Bo Glua in 1983, at the time the war against the communist insurgents began turning in Bangkok's favour, while the new H1256 road through the National Park from Pua was completed in the late 1980s. The H1081 road coming down the valley from the north via Sa Wa was only finished as recently as 1994/1995! To the east and west of the diminutive town, steep forested red sandstone slopes rise up, between which in the early morning Bo Glua can be blanketed under mist. The mountains to the west are the eastern edge of the Doi Pu Kha massif, while those to the east are the western edge of the Thai-Lao border ridge.

Trekkers hungry for a good meal should proceed about halfway down the main street to a modest but highly recommendable eating 'hut', which is situated on the right side close to the main salt well and the River Mang. Efficiently run by a cheerful tall lean lady with goofy front teeth and a couple of tall lean daughters, it serves both a fine *pat thai* and a toothsome dish of roast chicken on rice with ginger dip and soup. It is possible but not easy (in 1999) to find overnight accommodation in Bo Glua. There are rooms in people's houses (which I have sometimes used), and once, proceeding to a trek, we camped (with permission) in the grounds of the district office high up above the village on the east side. But until some villager opens up regular guesthouse-type accommodation, which must surely soon happen, you are probably better advised to stay at the Park HQ, unless you speak enough Thai or are sufficiently resourceful to ask for and get what you want. It is also possible to stay or camp at the temple.

Further down the main street is the monastery-temple (*wat*) with a cute, folksy, centuries-old main building in the old Lan-Na style. A singular feature of this dilapidated little building are the great cracks in its walls, the result of it having been hit by a shell during the communist insurgency. Incidentally, during that time the Thai Army, sitting on the mountains to the west of Bo Glua, and the CPT's PLAT, sitting on the ridge to the east, used to trade artillery fire across the Mang valley, over the heads of the villagers, who sat it out hidden in little bunkers.

Bo Glua obviously takes its name from the salt well in the village (the biggest such well of half a dozen in the locality) and from the salt-extraction carried out there, an important local industry that has been going on for hundreds of years, making this tiny town somewhat historic. Before salt became easily and cheaply available from other sources, merchants used to come long distances across the mountains from every direction to buy the scarce and precious Bo Glua commodity. Not least they used to come with caravans of pack animals, including elephants, from Pua, walking part of the trail that we trekked near the Park HQ and Pang Kob. Then they would return loaded up with salt, in columns typically 40-60 beasts strong and minded by 8-10 men, proceeding to Pua and on to Nan or even Chiang Mai, where in the 19th century Bo Glua salt was used as currency in the market, and where Yunnanese Haw traders bought it up to take on their far-ranging caravans. It is not known how long the wells at and around Bo Glua have been in existence or who first discovered them. Traditionally, it is said, they have been worked by the local Lua, as they still are, and it is thought that there is some connection between these wells in the north-east of Nan province and other similar wells in Sipsong Pan-Na (in China's Yunnan province) as well as in northern Laos. Now that salt is widely and cheaply available from other sources, you would have expected that salt-production in Bo Glua would have withered away. But exactly the opposite is the case. The village still produces salt, tons of it, but it is purchased by new takers – the growing number of Thai trippers who come to Bo Glua across the mountains in minibuses and pick-ups. They buy the 10-kg bagfuls of gleaming white salt as a useful souvenir. Remote tiny Bo Glua is becoming a tourist attraction!

In Bo Glua there are actually two wells. The first and principal one lies, as said, in the middle of the village, set back from the main street, near the river, while the second is down beyond the *wat*, on the eastern side of the street, set back, and next to a salt-producing cooperative. The salty water, once it has been drawn up from the 20 to 30-ft-deep wells, is transferred into a number of extraction sheds. In Bo Glua the salt is obtained not by drying out the water in reservoirs, but by evaporating the water off in the sheds in giant wok-like metal pans boiled over stoves fired by burning logs. In 1995 I counted two dozen such boiling pans in the village, i.e. a dozen pairs on a dozen double stoves, and today there are probably many more. Each pan, measuring 4 ft in diameter, produces an incredible 12 kgs of salt per evaporation (lasting 3-4 hours), making daily production alone a substantial quantity. The clay stoves or furnaces throw out a lot of heat, sweltering in the day, but making a warm cosy atmosphere in the sheds during cool evenings. I have given a more in-depth account of both Bo Glua and its salt-production in my cultural guidebook *Around Lan-Na*, to which the reader is referred.

Exiting: Bo Glua – Park HQ – Pua – Nan (Map 14)

From Bo Glua back up by *silor* to the National Park HQ costs about 20 baht and to Pua about 50 baht. If you are waiting for public transport down by Bo Glua, try hitch-hiking in case no *silor* comes or none comes for a long time. On the H1256 road, starting at its eastern end, you cross a bridge over the Mang river, pass Bo Glua hospital on your left, and climb steeply up past the Lua double village of Nam Pae (left) and past the beginning of the path for the Lua double village of Go Guang (right, about 8 kms from Bo Glua) to a pass (1650 m high, 13 kms from Bo Glua), marked by a fire prevention office. Then you go along a stretch of the road affording views of many groves of **'ancient' 'fishtail' palms**, a specimen of which was encountered earlier during the trek on the way to Pang Kob. Actually, the fronds of these primaeval-looking trees as much resemble pairs of wings as fishtails. Classified as *caryota sp*, and known in colloquial Thai as *tao raang yak* or 'giant tufted palm', the palms are a rare and endangered species. They are found only at an altitude of 1500-1700 m, and each palm grows to a height of 8-12 m, with fronds 2-3 m long. In Thailand the palms exist only in Doi Pu Kha National Park, but it is said that some more grow in Laos. *Caryota sp* is considered to be a mixture of *caryota ochlandra* and *caryota no*, and is thought to constitute a new kind of 'prehistoric' palm tree, suited to cloudy mountain terrain. During the communist insurgency in Thailand, guerrillas living in the mountains of Nan used to eat the fishtail palms, grinding up their trunks to make a kind of flour.

You pass, too, the famous **Chompu Pu Kha tree** or 'pink Pu Kha' tree (left, km 16), which can be viewed from a wooden platform. Not much to look at, even when it blossoms pink in February, this tree is nevertheless of considerable botanical interest. For a while, people claimed that it was unique, if not in the world, then certainly in Thailand. And so it was until a a very few other isolated specimens were found in Nan province, two near the village of Maniploek (see Trek 12). These extremely rare trees would seem to be related to similar or even identical trees found especially in south China (Yunnan province), but also reportedly in Vietnam and Laos. In China the species, classified as *Bretschneidera sinensis Hemsley*, was first discovered a century ago, growing at an altitude of 1524 m (5000 ft) – almost exactly the same as the Pu Kha tree (1540 m or 5052 ft). The Bretschneider *chompu* tree beside the road in Doi Pu Kha National Park is about 25 m high, 50-100 years old, has a medium-sized trunk with smooth greyish-brown red-veined bark, thin dark-green leaves, orange cherry-sized berries, and clusters of pink bell-shaped flowers, each spray of which is about 40 cms long. It is deciduous, produces mustard oils, and shows affinities to primitive plants, suggesting that it too, like the 'prehistoric' palms, might be a relic. Some research, comparing the leaves, fruit and flowers of the Nan *chompu* trees with those of their relatives up in Chinese Kunming suggests that the former might really differ from the latter, possibly having characteristics all of their own, which would mean that the Pu Kha trees are perhaps genuinely unique after all.

You come next to Laan Du Dao (km 17), and 5 kms further, after skirting the Lua village of Nam Dan (left, km 20), reach the turning for the Park HQ (right, km 22). If you are bikers who have left their machines there, retrieve them from the HQ, and then continue, assuming it is not too late, in the same way as *silor*-travellers. The rest of the exit journey back to

137

Pua and Nan is the same as the access journey on the way out, except in reverse. You pass the viewpoint (right), the turning (right, km 24) for the half dozen villages offroad north, the signs indicating the beginning (or in this case the end) of the National Park, various turnings to offroad settlements, and Na Lae. Coming down steeply off the mountains, you pass through some outlying rural Thai villages, before hitting a T-junction. Left goes to Nam Yao on the H1081 road, while right brings you after 200 m to the central crossroads in Pua (ca 50 kms from Bo Glua). At the crossroads go left to travel 60 kms south down the H1080 road via Ta Wang Pa to Nan town. Trekkers using *silor* will have to change onto a local bus in Pua in order to complete the journey back to Nan. The red buses go hourly and continue until reasonably late in the evening (fare a few baht). If you miss the last one, try taking a Pua-Nan *silor*. In 1999 I saw a new guest house in Pua, located on the main road at the southern end of the town, although it could be pricey. Allow a good hour to travel from the Park HQ to Pua, and the same from Pua to Nan.

Trek 10

Doi Pu Kha National Park HQ – Kiu Haen – Toei – Nam Pua Pattana – Charaeng Luang – Huai Por – Nam Choon – Bo Yuak

Parameters

trekking mode: basically a foot trek, but first part could be done as a motorcycle trek

core trek time: 2 days/1 night fastest time, 3 days/2 nights slowest

accessing time: from Nan town to the Park HQ via Pua allow about half a day using public transport and 2-3 hrs using your own hire motorcycle or jeep

exiting time: from Bo Yuak Tai to Nan via Bo Glua, the Park HQ and Pua allow at least half a day

overall trek time: from Nan to Nan about 3 days, including accessing and exiting time

degree of difficulty: as a walking trek: easy
as a biking trek: only moderately difficult dirt riding

guide(s): advisable for short central section between Charaeng Luang and Huai Por, but not strictly necessary

guide name(s): Taen & Waad (see photo)

tent: not absolutely necessary, but useful as a fallback

map(s): see 14 & 16

Overview

This varied trek, taking in numerous Lua (Htin) villages and negotiating all kinds of terrain, from dirt road to mountain forest, heads north up that long dirt side road that leaves the H1256 National Park road just west of the Park headquarters, proceeds to the end of the trail at Charaeng Luang, crosses one decent mountain ridge to reach the Lua village of Huai Por, and then descends eastish along a very rough foot and then vehicle trail via Nam Choon to Bo Yuak Tai, situated down in the valley on the H1081 road north of Bo Glua. In doing so, it cuts off a corner – as does Trek 9 – of the main northerly part of Nan province's Doi Pu Kha National park, albeit a corner bigger than that sliced off in Trek 9. The hike exits, again like Trek 9, by heading south down the backvalley H1081 road to Bo Glua, from where it returns up the H1256 road to the starting point at or near the Park HQ. It is an easy, although tiring, trek that you can do mostly, if not entirely, on your own. The only stretch for which you probably need a guide is the cross-country link between Charaeng Luang and Huai Por. But remember that, having no guide(s) for most or all of the way, you will have to carry the full weight of your baggage yourself. I did this trek in January 1998 with Nittaya Tananchai, and we hired the two (rather reluctant and expensive) guides Taen and Waad from Charaeng Luang for the morning's climb over the confusing central mountain link. This was an expedition which, when we did it, we had to radically recast on the hoof, aborting our original plan. Originally we had intended to trek from Charaeng Luang and Huai Por north to Pu Wae mountain, descending east to the valley of the H1081 road much further up. But in Huai Por no one knew the way to Doi Pu Wae, or they were unwilling to go, and so, stuck in Huai Por, we had to think how to make a new onward second part of the trek, deciding to cut east to Nam Choon and Bo Yuak Tai.

There is something in this outing for motorcycle trekkers. From Nan you could ride via Pua up to the Park HQ, turning left 2 kms just before the HQ into the northbound side road, and proceeding on hilly dirt as far as you can get – in 1998 as far as the new part of Charaeng Luang, called Ban Mai or Charaeng Mai. From here, you could either return to the H1256 and Nan, or you could walk on to Charaeng Luang, or you could camp overnight at nearby Nam Pua Pattana. I will consider these options below. Whether there is anything in this trek for bicyclists (on mountain bikes), I do not know. It would hardly be worth cycling just up and down the side road to Nam Pua Pattana or Charaeng Mai. And riding along the H1256 through the National Park (perhaps as part of a long loop from Nan) would surely be very tough and dispiriting because the way is so steeply up-and-down.

Strategy

Using Nan town as your overall base, you can kick off the actual trek in one of two places, which lie close to each other: either at the beginning of the northbound side road, where it leaves the H1256 National Park road, or at the Park HQ. Because the two starting points are so close to one another, just 2 kms apart, it does not matter much which you choose, but proceeding from the HQ will appeal if you want to use its facilities, for example staying overnight or leaving your motorbike there.

On Day 1, if you follow our schedule, you make your way during the morning either by hire motorcycle or by public transport from Nan via Pua to either the beginning of the side road or the Park HQ. Arriving here late morning, you leave your machine (if you have one) at the Park HQ. Then, starting respectively from the beginning of the side road or the HQ, you walk about 4½ hrs up the dirt side road to Charaeng Luang, passing many villages and settlements. The road progressively deteriorates (in 1999) until at the end you follow just a path. You could try hitch-hiking up this road, but on each of the two occasions that I have been along it I failed to get any lift, having to hoof the whole stretch. Perhaps a couple of trucks a day go some or most of the distance. But never mind, it is a pleasant walk. You spend the first night at Charaeng Luang. On Day 2 you take one or more guides from Charaeng Luang and trek during the morning 2½ hrs to Huai Por, where you have an early lunch. While the guides return to Charaeng Luang, you continue in the afternoon on your own about 1hr 20 mins to Nam Choon. From here you either walk or hitch-hike, as we managed to do, 5 kms down to Bo Yuak Tai and the H1081 road. Now you must return either by public transport or by hitch-hiking south to Bo Glua and then west to the vicinity of the Park HQ, where you can retrieve your motorcycle, if you have one, before returning via Pua to Nan.

It is unlikely that you will get back to the Park HQ, let alone Nan, before dark on Day 2, and so a likely problem towards the end of this trek is where to spend a second night. It would be logical to overnight at Bo Yuak Tai or Bo Glua or back at the Park HQ. We stayed in Bo Yuak Tai, but I do not advise this. Unless you can speak Thai, it is unlikely that you will be able to arrange accommodation, although you could, I suppose, just pitch a tent across the road on the banks of the River Wa. We arrived at Bo Yuak Tai late afternoon. We tried for a couple of hrs to get on to Bo Glua or the Park HQ both by public-transport *silor* and hitch-hiking, but failed miserably and were caught out by nightfall. In the end we stayed in the house of a man who lives in Bo Tuak Tai and who, seeing our plight, offered to put us up. Nor is Bo Glua, if you can reach it, an easy place to stay in (as of 1999), again unless you can speak some Thai. So my solution to the problem is: (1) either stay the second night at Nam Choon, which would give you the whole of the next day, Day 3, to return to the Park HQ and Nan, or (2) reschedule the whole trek. (1) The former is probably the better option. Nam Choon is a pleasant scenic Lua village, begging to be stayed in. Put up a tent or stay in its adult education centre. Undoubtedly, during your stay at Nam Choon you could, if you wanted, fix up a lift for the following morning. (2) In the latter case, you could recast the trek by bringing everything forward. Make your way to the Park HQ during the afternoon of the day preceding the actual trek, and stay there overnight. The next day, make your way during the morning, either by walking or by hitch-hiking or by a combination of both, to Charaeng Luang, and during the afternoon trek on to either Huai Por or Nam Choon, spending the night there. On the last day you have enough time from either Huai Por or Nam Choon to exit the trek. All things considered, the better places to stay are the Park HQ, Charaeng Luang and Nam Choon, and the less good places are Huai Por, Bo Yuak Tai and Bo Glua.

We did this trek without a tent, staying in people's houses in Charaeng Luang and Bo Yuak Tai, and because you overnight not out in the jungle, but in villages, a tent is not strictly necessary. If you are reluctant to stay in (hill-tribe) people's houses – an experience actually not to be missed – or in places such as adult education centres, take a tent with you. A tent gives you independence and privacy, and, even if you do not use it, constitutes a useful fallback. If you take no tent, ensure absolutely that you have a mosquito net with you!

The Lua people: background information

For brief background information on the Lua people, such as you meet at Nam Pua Pattana, Charaeng Luang, Huai Por and Nam Choon, see Trek 5.

Accessing and launching the trek (see Map 14)

Make your way to the vicinity of Doi Pu Kha National Park HQ. If you start from Nan town, you will travel on the H1080 and H1256 roads via Pua. An account of this access route can be found in Trek 9. Near the HQ decide whether you want to launch the actual trek from the HQ or the start of the side road. Decide too whether you need or want to spend a night at the HQ. For details about overnighting at the HQ complex or at its nearby annexe of Laan Du Dao – whether in a room or under canvas – likewise see Trek 9. If you have come from Pua by *silor*, and assuming you do not need to stay at the HQ, get off at the beginning of the side road. It is just beyond a rest place/viewpoint (left) and 2 kms short of the Park HQ, and is marked both by a large regular road sign indicating (in Thai) five villages left, together with their distances, and by a small wooden sign near a fir tree indicating 'Tontong Waterfall 850 m'. There is a *sala* or roofed open-sided waiting hut at the mouth of the road on the left side. The first few kms of the side road are paved, in 1999 to the far side of the second village, Toei Klang. Now start walking. Apparently the Pua *silor*, if it is worth their while, sometimes enter this side road, even going as far as the village of Ta Noi. If that is the case, you are in luck. Continue in the *silor* as far as you can get, saving your energy for the more interesting meat of the trek later.

If you are coming with your own transport, probably a motorcycle hired in Nan, leave it at the Park HQ. Of course, you could leave it at the first village up the side road, Kiu Haen, or indeed anywhere up the side road, but then you would have to return to that place after the trek to retrieve your machine, which would be inconvenient. This is what I once did, leaving my Honda Dream at the health centre in Kiu Haen (bottom end of village, right side), but the option, although possible, is hardly recommendable. So you leave own transport at the Park HQ. Having done this, now make your way to the side road. You can either walk 2 kms back along the H1256 to the start of the side road, or cut across country to it from the back of the HQ. There is a path which does this, issuing, I think, at Toei Hua Doi. I have not walked this link path, so I am not sure of its details – ask at the HQ. If you can sweet-talk the HQ officials, you might be able to get them to take you free in a truck to the beginning of the side road, or to Kiu Haen, or even further. And if you pay them, you might get them to take you to Ta Noi or beyond, an ideal scenario. A nice place from which to start walking on the side road is Toei Hua Doi.

If you are doing this expedition as a motorcycle trek, head off up the side road. If you are moderately skilled at riding on dirt, you should be able to get as far as Nam Pua Pattana 2 (used to be called Ban Ta) or to Charaeng Mai (= New Charaeng), but not to Charaeng Luang.

*

Trekking route detail (see Map 16)
Day 1: H1256/start of side road – Kiu Haen – Toei – Ta Noi – Nam Pua Pattana – Charaeng (Ban Mai) – Charaeng Luang

Aim to start walking from the junction by midday or 1pm at the latest, so that you reach Charaeng Luang after some 4½ hrs of walking by nightfall. By all means avail yourself of any passing lift (*silor* or private truck) to speed you on your way at the beginning. The hardest part of Day 1 is at the end, just when you are most tired, when you have to climb steeply up, fully laden, to Charaeng Luang. Save your energy for then.

Time log

Start/0 hrs	Set off along the side road, proceeding downhill on a cement-section surface, through a little defile in a kink in the way, to the first village:
ca ½ hr	**Kiu Haen** (Lua), with its health centre at the bottom end, right side. Continue past the Lua village of **Toei Klang** (according to the sign at the mouth of the side road, 3 kms from the H1256) and down to a bridge and river, where in 1999 the paved surface gave over to dirt. Climb up the other side of the valley to reach the Lua village of:
ca 1 hr	**Toei Hua Doi**, which is split into at least two parts. Just to confuse things further, this whole area is known as Huai Ngon. You reach a T-junction, marked by a *sala* or waiting hut. By the junction, on your right side, there is a shop (next to a phone box) which has drinks. From the *sala* you enjoy a new scenic view N across a second valley into the heart of the National Park. You will be heading to the right side of N, and you should be able to make out your dirt-trail route contouring ca NNE round the mountainsides, taking in villages on the way. From the T-junction, the way going left and to the left side of N proceeds ca 2 kms to Toei Noi (= little Toei) and then on to the village of Choon, which you can see in the distance at 330°, and from which you can continue to Sa Kaat (see Trek 11) and ultimately the H1080 road. After a rest, go right from the T-junction, past the shop and phone booth, out of Toei Hua Doi and downhill. For a while the route heads in a more easterly direction, before striking N again. Somewhere along here, I suspect, the cross-country path from the Park HQ connects with the dirt road. Follow the power lines.
ca 2 hrs	Right side of road, by a bridge: Waeng stream and waterfall, a slimy 100-ft chute reminiscent of Huai Khon waterfall (Trek 13). There is also a little drinking spring at Nam Tok Waeng. After another bridge, across the Huai Sa Khun (Sa Khun stream), and some 30 mins from the Waeng stream:
ca 2½ hrs	turning right (east) for the Lua village of **Ta Noi**, which lies some 300 m from the junction and has a hill-tribe education centre. A path continues from Ta Noi to the Lua village of Sa Khun, the Hmong settlement of Pang Kob and other villages (see Trek 9 & Map 14). Continue straight (north) from the turning and reach just a few minutes later:

143

ca 2½ hrs **Nam Pua Pattana 1**. This small backward Lua place of a dozen houses and no school is the first half of a double village, the two parts of which I have called Nam Pua Pattana 1 and 2. 'Nam Pua Pattana' is actually a new name recently bestowed by Thai officialdom to the 3-part village of Ta (at Ta Noi and at Nam Pua Pattana 1 & 2). Got it?

In the blazing sun, toil up the hill on a deteriorating road out of Nam Pua Pattana 1 and head into an amphitheatre of mountains to arrive 35 mins later at:

ca 3 hrs **Nam Pua Pattana 2**, also known as Ban Ta (= Ta village). The second larger half of Nam Pua Pattana, this relatively big, strung-out Lua village in a very attractive setting has a fine south-facing adult education centre, with a long balcony at the front, reached by wooden steps. On two separate occasions we have found the staff here very friendly and helpful. If you ask, they will allow you to cook up instant noodles or whatever in their kitchen in the back left corner of the building, and undoubtedly they would let you stay overnight at the centre. So solicitous was one teacher here that, after we had set off – unsure of the route – on our onward journey to Charaeng Mai, he motorcycled to that place to check that we had safely reached it. I have always liked Nam Pua Pattana, and if you are a less ambitious trekker or perhaps a motorcycle trekker who wants to go no further, you could have a nice time and good fun camping here, maybe using the village as a base for some local exploration. Look for a tenting spot down by the River Pua (from which the double village takes its name), which flows past nearby to the west. From Nam Pua Pattana you could make excursions on foot or by bike to Charaeng Mai (30 mins), on foot only to Charaeng Luang 1½ hrs), and on foot with a guide to Nam Pua waterfall (ca 3 hrs) (see Trek 12). Upstream along the River Pua and in the vicinity of the waterfall, there is some fantastic jungle, in which you could also tent, doing some 'Rambo' camping. It is at Nam Pua Pattana 2 that Trek 12 ends, exiting to Toei Hua Doi and the H1256 road after coming south from Lua Maniploek via Hmong Khang Ho and Nam Pua waterfall.

Proceed out of the rear upper end of Nam Pua Pattana 2, continuing N steeply up, to reach 30 mins later:

ca 3½ hrs **Ban Mai** (= New Village) or **Charaeng Mai** (New Charaeng), another Lua place in what seemed to us a rather bleak setting. In 1998 this was indeed, as its name suggests, a new village, sited at the very end of the dirt side road. People were building or had just built new wooden houses. The place seemed deserted, something of a ghost settlement, but probably that has all changed meanwhile. With night approaching, we could find no one to ask about the onward way to Charaeng Luang. But fortunately the teacher arrived on his motorbike from the adult education centre and put us right. The situation with Charaeng is that in the next few years (if it has not already happened) Charaeng Luang up in the mountains is to be moved out and down to New Charaeng. Beyond Ban Mai only a steep path goes on to Charaeng Luang. The road is planned to end at Ban Mai and not to be pushed through to Charaeng Luang. The authorities want to relocate Charaeng Luang to bring it somewhat out of the depths of the National Park and to a place where the inhabitants can be reached by road and where they, in turn, have better access to the outside world. The relocation brings a problem from the point of view of this trek. As the years go by and the village does move, guides for Huai Por, if required, will have to be found and hired in Ban Mai, not in old Charaeng Luang, and the next leg of the trek will have to be made from the new village, just as the first overnight stop will have to be made there. Thus at the time of writing the situation is fluid. In Ban Mai try to ascertain what the latest is, perhaps by attempting to locate guides Taen and Waad. If people, on seeing my photo of them, point up to Charaeng Luang, then probably old Charaeng is still inhabited, in which case you can press on.

In 1998 Ban Mai or New Charaeng was connected with Charaeng Luang by only a footpath, which people said was 3 kms long, although to us, tired from walking all the way from the H1256 road, it seemed much longer. The path begins by heading ENE. At a fork, branch left. Now the way swings left and then right to climb very steeply up the side of a ridge to reach one hour out from Ban Mai:

ca 4½ hrs **Charaeng Luang** (= big Charaeng).

In 1998 this small elevated traditional Lua village, attractively set and without electricity, comprised 32 houses as well as an adult education centre and little school, all spilled down the hillside. Every family had one of three surnames: Pa Paeng, Jai Ping or Na Shon. The headman's name was Boon Si, while the deputy headman, a knowledgeable forceful character, was called Gu – enlist his help if you need it. Evidently there is a waterfall nearby, called Nam Tu. We were amazed to find a couple of motorbikes in Charaeng Luang. How on earth did people manage to bike up paths that we could hardly drag ourselves up on foot? When we did this trek, we completed the last hour very slowly on our own in the dark with the aid of torches, an alarming experience not to be recommended. We arrived at the bottom end of the village to be greeted by howling snarling dogs. A party seemed to be in full swing upstairs in the adult education centre, to which we were taken, and where we were invited to stay and eat. The centre was run and taught by a lean sultry Thai beauty called Patcharaya Moon-ngoen, nickname Aep, who was sidelined in her own domain by the loud high-spirited crew partying, but who obligingly cooked up some food for us. She and her boyfriend may now be down at Ban Mai. In the thick of things, bombarding us with questions and suggestions, was deputy headman Gu, who fixed up for us the two guides Taen and Waad, who were to accompany us the following morning to Huai Por, portering our backpacks. If you hire guides in Charaeng (Mai or Luang), reckon on paying them each 150-200 baht per day, which is what it will take them to go to Huai Por and back.

Day 2: Charaeng Luang – Huai Por – Nam Choon – Bo Yuak Tai

The journey to Huai Por took us 2½ hrs, starting at 9.15am and arriving at 11.45am. It crosses one big ridge. Dark-skinned, hirsute Taen and bony-faced, Wa-eyed Waad led the way.

Time log

Start/0 hrs	Leave the village by going straight up behind the school, past the last house and a circular water tank.
	At a fork, go left.
	Heading NE, follow a stony path up to the top of a shoulder. The overall mountain ridge is called Doi Saam Sao. Continue climbing it.
40 mins	At a kind of clearing, fork left into woods, proceeding along the left (south) side of a hill.
	After a few mins you emerge into an open patch. Go N, leaving the patch on your extreme left (W), and leaving a wooded mountaintop exactly behind you. Incidentally, this commanding height was once, during the era of the communist insurgency, the site of a CPT/PLAT guerrilla base. A little path goes down through some bushes.
50 mins	After a few minutes you emerge into open countryside with a view of the path dipping and climbing the mountain ahead. Keep going north, and keep to the left side of a col.
55 mins	View westish (240°) over Charaeng Luang, with Ban Mai exactly beyond it.
1 hr 5 mins	An hour from Charaeng Luang, reach top of Doi Saam Sao ridge and end of climb.
	Pass through bushes, a defile, a ravine and woods to proceed downhill to an open knoll.
	In an open spot, bear right 30° (just E of N) into trees.
	You ascend a bit, and then again, to skirt round the right (eastern) side of a shoulder, before continuing steep down and along through tunnels of undergrowth and head-height bamboos.
1 hr 35 mins	View NE (45°) of Huai Por across a valley.
	Drop steep down through a small plantation of *miang* bushes (wild tea) to arrive at the:
2 hrs 5 mins	Huai Choon or Choon stream and a pool.
	Cross the stream and follow a path that climbs steeply up the far bank. Where the path contours, another path comes in from the left. The united track brings you to:
2½ hrs	**Huai Por.**

The Lua village of Huai Por lies at the end of a (in 1999) very poor dirt side trail striking approximately NW from the H1081 road down in the valley and taking in midpoint Nam Choon. When we trekked down the trail, the uppermost part was still impassable for vehicles, and so there were no trucks in Huai Por. More outlying bits of the village lie along this uppermost stretch, detached from the main part of the settlement. There is an adult education centre here, in which you could stay if you wanted, and in 1998 there was no electricity. The headman, called Wan, is the brother of deputy headman Gu in Charaeng Luang. While we were taking an early lunch, we formed a poor impression of Huai Por, which seemed to be in the grip of drunken exploitative people. It was in the village that we learned that the original plan we had for this trek – to reach the Lua village of Huai Kwaak and its nearby peak of Doi Pu Wae – was apparently unfeasible, compelling us to abort the project and redesign the trek on the hoof. The problem with going to Huai Kwaak, so we were told, was that no one used the path, that the path was therefore overgrown, and that no one would be able to find the way. We got the impression that the hearts of our Huai Por informants was not in the matter, although, to be fair, it is possible that the distance was very great. So we asked about alternative goals from the village. We could go from Huai Por to the Lua village of Huai Jaan, they said, which was an estimated 4 hrs' trekking away. But for this they wanted 300 baht per guide and would not go with fewer than 2 guides. They were not be budged from these inflated demands (150-200 would be more appropriate), 600 baht seemed to us too much to get to the next village, and so we decided to cut down to Nam Choon instead. This is a pity, as proceeding to Huai Jaan might be a fine continuation of this trek from Huai Por. Perhaps you will have better luck than we had and can check it out, thereafter either going even further north from Huai Jaan, or striking east to the H1081 road, in the manner that we are now about to do.

Time log

Start/0 hrs	It is hardly necessary to keep a time log or record details of the rest of this trek – you cannot miss the way and just keep walking down the track past Nam Choon to the 'main' road in the valley. It is about 4 or 5 kms from Huai Por to Nam Choon and the same from Nam Choon to the H1081 at Bo Yuak Tai.
	From Huai Por's adult education centre, go along a track, past the village entrance sign, and down over a makeshift bridge across a stream, heading broadly SE.
25 mins	An outlying piece of Huai Por. You can see that a road exists between Huai Por and Nam Choon, but that (in 1998) it is impassable for 4-wheel traffic and probably also for 2-wheeled. No doubt this way will be recut sooner or later and will ultimately be upgraded or paved – perhaps it already has been.
40 mins	You come down to a stream and a log bridge.
55 mins	Up left: houses near giant bamboos and a big tree with air roots.
1 hr 10 mins	Wooden bridge.
1 hr 20 mins	Reach **Nam Choon**.

Nam Choon is a medium-sized Lua village, set around a cement main street. The inhabitants all have the surname Jai Ping, and the headman is called Laa. In 1998 we found just one roadside shop, which sold a few provisions, but no soft drinks. There is an adult education centre, likewise situated beside the road (left/N side), which would make a good place to stay. Consider doing so. I like Nam Choon. It is a nice scenic place, and people are friendly. Traffic reaches here, although just a couple of vehicles a day. They say of Nam

Choon tobacco that when you smoke it, the geckos fall from the ceiling, and that if they don't, the tobacco cannot be from Nam Choon!

You will need to review your situation in Nam Choon. Should you continue down to the main road or spend a night up here? We arrived in the village at 3pm, tired from lugging heavy backpacks during the hottest part of the day. We decided that we would not continue down to the H1081 road on foot. We would get a lift if one was available, but, if not, would stay overnight in Nam Choon at the adult education centre, the following morning either walking or trucking out. By chance a pick-up with some medics was vaccinating villagers at the AEC, and our hopes were high that we could ride out with them after they had finished their work. It is lifts such as this that you have to learn to exploit. But it transpired that the medics, after their work in the village, were going to walk to another settlement south of Nam Choon to do more vaccinating, spending the night there before returning next morning. We were welcome to a ride next day! In the end we got a lift down late the same afternoon in the truck of a local hill-tribe development official, who was involved in some school building project – only to get stuck at nightfall in Bo Yuak Tai.

If you walk down to the main road, the distance is 4.7 kms or a long hour on foot. If you want to try your luck with a lift, the one or two vehicles that come to Nam Choon each day usually leave either early morning or late afternoon. If a lift is offered to you, try to establish where it is going to. If it is going to Bo Glua or even to Pua, take it – you have a chance of exiting the trek the same day, or at least of getting back to the Park HQ. But if the lift is going only to Bo Yuak or in the 'wrong' direction towards Huai Khon, and there is the danger that you might get stuck and benighted in Bo Yuak Tai, consider staying in Nam Choon, as suggested earlier, and walking or hitch-hiking out the next morning. Nam Choon is a nicer, easier and better place for you to overnight than in Bo Yuak or even in Bo Glua.

> Walk or hitch-hike from Nam Choon to the H1081 road. The distance is just under 5 kms. In 1998 parts of the dirt side road were in a dreadful condition, especially the bottom end, which winds very steeply down through deep bulldust. Drivers keep a pile of heavy logs down by the junction, which, when they come up to Nam Choon, they load into the back of their trucks, putting weight on the back axle to prevent wheelspin.
>
> About 1 km down the road, below Nam Choon, there is a second part of the village.
>
> At the end of the Huai Por/Nam Choon side road, which is also the end of the trek, you hit the H1081 road at a T-junction just south of **Bo Yuak Tai** (= South Bo Yuak), which as its name suggests is the southern part of Bo Yuak village. Left (north) goes to the main northern part of Bo Yuak, where there is a small functioning salt well, and on ultimately to Huai Khon, while right (south) proceeds to Sa Wa and Bo Glua. A marker stone near the junction reads 'km 94'. The bridge crosses the River Wa.

Exiting the trek (see Map 14)

Take a public-transport *silor* or hitch-hike the ca 17 kms south to Bo Glua. The *silor* fare should be about 30 baht. You pass through the village of **Huai Kaab** before reaching the upper or northern part of **Sa Wa**. From here the exit route and details are the same as for Trek 9 (see under 'Exiting' at end of Trek 9). For background information about Bo Glua, about its salt wells and salt-extraction, and about the 'prehistoric' palms and the famous Chompu Pu Kha tree on the H1256 road from Bo Glua back up to the National Park HQ, likewise see under 'Exiting' towards the end of Trek 9. If you get stuck in Bo Yuak Tai at nightfall, put up a tent across the road from the junction on the banks of the River Wa, and try again next morning. You should be able to find some food and drink a short distance north up the H1081 road at the main part of Bo Yuak, where there is a health centre (east side of road), at which you could get medical attention, if you needed it, and at which you could also probably stay overnight.

Trek 11

Nan – Pua – Ratchada – Pang Kae – Maniploek – Pang Kae – Kwet – Sa Kaat – Pua – Nan

Parameters

trekking mode: by motorcycle (possibly also by mountain bike)
trek time: 1 long day, or 2 days/1 night (by motorcycle)
trek distance: at least 250 kms
degree of difficulty: standard route: for average riders moderately difficult, for skilled bikers no problem
tent: only necessary if you break the journey and stay overnight at Maniploek
map(s):   see 17 & 18

Overview & strategy

Ushering in four treks revolving around the remote double-village of Maniploek, this scenic, varied and exhilirating motorcycle trek takes you into the heart of the main northern part of Nan province's Doi Pu Kha National Park. Starting from Nan town with its guest houses and facilities, and returning to Nan town, it is – in the standard form described below – 250 kms long, but can be shortened or lengthened, made easier or more difficult, at will. As such, it has something to offer biking travellers of all abilities. In its standard unmodified form, the outing proceeds over a mixture of paved and dirt surfaces, the dirt component consisting of a wild little 15-km loop near Maniploek and of a 35-km stretch contouring around the mountains past the Lua villages of Kwet and Sa Kaat (i.e. comprising 50 kms in total). Unless you have a bigger bike (not a Honda Dream, but an enduro machine of 200 cc or more) and/or are an experienced faster rider, the trek is rather far to be done comfortably in one day. If you do tackle it in one day, you will be undertaking it only for the pleasure of the ride, not for the ride plus any incidental diversions. Consider lengthening the trek from one day to 2 days/1 night by interpolating a night at, say, the forestry station at Maniploek, for which you would need a tent and some provisions. Then, not only would the trip be less rushed, but you could also include a spot of 'sightseeing' or make some additional hairy side rides. Thus you could check out some of the Hmong and Lua (Htin) villages en route, explore Pa Poeng Cave, visit a pair of extremely rare Chompu Pu Kha trees, or ride to

Khang Ho or Pong Tom. In its standard unmodified form, the trek is moderately difficult for riders of average or better ability on a Honda Dream and fairly easy for dirt freaks on enduros. I am speaking here of the dirt sections – the stretches on regular paved roads pose no problems for anyone. Only the loop near Maniploek could be considered problematic. I did this trek at Christmas 1998 in the company of Nittaya Tananchai, our daughter Tanya (aged 7), and Doug 'Birddog' Boynton. We rode on two 100cc Honda Dreams hired in Nan, two to a bike, and were additionally weighed down with backpacks and tents (this does not apply to the little loop near Maniploek, where Doug and I rode the bikes solo and unencumbered). If we, average biking folk, can do it, so can you!

More specifically, the trek takes you north from Nan ca 80 kms up the main 1080 highway via Pua to the village of Ratchada (Map 17), where you turn off east to head up a side road, at first paved and then dirt, some 16 kms to a junction. At this junction, which I shall call 'Magic Junction' because suddenly, in the mountains, you hit a dream highway in the middle of nowhere, you turn approximately NE to proceed 20 kms up the lonesome dream highway via the Hmong village of Pang Kae to far-flung Maniploek, or, more accurately, to Maniploek forestry station. From here you can continue just a short distance to the two parts of Maniploek village (one part Hmong and the other Lua). The journey from Nan town to Maniploek forestry is 115 kms and takes about 2¾ hrs (less on a bigger bike), riding fairly continuously and not making longer stops, e.g. for lunch. From the forestry station you make the short tricky loop via Maniploek 1 (the original Hmong part of the double-village) and Maniploek 2 (the new Lua part) to arrive back at the forestry post (Map 18). On this loop you can look at Pa Poeng Cave and you could make a detour to the Chompu Pu Kha trees. At the forestry you decide whether you want to spend a night camping, which would extend the trek from 1 day to 2, or whether you want to push straight on. To make the trek less of a rush, and to enable you to explore the interesting Maniploek locality more fully and at your leisure, I recommend you do spend a night under canvas there (or even two nights). The setting and atmosphere up at elevated Maniploek is magnificent. In any case you will need to break for a picnic lunch there.

From Maniploek, either in the afternoon of Day 1 or in the morning of Day 2, you backtrack 20 kms to 'Magic Junction' and turn left to proceed 35 kms along a scenic, seemingly endless, essentially contouring, dirt road around the mountains and valleys, passing through a number of villages (including the larger Lua places of Kwet and Sa Kaat), and ending down at a T-junction by Na Fang village. A short paved link road down in the valley brings you west back to the main 1080 road 5 kms north of Pua. From Pua you return to Nan, either 60 kms south down the 1080 road via Ta Wang Pa (the same way as you came on the outward journey, but in reverse), or, more circuitously and to vary the pattern, along the H1081 and H1169 roads via Nam Yao, Santisuk and Kiu Muang, which is rather slower. This trek is written with motorcycling and motorcyclists in mind, but I see no reason why some or all of it could not be done as a bicycling expedition, although it could only be done by tough and persevering cyclists on mountain bikes. Of course, everything would be slower and more leisurely, and you would need to take more food with you.

The trek could be truncated or extended in the following ways. You could shorten it slightly and certainly make it easier by cutting out the little loop from Maniploek (why not walk it in a morning or afternoon instead?) and by cutting out the long dirt trail round by Kwet and Sa Kaat. This would mean that almost the whole journey would be done on asphalt, while the latter modification would mean that you returned to Pua the same way as the route you came (via Ratchada). This option might appeal to less ambitious trekkers, to trekkers less sure of their riding abilities, and to trekkers more interested in mooching around the Maniploek area and perhaps in doing some camping than in blasting their way down dirt trails. The trek could be extended by making – or, rather, attempting to make – additional side trips offroad to the Lua village of Pong Tom and the Hmong pasturing settlement of Khang Ho (Map 18; more observations below). In both cases you would have to return the same way, as there is no exit by bike from either Pong Tom or Khang Ho. This option might appeal to, and could only be carried out by, very skilled bikers (dirt freaks).

Preparing for the trek
Where applicable, hire a Honda Dream (no other types of bike available) at one of the two hire shops in Nan, which should cost you about 150 baht per day. Take a tent along if you intend to camp at Maniploek – take one anyway both as a fallback and in case you change you mind underway. If you are doing the whole trek in one day, buy some food for a picnic lunch. Always carry some water with you in case you break down in the middle of nowhere. If you are spreading the trek over 2 days, camping at Maniploek forestry, take enough food for a lunch, supper, breakfast and another lunch, although one or both of these lunches could be taken at a noodle shop in Pua. Drinks and limited (snack) food are available at Pang Kae.

The Lua & Hmong peoples
For background information on the Lua (Htin) people, such as inhabit Maniploek 2, Kwet, Sa Kaat and other villages on the route, see Trek 5. For a thumbnail sketch of the Hmong people, such as live at Pang Kae and Maniploek 1, see Trek 16 under 'Santisuk'.

*

Trekking route detail / accessing Maniploek (see Map 17)
Ride north out of Nan town (= km 0) along the H1080 road 60 kms or about 1 hr to the small market town of Pua. On the way you pass Nan airport (right), the **Pa Toob Cave complex** (km 10, left) and **Ta Wang Pa**, another small market town (offroad left) lying just south of the H1080/H1148 junction. As you approach **Pua,**

you descend a hill, passing a Shell fuel station (right), a new guest house (left – could be expensive), and a new small supermarket (left) to arrive at Pua's central crossroads (km 60). The highway is divided here by a long central reservation with a ditch. Left at the crossroads takes you to Pua's shops and evening market, while right and then immediately left brings you to the H1256 National Park road and Park HQ. North of the crossroads (right side) is Pua's day market and share-taxi or *silor* stand, and opposite, across the highway, are a couple of shops where you can buy bottled water. If you are hungry, there is a recommendable noodle place just south of the crossroads on the left (west) side. From Pua, it about another 1¾ hrs to Maniploek.

Now continue north, still on the H1080 speed road, and proceed 18.7 kms past two turnings left (west) for Chiang Klang and past the village of **Ratchada** with its little crossroads to a turning right (east) and the beginning of the H1291 side road (km 78.7). Just before the turning there is a Cosmo Oil fuel station on the right side, where you should tank up before going up to Maniploek and Sa Kaat. A 'milestone' at the mouth of the H1291 reads 0 km. Turn into this side road and on a fine tarred surface head east towards the mountains of the Doi Pu Kha National Park massif, passing through the rural Thai villages of **Na Noon, Soi Prao, Den Tara** and **Pa Ruak**. At the junction in Pa Ruak, marked by a *sala* right, a side road left goes to Hua Nam Santa Na, while just beyond Pa Ruak the broad quality road gives over, as you enter foothills, to a thin winding way with poor pitted asphalt (in 1999).

You now climb up through fine vegetation, and a valley scene opens up, offering views of Pang Kae village and plantations of temperate fruit high up left. Coming up here, we have always encountered lots of bulbuls (black-crested birds with brown bodies). A turning left (km 92.2), marked by a 'highland development office' left, leads to the village of Nong Pla. Continue straight, and a couple of kms later you come to the junction that I have dubbed **'Magic Junction'**, owing to the fact that this big junction, set incongruously in the middle of nowhere, suddenly comes upon you as if by magic, also bringing you to the start of an unaccountable, spanking new, dream highway that goes through the mountains all the way to Maniploek. At Maniploek we enquired about the rationale of this brand-new highway in the sky or skyway. It had been built, so we were told, partly for security reasons, and partly because the local Hmong had wanted a decent access road. In this matter, they had directly petitioned the Thai Queen, suggesting that in the past they had helped the country, and that now, with royal support and patronage, the country could perhaps help them, whereupon the Queen had had the road built. 'Magic Junction' lies 15.8 kms from the H1080 road, 34.5 kms from Pua crossroads, and 94.5 kms from Nan.

Magic Junction is actually a kind of crossroads. Right goes on a dirt track 3 kms to Pang Kor. Straight is the beginning of the 35-km-long dirt road to Kwet and Sa Kaat that we will be biking later. And left is the start of the new 22-km-long 'dream highway' to Maniploek (the Hmong part). Go left, immediately passing a forestry conservation office on your left side. Now you climb up 6.5 kms to the Hmong village of **Pang Kae** (km 101), before the village passing a turning left for a 'forestry and watershed office', a paramilitary BPP camp right, and a turning left for the village school. Pang Kae has a 'wild-east' store selling food, drinks and fuel (right side of road). The road now continues 12.8 kms through marvellous mountain scenery, in one place ablaze with Mexican sunflowers, to a spirit house standing on a junction. Just beyond Pang Kae a turning left (west) marks the beginning of a bad dirt way which plunges down to Tung Chang, back on the

H1080 road. I have not explored this side trail. It is an optional extra route that might appeal to dirt biking fans. Not far short of the spirit house, a dirt side trail heads off right – it is, I think, the old route from Pang Kae first to Ban Nong and then to Maniploek. You may be able to directly access Khang Ho (see Trek 12) from this old route, but again, not having explored it, I cannot comment on the trail, which might likewise appeal to intrepid dirt-riding freaks. At the junction with the spirit house (km 113.8), straight on is a 1-km-long dirt track entering Maniploek 1 (the original Hmong part of Maniploek) by the backdoor, while right, the continuation of the dream highway, drops 1 km to a crossroads (km 114.8). Essentially, you have reached **Maniploek**. Straight over the crossroads you come immediately to the entrance to **Maniploek forestry station**, with a half-raised barrier at the entrance and with buildings beyond. Left (north) continues 1.6 kms on asphalt to **Hmong Maniploek 1**, while right proceeds 2.6 kms on a tricky dirt track to **Lua Maniploek 2**. Maniploek forestry, which you can use as a base, is 36.1 kms from the H1080 road, 54.8 kms from Pua crossroads, and 114.8 kms or some 115 kms from Nan.

Camping at Maniploek forestry station
On biking Trek 11, you might want – as suggested earlier – to break the journey and intercalate a night at the forestry station, perhaps to make the outing less of a rush, or to have more time to explore and enjoy the Maniploek locality, or just to do a spot of camping, or for all these reasons. In Treks 12, 13 and 14, which all start from Maniploek, you will have to stay at the double village, and I recommend that in each case you stay at the forestry station in a tent. You are welcome to do this (free of charge), and my trekking companions and I have camped there many times, perhaps a dozen memorable nights in all. Strictly speaking, this is not a forestry place, but a 'watershed development and security' station, which means that it does indeed plant trees in an effort to reforest denuded terrain, but also helps local Lua and Hmong tribespeople start up with crop-growing (cabbages, lettuces and temperate fruits etc. instead of slash-and-burn and hunting), and secures the remote and until recently troubled area by 'managing' these tribals, employing them to plant trees (in 1999 they were paid 105 baht/day) and, as said, aiding them with the cultivation of cash crops.

In December 1998, when we researched the four treks in this book based on Maniploek, the station was run by four young people (just workers really) – a man (called Maeo) and three girls. There must be some kind of 'boss', but we never saw him or her. The four live on site in huts, and while Maeo drives around in a lorry, getting supplies and ferrying equipment and tribal workers to and from the reforestation zones, the girls cook, tend plants and whatever. The foursome are reserved, but friendly and helpful, although they will not organize anything for you. Just get stuck in to whatever you want to do – pitching a tent, washing, resurrecting the fire, boiling water, making instant noodles or coffee – and don't stand on ceremony. They will soon tell you if some action is out of order. It has to be said that Maniploek forestry is poorly equipped and run, compared to other similar places, for example the forestry complexes at Mae Sa Nan or at Sa

Wang. It does have a generator (but apparently no mains electricity, although there is mains power at nearby Maniploek 1), but when we were there, this was never in use – there was no fuel for it! So there might be no light and you might have to get used to doing everything in the dark or by torchlight. The staff cook before dark, sit by the fire, and go to bed early. It's back to nature up here, which has its upside.

As you come past the barrier into the forestry station compound, which is attractively set in a basin, you see a large open-sided shed with a cement floor immediately to your right. You can camp on some grass between this and a pond with a little fountain in it. For politeness' sake, let the staff know your intentions, get their permission, and pitch camp. There is room for two or three tents. On the same side of the entrance driveway, but set further back (top right, relative to the entrance), there is a large new building on a knoll. It is something of a mystery and never seems to be used. Perhaps it is a symbolic showpiece HQ or the boss' quarters. Diagonally opposite the open shed and the 'campsite', on the other side of the driveway, are the huts where the staff live. Next to these, on the same side, is a little block with two *hongnam* cubicles, i.e. bathroom and toilet combined. I call these cement cubicles 'the jungle toilets', because their floors are artfully constructed out of rock slabs and fist-sized stones of different colours set into the ground, while pot plants, ferns, cacti and orchids adorn the walls, floor and spaces between the toilet and shower – a designer loo in the jungle! Beyond the bathroom block is a truck and lorry port, where you can park your bike(s) under cover. Some distance behind this – top left, relative to the entrance – is the cookhouse, and beside it are outdoor tables and benches, as well as a hearth with a permanently smouldering fire, surrounded by logs for sitting on.

In the cookhouse there are a couple of gas rings running off propane, which you can probably use, and trivets over the outdoor fire support two huge blackened kettles, which you can use for boiling up water for making coffee, tea, instant noodles, packet soups, or just hot water for washing with. Sounds idyllic? In a sense it is. Before retiring to your tent, you can have a great time by the hearth, sitting around the blazing logs, reviewing the day's trekking events, nipping at whisky or beer, warming your legs, and studying the incredibly bright stars. If other (Thai) visitors have come by, they congregate here with picnic suppers and guitars. It gets pretty cold in the night at Maniploek. During the winter the temperature in the early morning routinely drops to 6 or 7° C, as it did when we were there, and there can even be frosts, so make sure you have a decent sleeping bag with you. By the same token there are terrific dews, soaking your tent. Some days a market truck calls by in the early morning, usually between 8 and 9am. If you have come to Maniploek without your own transport, look upon it as a possible lift out. It was at Maniploek forestry that we found on the trunk of a tree an outsize yellow and brown moth, 6 inches long and with a 6-inch wingspan, and Doug did some great birdwatching round about.

Information about Maniploek and local features

Maniploek, once also known as Chong Pai, is a double village, consisting of a Hmong section (Maniploek 1) and a Lua section (Maniploek 2), the two set about 5 kms apart. The Hmong part is the original village, while the Lua part is new. When I first came here in January 1994 – before the road was built, necessitating a long ride on a dusty dirt track – there was, if I remember correctly, no Maniploek 2, which was established ca 1995-96, when Lua were moved from new Ban Ta (Nam Pua Pattana 2).

To reach the Hmong part, go north from the junction at the entrance to the forestry station and continue 1.6 kms, plunging down and up, to the end of the asphalt road, where you find **Hmong Maniploek 1**, set on the skyline on a saddle or col, with views both ways (see Map 18). A Blue Hmong place, identifiable by the blue pleated skirts worn by some women, it is a medium-sized, spread-out village with a school and a couple of little shops. It is a typical Hmong place. The wooden houses are built straight onto the ground, the bare earth often constituting their floor, and the settlement has a characteristic scruffy ravaged look. Lots of children, dogs, chickens, pigs and miserable ponies have the run of the place, and numerous pick-ups and motorcycles are in evidence, although there is little sign these days of traditional Hmong costume, except at the Hmong New Year. Readers of my other books on Thailand will know that, while I respect the Hmong, I do not like them much. Too many times all over northern Thailand they have ripped me off or attempted to do so. Migrants from southern China, these are Mongoloid, happy-go-lucky, independent, proud, impervious, businesslike, entrepreneurial, money-oriented people, who will make a buck or as much as they can wherever they can. If you hitch a ride in a Hmong truck to or from Maniploek, negotiate a fare with the driver before you hop aboard, to save yourself from an unpleasant surprise. Hmong rapacity extends to despoiling the environment. They are champion poachers and unscrupulous illegal loggers, and unfortunately you can see them in action around Maniploek. To balance up the picture, I must add that the Hmong can also, conversely, be unusually welcoming, hospitable and generous, famously so during their New Year celebrations. I once sent a party of young 'green' English travellers, who wanted a suggestion for a trip in Nan province, up to Hmong Maniploek from Nan town's *Doi Pu Kha Guest House*, and, stumbling on New Year festivities in the Hmong village, they had the time of their lives.

In connection with the Hmong, Maniploek 1 and the forestry station, I mention a story narrated to us one day in December 1998 at the forestry outpost by a group of local Thai people visiting and overnighting there, one of whom was a policeman. He said that the Hmong of Maniploek and of Pang Kae, in cahoots with a forestry official, were smuggling 'speed' (amphetamine sulphate) and 'ecstasy' from Laos. Just the day before, a consignment of 200,000 tablets had come across. Everyone knew about the shipment and who was involved, but it had proved impossible, as always, to catch the traffickers red-handed. In any case, so the lawman said, even if they had been caught, they would not have been stamped upon, because harsh treatment or real justice was never meted out. After a few weeks in prison the drug smugglers would have been let out again. This activity might account for some of the flash trucks, quite out proportion to the means of wheeler-dealer cabbage-growing Maniploek Hmong, that you see zipping into and out of the village, some driven by mere youngsters.

Between the forestry and Maniploek 1 lies **Tam Pa Poeng** or Bee Cliff Cave, which is of interest and worth a visit. From the crossroads in front of the forestry station, go 1.1 kms north towards the Hmong village. The cave lies at the bottom of the dip, on the left side, about 200 m from the road. A sign beside the road points towards it. You walk along a little path through jungle vegetation and past rocks and a stream to reach the cave. At the foot of a massive, awesome, perhaps 50-m-high, vertical rock face, is the equally massive and awesome, square, dark mouth of a cavern, which burrows west and downwards into the mountain.

Technically, the cave and its immediate surroundings (i.e. the whole depression at this end of the valley running up towards/just south of Maniploek 1) are, so my Danish geologist friend Soeren Skipsted tells me, with whom I first visited Tam Pa Poeng in January 1994, part of a stream sink dolina. A minor stream, now usually water-filled only in the rainy season, runs towards the cave and suddenly disappears through cracks and fissures in the limestone bedrock, forming a so-called stream sink. From here, the water seeps through small underground cavities, subsequently emerging at a much lower level somewhere deep inside the cave. The stream, besides directly causing the sink and cave, probably also indirectly caused the cliff at the entrance to the cave. The water, eating away underground at the limestone, created cavities, which, when they became large enough, left nothing to support the roof, which collapsed into the cave, causing the cliff. Alternatively, the water undercut the bedrock, creating overhangs, which, becoming unstable, likewise collapsed, causing the dolina rock face.

You can climb down into the dolina. The entrance chamber itself, beneath the cliff, is a huge cathedral-like feature, maybe 200 m long and so far among the biggest known single-room chambers in Nan province. Take a look at the big flowstone formations (a kind of dripstone created by water running down the wall surface) with small water-filled basins on the cave wall to the right just inside the entrance. From here you can continue further downwards into the cave, climbing over hugh boulders that have fallen from the roof. Proceeding more horizontally, the big chamber gives way to another similar narrowing chamber, ending in a tall corridor filled with dripstone formations on the walls. In the floor is a dangerous, narrow gaping hole with a 20 to 30-m vertical drop down to the practically unexplored lower level of the cave. Evidently, no one has ever been to the very bottom of the whole cave or knows where it goes or exits. To get deeper and further into it and then back out again, you would need caving equipment and ropes or ladders. Dogs have wandered in and died there. Reportedly local people once tried to explore Tam Pa Poeng, but got only so far, their torches running out and one of their number becoming unwell, either for psychological reasons or due to a lack of oxygen and a concentration of carbon dioxide in the cave atmosphere. Essentially uncharted and undeveloped caves such as Tam Pa Poeng are potentially seriously hazardous, especially during the rainy season. You could fall into a shaft or pass out and die from insufficient oxygen and CO_2 poisoning. If you investigate it, take great care, picking your way and checking the oxygen level with a cigarette lighter or kerosene lamp.

No less interesting than the interior of the cave is its mouth, where a great collection of jungle flora grows. In this cool corner, shafted through with beams of sunlight, clumps of banana palms brood in the silence, 100-ft-long air roots dangle from the cliff face, and you can find specimens of that rare and singular, 'prehistoric', 'fishtail' palm visible from the H1256 road through Doi Pu Kha National Park, and which we encountered in Trek 9 on the way to Pang Kob (for more information on this throwback palm, see Trek 9 under 'Exiting: Bo Glua – Park HQ'). Some of the 'ancient' palms grow in the most precipitous inaccessible places, and you wonder how they eke out an existence there, clinging to sloping ledges. In January 1994 the mouth of the cave had a ghostly appearance because all the banana palms had died, having been frosted. It is a cold spot. During the communist insurgency, many of the caves in Nan province (e.g. Tam Pa Daeng near Pong Tom, Huai Khon Cave, and the caves at Doi Pa Ji west of Nan town) were used by the CPT guerrillas as strongholds, in which they stored materials, slept, and sheltered from bombardment. But evidently Tam Pa Poeng was not so used because it is too chilly. Not far from Bee Cliff Cave, about 100 m from Hmong Maniploek 1, there is another smaller dolina, a collapsed dolina, where the roof of an underground cave could not support itself and fell in, leaving a steep-sided depression like the sunken crater of a volcano. The vegetation around and inside this smaller dolina is characteristically dense and intertwined.

To reach the Lua part of Maniploek (Maniploek 2), go south from the crossroads by the forestry station on a poor dirt track (see Map 18). After just a few hundred metres, where the trail swings east, you can see on your right (south) side, another 200-300 m offroad, a corner that I call the **'cliff idyll'**. Take a look in here. In the background there is an amphitheatre of vertical jungle-covered cliffs, at the bottom of which a stream wends its way in a curve through banana palms. In the foreground is a fertile area with huts, where Hmong cultivate lettuces and tend orchards. It is indeed an idyllic spot, and it would be beautiful to camp wild here, which perhaps you can. The rutted track climbs twice steeply up (follow the power lines), passes through woods, and – 2 kms from the crossroads – hits a T-junction. Right (south) goes to two Chompu Pu Kha trees (more below), to Khang Ho (see Trek 12) and to Doi Pu Wae (see Trek 14). Left (north), our route, continues 0.6 kms past half a dozen granaries to Lua Maniploek 2. When I once briskly walked this 2.6-km roundabout way from the forestry to Maniploek 2, it took me 35 mins. There is a shorter, quicker, more direct way to Maniploek 2 from the forestry station, a footpath cutting across country from the back of the compound, but I have never found it.

Lua Maniploek 2, the new part of the double village, is for me much more attractive and sympathetic than the Hmong part. Full of Yot On families, its wooden houses, raised on stilts, are not dispersed, as in Hmong Maniploek, but huddled together, giving a feeling of cosiness and community. Near the main southern entrance are some official buildings (a kindergarten, I think) and a little shop. Maniploek 2 spills down an east-facing hillside. The best thing about it is its splendid view SE (120°) of Doi Pu Wae, one of Thailand's most beautiful and spectacular mountains. Visible of this jagged tooth of a peak is a huge cliff on its west-facing side. You can climb Doi Pu Wae from Maniploek 2, as a few Thai people do each year, and as we shall do in Trek 14, hiring guides in the Lua village not just for the Pu Wae expedition but also for Treks 12 (to Khang Ho and Nam Pua Pattana) and 13 (to Pong Tom and Huai Sai Kao). As indicated earlier, most of the villagers at 'M2' were moved there by the Thai Army about 1995-96 from Ta village (at Nam Pua Pattana 2). A guiding friend of ours said that the new village's first crop of rice produced lush plants, but with no seed. The second season was a similar disaster, and it was only after three years that they got a satisfactory harvest. For two years the forced migrants starved and had to beg food from the authorities. For some background information on the dour but fascinating Lua (Htin) people and their culture, see Trek 5.

To view the **two Chompu Pu Kha trees** near Maniploek 2, rare siblings of the famous pink Pu Kha tree beside the H1256 road in Doi Pu Kha National Park, go back south from Lua Maniploek past a small reservoir at the village entrance 0.6 kms (5 mins on foot) to the junction, bear left (the way right takes you back to the forestry station) and follow a 4WD track. Walk a further 20 mins or 1.3 kms to a fork (see Map 18). Left at the fork is the beginning of a trail to the former village of Nam Poen (+ 1.2 kms) and ultimately Doi Pu Wae. Go right. Just past the fork, on the left side is the first of two locally-growing *chompu* or pink Pu Kha trees. Continue ca 200 m down the track. You quickly come to a second fork. The way left at this new fork is the start of the trail for Khang Ho (+ 7 kms) and Nam Pua Pattana. Just by the second fork, signed, is a second Chompu Pu Kha tree. When I looked at these trees in December 1998, they had orange cherry-sized berries. For more information about the celebrated pink Pu Kha Bretschneider trees, see Trek 9 under 'Exiting: Bo Glua – Park HQ'.

The little loop (see Map 18)

Here is a super little 10½-km or 6½-mile side loop that can be done from Maniploek forestry station either by motorcycle as an optional extra part of Trek 11 (this trek), or on foot as an additional bonbon for people who have come to do

Treks 12, 13 or 14, or who are just doing a spot of camping at Maniploek. It will take an hour or so by bike and a morning or an afternoon by shanks's pony. From the crossroads by the entrance to the forestry station (km 0) go north down and up the paved road, past Tam Pa Poeng or Bee Cliff Cave (left side, km 1.1), to a T-junction (km 1.6), which marks the beginning of Hmong Maniploek 1. Left is a back way into the village and, if you go backwards down it, links up with 'Dream Highway' by the spirit house. Go right to enter the main part of the village. There is a store down on your right and the village school down left. Proceed 400 m through the centre of the village to reach a second T-junction (km 2.0) at the top end. Left goes to the school, and right, our way, goes up towards half a dozen water tanks. At a fork, bear left, pass the tanks, and proceed very steeply up a mediocre rutted dirt track. If you are two-up on a Dream, one of you will have to get off and walk. At the top, you ride or walk high up on a 4WD track along the crest of a ridge, enjoying great views. Two kms further you come to a junction, known as Saam Yaek (= three ways), which is marked by a green metal sign (km 4.0). Left goes to the (former) Lua village of Pong Tom (apparently relocated mid-1999) and also to Pa Daeng Cave (see Trek 13), while right, our way, continues 3.8 kms on a beautiful sketchy track, negotiable by skilled riders, to the rear entrance of Lua Maniploek 2 (km 7.8 kms). The latter flattish little-used back stretch enters 'M2' above the village. Now the way is as described earlier. Pass 'M2', exit it by the little reservoir, and proceed south past the half dozen granaries 0.6 kms to a junction (km 8.4). Go straight on to take in the two Chompu Pu Kha trees, which are 20 mins' walk away or a few mins by bike (for directions and some notes on these trees, see just above and also Trek 9). To complete the loop, go right at the junction, follow the new power lines through some woods, go down two steep rutted inclines – rather tricky on a bike – to pass on your left a house and the 'cliff idyll' described earlier (km 9.9), after which the track swings north to bring you back to the crossroads by the forestry compound (km 10.4).

Dirt freaks looking for real offroad adventure might like to try to get through to Khang Ho, which these days is just a remote Hmong pasturing settlement, most of the former village having been moved out in early 1995. Although I have visited it (on foot only, as part of Trek 12), I have not ridden there, and so I have no comment on the side trip as a biking excursion. But in December 1998 the trail was badly deteriorated and in places seemingly almost impassable, although I did see small motorcycles at Khang Ho, so some people must get through. On foot and from Lua Maniploek 2, it is 9.5 kms or about 2 hrs 20 mins to the settlement. From 'M2', go south 600 m past the granaries to the junction, bear left, and then take the second left, by the second pink Pu Kha tree, for Khang Ho, which lies 7 kms from the second fork. For more details of the trail to the Hmong outpost, see the first part of the route detail for Trek 12.

Trekking route detail: Maniploek – Pang Kae – 'Magic Junction' – Kwet – Sa Kaat – Pua – Nan (see Map 17)
We come to the second and longer half of this motorcycle trek. From Maniploek make your way 20.3 kms back down 'Dream Highway' to 'Magic Junction'. Leaving the forestry compound, you climb 1 km up to the T-junction with the spirit house, go left to proceed 12.8 kms past the Mexican sunflowers to Hmong Pang Kae, and continue 6.5 kms down to 'Magic Junction'. At the junction, right continues down to Ratchada and the H1080 road, while straight across goes on a

160

dirt track to the village of Pang Kor. We go left, beginning our distance readings at km 0 again. It is the start of a scenic 35-km-long dirt road, contouring round the sides of a couple of valleys and passing through well-cultivated and fairly denuded countryside, as well as through half a dozen villages, all of which are Lua.

Almost immediately you come to the village of **Kok**, with its school (km 1.3). The paved surface ends here, giving over to a (in 1999) fair dirt road. Next comes **Shi** village (km 2.1), with a turning left, health centre and school. A settlement follows (km 5.8), after which you reach **Nong** village with its school left (km 6.3). At km 7.6 there is a house and a turning right, and 200 m further comes **Nong Mai** or New Nong (km 7.8). The long viaduct-like bridge at km 11.3 crosses a confluence, where the River Sa Toon on the right flows into the River Gon on the left. Now comes the larger Lua place of **Kwet** with its school right (km 13.2), a couple of useless shops and a nice piece of jungle. From Kwet it is 8 kms to Sa Kaat and 22 kms still to the paved road down at Na Fang. After a broken wooden bridge, you get a view of a big village (Sa Kaat) in the distance high up. Now a ford supervenes (km 18.1), followed by a second ford with a log bridge, after which, passing a patch of jungle, you come to the beginning of **Sa Kaat**, with its school left (km 20.9) and kindergarten up left. In the main part of this extensive village (ca km 21.6 - 22.1), there are big wooden houses, a phone box and fuel. Public-transport lorry *songtaew* service Sa Kaat, and from the village you can trek to Choon, Toei Noi, Toei Hua Doi and on out to Doi Pu Kha National Park HQ and the H1256 road (see Map 16). Apparently there are a couple of noodle soup places in Sa Kaat, but we were unable to locate them. A turning right towards the end of the village (km 22.4) goes to Pu Gok.

Now begins the rutted and very dusty descent off the mountains. At a 4-way junction just beyond Sa Kaat (km 23.1), go straight on down. Second left off the junction goes 500 m to southerly Sa Kaat Tai. Finally, you reach Na Fang school, **Na Fang** village, and a T-junction (km 34.8). Turn right into a paved road and proceed straight, crossing two wooden bridges and passing a village, to reach another T-junction and the H1080 highway (km 37.3). Right goes north to Chiang Klang, Tung Chang and Huai Khon, while left, our route, brings us south back to **Pua** and its central crossroads (km 42.9). From Pua you continue south 60 kms or an hour's riding on the H1080 main road via Ta Wang Pa to Nan town (103 kms from 'Magic Junction' and ca 125 kms from Maniploek). If you have time, an alternative way back to Nan from Pua, varying the pattern and taking a slower country way in preference to the traffic-ridden highway, would be to go left (west) off Pua central crossroads and proceed down the H1081 and H1169 roads via the villages of Tin Tok, Pa Tong, Tung Hao and Nam Yao almost to Santisuk, where at a crossroads (see Map 8) you turn right at the village of Pu Yaeng to continue via Kiu Muang back to Nan.

Trek 12

Maniploek forestry – Lua Maniploek 2 – Khang Ho – Khun Nam Pua w/f – Nam Pua Pattana 2 – Toei Hua Doi – H1256 road / Doi Pu Kha National Park HQ

Parameters

trekking mode:	on foot
core trek time:	2 days/1 night
accessing time:	from Nan town to Maniploek via Pua and Ratchada allow about half a day using a combination of public transport and hitch-hiking, and ca 2¾ hrs with your own hire motorbike
exiting time:	from the H1256 road (near Doi Pu Kha National Park HQ) via Pua allow at least 3 hrs using public transport or a combination of hitch-hiking and public transport
overall trek time:	from Nan to Nan, including access and exiting times, between 3 days/2 nights and 4 days/3 nights
degree of difficulty:	easy, but long and tiring
guide(s):	after Khang Ho impossible without guide
guide name(s):	Pae & Yod (see photo section)
tent:	required
map(s):	see 17, 18, 16 & 14

Overview & strategy

This satisfying expedition, the second of four treks based on Maniploek and the first of three treks hiking from Maniploek, strikes from north to south through the very heart of the main northerly part of Nan province's Doi Pu Kha National Park. A trek to be done on foot only (at least as far as Nam Pua Pattana 2), it passes – going mostly downhill – through a variety of terrain: pleasant open alpine country, gloomy jungle, and airy woodland. The core part of the hike, which takes you from Maniploek 2 (the Lua part of the double village of Maniploek) via the Hmong settlement of Khang Ho and Khun Nam Pua Waterfall to the village of Nam Pua Pattana 2 (also known as Ban Ta) and on out past Toei Hua Doi to the H1256 National Park road, hitting that road near the Park HQ, takes 2 days and 1 night, and incorporates a 'Rambo' overnight stop camping wild beside the River Pua in dense jungle. The trek is not hard, but involves two long tiring days of walking. In my view, it would be impossible to find your way after Khang Ho unguided.

162

TREK 12: MANIPLOEK 2 – KHANG HO – NAM PUA PATTANA 2

I did the trip mid-December 1998 as part of a party of six, which also included Nittaya Tananchai, our infant daughter Tanya, Doug 'Birddawg' Boynton, and two Lua guides, Pae and Yod, hired from Maniploek 2. A sign of the relative easiness of the trek is that daughter Tanya, aged 7½ at the time, was able to manage it effortlessly and without complaint, at the most having to be helped or carried across rivers by the guides. Responsible trekkers with resilient children take note: jungle trekking with your offspring *is* possible, assuming they can keep going for – in the case of this hike – 8 hrs at a stretch, stopping only for lunch. The information in this chapter should be read in conjunction with that in Trek 11, especially with the extensive material in the previous chapter relating to accessing Maniploek, camping at the forestry station there, and reaching the Lua part of the village (Maniploek 2) – I do not want to repeat here everything already said there.

More specifically, on the day before you start walking you make your way to Maniploek and camp overnight there probably at the forestry station (Map 17). On Day 1 of the actual trek, you walk ¾ hr round to Lua Maniploek 2 (Map 18), pick up your guides, and hike past two specimens of the rare Chompu Pu Kha tree 2½ hrs down to Khang Ho, where you have an early lunch. In the afternoon you march ca 5¼ long hrs to the River Pua (Nam Pua), to a jungle waterfall of the same name near the river's source (Khun Nam Pua w/f), and to a riverside campsite, which is really just a space made by clearing some of the jungle vegetation. Here you spend the first night (the second overall), before trekking on Day 2 during the morning 2¼ hrs to Nam Pua Pattana 2 (Ban Ta), where you take an early lunch, and which in a sense is the end of the trek, at least of its core part, the rest being a matter of exiting. During the rest of Day 2 you walk along a small dirt road from Nam Pua Pattana 2 some 2¼ hrs to Toei Hua Doi and another hour via Toei Klang and Kiu Haen to the H1256 National park road, hitting it just 2 kms west of the Park HQ (Map 16). Hoofing and sweating your way along this contouring dirt trail, you are repeating a stretch done in Trek 10, except in reverse. With luck you might be able to hitch-hike some or all of the way from Nam Pua Pattana 2 to the H1256 road.

Once you have arrived at the National Park road, you have two options. Which you choose will probably depend on what time it is. Either you can proceed by public transport (or a combination of hitch-hiking and public transport) via Pua back to Nan (Map 14), directly exiting the trek, which should take you some 2½ to 4 hrs; or you can spend another night (the third overall) at the Park HQ, making a virtue out of a vice and combining the trek with a stop at the HQ. In connection with the walking times mentioned above (and also in the time log below), I must say that the timings are probably somewhat distorted, being too generous because progress was slowed down by my daughter. Thus a good hour could no doubt be shaved off the walk from Maniploek 2 to the River Pua, and it might be possible, especially if you started early straight from 'M2' and not from the forestry station, to complete the whole stretch from M2 to Nam Pua Pattana 2 in about 9 hrs or by 5pm. This saving would either give you a night not by the River Pua but in Nam Pua Pattana 2, enabling you to make a more orderly and less rushed exit the next day to Nan, or, assuming you still camped by the Pua river, it would give you more time to explore Khun Nam Pua w/f, a highly recommendable prospect, which we neglected for lack of time.

Other ways of modifying the trek are as follows. You could truncate it by walking unguided 2½ hrs to Khang Ho, where you could have lunch, and either return to Maniploek the same day, or camp there overnight and return the next day. Expert bikers (dirt freaks) with enduro machines could attempt to ride from Maniploek to Khang Ho, returning the same way. Although the 9.5-km-long trail (from M2 to Khang Ho) is in places (in 1999) in a badly deteriorated condition, this should still be possible, indeed must be possible because when we walked to Khang Ho, we saw bikes in the settlement. You could radically alter the expedition by trekking on from Khang Ho (with a guide from either Maniploek or Khang Ho) to Doi Pu Wae, which would be a fusion of this trek (12) and Trek 14. You could reschedule the trek by starting from Maniploek in the afternoon and camping at Khang Ho. This would have the virtue that you would then reach Khun Nam Pua Waterfall by lunchtime on Day 2, which would in turn enable you either to explore the jungle fall at your leisure, camping there and pushing on to Nam Pua Pattana 2 on Day 3, or to reach Nam Pua Pattana 2 by nightfall on Day 2, giving you the whole of Day 3 to exit the trek to Nan.

Because Maniploek, the start of the trek, lies some 115 kms or 2-3 hrs' riding from Nan (making a round trip to Lua 'M2' of almost 250 kms or 6 hrs of riding!), it makes little sense to go there in advance to set up the trek guidewise, unless you happen to be in the area. The distance is too great. So you will need to arrive at Maniploek the day before the trek, ideally at lunchtime. This will then give you time to get round to Maniploek 2 to organize guides, as well as to familiarize yourself with the forestry station, with the layout of the locality, and with the way to 'M2'. By the same token, because Maniploek is so out-on-a-limb, it makes little sense to use a hire bike to access Maniploek and the start of the trek. After the trek, when you exit by the Park HQ and then Pua, you would have the lengthy and complicated process – in order to retrieve your machine – of getting all the way round and back up to Maniploek via Pua, Ratchada and Pang Kae, using a combination of public transport and hitch-hiking. It would only make sense to bike to Maniploek and to leave your machine there if you wanted to tack Trek 11 onto the end of this trek (12), i.e. if, after doing the Khang Ho and Nam Pua hike, you wanted to further explore the Maniploek area (visiting Hmong Maniploek 1 and Beecliff Cave, doing the 'little loop' etc.) and then ride out via Kwet and Sa Kaat. And this is what we did. It has the virtue that you can kill two birds or treks with one stone, you can see the guides safely back to Maniploek, and you have the comfort and convenience of both accessing and partially exiting the trek with your own transport. The downside, of course, is that your transport lies idle in Maniploek for a couple of days while you do the hike.

Accessing the trek (Map 17)
As with all the treks in this book in Nan province, you will undoubtedly ultimately launch Trek 12 from Nan town and its guest houses. Now, bearing in mind the considerations above, you must decide whether you are going to access Maniploek and the start of the actual hike by hire bike or by public transport and hitch-hiking. If you ride there with your own transport, the journey is, as said, 115 kms, and it took me on two separate occasions 2¾ hrs. For a full account of the trip from Nan to Maniploek, see Trek 11 under 'Trekking route detail / accessing Maniploek' and also Map 17.

If you proceed to Maniploek by public transport and hitch-hiking, ride from Nan town on a local red bus north up the H1080 road via the towns of Ta Wang Pa, Pua and Chiang Klang and the village of Ratchada to the junction of the H1080 and H1291 roads, which is 19 kms north of Pua central crossroads. After Ratchada, watch out for a 'Cosmo Oil' fuel station on the right side. The junction is imminent. Get out of the bus at the junction (it will probably stop there anyway). The H1291 side road for Maniploek heads off right (east) towards mountains. If on the bus you come to the town of Tung Chang, you have gone too far. For more detailed supplementary information about the route Nan/Pua/Ratchada/Maniploek, see Trek 11 under 'Accessing Maniploek' and Map 17. Now proceed by public-transport *silor* and/or hitch-hiking from the junction via the villages of Pa Ruak and Pang Kae to Maniploek, a distance of some 36 kms. Plenty of trucks go up to Pang Kae and Maniploek, although you might have to wait a bit. Try, if possible, to ride with some kind of official truck (forestry, highland development, BPP, school) – you do not run the risk of being ripped off and might well travel free. Most of the vehicles going up here are Hmong. If you ride with a Hmong pick-up, negotiate a fare before hopping in. Hmong people are shrewd entrepreneurs and will happily get out of you whatever they can. Haggle ruthlessly, and, rather than allow yourself to be overcharged, just wait for the next vehicle. A fair price from the junction to Pang Kae is 20 baht per person, and from Pang Kae to Maniploek another 20 baht. More than 50 baht/person from the H1080 to Maniploek is too much. These Hmong drivers are going that way in any case.

Arriving at Maniploek, camping at the forestry station, & information about Maniploek and local features (Hmong Maniploek 1, Tam Pa Poeng, the 'cliff idyll', Lua Maniploek 2, the Chompu Pu Kha trees, & the 'little loop')
For information about these topics, see Trek 11 in conjunction with Map 18. On the subject of tenting at Maniploek, do not rule out the possibility of pitching camp not at the forestry station, but at Lua Maniploek 2. This would have the advantage that you are right on the doorstep of the trek, which sets off from 'M2', and that you can fraternize with the guides before setting out. The Lua village is in any case an attractive place to 'hang out'.

The Lua & Hmong peoples

For background information on the Lua (Htin) people, such as inhabit Maniploek 2, Nam Pua Pattana 2 (Ban Ta) and other villages on the route, see Trek 5. For a thumbnail sketch of the Hmong people, such as live at Pang Kae, Maniploek 1 and Khang Ho, see Trek 16 under 'Santisuk'.

Preparing for the trek

Try to calculate how many days, nights and meals the trek, as you conceive of it, will involve, and buy provisions accordingly in Nan (with some food to spare). Drinks and limited (snack) food is available back at Pang Kae. Once you have set up camp at the forestry station and got to know the layout and (limited) facilities there, make your way late afternoon on the eve of the trek round to Lua Maniploek 2 to hire guides, organize the trek and familiarize yourself with the local geography. It is a good idea to go at that time, rather than in the morning or at midday, because during the day the guides, like many of the villagers, are out working in their fields or for the forestry, only returning home towards evening. Seek out Pae or Yod or Tayan, all Lua men who live in 'M2', with whom I have trekked several times. Ask for them, or show to the villagers my photos of them in this book. Pae (= goat) is a good person to deal with. Rather older than the other two (at the time of writing he is aged about 40), he is a sensible and sympathetic chap. All three, including (in 1998) 22-year-old Yod, know that you are coming and are willing to guide. Pae's house is situated centrally.

For this trek we hired Pae and Yod, paying them 200 baht each per day, for which they carried our backpacks while guiding. At the end of the trek you will have to pay your guides for the time it takes them to get round by road, via Pua, back to Maniploek 2, plus any public transport fares. Pay them the same rate, i.e. 100 baht per half day. However, it is possible that, once they have arrived in Nam Pua Pattana 2 (Ta village), they might want to stop there and return to M2 walking back the way you all came, via Khang Ho, in which case pay them for an extra day, which is the time it will take them to hike back home. If the guides do leave you in 'NPP2' to do this, it is no problem – you can easily find your way via Toei Hua Doi to the H1256 road and/or the Park HQ on your own, and actually their departure frees you up as you exit the trek.

*

Trekking route detail

Day 1: Maniploek forestry – Lua Maniploek 2 – Khang Ho – Khun Nam Pua Waterfall – campsite by River Pua

If you have camped overnight at Maniploek forestry station, make your way to Lua Maniploek 2. Either walk there on the roundabout track (see Map 18) (or directly on the cross-country path from the back of the forestry to M2), or, if you have come by bike, ride round to the village. The 2.6-km journey will take you about 10 mins by bike and some 40 mins, fully laden, on foot. Specific details are in Trek 11. If you have a bike at Maniploek, leave it under the lorry port in the forestry compound or, as the case may be, under Pae's house. You might be able to persuade the man at the forestry, called Maeo, to give you a lift round to M2 in his lorry, which would give you a flying start. If you are already in M2 because you camped overnight there, Bob's your uncle – you are already at the start of the expedition. We set off on the first leg of this trek at 9.30am (go earlier). I start the time log from M2.

Time log

Start/0 hrs	Head out from Lua Maniploek 2 south down the dirt track and past the small reservoir and granaries to come after 600 m to a junction.
5 mins	At the junction right goes back to the forestry station. Go left (straight) and follow the 4WD track for ca 1.3 kms.
25 mins	At a fork, left goes to the site of the former village of Nam Poen and ultimately to Doi Pu Wae. Go right (straight). Just past the Pu Wae turning, on the left side of the track, you can see one of the two Chompu Pu Kha trees growing locally. For more information on these very rare pink-flowering Bretschneider trees, which when we passed in December had orange cherry-sized berries, see Trek 9. Continue down the track. After another couple of hundred metres you come to a second fork. Left is our route, but if you go right (straight) and continue some 100 m further along the track, you come to the second pink Pu Kha tree (on the left, signed). We went to have a look, delaying the trek by 10 mins. Beyond the second tree, the trail continues, I think, to Ban Nong and Pang Kae, being the old way between Pang Kae and Maniploek.
35 mins	Back at the second fork, go left (E), as indicated, and proceed down a footpath. It is about 7 kms to Khang Ho. On your right you have a new view from behind of the second *chompu* tree. You now walk broadly S. View W of the Maniploek/Pang Kae road ('Dream Highway'). Path rejoins 4WD track.
45 mins	View left, almost due E, of Pu Wae mountain. Walk along a spine, with views both sides.
1 hr 35 mins	Descend S down a spur into a valley and cool woods.
2 hrs 10 mins	Log bridge.
2 hrs 20 mins	Arrive at **Khang Ho**, some 9.5 kms from M2.

Khang Ho is a Hmong settlement of just a few houses with 4 families. Largely deserted, most of its inhabitants were moved out in early 1995 to Pang Kae, and now it is little more than a place where the Hmong keep their cattle. We saw motorbikes here. Arriving in Khang Ho at 11.45am, we had an early picnic lunch, boiling up water in a villager's dwelling to make instant noodles. You can trek from here a scenic way to Doi Pu Wae. If I remember correctly, Doi Khang Ho is the high ridge E of the settlement. Less ambitious trekkers (or adventurous dirt bikers) could stop and even camp at Khang Ho, if you can stand the attention you will draw upon yourself, returning afterwards to Maniploek. We stopped for ¾ hr, setting off again at 12.30pm.

3 hrs 5 mins   Leave Khang Ho, proceeding S out of the hamlet, along just a footpath now, towards a small pointed mountain.
3 hrs 25 mins Reach a confusing place, going down into a little valley and up the other side, making your way S – towards the sun – through banana palms and brushgrasses.
3 hrs 35 mins Cross stream and continue through jungle. Here our guides, while hacking a way with their machetes, collected herbs and flowers for adding to *lao kao* (rice whisky) to make *lao dong*. The natural ingredients, when infused in the spirit, render it more potent and potable, or so Pae and Yod claimed.
4 hrs 20 mins Passing stands of bamboo and another stream, proceed through more jungle and then woodland.
4¾ hrs   Come to an old derelict and overgrown Hmong settlement in the lee of a high ridge left.
4 hrs 55 mins At a fork, branch left and go E.
5 hrs 10 mins On a tree trunk: two big crosses. Later: two more.
               You should now be heading towards two high twin peaks and a precipitous ridge, called Pa Waek.
5 hrs 40 mins Arrive at a dried-up riverbed. Stop for a rest among its boulders and many trees, some buttressed. The river is the Nam Pua.
               Contouring and slowly descending at the same time, proceed down a steep escarpment. On account of daughter Tanya, who rather lost her nerve here, we made slow progress, undoubtedly sacrificing quite a bit of time, perhaps half an hour. You will go quicker.
6 hrs 55 mins Descend a stepped streambed.
7 hrs   Arrive above the **Pua river**. It is rocky and in deep jungle. The waterfall is a few mins upstream. We break off the trek for about half an hour to visit it, climbing down the river bank and clambering upriver, sometimes on rocks and sometimes in the water. At an altitude of 920 m above sea level, attractive **Khun Nam Pua Waterfall** is on the Nam Pua river near the river's mountain source (*khun* = mountain). At the fall, the Pua river cascades over a ca 8-m-high limestone cliff covered with various plants and mosses. In front of the fall, there is a deep pool, which is great for swimming in. The waterfall is best visited between November and January.
               Back at where the trek was halted, continue downstream, mostly on the left (east) bank.
7 hrs 40 mins After just a few mins, arrive at the **Nam Pua 'campsite'**.

We reached the River Pua 'campsite' just after 5pm. You speedier hikers, unencumbered with children, will certainly arrive here earlier, perhaps at 4pm or even, if you do not break to visit the waterfall, at 3.30pm. If you set off bright and early from Maniploek 2, you could get to the campsite even before that. If so, you have the option either of exploring Khun Nam Pua Waterfall from the campsite at your leisure, or of pushing on to the village of Nam Pua Pattana 2 and the end of the core part of the trek. It is another 2¼ hrs to 'NPP2', also known as Ban Ta.

The overnight tenting place is not really a campsite at all. It is an arbitrary spot beside the path and just above the Pua river in deep dank jungle. Perhaps I was tired from the long march, but this camp seemed to me one of the wildest and least satisfactory sites that we have tented at. The guides slashed and cleared a flattish plot of undergrowth and laid down some 6-ft-long banana palm leaves, on which in the gloom we erected the tents.

My diary notes tell of the 'Rambo' reality of the campsite. In among the trees, lianas twist, loop and hang, and air roots dangle. Lateral roots in the humus of the jungle floor keep snagging our ankles and tripping us up. In the background is the sound of rushing water. We climb down to the river to wash ourselves and our clothes, everything being filthy and sweaty. In the failing light we juggle soap, soap tray, flannel, towel, comb, clothes and spectacles, putting them on the sand or on boulders or on a fallen tree, or hanging them on bushes. The water is cold and gritty, when we move in it we stir up a cloud of muddy particles, and we wash as best we can with a gloomy wall of vegetation looking on. We count the number of mosquito, midge and sandfly bites, rashes, grazes, lacerations and thorn pricks that we have collected on our arms and legs. Doug talks encouragingly of the danger of scrub-typhoid-carrying seed ticks. Night has fallen, a fire is burning, water is boiling in a pot, and we make macaroni packet soup by torchlight, with the smoke from the fire getting in our eyes. We eat standing up and try to dry some of the washed clothes either by holding them in our hands next to the fire or by hanging them on stick structures beside the fire, where they attract dozens of moths and insects. Some garments we put straight back on, while others we put on next morning. All are still damp and dirty. In turn, each of us has to go back down to the river in pitch darkness to get more water in the pot to make coffee and tea, and to boil water for drinking tomorrow. We retire into the tents. It is very cold in the night, and we wear socks, T-shirts, jeans and pullovers inside our sleeping bags. Outside there is a heavy dew, and drops fall from the trees onto the tents – into them if we unzip the opening. In the morning it is damp and cold, and we can see our breaths. It is difficult, crazy, absurd – why do we do it? – and yet memorable and exhilirating. In the middle of trying to establish order in the depths of the jungle, daughter Tanya's cyberpet peeps for attention!

Day 2: Nam Pua campsite – Nam Pua Pattana 2 (Ban Ta) – Toei Hua Doi – H1256 National Park road

Time log

Start/0 hrs	Set off on path downriver (we left at 9.20am), crossing and recrossing the Nam Pua.
25 mins	Cross a small stream. The path becomes easier now, and the Pua river valley broadens and flattens out.
35 mins	A peak on your left side is Doi Pamom, on the top of which is an old Thai Army position that used to be shot at by the CPT PLAT during the country's communist insurgency.
¾ hr	Log bridge.

1 hr 5 mins	Two Lua field huts and crops in the foreground of Doi Pamom. Leftish, as you look back, you can see a hint of the southern end of Doi Pa Waek, and far left Pa Kwang.
1 hr 25 mins	Increasing signs of civilization: the view ahead (W) is of cultivated hillsides with huts. Walk along valley floor past buffaloes and wet rice fields.
1½ hrs	On your left side: settlement of **Ban Na**, which looks pretty, especially set against the background of Doi Pamom. Bamboo bridge right.
1 hr 40 mins	A stile, then a log bridge with a handrail.
1¾ hrs	View left across the Pua river valley of the new village of Charaeng Mai on the hillside, which is on the route of Trek 10. Charaeng Luang, or, as the guides put it, 'Sa Laeng Luang', lies to the NE, and is the goal of the first day's hiking in Trek 10.
2 hrs	Another log bridge and the River Pua. The goal of this trek, Nam Pua Pattana 2 or, as it is also known, Ban Ta, is not far away now. Stopping by the river for a few mins, we learn that Ban Ta used to be located to the NW before it was moved down to the River Pua and 'NPP2'. Old Ban Ta was once the home village of guides Pae and Yod until they were resettled to Maniploek 2. For them, coming to NPP2 or New Ta is something of a homecoming, arriving at a place where former fellow villagers of theirs live. Down in the Pua valley are NPP2/Ta granaries and a confusing maze of trails.
2 hrs 10 mins	Cross the Pua river and climb steeply up the far bank to arrive at some houses relocated from old Ta, and, just beyond:
2¼ hrs	**Nam Pua Pattana 2** on a dirt road (see Map 16). It is the end of the core part of the trek, the rest of the expedition being a matter of exiting. We arrived at NPP2 at 11.35am.

Nam Pua Pattana 2, which like Charaeng Mai and Charaeng Luang also lies on the route of Trek 10, is the northerly, second and larger half of the Lua double village of Nam Pua Pattana, both parts – and indeed a third part (Ta Noi) further south – also being loosely known as Ban Ta. Strung out along the dirt road, it is a relatively big place in a very attractive setting. Occasional vehicles come here, the village has a shop (although in 1998 we found that it sold virtually nothing, even having run out of packets of instant noodles), and in the thick of things there is a fine south-facing adult education centre, with a long balcony at the front, reached by wooden steps. Both on this occasion and during Trek 10, we found the staff at the centre uncommonly friendly and helpful. Discovering upon arrival at NPP2 that we had run out of food, and that there was nothing to be bought from the shop, to our embarrassment we simply had to beg food from the teachers, but they did not mind at all and even gave us free rein of their kitchen, which is located in the back left corner of the education centre. If you ask, I am sure they will allow you to cook up instant noodles or whatever in the kitchen, and undoubtedly you could also stay overnight in their centre. I have always liked Nam Pua Pattana 2, and, if you are not in a hurry to exit this trek, you could have a nice time and good fun stopping the rest of the

TREK 12: MANIPLOEK 2 – KHANG HO – NAM PUA PATTANA 2

day and a second night in the village, either putting up in the adult education centre or pitching your tent somewhere down by the River Pua. You could even incorporate an extra bit of trek by walking 1½ hrs up to Charaeng Luang (and the same back).

Exiting the trek (see Map 16)

Before you go any further, you must divine the intentions of your guides. Are they coming with you, returning home to Maniploek 2 by the H1256 and H1080 roads via Pua and Ratchada, do they want to stop and stay with friends at Ban Ta, or do they intend to return directly across country to M2 via Khang Ho, going back the way you have all just come? If the latter two, pay them off, giving them extra lolly for their journey home. Don't worry about leaving them. Just don't worry about them. They have friends all over the place and are a million times more resourceful than you. Don't worry either about making your way to the H1256 road on your own and on out to Pua and Nan (or, as the case may be, back to Maniploek, if you have left you bike there). Exiting the trek is a piece of cake. There is a good chance that you can hitch-hike some or all of the way to the H1256. We found that we had to walk 2 hrs to Toei Hua Doi, where we got a lift the rest of the way to the National Park road and beyond. If you find that you have to walk the whole way to the H1256, it will take you about 3 hrs. If the day is quite far advanced, consider staying overnight at Nam Pua Pattana 2 and exiting the trek the next day. If it is mid-afternoon and you want to press on, but feel that you may not be able to get back to Nan (or Maniploek) the same day, consider walking out to the H1256 road and staying overnight at the National park HQ, which is just 2 kms E of where the dirt road hits the H1256.

Nam Pua Pattana 2 – Toei Hua Doi – Toei Klang – Kiu Haen – H1256 National Park road / Park HQ – Pua – Nan / Maniploek (Map 16)

After an hour for lunch at NPP2, we set off on foot on the last part of the trek at 12.35pm. The guides came with us, wanting to return to Maniploek by road, just as we wanted to in order to retrieve our bikes.

Time log

Start/0 hrs   From NPP2 proceed south 35 mins along the dirt road to descend a hill and arrive at:

35 mins   **Nam Pua Pattana 1**, which is the other smaller half of the Lua double-village, consisting of just a dozen or so houses.

40 mins   A few mins later, by a bridge over the Huai Sa Khun, you come to a turning left (E) for the Lua village of **Ta Noi**, which lies some 300 m from the junction and has a hill-tribe education centre. Beyond Ta Noi, a path continues E to the Lua village of Sa Khun, the Hmong settlement of Pang Kob and other villages (see Trek 9). Continue straight (S) from the turning and bridge to reach about 30 mins later another bridge over the:

1 hr 10 mins   Huai Waeng or Waeng stream. On the left side of the road, by the bridge, is **Nam Tok Waeng** or Waeng waterfall, a slimy 100-ft chute reminiscent of Huai Khon waterfall (Trek 13). It has a little drinking spring, at which the guides, if they are still with you, will doubtless refresh themselves.

After continuing S, the dirt road swings right (W) to climb up towards Toei Hua Doi. Some 30 mins out from Waeng w/f, a path heads off S from the left (S) side of the road by an electricity post on a bend in the road shortly before the first house of Toei Hua Doi. It is a short cut across the valley to the H1256. Your guides might take it. Ours did. We debated some time about whether to follow them or whether to continue by the dirt road via Toei Hua Doi and the other villages in the hope of getting a lift. In the end we decided to stick to the road and try to get a lift.

You come to the first houses of the village of Toei Hua Doi and a T-junction, at which you go right. Follow the road round to come to another junction, a *sala* or waiting hut, and the centre of:

ca 2 hrs   **Toei Hua Doi** village. Obliquely across from the *sala*, near the phone box, there is a store on the corner with soft drinks and even beer. Go on, you have earned it! While you are wetting your whistle at the waiting hut, admire the scenic view N across the valley into the heart of the National Park, out of which you have just trekked. NNE you can pick out the road just hoofed, contouring round the mountainsides. As you look out over the valley, the track heading approximately NNW relative to the *sala* proceeds ca 2 kms to Toei Noi (= little Toei) and then on to the village of Choon, which you can see in the distance at 330°, and from which you can continue to Sa Kaat (see Trek 11) and ultimately the H1080 road. The village of Toei consists of three parts: Toei Noi, just mentioned, Toei Hua Doi, where you are now standing, and Toei Klang, through which you must next pass. Just to confuse things further, the whole local area is known as Huai Ngon.

Our decision to exit by the dirt road via Toei Hua Doi and not by the short-cut path taken by the guides paid off because soon a truck came, which gave us a lift up to the H1256 road. It was a National Park fire-protection vehicle, and it took us free of charge with our guides not just to the National Park road, but on to Pua and even all the way back to Maniploek (which is where we all wanted to go) – an amazing stroke of luck.

If you cannot get a lift out, continue walking from Toei Hua Doi. It is about another hr up to the H1256 road.

Turn left (S) by the waiting hut and go down into a valley to a bridge and river. Now climb up the other side of the valley, say goodbye to the dirt road by picking up a paved surface, and pass through the Lua village of **Toei Klang**.

Continue on to **Kiu Haen** (Lua), passing a health centre (left side of road) at the beginning or lower end of the village.

Now walk the last couple of kms up the cement-section road, through a little defile in a kink in the way, to a:

ca 3 hrs   T-junction and the **H1256 National Park road**. The junction is marked by a waiting hut on the right side and by a large sign on the

TREK 12: MANIPLOEK 2 – KHANG HO – NAM PUA PATTANA 2

left side indicating (in Thai) the villages you have just passed through. Left (E) proceeds 2 kms to the Park headquarters (see Map 16) and ultimately Bo Glua, while right (W) exits to Pua and Nan (or Maniploek, if applicable).

If you need to go to stay at the Park HQ, either because you can get no onward lift and it is getting dark, or simply because you choose to intercalate a night there, go left and walk or ride past a viewpoint (left) 2 kms to the Park HQ (left side of H1256, up a driveway). For information about the HQ and about staying at it or at its nearby annexe of Laan Du Dao, see Trek 9. Otherwise go right and hitch-hike or take the first available public-transport *silor* (fare about 25 baht) ca 30 kms or 1 hr down the H1256 to Pua (see Map 14). You pass the signs indicating the beginning, or in this case the end, of the National Park, various turnings to offroad settlements, and the village of Na Lae. Coming down steeply off the Doi Pu Kha National Park massif, you then pass through some outlying rural Thai villages, before hitting a T-junction. Left goes to Nam Yao on the H1081 road, while right brings you after 200 m to the central crossroads in Pua. Here, right takes you N up the main H1080 highway to Chiang Klang and the Ratchada turn-off for Maniploek, while left takes you 60 kms S down the H1080 highway via Ta Wang Pa to Nan town.

If you are exiting this trek to Nan, you will now, in Pua, have to part company from your guides, assuming they are still with you. Pay them off if you have not already done so, and give them extra money for their fare home (I suggest 60-100 baht per guide). In Pua take the first available bus for Nan (journey time about 1 hr, fare a few baht). The local red buses go hourly and continue until reasonably late in the evening. If you miss the last one, try taking a Pua-Nan *silor*, or just hitch-hike. In 1999 I saw a new guest house in Pua, located on the main road at the southern end of the town, although it could be pricey.

If you are exiting the trek back to Maniploek, because you have left your bike there or because you want some more fun up there (at the same time escorting the guides home), take the first available bus or *silor* or thumbed lift north 19 kms to the Ratchada turn-off. Proceed as described earlier in this chapter under 'Accessing the trek' and as detailed in Trek 11 under 'Accessing Maniploek' (see also Map 17). If you are returning to Maniploek, stock up with fresh supplies in Pua at the market and supermarket near the crossroads.

Trek 13

Maniploek forestry – Maniploek 1 – Saam Yaek – Pong Tom – River Nan campsite (– Huai Khon w/f) – H1081 / Huai Sai Kao

Parameters

trekking mode:	on foot
core trek time:	2 days/1 night
accessing time:	from Nan town to Maniploek via Pua and Ratchada allow about half a day using a combination of public transport and hitch-hiking, and ca 2¾ hours with your own hire motorbike
exiting time:	from the H1081 road (near Huai Sai Kao) via Huai Khon, Tung Chang and Pua at least half a day using a combination of hitch-hiking and public transport
overall trek time:	from Nan to Nan, including access and exiting times, between 3 days/2 nights and 4 days/3 nights
degree of difficulty:	easy
guide(s):	recommendable, but you might be able to manage unguided
guide name(s):	Pae & Tayan (see photo section), also Yik
tent:	required
map(s):	see 17, 18, 19 & 20

Overview & strategy

This juicy little outing, the third of four treks based on Maniploek and the second of three treks hiking from Maniploek, strikes almost due north from the far-flung double-village of Maniploek (with its two Hmong and Lua parts) to cut through the northernmost part of Nan province's Doi Pu Kha National Park. Essentially it is a long but scenic descent into the valley of the River Nan – here beautiful and wild in its upper reaches – followed by a short stiff climb back out of the valley on the far side. From Maniploek the route leads to the remote Lua settlement of Pong Tom (if it is still there – more below), then down to the River Nan, where a night is spent under canvas at the water's edge, and finally up to the H1081 road, hitting it just east of the Lua village of Huai Sai Kao, which in turn lies just east of the big Tai Lue village of Huai Khon. Proceeding from the campsite by the Nan river, trekkers have the option of making a short 'Rambo' detour to take in inaccessible Huai Khon Waterfall (also known as Wangpian w/f).

TREK 13: MANIPLOEK – HUAI SAI KAO

The core part of the trek, from Maniploek to the H1081 road and Huai Sai Kao, can only be done on foot and takes 2 days and 1 night or, more accurately, a day and a morning with a night in between. If like most tribals you can fly along the trails lickety-split, you might be able to make it from Maniploek to Huai Sai Kao in one day, as the local Lua do. This not a difficult hike either physically or routewise, and you might be able to dispense with a guide. However, as always, guides ensure that you do not get lost, they carry your luggage, help strike camp, and provide security and company. I got up this mini expedition just before Christmas 1998 as part of a party of 6, which also included Nittaya Tananchai, our infant daughter Tanya, Doug Boynton, and two Lua guides, Pae and Tayan, hired from Maniploek 2. A sign of the comparative easiness of the trek is that daughter Tanya, aged 7½ at the time, was able to manage it effortlessly and without complaint, at the most having to be carried across the Nan river by the guides. She even exulted in paddling in the River Nan, in sleeping in a tent in the jungle under the stars, in tending the campfire, and in cooking over it. Responsible trekkers, therefore, with resilient children take heart: jungle trekking with your offspring *is* possible, assuming they can keep going for about 7 hrs, including stops, which is how long it takes to get from Maniploek to the River Nan campsite (the longest stretch). Much of what applies to this outing applies also to the two previous trips (Treks 11 and 12) and has already been set forth in those chapters. For obvious reasons, I do not want to keep repeating data already given elsewhere, and so the reader is referred to those two earlier chapters and should peruse the account here in conjunction with the texts of Treks 11 and 12, especially with the extensive material already given relating to accessing Maniploek, camping at the forestry station there, and reaching the Lua part of the village (Maniploek 2 or 'M2').

More specifically, on the eve of the trek you journey by bus and hitch-hiking or possibly with your own hire motorbike to Maniploek and camp overnight there probably at the forestry station (Maps 17 & 18). On Day 1 of the actual trek, you make your way first to a junction called 'Saam Yaek' (= three ways), which from the forestry complex can be reached either by walking via Hmong Maniploek 1 or via Lua Maniploek 2 (see Map 18). From Saam Yaek you walk 1¼ hrs to Pong Tom (if it has not been moved) and then about another 3 hrs down to the River Nan, stopping for lunch on the way. Now it is just 20 mins along the southern river bank to the campsite (Map 19). On the morning of Day 2, you continue along the southern river bank until the confluence of the Nam Ri and the River Nan, you cross the Nan river and climb steeply up until you pick up a flattish 4WD track, which brings you to the H1081 road (Map 19). The stretch from the campsite to the road takes ca 3¼ hrs. From the confluence you have the option of clambering adventurously down the River Nan a short distance to Huai Khon (or Wangpian) Waterfall. If you make this detour, you can either return to the confluence and then proceed as above, or continue downriver somewhat to pick up another northward-ascending path, which likewise brings you to the 4WD track and ultimately the H1081.

175

At the junction of the 4WD track and the H1081 road you snatch a picnic lunch while waiting for a lift west to Huai Sai Kao and Huai Khon. Both villages are not far from the junction, and in the absence of a lift on the little-used H1081 road it would be possible to walk the 2.8 kms to Huai Sai Kao and then the further 5 kms to Huai Khon (Map 20). You have now reached the exiting stage of the trek, although many trekkers might want to intercalate a second night at interesting Huai Khon, where in 1999 there was a new guest house. From Huai Khon, which is serviced by regular public-transport *silor* or share-taxis, you hitch-hike or travel by *silor* west and then south along the H1080 road to the village of Pon (or beyond), where you can pick up buses heading south for Nan town (Pon is the northerly end-stop of the local Nan-Pon bus route) (Map 20). From Pon you ride south either by bus or still in your hitch-hiked lift to Tung Chang, Ratchada, Chiang Klang, Pua and Nan. Near Ratchada, your guides, if you hired any and if they are still with you, will alight at the junction of the H1080 and H1291 roads to hitch-hike east up the H1291 side road back to Maniploek, as you will do too if you have left a motorbike there or if you want to return there for more fun (Map 17 again). There should be no problem exiting the trek from Huai Sai Kao or Huai Khon to Nan town or back to Maniploek in the afternoon of Day 2 (Day 3 overall), but be warned: the distances up in this far-flung north-easterly corner of Nan province are quite great. It is almost 30 kms from Huai Khon to Pon with its bus terminus, and it is some 135 kms from Huai Khon to Nan town (or getting on for 150 kms to Nan from where you first hit the H1081 road and snatched a picnic lunch).

The trek can be modified, as said, in two ways: by delaying the exit and spending a second night at Huai Khon, and by incorporating a visit to Huai Khon Waterfall (more info during the trekking detail below). But it can be modified in other ways, too, as follows. You could drastically truncate it by proceeding only as far as (the site of former) Pong Tom. Here I must enter a note about this place. At Christmas 1998, when we did this trek, Pong Tom (or Prong Tom or Prong Tom Mai) existed as a small village. However, by mid-1999, so Doug reported, it had been relocated to within 2 kms of Lua Maniploek 2 and no longer existed. There can be few villages that have been more shunted around by the authorities or which more keep returning to their former site despite resettlement than Pong Tom. So currently its status is dubious. It may have vanished from its former site, you might find it elsewhere, it may have half moved, with some people remaining at the former site, or it may have moved from its new (newest) site back to its former site. Accordingly, I shall cite the Pong Tom we passed through as virtual 'Pong Tom'. Whatever the case, there should still be a small new forestry office at 'Pong Tom', and of course the skeleton of the place will still be there.

At 'Pong Tom' you could either simply walk back to Maniploek the same day, or you could spend a night there, either pitching a tent somewhere or trying to stay at the little forestry office. Skilled bikers could even reach 'Pong Tom' by biking along the forest trails from Maniploek. If your plan is to hike only to 'Pong Tom', you could also perhaps take in nearby Tam Pa Daeng or Red Cliff Cave. This truncation of the trek might appeal to less ambitious trekkers or to those wanting to base themselves on Maniploek forestry, making a series of little explorations of the local area. Another option, also truncating the trek but not so drastically, would be to proceed to the River Nan, camp there, perhaps explore Huai Khon Waterfall from the campsite, and then return via 'Pong Tom' to Maniploek. This would have the virtue of cutting out the roundabout exit by road via Huai Khon and Pon, and would mean that you could use a hire bike to access Maniploek because you would be returning there to retrieve it. Even as I write this, this compromise option seems to me an excellent idea.

There are other possibilities, which I cannot comment on because I have not looked into them. Thus Pae told us that from the confluence of the Ri and Nan rivers you can walk up the Nam Ri to Kiu Jaan (Map 19), a Lua village on the H1081 road well east of Huai Sai Kao, which would mean that the trek would then terminate at Kiu Jaan. Trek 13 is altogether a flexible trip with several variations. Looking at things more grandly, a final modification would be to combine this trek with the previous one, Trek 12 (from Maniploek south via Khang Ho, Nam Pua Pattana 2 and Toei Hua Doi to the H1256 road). The result would be one long trek, running on a north-south or south-north axis, which would pass clean through the whole of the main northerly heartland of Doi Pu Kha National Park. However, to undertake such a magnificent combined trek, you would have to start not from Maniploek, but either from the Park headquarters in the south or from Huai Sai Kao in the north. Furthermore, you would first have to pick up guides from Maniploek and bring them round to the southerly or northerly start of the trek. In the middle of the combined supertrek you would pass through Maniploek. From Nan to Nan such an expedition would take at least 4 days and could easily be stretched out to last a week.

Because Maniploek, the start of the trek, lies some 115 kms or 2-3 hrs' riding from Nan (making a round trip to Lua Maniploek 2 or 'M2' of almost 250 kms or 6 hrs of riding!), it makes little sense to go there in advance to set the trek up guidewise, unless you happen to be in the area. The distance is too great. So you will need to arrive at Maniploek the day before the trek, ideally at lunchtime. This will then give you time to get round to Maniploek 2 to organize guides, as well as to familiarize yourself with the forestry station, with the layout of the locality, and with the way to M2. By the same token, because Maniploek is so isolated, it makes little sense to use a hire bike to access Maniploek and the start of the trek, unless you are planning to return there. After the trek, when you exit via Huai Sai Kao, Huai Khon, Pon, Tung Chang, Ratchada and Pua, you would have the awkward process at Ratchada of hitch-hiking all the way up the H1291 side road via Pang Kae to Maniploek (an then back out again) to retrieve your machine. It would only make sense to bike to Maniploek and to leave your machine there if, as said, you planned to truncate the trek, returning from

'Pong Tom' or the River Nan to Maniploek, or if you wanted, say, to tack motorcycle Trek 11 onto the end of this trek (13), i.e. if, after doing the 'Pong Tom' and Huai Sai Kao hike, you wanted to further explore the Maniploek area (taking a closer look at the Hmong tribals of Maniploek 1, visiting local Beecliff Cave with its stream sink dolina, taking a peek at the two rare Chompu Pu Kha trees near Maniploek 2, and so on) and ride out via Kwet and Sa Kaat. And there is a lot to be said for this. It has the virtue that you can kill two birds or treks with one stone, you can see any guides (if you have hired them) safely back to Maniploek, and you have the comfort and convenience of both accessing and partially exiting the trek with your own transport. The downside, of course, is that your transport lies idle in Maniploek for a couple of days, while you do the hike.

Accessing the trek
As with all the treks in this book in Nan province, you will undoubtedly ultimately launch Trek 13 from Nan town and its guest houses. Now, bearing in mind the considerations above, you must decide whether you are going to access Maniploek and the start of the actual hike by hire bike or by public transport and hitch-hiking. If you ride there with your own transport, the journey is, as said, 115 kms, and it took us on two separate occasions 2¾ hrs. For a full account of the trip from Nan to Maniploek, see Trek 11 under 'Trekking route detail / accessing Maniploek' and also Map 17.

If you proceed to Maniploek by public transport and hitch-hiking, ride from Nan town on a local red bus north up the H1080 road via the towns of Ta Wang Pa, Pua and Chiang Klang and the village of Ratchada to the junction of the H1080 and H1291 roads, which is 19 kms north of Pua central crossroads. After Ratchada, watch out for a 'Cosmo Oil' fuel station on the right side. The junction is imminent. Get out of the bus at the junction (it will probably stop there anyway). The H1291 side road for Maniploek heads off right (east) towards mountains. If on the bus you come to the town of Tung Chang, you have gone too far. For more detailed supplementary info about the route Nan/Pua/Ratchada/Maniploek, see Trek 11 under 'Accessing Maniploek' and Map 17. Now proceed by public-service *silor* and/or hitch-hiking from the junction via the villages of Pa Ruak and Pang Kae to Maniploek, a distance of some 36 kms. Plenty of trucks go up to Pang Kae and Maniploek, although you might have to wait a bit. Try, if possible, to ride with some kind of official truck (forestry, highland development, BPP, school) – you do not run the risk of being ripped off and might well travel free. Most of the vehicles going up here are Hmong. If you ride with a Hmong pick-up, negotiate a fare before hopping aboard. The Hmong are shrewd businesspeople and will happily get out of you whatever they can. Haggle ruthlessly, and, rather than allow yourself to be overcharged, just wait for the next vehicle. A fair price from the junction to Pang Kae is 20 baht per person, and from Pang Kae to Maniploek another 20 baht. More than 50 baht/person all the way to Maniploek is too much. These Hmong drivers are going that way in any case.

TREK 13: MANIPLOEK – HUAI SAI KAO

Arriving at Maniploek, camping at the forestry station, & information about Maniploek and local features (Hmong Maniploek 1, Tam Pa Poeng, the 'cliff idyll', Lua Maniploek 2, the Chompu Pu Kha trees, & the 'little loop')

For information about these topics, see Trek 11 in conjunction with Map 18. On the subject of tenting at Maniploek, do not rule out the possibility of pitching camp not at the forestry station, but at Lua Maniploek 2. This would have the advantage that you start the trek directly from where the guides live, and that you can fraternize with them before setting out. The Lua village is in any case an attractive place to 'hang out'.

The Lua & Hmong peoples

For background information on the Lua (Htin) people, such as inhabit Maniploek 2, Pong Tom and Huai Sai Kao, see Trek 5. For a thumbnail sketch of the Hmong people, such as live in Pang Kae and Maniploek 1, see Trek 16 under 'Santisuk'.

Preparing for the trek

Try to calculate how many days, nights and meals the trek, as you conceive of it, will involve, and buy provisions accordingly in Nan (with some food to spare). Drinks and limited (snack) food is available back at Pang Kae. Once you get to Huai Khon, plentiful food and drinks are available. When you have set up camp at the forestry station and got to know the layout and (limited) facilities there, make your way late afternoon on the eve of the trek round to Lua Maniploek 2 to hire guides (if you want any), organize the trek and familiarize yourself with the local geography. It is a good idea to go at that time, rather than in the morning or at midday, because during the day the guides, like many of the villagers, are out working in their fields or for the forestry, only returning home towards evening. Seek out Pae or Yod or Tayan, all Lua men who live in 'M2', with whom we have trekked several times. Ask for them or show my photos of them in this book to the villagers. Pae (= goat) is a good person to deal with. Rather older than the other two (in 1999 aged ca 40), he is a sensible and highly sympathetic character. All three, including (in 1998) 22-year-old Yod, know that you are coming and are willing to guide. Pae's house is situated centrally.

For Trek 13 we hired 'mountain goat' Pae and bespectacled urbane Tayan, paying them 200 baht each per day, for which they carried our backpacks while guiding. For the 2-day trip they got 450 baht each, which included a 50-baht tip (900 baht for the trek all told). If either or both of them are unavailable, ask in M2 for someone called Yik, whom we have never met, but who knows the trail to Huai Sai Kao (which he does in 5 hrs flat!) because he has relations there. Actually, on this trek it was Tayan who led the way, not Pae, who followed behind. Never having been to Huai Sai Kao, Pae did not know the route at the time, although he does now. Tayan, by contrast, grew up in Pong Tom, and his mother, whom he sometimes visits, lives in Huai Sai Kao, so he knows the path well.

Incidentally, after growing up in Pong Tom (at the village's oldest and original site down by the River Nan), Tayan lived for a while in Nam Pua Pattana 2 (Ban Ta), before moving to Maniploek. It all shows how these Lua get about, leading disruptive lives, often because they are moved around by Thai officialdom. Tayan has two children, in 1999 aged 9 and 4, and grows rice and cabbages etc., when not working for the forestry authority.

It is possible, but unlikely, that the guides, after having led you to Huai Sai Kao, will return to Maniploek the way they and you have come, which would have the advantage that you would have more freedom of manoeuvre when exiting the trek. However, when we asked Pae and Tayan if they wanted to do this, they replied: "No way! The climb up from the River Nan back to Pong Tom is too much of a killer." If you still have guides with you after Huai Sai Kao, you will have to pay them, of course, for the time it takes them to get round by road, via Huai Khon, Tung Chang and Ratchada back to Maniploek 2, plus any *silor* and bus fares. Pay them the same rate, i.e. 100 baht per half day.

*

Trekking route detail
Day 1: Maniploek forestry – Lua Maniploek 1 (or 2) – Saam Yaek – 'Pong Tom' – campsite by River Nan
The trekking notes in my diary begin from the Saam Yaek junction (see Map 18). This is because we persuaded Maeo, who manages Maniploek forestry station, to drive us there together with the guides in his lorry, thus allowing us to get off to a flying start. But you, unless you can also get a lift, will have to walk from the forestry compound to Saam Yaek. There are two ways of doing this. You can go either via Hmong Maniploek 1 or via Lua Maniploek 2. Each has something to recommend it. (1) Proceeding via M1 is shorter. It is 1.6 kms to M1 and then 2.4 kms from M1 to Saam Yaek, making 4 kms in total from the compound to Saam Yaek – perhaps an hour's walk. But to go this shorter way, you will have to get the guides to come from M2 to meet you at the forestry. It also involves more down-and-up climbing. For the guides it makes more sense to go direct from M2, their home village, to Saam Yaek. So consider the other way to Saam Yaek. Indeed, a neat solution for this trek would be to camp on the eve of the expedition in M2, so that both you and the guides can start fresh together from M2. Of course, if you have come to Maniploek by bike, you can easily ride round to M2, saving yourself and the guides a walk. (2) From M2 to Saam Yaek is 3.8 kms, moreover on a flattish trail. From the forestry to M2 via the roundabout dirt track is 2.6 kms, unless you can find the little path which runs directly cross-country from the back of the forestry compound to M2 (I have never found it). Thus the other way – to Saam Yaek from the forestry via M2 – is 6.4 kms or 4 miles long, which might take you 1½ hrs. Now I will detail both ways of getting from the forestry station to Saam Yaek.

(1)   From the crossroads by the entrance to the forestry, go N down and up the paved road, past Tam Pa Poeng or Bee Cliff Cave (left side, km 1.1), to a T-junction (km 1.6), which marks the beginning of

TREK 13: MANIPLOEK – HUAI SAI KAO

Hmong Maniploek 1 (Map 18). Go right to enter the main part of the village. Proceed 400 m through the centre of the village to reach a second T-junction (km 2.0) at the top end. Go right again up towards half a dozen water tanks. At a fork, bear left, pass the tanks, and proceed very steeply up a rutted dirt track. Follow the elevated 4WD track along the crest of a ridge 2 more kms to Saam Yaek junction, marked (in 1998) by a green metal sign (km 4.0). Left, our route, continues to 'Pong Tom', while right is the way to and from M2.

(2)   From the crossroads by the entrance to the forestry station, go S on a poor dirt track and follow the electricity posts and wires to M2 (Map 18). After just a few hundred metres, the trail swings left (E), and on your right (S) side you can see, some 200-300 m offroad, a lovely corner, backgrounded by a scarp, that I call the 'cliff idyll' (see Trek 11 for details). The rutted track climbs twice steeply up and passes through woods to hit a T-junction (2 kms from the forestry crossroads). Turn left (N) and continue 600 m past half a dozen granaries to reach M2 (2.6 kms). Unladen, I once briskly walked from the forestry station to M2 in 35 mins. Now, having linked up with your guides (if you have decided to take them), continue N behind the village at its upper end and leave M2. Walk 3.8 kms on a sketchy flattish elevated track to reach Saam Yaek (6.4 kms from the forestry). In 1998 the junction was marked by a green metal sign. Left is the way to and from Hmong Maniploek 1, and right is your way to 'Pong Tom'.

Time log

Start/0 hrs   At **Saam Yaek**, go left for 'Pong Tom' if you have come from M1, and go right for it if you have come from M2. We set off from the Saam Yaek junction at 9.30am and, trekking at a leisurely pace and making a generous pause in 'Pong Tom', took 5½ hrs to reach the campsite by the River Nan. You can add to this however long it took you to hike from Maniploek forestry to Saam Yaek to arrive at an estimate of the overall trek time on Day 1.
View NE (50°) across valley to Lua village of Huai Gaan, with the H1081 road visible just beneath it.
Cattle gate across track.
View back left of school at Hmong Maniploek 1.

35 mins   Take a footpath right, which cuts off a corner of the 4WD track, rejoining the track at a clearing.

40 mins   Clearing in trees.
Continue up 4WD track, walking uphill and down dale.

1 hr 5 mins   Ca 4.3 kms out from Saam Yaek, you come to a 3-way junction. Left (straight) is the path to **Tam Pa Daeng** or Red Cliff Cave, which lies about 4.4 kms from the 3-way junction (you will need guidance to find the cave, in which a hermit lived when I last visited), while right, our route, goes very steeply down to 'Pong Tom', sited before you against an attractive panorama. Prior to descending, admire the fine view, characteristic of this north-eastern corner of Nan province, backing up to the Lao border. The modern building and curious

raised cement structure at your feet is a new forestry office with water tower. Due N, in the distance, the new border road from Huai Khon to Laos is visible. Below the forestry building, go straight (not right) and up to the (site of the former?) village of:

1¼ hrs   'Pong Tom' or 'Pong Tom Mai' (New Pong Tom).

As said, this place may by now have (partially) vanished or moved to a new site nearer Maniploek. But at Christmas 1998 we found here a small Lua settlement, consisting of some 20 shacks. It was one of the most cut-off, backward and impoverished of the dozens of Lua villages that I have seen. The inhabitants' fields lay miles away, and a sign of its remoteness was that the people, upon our arrival, seemed distinctly fearful of us. The site was fairly new. Original or old Pong Tom, which had comprised some 100 houses, used to be located near the Nan river, but had been broken up a few years earlier, with the villagers being forcibly dispersed to New Pong Tom, Nam Ri and Huai Sai Kao. A smidgen of controversy attached to Pong Tom Mai. The Pong Tom Lua who had been resettled by the authorities to Nam Ri, a relocation intended to consolidate Doi Pu Kha National Park, had then moved back to New Pong Tom of their own accord, maintaining that Nam Ri was unsuitable for them, while Pong Tom Mai was suitable. When I first came here in January 1994 with my Danish geologist friend Soeren, these people had just decamped 'illegally' back to New Pong Tom, and the place was full of recently constructed houses and seemed to be bigger than in 1998. In my diary for 1994, I noted that there were about 300 people in Pong Tom Mai. It must have been the case that in the 4 years following many of them had acquiesced after all and remained elsewhere. Where the new forestry office now is, on a knoll above the village, Soeren and I found the remains of an old Thai Army camp, which had been used to secure the area during the struggle against the communist insurgents. If you intend to go no further than 'Pong Tom', consider staying there. You might be able to sleep inside the new forestry building, or pitch a tent near it or just anywhere. We spent ¾ hr at 'Pong Tom', partly because the guides 'went visiting', and partly because we took a good look around. We left at 11.30am.

2 hrs   Set off again at the far end of 'Pong Tom' on a footpath leading NNE (40°) past two rocks, through trees and contouring on the left side of a small valley. After rising slightly, the path then decends.
To your right there is a great view across a valley down onto Huai Gaan, while, looking N, you can enjoy a fantastic vista of successive mountain ridges extending far into Laos.
Now begins a long descent N along a well-worn path in the direction of Huai Khon.
Cattle gate.

2 hrs 20 mins   Twenty mins out from Pong Tom, fork right by a boulder and a pen with cattle and ponies.

2½ hrs   Muddy streamlet and logs.

TREK 13: MANIPLOEK – HUAI SAI KAO

2 hrs 35 mins The village visible right at 120° in the far distance, just below the skyline, is Buak Ya (Lua), close to the Lao border. Below it a path snakes down to Piang Ko in the Nan river valley on the H1081 road.

3 hrs   Come to a clearing with two cement tanks, some banana palms and a fine tree with little green leaves and 'cotton' fluff. The tanks are marked with '323', probably indicating a former Thai Army camp, N° 323. Our guides told us that Old Pong Tom used to lie hereabouts. We reached the clearing at 12.30pm and made a 40-min lunch stop in it.

3 hrs 40 mins Set off again, descending steeply.
3¾ hrs   Pass the Huai Haat (Haat stream) and a mini chute of water.
             Proceed through bamboo tunnels and into an open valley.
             The gash of the H1081 road is plainly visible.
4 hrs 25 mins Come down to stream and a small side valley filled with banana palms. There used to be a settlement here, possibly Old Pong Tom.
4½ hrs   Cross a field with two granaries and a tree. We stopped here for a 15-min rest.
             Continue down the little valley, bear left in some bamboos, and then walk down an old paddy field.
4 hrs 55 mins Reach a path and the **River Nan** (now see Map 19). The path runs above the river on the (left) south bank. Elated, we stopped again for 15 mins. The river, some 5-10 m wide, has rocky banks of pink-brown boulders, and flows through a fairly steep-sided valley of brilliant green vegetation.
5 hrs 10 mins Walk 20 mins downstream on a good path on the south bank of the Nan, sometimes high above the river, to reach the:
5½ hrs   **Campsite by the River Nan**, where you stop for the night.

We arrived at the River Nan campsite at 3pm, after plentiful stopping en route. The site lies between two sets of shallow rapids, has a sandy 'beach', and can be identified by a crucial little spring. The spring is important, especially for the guides, because it is the only spring locally with good drinking water. You should not drink water from the River Nan because several villages lie upstream, contaminating it. Use the good spring water, in your case also boiling, filtering or purifying it. A couple of better camping places can be found 25 mins or so further downstream, the first at the confluence of the Rivers Nan and Ri, but they suffer precisely from the fact that they have no springs of good water, which is why you should camp where you do camp. At the campsite, there is a place to pitch a couple of tents beside the path, just up from the river, 6 or 10 ft above the 'beach'. As we erected our tents amid the sand, rock and bushes, four surprised Lua fishermen, one of them strikingly moustachiod and looking like an Indian, went past, slowly trawling their way upstream and pausing to watch us. The guides established their home from home nearby, likewise on a kind of ledge, under an overarching canopy of bushes. Here they lit a fine fire, on which they cooked fish in bamboo tubes, and beside which they slept, to keep warm, the smoke fending off mosquitoes, or so they hoped. When they went off fishing, we likewise got a fire going for cooking, boiling water, drying clothes, making light after it had got dark, and keeping Tanya amused. While she paddled and splashed in the Nan, we washed and rinsed through the clothes. I remember this camp as being an agreeable one, and we spent a fun evening and night there.

Day 2: River Nan campsite – confluence of Rivers Nan & Ri (– Huai Khon Waterfall) – H1081 road – Huai Sai Kao (Map 19)

From the campsite by the River Nan to the H1081 road takes about 3¼ hrs, not including any visit to Huai Khon Waterfall, which will distort your timings. We started Day 2 at 8.50am. To be honest, you would not be missing so much trekwise, and you would save yourself some exiting trouble with the guides, if, as suggested earlier, you simply turned round at the campsite and hiked back to 'Pong Tom' and Maniploek. Thus, consider doing so, perhaps spending a second fun night by the Nan and/or visiting Huai Khon Waterfall, which lies about an hour downstream from the campsite.

Time log

Start/0 hrs   Set off on the path, continuing westish downstream along the left (south) bank of the River Nan, passing through some infuriating bamboo tunnels (they are not high enough to let you walk through head bent forward, and not low enough to make you crawl on hands and knees), and walking in places high above the river.

25 mins   You come to the **confluence of the Rivers Nan and Ri**. The Nam Ri flows into the Nam Nan on the opposite northern bank from the right (NNE). Except for the problem with good water, you could also camp satisfactorily near the confluence. It is possible, as said and as our guides told us, to trek up the Nam Ri to Kiu Jaan (Lua), situated on the H1081 road (not having done this, I do not know how long it would take). Now is decision time. By the mouth of the Nam Ri, on the far bank of the River Nan, a path climbs up steeply, heading N. It is the quickest way to the H1081 road and Huai Sai Kao. Take it, crossing the Nan, if you want to press on to the end of the trek. If you want to make an adventurous detour to take in Huai Khon Waterfall, continue downstream[1].

---

[1] The fall lies some 30 mins and three bends of the River Nan west downstream. It is by no means easy to get to. In 1994, at the end of January, I managed to visit the fall from Pong Tom, coming this way with my Danish friend Soeren Skipsted. But at Christmas 1998, during Trek 13, we were unable to reach the fall. There were places where we would have had to wade through fast-flowing chest-high water, which would have been very difficult with daughter Tanya. On her account, the guides dissuaded us from attempting to visit the fall. Huai Khon Waterfall, also known officially as Wangpian Waterfall, is located inaccessibly in a part of the Nan river where there are cliffs on both sides. There is no path or proper way to it from either end. Of the two approaches, that from the west (the far side, relative to us) is said to be easier, while the access from the east (our way) is the more difficult. You cross and recross the Nan a couple of time and clamber to the fall Rambo-style over slabs of rock, through the water, and up and down the banks. Situated on the left (south) side of the River Nan, Nam Tok Huai Khon consists of half a dozen cascades tumbling some 50 m down a slimy escarpment into the river in deep jungle. It is as impressive as it is creepy. Once at the fall, you do not need to return to the Nam Ri/Nam Nan confluence to

184

TREK 13: MANIPLOEK – HUAI SAI KAO

We got into a time-wasting pickle of indecision near the confluence. We started for the waterfall, but then, hearing from some local Lua fishermen, that we would have to wade through swirling chest-high water to reach it, aborted the idea. Still on the south bank, we climbed up somewhat and walked along a path round a further bend of the river to an open sandy cove. This would also make a nice spot to camp, except, again, there is apparently no sweet water to drink here. After speaking to some fishermen at the cove and, after some shilly-shallying, aborting the detour to the fall in favour of striking for Huai Sai Kao, we crossed the river and on the northern bank opposite began climbing steeply up a shoulder. In a killer ascent, it rises to meet the first path up from the confluence.

1 hr 25 mins   Join the other original proper path (from the confluence), which comes in from the right. Actually, there are many paths that go up from and down to the River Nan in this area. Almost any one will do, as long as it brings you to a key clearing at the top of the ascent. Conversely, from the clearing, numerous paths fan out to descend into the valley to the River Nan. They are used by fishermen from Huai Sai Kao. The fishermen park their motorbikes in the bushes all around the clearing.

1 hr 55 mins   On a knoll we encountered the first parked motorbikes.

Two mins later arrive at a clearing, the key clearing mentioned above and in Footnote 1. More parked motorbikes. From the clearing, the main way out (N) is the 4WD track to the main 1081 road and Huai Sai Kao. (The way left goes down 3 kms to the Nan river, passing near the bottom a curious latrine block with three toilets. This used to be a regular track, but in 1999 was overgrown. There are plans to rehabilitate this way down to the Nan. At the bottom you go left (east) upstream to access Huai Khon Waterfall from the west.) We rested 15 mins at the clearing.

2 hrs 10 mins   Set off N along the 4WD dirt track towards the main road, 5 kms away. Walking on the level, you pass granaries at almost every corner. Looking NE, you can glimpse across the Nam Ri valley a corner of Kiu Jaan village on the skyline.

2 hrs 35 mins   A fine view due S to Doi Pu Wae with its west-facing cliff in the far distance (we go there in Trek 14).

3¼ hrs   Hit the main **H1081 road** at a T-junction. Right goes to Kiu Jaan and eventually Bo Glua, while left, our route, proceeds 2.8 kms to Huai Sai Kao and then 5 kms further to Huai Khon. At the junction there is a tin-roofed hut and a brown sign pointing back down the dirt side track and indicating 'Wangpian Waterfall 7 kms' (= Huai Khon Waterfall).

---

continue the trek. Make your way further downstream a few mins, round a bend, and you come to a place where an overgrown track climbs steeply up, past a quaint three-toilet building, 3 kms or about 30 mins' walk to a clearing. The way swings first left, then right, and at the top right again, bringing you to the clearing. At the clearing, you rejoin the other way up from the River Nan and pick up a 4WD track that brings you after some 5 kms to the H1081 road. Our guides spoke of yet another possibility (untrekked by myself and hence unverified). Apparently you can walk further along the Nan river, downstream away from the waterfall, to a place where you come to issue by Old Huai Khon and the new district office (see below under 'Exiting') – strictly for explorer-adventurers only!

185

Exiting the trek (see Map 20)
You have reached the end of the core part of the trek. Now you must make your way via Huai Sai Kao to Huai Khon and on out via Pon to Ratchada, where some trekkers might want to return to Maniploek (the guides certainly will, if you have them and they are still with you), after which you exit via Pua to Nan town. I think there are no *silor* on this stretch of the H1081, so start hitch-hiking. You might have to wait some time for a lift because traffic is pretty infrequent in these remote, very sparsely populated outreaches of Nan province. We arrived at the junction at midday and had to wait two full hours by the roadside in the blazing sun and heat for the first truck to come along. During that time we had a picnic lunch, eating up our last provisions, and Tayan walked on to Huai Sai Kao to see relatives and friends, Pae remaining with us. You can likewise trek on to the small Lua village, but you gain little, although you might be able to get some soft drinks there, and it will be a shadier, more comfortable place to wait. From Huai Sai Kao you will still have to hitch-hike a lift with a passing pick-up. In the end, picking up Tayan in Huai Sai Kao, we all six, a sweaty dishevelled crew, got a ride in a truck driven by a curious coquettish lady, wearing white gloves and many silver bracelets, and a kind of toyboy, who was ostensibly from the agriculture department. They whisked us through Huai Khon, Pon and Tung Chang to the Ratchada turn-off, twice stopping briefly on official business at the new district office near Huai Khon and and at the district office (*ampoe*) in Tung Chang. Then we hitch-hiked back up to Maniploek, arriving at nightfall. I mention all this to illustrate how things can and often do turn out.

If things go wrong at the junction, either because no lift comes or because you get caught out by nightfall, walk the short distance of 2.8 kms to **Huai Sai Kao** (= white sand stream) and put up your tent there somewhere, or stay overnight in some official building or villager's house. I can tell you little about this small and attractive, but meagre village because I have never stopped there except to thumb a lift, but it has a little shop. If the worst comes to the worst, walk a further 5 kms on to Huai Khon, which is a relatively large and civilized Tai Lue place with shops, eating places, public transport and even accommodation. Thus, by hitch-hiking or by walking you reach Huai Khon via Huai Sai Kao. On the way you pass 1 km after Huai Sai Kao a turning right to the new district office of *ampoe* Chaloem Pra Kiet, set back from the road. Behind it and slightly to the east lies a jungle *wat* or monastery and also **Huai Khon Cave**, both worth a visit. This is not the place to describe these incidental offroad features, and for details of them the reader is referred to my cultural guidebook *Around Lan-Na* (Chapter 15). Opposite the new district complex, on the other, south side of the 1081 road, is the site of Old Huai Khon, before the village was moved to its present location during the CPT insurgency. The area was once both a communist stronghold, based on Huai Khon Cave, and the scene of a major battle between the Thai Army and People's Liberation Army of Thailand (PLAT) guerrillas.

Huai Khon is such an interesting and pleasant place that, especially if you are unhampered by guides, you might consider breaking your exit journey there to spend a night. On the eastern edge of the village, just before you descend a steep S-bend to arrive at the pitlike centre, you pass headman Leng's house (right), a military camp (left) and a kind of guest house (right), started in 1997. Called in Thai *Baan Pak Chom View Huai Khon* ('Huai Khon Viewpoint Resting House'), it is sited in an elevated position and enjoys a nice view west over Huai Khon. Apparently built by Bangkok people, but run by locals, it consists of two green-roofed bungalows, divided up into three rooms apiece. I once spent a pleasant couple of days in the lodging. At 300 baht a night, the rooms are rather expensive (bargain the tariff down to 200 baht), but they are relatively well-equipped, each coming with a hot shower, fridge, fan, mirror, fresh bottled water, night light, and a little balcony with tables and chairs.

A large place spread over several hillsides and still expanding, Huai Khon (pronounced 'kawn' or 'corn') has flourished recently for a number of interconnected reasons. One is the opening of the Thai-Lao border at a spot just a few kms away from the village. Another is the construction at that spot of the new cross-border road to Hong Sa in Laos. A third is the drastic re-engineering of the H1080 highway from Nan town to Huai Khon, which has much improved access to the village, and which was carried out to feed the new cross-border road and as a function of the opening of the border. A fourth is the advent of a popular border market, held early every Saturday morning at the frontier, where the road crosses from Thailand into Laos close to Huai Khon.

The village is a Tai Lue place. In fact it is the largest settlement of Lue people in Thailand. The Lue are one of the many ethnic groups that belong to the Tai family of peoples, which also includes, for example, the Tai Yuan (the Lanna Tai of northern Thailand), the Tai Yai (Shan), the Tai Lao, the Tai Dam (Black Tai) and the Tai Daeng (Red Tai). They are related, therefore, to the Tai of Thailand, to the *khon muang* or ordinary local people of northern Thailand, and in consequence there is nothing 'hill-tribish' about them. The Lue of Huai Khon have migrated during the last century or so from Muang Ngoen, which lies not far away in Laos' Sayaburi province. Ultimately all the Tai Lue have come from Sipsong Pan-Na, in the southern Chinese province of Yunnan, where the majority of Lue still live.

Huai Khon, like the Lue in general, is famous for its weaving and textiles. Under every second house, in among the stilts of the raised dwellings, the women can be seen working at large wooden hand looms. They produce (mostly to order) especially textiles featuring characteristically Lue geometric designs, including the celebrated *lai nam lai* or flowing water motif, which is so sought after by fashion-conscious middle-class Thai ladies, and which has become known, wrongly, as the Nan style. For further information about Huai Khon, the border market, the Tai Lue, and their history, culture and weaving tradition, see again my *Around Lan-Na*.

With your lift you may well, as we did, blast straight through Huai Khon, perhaps to Tung Chang or even Nan. Or you might be dropped off at the Tai Lue village, or have opted to break the journey there. You can exit Huai Khon either by further hitch-hiking or by public transport. The best place to wait is in the central 'pit' of the village, with its cluster of stores, where all the trucks stop and from where all the vehicles, including *silor*, go. There is an intermittent *silor* service from here to the village of Pon, from where an hourly bus service runs to Nan town. The last share-taxi pick-up may well leave Huai Khon at around teatime or earlier, and the last bus leaves the terminus at Pon at, I seem to remember, 5 or 6pm. Don't rely too much on the *silor* down to Pon, and don't start your exiting too late. Hitch-hike if necessary. Nor should you underestimate the distances and travelling times up in this obscure corner of Nan province. From Huai Khon it is some 30 kms to Pon, 65 kms to Pua, and a cool 135 kms or 85 miles to Nan town. The *silor* fare to Pon is about 30 baht, and a bus ticket from Pon to Nan something similar.

You travel out of the western end of Huai Khon (now on the H1080 road), up a steep hill and past the big village school (left). Almost at once you come to a junction. The way right (north) is a new stretch of road which proceeds 6 kms to the border, to the location of the Saturday border market, and to Laos. From the border it is 35 kms to Hong Sa, while China lies just 250 kms distant. But you continue straight, passing a number of backwoods villages, some of them hill-tribe. **Sob Pang** (left), also known as Mai Chai Tong Rat, is Khmu, **Sob Poen** (offroad, left) is Lua, **Pin** (right) is apparently Lua, **Pang Hok** is mixed Lua and Tai Lue, **Nam Liang** is mixed Khmu and local Nan people, and **Nong Kham**, just before Pon, is Lua. Between Pin and Pang Hok the road swings south, after Pang Kok coming down off the mountains. At Nong Kham you are back down in lowland country with its cultivated fields and other trappings of 'civilization'. Just offroad right (west) of Nong Kham is **Lai Tung**, another big weaving village inhabited by Tai Lue. It is the best place to buy examples of Lue handweaving if this art interests you, having two shops well-stocked with textiles. And then you reach **Pon**, just a small place where the local red buses from Nan terminate.

If you are in a *silor*, or if you get dropped in Pon by your lift, change onto one of the buses and ride a good 100 kms or 2-3 hrs back south to Nan. If you are still in a vehicle you have flagged down, continue as far as you can get. Where your lift runs out, you can change onto a bus. Now you speed south down the H1080 road, past half a dozen rural Thai villages, to the small district town of **Tung Chang**. Just beyond Tung Chang you can see a monument right (east) commemorating the Thai, KMT, Wa and other soldiers who fought in Nan province against the communists during the insurgency, many losing their lives. The next stop is the turning left (east), just north of Ratchada village, for Pang Kae and Maniploek. If you have guides with you, or if you intend to return to Maniploek, they/you must alight here from the bus. If you see the 'Cosmo Oil' fuel station on your left, you have overshot the turning. Make the bus driver aware of what is going on, in case he speeds on to offroad Chiang Klang. For details about getting from the junction up the H1291 side road to Maniploek, see towards the beginning of this chapter under 'Accessing the trek', and see also Trek 11 under 'Trekking route detail / accessing Maniploek' as well as Map 17. Otherwise sit tight on the bus or in your lift and proceed another 19 kms south to Pua and then a further 60 kms to Nan town.

Trek 14

Climbing Doi Pu Wae (1)

(from Maniploek, approaching from the south-west)

Maniploek forestry – Lua Maniploek 2 – Nam Hoem – 'Campsite 3' – Doi Pu Wae summit – Nam Hoem / 'Campsite 1' – Lua Maniploek 2

Parameters

trekking mode:	on foot
core trek time:	2½ days/2 nights
accessing time:	from Nan town to Maniploek via Pua and Ratchada allow about half a day using a combination of public transport and hitch-hiking, and ca 2¾ hours with your own hire motorbike
exiting time:	from Maniploek to Nan town via Ratchada and Pua allow about half a day using a combination of hitch-hiking and public transport, and ca 2¾ hrs with your own hire motorbike
overall trek time:	from Nan to Nan, including access and exiting times, 3½ days/3 nights
degree of difficulty:	medium difficult, semi-'Rambo', no rock-climbing
guide(s):	required
guide name(s):	Pae & Yod (see photo section)
tent:	required
map(s):	see 17, 18, 21 & 22

Overview & strategy

On this expedition, which involves some excellent jungle camping, you climb Doi Pu Wae or Pu Wae mountain, one of northern Thailand's most spectacular and beautiful mountains. The traffic-ridden hump of Doi Intanon near Chiang Mai, Thailand's highest peak, which we pass in Trek 23, holds little interest for the trekker (even if much for the birdwatcher). Doi Pahom Pok, the Kingdom's second-highest mountain and the goal of Trek 3, is secluded and offers scenic views, but is similarly round-topped and rather unspectacular. Doi Chiang Dao, the country's third-highest peak and the goal of Trek 4, is certainly an impressive, steep-sided, monolithic block, but it lies close to civilization and is fairly frequented. But Mount Pu Wae, 1837 m high (6027 ft) and set remotely in the heart of Nan province's Doi Pu Kha National Park, looks like a real mountain, although is little visited. Lying at the northern end of a N/S-running ridge, it is a veritable horn or tooth of a peak, and on its west side has something of an Eiger-like face, with cliffs falling precipitously into the Hoem river valley, while on its south side a grassy field slopes away down to the saddle of the ridge, the field resembling the concave canvas back of a deckchair that a giant might comfortably recline in. From the summit there are fabulous views in every direction, especially east to the Thai-Lao border ridge, dotted with Lua (Htin) villages.

This trek is the last of four based on Maniploek and the third of three hiked on foot from this far-flung double village with its two Hmong and Lua parts. It is also the first of two ascents of Doi Pu Wae, the second being the subject of Trek 15. Here, in Trek 14, we climb Pu Wae from Maniploek 2 (the Lua half of the double village), approaching the peak from the south-west. In Trek 15 we climb it from the villages of Dan and Huai Poot (over by the Lao border and north of Bo Glua), approaching from the north-east. Both tacks have much to be said for them, but they are rather different cups of tea, and you should choose which is better suited to your needs, interests, ambitions and capabilities. The relative merits of the pair are as follows. Trek 14, approaching from Maniploek and the SW, is slower, longer, more roundabout and difficult, passes through jungle, involves camping wild, and is the more adventurous and less used of the two routes. Trek 15, accessing from Huai Poot and the NE, is quicker, more direct, easier, cleaner, passes through woodland, involves camping in a Lua village, and is the regular well-trodden way up Pu Wae. Both hikes, as I did them and have written them up, backtrack the way they came, although in Trek 15 it is possible to make a little loop. For this reason it makes good sense to access and exit the treks with your own transport, hiring a motorbike in Nan town and riding it to and from Maniploek (or, in Trek 15, Ban Dan), if you can and so wish. But back to this expedition, Trek 14.

The core part of the trek, from Maniploek to Pu Wae and back, can be done only on foot and takes, as things panned out when I did it, 2½ days (2 days plus the morning of a third day) and 2 nights, although, if you pushed yourself, you could complete the outing in 2 days and 1 night. To this, of course, must be added the access and exit times, making the overall trek time about 3½ days and 3 nights. I did this expedition in mid-December 1998, accompanied by Thai girl Nittaya Tananchai, US birding boy Doug Boynton, and two Lua guides, Pae and Yod, hired from Maniploek 2. In my estimation guides are necessary for the trip. Although Pu Wae looms large in the landscape and you rarely lose sight of it, it is doubtful whether, without guides, you could find your way to or locate the campsites. There are dangerous cliffs in the vicinity of Lua Maniploek 2, and the way that would seem to be the obvious direct route to the mountain leads straight over them, while the correct way is indirect and not at all obvious. The trek is nowhere physically very difficult, and no actual rock-climbing, scrambling or use of ropes is involved. Nevertheless, I have graded it as moderately severe and in particular as semi-'Rambo' in quality. This is because you have to bust your way through acres of high grasses, bamboo tunnels, dense vegetation and thorns, and have to camp wild in the jungle twice, fending for yourself. When we got back to Maniploek 2 ('M2') at lunchtime on Day 3, we all felt bushed.

On both ascents of Doi Pu Wae, first from Maniploek (Trek 14) and then from Dan and Huai Poot (Trek 15), my climbing parties and I met no one on the summit and no other trekkers on the way up or down. But this is not to say that you won't. Because the mountain is so alluring, it *is* climbed sporadically, by groups of Thais. It is even, horror of horrors, sometimes visited by lazy, contemptible, ecologically unenlightened Siamese flown in by helicopter to a spot near the summit. Pu Wae is ascended mostly from Ban Dan (Dan village), and only occasionally from Maniploek, which is a reason to trek it from the latter. In the winter of 1997-98 guides from Lua Maniploek 2 took five parties of some 10 Thai people each from 'M2' to the summit. The parties used about 10 guides, one per trekker, and according to Pae, who was involved, the guides spent their whole time running backwards and forwards, shuttling food and water. In the winter of 1998-99 we were the first group to trek to the peak from M2.

Much of what applies to this outing applies also to the three previous trips (Treks 11, 12 & 13) and has already been set forth in those chapters. For obvious reasons, I do not want to keep repeating information already given elsewhere, and so the reader is referred to these earlier chapters and should study the account here in conjunction with the texts there, especially with the material already given relating to accessing Maniploek, camping at its forestry station, and reaching the Lua part of the village (Maniploek 2).

More specifically, on the eve of the trek you journey by bus and hitch-hiking or ideally with your own hire motorbike to Maniploek and camp overnight there, probably at the forestry station. On Day 1 of the actual trek, you hike 3 hrs down to the Nam Hoem or Hoem river, where you have lunch, and in the afternoon you climb up 1½ hrs to a campsite that I have dubbed 'Camp 3', because it is the third and last of three possible overnight tenting places on the way to the summit (see Map 21). Where you can camp is determined by the availability of water, and water is available in three places: at the River Hoem (Camp 1), high up at Camp 3, and between the two latter places (Camp 2). There is no water on or near the summit, and so the summit does not make a suitable camping place. But it is inadequate for other reasons. The summit is rocky (with tufted grass) and has no flat areas for pitching a tent. You could, if you wanted, camp at a place just below the summit (15 mins' climb from the top), and people do stay there, but it has no water, and you would have to bring or fetch water from Camp 3, which is the place nearest to the summit with water. It is no disadvantage to tent at Camp 3. On the contrary, of all the sites camped at in this book this is one of the nicest.

TREK 14: CLIMBING DOI PU WAE FROM MANIPLOEK

On Day 2 you climb 2 hrs 20 mins from Camp 3 to the summit, spend an hour on top admiring the view and having a picnic lunch, and descend 2 hrs back to the River Hoem and Camp 1, down in the valley. Here you spend a second night under canvas, although, time permitting, you could push on back to M2. Arriving at Camp 1 mid-afternoon, we contemplated doing this, but there seemed no point in it because then you would simply end up spending the second night at M2 instead, compared to which another night camping out in the wilds seemed much preferable. On the morning of Day 3 you trek 3 hrs back up to Maniploek 2, arriving at lunchtime. This is a good time at which to return in that, unlike hitting M2 at 6pm the previous evening, it leaves you the afternoon in which to make an orderly exit to Nan, which can certainly be done by motorcycle, and could also perhaps be done by hitch-hiking and public transport.

The route just outlined is a relatively long and circuitous way to climb Doi Pu Wae. Relative to M2, the mountain lies almost due east, directly opposite the village, across the Hoem river valley (Map 21). But from M2 you go first south, slowly descending to the Nam Hoem, and then SE to climb out of the Hoem valley and up to Camp 3, finally swinging NE to Pu Wae (i.e. approaching from the SW). It would appear logical to head directly for the mountain ESE (120°) from M2 (i.e. approach from the WNW). We suggested doing this to the guides. But they explained the impossibility of such a route. First, as mentioned, there are the cliffs just east of M2 (the west side of the Hoem valley), which you cannot climb down, and, second, on the east side of the valley, there is the west-facing Eiger-like cliff of Pu Wae, which you cannot climb up. Further, once you have crossed the little river of the Hoem down in the valley, there is no more water. We put it further to the guides that it would also seem logical to approach Pu Wae from the NW or NNW, climbing gradually up a long gentle spur. But on that route, too, there is no water and no path either, or so the guides said. And thus, apparently, you are obliged to take the roundabout route set out above and also below.

The trek can be modified as follows. It would be possible to lengthen it by proceeding from M2 not down to the River Hoem and then up the far side of the Hoem valley, but by hiking south 2½ hrs to the Hmong settlement of Khang Ho, then ascending the west-facing flank of Doi Khang Ho (1918 m), and finally trekking north up the ridge to Pu Wae. The first part of this alternative approach, as far as Khang Ho, is the same as the first leg of Trek 12, and is detailed in that chapter. The rest of the way I have not done and so cannot comment on it. But guides Pae and Yod said that it is more beautiful than the shorter way via the Nam Hoem and Camp 3. If that is the case, it must be beautiful indeed because our way is already very attractive.

Looking at things more grandly, a second drastic modification would be to combine this trek with the next one, Trek 15 (to Pu Wae from Dan on the H1081 road via Huai Poot). The result would be one long trek, passing from west to east clean through the heart (the main northerly part) of Doi Pu Kha National Park. You would not return to Maniploek, but would descend from the summit NE to the elevated Lua village of Huai Poot, from where you would go down to Dan village on the H1081 road. Our original plan when climbing Doi Pu Wae had been to carry out this combined 'supertrek', but we were thwarted because the guides did not know the way from the summit to Huai Poot, incredibly never having been to the village and not even knowing its name, although it neighboured Maniploek 2. Thus, because I have not trekked right through in one go, I cannot detail this combined W-E route. The supertrek would only be suitable for hikers who had accessed Maniploek without their own transport, because you would exit it far from M2 in quite another part of Nan province. If you had taken a motorbike to Maniploek, leaving it there, it would be a ridiculous and complicated journey to return from Dan, where you would end up, to Maniploek to retrieve your machine. The same rather applies to guides. If you took them from M2 as far as Dan, they would have the problem of going half way round the National Park (no matter whether they went south via Bo Glua and Pua, or north via Huai Khon and Tung Chang) all the way to Ratchada, from where they would still have to travel 40 kms back to M2. Nevertheless, the combined trek would still be possible, perhaps by settling on a compromise solution. You descend with the guides as far as Huai Poot, after which they return to M2, while you continue down to Dan on your own. This is less of a problem than it might sound. Huai Poot lies not so far from the summit, you can clearly see it from the top, and it should not be difficult to orienteer your way to the village. To do so, you would have to read backwards my notes in Trek 15 for the leg Huai Poot to the summit of Pu Wae. And it would be good for Pae and Yod, or whoever you hire from M2, to learn this key link. The leg from Huai Poot to Dan is very clear. You could not possibly lose your way, and people go up and down that path all the time. Again, you would have my notes on the leg to help you, which you would likewise have to read backwards.

Because Maniploek, the start of the trek, lies some 115 kms or 2-3 hrs' riding from Nan (making a round trip to Lua Maniploek 2 of almost 250 kms or 6 hrs of riding!), it makes little sense to go there in advance to set the trek up guidewise, unless you happen to be in the area. The distance is too great. So you will need to arrive at Maniploek the day before the trek, ideally at lunchtime. This will then give you time to get round to M2 to organize guides, as well as to familiarize yourself with the forestry station at the double village, with the layout of the locality, and with the way to M2. By the same token, because Maniploek is so out-on-a-limb and complicated to reach by public transport and hitch-hiking, it does make sense, as indicated, to use a hire bike to access Maniploek and the start of the trek. This is all the more so the case because in this trek, in its standard form, you return to your starting point, unless you plan to try to reach Huai Poot and Dan. When you return to Maniploek, your bike is waiting for you and you can comfortably and speedily exit the trek. Further, having a hire bike in Maniploek would enable you, if you wanted, to tack motorcycle Trek 11 onto the end of the Pu Wae trek, i.e. you could take in Kwet and Sa

Kaat as you exit, killing two birds with one stone. With a bike you could also roam around the Maniploek area, visiting the local 'sights', such as Hmong Maniploek 1, Tam Pa Poeng (Beecliff Cave) with its stream sink dolina, and the two rare Chompu Pu Kha trees near Maniploek 2.

Accessing the trek

As with all the treks in this book made in Nan province, you will undoubtedly ultimately launch Trek 14 from Nan town and its guest houses. Now you must decide whether you are going to access Maniploek and the start of the actual hike by hire bike or by public transport and hitch-hiking. If you are at all competent with a bike, use one. You can ride quickly and conveniently to your destination, and can do the same back to Nan. The distance to Maniploek is, as said, 115 kms, and on two separate occasions the journey took us on a little Honda Dream 2¾ hrs. For a full account of the trip from Nan to Maniploek, see Trek 11 under 'Trekking route detail / accessing Maniploek' and also Map 17.

If you proceed to Maniploek by public transport and hitch-hiking, ride from Nan town on a local red bus north up the H1080 road via the towns of Ta Wang Pa, Pua and Chiang Klang and the village of Ratchada to the junction of the H1080 and H1291 roads, which is 19 kms north of Pua central crossroads. After Ratchada, watch out for a 'Cosmo Oil' fuel station on the right side. The junction is imminent. Get out of the bus at the junction (it will probably stop there anyway). The H1291 side road for Maniploek heads off right (east) towards mountains. If on the bus you come to the town of Tung Chang, you have gone too far. For more detailed supplementary information about the route Nan/Pua/Ratchada/Maniploek, see Trek 11 under 'Accessing Maniploek' and Map 17. Now proceed by public-transport *silor* and/or hitch-hiking from the junction via the villages of Pa Ruak and Pang Kae to Maniploek, a distance of some 36 kms. Plenty of trucks go up to Pang Kae and Maniploek, although you might have to wait a bit. Try, if possible, to ride with some kind of official truck (forestry, highland development, BPP, school) – you do not run the risk of being ripped off and might well travel free. Most of the vehicles going up this way are Hmong. If you ride with a Hmong pick-up, negotiate a fare before hopping aboard. The Hmong are shrewd businesspeople and will happily extract from you whatever money they can. Haggle ruthlessly, and, rather than allow yourself to be overcharged, just wait for the next vehicle. A fair price from the junction to Pang Kae is 20 baht per person, and from Pang Kae to Maniploek another 20 baht. More than 50 baht/person all the way to Maniploek is too much. These Hmong drivers are going that way in any case.

Arriving at Maniploek, camping at the forestry station, & information about Maniploek and local features (Hmong Maniploek 1, Tam Pa Poeng, the 'cliff idyll', Lua Maniploek 2, the Chompu Pu Kha trees, & the 'little loop')

For information about these topics, see Trek 11 in conjunction with Map 18. On the subject of tenting at Maniploek, do not rule out the possibility of pitching camp not at the forestry station, but at Lua Maniploek 2. This would have the advantage that you start the trek directly from where the guides live, and that you can fraternize with them before setting out. The Lua village is in any case an attractive place to 'hang out'.

The Lua & Hmong peoples

For background information on the Lua (Htin) people, such as inhabit Maniploek 2 and Huai Poot, see Trek 5. For a thumbnail sketch of the Hmong people, such as live at Maniploek 1, see Trek 16 under 'Santisuk'.

Preparing for the trek

Try to calculate how many days, nights and meals the trek, as you conceive of it, will involve, and buy provisions accordingly in Nan (with some food to spare). Drinks and limited (snack) food is available back at Pang Kae. Once you have set up camp at the forestry station and got to know the layout and (limited) facilities there, make your way late afternoon on the eve of the trek round to M2 to hire guides, organize the trek and familiarize yourself with the local geography. It is a good idea to go at that time, rather than in the morning or at midday, because during the day the guides, like many of the villagers, may well be out working in their fields or for the forestry, only returning home towards evening. Seek out Pae or Yod or Tayan, all Lua men who live in M2, with whom I have trekked several times. Ask for them, or show to the villagers my photos of them in this book. Pae (= goat) is a good person to deal with. Rather older than the other two (in 1999 he was aged about 40), he is a sensible and sympathetic character. All three, including (in 1999) fresh-faced, 22-year-old Yod, know that you are coming and are willing to guide. Pae's house is situated centrally.

For Trek 14 we hired mountain goat Pae and young buck Yod, paying them the usual 200 baht each per day, for which they carried our backpacks while guiding and prepared the campsites etc. For the 2½-day trip they got 600 baht each, which included a 100-baht tip on account of their sterling work (1200 baht for the trek all told, spread between the three of us). If either or both of them are unavailable, there must be plenty of other people in M2 who know the way, because from time to time villagers lead quite big parties of Thais to Pu Wae. If you decide not to return to Maniploek, but to continue from the summit to Huai Poot and Dan, and if consequently you send your guides back from the summit or Huai Poot, pay them at least a day's wage for the time it will take them to get back home.

*

196

Trekking route detail (Map 21)
Day 1: Maniploek forestry – Maniploek 2 – Nam Hoem – 'Campsite 3'

If you have camped overnight at Maniploek forestry station, make your way to Lua Maniploek 2. Either walk there on the roundabout track (see Map 18) (or directly on the cross-country path from the back of the forestry compound to M2), or, if you have come by bike, ride round to the village. The 2.6-km journey will take you about 10 mins by bike and some 40 mins, fully laden, on foot. Specific details are in Trek 11. If you have a bike at Maniploek, leave it under the lorry port in the forestry compound or, as the case may be, under Pae's house. You might be able to persuade Maeo, the man at the forestry, to give you a lift round to M2 in his lorry, which would give you a flying start. If you are already in M2 because you camped there overnight, Bob's your uncle – you are already at the start of the expedition. We set off on the first leg of this trek at 9.30am. I start the time log from M2.

Time log

Start/0 hrs	Set off from the bottom eastern end of Lua Maniploek 2, by the last electricity pole, following a well-worn track.
	After a couple of mins, where the track goes up, fork left onto a footpath with red-and-white marker stones. Head towards a tin-roofed building and Doi Pu Wae.
	Fork right just before the building and descend through brushgrasses, the path swinging S.
25 mins	Enter copse.
	Stream.
¾ hr	Second copse.
1 hr	Fork right.
	Descend into the valley of the River Hoem through airy woodland.
	Make a sudden surprising turn right to pick up a densely overgrown path with chest-high grasses.
1 hr 20 mins	Looking almost N (30°), you can glimpse the village of Nam Ri in the distance.
	Wade through 10-ft-high grasses!
	Up and over a little shoulder.
1½ hrs	View due E across Hoem valley of Pu Wae, forested almost up to the west-facing cliff. The route to the summit runs in from the right, just below the ridgecrest and the little pyramid peak (= Doi Pu Wae Noi).
2 hrs	Stop for a rest on a knoll with a forest shelter.
	Descend into a jungle corner and cross a dried-up streambed.
2 hrs 5 mins	Another view left to Nam Ri. Pu Wae and its cliffs loom ever larger.
	Steeply descend a shoulder to a dried-up streambed (Nam Poen?).
	At this point we all got lost for 20 mins in a grove of banana palms, which has probably distorted the timings somewhat.
3 hrs	Arrive at the **Nam Hoem**, a big stream or small river flowing from S to N at the bottom of the Hoem valley. Stop for an atmospheric lunch in the boulder-strewn creek amid gloomy mossy jungle and surrounding forest. We arrived here at 12.30pm and stayed for ¾ hr. While we munched on peanut butter sandwiches, the guides caught five freshwater crabs, which they roasted on a fire of twigs and ate with sticky rice. Camp 1, where we stay on the return journey, is in the immediate vicinity, beside the Hoem river.

3¾ hrs   Set off again (we left at 1.15pm) on far eastern bank of the River Hoem, beginning the actual ascent of the Pu Wae ridge. The way goes steeply up, allowing glimpses left through the treetops of the rocky fortress of Pu Wae.

Climb SE up a shoulder through woods. Somewhere up here is the site of Camp 2. When we ascended the shoulder, we were the first trekking party of the season, and we made slow progress in places because the path was overgrown, the guides having to hack a way with machetes.

5 hrs   Pick up a traverse path (tomorrow's path), running SW/NE. Left (NE) heads under ridgecrest cliffs towards Pu Wae, while right (SW) goes to Camp 3. Go right.

5 hrs 10 mins Ten mins from the junction, view left (140°) of some 'ancient' 'fishtail' palms high up near the ridgecrest. These 'prehistoric' palms grow in various pockets of Doi Pu Kha National Park, especially beside the H1256 road a few kms east of the Park HQ. For more data on the throwback relic palms, see Trek 9 under 'Exiting'.

5¼ hrs   Fifteen mins from the junction of the two paths, reach **Camp 3**.

Camp 3 is an especially nice camping spot, and you could have a pleasant time tenting for 2 or 3 days at it, living wild and exploring the area, perhaps climbing up to the 'ancient' palms, roaming south to Doi Khang Ho, and of course scaling Pu Wae. People come to the vicinity to hunt and stay at the campsite and in shelters dotted throughout the area. The campsite is in a copse, near an envined tree and a big boulder, and revolves around a tiny trickling streamlet, which features a length of bamboo, split in half lengthways to form a conduit and spout. Here you can wash in nature and get water for cooking and making hot drinks. The actual tenting spot is just north, slightly above the streamlet. It is level, in grasses and among trees. After pitching camp and washing, we got a fire going, gathered three large stones to make a trivet, and boiled water in a pot on it. Later, in our elation camping at this idyllic site, we whooped it up with a fireside supper of 'Ma-maa' instant noodles, a box of Californian raisins, mugs of coffee, and a half bottle or 'flattie' of Regency (a tasty Thai brandy). The guides, who slept by the streamlet and envined tree beside a fire of their own, went off hunting and came back with two squirrels. They cooked the meat in bamboo tubes and ate everything, including the entrails.

We arrived at Camp 3 at 2.45pm. It is about 2 hrs 20 mins further to the summit of Pu Wae. You could undoubtedly push on and still reach the top on Day 1. You would arrive at about 5pm and could camp at the spot just below the summit, but you would have to take water with you from the streamlet at Camp 3. In my diary I noted that the hike from M2 to Camp 3 was enlivened by encounters en route with wild plum trees, a fig tree by the Nam Hoem laden with thousands of green figs, round knobbly 'turd' fruits, anthills, birds, a kind of hopping-flying grasshopper-dragonfly creature, and a 12-inch-long black earthworm.

TREK 14: CLIMBING DOI PU WAE FROM MANIPLOEK

Day 2: 'Campsite 3' – Pu Wae summit – Nam Hoem / 'Campsite 1'

From Camp 3 to the summit is about 2 hrs 20 mins. If you get away in good time and do not spend hours on the summit, you could, if you wanted, easily make it back to Maniploek 2 by nightfall, not spending a second night camping out by the Hoem river. We were all ready to go bright and early, but could not set off because the guides were not ready, an unusual situation because normally it is we who hold them up. They had not hunted anything for breakfast, and one of them was still out with his gun. Finally Yod returned holding three green parrotlike birds with red feet (probably green wood pigeons). He and Pae irritated us further by then sitting down to eat not the birds, but the rest of the squirrel stew, warmed up, from the previous day, when they could have eaten that in the first place. Yod was also bearing pieces of some tree stem he had found, which has medicinal properties and treats stomach ailments. We finally set off at 9.40am.

Time log
Start/0 hrs — From Camp 3, set off N back along the traverse path used the previous day to reach the campsite.
After 15 mins, near the path junction, drop off and hide your tent, backpacks and anything that you do not need for the summit. Of course, if you are contemplating striking through from the summit to Huai Poot, with a view to exiting via Dan village, do not do so, but take everything with you.
At the junction continue broadly N.
The contour path rises through woodland.
50 mins — On a tree stump: two arrows.
Climb steeply up through treeline towards skyline. Watch out for holes!
1 hr 5 mins — Time for a rest by some rocks, near two palms on the skyline. View NNE (310°) of Maniploek 2 (starting point of trek). Also visible is the path from M2 to Khang Ho on a shoulder across the Hoem valley. Climb through open grass towards two more palms, the 'real' two, which you have been seeing from afar.
1 hr 20 mins — Reach the two palms (second pair). You are presented with a magnificent close-up view of Pu Wae's perpendicular west-facing cliff, seen now in profile from the S.
1 hr 40 mins — Reach skyline and the saddle or spine of the ridge. On its eastern side, the ridge falls away in a small cliff. Enjoy a grand view E of Lua villages such as Sa Kieng, of the Thai-Lao border, and of Laos.
Just below the summit, at the foot of the final grassy cone, there are a couple of sleeping places and a level spot big enough for one tent. Surprisingly, the area is littered with dung. Cattle wander up here, presumably from Huai Poot. Apparently, some years ago there was no grass on the summit at all because the cattle had eaten it. They must have a taste not just for mountain grass, but also for heady views.
2 hrs 20 mins Reach **summit of Doi Pu Wae**, 1837 m high (6027 ft).

After our late start, we arrived on top at midday, spending an hour up there studying the all-round view and eating some lunch. The 2¼ hrs it took to reach the summit included some stops to take photos, as well as the normal resting stops. The first time we stood on Pu Wae, the sky was overcast, and

Doi Khang Ho to the south was shrouded in mist and clouds. The second time, we were bathed in brilliant intense sunshine under a deep blue sky. Pu Wae seems to have its own microclimate, and it is often windy on top. The summit is tufted grass interspersed by sharp pieces of rock. It is perhaps 10 m across and falls away on all sides.

This is what you can see from the summit, going clockwise from N (see Map 22). If you look just E of N (20°), you can see the Lua village of Huai Gaan in the distance, with the H1081 Huai Khon/Bo Glua road passing beneath it. The village close to you at 40° is Huai Poot. It is from this Lua place that you climb Pu Wae approaching from the NE, and to which you must continue if you want to exit via Ban Dan. Two villages close to each other at 60° and 65° are Huai Saek and Buak Om, both Lua, like all the other settlements visible. Due E (90°) lies the big village of Piang Sor just below the top of a mountain ridge, which is the Thai-Lao border ridge. Below Piang Sor is another, small village, which is Huai Fong, I think. Looking at 110°, you can see Sa Kieng, another village lying high up, close to the border. To its right, at 130°, is Sa Chook, lower down and on a dirt road. The prominent gash of the dirt road links Sa Chook and Huai Fong, beyond Huai Fong descending NW to the H1081 road and hitting it 3 kms south of Dan. Looking E and SE from Pu Wae, you cannot see the main H1081 road down on the Nan river valley floor. Due S (180°), along the ridge you are standing on, lies first, close by, Doi Pu Wae Noi or Little Pu Wae mountain (ca 1682 m – the 'pyramid' peak), and in the distance Doi Khang Ho (relatively high at 1918 m). This side of it, coming back to yourself, are two cliffs. The farther one is the cliff above Camp 3. To your W, running the whole way from SSW to NNW, is, below you, the forested valley of the Nam Hoem and, beyond it, a ridge and escarpment, the northern end of which falls as cliffs into the Hoem valley near Maniploek 2. M2 can be sighted at 300° behind the cliffs. Now you can appreciate why you cannot march in a straight line from M2 to Pu Wae!

If it is your intention to try to exit Pu Wae and this trek by proceeding to Huai Poot, descend a short distance from the top down the summit cone in a westerly direction (270°) and then swing right (N). There is a path. Follow it, going broadly N and NE to Huai Poot. You will have to try to read my notes for Huai Poot to Pu Wae (in Trek 15) backwards. You will know if you have descended too far W from Pu Wae summit: you will fall over the Eiger-type cliff! But we exit Pu Wae by the way we came, going back to M2 via the Nam Hoem.

3 hrs 20	After an hr or so on top, set off back down again, retracing your steps (we started at 1pm).
4 hrs 20 mins	After 1 hr, reach the tent/backpack drop and the junction of the two paths. Go right and climb back down to the Hoem river. Somewhere near the site of putative Camp 2, we passed a posse of 4 Lua hunters.
5 hrs 5 mins	After ¾ hr of descending, you reach the **Nam Hoem and Camp 1**. The campsite is on the western bank under a huge fig tree.

Camp 1 is a pretty desperate place to stay overnight. It is damp and dark, and thick with rank vegetation. It teems with every kind of insect and other creepy-crawly, and after dark with dozens of moths. If you don't fancy all this, and if you have time in hand, you can still press on to Maniploek 2 and the forestry station. From Camp 1 to M2 is about another 3 hrs. If, on the other hand, you revel in jungle camping, this is the place for you. Pitch your tent below the fig tree. We arrived at Camp 1 at 2.45pm and debated for a while about whether to push on or stop. To return to M2 would have meant arriving there at about 6pm and nightfall, and the forestry station would have been reached well after dark. Pitching camp late and in the dark is never a happy experience. So we decided to erect the tents and get cleaned up at Camp 1, while it was still light. What clinched the matter for us was that, in pressing on for M2, you gain nothing, because you have to spend a night there anyway. So you might as well spend that night in more interesting surroundings – at Nam Hoem. Further, as said earlier, if you arrive at M2 at midday of Day 3 (tomorrow), you can comfortably exit M2, the forestry and the whole trek during the afternoon, something you cannot do at 6pm on Day 2 (today). The water in the Hoem river was so icy cold that we could hardly bring ourselves to wash more than our hands and faces, and hair-washing went by the board for yet another day. All night long figs from the tree fell on our tents.

Day 3: 'Campsite 1' / Nam Hoem – Maniploek 2

Time log

Start/0 hrs	Set off from Camp 1 (we left at 9.30am), climbing up through the banana grove and on up the shoulder.
30 mins	Reach resting knoll.
	Breast your way back through those accursed grasses and thorns.
1 hr	Streambed (that of the Nam Poen, I think).
1¼ hrs	Come to second knoll and lean-to shelter.
	Contour through more high grasses. At this point in our trek, it started to rain, and the top of Pu Wae disappeared in clouds (the microclimate at work).
	Proceed up and over ridge.
2 hrs 10 mins	Where the path divides, branch right.
2¼ hrs	A couple of mins later, reach a mini pass with stones.
	Field with orchard left.
2½ hrs	M2 visible.
3 hrs	Climb up to arrive back at M2. End of trek. Reaching M2 at 12.30pm, we ate up the rest of our provisions in the village, also getting Pae to boil water so we could make instant noodles, before exiting.

Exiting the trek (see Maps 18 & 17)

Exiting Maniploek 2 and the forestry station for Nan is exactly the same as accessing the trek, except in reverse – simply retrace your steps. If you have come to Maniploek by hire bike, which is an ideal thing to do on this trek precisely because after Pu Wae you return to your starting point at Maniploek, you have the option during the return journey of including the dirt loop via Kwet and Sa Kaat, thus tacking the second half of motorcycle Trek 11 onto the end of this trek. Only consider doing this if you have plenty of time and are an experienced rider.

But first you must return from M2 to Maniploek forestry, a distance of 2.6 kms. By bike this will take you 10 mins or so, and on foot about 40. Proceed south out of the village on the dirt track past the half dozen granaries 600 m to a junction. Here turn right, follow the new power lines through some woods, go down two steep rutted inclines – rather tricky on two wheels – to pass on your left a house and a pretty corner that I call the 'cliff idyll' (for details see Trek 11), after which the track swings north to bring you back to the 'crossroads' in front of the forestry complex.

Now exit the forestry and Maniploek altogether. If you are returning to Nan by bike, allow about 2¾ hrs to cover the 115 kms to Nan going the direct way via Ratchada (it is about 1 hr to the H1291/H1080 junction by Ratchada), and a good half day going the longer indirect way via Kwet and Sa Kaat. If you are returning to Nan by a combination of hitch-hiking and public transport, allow at least half a day. Hitch-hiking from the forestry crossroads should not be too difficult. Plenty of Hmong trucks and bikes go from M1 to Pang Kae and on down to the H1080 road for Pua or Tung Chang, especially early morning. The lorry from the forestry station sometimes flits in that direction, and intermittent market trucks come visiting at Maniploek, with which you could also ride, although they also mostly come and go early morning. But, of course, having your own transport is much quicker and more convenient. Before hopping into a Hmong truck, always negotiate a fare with the driver, so as to avoid any unpleasant surprises or awkward situations. A fair price at the time of writing is 20 baht per person to Pang Kae and another 20 from Pang Kae to the main H1080 road.

First you make your way 20.3 kms back down the elevated 'dream' road via Pang Kae to the junction ('Magic Junction') below Pang Kae. Leaving the forestry crossroads, you climb 1 km up to the T-junction with the spirit house, go left to proceed 12.8 kms past the Mexican sunflowers to Hmong Pang Kae, and continue 6.5 kms down to 'Magic Junction'. Here you go left if, as a biker, you want to include the scenic 35-km dirt loop via Kwet, Sa Kaat and Na Fang, issuing just north of Pua (for details see the end of Trek 11 and Map 17). Otherwise go right, drop down on the poor winding road to Pa Ruak, and speed to the Ratchada junction ('Magic Junction' to the H1080: 13.5 kms). At the Ratchada T-junction and the H1080 road, right goes north to Tung Chang and Huai Khon, while left, your route, brings you south 19 kms back to Pua. If you are hitch-hiking and without your own transport, you can pick up public transport down at this T-junction. Take the first available *silor* or bus heading south. Local red buses pass once an hour and will take you all the way back to Nan. The last one leaves relatively late, perhaps early evening. Should the public transport be finished, resort to hitch-hiking. If you take a *silor*, change in Pua onto the bus or another Nan-bound *silor*. From Pua central crossroads it is a further 60 kms or an hour's ride south on the H1080 main road via Ta Wang Pa to Nan town.

Trek 15

Climbing Doi Pu Wae (2)

(from Dan & Huai Poot, approaching from the north-east)

Dan – Huai Poot – Mount Pu Wae summit – Huai Poot – Dan (or looping back from summit to Dan via Pu Du & H1081)

Parameters

trekking mode: on foot

core trek time: 2 days/2 nights

accessing/exit mode hire motorcycle recommended, owing to distances and complication involved in reaching Dan

accessing distance from Nan town to Dan via Pua and Bo Glua ca 145 kms (90 miles)

accessing time: from Nan town to Dan via Pua and Bo Glua allow ca 4 hrs with your own hire motorbike and 1 day using a combination of public transport and hitch-hiking

exiting distance from Dan to Nan town via Bo Glua and Pua ca 145 kms (90 miles); via Huai Khon, Tung Chang and Pua ca 176 kms (110 miles)

exiting time: from Dan to Nan town via Bo Glua and Pua allow ca 4 hrs with your own hire motorbike and 1 day using a combination of hitch-hiking and public transport; from Dan to Nan town via Huai Khon, Tung Chang and Pua by hire bike allow the best part of 1 day (plus any time spent in Huai Khon)

overall trek time: by motorbike from Nan to Nan, including access and exiting times, at least 3 days going and returning via Bo Glua and about 4 days going via Bo Glua and returning via and staying a night in Huai Khon (i.e. doing the 'north-eastern loop')

degree of difficulty: easy, no rock-climbing

guide(s): advisable only from Huai Poot to summit

guide name(s): Num, Sug & Bun (see photo section)

tent: advisable, but not essential

map(s): see 23, 24, 22, 14 & 20

Overview & strategy

This trek is the second of two superb ascents of Doi Pu Wae, one of northern Thailand's most spectacular and beautiful mountains (the other ascent is detailed in Trek 14). The traffic-ridden hump of Doi Intanon near Chiang Mai (Thailand's highest peak), which is incidentally visited in Trek 23, holds little interest for the trekker, although has much to offer the birdwatcher. Doi Pahom Pok, the Kingdom's second-highest mountain and the goal of Trek 3, is secluded and offers scenic views, but is similarly round-topped and rather unspectacular. Doi Chiang Dao, the country's third-highest peak and the goal of Trek 4, is certainly an impressive, steep-sided, monolithic block, but it lies close to civilization and is fairly frequented. But Mount Pu Wae, 1837 m high (6027 ft) and set remotely in the heart of Nan province's Doi Pu Kha National Park, looks like a real mountain, although is little visited. Lying at the northern end of a N/S-running ridge, it is a veritable horn or tooth of a peak, and on its west side has something of an Eiger-like face, with cliffs falling precipitously into the Hoem river valley, while on its south side a grassy field slopes away down to the saddle of the ridge, the field resembling the concave canvas back of a deckchair that a giant might comfortably recline in. From the summit there are fabulous views in every direction, especially east to the Thai-Lao border ridge, dotted with Lua (Htin) villages.

In the previous trek (14), we climbed Doi Pu Wae from the double Hmong-Lua village of Maniploek, approaching the peak from the SW. Here, in Trek 15, we climb the mountain from Dan and Huai Poot (two villages in the far north-eastern corner of Nan province, near the Lao border and well north of the little town of Bo Glua), approaching from the NE. Both tacks have much to be said for them, but they are rather different cups of tea, and you should choose which is better suited to your interests, ambitions and capabilities. The relative merits of the two are as follows. Trek 15, accessing from Huai Poot and the NE, is quicker, more direct, easier, cleaner, passes through woodland, involves camping in a Lua village, and is the regular, fairly well-trodden way up Pu Wae. Trek 14, approaching from Maniploek and the SW, is slower, longer, more roundabout and difficult, passes through jungle, involves camping wild, and is the more adventurous and less used of the two routes. Both hikes, as I did them and have written them up, return to their respective starting points, i.e. backtrack the way they came, although in Trek 15 it is possible to vary the way back to Dan by making a loop via the village of Pu Du (see Map 24). For this reason it makes good sense to access and exit both treks with your own transport, hiring a motorbike in Nan town and riding it to and from Dan (or, in Trek 14, Maniploek), if you can and so wish. But back to this expedition.

It makes all the more sense to access/exit the trek by hire bike (or even jeep) because the starting/ending point at Ban Dan (Dan village) lies far away from Nan town, which is undoubtedly the place – with its guest houses and facilities – from which you will ultimately launch the trek. The shortest way from Nan to Dan, via Pua and Bo Glua, is about 145 kms (90 miles), much of which is through the mountains. Further, the journey to Dan, whichever way you go, is quite complicated, and especially with public transport would be problematic and time-consuming, although feasible. On the positive side, the journey to Dan is so scenic and interesting that, if you are a biker, it is worth going there just for the ride. By contrast, Dan and the start of the trek is so far-flung, and the trek itself so relatively short and sweet, that, to make the outing fully worthwhile, it would be a good idea to combine it with something else. My suggestion is to exit the trek not by riding back to Nan via Bo Glua, but by continuing N from Dan and returning to Nan via Huai Khon, perhaps spending a night there, which would mean that in addition to the foot trek you would do a motorcycle trek around the great loop NE of Nan. Other suggestions as to what you could do up in this fascinating obscure corner can be found in my book *Around Lan-Na*.

I did this expedition at the beginning of January 1999 in the company of Nittaya Tananchai, our daughter Tanya (not quite 8 at the time), Doug Boynton and three guides hired in Dan. The core part of the trek, from Dan to the summit of Pu Wae, can only be done on foot – in 1999 there was no way of getting a motorbike up to Huai Poot. This walking part is nowhere physically difficult, and no actual rock-climbing, scrambling or use of ropes is involved, hence my grading of the trek as easy. It is a fine little hike, but an added bonus is that you can do an agreeable spot of camping in midpoint Huai Poot (Lua). As it is a village, you could dispense with a tent here, staying in a villager's house or in the school. Although, therefore, a tent is not strictly required on the trek, nevertheless I recommend taking one. We so much enjoyed tenting in elevated Huai Poot, with its direct view of Pu Wae, that on our descent from the summit we regretted not returning via the village, when we could have spent a second night there. On both ascents of Doi Pu Wae, first from Maniploek (Trek 14) and then from Dan and Huai Poot (this trek), we met no one on the summit and no other trekkers on the way up or down. But this is not to say that you won't. Because the mountain is so alluring, it *is* climbed sporadically, by groups of Thais. It is even, horror of horrors, sometimes visited by lazy, contemptible, ecologically unenlightened Siamese helicoptered in to a spot near the summit. Pu Wae is ascended mostly from Dan, and only occasionally from Maniploek. During the winter season of 1997-98, guides from Maniploek took five parties of Thai people from Maniploek to the summit, while in early 1999 the guides we hired in Dan said that each year the peak was climbed 'several times' from Dan 'mostly by groups of Thais' with guides from Dan.

Because there are so many variables in this trek relating to the chosen mode of transport and the exit route (both from the summit and from Dan), it is not easy to give estimates of the time needed either for the overall trek or for its core part. I will tell you how things panned out timewise for us and how they might pan out if I were to do the trek again, undertaking it as

I can now see how it should be done. Overall the trek took us 3 days and 2 nights. On Day 1 we rode by motorcycle from Nan via Pua and Bo Glua to Dan, where we hired our 3 guides, and then walked up to Huai Poot, arriving late afternoon. We spent a first night there, and on Day 2 walked (taking our tents and backpacks) up to the summit of Pu Wae, where we had a picnic lunch. In the afternoon we descended from the summit not via Huai Poot, but, wanting to vary the walk, via the small Lua village of Pu Du. We had half intended to stay the second night there, but, finding it uncongenial, decided to continue on down to the H1081 road in the Nan river valley. This is where things began to unravel for us. From the summit we should have returned to Huai Poot (more interesting than Pu Du), and, failing that, should indeed have stayed in Pu Du, completing the rest of the trek and the return journey to Nan the next day. But we pressed on and reached the road about 5pm. Now we all had to hoof it 3 or 4 kms up the main road (no lifts) back to Dan, where we had left our motorcycles, and which we reached at nightfall. We could have stayed in Dan, but preferred to press on, riding back south in the dark to stay with friends near Bo Glua, where we spent the second night. On the morning of Day 3 we rode back to Nan.

But now I give you a schedule, fleshed out with more specific information, of how I believe the trek should really be done, a schedule that I recommend you follow and which I would follow if I were doing the trek again. On Day 1 you make your way ideally by bike (ca 4 hrs) or conceivably by public transport and hitch-hiking (allow all day) from Nan via Pua and Bo Glua to Dan. If you have a bike, you leave it in Dan. Mid-afternoon or earlier, you climb on your own 1¼-1½ hrs up to Huai Poot. You do not need guides for this, as the way is clear. You camp overnight in Huai Poot, organize guides if you want them, and on the morning of Day 2, leaving your tents and backpacks in Huai Poot, climb up 2¾ hrs to the summit. In the afternoon you return ca 2½ hrs to Huai Poot, where you spend a second night. (You could, if you wanted, descend, as we did, 2¼ hrs to Pu Du, where you likewise spend Night 2, completing the remaining ¾ hr of descent to the main road and the ½-hr walk back to Dan on the morning of Day 3. But in this case you would have to take your tent and backpack with you to the summit.) On the morning of Day 3, you walk 1 hr quickly back down to Dan, retrieving your bike if you have one. Now, if you do not return to Nan the way you came (via Bo Glua and Pua), you exit the trek by going N and W 41 kms along the lonely mountainous H1081 road to Huai Khon (see Map 23). Really this should be done by bike, although you might with luck manage to hitch-hike the stretch (no public transport). You spend Night 3 at the interesting Tai Lue village of Huai Khon, where there is a guest house, before returning on Day 4 to Nan via Tung Chang and Pua, thus completing the big north-eastern loop. If you have made it to Huai Khon by hitch-hiking, there is public transport from Huai Khon back down to Nan. This combined best-case outing 'knocks off' Pu Wae, two nights of camping at Huai Poot, Huai Khon and the big loop all in one go, and even as I write these words I thrill at the prospect of it.

TREK IT YOURSELF IN NORTHERN THAILAND

Concerning guides, we hired three local Thai (*khon muang*) men in Dan village: older man Num, not-so-old Sug or Saak, and youngster Bun or Pan (see photo section). We got hold of them by asking in a Dan noodle soup place, where we happened to be snacking a lunch. The speed at which the lady owner convened the three suggested that it was common for guides to be hired in Dan to climb Pu Wae, and indeed we got the impression that the trio, especially the older man, had done the trip many times before. Although they did everything we asked of them, I cannot say that they were the most satisfactory guides I have hired. They seemed uncommunicative, sulky, even importunate. This may have been because they were regular, if rural, Thais, rather than robust tribals, and felt put upon or demeaned portering for us. The only one who spoke during two days was the older man, who was as if the leader, through whom any communication was channelled. Thus it was he who kept coming to us up in Huai Poot applying for extra money to buy first rice, then four tins of sardines, and then even a bottle of *lao kao* (rice whisky), which added to their fee. Food they could easily have brought with them from home, as have done all the many other guides I have hired, or they could have arranged the provisions issue with us down in Dan, where there are shops. But no matter, it was no big deal. However, you do not really need guides from Dan anyway, unless you want them to carry your stuff up to Huai Poot. The way from Dan up to Huai Poot is short and clear, and you can easily find it yourself. So dispense with guides from Dan and hire them, if you need any, in Huai Poot. I am afraid I do not have the names of any Lua guides in that village, but apply to the headman. He will easily be able to find someone – probably everyone in Huai Poot knows the way to the top of Doi Pu Wae. We agreed to pay our taciturn threesome 150 baht per day each, and gave them 250 baht each for 1½ days (a short afternoon and a full day), on top of which came their extras.

The only way the trek can really be modified is by choosing to descend from Pu Wae not back to Huai Poot, but to Pu Du and the H1081 road south of Dan, thus making the trek into a little circuit. I will outline this option below under the trekking detail. Because Dan, the start of the trek, lies some 145 kms or at least 4 hrs' riding from Nan (implying a round trip to Dan from Nan of almost 300 kms or 8+ hrs of riding!), it makes absolutely no sense to go there to set up the trek in advance, seeking out guides or studying the lie of the land. The distance is too great. So you will just have to set off and organize things as you go along. Aim to arrive at Dan by lunchtime or early afternoon, to give yourself time to familiarize yourself with the layout of the village, find somewhere to leave your bike (if applicable), locate the start of the trekking path, and collar guides (if you want).

The Lua people
For background information on the Lua (Htin) people, such as inhabit Huai Poot and Pu Du, see Trek 5.

TREK 15: CLIMBING DOI PU WAE FROM HUAI POOT

Preparing for the trek

Food is perhaps less of a problem on this trek. When you access it, you can have a good meal in Bo Glua, and you can find a couple of rudimentary noodle soup places and food stores in Dan. When you exit, you can find food aplenty in Huai Khon, if you go that way, and there are eating places in Bo Glua if you return the same way. So you really only need food for the time you spend in Huai Poot and climbing Pu Wae from there: I make that 2 suppers, 2 breakfasts and 1 picnic lunch – say 5 meals. If you want to get hold of Num, Sug and Bun, ask for them in the main street of Dan, showing my photo of them in this book.

Accessing the trek (see Maps 14 & 23)

As with all the treks in this book made in Nan province, you will undoubtedly ultimately launch Trek 15 from Nan town and its guest houses. Now you must decide whether you are going to access distant Dan and the start of the actual hike by hire bike or by public transport and hitch-hiking. Hire bike is strongly recommended. Use one if you are at all competent with a small, step-through, clutchless motorcycle. You can ride swiftly and conveniently to your destination, and can do the same back to Nan. The distance to Dan is, as said, ca 145 kms across the mountains, and on a 100-cc Honda Dream will take about 4 hrs, excluding any eating stop in Pua or Bo Glua.

   With transport of your own, take the main H1080 road north from Nan to the small market town of Pua, passing Ta Wang Pa on the way, 16 kms before Pua. The 60-km journey should take you about 1 hr. In the centre of Pua you need to turn right at the crossroads, negotiating the exasperating new elongated reservation in the middle of the highway. If you have not already tanked up at the Shell station on the run-in to Pua, do so now at the fuel place near the beginning of this road going right (approximately SW), which is the H1081. Almost immediately, after just 200 m, turn left into the H1256 National Park road. Going downhill, you should find a temple on your left.

   Now ride clean through the National Park, across the Doi Pu Kha massif, to Bo Glua (Map 14). The exhilirating ca 50-km-long stretch will take you about another 1½ hrs. You head out through some outlying rural Thai villages, before beginning a great climb up into the mountains. Ride straight through, following the 'main' road and ignoring any side turnings. The main features of the route are the village of Na Lae (on a hill, left), three big signs indicating the entrance to the National Park, a side road going left (north) to half a dozen Lua villages (see Treks 10 & 12), a viewpoint on the left side, the turning left for the Park HQ, the Lua village of Nam Dan (right, nothing to do with our destination village of Dan), Laan Du Dao (right, extension of the Park HQ), the celebrated Chompu Pu Kha tree (right), groves of 'prehistoric' 'fishtail' palms (both sides of road), a fire prevention office by a pass, and the steep descent past the Lua village

209

of Nam Pae (offroad right) to the little town of Bo Glua. As you approach Bo Glua, you pass a hospital (right), cross a bridge, pass a turning (right) that takes you into Bo Glua's main street with its shops and eating places, and hit a T-junction, marked by a police box. For information on the Park HQ and Laan Du Dao, see Trek 9 under 'Strategy & accommodation', and for information about Bo Glua, its facilities, its famous salt wells and historic salt-production, as well as about the Chompu Pu Kha tree and the 'ancient' palms, see also Trek 9 under 'Exiting the trek'. Eat in Bo Glua.

At the T-junction turn left and proceed north 35 kms up the small, winding, and in places patchy H1081 road to Dan, which will probably take you a further hour (now see Map 23). On the way you pass Huai Pong, Pu Yoen (offroad left), Nong Nan (offroad left), the turning right for Sa Pan, lower Sa Wa (the main part of the double village), upper Sa Wa, Huai Kaab, the turning left at Bo Yuak Tai for Nam Choon and Huai Por (see Trek 10), the main part of Bo Yuak with its salt well and small salt works (right, down behind the health centre – perhaps visit the place on your way back), Sa Lae, Na Koen, Na Bong (just a couple of roadside shops), Waen, Na Hin, Na Ku and Dan, which lies mostly offroad right. The entrance to the main street with its rudimentary stores and noodle places can be found at the far northern end of the village, branching off right (E) opposite Dan's health centre (left side of main road). The path for Huai Poot starts behind this health centre. Leave your bike at the centre, or at the shop just south of it, or at a house in the main part of the village.

If you are accessing the trek without your own transport, proceed as above, but use buses and *silor*, probably resorting to your thumbing a lift after Bo Glua. As early as you can, take one of the hourly local red buses from Nan to Pua, getting off in the centre of Pua by the crossroads (the buses continue N). The journey should take about 1 hr. Cross the highway with its median strip, and look where the *silor* or *songtaew* (public-transport pick-ups) bound for Bo Glua congregate. Traditionally this has always been in front of the day market, just NE of the central crossroads. Take the first available vehicle to Bo Glua (fare about 50 baht). *Silor* (= four wheels) or *songtaew* (= two benches) (*silor* and *songtaew* are the same thing) leave Pua for Bo Glua fairly regularly until about 11am, after which they depart when enough people have gathered. They move rather slowly, stopping frequently and sometimes going round the houses, and it may take 2 hrs to reach Bo Glua. Some of these *silor* may continue from Bo Glua north in the direction of Ban Dan, in which case you are in luck. Otherwise look for another one – I think they wait diagonally opposite the police box and adjacent 'restaurant' on the T-junction. If everything seems to be happening very slowly, just start hitch-hiking, which is often much quicker. From the T-junction of the H1256 and H1081 roads (by the police box) you might have to begin hitch-hiking anyway. Proceed north 35 kms to Dan in whatever way you can.

*

Trekking route detail (Map 24)
Day 1: Dan – Huai Poot

The hike up to Huai Poot takes a long hour, so you can afford to set off as late as about 4pm, although it is not advisable to start later than that in case you lose your way. Nor do you want to arrive in Huai Poot in the dark. It took us 1 hr 10 mins to do the climb, but we were not carrying our baggage. We set off at 2pm and arrived just before 3.15pm, a good time to hit a village where you plan to camp.

Time log

Start/0 hrs	Locate Dan health centre, which lies beside the H1081 road (west side) at the far northern end of the village, opposite a waiting hut and the way into the main street and main part of the village. Some signs (in Thai) near the health centre point W to Doi Pu Wae, Tam Nam Hoem (River Hoem Cave) and Huai Poot. Immediately behind the middle building of the health centre is the start of a well-trodden path to these places. Take it and climb steeply up in a series of scorching zigzags through woodland.
35 mins	Come to a *sala* – time for a little rest.
¾ hr	If you look WSW (240°), you can see on the skyline a triple hump, which is Doi Pu Wae.
	Fork left.
55 mins	View back E of Buak Om village across the Nan river valley.
1 hr	View ESE (120°) of village of Piang Sor very high up on opposite ridge, just below crest. Sa Kieng and part of the dirt road from the H1081 up to Huai Fong are also visible.
1 hr 5 mins	Village sign announces: Huai Poot.
	At the division of the path, both ways to the village. Go rightish.
1 hr 10 mins	Arrive at **Huai Poot**. Walk through village to top end.

Huai Poot is a traditional Lua (Htin) village, spread out on the mountainside and facing E. In 1999 it had no electricity and no access road or even track, just the walking path. Because of its position, it enjoys a magnificent panoramic view E of the border ridge opposite, studded with a number of Lua villages. Huai Poot is full of Jai-ping and Oon-tin families, and the headman is called Duang Jai-ping. He said that the village contained some 28 houses and 50 families, but it was not clear to us whether or not this reckoned in the houses and families living in the Lua satellite settlements of nearby Pu Na and more distant Nam Hoem and Huai Pim. The village school is situated at the top end of Huai Poot, and we camped near it on the left or SW side of a volleyball pitch, directly before the peak of Pu Wae. Next morning it was a great sensation to emerge from the tents at an early hour and to gaze at Pu Wae, looming to the SW full in the early morning sun. Various buildings abut the volleyball pitch. Going clockwise from the long schoolhouse, you find a kind of stockade open-air bathroom (in which you can wash, if you can stand the freezing water), a classroom, a rice bank, and a teacher's hut. During our visit, a wandering monk seemed to have taken up residence in the eastern wing of the main school building. There is wood lying around. Get a fire going and brew up. We managed to obtain some home-distilled Lua *lao kao* at 25 baht a bottle. The level elevated pitch with its scenic views is a nice place to stay and we much enjoyed camping beside it at Huai Poot.

Day 2: Huai Poot – Doi Pu Wae summit – Huai Poot (or: summit – Pu Du – H1081 road – Dan)

From Huai Poot to the summit of Pu Wae is about 2¾ hrs. In Huai Poot, before setting off for the summit, you must decide if you are descending from the summit back to Huai Poot or down to Pu Du. I recommend the former, in which case you can leave your tent and backpack in Huai Poot, returning to spend a second night. If you decide on the latter, you will have to pack up your tent and backpack, and take them with you. You should also hire a guide, as the way off Pu Wae for Pu Du is not clear. It is advisable to collar a couple of boys to show you the way to the summit even if you are simply returning to Huai Poot, although you might be able to orienteer your way to the summit. Apply to headman Duang or a teacher.

Time log

Start/0 hrs	The path for Doi Pu Wae leaves from behind the school. A well-worn trail, it skirts round the right north-western side of the village to ascend a spur, for some way running alongside a fence enclosing a huge field.
ca 5 mins	Fork left and follow a contour path heading broadly SW.
¼ hr	At another fork go left (straight) to pass a dried-up pond in woodland. Path climbs.
55 mins	A camping spot.
1 hr 5 mins	Reach top (northern end) of the ridge on which Pu Wae lies somewhat south. The ridgetop is open and covered with scrub. There is a fine view north. Huai Gaan village is plainly visible at 30° or just E of N. A bit further along the trail, you can also enjoy a view W of Lua Maniploek 2 just below the distant skyline and of cliffs in front of the village. It is on Maniploek 2 that Treks 11, 12, 13 & 14 are based, and it is from the village that the other ascent of Pu Wae (in Trek 14) is launched, approaching the summit from the SW. Bear left and descend steeply through scrub to a pond.
1 hr 25 mins	Pond. From the pond head S towards the high part of the Pu Wae ridge through an open area with cattle droppings. Continuing S, navigate you way through a little maze of trails made by the cattle, passing annoying plants with thorns.
1 hr 50 mins	Arrive at the foot of the summit 'massif' of Pu Wae. Blocks of water-sculpted rock lie dotted around. To your right (W) the Nam Hoem or Hoem river flows in the bottom of the valley. Now climb steeply up between two lesser peaks or outcroppings towards a double col divided by a third peak-outcropping in the centre. All three mini peaks have palms and rock pinnacles on top. They make an intriguing landscape in the fierce light. Skirt round the central outcropping on its right (W) side, i.e. of the twin cols opt to go towards the right-hand one.

212

You gain a view the grassy summit of Pu Wae. When we spied this final peak in the summit block, we found ourselves surrounded by cattle!

The path climbs up round the W side of the summit through grass to the top.

2¾ hrs Reach **summit of Doi Pu Wae**, 1837 m (6027 ft) high.

Starting from Huai Poot at a leisurely 10am, we arrived on top at 12.45pm, spending a short hour up there studying the all-round view and eating some lunch, before beginning our descent at 1.35pm. The summit is tufted grass interspersed with sharp pieces of rock. It is perhaps 10 m across and falls away on all sides. This is what you can see from the summit, going clockwise from N (see Map 22). If you look just E of N (20°), you can see the Lua village of Huai Gaan in the distance, with the H1081 Huai Khon/Bo Glua road passing beneath it. The village nearby at 40° is Huai Poot, from where you have just come. Two villages close to each other at 60° and 65° are Huai Saek and Buak Om, both Lua, like all the other settlements visible. Due E (90°) lies the big village of Piang Sor just below the top of the Thai-Lao border ridge. Below Piang Sor is another, small village, which is Huai Fong, I think. Looking at 110°, you can see Sa Kieng, another village lying high up, close to the border. To its right, at 130°, is Sa Chook, lower down and on a dirt road. The prominent gash of the dirt road links Sa Chook and Huai Fong, beyond Huai Fong descending NW to the H1081 road and hitting it 3 kms south of Dan. Looking E and SE from Pu Wae, you cannot see the main H1081 road down on the floor of the Nan river valley. Due S (180°), along the saddle of the Pu Wae ridge, lies first Doi Pu Wae Noi or Little Pu Wae mountain (ca 1682 m) and in the distance Doi Khang Ho (relatively high at 1918 m), with a couple of cliffs this side of the latter. To your W, running the whole way from SSW to NNW, is, below you, the forested valley of the Nam Hoem and, beyond it, a ridge and escarpment, the northern end of which falls as cliffs into the Hoem valley near the village of Maniploek 2, which can be sighted at 300° behind the cliffs.

Descent from summit of Doi Pu Wae

Option 1: via Huai Poot

If you follow the standard version of this trek, descending from Pu Wae via Huai Poot, as I have recommended, you will probably be back at Huai Poot and your tent within 2 hrs or so. Spend a second night there, before climbing back down on the morning of Day 3 an hour to Dan, from where you can exit the trek. I think it is preferable to stay again at Huai Poot than to camp Night 2 down at Dan, although you would have time enough from the summit to return to Dan by nightfall. Of course, the way back is the same as the way up, except in reverse, so there is nothing to say about this option. Simply retrace your steps. You leave the summit by dropping down a short distance in a westerly direction (270°) and then swinging right (N). You will know if you have descended too far W from the summit cone because you will tumble over Pu Wae's Eiger-like west-facing cliff!

Option 2: via Pu Du

This alternative way of descending from Pu Wae, which we took, but which I do not entirely recommend, goes via the Lua village of Pu Du and is an option worth following if you want to vary the route back down and/or spend the second night in a different place. From the summit it is about 2 hrs 10 mins to Pu Du and then, if you wanted to press on to the H1081 road, a further 30 mins – allow a good 3 hrs all the way down to the road.

Time log

Start/0 hrs	Go W off the summit cone and descend fractionally (as if for Huai Poot), but instead of turning right (N) for Huai Poot, swing left (S) and slip down a grassy path 10 mins to a place in trees that rather resembles a campsite, and which is indeed occasionally used as such, although there is no water there.
10 mins	At the little camping place there are a couple of sleeping places and a level spot big enough for one tent. Dung indicates that cattle also like to dally here. From the 'campsite', zigzag E down through the trees. Bear rigorously left (NE) to proceed gradually down the left side of a gulley. Pass primitive tree ferns (cycads).
35 mins	Cattle gate with stile. Steeply descend shoulder, aiming for a pointed knoll visible dead ahead.
55 mins	Clear view NE of Huai Poot across an intervening valley.
1 hr 25 mins	Reach foot of pointed knoll. Climb up over it!
1 hr 35 mins	Reach foot of second pointy knoll, and climb up over that too!
1 hr 40 mins	Airy view down onto cute Pu Du village. Now, too, you have an uninterrupted view across the Nan valley, with a glimpse of the paved 1081 road in the bottom of it. Cross some mountain rice fields.
2 hrs 10 mins	Arrive at **Pu Du**, a small Lua village of some 20 houses set on a brown patch amid deforested hills. At the top end is a school with a volleyball pitch and two white water tanks. We found Pu Du unattractive, although its inhabitants, a stream of whom we passed on the path down to the road as they were coming up from fishing in the Nan river, were uncommonly friendly. Accordingly, we decided to press on to the valley floor. If you want to stay in the village, pitch camp near the school on a corner of the volleyball pitch, or apply to deputy headman Paeng (there is no headman here – the headman lives in Huai Poot, overseeing both villages). On the morning of Day 3, continue as below down to the road and on (as the case may be) to Dan. We stopped 15 mins in Pu Du.
2 hrs 25 mins	The path down to the H1081 road leaves Pu Du at its bottom end. Walk steeply – in places very steeply – 35 mins down to the road. Coming up this path, which would take about an hour to Pu Du, must be some killer ascent.

3 hrs   You hit the road by a *sala* (right/south), a bridge over the Huai Suai (which flows into the nearby River Nan), a kind of dam construction (right), and, across the road, the start of a dirt way up to Huai Fong, Sa Chook, Piang Sor and Sa Kieng. The bridge is marked 'km 109.7', and it is just over 3 kms left (N) back up the road to Dan, passing roadside km-stones 110 and 111.
    If you have left your bike in Dan and/or want to exit the trek via Huai Khon, proceed N up the H1081 about 30 mins to Dan. Otherwise start hitch-hiking S towards Bo Glua. On the way to Dan, beyond km-stone 111, you pass on your left side another, now little-used way up to Huai Poot. It starts near a bridge (over the Poot stream) and opposite a Buddha figure looking out from a derelict *wat* over the floor of the Nan river valley towards the border mountain ridge.

ca 3½ hrs   Arrive back at Dan village (right, down, offroad), the health centre (left), and your motorcycle, if you came on one from Nan.

Exiting the trek (see Maps 23 & 20 if going north via Huai Khon, and 23 & 14 if going south via Bo Glua)
If you followed the standard recommended version of this trek and stayed a second night in Huai Poot, or if you followed the non-standard alternative version and stayed Night 2 in Pu Du, you should in both cases reach Dan early to mid-morning on Day 3, a favourable time to exit the trek. Now decide whether you want to exit by returning to Nan via Bo Glua and Pua (the way you came), or whether you want to return to Nan via Huai Khon, which I warmly recommend, especially if you have a motorbike with you. In the former case, ride or hitch-hike or take a *silor* (if there is one) from Dan 35 kms S down the H1081 road via Bo Yuak, where you could consider stopping briefly to visit the little salt-producing plant (SE of the health centre), to Bo Glua, where you could take some lunch in the main street and perhaps likewise look at the salt well and extraction facilities (*bo glua* = salt well). If you have no hire bike, you can pick up public transport in Bo Glua for the 50 kms to Pua, after which you can take a bus the final 60 kms back to Nan. Otherwise continue the backtracking journey by bike or hitch-hiking. Detailed information about exiting from Bo Glua, about the little 'town' and its salt-production, and about the route W through Doi Pu Kha National Park, can be found in Trek 9 under 'Exiting the trek' and also (starting at Bo Yuak Tai) at the end of Trek 10.

In the latter case, which completes the loop round the remote north-eastern corner of Nan province and around the main northern part of Doi Pu Kha National Park, ride N and then W up the H1081 road 41 kms to Huai Khon, where I suggest you break the exit journey and spend a third night in this interesting Tai Lue village. There is accommodation in Huai Khon, as well as shops and food, and from it an intermittent *silor* service goes down to Pon, from where buses go S to Nan. The stretch from Huai Khon to Nan is a lengthy 135 kms, and from Dan to Nan via Huai Khon a cool 176 kms or 110 miles! You might be able to exit to Huai Khon from Dan without your own transport. However, there are so few settlements up this way that no public-transport *silor*, I feel sure, ply the route, so you will have to hitch-hike. So little transport of any kind proceeds N beyond Dan that you might have to wait hours for a lift, and you could wait all day for a ride through to Huai Khon. On the other hand, you might be lucky and intercept a through lift within minutes. Perhaps you should set yourself a time limit and say to yourself that if you have not got a lift by then, you will exit the other way via Bo Glua. Most vehicles will be bound for villages on the way, for example Huai Gaan or offroad Nam Chang and Nam Ri (see Map 23), so make sure that you are hopping into a vehicle bound for Huai Khon – unless you want a little adventure. Actually, if you have a tent with you, you cannot go far wrong. But I am assuming that you will exit by motorcycle. All the places up in this obscure 'adventure-playground' corner of Nan province, especially Nam Chang and Nam Ri, I have explored in my guide *Around Lan-Na*.

Dan is the last regular village on the H1081 road as you strike N from Bo Glua and is likewise the last before Huai Khon. Make sure you have enough petrol in your tank to get to Huai Khon. **Piang Ko**, 3 kms beyond Dan is just a settlement beside the River Nan that has an end-of-the-world feeling, although you could do a nice spot of camping there on the banks of the youthful Nan river. Now you climb up in a series of curves out of the Nan river valley into the hills on a new mountain highway, passing two turnings right for offroad **Huai Gaan**, an impoverished Lua village that runs down a spur amid a marvellous mountain setting. Beyond Huai Gaan, at the head of the valley, you come to a new and elevated reforestation complex, which in an emergency would be a place to stay overnight, before reaching a junction, 17 kms out from Dan. Right goes down the H1307 dirt road to Lua Nam Chang (10 kms from the junction) and Lua Nam Ri (16 kms from the junction), while left (straight) continues on a paved surface towards Huai Khon. Soon the little-used highway swings W to come next, 24 kms from Dan, to **Kiu Jaan**, a relatively new, rather ugly Lua village, straggling along a ridgetop. The turning left (S) 9 kms further (33 kms from Dan) goes down to Huai Khon Waterfall (also known as Wangpian w/f) and is where Trek 13 ends. The rest of the exit journey to Huai Khon and Nan is the same as that in Trek 13, and for detailed information about the remaining exit route, about Huai Khon and about staying in a guest house there, see the end of that trek under 'Exiting the trek' as well as Map 20. Three kms after the turning you come to the meagre but attractive Lua village of **Huai Sai Kao** (36 kms from Dan), then you pass a turning right for a new local district office and for Huai Khon Cave, following which you descend to **Huai Khon** (41 kms from Dan), passing the above-mentioned guest house (right) just before you go down a steep hill to the village centre. Now, as said, look at the data at the end of Trek 13.

Above: (Trek 3) Summit of Doi Pahom Pok with cliff viewed from W
Below: (Trek 3) Camping on summit of Doi Pahom Pok

Above: (Trek 4) Summit of Doi Chiang Dao viewed from SW
Below left: (Trek 4) Doi Chiang Dao summit viewed from S from poppy field
Below right: (Trek 12) View N of Doi Pamom foregrounded by Lua field hut

Above: (Trek 4) Som and Nittaya on summit of Doi Chiang Dao
Below: (Trek 4) View WSW of Saam Pinong from Doi Chiang Dao summit

Above: (Trek 6) River Wa near Huai Dua
Below: (Trek 7) Huai Miang near campsite

Above: (Trek 12) Jungle-bound Khun Nam Pua Waterfall
Below: (Trek 13) Huai Khon Waterfall cascading into River Nan

Above left: (Trek 5) Mae Sa Nan Waterfall
Above right: (Trek 18) Mae Rit Waterfall near Mae Waen
Below: (Trek 7) Camping at Kiu Lom ('Windy Col')

Trek 8: Descending Huai Pla Jaad w/f – four shots of four component falls
Above left: Double fall at top end (first main fall)
Above right: Triple fall in upper middle section
Below left: Fall in lower middle section, part of another triple fall
Below right: 7th and last main fall at Nam Mao Mork, looking back up

Above: (Trek 15) Camping at Huai Poot with view SW of Doi Pu Wae
Below: (Trek 15) Lua house at Huai Poot with view SW of Doi Pu Wae

Trek 14: Climbing Doi Pu Wae from Maniploek 2, approaching from SW
Above: View E of Pu Wae ridge across Nam Hoem valley from Maniploek 2
Below: Close-up view NE of Pu Wae summit and cliff from Doi Pu Wae Noi

Above: (Trek 16) First broken bridge between Pi Nuea & Santisuk (Doi Pa Ji)
Below: (Treks 12 & 14) Lua guides Yod (L) and Pae (R) from Maniploek 2

Trek 16: Between Pi Nuea and Santisuk (Ban Doi Pa Ji)

Above left: (Trek 5) Lua guide Wan of Mae Sa Nan beside Nam Nae
Above right: (Trek 18) Pwo Karen woman in everyday dress at Ton Ngiu Nuea
Below: (Trek 18) Pwo Karen women in everyday dress at Ton Ngiu Nuea

Above left: (Treks 1 & 2) Ulo-Akha woman at Hin Taek market
Above right: (Treks 18 & 19) Pwo Karen woman Na Pi Kloe at Mae Pae Luang
Below: (Treks 1 & 2) Akha girls Mi Yu in Pami costume (L) and
Bu Ga in Loimi costume (R) at Mae Salong

Treks 18 & 19: Pwo Karen woman Na Pi Kloe in best costume at Mae Pae Luang

Treks 18 & 19: Pwo Karen woman Na Moeng Mi in best finery at Mae Pae Luang

Above: (Trek 23) Lawa woman weaving at Ho Gao
Below: (Treks 18 & 19) Pwo Karen girl weaving at Huai Hia

Trek 23: At Lawa village of Ho Gao
Above: Traditional Lawa house – notice the *galae* or V-shaped gable-ends
Below: Headman Moen's wife cooking in her kitchen

Trek 23: Four Lawa lasses from Ho Gao and Pae in their best costumes

Trek 23: At Ho Gao – two groups of 5 and 3 Lawa women in their best attire

Trek 23: Lawa woman in her best costume at Ho Gao

Trek 23: Older Lawa lady in her festive attire at Ho Gao

Trek 23: Lawa man Joo at Ho Gao

Above left: (Trek 23) Lawa man Joo in traditional costume with sword at Ho Gao
Above right: (Trek 22) Older Lawa man at Mae La Oop
Below: (Trek 24) 'Old Elephant Trail' country, looking N/NE from Doi Yao

Trek 24: 'The Old Elephant Trail' crossing Doi Yao

Setting out on a jungle trek, boating down the River Wa in the early morning with the mist lifting. With Nittaya, Soeren and three Lua guides

Above: (Trek 5) Wan (L) and Yook (R) breakfasting at 'Sandy Cove' campsite
beside the River Wa
Below: Lua guides Wan (L) and Yook (R) from Mae Sa Nan

Above: (Trek 6) Nit (L) and Kham (R) at Huai Dua campsite beside River Wa
Below: (Treks 6 & 7) Lua guides Nit (L) and Kham (R) from Mae Sa Nan

Trek 3: Chinese-Wa guide Joy from Pu Muen

Above: (Trek 8) Stopping for a rest near top of Hill 1700
Below: (Trek 8) Lua guides Nguan (L), Sutat (centre) and Niran (R) from Sa Wang

Trek 8: Climbing down Huai Pla Jaad Waterfall
Above left: Second main fall and biggest single component cascade
Above right: Chute in middle section
Below left: Looking down a stretch of Huai Pla Jaad in middle section
Below right: Sixth main fall, in lower section

Above: (Trek 14) View N past summit cliff of Doi Pu Wae up Nam Hoem valley
Below: A public-transport *songtaew* ('two-bencher') or *silor* ('four-wheeler')

Above: (Trek 14) Lua guides Pae (L) and Yod (R) from Maniploek 2
on summit of Doi Pu Wae in clouds, view S
Below: (Trek 13) Lua guides Tayan (L) and Pae (R) from Maniploek 2

Above: (Treks 20 & 21) Author and Lawa girl at Chang Mor
Below: (Trek 18) Two Pwo Karen nymphets at Ton Ngiu Nuea

Above: (Trek 15) Three guides from Dan village – Num (L), Sug , and Bun (R)
Below: (Trek 10) Two Lua guides Taen (L) and Waad (R) from Charaeng Luang

Trek 24: Along the 'Old Elephant Trail' from Mae Hong Son to Chiang Mai
Above: Karen guides Lor Sor (L), Loe Mo Po ('Mr Nice Guy'), & Cha Tu (R)
Below: Second set of Karen guides – 'Mr Nice Guy' Loe Mo Po (L),
Surasak (centre) and Sae Ri (R)

Trek 17: Through Mrabri country, near Huai Yuak
Above: 'Yellow Leaf' Mrabri man Muang and family 'at home'
Below: Mrabri man Gu with his two wives Ying (L) and Sorng (R) & family

Part 2c

Treks 16-17: In Nan province, west of Nan town, in Mrabri country launched from Nan town

Trek 16

Nan – Pi Nuea – Santisuk (Ban Doi Pa Ji) – Sob Khun – H1148 & H1080 – Ta Wang Pa – Nan

Parameters

trekking mode: on foot, possibly by motorcycle

trek time: on foot, 2 days/1 night fastest time, 3½ days/3 nights slowest

degree of difficulty: as a walking trek: easy, but long and tiring
as a biking trek: difficult, for skilled offroad riders only (it is doubtful whether this trek can still be done by motorcycle)

guide(s):   not required

tent: not absolutely necessary, but recommendable

map(s):   see 25, 26 & 27

Overview & strategy

This meaty arduous two-day hike, carried out on Nan's doorstep just west of the town, passes through Doi Pa Chang Wildlife Sanctuary, breaking the journey at the isolated White Hmong village of Santisuk, also known as Ban Doi Pa Ji or Mount Pa Ji village. It is the first of a pair of loop treks done either side of the H1091 Nan-Chiang Muan road. The first, this trek, takes place north of that road, starting in Nan and passing through the villages of Pi Nuea, Santisuk and Sob Khun, before looping back to Nan town via Ta Wang Pa along the H1082, H1148 and H1080 roads (see Map 25 for an overview). The second, Trek 17, takes place south of the road, likewise starting in Nan, but passing through Du Tai, Tam and Huai Yuak, before looping back to the provincial 'capital' on the H1091 Chiang Muan road. Both outings trek through Mrabri country, through the landscape and habitat of the celebrated *pi tong luang* people, the nomadic 'Spirits of the Yellow Leaves'.

The hike is best done as a foot trek, although it could possibly be done in part or in total on a motorbike. The status of the route, especially of the first leg from Pi Nuea to Santisuk, keeps changing. Sometimes you can get through on two wheels, and sometimes you cannot. At the time of writing the first leg was unbikable again. But even if bits or all of (the core of) Trek 16 are bikable, they can be handled only by very skilled offroad riders with the right kind of (enduro) machine (more below). So it is questionable whether you can do the expedition on a bike, and the trip is best considered a walking trek. I recommend that you do it as such, and in this account I shall treat it from the perspective of a foot trek.

If you carry out the hike as I have written it up here and as I did it myself (standard form), it will take you 2 days and 1 night, the night being spent at midpoint Santisuk. However, these are two days of prolonged exhausting walking, and in its standard form the outing is not for the faint-hearted. A bonus is that you can do the trek on your own, without guides. I did, having no hill-tribe guide or even Thai-speaker with me, just a couple of *farang* friends. Of course, without guides, you will have to carry your tent and backpack yourself, all day, up hill and down dale, in the blazing sun. I first trekked this route in mid-February 1997 in the company of US couple Pete Alcorn and Kelly Martin. Later, in March of the same year, I re-did the first leg of the trek (as far as Santisuk) by motorbike, accompanied by Thai girl Nittaya Tananchai and Swiss boy René Reinert, and going back the same way (via Pi Nuea). As indicated, I shall return to the vexed question of the trek as a motorcycle excursion presently.

More specifically, you tackle this trek (as a foot trek) as follows. On Day 1 you travel by public transport 43 kms west from Nan town on the H1091 road to the start of the H1172 road, which lies just before Ban Luang (see Maps 25 & 26). You hitch-hike or ride by *silor* (public-transport pick-up or share-taxi) north a few kms to the village of Pi Nuea, which marks the start of the trek proper. Now you walk a mere 23 kms (nearly 14½ miles) north along a dirt road and then country trail to Santisuk or Doi Pa Ji village, which should take you 7-8 hrs. On the way you pass half a dozen broken bridges, Huai Fai forestry outpost, and a fine stretch of jungle. The way is basically flattish or undulating, and cuts through Doi Pa Chang Wildlife Sanctuary, formed in 1979. You spend the night in the remote White Hmong village of Santisuk, either in someone's house, or at a sanctuary office in the village, or in a tent. From Santisuk you have views of Pa Ji mountain, from which the Hmong village used to take its name before it was rechristened 'Santisuk' by the authorities, and of Doi Pa Chang, the mountain from which the wildlife reserve takes its name. On Day 2 you strike NE from Santisuk over the hilltops 20.5 kms (12¾ miles) to the far-flung Hmong village of Sob Khun (Map 27), a hike through dry country (no water on the way!) that should take you about 7 hrs. Sob Khun lies at the south-western end of the scenic H1082 road, and from it you hitch-hike late afternoon to the H1148 and then H1080 roads, hitting the H1080 near Ta Wang Pa, from where you take a bus south ca 45 kms back to Nan town, probably arriving after dark in the early evening.

Accomplished thus, the trek takes 2 long days and 1 night. But this is an ideal schedule, involving quite a bit of luck. If we managed the expedition within this 2-day time-frame, it was because, luckily, we soon got a lift from the H1091/H1172 junction to Pi Nuea, because a forestry truck then took us a couple of kms from Pi Nuea up the start of the dirt trail to Santisuk, because we were able to ride the trail's last few kms to Santisuk in a Hmong lorry returning home from the fields, and because in Sob Khun we got a lift almost immediately all the way to Ta Wang Pa. But things might not go so swimmingly for you, although you could have even better luck. What happens if things go wrong? Here is a schedule for an accidental worst-case scenario or if by design you merely want to spin out the trip.

You take too long getting away from Nan, arrive rather late at the H1091/H1172 junction, only slowly get a lift to Pi Nuea, set out too late for Santisuk, and realize that you will never get there by nightfall. Well, spend the first night at Huai Fai forestry office (Map 26), for which you should have a tent and, of course, food. On Day 2 you trek on to Santisuk, comfortably reaching it the same day. You spend Night 2 in Santisuk, and on Day 3 hoof it to Sob Khun. You must get to Sob Khun in one day, as there are no villages on the way where you could stay, and no water either. But, let us say, you arrive late at Sob Khun and/or fail to get a lift out to the H1080 main road. In this case, stay a third night at Sob Khun, and during the morning of Day 4 hitch-hike out of the village, as you will certainly be able to do, possibly with public transport, and return to Nan, reaching it by lunchtime. With this slowest schedule, you will have got in plenty of camping and have had an eyeful of the Hmong people.

It is clear that this trek, unlike most of the expeditions in this book, cannot be modified – truncated or extended – in any way, unless you walk from Santisuk back to Pi Nuea the way you came. It is, after all, a loop trek. However, it can be modified as a motorcycle trek, assuming that the trip is bikable at all. And now I come to the problem of Trek 16 as a biking excursion. There used to be a small proper road from Pi Nuea to Santisuk, but some years ago the half dozen bridges crossing the rivers en route were burnt and destroyed in mysterious circumstances (more below), never to be rebuilt. As you pass along the trail, the ruins of the substantial bridges are plainly visible. In places the people of Pi Nuea and the Hmong of Santisuk built makeshift replacement bridges of logs and bamboo, and it was possible on a bike to cross the rivers and streams on them, otherwise simply fording the water. But these makeshift bridges break up with use or get washed away in the rainy season, when streams can become raging torrents, and the bridges may or may not get repaired. So at any one time it is impossible to say if you can bike from Pi Nuea to Santisuk. In the early and mid-1990s my Danish geologist friend Soeren Skipsted, who spent several years exploring Nan province, said that the route was impassable. On the one occasion when he did manage to get through, his trip ended in fair disaster. He and his fellow rider had to lift their motorbike over some streams and deep streambeds where the bridges were gone. He got caught out by nightfall and, unable to go back, had to ride out in darkness all the way via Santisuk and Pong back to Nan, which should be a warning to any would-be adventurers. But in March 1997, Nittaya Tananchai, René Reinert and I got through from Pi Nuea to Santisuk on two Honda Dreams without much difficulty, returning the same way the same day. The trip took us 2 hrs each way. Further, other (skilled) bikers I spoke to in Nan's two principal guest houses, said that they had also managed the trip (on larger enduro machines), some having even managed to bike out by Sob Khun. However, in December 1998 René said, after having attempted it anew, that the Pi Nuea-Santisuk stretch was again impassable, the bridges being completely broken down and the trail overgrown.

The message in all this is that as a biker you should never or no longer expect to be able to blaze an offroad trail from Pi Nuea through to Santisuk. By all means go and have a look, and see if you can get through. With a bike you will not lose much time if your reconnaisance turns out to be futile. If it does, consider trying from the other end, from Sob Khun. But be warned: of the three ways to and from Santisuk, this has always been the most difficult, or so everyone has always said, and certainly when we walked out from Santisuk to Sob Khun I found myself muttering that it would be impossible to ride the stretch on a bike, although it has been done. The problems are at each end. Leaving Santisuk, there is a disastrous long rutted upgrade, and approaching the forestry office and checkpoint 2 kms short of Sob Khun there is a fiendish rocky downgrade. Incidentally, the third way to and from Santisuk, involving Pong, is the easiest. In fact, it is the main and only regular access to the Hmong village. Thus, to come back to modifications of the trek, you could as a biker proceed from Pi Nuea to Santisuk (assuming you can get through) and exit not via Sob Khun, but via Pong. Or you could attempt to reach Santisuk from Sob Khun, exiting either via Pi Nuea (if that is possible) or via Pong. Try to ask at each respective starting point (Pi Nuea and Sob Khun), and ask again in Santisuk. The locals know the (im)possibilities.

The Hmong people
For some brief background information on the Hmong people, such as inhabit Santisuk and Sob Khun, see below, under 'Santisuk'.

Preparing for the trek
Take a tent with you, especially if you think that you will spend more than one night during the trek. Otherwise be prepared to stay in Hmong houses, forestry offices or teachers' houses, in which case you should take and use a mosquito net. In Nan buy food for however long you suspect the trip might last. There is some limited food in Santisuk and Sob Khun in the rudimentary stores there. On the second leg of the trek from Santisuk to Sob Khun it is essential that you have a fair amount of drinking water with you, which presupposes that you have brought along a suitable container (water bottle). I suggest that you carry at least 2 litres of drinking water per person on each leg of the trip. As accessing Pi Nuea from Nan is really part of the trek itself, I include is no separate section on accessing, which is subsumed under the trekking route detail. As said earlier, the route detail is given from the point of view of the trek being walked.

*

Trekking route detail (Maps 25 & 26)
Day 1: Nan – Pi Nuea – Huai Fai forestry – Santisuk (Ban Doi Pa Ji)

First you must make your way from Nan town to Pi Nuea. Try to do this as early as possible if you want to complete the first leg of the trek (all the way to Santisuk) on Day 1, not breaking it at Huai Fai forestry. You begin by journeying some 43 kms W from Nan along the H1091 road in the direction of Chiang Muan and Payao. This can be done by either *songtaew* (those public-transport pick-ups with two benches in the back), or by bus, or by hitch-hiking. Check out the day before the trek in Nan where from and at what time the buses and *songtaew* leave. The *songtaew* for Ban Luang (near Pi Nuea) depart from the site of Nan's evening market, which is centrally located quasi opposite the *Dheveraj Hotel*. Buses bound for Chiang Muan and Payao depart from the main bus station next to Nan's large day market. If you cannot sort all this out, or if you want to hitch-hike, walk to and station yourself at the beginning of the H1091 road on the W side of town, and wait for the first *songtaew*, bus or lift to come by. We took a lorry *songtaew* from the evening market at 10am (too late) for a fare of 25 baht per person (1997 prices).

Journey out along the scenic H1091 road past the Yao village of **Nam Kong** and the big Hmong village of **Song Kwae** 43 kms to the turning right (N, the H1172 side road) for Pi Nuea. Shortly before the turning, you make a very steep descent – the downgrade is an accident black spot! If you reach Ban Luang, 2 kms beyond the turning, you have gone too far. The turning itself is marked by a police box and, opposite it, some road-construction buildings. We arrived here at 11.20am after a ride of 1 hr 20 mins. Alight from your vehicle at the junction and hitch-hike N up the 1172 road towards Pi Nuea. It may be the case that your *songtaew*, if you are on one, takes in Pi Tai and even Pi Nuea, in which case you are in luck and off to a flying start. You come first to **Pi Tai**, the southern part of Pi village, at the entrance to which there is a junction marked by a *sala* or waiting hut. Go right at the junction for Pi Nuea, the northern part of Pi village. If your lift stops at Pi Tai, wait at the *sala* for another lift to Pi Nuea or start walking. At the entrance to **Pi Nuea**, which lies 6.5 kms from the H1091 road, you have a similar junction arrangement. Straight on goes to the centre of the village, while right continues towards Santisuk, skirting Pi Nuea. Take either way – the two routes join up again beyond the village. Pi Nuea is a rural Thai (Nan *khon muang*) place with shops and petrol, and its headman's name is Laam. A few years ago there used to be a kind of camp, situated E of the road skirting Pi Nuea, where some 'Yellow Leaf' Mrabri people 'lived', convened there by unscrupulous entrepreneurs wanting to 'show' these 'Stone Age' nomads to tourists.

On the far side of Pi Nuea the paved road ends at a bridge (6.7 kms from the H1091 road). Now a very poor dirt way, interspersed with fords, mud holes and large puddles, lurches out through rice and cotton fields. We arrived at the bridge at 11.45am and immediately got a lift with some official in a 4WD truck to the first broken bridge on the way to Santisuk (see Map 26). Do the same if you can. Take any ride on the way from Pi Nuea to Santisuk – the distance to be covered is so great. This little bonus lift has caused my timings to be messed up. We rode slowly 15 mins in the truck, arriving at broken bridge 1 at midday. I estimate that it would have taken 30-40 mins to walk from Pi Nuea to this first broken bridge. Accordingly I will start my time log from this bridge, rather than from Pi Nuea. Just before the broken bridge you come to a fork. Right continues to the bridge, terminating there because the bridge is destroyed, while left drops down on an orange dirt trail to a small river, which you cross. In 1997 there was a tiny flimsy bamboo pontoon bridge across the river, which, on our bike trip to Santisuk, we managed to (had to) ride over.

222

Time log

0 hrs   Almost immediately after broken bridge 1, you come to a second broken bridge, whose overgrown concrete supports tilt drunkenly. The first bridge is on your right, the second on your left. At the same time you come to the river again, which must be recrossed.

Now an old paved road, whose surface is mostly broken up these days and which has largely reverted to dirt, heads approximately N up a beautiful valley, flanked in places by cliffs and outcroppings. Along here, right of the track, there used once to be another Mrabri camp, 'Soon Pattana Lae Anuraak Ka Tong Luang' or 'Yellow Leaf People's Development and Conservation Centre'.[1]

I well remember how hot and sticky it was walking, fully laden, up this valley and toiling up the upgrades on the deteriorating road.

¾ hr   Pass a sign (left) announcing 'Doi Pa Chang Wildlife Sanctuary 200 m), after which you come immediately to a barrier across the way, a checkpoint, and some forestry/sanctuary conservation buildings up right, which are the **Huai Fai forestry** office. The isolated sleepy outpost lies 13.5 kms from the H1091 road and 7.5 kms from Pi Nuea. We arrived here at 12.45pm and stopped for a quick 25-min snack lunch. A couple of forestry boys appeared, but took little interest in us. We ate in flattening midday heat and in a silence that was only interrupted by the passage of two vehicles. One was an old motorcycle ridden by a Hmong man with a granny as pillion passenger, and the other was a Hmong truck with 10 people aboard. Both were going in the, for us, wrong direction, to Pi Nuea. So as recently as 1997 four-wheeled vehicles were sometimes negotiating this track. If you arrive at Huai Fai later than 1pm, consider spending your first night at Huai Fai. The forestry boys will not mind, will even welcome you as a distraction. Things look pretty basic here, so be prepared to slum it. Nevertheless, you could have a pleasant time camping in nature.

---

[1] Run by US missionary Eugene Long (widely known locally as 'Boonyeuan') and his wife and family, it was in full swing in the winter of 1997-98, with some 45 'Yellow Leaf' people in residence. The missionary family, which prior to this time for many years ran a similar colony in Prae province, had apparently been invited by the governor of Nan province to come to Pi Nuea and set up the camp. They built a large house, encouraged Mrabri to come and live on the adjacent hillside, cared for them and taught them skills that would better equip them for life in modern Thailand. But by December 1998 the camp was deserted, the house abandoned, and the Mrabri gone, and Boonyeuan had returned in disgust to Prae. He had been threatened by Hmong tribals and others with a powerful vested interest in the crowd-pulling money-spinning 'Yellow Leaves', and had needed military protection. In December 1998 his vacated Pi Nuea camp was still being guarded by troops. But it was also the case that the missionary's fortune had changed. He no longer enjoyed the patronage of the governor of Nan. With a change of governor, the welcome he had once enjoyed turned to resentment. Not least the new governor was incensed that Boonyeuan's colony had been built within the Doi Pa Chang Wildlife Sanctuary. Such are the whims of Thai officialdom, and the whole story is an insight into Nan provincial politics. You can see the former camp from the 'road' – perhaps when you walk past the Long family and the Mrabri will be back in residence again!

TREK IT YOURSELF IN NORTHERN THAILAND

1 hrs 10 mins	Set off again after a 25-min lunch rest.
Cross river, passing third broken bridge.
Hike uphill and down dale through jungle.
Paved upgrade.
Toil uphill for about an hour, then proceed along a ridgecrest through typical Mrabri country.
Some fine jungle.
2½ hrs	Log bridge.
Giant ferns.
3 hrs	Another log bridge and a stream, from which, if you have a filter with you, you can fill up your water bottle.
Signs of land cultivation.
3½ hrs	Down to broken bridge 4 and makeshift replacement log crossing.
3¾ hrs	Bamboo cattle gate.
Field huts.
4 hrs	View NNE (30°) of serious toothlike mountains in distance: they are Doi Pa Chang and Doi Pa Wua beyond Santisuk.
4 hrs 5 mins	Log bridge over stream. On our trek we passed Hmong people in fields here.
5 hrs	Streamlet and drinking fountain (left).
5 hrs 10 mins	Broken bridge 5, stream and log crossing.

When we got to this point, it was already 5.10pm. We were very tired, and Santisuk was still some way off. We feared that we would arrive after dark and would have to walk in the dark. When a Hmong lorry came along, returning to Santisuk from the fields, we had no hesitation in jumping aboard, even though I knew that it would mess up these trek timings. By all means do the same if you have the opportunity, especially because the Pi Nuea/Santisuk leg is so long and because it is no fun trekking in the dark and arriving at a strange place after dark. If you do end up walking this last section in the dark, it is not such a big problem – the way is easily followed. Our Hmong lorry was piled high in the back with brushgrasses, on top of which were perched 10 Hmong people. We bumped and swayed along with them atop the stack. It was a feat of navigation how the driver got the lorry over the remaining makeshift bridges, precisely positioning the wheels on the logs and guiding them slowly across. We arrived at Santisuk 20 mins later at 5.30pm, and I reckon that the timely lift cut about an hour off the trek, which means that, starting from broken bridge 1 at midday, we would have reached Santisuk after 6pm, at nightfall, after a good 6 hrs of hiking. During the final section of the trail, we passed one more big broken bridge (the 6th) and three more little log bridges.

You hit **Santisuk** at a T-junction. The way left goes to Pong and is the main regular way to and from the Hmong village. The way right curves round anti-clockwise to the centre of Santisuk and its school, passing the village health centre on the way on a corner of the school playing field. Just before the T-junction, you find a Doi Pa Chang Wildlife Sanctuary office on your right, positioned on top of a knoll. Nearby is a workers' accommodation block, where we stayed.

Santisuk

The White Hmong village of Santisuk or Ban Doi Pa Ji, as it is also known, is a large populous place of some hundred houses, very much cut off from the outside world. It lies 23 kms from Pi Nuea and nearly 30 kms from the H1091 Nan-Chiang Muan road, more than 20 kms from Sob Khun, and ca 36 kms from Pong. Set in a basin, it has a big school, in 1997 had no electricity, and has a couple of poorly provisioned shops selling soft drinks and packets of 'Ma-maa' instant noodles. People are friendly, although for obvious reasons they are not used to seeing *farang* in their village. Santisuk dates back to 1984-85 and is inhabited by former 'Red Hmong', that is by Hmong who during Thailand's communist insurgency sided and fought with the CPT. The village is composed of people on the one hand from former 'red' settlements that used to exist locally and which following the insurgency were wound up and centralized at Santisuk, and on the other from the 39 hill-tribe villages in the Doi Pa Chang area that have been or are in the process of being relocated out of the wildlife sanctuary.

As said, 'Santisuk' is the new sanitized name given by officialdom to a village that is also known, especially by the Hmong, as Ban Doi Pa Ji (the 'Ji' is pronounced as a short 'jih'). It takes its other unofficial name from Pa Ji mountain, a lesser peak near the village, conical in shape. Doi Pa Ji can be seen lying roughly SE (120°) relative to the village, and I remember that there is a good view of it from the sanctuary office, looking eastish. To the NNE of the village you can see a bigger double-mountain. This consists of Doi Pa Chang (= elephant cliff mountain) on the right, from which the sanctuary has taken its name, and Doi Pa Wua (= cow cliff mountain) on the left. It would be fun to climb in particular Pa Chang mountain, if it is safe to do so (there may be old mines from the insurgency lying around).

In 1997 we stayed overnight at the sanctuary office near the T-junction. This was in the days before I always took a tent with me on treks (the perfect solution to the accommodation problem, which I have meanwhile adopted). Having no tents, Pete, Kelly and I thought that we would stay in the office itself, the new building on the knoll. But it transpired that it was totally deserted, having not a stick if furniture in it, was fairly dilapidated, and had no water. Perhaps it is serviceable now. Seeing us poking around up there, some sanctuary-conservation boys came and invited us to stay in their quarters, somewhat SE of the office building, one of them vacating his room. This was a squalid billet in a row-block of workers' rooms. We hung up our mosquito nets amid dirty clothes, pin-ups, toothbrushes, tools and drums of chemicals, and all night long a mouse nibbled at a rice sack in a dark corner. The camp had lots of guns and a generator. We washed in the dark from a tap in the base of a large cement water tank. But we had a grand time with the boys, cooking over a fire and tippling Hmong *lao kao* with them until late into the night under the stars. Consider staying here yourself, or stay with the schoolteachers in one of their houses (they will be more than willing to help), apply to the *pu yai baan* or headman, or just put up your tent in a suitable discreet corner. Undoubtedly one or two Hmong in Santisuk speak some English, and they may well take you in hand, if you can find them. The village has connections with the wider world (outside Thailand), some inhabitants even having been to the UK and the US. In the upper northern part of the village, we saw sunnily written on the wall of a house: 'I have been to England. I am fine. Have a good time.'

Traditionally the Mrabri or in popular Thai parlance the *pi tong luang* ('Spirits of the Yellow Leaves') have lived in the Doi Pa Ji area, or, rather, it was one of the places they visited in their nomadic wanderings. They have not been there recently. The fighting at Doi Pa Ji during the communist insurgency, during which a few of them were injured or killed by mines, frightened them away. But reports say that the shy fragile 'Yellow Leaves' are now beginning to return to the area. If they are, you might be able to visit them from Santisuk, but you would need a Hmong guide to bring you into contact with them. For some background information on the 'yellow-leaf' Mrabri, see Trek 17 under 'Huai Yuak'.

During the communist insurgency, the Doi Pa Ji area was one of the largest and best-organized CPT/PLAT strongholds in the whole of northern Thailand. It was also the scene of a major battle between PLAT troops and the Thai Army with its KMT/Wa auxiliaries. Two big caves near Santisuk village were used by the communists, one housing a hospital and the other a communications centre. You can visit these caves, but you would need to spend an extra night in Santisuk to do so. The CPT stronghold was attacked by heavy artillery and helicopters, and in 1974 three Thai Army helicopters were shot down by the communists over Doi Pa Ji. The machines crashed into the mountain and rolled down the mountainside. The wreckage is still there. The 'Red' Hmong insurgents at Doi Pa Ji laid down their arms in 1982, after which they were sent down for political re-education in lowland towns in Nan province. Between 1984-85 they were resettled in Santisuk. Prior to that time there had been no village actually at the site of present Santisuk. The site had been no more than jungle and CPT hideouts. But there had been three Hmong villages in the local area: Eggarat, Tong Daeng and Dor Su, to give them their PLAT guerrilla names, meaning respectively 'Independence', 'Bronze' and 'Fighting Village'. These settlements were wound up and their inhabitants, following rehabilitation, relocated to the new centralized village of Santisuk. They were joined by Hmong from Kiu Khan (a village up near Chiang Khong), and these families live in their own section of Santisuk.

Santisuk is a somewhat controversial place not just on account of its insurgent past. It harbours a dark secret that, despite frequent questioning both of the local Hmong and of teachers and sanctuary officials, friends and I have never been able to fully fathom. Which brings me to the vexed question of the 7 destroyed bridges. These well-constructed bridges, lining the Pi Nuea to Santisuk trail, were mysteriously all burnt down, as everyone agrees, during one and the same night. It seems that they were razed, in what must have been a concerted well-organized action, in 1989, although in 1997 some people thought that it had happened '4 years ago' or '3 years ago' or '5-10 years ago'! But why were they burnt down, and by whom, and why have the concrete and railway-sleeper bridges never been rebuilt?

A wildlife sanctuary man thought that the Hmong had burnt down the bridges to stop consolidation of the wildlife reserve and to prevent the authorities coming into the area, who would have implemented a logging ban. But why would the Hmong, in downing the bridges, have wanted to destroy a – for them – vital link with the outside world, making their lives more difficult and preventing them getting easily to Nan town? As if disproving this idea, they have even gone to considerable trouble replacing the burnt bridges with makeshift log crossings. Some Hmong people said that *anuraak* people, from the forestry and sanctuary authorities, had done the deed to consolidate the wildlife reserve, frustrate logging, and prevent traffic from going out of the sanctuary from Santisuk on all ways except that to Pong. But why should the authorities start destroying well-engineered bridges, and why should the *anuraak* burn down something that either they or some other authority had just built? Just to frustrate logging and traffic? If they had wanted to do that, they could easily have done it with a couple of checkpoints, of the kind that exists at Huai Fai. And, in any case, some minimal traffic was still using the way out to Pi Nuea, both two- and four-wheeled, as we saw in 1997. We learned, too, of some killing(s). Nobody liked to speak about this, but it seems that one or possibly more *anuraak* officials were killed by the Hmong. But why? And why was a kindergarten in Santisuk, as well as the bridges, also burnt down?

What seems to have happened is this. A dispute arose between the authorities and the local Hmong, probably over logging. In the heat of the moment an official was murdered. The authorities retaliated by burning down the bridges. And the Hmong in turn retaliated by torching the nursery. This animosity between the two parties would explain the arsenal of weapons at the *anuraak* camp, where we stayed. But why have the bridges never been rebuilt, and why has the road out to Pi Nuea been allowed to deteriorate? Theories ranged from 'there is no money for the job' to 'no one can agree whose responsibility the road is'. There is some sense in the latter because the road appears to run through bits of both Nan and Payao provinces. Perhaps Payao is not interested in a troublesome trail on the edge of its area of jurisdiction. But it is more likely that the killing and destruction of the nursery still rankles with the authorities, and that they feel disinclined to repair the bridges for the Hmong. This would tie in with the paramount consideration, which is that the authorities do indeed want to consolidate the wildlife sanctuary and frustrate logging, and that it makes no sense to repair the bridges and have a busy road running through the middle of it. Even more so than the country's National Parks, designated wildlife reserves are taken very seriously in Thailand. The failure to rebuild the bridges and the deterioration of the Pi Nuea/Santisuk and Santisuk/Sob Khun trails may be bad news for the Hmong, and unwelcome for biking trekkers, but it is good news for foot trekkers.

The route to and from Santisuk via Pi Nuea has already been detailed in the first leg of this trek. For reference for bikers, the way to and from Santisuk via Sob Khun is the most difficult of the three ways radiating from the village. The worst section of the Sob Khun route is at the Sob Khun end, although the climb up from the river near Santisuk is awful enough. If you exit Santisuk to Pong, the way is worse at the Santisuk end than at the Pong end. In Santisuk, from the T-junction beside the wildlife office, it is 13.8 kms in the direction of Pong to Doi Pa Chang Wildlife Sanctuary HQ, a further 4.2 kms to a sign marking the entrance/exit of the sanctuary, another 2.3 kms to the village of Khun Kamlang, then 1.7 kms to a junction and the H1188 road at Nam Om village. From there you go W another 14 kms along the H1188 to Pong (total Santisuk to Pong: 36 kms), which lies N of Chiang Muan on the H1091 Nan/Payao road. If you go NE up the H1188 via Nam Puk, you come to the H1148 Chiang Kham/Nan road.

Brief background information on the Hmong people
Before we continue our trek, I interpolate here a thumbnail sketch of the Hmong people, whom we encounter not just during Trek 16 at the villages of Santisuk and Sob Khun, but during many of the other treks in this book at numerous villages. Also known in Thailand – incorrectly – as Miao or Meo, the Hmong are an ancient Asian people who have migrated from China. In fact they are the most widely dispersed of the many tribal groups to have come out of that land. If some 6 million Hmong exist worldwide, about 5 million still live in south China, ca 400,000 in northern Vietnam, some 150,000 in Laos, ca 100,000 in Thailand, and many in 'Western' countries, especially the USA. Thailand's Hmong came from Laos, first migrating across the Mae Khong (Mekong river) in the late 19th century. In the Kingdom they are the second most numerous minority group after the Karen, accounting for about 15% of the country's hill-tribe populace. The Hmong are not (as are, say, the Lua) a group from the Mon-Khmer ethnic stable, but are a Mongoloid, Sinitic, 'slit-eyed' and relatively smooth-skinned people. Their tongue is usually classified as one of the Hmong-Yao languages within the Sino-Tibetan linguistic family.

The tribe is divided into several sub-groups, including the White Hmong, the Blue, Red, Black and Striped Hmong. These distinctions are based on the costumes worn especially by the women of the different sub-groups. In Thailand only Blue and White Hmong are encountered, and they are easily told apart. Blue Hmong women wear as part of their traditional tribal costume an indigo blue, accordeon-pleated, knee-length skirt made of handwoven hemp or cotton. White Hmong women do not wear such a skirt, but dress in loose black trousers with a kind of rectangular apron, worn front and back, which is black in colour and generously edged with azure. This makes the name of their sub-group something of a misnomer. However, the White Hmong do have a heavily pleated, white hemp skirt, from which they derive their name, although it is seldom seen, being worn especially by girls only at the Hmong New Year celebrations.

As with the Yao, some typically Sinitic traits and practices can be observed in the Hmong and their culture, which is the result of the tribe having lived during its history for hundreds of years alongside the Chinese and Yunnanese. For example, the Hmong are money-oriented, strive for wealth, gamble, worship their ancestors, smoke water pipes, and have bare earth floors in their houses. They like their freedom and independence, and amass wealth, which they are good at doing, in order to guarantee this. The Hmong are born entrepreneurs, businesslike in their dealings, and relatively impervious. The downside of their character and qualities is that they can be rapacious and overproud, have scant respect for the authorities, and make unscrupulous loggers and poachers. The upside is that in their villages, given the right occasion (e.g. New Year), they can be exceptionally hospitable vis-à-vis the outsider.

Traditionally, the Hmong of Thailand have been more involved in poppy cultivation and opium production than any other of the country's hill tribes. A few villages are still thus engaged, but most have now turned mainly or wholly to growing other cash crops, such as cabbages and temperate fruits. The Hmong were the first of Thailand's hill tribes to embrace modern technology and dip their toes into local urban economies. Many Hmong men now own pick-ups, with which they operate flourishing transport businesses, while their womenfolk can be found selling their exquisitely embroidered and appliquéd needlework far and wide, even on the streets of Chiang Mai and Bangkok. For further information on the Hmong people, their history and culture, on their role both in the 'Secret War of Laos' (1961-73) and in the communist insurgency in Thailand, on their flight post-1975 from communist Laos to refugee camps in Thailand, and on their subsequent dispersal throughout the world, see my book *Around Lan-Na* (Chapter 11 and elsewhere).

Day 2: Santisuk (Doi Pa Ji) – Sob Khun – Ta Wang Pa – Nan (Map 27)

In 1997 we were told that a lorry a day went from Santisuk to Sob Khun. This might still be true, although no vehicle passed us when we hiked this second leg of the trek. If it is, you might be able to hitch-hike some or all of the protracted way to Sob Khun. We set off on the 20.5-km-long march (12¾ miles) at 9am, arriving at Sob Khun at teatime. The route heads NE and is, indeed, worse than the Pi Nuea to Santisuk way. Hmong people in Santisuk warned us that there was no water on the all-day walk to Sob Khun and that we should carry plenty of water. We took 2 litres each and drank it all. You should likewise heed the warning. Boil up drinking water during the evening of Day 1 in readiness for the morning of Day 2. On Day 2, in contrast to Day 1, when the going was hot and humid, we trekked under an overcast sky and in a fresh wind, which made the going cooler and much pleasanter.

Time log

0 hrs	The trail begins E of Santisuk school, on the far side of the playing field, near the health centre. Over in this corner you find a river and broken bridge 7. Cross the river and head E.
20 mins	Toil continuously up a steep rutted track, following the tyre marks! You come to a first cattle gate, made of bamboo, and ahead of you lies an outcrop.
¾ hr	Second cattle gate. On your right: Doi Pa Ji, forming a fine cone.
1½ hrs	The climb seems to end, but there is more to come.
1¾ hrs	Cattle gate 3.
	You pass through a col and down into a flatter landscape.
	Drop down into a hot arid bowl, which is followed by an enervating drag up.
3 hrs	Cattle gate 4.
	Now you pass through tunnels of elephant grass.
3 hrs 20 mins	At a fork, go right and down.
	Along here we passed Hmong women cutting brushgrasses.
4 hrs	Lunch stop in the shade of some elephant grass. We stopped at 1pm for 30 mins.
4½ hrs	Set off again.
	Long downhill.
ca 5 hrs	After some 5 hrs we gained a view across a wide valley. On the far side, in the distance, miles and miles away, we spotted a dirt road and, I think, a village. We imagined it was the continuation of our route and Sob Khun and, feeling exhausted and baulking at the seeming impossibility of trekking on so far, threw ourselves down by the roadside, ready to give up. It looked as if we had bitten off more than we could chew. What we did not know was that Sob Khun lay nearby, hidden down in the valley. We rested quite some time in the trackside grass, cooling off, regaining strength, thinking what to do, and drinking our water bottles dry, which also alarmed us. Suddenly Pete noticed a tall mast not far away. Where there was a mast, there might be other civilization, in the form of buildings or people. Pete went to investigate, optimistically taking the water bottles. Presently he returned with water and the news that just 200 m away there was an *anuraak* checkpoint, three buildings, the easterly entrance/exit to Doi Pa Chang Wildlife Sanctuary, and a couple of paramilitary soldier boys. Ironically, we had all but given up just a few steps from the outpost and, indeed, from the end of the trek. Now we stumbled hotfoot to the outpost. Here, taking another long rest and drinking copious amounts of *anuraak* water, we learned from the boys that Sob Khun lay just a further 1.8 kms away.
ca 6¾ hrs	Set off on the remaining stretch for Sob Khun. Just beyond the checkpoint is a river, a broken bridge and a replacement log bridge.
	It is followed by a second log bridge and also a streamlet and 'drinking fountain'.
	Now at last you can see the paved road linking Sob Khun with the outside world.
7 hrs	Arrive at **Sob Khun**.

We reached this big Hmong place with lots of tin-roofed houses at 4pm, although, if we had better known the lie of the land and had not stopped for so long, we might have reached it half an hour earlier. There are shops in the village, and we quaffed soft drinks and, in our elation at having arrived, even large bottles of beer. As we relaxed and rehydrated, it seemed certain that we would get no lift out towards Nan that day and would have to spend the night in Sob Khun. But suddenly a truck approached, we flagged it down, and by good fortune got a lift lickety-split all the way to distant Ta Wang Pa, from where we caught the first bus to Nan, arriving about 6pm.

Exiting Sob Khun to Nan (See Map 25)
Now you must emulate our exit. From the main shop or from a waiting place at the easterly end of the village's main street, hitch a ride out of Sob Khun. Most lifts will probably go to Ta Wang Pa, the nearest town. If towards nightfall you have still got no lift, contemplate spending the night in Sob Khun and start looking for somewhere to pitch your tent. I think end-of-the-road Sob Khun is a better place to stay than other villages further down the road. Undoubtedly, you will then get a ride the next morning, possibly by *silor*. On the way out along the scenic H1082 road, you pass the Hmong village of Doi Tiu and Huak, as well as (in 1997) three checkpoints. I imagine that Sob Khun and Doi Tiu are settlements that have been moved out of the wildlife sanctuary. At Na Noon Song you hit the main H1148 Chiang Kham/Nan road. Go right (E) and continue in your lift, or in a new lift, to another T-junction. You have reached the main H1080 highway N from Nan. Left (N) proceeds 16 kms to Pua and then Tung Chang, while right (S) goes a short distance to Ta Wang Pa and then 44 kms to Nan town. If your lift is heading for Nan, stay aboard of course, otherwise alight and take the first available bus (or hitch-hike) S to Nan. There is plenty of traffic, including public transport, on the 1080 highway, so you need not worry about returning to Nan once you have got this far. From Ta Wang Pa we got a local red bus to Nan for (in 1997) 12 baht!

Trek 17

Through Mrabri 'Yellow Leaf' country

Nan – Du Tai – Ban Tam – Huai Liep/Pa Pae – Mae Ka Ning forestry – Ta Kien Tong – Huai Fai – Huai Na Ngiu – Huai Yuak – Pang Poei – H1091 – Nan

Parameters

trekking mode: on foot or by motorcycle

trek time: on foot 3 days/2 nights maximum, by motorbike 1 day

trek distance: core part of trek from Tam to H1091 road ca 40 kms, overall trek Nan to Nan ca 91.5 kms via Huai Liep, and ca 94 kms via Pa Pae

degree of difficulty: as a walking trek: easy, but long
as a biking trek: moderately difficult, for skilled dirt riders only

guide(s): not required

tent: recommended, but not absolutely necessary

map(s): see 28

Overview & strategy

This splendid and varied trek, carried out on Nan's doorstep just west of the town, passes through fine mixed terrain and a pot-pourri of settlements inhabited by Hmong, Yao, Lua and Khmu tribal people. It is the second of a pair of loop trips done either side of the H1091 Nan to Chiang Muan road. Where the first (Trek 16) took place north of that road, traversing in a north-easterly direction a right-angled segment between the westbound H1091 and northbound H1080 roads and taking in the villages of Pi Nuea, Santisuk and Sob Khun (see Map 25), the second, this trek, takes place south of the H1091 road, traversing a right-angled segment between the southbound H101 and westbound H1091 roads and passing in a broadly north-westerly direction through the villages of Du Tai, Tam and Huai Yuak (see Map 28). Starting in Nan town and looping back clockwise to the provincial 'capital', both outings, and especially this one, trek through Mrabri country, through the habitat of the celebrated *pi tong luang* people, the nomadic 'Stone Age' 'Spirits of the Yellow Leaves'.

232

TREK 17: NAN – BAN TAM – HUAI YUAK – NAN

The trek can be undertaken either on foot or by motorcycle. Done on foot, it will take the best part of 3 days and 2 nights. Biked, the excursion can be managed inside a day. The core part of the trek, from Tam village to Pang Poei, is basically on a 4WD dirt track which, while easy enough on a bike for most of its length, is in places problematic. Thus, unless the track has been upgraded since I last passed along it, the trek should only be biked by experienced riders with dirt skills. Novice or inexperienced bikers casually hiring a Honda Dream in Nan be warned. If you try to ride through this obscure corner, you are almost bound to get into difficulties or take a tumble. Accordingly, I recommend, generally speaking, that the trek be done on foot, and I have written it up from the point of view of a foot trek (experienced bikers can look after themselves anyway). If, following my schedule, you walk the 40-km-long hike at the heart of the trek (from Ban Tam to Pang Poei and the H1091 road), it will take you 2 days plus the morning of Day 3, and also 2 nights, the nights being spent at Mae Ka Ning reforestation centre and at the Hmong village of Huai Yuak. Considering that the two nights are spent at a forestry place and at a village, you can get away on Trek 17 without taking a tent with you, although you should then take a mosquito net and, of course, a sleeping bag. Nevertheless, I recommend, as always, that you take a tent, which gives you flexibility, freedom, independence, privacy and the reassurance that you know you have fallback accommodation with you.

You can easily do the trek unguided on your own (the way is clear), but this means that you have to carry your backpack, tent, food, water and camera yourself, making a hike that is already prolonged and tiring even more exhausting. Thus the outing, walking fally laden, uphill and down dale, in the blazing sun, is not for the faint-hearted. It does not really matter which way round the loop you go, either clockwise from Du Tai on the H101 road up to Pang Poei and the H1091, or anticlockwise from the H1091 and Pang Poei down to Du Tai and the H101, but clockwise (as the trek is written up) is, I think, better because, as you hike NW, you mostly have the sun behind you, which means that you do not have it in your face and that the scenery is nicely illuminated in front of you. I have trekked this route several times both on foot and by motorcycle. The last time I hoofed it was in early 1996 with Nittaya Tananchai, and the last time I biked it was in early 1998. The area and villages through which this hike passes are sporadically trekked by Nan's only trekking agency, a modest low-impact outfit called *Fhu Travel*. However, it is unlikely that you will run into Fhu's groups of 3 or 4 'trekkies' as they do their rounds – I have never done so.

Now for a more specific outline of the expedition, seen from the perspective of the foot trekker (see Map 28). On Day 1 you make your way by whatever form of transport you can muster from Nan town via Du Tai to Tam village. From Ban Tam you walk ca 3 hrs and 11.5 kms over a ridge to the Lua village of Huai Liep, where you have a picnic lunch, if you have not already done so. Then you walk 45 mins or ca another 3 kms to Mae Ka Ning reforestation centre, arriving there about mid-afternoon. The hiking on

Day 1 thus totals some 4 hrs and 14.5 kms maximum. After spending the night either in the main forestry building or in a tent, you continue walking on Day 2 ca 3 hrs or 12.5 kms to the Hmong village of Huai Yuak, passing Ta Kien Tong (Hmong), Huai Fai (Yao) and the double village of Huai Na Ngiu with its southerly Yao part and northerly Hmong part. You arrive at Huai Yuak at lunchtime and spend the rest of the day and also Night 2 there. On Day 3 you march some 2¼ hrs to Pang Poei (Hmong) and then a final hour up to the H1091 road (13 kms in all). Reckoning in a break at Pang Poei, it takes 4 hrs from Huai Yuak to the 1091 road, which you reach at lunchtime. You eat a roadside picnic lunch while you hitch-hike a lift or take the first available bus or *silor* E 31 kms back to Nan. According to my calculations, the complete loop Nan-to-Nan (via Huai Liep) is 91.5 kms; the section between the two main roads (the H101 at Du Tai and the H1091 near Pang Poei) is 55 kms; and the central walking section (from Tam village to the H1091) measures, as said, 40 kms or 25 miles, which is done in a leisurely total of some 11 hrs.

From the biker's point of view, the trek is exactly the same except that from Ban Tam you proceed to Mae Ka Ning forestry not directly over the ridge via Huai Liep, but indirectly via the villages of Pa Pao and Pa Pae. Unless you went backwards from Mae Ka Ning to Huai Liep, you would miss out the Lua village, but by way of compensation you take in the mixed Khmu and Yao village of Pa Pae. It used to be possible to bike the way from Tam over the ridge to Huai Liep, although this was always very difficult and may now have become virtually impossible. People simply ride or drive via Pa Pae. However, in 1998 the stretch from Pa Pae to Mae Ka Ning was also on two wheels far from being a piece of cake. Adding in the extra distance biked via Pa Pae increases the total distance of the trek (Nan to Nan) from 91.5 kms by a couple of kms to 94 kms – let's say 100, allowing for little errands, deviations and mistakes.

Unlike most of the expeditions in this book, Trek 17 clearly cannot really be modified. It is, after all, a loop trek, and is thus little amenable to being truncated or extended. As just said, the beginning of the core part of the expedition (from Ban Tam via Huai Liep to Mae Ka Ning forestry) can be varied to proceed via Pa Pae, but while it makes sense to go this slightly more roundabout way by bike, it does not do so on foot. On a bike you could truncate the trek by proceeding from Nan only as far as Mae Ka Ning, returning the same way. This would suit less ambitious bikers and would make a pleasant 75-km-long day trip out from the guest houses of Nan. The scenery from Tam to Pa Pae and Mae Ka Ning is beautiful, and you would take in the Khmu-Yao village of Pa Pae. From the Yao part of Pa Pae, called Huai Rai, you can walk apparently an hour to Huai Waen waterfall. You could even camp at Mae Ka Ning forestry, before returning to Nan. The trip (as a foot trek) could also be modified by speeding it up and doing it in 2 days. Assuming you can get to Ban Tam in good time, you could march ca 7 hrs to Huai Yuak, eliminating the night at Mae Ka Ning forestry, stay overnight in the Hmong village, and on the morning of Day 2 hike out 3 hrs from Huai Yuak via Pang Poei to the H1091 road, not stopping in Pang Poei. You would be back in Nan well before the end of Day 2. Or, if it too far to get to Huai Yuak by nightfall on Day 1, you could break the journey and stay overnight at another village, between Mae Ka Ning and Huai Yuak, for example at Huai Fai or Huai Na Ngiu. This would still give you time on Day 2 to trek out via Huai Yuak and Pang Poei to the H1091 and back to Nan. With these two alternative schedules you would be more rushed. The virtue of doing the trek as I describe it, in a leisurely 3 days and 2 nights, is that you have plenty of time for stopping and exploring the villages and peoples en route.

One final consideration: Thailand has a policy, which is being slowly implemented, of providing every hill-tribe village with decent road access. At present the settlements dotted along the core stretch of the trek do have vehicle access, although it is poor. But all that could change in the future, and access at each end, to Pa Pae from Tam and to Pang Poei from the H1091, is already good, on a metalled surface. The status of the track through Huai Liep, Ta Kien Tong, Huai Fai, Huai Na Ngiu and Huai Yuak, is uncertain. Apparently, it was cut by the peoples of these villages themselves, and/or falls under the jurisdiction of the forestry authorities, but not under that of the highways department, which is why it has never been improved. If the 4WD track is upgraded, all will not be lost. The stretch might become less attractive as a route for walking along, but it will be better for biking along, in which case Trek 17 will turn into more of a motorcycle outing.

The Hmong people
For some brief background information on the Hmong people, such as inhabit Ta Kien Tong, Huai Na Ngiu Nuea, Huai Yuak and Pang Poei, see Trek 16 under 'Santisuk'.

Preparing for the trek
In Nan buy food for however long you suspect the trip might last. After Ban Tam, only Huai Yuak really has (rudimentary) stores, at which you can purchase provisions. As accessing Tam village from Nan and exiting to Nan along the H1091 road are part of the trek itself, there are no separate sections on accessing and exiting, which are subsumed under the trekking route detail. As said earlier, the route detail is mainly given from the perspective of the trek being walked.

*

Trekking route detail (see Map 28)
Day 1: Nan – Du Tai – Ban Tam – Huai Liep/Pa Pae – Mae Ka Ning forestry station
First you must make your way from Nan town 20 kms to Tam village (Ban Tam or Tham), which will require a modicum of initiative. You start by proceeding 5 kms

TREK IT YOURSELF IN NORTHERN THAILAND

S from Nan down the main H101 Nan-Prae-Bangkok highway to the village of Du Tai. You can do this either by *songtaew* (those public-transport pick-ups with two benches in the back, also known as *silor*), or by bus, or by hitch-hiking. The day before the trek, check out in Nan where from and at what time the buses and *songtaew* leave. If you can identify it, there is, apparently, one red *songtaew* that goes each day specifically to Ban Tam. *Songtaew* for the villages surrounding Nan depart from the site of the town's evening market, which is centrally located just down the side street opposite the *Dheveraj Hotel*. If you want to use a bus for the paltry 5 kms to Du Tai, don't bother with the big long-distance buses for Bangkok, Chiang Mai, Sukotai or whatever. Take a small local bus bound for Wiang Sa. Such buses depart, I think, from the bus station beside Nan's main day market. If you cannot sort all this out, or if you simply want to hitch-hike, walk to and station yourself at the beginning of the H101 road (km 0) on the south side of town, and wait for the first *songtaew*, bus or lift to come by. The fare to Du Tai will be just a few baht.

You can tell when you have reached **Du Tai** and the turning right (W) for Ban Tam because there are half a dozen tall telecoms masts to the right of the H101 on a hill. If you are in a *songtaew* or bus heading for Wiang Sa, get out at the junction and proceed another 15 kms by hitch-hiking or in another *songtaew* to Tam. As you head up this side road, you pass through the rural Thai villages of Na Sao, Pa Ka, Muang Jaroen Rat and Na Mon. Some 4.4 kms from the Du Tai junction, bear right at a confusing fork (9.4 kms from Nan), and 3.4 kms later at the crossroads in **Muang Jaroen Rat** (12.8 kms from Nan) go left past an Esso fuel station. Now proceed straight, ignoring three turnings to the left, until you reach the drawn-out village of **Tam** (centre ca 18.7 kms from Nan). There are shops in Ban Tam for stocking up with any food or drink that you have not already obtained in Nan. Continue in your lift or walk from the centre of the village a short distance to the top end of Tam and a checkpoint on the left side of the road (20 kms from Nan and 14.8 kms from the H110/Du Tai junction).

By the checkpoint at the far end of Tam comes the parting of the ways. Foot trekkers go right, leaving the road, to begin their hike (see below). Bikers, by contrast, continue 8 kms along the paved road to the small village of **Pa Pao** (km 27.9) and then a further km to a T-junction (km 28.8). At the junction, which is marked by a temple opposite you, left goes to Wiang Sa, while right brings you immediately to **Pa Pae** (km 29). This friendly sizeable village has shops and a large school, and is inhabited mainly by relatively assimilated Khmu people, although at its top end, on the left side of the road, there is an unmarked Yao settlement called Huai Rai. Beyond Pa Pae, a (in 1998) very poor dirt track continues to a junction (36.4 kms from Nan), on the left side of which, set back, lies Mae Ka Ning reforestation centre. As you negotiate the 7.5-km-long stretch, bear right at a fork – the way left goes down to a river, rejoining your right-hand way later. For more on Mae Ka Ning and the rest of the trek, see below, when the biking and walking routes rejoin each other. But now back to the walking route.

Time log

0 hrs   At the checkpoint on the far side of Ban Tam, turn right off the paved road to pick up opposite the checkpoint an old dirt track in a dreadful condition. When we walked this trek, we started out from here at 10.15am. As a dirt biker with a suitable machine, you might still be able to get up this trail. Before the road was built round by Pa Pae,

the 4WD track was used in both directions (treacherous coming down) by locals and also by the odd *farang* motorcycle trekker from Nan's guest houses (myself included).

Climb steeply up the winding trail.

¾ hr   You emerge at some fields and huts.

Continue walking and climbing at a leisurely pace in the blazing sun.

2 hrs   Finally the climb ends. From the top there is a grand view W of the ridge marking the provincial boundary between Nan on this side and Prae and Payao on the other.

Now you go down and down.

2½ hrs   Arrive at a ford.

3 hrs   Come to a second ford.

ca 3¼ hrs   10 mins later, reach **Huai Liep** with its health centre near the road (11.5 kms from Tam checkpoint, 31.5 kms from Nan).

Huai Liep is a Lua (Htin) village isolated from almost all the other Lua villages in Thailand, which are situated E and NE of Nan town, mainly in Doi Pu Kha National Park and down the Lao border. With its 60 families, many having the surname Ka-lek, it is also, like Khmu Pa Pae, a relatively assimilated place, and, unless you have not seen a Lua village before, is not especially worthy of attention (for some brief background information on the Lua people and their culture, see Trek 5). The wooden houses are robustly constructed high off the ground, and a couple of them conceal rudimentary shops. It seems that the inhabitants were resettled to Huai Liep some years ago from Na Kok (a village SE of Bo Glua). The health centre by the 'road' is run during the week by a friendly, helpful, chubby-faced Hmong man from Huai Yuak, called Somboon Saelao, who will doubtless allow you to stay at the centre, if you want to and he is there. Another overnight accommodation possibility in Huai Liep, if you do not want to press on to and stay at nearby Mae Ka Ning forestry office, is the school on the far side of the village, right of the 'road'. The teachers are a lively hospitable crew and will surely sort you out lodgingswise and in other ways. When we passed by, they helped us cook up instant noodles for a late lunch, even though they had already finished their midday break.

When we walked this route, we spent a tardy 1½ hrs at Huai Liep, first looking round the village and then involved with the teachers. Arriving well after 1pm, we left at 3pm. The school lies just beyond the village, E of the 'road'. From here it is just 3 kms or 45 mins' walk to Pamai Mae Ka Ning (*pamai* = forestry). My time log below for the short final hop on Day 1 does not reflect time spent in Huai Liep.

ca 3¼ hrs   After the school, go left at the junction, cross a wooden bridge, and at the next junction go straight, to arrive immediately at Mae Ka Ning reforestation centre on your left. The track coming in from the left at the junction and just before the centre is the other way to this point, proceeding via Pa Pae, which lies 7.5 kms back down the track. Here, therefore, the alternative way from Ban Tam to Mae Ka Ning, used

237

ca 4 hrs

by people biking this trek, rejoins our walking route. Henceforth the biking and walking routes coincide.
Reach **Mae Ka Ning reforestation centre** (ca 34.5 kms from Nan and 14.5 kms from Tam checkpoint).

When we trekked through here in 1996, Mae Ka Ning reforestation centre was still being built, although by now it must certainly be finished. Actually, the station comprises not just a reforestation centre, but also 'Mae Ka Ning River Management'. The complex is set in a bowl, around the floor of which the Ka Ning river flows, and its various buildings are adjoined by extensive nurseries with thousands of seedlings and saplings, destined to reforest the denuded sides of the bowl and the whole area. The staff are doing a painstaking, highly laudable job, and you can encourage them by expressing an interest in their work. We stayed in the centre's – at that time – still unfinished visitors' building, sleeping on cushions snatched from a set of armchairs and laid out on the bare cement floor. Undoubtedly you will likewise be welcome to stay in the meanwhile completed visitors' building. Otherwise pitch a tent on some suitable patch. In January we found it decidedly chilly in the Mae Ka Ning basin after dark, but soon the Lua nurserymen and -women of the complex had a roaring fire going, and we went on to spend a hilarious evening there with them, being plied with *lao tho* (a kind of milky, sour-and-sweet, semi-fermented rice wine) and buffalo tartare. The raw ground meat, spiced with chilli, was quite a delicacy compared to some grilled intestines that were also urged on us!

Day 2: Mae Ka Ning forestry station – Ta Kien Tong – Huai Fai – Huai Na Ngui – Huai Yuak

The second leg of the trek, from Mae Ka Ning forestry to the Hmong village of Huai Yuak, covers ca 12.5 kms and takes about 3 hrs on foot (we set off at 9.30am and arrived at 12.30pm). The modest trekking duration of just 3 hrs gives you plenty of time during the day for exploring the settlements en route (which will, of course, add to the 3 hrs).

Time log

0 hrs   Continuing up the 4WD dirt trail from the forestry complex and its nearby junction, you come after just a 20-min walk to:

20 mins   **Ta Kien Tong** (km 36). A small, attractive, slightly down-at-heel White Hmong place with a kindergarten and school, the village – in true Hmong style – has grass-roofed houses built straight onto the ground, not on stilts as at Huai Liep. We noticed here tiny women, scarcely 4 ft high.
The route continues 3 kms up and over a small hill to arrive at:

¾ hr   **Huai Fai** (km 39), which is a small Yao (or Mien) village of some hundred souls.[1]

---

[1] It is instantly recognizable as a Yao place by the traditional costume of some of its female inhabitants – opulent red ruff, black tunic, heavily embroidered trousers, and a big black

TREK 17: NAN – BAN TAM – HUAI YUAK – NAN

In Huai Fai, cross the bridge and go left at the T-junction. You pass the village school, before continuing up over another small ridge.

1½ hrs   The next goal and venue of the second overnight stop, Huai Yuak, can be seen in the distance.

Cross a further small hill, to arrive at a ford and:

1¾ hrs   **Huai Na Ngiu** (km 43). This is actually a double village. Huai Na Ngiu Tai (*tai* = south), the first part reached, with the school, is another Yao settlement. A second part, Huai Na Ngiu Nuea (*nuea* = north), set behind the first, is Hmong. Together, so it seemed to us, they form a rather scruffy place, where tribal costume is dying out. In 1996 we found here a makeshift shop run by traders from Nan town. Huai Na Ngiu Tai would be a suitable place to stay overnight (as an alternative to Huai Yuak) if you so wished. Try the school, where, assuming the teachers are present, you could sleep on the floor of one of the classrooms. Or perhaps a teacher will invite you into his or her house. Otherwise pitch a tent somewhere.

Leave Huai Na Ngiu Tai by going W out of the village and crossing two fords. It is another 4 kms to Huai Yuak. Not far short of the Hmong village, we once found a small poppy field on the left side of the road, across the stream. In early February some of the opium poppies were in flower, while others already had scored pods.

2¾ hrs   You reach a junction (km 46.5). Straight on continues to Pang Poei, while right climbs steeply up to offroad Huai Yuak. In past years there has been a sign at the junction giving in Roman letters the Hmong name of the village, 'Zoshib Yuas'. Go right (E) and toil 500 m up the side trail to:

3 hrs   **Huai Yuak**, elevated on a shoulder.

Huai Yuak (= palm heart or plantain stream) is a well-established White Hmong village. It is a typical Hmong place, with big squat wooden houses dotted around a central compound of dusty brown earth. Dogs, black pot-bellied pigs, chickens and buffaloes wander around, and if you go into any house, you do not ascend a wooden ladder, but step straight onto a tamped earth floor. There is a school at the top end of the village, and, especially near the entrance, some relatively well-stocked shops. Apparently, the people of Huai Yuak originally came from Laos 'a couple of generations ago'. A sign of the prosperity of the place, several men in the village have

---

turban. If you look around the settlement, you will undoubtedly come across at least one group of costumed women sitting on three-inch-high stools busy at their favourite occupation, needlework, which is done 'back to front'. A doubly bespectacled granny we spoke to, called Jiawsing Saejao, said that it took three months to embroider a 'simple' pair of trousers and a year to do a complicated pair. The Yao are the most sophisticated and self-assured of all Thailand's ethnic minority groups, and the least fazed when visitors such as you or I turn up in their midst. Their composure and studied politeness can even seem stand-offish to *farang*. Yao culture is considerably sinicized, the result of its people having lived many centuries during the tribe's history alongside the Chinese. Most Yao still live in China, in the south, but others, having migrated, can be found in Vietnam, Laos and northern Thailand, where about 40,000 inhabit especially the provinces of Chiang Rai, Payao and Nan. For more background information on the Yao people, see my cultural guide *Around Lan-Na* (Chapter 13).

239

two or three wives. Try staying here either at the school or in the house of Hmong man Somboon Saelao, or just put up a tent in a quiet flat corner, even down by the Yuak stream. Because of all the animals and because the village lies tipped down an incline, it may be problematic pitching camp in Huai Yuak, and staying at the school presupposes that the teachers are present, i.e. that you do not arrive at the weekend or in the school holidays. On different occasions I have stayed both at the school and in Somboon's house. Somboon is the chubby-faced chap (sometimes with a small moustache) mentioned earlier, who often during the week works at the health centre in Huai Liep. If he is still working there, you are most likely to run into him at Huai Yuak at the weekends, from Friday evening through to Monday morning. He is a likeable, helpful, *farang*-friendly fellow. As you enter the Hmong village, going up the steep access way, his house lies immediately left and then left again. If Somboon is absent, try his brother Mongkhon, who should also be able put up or arrange accommodation for trekkers. One of Somboon's children is a handicapped boy, which might make his house more identifiable.

If you manage to stay in Somboon's house, or indeed in the house of any other Huai Yuak family, you will need to be able to 'rough it'. It is a typical Hmong affair, the inside rather resembling a farm outhouse. On the other hand, a night there will provide you with an unparalleled insight into Hmong circumstances. The sleeping compartments are cramped and scruffy. The guest platform is likely to be littered with sacks, baskets and agricultural implements. Maize hangs from the ceiling. Fires smoke. Dogs and chickens do their best to infiltrate the place, and at night rats climb around in dark corners, trying to get at the grain. There is a constant coming and going of adults and children. Against one wall is the family altar, and near it is a table with two benches. In one corner, on a large clay stove, a giant wokful of pig food bubbles, while at another fire, smouldering on the ground, a wizened old granny washes, naked to the waist. Her fire is shared by dogs, lying with their snouts in the ashes.

If you have the time, energy and inclination, and if you do not mind a rather awkward voyeuristic experience, Somboon, like his brother Mongkhon and other villagers in Huai Yuak, may well be willing – for 50 or 100 baht – to take you to visit the Mrabri or 'Yellow-Leaf' people, some of whom can always be found in the hills surrounding the village. Certainly, he has guided me several times to the 'Maku', as the Hmong call the 'yellow-leaf' Mrabri. At any one time many Hmong in Huai Yuak know where families and bands of the nomadic 'Stone Age' people are living locally, and intermittently the Mrabri labour for the Hmong villagers on the latter's fields. But how is your Thai or Hmong or even Mrabri?! Actually, you hardly need to go to the trouble of engaging a Hmong guide because there is a good chance, if you keep your eyes open, that you will see Mrabri at or near Huai Yuak without even going to look for them. They like to come to the shops to buy sweeties, medicines and whatever, and they can often be found on the 'road' N and S of the village or working in the fields just either side of the road. During the Hmong New Year they hang around in Huai Yuak in droves. The village enjoys a splendid view W across the valley to the ridge of Doi Huai Yuak (or Doi Na Ka) and Doi Pu Kaeng (1403 m, 4600 ft). The ridge is a favourite dwelling place of the Mrabri when they are not working close at hand for the Huai Yuak Hmong or doing their rounds, visiting other of their preferred sites. After dark you can often see the fires of Mrabri camps on Doi Na Ka, faint distant pinpoints of flickering light.

Some brief background information on the Mrabri

The Mrabri are one of the most 'primitive', interesting, obscure and rare tribes alive today. A tiny celebrated group of elusive, nomadic, so-called 'Stone Age' hunter-gatherers, they are widely known in Thailand as the *pi tong luang* (pronounced 'pee torng leuang/loe-ang'), although they call themselves 'Mrabri', which in their language means 'forest people'. *Pi tong luang* means in Thai 'yellow leaf spirits' or 'spirits of the yellow leaves' and is a graphic, sensation-mongering Siamese name for the Mrabri which the tribe finds pejorative and dislikes because, the forest people complain, 'we are not spirits but human beings'. The logic of the Thai appelation *pi tong luang* is well-known: the Mrabri build temporary shelters for living in, which are roofed with banana leaves (*tong*), and which they abandon after a week or so, when the leaves turn yellow (*luang*), going to a new site, where they build a fresh shelter roofed with green leaves. The *pi* (= spirits) part of the name derives from the fact that the Mrabri, being shy folk, always lived spectrally deep in the jungle and used to run away and hide whenever strangers approached, and so were rarely, if ever, seen by Thai or other hill-tribe people, having more the reality of spirits. Further, local people, walking or hunting in the mountains and jungle, sometimes came across the disused yellowed shelters, but never encountered the beings who built them, so, they concluded, the shelters must have been built by and be inhabited by spirits. Until a few decades ago it was seriously doubted that the Mrabri existed at all, except as *pi*. Striking about these gentle, timid, fragile folk, as everyone observes who sees photos of them or meets them in the flesh, is their bushy tousled hair, like black straw, and the haunting, melancholy, strangely beautiful look on their faces.

It is generally maintained in the guide books on Thailand as well as in newspaper articles and more scholarly literature on the Mrabri that the 'Yellow Leaves' have dwindled in number to just some 140 souls. This figure needs qualifying in two ways. First, the number is probably higher. The American missionary Eugene Long, who has lived with and cared for the Mrabri for many years and who must know them better than anyone else, estimates their population at 240-250. Nevertheless, the number of 'Yellow Leaves' is so small that the tribe faces extinction, with a gene pool scarcely sufficient to allow survival. Second, this figure applies only to the Mrabri of Thailand. There are more of the forest people in Laos, in

Sayaburi province (opposite Thailand's Nan province), a fact that is not at all well-known. This second group may comprise another two or three hundred people. The second group live only 100-150 kms away from their 'Thai' counterparts, who now live exclusively in the provinces of Nan and Prae. The two groups do not visit or even know of each other, although it must be the case that quite recently, possibly in the early decades of the 20th century, they were all part of the same group. In Thailand the Mrabri are now found, as said, only in Nan and Prae provinces, especially in three or four locations based on some Hmong and a Yao village. Specifically, they gravitate in their wanderings to the vicinity of: the Hmong village of Huai Yuak (W of Nan town), the Hmong village of Bo Hoi (NE of Rong Kwang in Prae province), the Hmong village of Khun Satan (on the H1216 road between the towns of Rong Kwang and Na Noi, the Yao village of Nam Kong (on the H1091 road W of Nan town), and the Hmong village of Santisuk or Ban Doi Pa Ji (NW of Nan town, N of the H1091 road)(see Trek 16). Evidently the Mrabri used to be quite widespread in northern Thailand, roaming far and wide until they were progressively squeezed by developing Siam and by hill tribes migrating into Lan-Na from Laos and Burma. The first sightings of and reports on the forest people and their shelters date to the first half of the 20th century, and the first serious expeditions to, contact with and scientific study of them did not come until the early 1960s.

The Mrabri tongue is classified as belonging to the Mon-Khmer branch of the Austro-Asiatic linguistic family, and is related to Lua (Htin), Lawa, Wa, Khmu and the other languages of this branch. The Mrabri people would seem to be an extreme example of a tribe that has been compromised by the process of fission and entropy that over the centuries has affected so many of the Mon-Khmer peoples. Mysteriously, they remain stuck at the first hunter-gatherer stage of human development. They seem not to have gone through and then declined from an earlier flourishing civilization, like, say, the Lawa. Nor have they progressed like the Lua and Khmu to farming and animal husbandry. The Mrabri keep and raise no pigs or chickens or buffaloes, plant no rice, and till no fields, but on the threshold of the third millennium are still hunting squirrels and gathering yams, or just scrounging from the Hmong. They have little or no religious system, no agriculture, no real housing, no art, no monuments to their past, no writing or literature, and apparently no aspirations. They have known no Stone Age, and have apparently passed through no palaeolithic or neolithic phases. They are still in a 'bamboo age', or rather have suddenly been catapulted in the last few years from a hunter-gatherer bamboo age, missing out all the intervening Stone, Iron and Bronze Ages, straight into the Atomic or IT Age.

The 'yellow-leaf' people mostly wear loincloths (men) and old tattered cast-off clothes (men and women) obtained from the Hmong. They live in automonous bands of two or three families or 10-15 people, and have no king or clan chiefs or headmen. In their bands, at each camp, they live one family to a shelter. The shelters, typically sited quite high up on a hillside, are simple lean-to constructions backing on to the slope. Two wooden or bamboo uprights and a crosspiece support the outer end of a bamboo-and-leaf roof, the inner end of which rests on the ground or hill slope. The family sit, squat and lie in the mouth of this shelter, looking out over the valley and countryside, and with a fire before them. At night they sleep in their shelters on the ground with their heads at the upper back end of the lean-to and their feet at the front end by the fire.

The fact that they build not proper houses but only temporary shelters is a function, like their nomadism, of their hunter-gatherer lifestyle. As hunter-gatherers, they stay in a particular location until they have exhausted the food to be had there. Traditionally, this was about seven days or the amount of time it took for the green banana leaves on the roofs of their shelters to turn yellow. Because they move on when they have exhausted the local food supply, it makes no sense to construct a permanent wooden or even stone dwelling, and by the same token it makes perfect sense to build a quickly erected, 'throwaway' shelter of bamboo and banana leaves. These days the Mrabri are tending to stay ever longer in one place, slowly losing their nomadism. This is not at all because the food supply is becoming endlessly abundant, but because they are increasingly working (most observers would say slave-labouring) for the Hmong. They are doing this, and in general hanging around on the fringes of Hmong society, precisely because their natural food supply is becoming ever more meagre. This, in turn, is a result of their foraging territory and living or wandering space being progressively diminished on account of logging, the construction of access roads, the expansion of Hmong and other hill-tribe farming, and the general encroachment of burgeoning Thai society.

Traditionally, the Mrabri have supplemented their subsistence 'economy' by bartering, especially with the Hmong. They exchange honey, beeswax, rattan mats and baskets, jute slingbags, and other jungle produce for things like pork, clothes, salt, tobacco, matches and rice. Incidentally, in respect of the jungle and its flora, they have an immense knowledge about the medicinal uses of plants, as well as about survival in nature in general. New things are being learnt from the Mrabri herbal pharmacopoeia all the time. But as the demand of the Hmong for what the forest people can offer declines, and as the Mrabri, through their contact with the Hmong and the outside world, aspire to more and more consumer goods, the bartering is breaking down, and the Mrabri, in order to obtain what they want, have to rely increasingly on toiling for the Hmong and simply on begging. The 'Yellow Leaves' are inveterate beggars, and this begging, which has now come to include importuning tourists coming to 'see' them in a recent little wave of 'exotic' tourism in Nan, is nothing new. By all accounts it goes back, like their bartering with local people, quite some time.

The predicament of the Mrabri, in which they are being geographically squeezed, are losing their nomadism, and are becoming less reliant on their hunting and gathering and more dependent on working for and begging

243

from other people, is being exacerbated by different kinds of reprehensible exploitation. It may be true that ultimately the Mrabri are not forced to toil for the Hmong, to some extent choosing – rather like willing slaves – to do so, but the fact that a 'yellow-leaf' family has to slash whole mountainsides for days on end in the sweltering sun for a truck-owning Hmong farmer merely to obtain a small pig (value 300 baht) can only be described as exploitation. In recent years the 'exotic' 'primitive' *pi tong luang* have been exploited too as a tourist draw, rather like the 'sensational' Padaung 'long-neck' women of Mae Hong Son province, by unscrupulous touring agencies, operators, middlemen, corrupt policemen and their families, and upmarket hotels such as the *Dheveraj* in Nan and the *Nakhon Prae* in Prae, all wishing to cash in on the money-spinner represented by the Mrabri. Many people in Nan and Prae provinces, and at the more local level in villages such as Huai Yuak and Bo Hoi, have powerful vested interests in the 'Stone Age' people, which can make it a fraught business trying to visit them freelance. In the light both of this and of the exploitation, with its 'human zoo' implications, it would be understandable if, not wanting to aggravate their plight, you preferred not to try to 'see' the Mrabri.

The prognosis for the forest people is, thus, rather dismal. In the short term the danger for them is decline into slavery or peonage especially to the Hmong. In the longer term their problem is of being assimilated by especially the Hmong. This process has already started. The Mrabri already work for them and hang around their villages as ragged scroungers, some have settled in huts on the fringes of Hmong villages, and others have started intermarrying with Hmong and adopting their dress and customs. It seems to me that the fate of the 'Spirits of the Yellow Leaves' will probably be to become Hmong, disappearing as Mrabri back into the spectral status that they originally held. Readers requiring further information about this very interesting tribe, about their culture, exploitation and predicament, are referred to the long account I have included in my guide *Around Lan-Na* (Chapter 22), in which I also describe visits I have made off my own bat to the Mrabri.

Day 3: Huai Yuak – Pang Poei – H1091 road – Nan

The third and last leg of the hike, from Hmong Huai Yuak via Pang Poei to the H1091 road (from where you take transport back to Nan town), covers some 13 kms and takes about 3¼ hrs on foot (we set off at 8.45am and arrived at 1pm, spending an hour in Pang Poei). The modest walking duration of just over 3 hrs gives you plenty of time during the morning to look at Pang Poei, perhaps even to take an early lunch there, and the whole afternoon to make your way back to Nan. The first 10-km section to Pang Poei took us, laden with backpacks and camera equipment, but setting out fresh in the early morning, a good 2¼ hrs.

Time log

0 hrs   Go back down the steep side road from Huai Yuak village to the junction and turn right (N) into the 'main' trail again. The route goes over hill and dale, past typical Mrabri country, through pleasant

woods, and mostly downhill. Along here we encountered a couple of 'Yellow Leaf' people at the roadside and others working in fields and clearings near the road. Keep your eyes peeled, and you might, too. The way is clear. Just follow it, avoiding any turnings right or left.

A couple of drawn-out rutted descents, virtually impassable in the rainy season and problematic if there has been a recent shower, can cause difficulty for people on two wheels, even to skilled riders.

2 hrs Reach the valley bottom, fields, a ford and a pond, and then:

2¼ **Pang Poei** (km 56). This regular Hmong village, with basic shops and set down in a valley, has been somewhat spoiled by Nan's Fhu trekking agency. As soon as we strolled in, women came rushing out to try to sell us needlework – always a sign that tourists drop by and are expected by the locals! Nevertheless, stop for a rest in Pang Poei and have a look around. We spent an hour there, eating a mid-morning snack meal. A friendly lady with a small shop made us some noodle soup and talked about her husband, who had been 4 years in the US and spoke good English. Hunt him out if you need help or want to stay in the village.

3¼ hrs After an hour or so in Pang Poei, set off again. The last 4-km section of the route, from Pang Poei up to the main H1091 road, has recently been paved, so you must hoof the final part of the trek for an hour on asphalt. The way passes Pang Poei Alliance Church, a hill-tribe development centre, and a school. At a fork, branch left – just follow the tarred road – and climb up out of the valley.

4¼ hrs After an hour's march, you arrive at a T-junction and the **H1091 road** (km 60). Left (W) goes to Ban Luang and Chiang Muan, while right (E) goes 31.5 kms to Nan. (Anyone doing this trip in reverse should look out for the turning for Pang Poei and Huai Yuak about 31.5 kms out from Nan. The junction, between km-stones 30 and 31, is marked on the left/south side by a little waiting hut and several signs in Thai. *Silor* ply the H1091 road from Nan to Ban Luang three times a day, leaving Nan from the site of the central evening market, opposite the *Dheveraj Hotel*.)

Now you must get back to Nan. The 32-km-long stretch is too far to walk, so you must ride in a vehicle. Sooner or later a Nan-bound bus or *silor* will come along, but if you tire of waiting, just start hitch-hiking, boldly flagging down any lorry or pick-up. While you are waiting in the little *sala*, eat up your provisions in a picnic lunch. After we walked this trek, we got a lift in an empty cattle truck right to our guest house door. About 30 baht per person would be an appropriate fare (in 1999).

The way back to Nan town is scenic, especially the first part, which dips and dives like a roller coaster along the crest of a ridge, affording splendid views S towards Doi Luang and N towards Doi Pa Ji (see Trek 16). Coming off the mountains, the road reaches (km 71.5, or 20 kms out from Nan) the extensive and developed Hmong village of **Song Kwae**, which is inhabited by people who have been moved out of the Doi Pa Chang Wildlife Sanctuary and Doi Pa Ji area. Following Song Kwae, it passes through the Yao village of **Nam Kong** (km 75.5, or 16 kms from Nan), after which the H1091 broaches orange orchards and cotton fields, and then increasing signs of 'civilization', until it brings you back to Nan (km 91.5).

Part 3a

Treks 18-19: South-east of Mae Sariang, in Mae Hong Son province in Pwo Karen country ultimately based on Mae Sariang town

Trek 18

Mae Waen – Mae Rit w/f – Kong Pae Nuea – Kong Pae Tai – Ton Ngiu Nuea – Huai Hia – Mae Pae Noi – Mae Pae Luang – Ta Fai – Kong Koi – Tung – Mae Waen

Parameters

trekking mode:	on foot
core trek time:	2½ days/2 nights
accessing time:	from Mae Sariang town to Mae Waen (43 kms) allow up to half a day using a combination of public transport and walking, and ca 1½ hrs with your own hire motorbike
exiting time:	from Mae Waen to Mae Sariang town (43 kms) allow up to half a day using a combination of walking and public transport, and ca 1½ hrs with a hire bike
overall trek time:	from Mae Sariang to Mae Sariang, including access and exiting times, between 3 days/3 nights and 4 days/4 nights
degree of difficulty:	easy, but quite long and tiring
guide(s):	necessary as far as Kong Pae Nuea, after which you should be able to find your way unguided if you want
guide name(s):	Mr Pan II (Pan Kapaap)
tent:	advisable, but not essential
map(s):	see 29, 30 & 31; refer also in part to 32, 33 & 34

Overview & strategy

This trek, the first of six trips (18-23 inclusive) based on Mae Sariang, ventures into the largely unvisited and unexplored, mountainous territory lying ESE of that westerly town. The territory is inhabited by colourful Pwo Karen people, a sub-group of the Karen tribe, and probably the main reason to do the trek is to be among the Pwo Karen, visiting some of their 20-30 villages in this corner of northern Thailand. The outing is the first of a pair (the other being Trek 19), both of which roam in this territory. The principal difference between them is that this trek (18) is a foot trek, indeed can only be done on foot, while the other (19) is a motorcycle hike, which is sensibly done only on two wheels. The complementary pair of outings to some extent duplicate each other, so, if you have done the one, you may not want to do the other. Trek 18, like the next four or five expeditions, is ultimately best launched – and I recommend you do launch it – from Mae Sariang, with its guest houses, shops, restaurants and other facilities, although in the case of Trek 18 you could launch it, I suppose, from distant Chiang Mai.

Locally, the hike starts from and is based on the village of Mae Waen and a kind of 'guest house' there called *Pan House*. Mae Waen lies 43 kms from Mae Sariang. The trek is a loop excursion, proceeding from Mae Waen and this 'guest house' in an anticlockwise direction back to the 'GH'. I did this trek in February 1998 on my own (without Thai or *farang* friends), accompanied and aided only by Mr Pan of *Pan House*. If you undertake it as I did it, you will have to carry your own stuff and walk for 2½ days (2 days and the morning of a third day), although the distances and times on Days 2 and 3 are modest. To this core trek time can be added the time needed to access and exit Mae Waen. I managed the outing without a tent, staying in houses in Pwo Karen villages, and you could do the same, but I recommend that you take a tent (if you don't, then you should take a mosquito net). In my opinion you could dispense with the services of 'guide' Mr Pan once you have got to Kong Pae Nuea at lunchtime on Day 1, sending him back to Mae Waen. After Kong Pae Nuea you should be able to find the way on your own.

Now for a more specific outline of the expedition. You make your way from Mae Sariang or possibly Chiang Mai to Mae Waen (details below under 'Accessing'). If you have a hire motorbike and are in Mae Sariang, consider visiting Mae Waen and *Pan House* in advance to sound out Mr Pan and set up the trek. You stay overnight at extremely basic *Pan House*, and set off next day, on the morning of Day 1 of the actual core trek, for Kong Pae Nuea. On the way, 45 mins out from Mae Waen, you take in Mae Rit Waterfall, after which you walk another 2¼ hrs to the Pwo Karen village of Kong Pae Nuea, where you stop for lunch (see Maps 30 & 32). Here, as said, you could consider dispensing with Mr Pan. In the afternoon you hike via Kong Pae Tai ca 2½ hrs to Ton Ngiu Nuea (both Pwo Karen villages). Before Ton Ngiu Nuea you must cross the deep valley of the Mae Rit (River Rit), plunging down and up – an exhausting business. You spend Night 1 of the actual hike (second overall) under rather primitive conditions at Ton Ngiu Nuea, either tenting or in someone's house. Day 1 thus involves some 5½ hrs of marching or about 7¼ hrs including lunch and other stops.

On the morning of Day 2, continuing to walk as if round a huge bowl, you hike from Ton Ngiu Nuea ¾ hr to Huai Hia, then 1½ hrs to Mae Pae Noi, and finally 1 hr to Mae Pae Luang (all Pwo Karen places). You spend Night 2 (third overall) in Mae Pae Luang, which as its name suggests (*luang* = big) is a large village, complete with a missionary station and a store selling beer, soft drinks and snacks. You stay with the headman or in some villager's house, or you pitch a tent somewhere. You might even get invited to lodge with the missionaries! Day 2 comprises about 3½ hrs of actual marching or some 5¼ hrs of trekking including lunch and other stops.

TREK 18: MAE WAEN – TON NGIU – MAE PAE – MAE WAEN

On the morning of Day 3 you return from Mae Pae Luang to Mae Waen, walking 1¾ hrs via Ta Fai (Ka Fai) to Kong Koi (Go Goi), and then about 35 mins via Tung village to Mae Waen (rather as in Maps 33 & 34). You can eat a mid-morning noodle soup in Kong Koi, and you reach Mae Waen about 1pm. Trekking on Day 3 comprises about 2½ hrs of actual marching or some 3 hrs including food and other stops. Adding all these times up, you trek for ca 12 hrs during the 2½ days (straight walking) or some 15½ hrs including stops. With the trek ending back in Mae Waen at lunchtime on Day 3 (the fourth overall, since Mae Sariang), you have sufficient time to exit it back to Mae Sariang the same day; or you could spend the afternoon of Day 3 and Night 3 (the fourth overall) at *Pan House*, exiting next morning; or you could do either of these options, proceeding (if you have a motorcycle) to another expedition, say Trek 20 or perhaps 21.

The trek could be modified as follows. It could be extended almost at will. There are dozens of – mostly Karen – villages in the quarter SE of Mae Sariang and S or SW of Mae Waen, and you could include any of them on a prospective itinerary. I have hardly begun to map out all these settlements and the labyrinth of trails interconnecting them. For suggestions and advice, you could ask the missionaries in Mae Pae Luang, who know the whole area. Or you could try to involve local Karen, hiring them as guides. The trek could be truncated by proceeding from Kong Pae Nuea not to Kong Pae Tai, Ton Ngiu Nuea and Huai Hia (Map 32), but directly to Huai Hia, from where you would pick up the standard trail again. For a while, between Kong Pae Nuea and Huai Hia, this option would follow the route taken in motorcycle Trek 19 (see details there). It could be drastically truncated by going only as far as Mae Rit Waterfall and then back to Mae Waen. This option might appeal to travellers intending to do no more than stay in Mae Waen at *Pan House*, but wishing to make one or more little excursions from Mae Waen. The expedition could be slightly recast by spending Night 1 of the actual trek not at Ton Ngiu Nuea, but below it and just short of it on the banks of the Rit river (Map 30). When I passed through, I made a mental note to myself that the spot where you cross the river en route for Ton Ngiu Nuea would make a beautiful and excellent place for doing a spot of wild camping. For this, of course, you would need a tent. From there you could backtrack via Kong Pae Tai and Kong Pae Nuea to Mae Waen, or you could exit from Kong Pae Nuea to the H108 road via Huai Goong, following in reverse a stretch done in Trek 19 (Map 32). Finally, the trek could be modified by proceeding from Ton Ngiu Nuea not to Huai Hia, Mae Pae Luang and back to Mae Waen, but by exiting directly to the H108 road. This possibility, which I have not checked, was mentioned to us at Ton Ngiu Nuea by the villagers there, who said that you reach the H108 at a mountain or place called Doi Liam.

Accessing the trek & staying at Mae Sariang and Mae Waen
It is probable that you will ultimately launch this trek and access Mae Waen from Mae Sariang, a strategy I recommend. However, you might do so from

faraway Chiang Mai, proceeding either by bus or hire motorcycle along Highway 108 via Chom Tong, Hot and Kong Loi. If you do this, set off not too late, as the distance is reasonably long. You journey some 90 kms to the town of Hot, and then a further 65 kms to the turn-off for Mae Waen (total ca 155 kms). From the turn-off it is a further final 5 kms to Mae Waen. As you sit on your Chiang Mai/Mae Sariang bus or on your motorbike you can gauge your proximity to the turn-off by the km-readings on the roadside 'milestones', which increase, starting at 0 km in Hot. The Mae Waen turn-off (left/S) is just after km-stone 65, i.e. 65 kms out from Hot.

If you are accessing the trek from Mae Sariang, you will have already established yourself in that westerly town not far from the Thai-Burmese border, having arrived there by bus or motorcycle or jeep either from Chiang Mai via Hot and the H108 road as outlined above, or from Mae Hong Son via Khun Yuam and the H108 road, or just conceivably from Mae Sot via Mae Salid and the dangerous H1085 (H105) road. **Mae Sariang** is an appealing comfortable little nest with everything the trekker-traveller needs in the way of guest houses, restaurants and shops. I have painted a fairly detailed picture of it in my adventure travelogue *Three Pagodas: A Journey down the Thai-Burmese Border* and so, not wanting to repeat all that, will confine myself here to essentials. The population of the place is an ethnic mix, reflected in the buildings, of Thais, Shan, Karen, Chinese and Muslim Indo-Burmese. The number of gold shops and flash Audis, Volvos and Mercedes, disproportionate for such a backwater town, betrays that it is a flourishing trading centre, living off a cross-border trade – channelled through nearby Mae Saam Laep – which sees consumer goods flowing from Thailand into Burma (specifically Kawthoolei or the Karen State) and teak and cattle coming in an endless stream out of Burma into Thailand. Of an evening you can see convoys of laden cattle trucks setting off from Mae Sariang on the overnight journey to the slaughterhouses of Chiang Mai and Bangkok. There is a big covered day market in town as well as a couple of small supermarkets, in which you can buy provisions for trekking. These days a regular trickle of *farang* or foreign travellers pass through Mae Sariang. They are mostly doing, either clockwise or anticlockwise, the Chiang Mai/Mae Hong Son loop and usually stay just a night in town, breaking their journeys. From Mae Sariang you can visit, if it is open to *farang*, the controversial border village of Mae Saam Laep, which is located W of town, down on the River Salween. This is the place through which much of the teak and cattle are funnelled. Traditionally it has been an important place for the rebel Karen military and for Burmese Karen in general, and it has been fought over by the Karen National Liberation Army and the Burma Army. It was recently attacked and half burnt to the ground by the DKBA, a pro-Rangoon Buddhist Karen splinter faction. Otherwise you can visit the ancient Lawa people and the Pwo Karen, as we are doing in Treks 18-23, to be found in the mountain country respectively NE and SE of Mae Sariang.

The town has quite a number of guest houses and hotels, but they are all, in my opinion, of mediocre quality. Most *farang* stay in one of the three following establishments: *Riverside GH*, *Mae Sariang GH* and *See View GH*. The tucked-away *Riverside*, overlooking the Yuam river, is a typical traveller hang-out and has a nice elevated reception-cum-eating area, but dismal rooms below stairs. Nearby *Mae Sariang GH* is an acceptable place with cold-water rooms around a compound. Accommodation at both the latter go for the usual prices. *See View*, across the River Yuam, which is not as good as it might at first appear, has rather seedy hot-shower rooms in a motel block for 120 baht (1998 prices) and a ranch-style restaurant. This is the place whose owners tout for business around town on motorbikes, intercepting *farang* and trying to lure them to *See View*. Once they get you there, they tend to overorganize you, beers are overpriced, and it is all a bit of a hard sell. On the plus side, the staff will pick you up from and run you to Mae Sariang's bus and *silor* stations free of charge in a truck. Currently, my preferred lodging in Mae Sariang is a place called *Lotus GH*, which is located towards the eastern end of the town's long main street, the E/W-running Wiang Mai Road, not far short of the big four-way junction at the bottom south-easterly end of Mae Sariang, where the ways go variously to Hot, Mae Hong Son and Mae Sot. Not really a proper GH, but just rooms to be rented by the night or hour, *Lotus* is set in the seedy run-down surroundings of a former brothel complex. But the rooms, although a tad prisonlike, are clean and OK, with their own bathroom and hot shower, and represent good value. The staff at reception will automatically try to overcharge you when you enquire about room prices. Ruthlessly bargain them down from 250 baht, 200 baht or whatever, even making as if to walk away – 150 baht (in 1999) is enough for a room here. Easily the best and most popular place to eat in Mae Sariang is *Intira Restaurant*, which can be found in the centre of town towards the western end of the long main street, near the central crossroads. The food in this no-nonsense establishment is very good, freshly cooked, quickly served and very fairly priced. Fill up your stomach here before heading off on a trek.

Accessing Mae Waen from Mae Sariang (Maps 29 & 34)
This is easily done. By public transport, take a bus bound for Hot or Chiang Mai from the bus station and proceed E along the H108 road 38 kms to the turn-off for Mae Waen. The ride is scenic, and you get many good views right (S) into the mountainous territory of the Pwo Karen. The Mae Waen turn-off lies just short of km-stone 65 and is marked by a *sala* or waiting hut and a sign for *Pan House*. You can anticipate the turning by counting downwards the km-markers. When you get to 66, you are nearly there. As you approach the turning, you cross a viaduct-style bridge, a turn right for a village, and an aerial in a forestry office compound. Get out of the bus at the Mae Waen turning – it may well stop there anyway. Apparently one or two *silor* (public-transport pick-ups) go everyday from Mae Sariang to Mae Waen at about 4pm. They will leave from the vicinity of the covered day

market, where you should ask about departures (preferably in advance). Presumably the *silor* complete the 43-km journey in 1-2 hrs before nightfall. A motorcycle makes a good way of conveniently accessing and exiting this trek. If you have transport of your own, proceed as above – as if you were on the bus – to the Mae Waen turn-off. My km readings start at km 0 at the complicated junction where Mae Sariang's main Wiang Mai Road joins the H108 Mae Hong Son/Hot highway at the bottom south-eastern end of town (the junction which also marks the beginning of the Mae Sot road). Incidentally, a large fuel station on the main highway just 1 km N of this junction makes a good place at which to tank up. Ride 38 kms to the Mae Waen turn-off, passing after 13 kms the turning left, which is the beginning of motorcycle Trek 21, and after 30.7 kms the turning right (by a police box), which is the start of biking Trek 19.

From the junction proceed S 5 kms to Mae Waen along a flattish dirt side-road, which gently descends to the valley, fording a stream shortly before Mae Waen (km 43). At a fork go right onto a cement road, then in the village right again, and left at a T-junction by a corner shop and *sala*. *Pan House* lies almost immediately on your right, slightly elevated (km 43.2). If you have used the bus to reach the Mae Waen turning, you can easily walk the 3¼ miles from the H108 road to *Pan House*, which should take you a long hour. Otherwise, try hitch-hiking. This should not be too difficult because a fair amount of traffic goes to Mae Waen or passes through it on the way to various villages beyond (including Bo Sa Li, Tung, Kong Koi, Ta Fai and Mae Pae Luang).

I feel somewhat apologetic about bringing reader-trekkers to **Mae Waen and *Pan House***. Both are unprepossessing. Mae Waen is just a rural Thai village like thousands of others. It has a little network of streets, shops and a *wat* or monastery-temple up on a hill. The people are mostly small farmers. One household even has a daughter who has married a *farang*. On the other hand, it is a quiet, authentic, backwater place, which makes a good retreat, where you can relax and from which you can observe a typical *khon muang* agricultural community with its leisurely pace of life, virtually unchanged for centuries. For the right kind of person it is as good a place as any just to 'hang out'. On the far side of Mae Waen, at a crossroads (see Map 34), the way left (E) goes to Hot and is an alternative access to Mae Waen; the way straight across (S) goes to the assimilated Lawa village of Bo Sa Li, beyond which a path goes to the Pwo Karen settlement of Mae Tien; and the way right heads approximately SW to a string of villages, including Tung, Kong Koi, San, Ta Fai and Mae Pae Luang (Map 33).

Pan House is a big old teak dwelling, raised on stilts, which is the home of the small family of Mr Pan. Mr Pan, real name Pan Kapaap, is really Mr Pan II. It was his cousin, the original Mr Pan, who put *Pan House* on the map, starting a little guest house in Mae Waen, encouraging travellers to drop by and stay, and organizing some trekking locally. This man, Weerapan, by all accounts spoke good English and was clued-up, but he went to work in Chiang Mai in the tourist/trekking industry. His place and *Pan House* were then taken over by Pan II. The latter, a small thin man, aged 33 in 1999, can also speak some – rudimentary – English, which he has learnt from a dictionary. But he is not really a replacement for the original Mr Pan. Pan II is basically a local farmer who does a small amount of guest-housing and trekking as a side line. He is married to a local Lawa girl, called Lam Duan, who in 1999 was aged 29. When I visited, they had one child, a small boy. At *Pan House* there is just one room for visitors, for which Mr Pan charges 50 baht per person. Presumably, if more guests turn up than can fit into this single wooden-box room, they have to sleep on the covered balcony. In 1998 breakfast was 20 baht, lunch 30, supper 40, and a coffee 10 baht. Do not expect much at this very modest, low-key place. Everything, from the room to the washing facilities to breakfast is extremely basic. Not that many visitors do call by, despite the sign up on the H108 road. In 1996, according to the visitors' book, only 6 people stayed, and in 1997 no one.

So far so good. Now, at the risk of sounding mean and gossipy, I come to the downside of *Pan House*. I can imagine that travellers coming here, lured by the sign up by the H108, might be decidedly disappointed, and the longer I stayed the more irritated I grew. Unless they have been improved meanwhile, the washing facilities consist of an old oil drum filled with icy cold water in a cramped outdoor cement cubicle with no lighting. Washing is with a plastic dipper, with which you pour the icy water over your body, and there are no nails or hooks in the cubicle on which to hang clothes, towels or washing bags. The 'bathroom' is primitive even by Thai and hill-tribe standards, and yet this is a place which masquerades as a guest house. During my visit, Mr Pan had to do everything, ready my room and prepare, cook and serve all the meals. His wife did precisely nothing, neither welcome her guest, sweep the dirty stairs, wash up the dirty cups lying around, or offer to see to my washing. A pleasant enough lass, she was ultimately just a peasant girl who in 4 or 5 days did nothing more than sit in the sun examining her fingernails. I don't think I have ever seen a person do less. Guests eat alone at *Pan House*, not with the family. A bonus is that free China tea is served with all meals, but the food was always the same: fried noodle, vegetable and fat meat, swimming in oil and too salty. Mr Pan confuses breakfast with lunch, and tried to charge me extra for things which were included, e.g. coffee at breakfast, and for things which he did not provide or which I had to buy at a village shop. You get the picture.

On the guiding front, things were not hugely different. As a trekking guide, the new Mr Pan normally charges 400 baht/day for one person and 600 baht per day for two, although I bargained him down a bit. He has a couple of treks near Mae Waen on his books, but is hazy about the wider area. When I took him on the trek described in this chapter, on paths and to villages not part of his stamping ground, he started talking about hiring Karen guides, showing little personal initiative and making himself redundant. Nor did he seem to have much stamina. When we reached Kong Pae Tai, after just 3½ hrs' walking, he wanted to call it a day and spend the

253

night there. After Kong Pae Nuea he did not appear to know the way, and there is a sense in which, after the first morning, I led him, asking the way in my broken Thai. But do not let these harsh detractions put you off staying at *Pan House* and trekking with Mr Pan. It remains a useful pied-à-terre, and he is a pleasant and obliging enough chap. Coming as a group of two or three people, you will be better able to laugh off the shortcomings. For this trek I paid Pan 800 baht for the trip, or 300 baht for each of the two full days spent walking and sleeping away from Mae Waen, plus 200 baht for the morning of Day 3. He did not carry my backpack, but did put our food into his. In the matter of guiding, it is usually not as easy to bargain down a regular Thai person as it is a hill-tribe man. As already indicated, you could consider dispensing with Mr Pan and his guiding services after Kong Pae Nuea, once he has shown you the way via Mae Rit Waterfall to that village. After Kong Pae Nuea you should be able to find the way yourself, and he can return to Mae Waen.

Some brief notes on the Pwo Karen
The Pwo Karen are a sub-group of the Karen people (the stress is on the second syllable: Ka-*ren*). The Karen race includes a number of sub-groups, including the S'gaw Karen, the Pwo Karen, the Karenni (or Kayah Karen, or 'Red Karen', or Bwe), the Pa-O (or 'Black Karen') and the Padaung 'Long Neck' Karen. In Thailand only the S'gaw and Pwo Karen are represented in substantial numbers, the latter three sub-groups existing in very small numbers. Accordingly, the S'gaw and the Pwo are the two major divisions of the Karen in Thailand, and are the subject of our interest, while the Karenni, Pa-O and Padaung are peripheral and need not detain us further (for an account of the celebrated 'Long Neck' Karen see my *Three Pagodas*, Chapter 7). It is estimated that the Karen race as a whole, which lives in Burma and Thailand, comprises some 4 million people, of which the vast majority inhabit Burma. Nearly 300,000 Karen live in Thailand, accounting for fully 50% of the country's ethnic minority or 'hill-tribe' population. As such, the Karen are easily the Kingdom's most populous highland tribal group. In Thailand, the Karen live all down the country's western border with Burma, broadly from the latitude of Chiang Rai town to that of Ratchaburi. Of these 300,000 'Thai' Karen, about 80% are S'gaw and 20% Pwo. Thailand's Pwo Karen live south of a line drawn between the towns of Mae Sariang and Hot (i.e. south of the H108 road). Some 20-30 Pwo villages lie immediately south of that line, and there are other pockets of Pwo Karen down in Tak and Kanchanaburi provinces. In Thailand the Karen are referred to by the Thais as 'Kariang/Kaliang' or just 'Yang'. Apparently they do not have a name, such as Karen, for their race as a whole. The S'gaw Karen call themselves 'the S'gaw people' and call their Pwo cousins 'the Pwo people'. However, the Pwo Karen know themselves as the 'Plong' or 'Plong Su' people.

TREK 18: MAE WAEN – TON NGIU – MAE PAE – MAE WAEN

The Karen languages are usually classified as belonging to the Karennic branch of either the Tibeto-Burman or Sino-Tibetan linguistic family. The S'gaw and Pwo sub-groups have their own languages, which are considered to be mutually unintelligible. The origins of the Karen are obscure, and are thought to lie in south-west China or south-east Tibet. The Karen may have come a very long time ago from the Gobi Desert area. Certainly they have been living for many centuries in Burma and even predate the Burmans. A sign of this long 'Burmese' residency and of the fact that they cannot have lived in Chinese space for a considerable period is that, generally speaking, Karen culture – unlike that of, say, the Yao or Hmong or Wa – shows no Sinitic influence or evidence of association with the Chinese. Rather it bears, if anything, traces of contact with the Burmese, Mon, Lawa and British. Following a residency of one or even two thousand years in 'Burma', some Karen began migrating eastwards, crossing the Salween river, evidently in the 18th century. Reaching territory that is now Thailand, specifically Mae Hong Son province, they found themselves entering land occupied by the ancient declining Lawa people (for a brief account of the Lawa see Trek 23). They managed to settle among and live peacefully with the Lawa, and today both S'gaw and Pwo Karen live cheek by jowl with the Lawa, continuing to get along with them and even intermarrying with them. You can see this both south and especially north of the H108 road. In these areas there is considerable evidence of Lawa influence in the costume, ornamentation and implements of the Karen. The ethnographers Paul and Elaine Lewis report that the Pwo, according to the testimony of their own folk tales, regard themselves as the guardians of the entire Karen culture. Further, they consider their more numerous S'gaw cousins to be, as it were, the male lineage of the Karen tribe, whereas they are the female lineage. Perhaps this accounts for the noticeable tendency of the Pwo, among both females and males, to beautify themselves in terms of their costume, accoutrements and cosmetics! In this brief account, it is the Pwo, rather that the S'gaw or the Karen as a whole, who interest us, and so in the following I shall confine myself basically to the Pwo. For an extended account of the S'gaw Karen such as live actually on the Thai-Burmese border, of the Karen in general, of their history and culture, and of their long-standing bloody struggle against Rangoon for an independent state, the reader is referred to Chapter 9 of my *Three Pagodas*.

The Pwo Karen, like their S'gaw counterparts, live in villages that can be sited both in the lowlands and in the low highlands. The Karen do not live high up, like many Akha, Hmong and Lua (Htin). Most Pwo just south of the H108 road, around the village of Mae Pae Luang, live at a medium elevation of around 500 metres above sea level, although you can find a few in valley villages such as Ta Fai. Pwo settlements, like S'gaw, tend not to move, as do traditionally those of many migratory hill tribes, but are basically permanent. Some Karen villages are one, two or more hundred years old. This is because (or is perhaps the cause of the fact that) they practise wet rice cultivation in established terraced paddies even with irrigation, and grow orchards. There is a sense in which the Karen, not living high up, not continually moving their habitations on, and not relying mostly on slash-and-burn agriculture and on dry rice cultivation, are not highlanders or a hill-tribe at all, but sedentary lowland farmers. Pwo houses are raised off the ground on stilts, are made of wood and split bamboo with grass roofs, and have spacious, partly covered verandas that are used for preparing food, sometimes eating, chatting, weaving, and accommodating guests overnight.

Most households are nuclear, consisting of a husband and wife plus their unmarried children, but not three-generational, as in other ethnic minorities. Marriage is monogamous and for life, divorce and adultery are frowned upon, and pre-marital sex is abnormal. Kinship, unusually among the hill tribes, is matrilineal, and residence matrilocal. As indicated, the Pwo, like the Karen in general, tend to practise an ecologically informed crop rotation, rather than slash-and-burn agriculture, and where feasible prefer to develop terraced wet rice fields. They raise livestock, for sacrificing, eating and selling, but do not traditionally, like the Karen as a whole, grow opium. All Karen women are consummate weavers, creating their cloth, from which they make their clothes, shoulder bags and blankets, on simple backstrap looms. The Karen are the only tribal people in Thailand (with the exception of a very few Lawa) who own and use elephants, although I cannot say that I saw any evidence of this in the Pwo villages around Mae Pae Luang. All over Thailand and South-East Asia the Karen are famed as mahouts, and in Karen society elephant owners enjoy high status. In my opinion, based on extensive travelling over many years among the S'gaw all down the Thai-Burmese border, the Karen are the most hospitable of all Thailand's minority peoples. However, based on my limited experience of the Pwo, I cannot say that this applies to them. Many border S'gaw, I have found, will give you food and possessions down to their last penny, but the Pwo, it seemed to me in many cases, would not give except in exchange for money. This impression was backed up by a missionary I met who has worked several years with the Pwo. He said of the Pwo that they would not do anything for nothing, and told me the story of a Pwo man who travelled with a gravely ill friend to Mae Sariang hospital, but who would only give the friend a life-saving transfusion of his blood if the friend paid him handsomely for it! Karen hospitality is at its peak, needless to say, during their New Year celebrations, which are in February.

A key figure in a Karen village, much more so than the headman, who often has little more to do than fulfil the thankless task of interfacing with the Thai authorities, is the priest or shaman, whose position is essentially hereditary. He is the ritual and spiritual leader of the village, fixes dates for and officiates at important annual village ceremonies, watches over the moral conduct of the villagers, requires sacrifices when the moral code has been broken, arbitrates in disutes, has a say in the allocation of fields, and generally arranges for and guarantees the harmony of the community, a striving for and the preservation of harmony both within the village and between the village and the spirit world being a basic theme of S'gaw and Pwo life and a paramount desire among the Karen. The shaman is, of course, an animist, and most Karen in Thailand, including the Pwo, are animists. Some Karen down the Thai-Burmese border and in Burma are Christians, especially Baptists, and missionaries have had a long and successful record of converting the Karen. Most Karen in Burma are Buddhists. The Karen of both Burma and Thailand have experienced a number of millennial and messianic movements, and their culture has spawned religious cults. These movements and cults capitalize on the general feeling of the Karen of inferiority, of impoverishment, of being downtrodden, and of having an orphan status, by promising a future of peace, prosperity, harmony, happiness, fulfilment, and a triumphant our-day-will-come deliverance.

The most striking and perhaps interesting aspect of the Pwo Karen, especially from the trekker's point of view, is their costume, which is different from that of the S'gaw. Unmarried Pwo girls wear a long white cotton shift, embellishing it more heavily than S'gaw maidens do their shifts. The adornment is in red or shades of pink and often takes the form of an all-over lozenge pattern on the lower portion of the dress, or panels across the collar bones and breast, or yoke-like strips down the shoulders. Girls used to wear their hair long and tied in a knot on top of the head, like their mothers, but now they mostly wear it short in the style of the ubiquitous bobcut of all schoolgirls in Thailand. Women, as said, wear their hair long and twisted up in a topknot, concealing the bun under a turban often of white or green or red material, or of terrycloth in any colour. When they are not wearing a turban, their hair is often generously decorated with silver hair clips.

Married Pwo women wear sarongs and sleeveless or short-sleeved overblouses or smocks. The sarongs are tube skirts of a plain red or cerise or pink colour with more or less horizontal banding. The smocks are typically in wine red and often with bold patterning. All the Pwo women I saw in the Mae Pae Luang area had smocks that were a fairly plain red except for the yokes, which were ornately patterned. They also wore detached black sleeves to protect their arms, and Akha-style 'anklets' on their lowers legs from knee to ankle. Their arms are laden with dozens of twisted bronze or silver bracelets, worn in two places: on the forearm, especially above the wrist, and on the upper arm, above the elbow. In this respect, the Pwo are reminiscent of the Padaung 'Long-Neck' women.

These days, most Pwo men simply wear casual western-style clothing, such as has been largely adopted by both tribal and Thai men all over the Kingdom. Traditionally and on special occasions they wear sleeveless V-necked smocks in red or red-and-white, and a sarong or Thai peasant-style trousers. An old Pwo man I stayed with in Ton Ngiu Nuea wore such a shirt in dark brick red with short sleeves. Traditionally, young Pwo bachelors have worn their hair long and pulled across the head to be tied at one side, rather in the fetching manner of the male cultists of the Karen jungle sect at Lae Tong Ku, south of Um Pang. Many Pwo men are densely tattooed from waist to knee, and some women are tattooed too.

All the Pwo women I saw during Treks 18 and 19 wore around their necks multiple strands of silver beads reaching down to about mid-chest or elbow level. They also sported chokers of black or white beads, from the front of which a furry tassel sometimes dangled. Some women wore earrings with long dangles of multicoloured fluff and pompoms. Altogether, Pwo women cut quite a dash, especially when got up in their best costume and liberally made up with lipstick, which they even apply to their cheeks to make marks like duelling scars. No self-respecting Karen, either Pwo or S'gaw, and no matter whether man or woman, would be seen without their little silver-embellished tobacco pipe and, going walkabout, without their shoulder bag. Pipe-smoking, combined with betel-chewing, leads to a favourite habit of the Karen, rather off-putting to the *farang* trekker, of spitting through the cracks in the slatted floors of their houses!

*

Trekking route detail
Day 1: Mae Waen – Mae Rit w/f – Kong Pae Nuea – Kong Pae Tai – Mae Rit – Ton Ngiu Nuea

Time log

0 hrs	Set off (we started at 10am), leaving Mae Waen village by its SW corner near a rice field, some tall bamboos and a well.
	Cross field, a stream and a second field, heading W.
	Walk uphill, bearing SW along a streamlet through some young trees, and then W.
	Path joins from right.
	Direction settles down to SW.
25 mins	Come to a farm track from Tung village. Join it, turning right, and follow it.
	Go along a cement conduit round the top end of a cabbage field, before swinging left across paddy fields and a valley.
	Cut across fields and valley to the Mae Rit or Rit river.
35 mins	Reach River Rit.
	Go upstream along northern bank.
	Path high up, right.
	Left: mini waterfall.
¾ hr	Reach **Mae Rit Waterfall**, a single fall ca 50 ft high. It is a pleasant spot, and you could spend an enjoyable day out here from Mae Waen, paddling and having a picnic or just whiling the hours away. We came across three Pwo Karen women shrimping. Characteristically, their arms were covered in bracelets and they were smoking silver-banded pipes.

1 hr	After a 15-min rest, set off again, crossing the river and climbing very steeply up in the corner on the left (S) side of the w/f. You scramble up a ravine and round to the top end of the fall. (Apparently there is an easier way up, going round the right side of the w/f.) Proceed upriver.
1 hr 25 mins	Leave river by left side.

Just after a bend, an indistinct short-cut path soon leads up to an irrigation water channel.

Go right ('upstream') one minute to a little log bridge, cross it, and follow path up.

Come to farm track. Go left, then right.

On a knoll turn right and come to a:

1 hr 40 mins Dirt road. Left goes down to Kong Koi village, right goes up to the main 108 road. Go right and up.

Due E (90°): view of Mae Waen.

By a spirit house go left.

A short cut branches right. You can take it or stay on the main route – they meet up again. We followed the main route.

Proceed up through a conifer wood.

After the hot slog up the track, stop for a well-earned 10-min rest in the shade of the trees.

In an open area, don't go left, which is a way to rice fields. Follow main route, the path levelling off.

2 hrs 40 mins Due S: unobstructed view of Mae Pae Luang in distance, where the Night 2 is spent.

2¾ hrs View SW (220°) across valley to Kong Pae Nuea, which is not far away now.

Come into more open scenery.

2 hrs 50 mins Just after a bend to the right in the main track, a path descends left (220°), unmarked by any sign. Take it, climbing steeply down.

Path skirts round hillside, then climbs up a bit to reach:

3¼ hrs **Kong Pae Nuea.**

Apparently called 'Glom Pae Nuea' in Karen, Kong Pae Nuea is the northern part (*nuea* = north) of the double village of Kong Pae, the southern part of Kong Pae Tai (*tai* = south) lying nearby to the south. Mr Pan and I arrived here at 1.15pm, meaning that Kong Pae Nuea is about 3 hrs of hiking from Mae Waen (excluding longer stops). It is a Pwo Karen place and in early 1998 still had no electricity. We spent an hour in the village, having lunch and cooking up packets of instant noodles in someone's house. On the west side of Kong Pae Tai there is a health centre and three water tanks beside a crossroads. At the crossroads (see Maps 30 & 32), as you face roughly west with the health centre on your left and the village behind you, the way right goes up to Huai Goong (Kung) and the main H108 road, the way left goes directly to Huai Hia, and straight across (our route) proceeds to Kong Pae Tai and Ton Ngiu. The way going from right to left (N to S, from Huai Goong to Huai Hia) is part of the motorcycle way taken in Trek 19. It is also a (poor) vehicular access to Huai Hia as well as Ton Ngiu. From the crossroads and from the track to Kong Pae Tai, you can see many of the remaining villages on the trek as well as the route linking them. They lie dotted as if around a huge bowl, and the route quasi skirts round the rim of this bowl in an anticlockwise direction. Kong Pae Tai lies nearest, Ton Ngiu Nuea is beyond it to the left, Huai Hia lies left of that, and Mae Pae Luang can be seen further left in the far distance.

4 hrs 20 mins Allowing an hour for lunch and looking around in Kong Pae Nuea, set off again (we left at 2.20pm). Go straight across the crossroads, heading roughly W, and walk along a contouring dirt road (Map 30). Path joins from right –possibly it goes up to the main 108 road.

4¾ hrs After just 25 mins reach **Kong Pae Tai**, the southern part of Kong Pae. The day we came here, the Pwo Karen were celebrating the last day of their New Year, and we saw many fine costumes. This was the place beyond which Pan did not know the way. He wanted already to stop for the night. When I insisted we go on, he then wanted to hire a Karen guide from the village, but because of the celebrations none was interested, so we could find nobody. I suggested we could find the onward way ourselves, which we did. If we were able to do this, so can you! We spent 25 mins deliberating in Kong Pae Tai.

5 hrs 10 mins Leave the village at its far end (we set off again at 3.10pm).
At a fork go left past the school.
At another fork go right and past a pond.
The path skirts the left side of a ridge.
At a further fork go right, maintaining your height and keeping always to the bigger or main path.

5 hrs 40 mins Walk along crest of ridge, proceeding SE.
Far below you on your right side is a river, the Mae Rit.
Branch right off the ridge crest, to descend slowly to the river.

6 hrs 10 mins In valley bottom reach **Mae Rit**, here flowing from E to W. The spot, which is downstream of Mae Rit Waterfall, would make a nice campsite. If you are more interested in wild camping than staying in hill-tribe villages, consider stopping for the night here, pitching a tent (if you have one), getting a fire going, and washing in the river.

6 hrs 20 mins After a 10-min rest, cross the river and set off on the path directly opposite. You climb up a well-trodden way. It is a killer ascent, especially at the end of the day's trek, so take things nice'n'easy.
The path skirts round the left side of a shoulder.
A little path joins from the right.
Fork left, cross a trickle, and continue uphill. We went slightly astray here in a maze of paths. But by now you will already be able to hear the sounds of cowbells and human voices. Make for the sounds, which are near and among the houses of:

7 hrs 10 mins **Ton Ngiu Nuea**, which we reached at 5.10pm.

The Pwo Karen place of Ton Ngiu Nuea is the northern part of the double village of Ton Ngiu, its southern counterpart Ton Ngiu Tai lying about 2 kms away to the south. In 1998, when I visited, the settlement consisted of some 80 houses spilled down a hillside. I was surprised at how backward things were. There was still no electricity, most of the dwellings were of wood and split bamboo with grass roofs, and they had no toilets. From Kong Pae Tai the village could be reached only on foot, although from Huai Hia it could be accessed by a problematic motorcycle track. I was also taken aback by how 'hill-tribish' everything was with these Pwo Karen, just as I was to find the situation to be in nearly all the other Pwo villages I subsequently visited. I was surprised because all the other Karen I had ever visited had always seemed to me relatively developed, 'civilized', urbane and informed about the modern world. But then these other Karen had been the S'gaw Karen of the Thai-Burmese border area. In keeping with this distinction, the Pwo of Ton Ngiu Nuea spoke a dialect of Karen that even to my untrained ear sounded different from that of the border S'gaw Karen.

In their daily grind as impoverished hill-farmers, the Pwo of Ton Ngiu Nuea were friendly towards me and so interested that, when I took an evening wash at one of the standpipes dotted around their village, they gathered in a fair-sized crowd to gaze at the *farang* stripped to the waist and flannelling himself. I don't think I have ever been so much stared at while washing on a trek, not even by the Lua, which is saying something because the Lua themselves are champion gawpers at *farang* visitors. The attention was rather strange because I learned that *farang* trippers sometimes come to the village as part of an organized tour from Chiang Mai. But evidently they do not stay, but move on to look at the nearby cave. A sign of the place being tainted by such 'tourists' was that villagers tried to sell me a Coke at the exorbitant price of 20 baht. I have not been to the cave, but it is said to be a large one, some 500 metres long, with a stream going through it, and capacious enough to drive an elephant through it. Check it out!

In Ton Ngiu Nuea, look for a place to put up your tent for the night, or get invited to sleep on the platform of some villager's house. I stayed overnight in the house of an old Pwo couple, Lung Jor and his costumed wife Wila. It was still the last day of the Karen New Year festival, and in every house home-brewed rice whisky was being drunk. Mr Pan and I had to do the rounds, tippling in every shack, although Lung Jor's *lao kao* was the cleanest, strongest and best. It was in Ton Ngiu Nuea that I discovered that most Pwo don't like to be photographed, a pattern that repeated itself in the other Pwo villages we passed through. If you want pictures of Pwo Karen women and men in their colourful and fetching costume, you may well have to pay them.

Day 2: Ton Ngiu Nuea – Huai Hia – Mae Pae Noi – Mae Pae Luang

The second day is the easiest, comprising – if you follow my schedule – about 5¼ hrs of trekking (including stops) or just 3½ hrs of actual marching. You hike first 50 mins to Huai Hia, then 1½ hrs to Mae Pae Noi, and finally an hour to Mae Pae Luang. We started from Ton Ngiu Nuea at 9.45am and arrived in Mae Pae Luang just after 3pm.

261

Time log

0 hrs	Set off from Ton Ngiu Nuea on a path that leaves the village on its S side and which curves left (E).
	Soon you can enjoy a nice view back to Ton Ngiu Nuea and your overnight stop. The white building above the village is a small school, which in 1998 had one teacher. If you look ENE (70°), you can see Huai Hia, the next port of call, and behind it, in line, Kong Koi in the far distance, also on your route.
35 mins	View due N to Kong Pae Tai with its outlying school.
¾ hr	At a fork (both ways go to Huai Hia) go left on the lower way.
50 mins	Arrive at the Pwo Karen village of **Huai Hia** (apparently also known as Huai Kia in Karen). We spent ¾ hr there, snacking and watching girls weaving.

1 hr 35 mins	Leave Huai Hia by a path going up due S from two cylindrical water tanks.
	Follow main path.
	Path joins from left.
	Proceed down and curve left.
1 hr 55 mins	View of hidden rice fields on valley floor by a small river.
	Now take a grey-brown dirt path which zigzags steeply up S/SSE on the far side (but not the yellow-brown path branching left/E, which goes to some fields).
	Fork right.
2¼ hrs	Reach top of first of two hills that have to be crossed this morning (we got here at midday).
	Follow path down, climbing round right side of second hill.
	At a derelict threshing hut, go straight, not left.
2½ hrs	Reach top of second hill. Looking back (270-290°), two sets of houses visible in trees are Huai Hia Noi or Little Huai Hia. Looking onward (70°), you can see Kong Koi school and villages extending towards Mae Waen.
	Follow farm track a few metres and turn right (W) to proceed along crest of ridge (farm track).
	Cut through to village. Path dips a bit, crossing a streamlet (or follow the higher farm track).
	Come to new school (left) and:
3 hrs 5 mins	the Pwo Karen village of **Mae Pae Noi** or Little Mae Pae (*noi* = small, *parva*). It is a small scruffy place amid trees, with vehicular access. Arriving here at 12.50pm, we stopped for 1 hr 20 mins, eating lunch and snoozing, before continuing at 2.10pm.

4 hrs 25 mins	Leave Mae Pae Noi by dirt road at bottom of village by big clumps of giant bamboos.
	Walk for 50 mins some 4 kms along the dirt road.
5¼ hrs	Reach a crossroads, which is just 2 mins from Mae Pae Luang (see Map 31). Left goes to Ta Fai, Kong Koi, Tung and Mae Waen. Not used by us on this walking trek (we exit Mae Pae Luang for Mae Waen by another route), it is the new 'main' way between Mae Pae

Luang and Mae Waen and the outside world. Right goes to Pa Yoe and many other Pwo Karen villages. It is the 'main' way to Huai Hia and Ton Ngiu, used by motorcycles and 4WD vehicles. (On Trek 19 we bike across this crossroads from right to left on our way from Huai Hia via Mae Pae Luang to Ta Fai and Mae Waen.) Straight over brings you after a couple of mins to the centre of Mae Pae Luang. In 1998 Mr Pan and I were stunned at this crossroads to come across three turbanned *farang* kids roaming around on bicycles and speaking fluent Karen. It turned out that they were the children of a US missionary family stationed in Mae Pae Luang.

5¼ hrs   Reach **Mae Pae Luang** (we got here at 3pm).

Mae Pae Luang or Big Mae Pae (*luang* = large, *magna*) is another Pwo Karen place and, as its name suggests, is indeed an extensive village. Numbering some 600-700 inhabitants, it is said to be the largest Karen settlement in Mae Hong Son province, but that might mean Pwo Karen. After the likes of Ton Ngiu Nuea and Huai Hia, it is a developed well-sorted place, with an unexpected cement main street and side roads, and a regular little shop in the centre stocked with soft drinks and snacks. In its elevated position, the village offers fine views. If you look broadly E, you can see across the valley the villages of Ta Fai, Kong Koi and Tung, all on our route, and if you search NNE (30°), you can espy far off the broad hump of Doi Intanon, Thailand's highest mountain. In the village, enjoy the spectacle of the Pwo Karen women. Many have the big, broad, rather plain, square-jawed faces characteristic of the Karen, smoke little silver-embellished pipes, have their hair twisted up into a topknot under a turban of green material or of any-colour terrycloth, and wear a striking costume featuring a wine-red smock and skirt (unmarried girls have a long white shift), swathes of silver-bead necklaces, and multiple bronze bangles around their arms.

When you come to look for somewhere to spend the night, try the headman, who has a large house some distance from the central shop (I have not stayed there, so cannot comment on it), or erect your tent in a quiet corner, perhaps even on the patch of ground beside the shop and just down from the missionaries' house. If you strike gold, you might just get invited to stay and/or eat at the missionaries', although clearly you should not go angling for this. Both the missionary parents and the children are much in evidence in the village, and as a visiting *farang* you will soon be spotted. They will be able to point you to the headman's house, to a spot where you can camp, or to the house of one of their flock who might be willing to put you up. In 1998 I stayed at the missionaries' house and was made most welcome. Buddhist local boy Mr Pan, far too frightened to sleep in the house of *farang*, let alone of Christian evangelists, put up at the headman's.

The missionary family in Mae Pae Luang comprises Scott McManigle, his wife Annette, their three young boys, and a little Pwo Karen girl they have adopted. They are an American family from the Florida New Tribes Mission and have been in the village for eight years (in 1999). Scott, who is known locally by his Karen name of Jowan (Jor Waan), and Annette are youngish people, affable, engaging, extremely hospitable, and not at all the sanctimonious goody-goodies that you might expect of missionaries. They have some 50 converts in the village, and besides their pastoral work are involved in all sorts of laudable projects to help the Pwo. They have started a chicken egg producing scheme, are initiating a fish farm, run a small dispensary, have helped cut tracks to outlying settlements, and ferry sick tribals to hospital in their people-carrier vehicle. The little Pwo girl they have adopted was virtually an orphan. When her mother died, there was no one to look after her, her father being an opium addict. She is a sweetie-pie and a scream. Rattling along in the Pwo language, she suddenly switches to American, and out of her little hill-tribe mouth you hear around the house 'Mommy' and 'Daaady'. If you need help or information about local routes, the area or the Pwo Karen, apply to Scott, who is knowledgeable in this respect. His house, an extensive wooden affair, is just up from the centre of the village and the shop, and is easily identifiable by its enduro bikes, truck and people carrier. It was helpful Scott who, when he heard that I was having difficulty getting photographs of Pwo women in their best costume, went to some trouble to organize for me two Mae Pae Luang girls, Na Moeng Mi and Na Pi Kloe (*Na* means something like 'Mrs').

In the McManigle household I was treated to the guest bedroom, far better than any guest house, and while Mr Pan was no doubt picking at sticky rice and chilli dip at the headman's, I was regaled by Annette with a supper of spaghetti bolognaise, salad, two kinds of dressing and fresh real coffee, and a breakfast of pancakes and maple syrup – a veritable feast after the poor trekking fare of the past two days. It is amazing what you can stumble upon in the wilds! As I took my fill in the kitchen of these victuals, I could not help smiling at the corny homey signs on the walls: 'The McManigle Homestead est. 1986', 'Mom's Kitchen Open 24 hrs', 'Bathroom: Clean Water 5 cents extra', 'Home Sweet Home' and 'May God Bless'.

Day 3: Mae Pae Luang – Ta Fai – Kong Koi – Tung – Mae Waen

On the third day, which involves walking only in the morning, you are on the home stretch. Setting off late at 10.30am (because I got held up taking photos of Pwo Karen costumes), we hiked 1¾ hrs from Mae Pae Luang to Kong Koi, and then 35 mins from Kong Koi on to Mae Waen, arriving there at 1.15pm. Thus we trekked 2 hrs 20 mins altogether, or about 2¾ hrs including food and rest stops.

Time log

0 hrs   With the little shop at your back and Scott's house on your left, set off on the main village street to leave Mae Pae Luang descending broadly N.
At a bend, leave the cement road and continue on down in a northerly direction on a track. You are following the old way to Ta Fai.
At a fork, take the path – it subsequently rejoins the farm track.

	Fork left, down path, with a rice paddy on your left.
	Fork left again, heading for a white cliff feature.
	Cross streamlet and proceed down to a riverbed.
25 mins	Reach riverbed.
30 mins	Reach lower white cliff and a mine with a house.
	Follow dirt road from mine.
	Come to second mining camp.
	At a junction, by a *sala*, go straight (not left).
	Branch left away from main dirt road onto path – path rejoins dust road further on.
1½ hrs	Arrive at **Ta Fai** village.
	Cross the Mae To river.
	Not walking on the road, we follow an old direct way to Kong Koi, which emerges at a rickety bridge just short of Kong Koi on the way to San village (see Maps 33 & 34).
1¾ hrs	Reach centre of **Kong Koi** village (also known as Go Goi). There is at least one noodle soup shop in Kong Koi. Go on, 'spoil' yourself with an early lunch (we stopped for 25 mins doing this).
2 hrs 10 mins	Now leave Kong Koi, following the main way (see Map 34). You cross a river and a bridge, on the right side of which, set back, is a small dam and weir. Then you cross open fields to arrive, just 10 mins from Kong Koi, at:
2 hrs 20 mins	the village of **Tung** (Toong), apparently an assimilated Lawa place. Pass through Tung, turning right at a T-junction by a *wat*, and then crossing another bridge.
	At a fork not far beyond the bridge, go left on a short cut straight to Mae Waen (or, at the fork, go straight on to a crossroads, where you turn left, to arrive by an indirect way likewise at Mae Waen). After 25 mins of walking from Tung, arrive by the 'back door' at:
2¾ hrs	**Mae Waen.**

Exiting the trek (Maps 34 & 29)

If you arrive back at Mae Waen late morning or, as we did, at lunchtime, you have the whole afternoon – plenty of time – to exit the trek. This applies regardless of whether you have your own transport or not. Alternatively, you could hang out another night in Mae Waen at *Pan House*, exiting on the morning of the next day. Probably you will exit by returning to Mae Sariang, but you could, especially if you depart the next day, exit to Chiang Mai or even, if you are on a motorcycle, start out on another trip, for example Trek 20 or 21. Make your way from Mae Waen back up to the main 108 highway, crossing the fords just beyond the village. If you walk, it will take you 1-1½ hrs to cover the 5.2 kms, hiking fully laden along the hot dirt road gently uphill. You could try hitch-hiking – every day a trickle of traffic leaves Mae Waen or passes through it from outlying villages, most of it bound for either Mae Sariang or Hot. If you are exiting in the early morning, a couple of blue *silor* likewise leave Mae Waen every day bound for Mae Sariang and Hot. They set off bright and early, around 7 or 8am. Listen for the tooting of their horns (a sign that they are about to depart), or get Mr Pan to tell them that you want a ride. Once you are up on the H108 road by the *sala*, go left (W) for Mae Sariang and right (E) for Hot and Chiang Mai. Regular buses go past in each direction. Take the first one available, or try hitch-hiking. It is 40 scenic kms or a long hour's ride to the centre of Mae Sariang and 65 kms to Hot (150 to Chiang Mai). If you intend to proceed straight to Trek 20, go right (E) from the Mae Waen turning 10 kms to Kong Loi; to start Trek 21, go left (W) 25 kms to a right-hand turn-off (13 kms short of Mae Sariang), marked by a *sala* and many signs.

Trek 19

H108/Huai Goong – Kong Pae Nuea – Huai Hia – Huai Mu Nuea – Mae Pae Luang – Ta Fai – Kong Koi – Tung – Mae Waen – H108/km-stone 65

Parameters

trekking mode:	by motorcycle
trek time:	can be done as a one-day round-trip from Mae Sariang; 2 days/1 night if you stay overnight in a village
trek distance:	core trek offroad from Huai Goong turn-off to Mae Waen turn-off: 42+ kms; from Mae Sariang to Mae Sariang: 114+ kms
degree of difficulty:	for average riders moderately difficult and taxing in places, for skilled bikers some nice dirt trail riding
tent:	only necessary if you break the journey and stay overnight e.g. at Huai Mu
map(s):	see 29, 32, 33, 31 & 34

Overview & strategy

This trek, which is launched from the westerly town of Mae Sariang, is a motorcycle hike that ventures into little frequented mountainous territory inhabited by colourful Pwo Karen people, a sub-group of the Karen tribe. It is the second of two outings heading ESE from Mae Sariang into Pwo country, the first being walking Trek 18. The two treks intertwine and to some extent duplicate each other, so that if you have hoofed Trek 18, you will probably not want to ride Trek 19 (unless you want to return to the quarter to make further explorations on two wheels), and vice versa. At the same time the trek is the second of altogether six expeditions made into the mountains east of Mae Sariang (Treks 18-23 inclusive), and the first of a series of five motorcycle trips (Treks 19-23 inclusive) in the same area. It has to be said that the mountain plateau lying SE of Mae Sariang, peopled by the Pwo Karen, and the mountain plateau lying NE of the town, peopled by the Lawa and also by regular Karen, lend themselves especially to exploration by motorcycle. This is because these two quarters south and north of the 108 Mae Sariang/Hot highway are extensive and because the many villages in them are linked by a network of dirt roads and trails that are eminently bikable, but which are not very sensibly walked.

The trek can be done as a round trip from Mae Sariang in one day. You ride 32 kms from the centre of Mae Sariang east along Highway 108 to a junction at the village of Huai Goong (see Map 29). Then, turning right (south), you proceed on a dirt road to Kong Pae Nuea. From here you continue on a (in 1999) deteriorating dirt trail to Huai Hia (see Map 32), after which you ride along ridgetops towards the triple Pwo Karen village of Huai Mu, with its northern, middle and southern parts, in any of which you could stay. Now you make your way via Mae Pae Luang, where you could also stay, to Ta Fai (see Map 33), after which you pass through the more regular rural Thai villages of Kong Koi, Tung and Mae Waen, at the last of which you could stay at *Pan House*, before rejoining the main 108 road and exiting the offroad dirt part of the trek at km-marker 65 (see Map 34). The offroad loop (from Huai Goong to km-stone 65) is a manageable 42 kms long, excluding any side trips to, for example, Huai Mu. From the H108/Mae Waen junction you ride 40 kms back to Mae Sariang centre (see Map 29), making a total distance for the trek of at least 114 kms.

The main reasons to undertake this trek are, of course, to do some biking, but also to be among the Pwo Karen, who have some 20-30 settlements in this corner of northern Thailand. You could visit the Pwo at Kong Pae (either the northern or southern part), at Huai Hia, at Huai Mu, at Mae Pae Luang, or at any other Pwo village on or off the route. The best way to come into closer contact with the Pwo Karen, or with any other hill tribe, is to spend a night in one of their villages. This will extend the trek from the inside of one day to approximately 2 days and 1 night. If you decide on this option, you could camp in a tent, in which case you should take a tent with you, or you could stay in a villager's house, in which case you should take a mosquito net. Naturally, you will also need a sleeping bag and food.

Besides extending the trek timewise, intercalating a night or longer in a Pwo habitation, you could extend it distancewise by taking in the Pwo double village of Ton Ngiu (see Map 32) and/or any one of the three parts of Pwo Huai Mu: Huai Mu Nuea (*nuea* = north), Huai Mu Glang (*glang* = middle), and Huai Mu Tai (*tai* = south). More generally, you could use the route detail given below for this trek as a basis for further exploration of the trails and villages in the area. There are a score or more of Pwo settlements locally, interconnected by a labyrinthine network of dozens of motorcycle trails, which means that you could extend the trek at will. As yet, I have only scratched the surface in a wider exploration of these villages and trails, but the locality looks promising as an area in which to roam around on a bike. After the trek, instead of returning to Mae Sariang, you could either exit to Chiang Mai, perhaps by proceeding via Mae Chaem and across Doi Intanon National Park, or you could embark on Trek 20 or possibly 21. You would need to be properly prepared before starting out on one of these longer expeditions.

I did this trek in January 1999 in the company of Nittaya Tananchai and Doug Boynton. We broke the journey in Huai Mu Nuea, staying overnight in a villager's house. We rode on two little 100-cc Honda Dream bikes, hired from Mae Hong Son for 150 baht per day. As far as I am aware, there is as yet no motorcycle rental place in Mae Sariang, so, to do the trip by bike, you will have to bring a machine from Mae Hong Son or Chiang Mai. I am not at all sure whether it would be possible or advisable to try this trek by bicycle. The way is in places very steep and rough. I suppose tough guys with sturdy mountain bikes might manage things. For average to experienced motorcyclists, the (offroad) route is moderately difficult. There is only one undeniably difficult passage, which (in 1999) comes between Kong Pae Nuea and Huai Hia. Here you must negotiate a short disastrous downgrade. We ended up wheeling our bikes down. If you can reach Huai Hia, the worst is already behind you, and you should be able to manage the rest. You can alleviate the problem by doing the trek backwards (it is always easier riding up steep gradients than down), or avoid it by accessing the trek via Mae Waen and returning the same way. Skilled offroad riders with the right kind of machine (e.g. 200-cc enduro) and dirt freaks will find the trek a pleasant trip out. Make sure you leave Huai Goong with a full tank. As you come from Mae Sariang, there is a fuel station (left side) not far short of the Huai Goong junction.

About Mae Sariang and accommodation + food there
Trek 19, as said, is best launched from Mae Sariang, with its guest houses, shops, restaurants and other facilities. For information on the town, on staying in guest houses there, and on eating out, see Trek 18 under 'Accessing the trek'.

Brief notes on the Pwo Karen
For some outline information on this sub-group of the Karen, likewise see Trek 18.

*

Trekking route detail
As this is a round-trip trek from Mae Sariang, I will include here, in the main trekking route detail, the details of accessing the core offroad part of the trip, i.e. along Highway 108 as far as Huai Goong (and also, later, the details of exiting the core part of the trip, from the Mae Waen turn-off back along the 108 road to Mae Sariang). From the centre of Mae Sariang, ride up the town's long W/E-running Wiang Mai Road, past *Intira Restaurant* (right), the post office (right) and *Lotus Guest House* (right), to the complicated 'crossroads' at the far south-eastern end. Left goes N on the 108 road to Khun Yuam and Mae Hong Son. Just a few hundred metres up here is a big fuel station, a good place to tank up. Right goes a great distance down the Thai-Burmese border to Mae Salid and Mae Sot. Straight (eastish) is our route along the 108 highway towards Hot and Chiang Mai.

From the 'crossroads' proceed E along the H108 road 30.7 kms to the turn-off for Huai Goong (or Huai Kung) (see Map 29). The ride is scenic, and you get many good views right (S) into the mountainous territory of the Pwo Karen. You pass, 13 kms out from the crossroads, at km-stone 90 (measured from Hot), a turning left (N) for Om Long, Pa Pae and other villages. The junction is marked by a *sala* or waiting hut and many signs, and is the beginning of motorcycle Trek 21. Between this junction and the Huai Goong junction there is another fuel station (left), at which you should tank up if you have not already done so. Top up anyway. At a distance of 30.7 kms from the crossroads, or some 32 kms from Mae Sariang centre, you arrive at the Huai Goong turning. It is marked by a police box, a *sala*, and a couple of shops, one of which serves a noodle soup. The shops are part of Huai Goong village, which lies not far to the rear. It should not take you more than an hour to reach this junction. Do not leave the 108 road to embark on the core part of our trek without a fairly full tank of petrol. Undoubtedly you can top up at one of the shops near the police box or in Huai Goong village.

Turn into the side road (junction by police box = km 0) and proceed a short distance, before branching left onto a new dirt road (see Map 32). In 1999 this was still under construction and involved riding through a sea of brown powder. Follow the dirt road S, passing a turning left at km 4 for the village of Pong Soong, 800 m offroad, a couple of minor side turns left and right, and another turning left at km 5.3. This latter side trail may well link up with the villages of San and Kong Koi (see Maps 33 & 34). Or perhaps it was the previous Pong Soong side trail. I am not sure; I have not checked these two ways. A couple of kms further you come to a 'crossroads' (km 7.6), marked on the left side by a health centre and 3 water tanks (see Map 30). Consider the centre a place to stay or a source of help in an emergency. You have arrived at Kong Pae.

This is a double Pwo Karen village. The northern part, **Kong Pae Nuea** (*nuea* = north) lies to the left of the crossroads. Go in and have a look around if you want. If you go right off the crossroads, you can proceed a couple of kms along a contouring track to **Kong Pae Tai**, the southern part of the village (*tai* = south). By all means ride in and have a look at that too, although it might mess up your odometer readings. From the crossroads you can enjoy fine views SW into Pwo country. Panning anticlockwise, you can espy to the W Kong Pae Tai, left of that and set back Ton Ngiu Nuea, further left or south-westish Huai Hia, our next port of call, and approximately S, in the far distance, Mae Pae Luang, another place on our route.

Now go straight across the crossroads, continuing S, and brace yourself for the problematic passage. The dirt road proceeds to a junction (km 11.4), with a turning left going to I know not where, perhaps to Mae Pae Noi, after which it seriously deteriorates. For a few hundred metres the way descends steeply on a (in 1999) disastrous surface, which we were unable to ride down, first 'paddling' our bikes down with our feet, and then simply wheeling them down. Don't be too proud to do the same – it is better than crashing. And remember that if you lock the front wheel, you will inevitably slide and tumble. At the bottom you come to a river and ford (km 12.1). The river must be the Mae Rit. On the far side you ride up to the Pwo Karen village of **Huai Hia**. You pass first a lower part on your left side with a health centre (km 14), after which you reach a junction (km 14.8). Right goes a few kms along a 4WD track to the Pwo double village of Ton Ngiu (see Trek 18). If you have time and inclination, go and visit it. Left, our route, curves round an upper part of Huai Hia, before heading off into the wilds. Take a look at Huai Hia, too, if you wish.

Now the trail twists and turns for some distance, not seeming to go anywhere in particular. So much so was this the case when we rode along here that we felt that we had got lost. In part the track follows the crests of the ridges, offering fine views all round. A couple of settlements left would seem to be Mae Pae Noi and possibly Huai Hia Noi. We saw no one to ask. At km 19.3 a turning left does indeed go to Mae Pae Noi or Little Mae Pae (*noi* = small). Just one km further (km 20.2) you come to a junction. Right proceeds down to the triple Pwo village of Huai Mu, with its northern, middle and southern parts, while straight or left continues to Mae Pae Luang. Consider investigating and stopping the night, as we did, at unvisited and unspoilt **Huai Mu**.

Side trip to Huai Mu Nuea

You gradually descend a side trail 1.8 kms to Huai Mu Nuea or Northern Huai Mu (Mor) (km 22). A couple of kms beyond this settlement lies Huai Mu Glang or Middle Huai Mu, and somewhere beyond that is Huai Mu Tai or Southern Huai Mu. After we had already decided to stop at the northern part and had already installed ourselves, we discovered that the middle part was a bigger village, more traditional and with many more Pwo costumes in evidence, i.e. it would be a better and more rewarding place to stay. Profit from our mistake, and go and check it out. At the time of our visit Huai Mu Nuea consisted of some 20 houses and resembled a big farmstead and yard. Traditional Pwo costumes were visible, and many women were weaving at looms as well as carding and spinning cotton. It was a poor place, but the villagers were friendly. We were taken in hand and allowed to stay in the house of a girl called Yupa (in Thai) or Mpri (in Karen, meaning 'small'). Her orderly wooden abode lay in the far northern corner of the village and had a substantial cement water tank behind it. Mpri was an alluring tall, thin, dark-skinned girl, who had been married 5 years and in 1999 was aged 23. Her husband worked in San Patong (just south of Chiang Mai) and she herself worked in Chiang Mai. At the time of our visit she had returned to her village to see her parents. She was their oldest child and had younger brothers and sisters in Huai Mu Nuea. Perhaps because she was familiar with the outside world, she seemed well-disposed to us visitors/foreigners. I feel sure you could stay on the floor of her living room irrespective of whether she is there or not – it might even be easier to stay if she is not. Otherwise try staying in another house, or put up a tent somewhere. Actually, we could see no level spot anywhere in the village. Perhaps you are, indeed, better off going to Huai Mu Glang.

We had a slight disappointment in Huai Mu Nuea. I wanted to get some serious photos of Pwo villagers in their best costumes, partly to illustrate this book. Indeed, there was a sense in which we came to Huai Mu and even spent a night there with this aim in mind. Through our hostess Mpri, we arranged that some people would be ready for a little photo session the next morning. The whole idea generated considerable interest in the village, and more and more people said they would don their best garb and make themselves up, including some youths. A group of Pwo women and men in their full get-up is a fine sight. But the next morning not a single volunteer 'model' was to be found, Mpri had gone all lame, and it was as if the conversations and arrangements had never happened. Usually hill-tribe people are willing and proud to show their traditional attire, especially if they learn that your interest in it is a serious one. All the more inexplicable and disappointing was it, therefore, that no one showed up or kept their word. It seemed to fit in with my finding in Trek 18, that the Pwo Karen are simply reluctant to be photographed, although not for any spiritual reasons. When I later discussed the matter with Scott McManigle, the missionary in Mae Pae Luang, who has considerable experience of the Pwo, he was not at all surprised and said simply that they would not do anything for no money.

I resume the route detail 1.8 kms back up the Huai Mu side trail at the junction where it joins the 'main' track from Huai Hia to Mae Pae Luang. Km-readings continue from 20.2, as if we had made no diversion to Huai Mu (see Map 33). Two hundred metres further you come to another turning right (km 20.4), which may go to Huai Mu Tai. One km beyond this, you reach a relatively important junction (km 21.2). Right goes to Pa Yoe and other Pwo villages, while left or straight, our route, continues towards Mae Pae Luang, which is now 3½ kms away. You pass a couple more turnings right, before you come to the first entrance (right, km 24.5) to Mae Pae Luang. Just beyond the first entrance, you come to a crossroads. At it, the way left goes ca 4 kms to Mae Pae Noi (*noi* = little, *parva*), straight across is our onward route to Ta Fai, and right is a second entrance to Mae Pae Luang or Big Mae Pae (*luang* is large, *magna*). Go 100 m down either of the two right-hand entrance ways to reach the centre of **Mae Pae Luang** (km 24.6). Incidentally, the house of US missionary Scott McManigle and his family is a large wooden affair sandwiched between these two entrance ways.

Mae Pae Luang is, as its name suggests, a large (Pwo Karen) place, reputedly the biggest Karen settlement in Mae Hong Son province. Besides a missionary station, it has a relatively well-stocked shop with drinks. Consider staying a night here, although, because the village is quite developed, you may not have such an 'authentic' experience as at a more 'primitive' place such as Huai Mu. Put up either in a tent, or with the headman, or in a villager's house. Enlist Scott's help with this last, and apply to him, too, if you want to explore deeper south into Pwo territory – he knows all the villages and trails. Apparently the southernmost Pwo settlements in the area are Huai Bong and Huai Wok (= monkey stream). For more on Mae Pae Luang, see Trek 18 and also Map 31.

Back at the crossroads just outside Mae Pae Luang, go N through the crossroads in the direction of Ta Fai. You descend to a river bed and then, 5 kms from Mae Pae Luang crossroads, come to a division of the way (km 29.6). Go left – in fact, the two routes meet up again. At km 31.1 you reach a bridge, after which on paved sections you arrive at the mixed Pwo and rural Thai village of **Ta Fai** or Ka Fai (km 32.2). Henceforth you are back in comparative civilization. Pass through Ta Fai and follow a cement road 1.8 kms to arrive at the village of **Kong Koi** or Go Goi (km 34). At a central crossroads marked by a monastery-temple (*wat*) and also a water tower, the way left (W) takes you over a rickety wooden bridge uphill to San village and a health centre, beyond which a poor trail leads, I believe, back to the vicinity of Kong Pae. The way right (E) passes through the rest of Kong Koi (see Map 34). There are several stores in the village with soft drinks and beer, and at least one noodle soup shop. Towards the end of the main street, a road right leads a couple of kms up to a large new hilltop school, which is the gleaming white building clearly visible from many directions from afar. Look upon it as a possible place to stay overnight, if you want, and especially as a flat elevated secluded (during the night) spot to pitch a tent. As you leave Kong Koi, you cross a river and a bridge, to the right of which the water has been backed up by a kind of dam or weir (another possible camping place).

Now a regular dirt road crosses some open fields to arrive almost immediately at **Tung** or Toong (km 34.7), said to be an assimilated Lawa village. Other villages around here are reported originally to have been Lawa, including Bo Sa Li (just S of Mae Waen), Kong Loi (10 kms E of Mae Waen on the 108 road) and Bo Luang (also on the H108, E of Kong Loi). When Englishman Holt Hallett passed through this area in 1876 on a fact-finding mission, subsequently publishing his travel experiences and observations in his *A Thousand Miles on an Elephant in the Shan States* (1890), he expressly mentions Bo Sa Li, Kong Loi and Bo Luang as Lawa villages. Visiting each, he even photographed Lawa in Bo Sa Li (for more on the ancient Lawa people, see Trek 23). On the far side of Tung, at a T-junction by a *wat* (left), go right and over a bridge. Follow the dirt road until a fork. Straight (right) goes to a crossroads just S of Mae Waen, near which is the aforementioned Lawa village of Bo Sa Li (1.7 kms south of Mae Waen). At that crossroads go left for Mae Waen (see Map 34). Left at the fork, our route, is a less roundabout short-cut way to **Mae Waen**, bringing you across some fields to that village, entering it by the back door (km 36.6). For some information about Mae Waen as well as about *Pan House* in the village, which is a kind of 'guest house' where you could possibly stay, see Trek 18 under 'Accessing Mae Waen'.

From Mae Waen ride 5.4 kms N up a dirt road, fording a river just beyond the village, until you hit the main 108 highway at a T-junction (km 42) near km-stone 65. Right goes 65 kms to the town of Hot, 10 kms to Kong Loi, and ca 150 kms to Chiang Mai. If you are contemplating moving on to do motorcycle Trek 20 or planning to proceed to Chiang Mai, both of which you should really embark upon in the early morning, go right (E) here. Otherwise go left (W) for Mae Sariang, the centre of which lies 40 kms or a good hour's ride away. On the way you pass after 7.3 kms the Huai Goong turning by the police box and after 25 kms (13 kms short of Mae Sariang's south-easterly 'crossroads') the turning right for Om Long and Pa Pae, which is the start of motorcycle Trek 21. After 38 kms (from the Mae Waen turning) you reach the key four-way junction at the bottom end of Mae Sariang. Take the second left to enter the town's long main street, at the far end of which, after two more kms, you are back at the centre of Mae Sariang.

Part 3b

**Treks 20-23: four motorcycle treks north-east of Mae Sariang
in Mae Hong Son & Chiang Mai provinces
on the Ob Luang plateau in Lawa country
based on Mae Sariang town**

Trek 20

Mae Sariang – Kong Loi – Lao Li – Chang Mor – Saam – La Ang

Parameters

trekking mode:	by motorcycle
trek time:	variable as trip must be combined with another trek, either Trek 21 or 22 or 23. Combined with 21 or 22, could be done in one long day as a loop excursion from Mae Sariang, although interpolating a night stop is recommended; combined with Trek 23, allow at least 2 days/1 night
trek distance:	Mae Sariang centre to Kong Loi 50 kms, plus Kong Loi to La Ang 68 kms (total 118 kms), to which can be added the distances of Treks 21, 22 or 23, whichever you choose. Reckon on long overall distances.
degree of difficulty:	moderately difficult for average to experienced riders; no problem for skilled offroad bikers or for dirt freaks with enduro machines; the problem with all these treks is less with the difficulty and more with their sheer length
tent:	not strictly necessary, but advisable, not least as a fall-back
map(s):	see 35, 29, 36 & 37

Overview & strategy

With this trek we come to the first of four substantial motorcycle expeditions (Treks 20-23 inclusive) NE of Mae Sariang in Lawa country (see Map 35). At the same time we reach the third of altogether six outings launched from this westerly town (Treks 18-23) into the mountains lying to its east, and the second of five biking excursions (Treks 19-23) into the same plateau area. Trek 20 rides east from Mae Sariang 50 kms along Highway 108 to Kong Loi, climbs up approximately NNW via Lao Li on the H1270 dirt road 41 kms to the far-flung elevated Lawa village of Chang Mor, and then strikes further NNW another 27 kms along an incredibly remote dirt way to the isolated mountaintop Lawa outpost of La Ang (total distance from Mae Sariang 118 kms). As with the other three expeditions into Lawa territory, the trek involves some magnificent offroad biking in fabulous terrain.

The trip is a motorbike hike only. Because the distances involved are so great, and because the villages of the plateau of the Lawa are fairly well interconnected by dirt roads and trails, it makes little sense to walk it, or to walk part of it, or, more generally, to walk on the plateau. Like the mountainous area south of the 108 Mae Sariang/Hot road and SE of Mae Sariang, which is peopled by the Pwo Karen (Treks 18 & 19), Lawa country, sometimes referred to as the Ob Luang plateau, lends itself especially to exploration on two wheels (or in a jeep). I suppose Trek 20, in company with Treks 21-23, could possibly be managed on a bicycle, but the bicycle would have to be a very sturdy mountain bike, and the rider would have to be exceptionally tough, intrepid and persistent (no liability assumed, and no comeback, please).

As La Ang lies in the heart of Lawa country, far from anywhere, the trek does not end there. From it you must escape either by proceeding via Mae La Oop and Mae La Noi back to Mae Sariang, or by continuing via Ho Gao in the direction of Mae Chaem and ultimately Chiang Mai, or by going back the same way, a return journey to Mae Sariang that you could vary by riding from Chang Mor not via Lao Li and Kong Loi, but via Pa Pae. These three escape routes from pivotal La Ang on the one hand clearly add considerable distances to the overall journey, and on the other cross over to the other three treks in Lawa country, respectively to Treks 22, 23 and 21 (see Map 35). Combining Trek 20 with Trek 22 (via Mae La Oop and Mae La Noi back to Mae Sariang) would add 72 kms to the 118-km distance already travelled, making an overall round trip from Mae Sariang to Mae Sariang of 190 kms. Combining it with Trek 23 (via Ho Gao and Mae Chaem) would add 52 kms to the 118 kms already travelled to make an overall trip of 170 kms as far as Mae Chaem, or add 170 kms to the 118 already travelled to make an overall trip of 288 kms as far as Chiang Mai. Combining it with Trek 21 (back to Chang Mor and then via Pa Pae) would add 88 kms to the 118 kms already travelled, making an overall round trip from Mae Sariang to Mae Sariang of 206 kms. On a small bike, such as a Honda Dream, which is what can be typically hired in the tourist centres of Chiang Mai or Mae Hong Son, these are ambitious distances to be covering in one day on problematic mountain 'roads', and so it makes sense to spread the combined overall treks over two or more days, spending a night or nights at places en route (more below).

To make a more general observation, Trek 20 and Treks 21-23 can, of course, be permuted at will. Thus you can combine any one with any other, and you can ride them in any direction, 'backwards' as well as forwards. Accordingly, the way in which I have ordered Treks 20 and 21-23 in their respective chapters (e.g. in Trek 20 to start in Mae Sariang, proceed via Kong Loi, Chang Mor and La Ang, and perhaps to exit via Mae La Oop and Mae La Noi) is only nominal, and could be rearranged by you to suit your inclinations. However, you would then correspondingly have to pick and choose among the four chapters, sometimes having to read the maps and text backwards. Clearly I cannot detail all the possible permutations in separate chapters. But back to the trek in hand.

TREK 20: MAE SARIANG – KONG LOI – CHANG MOR – LA ANG

With Trek 20 my suggestion is, as said, to proceed from Mae Sariang 50 kms to Kong Loi, then go offroad 68 kms via Chang Mor (officially renamed as Santi Tam, I think) to La Ang. From here I suggest you go down via the big Lawa village of Mae La Oop to Mae La Noi in the Yuam river valley, and from there return S down the H108 road to Mae Sariang. The anticlockwise loop crosses over from Trek 20 to 22 at La Ang and is 190 kms long. From Kong Loi to Mae La Noi, a distance of some 110 kms, is nearly all dirt (in 1999). Needless to say, you could do the loop in reverse (clockwise), reading my maps and route detail backwards. I first did this loop in February 1998 with 'Mr Pan' of *Pan House* in Mae Waen (see Trek 18). On small bikes, we completed the journey in one long tiring day. In January 1999, I redid it with Nittaya Tananchai and Doug Boynton. We rode on two little 100-cc Honda Dreams and took a very leisurely 3 days, breaking the journey and spending nights at Ho Gao and Mae La Oop, although the loop could be comfortably done in 2 days/1 night, staying perhaps at Ho Gao (near La Ang). I suggest that you likewise spread the trip over 2 days (or longer). On stony dirt, the further you go in one day, and the more tired and careless you get, the greater is the chance that you will crash, as Nittaya, Doug and I all know to our cost! But apart from this, taking 2 or more days over the trek allows you to stop and look at things on the way, experience the Lawa and some of their villages, do a spot of camping, unhurriedly enjoy the marvellous scenery, do some bird-watching à la Doug, and generally take it easy and have a good time. Stay in Mae La Oop, or at Chang Mor, or in the attractive traditional Lawa village of Ho Gao (16 kms from La Ang, near the start of Trek 23, see Map 35), or in any village or place. Central pivotal La Ang is the obvious place to break the journey and stay overnight, but I have never found it so congenial.

You can modify the expedition, as already indicated, by crossing over at La Ang not to Trek 22 (continuing to Mae La Oop), but to Trek 23 (proceeding to Ho Gao and Mae Chaem). But another way of modifying it would be to involve Trek 21, which goes via Pa Pae (see Map 35). You could do this in two ways. Either you could access Chang Mor not via Kong Loi, as in the first part of Trek 20, but via Pa Pae, incorporating Trek 21 into Trek 20, i.e. you would use a different feeder route to Chang Mor, after which the way to La Ang would be as before. Or you could proceed from Mae Sariang via Pa Pae to Chang Mor (Trek 21), after which you could ignore the Chang Mor/La Ang stretch and go down via Lao Li to Kong Loi, finishing by returning to Mae Sariang. This would combine Treks 21 and 20 only, would shorten Trek 20, and would form a loop from Mae Sariang – albeit a shorter one than the great loop outlined above (it would comprise 15 + 46 + 41 + 50 = 152 kms). Trek 21, the feeder route to Chang Mor via Pa Pae, is more difficult, spectacular and slower than the feeder route to Chang Mor via Kong Loi (first part of Trek 20), and so, if you are planning to try this new combination, it is advisable to tackle that stretch first, i.e. do the modified trek clockwise, rather than the other way round, anticlockwise. The logic of this is that you should tackle the more problematic Pa Pae route while you are still fresh and have the whole day before you, and that, with the Pa Pae way to Chang Mor ascending, you should ride up the problematic stretch, which is easier than riding down it.

On the subject of difficulty, Trek 20, in its standard form (via Kong Loi to Chang Mor and on to La Ang), is in my estimation moderately difficult for average or experienced riders. The same applies if Trek 22, from La Ang via Mae La Oop to Mae La Noi, is tacked on to it. The dirt offroad stretches are mostly stony or gravelly, but with some bulldust passages and with some steep and/or rutted sections. Because of this, and because of the length and remoteness of the trails in Trek 20 (and also in related Treks 22 and 21), the expedition is not for inexperienced bikers or for novice riders who have casually hired a stepthrough Dream townbike in Mae Hong Son. Quite particularly the 27-km-long onward route from Chang Mor to La Ang is very remote (one of the remotest trails in Thailand) and lonely, unused by any traffic. As it goes on and on, it will give even the most experienced motorcycle trekkers a frisson of excitement and anxiety. Good nerves are needed for this stretch and for the link down from La Ang to Mae La Oop. Heaven help you if you crash or break down here, in the back of beyond. Unless you know what you are doing, it would be foolhardy to undertake either Trek 20 or Treks 21-23 as a solo biker. Go with a friend and preferably with two or more bikes/bikers. In view of the above, carry water and some food (and even a tent) with you on this trek, as you should on any such expedition, in case you break down, get a flat tyre, or crash, and have to spend a long time waiting for or going to get help. Obviously other bikers and bikes can be invaluable when such mishaps occur.

About Mae Sariang and accommodation + food there
Trek 20 is launched, as said, from Mae Sariang, with its guest houses, shops, restaurants and other facilities. For information on the town, on staying in guest houses there, and on eating out, see Trek 18 under 'Accessing the trek'.

Brief notes on the Lawa
During Trek 20 and in related Treks 21 or 22 or even 23, you encounter Lawa people at Chang Mor, Om Pai and La Ang, as well as at variously Pa Pae, Mae La Oop and Ho Gao. For some outline information on this ancient and very interesting ethnic minority group, see Trek 23.

*

Trekking route detail
Mae Sariang – Kong Loi – Lao Li – Chang Mor
From the centre of Mae Sariang, ride up the town's long W/E-running Wiang Mai Road, past *Intira Restaurant* (right), the post office (right) and *Lotus Guest House* (right), to the complicated 'crossroads' at the far south-eastern end. Left goes N up the 108 highway 30 kms to Mae La Noi, 98 kms to Khun Yuam and 168 kms to

TREK 20: MAE SARIANG – KONG LOI – CHANG MOR – LA ANG

Mae Hong Son. Just a few hundred metres up here is a big fuel station, a good place to tank up. Right goes a great distance down the Thai-Burmese border to Mae Salid and Mae Sot. Straight (eastish) is our route along the 108 road towards Hot and Chiang Mai. From the 'crossroads' proceed E along the H108 road 48 kms to Kong Loi (50 kms from the centre of Mae Sariang) (see Map 29). The ride is scenic, and you get many good views right (S) into the mountainous territory of the Pwo Karen (the venue of Treks 18 & 19). You pass, 13 kms out from the crossroads, at km-stone 90 (measured from Hot), a turning left (N) for Pa Pae and other villages. The junction is marked by a *sala* or waiting hut and many signs, and is the beginning of motorcycle Trek 21. The way issues after 46 long kms at Chang Mor, is an alternative and more difficult way of accessing Chang Mor, was in a parlous state in 1999, and should only be contemplated by experienced skilled riders (see Trek 21). At a distance of 30.7 kms from the crossroads (32 kms from Mae Sariang centre), you pass a turning (right) near the village of Huai Goong. It is marked by a police box and a couple of shops, one of which serves a noodle soup. The junction is the beginning of motorcycle Trek 19. After a further 7.3 kms (38 from the crossroads and 40 from Mae Sariang centre), you pass a turning (right or S) for Mae Waen. The junction, near km-stone 65 (measured from Hot) is marked by a *sala* and a sign indicating *Pan House*, and is the access to walking Trek 18 as well as the exit point for biking Trek 19. Continue a further 10 kms to arrive at Kong Loi, 48 kms from the crossroads and 50 kms from Mae Sariang centre.

Kong Loi stands on the junction of the main 108 highway and the 1270 side road (our route) N to Lao Li and Chang Mor. If you continue E from Kong Loi along the H108 away from Mae Sariang, you come after another 55 kms to the town of Hot, and a further 90 kms beyond Hot ultimately to Chiang Mai. Just before or W of the junction, there is a fuel station, at which you should tank up prior to going offroad. Kong Loi is an old but now assimilated Lawa place. The English explorer Holt Hallett, marching through here in 1876 on an expedition from Moulmein in Burma via Mae Sariang and Chiang Mai to Chiang Saen, speaks in his book *A Thousand Miles on an Elephant in the Shan States* of Kong Loi as a Lawa village, which like others locally was involved with the production of iron and metal goods. Turn left into the H1270 side road. My km readings start at 0.0 kms at the junction (see Map 36).

Now ride 16 kms to Lao Li and 41 to Chang Mor. The road, which heads roughly NNW, ascending gradually, is an alternation of paved and dirt sections as far as about Saya Goh or Mae Aeb (km 23). In 1999 it was still mostly dirt, some of the paved sections even deteriorating to dirt again, but clearly the road is slowly being worked upon, so in the future expect more and more of it to be asphalted. There is a fair amount of traffic as far as about Lao Li. You pass through one or more regular rural villages, including Ban Mai or New Village, which apparently is assimilated Pwo Karen. Crossing a bridge, you then climb up to the regular (S'gaw) Karen village of **Kong La** or Gong La (right or E side of road, km 13), pass an entrance (right/E) to Mae To National Park and to a Park office just offroad (ca km 16), and then, just a few hundred metres later, reach **Lao Li** (km 16.2). If you want or need to stay locally, perhaps because you are doing the trek the other way round and get caught out by nightfall here, consider staying at Lao Li (ask around or try the health centre) or at the National Park office.

Lao Li, also known as Mae To, by which the whole area is generally known, is a weird 'wild-west' staging post of a village with numerous roadside stores and eating places, at which you can get a noodle soup or fried rice. It is populated by an ethnic hotchpotch of Hmong, Karen, Lawa, Chinese and Thai. The Chinese are KMT (Kuomintang) Nationalists from Yunnan. The oldest of them (not their descendants) left China in 1949 with the KMT 3rd and 5th Armies, when Mao Tse-tung's communist People's Army vanquished Chiang Kai-shek's nationalist KMT forces, made their way down through Burma, and entered Thailand around 1961. The Chinese of Lao Li village are KMT 3rd Army people. More than 30 years ago, so an old man said, he and some others came here on business and simply stayed. The name of their leader, Gen. Lao Li, the celebrated commander of the 3rd Army, came to be given to the village.

On the far northern side of Lao Li, two turnings left (W) go 1 km to the Karen and Hmong village of Mae To Noi with its *wat*, and 500 m to San Bo Lek. Now the way goes behind a ridge, descends into a valley, and describes a big curve W, N and NE, offering new views N and NE of the mountains and valleys of the plateau of the Lawa. You pass two roadside settlements (ca km 18), which I think are outlying Karen bits of Lao Li/Mae To, before resuming the climb. A section of new asphalt around km-stone 23 speeds you on your way to the Karen village of **Saya Goh** (km 23.6), which seems also to be known as **Mae Aeb**. Mr Pan of Mae Waen's *Pan House* told me that from here you can walk 2 days and 1 night across country to Mae La Oop. Evidently it is a route sometimes used by trekking parties and passes through Huai Haak Mai Tai, Huai Haak Mai Nuea and Huai Gai Dam. He is willing to guide the likes of you and me along this route. Contact him at *Pan House* if you are interested (see Trek 18) or hire some Karen guides on the spot at Mae Aeb. On the eve of such a trek you could put up at Mae Aeb forestry office. I am slightly sceptical whether the path really does start from Mae Aeb. It might also leave from Ko Ta, higher up the road. Perhaps you can walk to La Oop from both places. Check the situation out!

Just 200 m beyond Saya Goh/Mae Aeb, a way goes left (W) (km 23.8) 1.5 kms to the Karen village of Mae Aeb and a waterfall. One km further, another way goes left (km 24.8, near km-marker 25) to Mae Aeb forestry conservation office, sited above the road. Then a way right (E) goes to the offroad village of Taab. At km 27.5, just short of km-marker 28, you come to the Karen village of **Ko Ta** or Koe Ta to the right side of the road. A man here once said that you can walk from Ko Ta a whole day via Karen Mor Wiang to Mae La Oop. Then, 6.8 kms further, you come to **Om Pai** (km 34.3), the first real Lawa village on this trek – discounting Kong Loi – and a significant one. It lies to the right (E) of the road and has a motorcycle repair place by the road, which I once made use of, getting a useless gear-changing pedal fixed. The surrounding countryside is noticeably agriculturally developed, a sign of Lawa diligence but also of outside aid. When I once looked over Om Pai in early 1993, I found a combined UNICEF/Royal Agricultural Project operating full-swing out of the village. It was aiding six villages from here, encouraging them to grow kidney beans, coffee, cabbages and other temperate produce instead of opium poppies. In keeping with the project, Om Pai had been transformed into a developed model village, with a generator, lighting, well-stocked shop and canteen – things which the surrounding settlements did not have at the time. Much earlier, a century and a quarter ago, so we learn from Holt Hallett's *A Thousand Miles on an Elephant*, the Lawa used to mine iron ore (red

TREK 20: MAE SARIANG – KONG LOI – CHANG MOR – LA ANG

oxide of iron) in the mountains near Om Pai (or 'Oon Pai', as he puts it), smelting it at the village and transporting the metal ingots by elephant two days down to places such as Bo Luang (on the H108), where it was further worked by Lawa into manufactured metal goods that were sold throughout Siam.

One km beyond Om Pai (km 35.4) comes Om Pai Nuea (*nuea* = northern), which also goes by the name of **Tam Chai** or Tam Sai, another Lawa place, which lies on each side of the road, but mainly on the left (W) side. Riding on a further 5.6 kms, you come to a mountaintop junction (km 41), just before which a prominent large new health centre lies on your left side, splendidly perched above the road on a knoll. The junction lies just a stone's throw from the Lawa village of **Chang Mor** or **Santi Tam**, as it has recently been officially renamed (I think). At this key junction, right (our route) continues another 27 kms to La Ang, while left proceeds 46 kms via Huai Haak Mai, Goh Mai Lu, Pa Pae, Om Long, Om Pok and Rai Lor back down to the 108 road, issuing 15 kms E of Mae Sariang town centre (see Maps 35 & 38). It is here, therefore, that Trek 21 joins Trek 20, coming up the Pa Pae trail the other way round and constituting an alternative feeder route to Chang Mor. Beyond Chang Mor, Treks 20 and 21 unite, going the same way, or, rather, Trek 21 crosses over into 20. The way left to Pa Pae and the many villages on and off the route looks harmless enough, rather resembling a fine dirt highway. And so it is for the first 14 kms to about Go Mai Lu. But do not venture lightly down here. Beyond Pa Pae the way deteriorates into a very poor and taxing trail (in 1999), on which unskilled bikers will get into difficulties. If you must go via Pa Pae, come up this route, as indicated earlier and as detailed in Trek 21 – riding up it is easier than riding down. Consider staying a night in Chang Mor, either sleeping at the health centre, or putting up with the headman, or tenting somewhere, perhaps at the health centre or at Chang Mor school (see Map 37). If you are doing the big loop from Mae Sariang via Kong Loi, Chang Mor, La Ang, Mae La Oop and Mae La Noi back to Mae Sariang (Treks 20 & 22), you are now nearly halfway.

Some confusion attaches to Chang Mor. It seems to be split into two parts. The first part lies, broadly speaking, to the right (E) of the junction, and a way to this section can be found 500 m beyond the junction (km 41.5) (see Map 37). The second part lies offroad (also right) 500 m down a side track which starts rather further beyond the junction (at km 43.2) and which is marked at its beginning by a *sala*. I had always thought that the first visible part near the junction was Chang Mor Luang (*luang* = big) and that the second hidden part was Chang Mor Noi (*noi* = little), but it might be the other way round. Further, the Thai authorities seem to have renamed Chang Mor 'Santi Tam', but that could be 'Santisuk', or it might be that one part is Santi Tam and the other Santisuk. But let us stick with Chang Mor, which is the original authentic name, and eschew the inauthentic unimaginitive euphemistic Thaiizing latterday dubbings such as Santisuk that officials cannot help sprinkling all over the place, wherever they get to.

Exploring Chang Mor once, back in early 1993, I stayed a night in the village in a Lawa house. The experience was so primitive that I regretted not putting up at the school ('Santisuk School'), to which people had directed me. This lay, as it still does lie, about a km beyond the first part of Chang Mor, down a steep little way going off left from the 'main road' (turning: km 42.2). Besides the school, there were some dozen houses also down here, and the whole complex may have been called Santisuk. One of the houses used to be a special house near the river, where *farang* stayed when they came visiting Chang Mor. Perhaps this house and the arrangement still exists, and you can stay down by the school. Check it out if you want to break your journey here. My diary tells me that the houses of the part of the village by the big junction (near the new health centre) were wooden affairs, raised well off the ground, with tin or shingled roofs, and were broadly arranged in a horseshoe shape. From them you could enjoy great mountain views across wooded plateau country. In the distance Doi Intanon, Thailand's highest mountain, was visible, while in valley pockets paddies nestled, ingeniously terraced in a way reminiscent of Nepal or India.

It was a traditional and in some ways still backward place. Most women wore the Lawa ladies' costume of a handwoven blue and red tube skirt, a smock, leggings or anklets around the lower leg, multiple strands of orange beads, and cupped silver earrings. Not wearing the best version of this traditional costume, they were dressed in a workaday form, which was filthy, as were the clothes of the men and children. Everyone, men and women, were smoking pipes all the time. From the tobacco smoke, and also from the smoke of the fires, candles and oil lamps in the houses, but also from ill health, all the children had hacking coughs. Dogs, chickens and other animals ran all over the village, up onto the balconies of the houses, where women sat weaving, and into the dwellings. Sleeping on one of these balconies, I was served stewed squash, cold rice and chilli dip for breakfast, the same as for supper the previous evening. The headman of Chang Mor said that his father had been a Khmer trader, who had come over this way, married and settled. This conformed to ancient migratory, trading and communication patterns, for the Khmer, like the Lawa and other fragmentary peoples of Mon-Khmer stock, had a history of visiting their Lawa cousins. The headman himself used to work in a tin mine near Om Koi (40 kms south of the 108 Mae Sariang/Hot road), which again was true to type because, as said, the Lawa have a celebrated history of metal mining, smelting and working (for more information on the Lawa, see Trek 23).

Chang Mor – Saam – La Ang
We continue our journey N from Chang Mor junction towards La Ang (km readings resume as if from Kong Loi) (see now Map 37). After the junction (km 41), you pass a turning right for the first part of Chang Mor (km 41.5), followed by km-stone 42, and then two turnings left, the second of which (km 42.2) goes steeply down to Chang Mor school, which is a possible place to stay overnight. One km later, at km 43.2, a side trail right (E) goes 500 m to the second part of Chang Mor, the start of this trail being marked by a *sala*. Until recently the H1270 road from Kong Loi up to Chang Mor used to end about here, and there was no dirt road through to La Ang. But now an incredible new dirt route has been blasted

through the 27 kms of wilderness lying between Chang Mor and La Ang. It is incredible partly because of the way's remoteness and isolation, and partly because it basically passes no onroad villages until Saam at the La Ang end, but mainly because it seems to go nowhere (Saam and La Ang can be accessed from Mae La Oop) and is used by no vehicles. On the two occasions that I have ridden along here, I saw zero traffic. Even as the link has been forged, it is becoming overgrown and is falling to pieces. Do not set off for La Ang unless you are sure you have enough petrol for the journey and also have drinking water with you. I think the logic of this very lonely new 'road' must be that it is, exactly as said, a link, crucially connecting the Mae Sariang/Hot road with the proposed new way from Mae La Noi via La Ang and Mae Hae Tai to Mae Chaem, a three-way opening up of the Lawa plateau in line with the configuration of routes in Map 35.

Near km-stone 47 the first of two side trails goes off right (E) to the remote Karen village of Om Raed (ca 40 houses), which lies across the valley and behind the ridge you can see. A couple of kms further, you pass the second way to Om Raed (km 48.9). Near km-marker 54, a turning left (W) leads 800 m up to the midpoint Karen village of **Por Mae Cho**, also known as Huai Pak Pai (km 53.9). Locals both here and in Mae La Oop say that a motorcycle trail runs from Por Mae Chu directly to Mae La Oop via the villages of Dong Mai and Dong Gao, respectively New and Old Dong! I have not been down that way, so I do not know the distance and the route is unverified. Do not attempt it unless you are a highly experienced biker. Apply to Por Mae Chu if you break down or have problems in the middle of the Chang Mor/La Ang leg. You proceed now down to a bridge and a river (km 56), after which you embark on an extended uphill stretch that winds up near Saam, and which offers some magical views W of terraced paddy fields down in the river valley and of a village across the valley. The village, to which there seems to be no access way, must be Huai Ha Mai. As you skirt it at a distance, it seems to tease you by inviting you across to visit full in the knowledge that you cannot. A way left (W) at km 63.4 would seem, in fact, to go to the coquettish village. Apparently there is another direct motorcycle trail to Mae La Oop from Huai Ha Mai (*mai* = new). It goes via Huai Ha. Again, I have not been down this route, do not know the distance, cannot vouch for it, and do not recommend any but very experienced riders to try it.

Just 100 m further (km 63.5), a turning right (E) goes 500 m to **Saam**, a regular Lawa village. Take a look in here, if you want. You pass a health centre (left) and a turning for a school (also left). Consider breaking your journey at Saam, staying overnight possibly at the health centre or at the school, either in the building or in a tent pitched in the grounds. Undoubtedly the Lawa of Saam will be thrilled to see you once they have processed the shock of *farang* turning up in their midst. A couple of kms beyond the Saam turn-off, you pass a turning left (W) (km 66.1) for the Karen village of Mae Lae, 200 m offroad. Just a km or so further, you wind up at a key junction in an open area (km 67.2). It is marked by a monastery-temple, called Wat Santikiri. At the junction, a trail right goes to Karen Sae To Sa, Karen Mae Hae Tai, Lawa Ho Gao and many other villages, and ultimately to Mae Chaem and Chiang Mai. From the junction it is 16 kms further to Ho Gao, a nice place to stay (see Trek 23). Left at the junction goes half a km to **La Ang** (km 67.7 entrance, km 68 centre).

La Ang has always seemed to me a rather scrappy place. Its importance is out of proportion to its size. It is an important pivotal little village because of its siting by the key central three-way junction or *saam yaek*, the arms of which go variously west to Mae La Oop and Mae La Noi, south to Chang Mor and Kong Loi, and east to Mae Hae Tai and Mae Chaem. Perhaps because of its strategic location, it has always had petrol, both ordinary and super. It is an elevated hilltop place with fine views and a stark light. The inhabitants are mostly Lawa people, intermixed with some Karen. Karen boys marry Lawa girls and then, following the practice of Karen matrilocality, go to live with their new Lawa wives, in this case in La Ang. Most of the village lies each side of the main street, consisting of some 30 relatively well-built wooden houses and a couple of stores, at which you can buy soft drinks, beer and whisky. At the south-eastern end of the main drag, a regular school is perched on a knoll. But in 1997 it had only 30 schoolchildren, the year electricity was scheduled to come to the village. Consider the school as a potential place to stay, either in the building or in a tent in its grounds.

On the three occasions I have passed through La Ang, I have bought packets of instant noodles and got the villagers – each time in a different house – to cook them up for me, which they have willingly done. It is a good way of getting into someone's house and of making contact with the Lawa. Try the same, perhaps at the headman's house, which lies midway down the village street on the E side. His womenfolk are obliging and attentive. Perhaps you can stay in the house of the *po luang* or headman. In 1999, when we lunched with him, he was in a poor state. Doing some building work on his house, he had fallen through the roof, injuring his back and ribs, and was in considerable pain. I think they all feared he would die, and he seemed heartened when we worldly *farang* expected that he would get better if he rested a lot and sought the help of the health centre at Mae Hae Tai. It is said that the Lawa people of La Ang cannot or can only imperfectly understand the Lawa people of Ho Gao or Pae, two villages only a few kms away. Their vocabulary and expressions are reportedly different. If true, this is a situation similar to the dialectal differentiation even in neighbouring villages among the Lua – people of the same stock as the Lawa – of Nan province. In La Ang, notice the characteristic Lawa design of the women's handwoven tube skirts: cerise or wine-red banding on a black or indigo ground, sometimes with blue warp *ikat* decoration (for more on Lawa culture see Trek 23).

Continuing from La Ang and staying the night locally
At La Ang you will have to choose how to continue your journey. Your options are: (1) to proceed to Mae La Oop, down to Mae La Noi and thence either back to Mae Sariang or on to Khun Yuam and Mae Hong Son; or (2) to proceed to Ho Gao and then to Mae Chaem; or (3) to return to Chang Mor. With option 1, Trek 20 crosses over to Trek 22, and the reader is referred to that trek. With option 2, Trek 20 crosses over to Trek 23, and you are likewise referred to that trek. With option 3, you are, of course, doing Trek 20 in reverse. If you are opting to proceed from La Ang to Chang Mor and on to Kong Loi, probably because you have approached La

TREK 20: MAE SARIANG – KONG LOI – CHANG MOR – LA ANG

Ang from Mae La Oop (doing Trek 22 in reverse) or because you have approached La Ang from Mae Chaem and Ho Gao (doing Trek 23 in reverse), the distances are as follows:

> La Ang – Saam turning: 4.5 kms
> La Ang – Por Mae Cho (Huai Pak Pai) turning: 14 kms
> La Ang – Chang Mor junction: 27 kms
> La Ang – Om Pai: 33.5 kms
> La Ang – Lao Li (Mae To): 52 kms
> La Ang – Kong Loi & H108: 68 kms
> La Ang – Mae Sariang via Kong Loi: 118 kms

If you opt to proceed from La Ang to Chang Mor and then continue not to Lao Li and Kong Loi, but via Pa Pae (doing part of Trek 20 and then Trek 21 in reverse), the distances are as follows:

> La Ang – Chang Mor junction: 27 kms
> La Ang – Pa Pae: 46.5 kms
> La Ang – H108 via Pa Pae: 73 kms
> La Ang – Mae Sariang via Pa Pae: 88 kms

If, having arrived at La Ang, you want to break your journey and spend a night hereabouts, you could of course try staying at La Ang, perhaps putting up with the headman or at the school or even at the monastery on the junction outside the village, or you could try staying at nearby Saam village (see earlier). I have tried none of these possibilities, never having been tempted to stop overnight in La Ang or Saam. My real recommendation is that you continue either to Ho Gao or to Mae La Oop and stay a night there, where you are much better served. It is a further 16 kms to Ho Gao, and 17 kms to Mae La Oop. With my various trekking companions, I have spent many enjoyable nights in the traditional Lawa village of Ho Gao and many satisfactory nights in the large established Lawa village of Mae La Oop. The people in Ho Gao are very friendly, and the headman there is willing to put you up, is even expecting *farang* motorcycle trekkers to come by. For details of how to get to Ho Gao and of staying there, see Trek 23. For details of how to proceed to Mae La Oop and of accommodation there, see Trek 22.

Trek 21

Mae Sariang – H108/km 13 – Pa Pae – Huai Haak Mai Tai – Chang Mor – La Ang

Parameters

trekking mode: by motorcycle

trek time: variable as trip must be combined with another trek: with second part of Trek 20 and then with either Trek 22 or 23. Combined with 20 and 22, could be done in one long day as a loop excursion from Mae Sariang, although interpolating a night stop is recommended; combined with Treks 20 and 23, allow at least 2 days/1 night

trek distance: Mae Sariang centre via Pa Pae to Chang Mor 61 kms, plus Chang Mor to La Ang 27 kms (total 88 kms), to which can be added the distances of Treks 22 or 23, whichever you choose. Reckon on long overall distances.

degree of difficulty: first stretch via Pa Pae to Chang Mor difficult and only for skilled riders with dirt experience; the rest moderately difficult for average to experienced riders; the problem with all these treks is not so much with their difficulty, but more with their combined length

tent: not strictly necessary, but advisable, not least as a fall-back

map(s):   see 35, 29, 38 & 37

Overview & strategy

This trek is the second of four substantial motorcycle expeditions (Treks 20-23 inclusive) NE of Mae Sariang in Lawa country (see Map 35). At the same time it is the fourth of altogether six outings launched from this westerly town (Treks 18-23) into the mountains lying to its east, and the third of five biking excursions (Treks 19-23) into the same plateau area. Trek 21 rides E from the centre of Mae Sariang a short distance of about 15 kms along Highway 108, turns N at a junction, and then climbs up approximately NE via the isolated villages of Pa Pae, Goh Mai Lu and Huai Haak Mai Tai on a problematic dirt way 46 kms to the far-flung elevated

Lawa village of Chang Mor. From Chang Mor it strikes NNW another 27 kms along an incredibly remote dirt way to the isolated mountaintop Lawa outpost of La Ang (total distance from Mae Sariang via Pa Pae to La Ang some 88 kms). In doing so, it joins Trek 20 and from Chang Mor repeats the latter part of Trek 20. As with the other three trips into Lawa territory, the expedition involves some magnificent offroad biking in fabulous terrain.

The outing is a motorbike hike only. Because the distances involved are so great, and because the villages of the plateau of the Lawa are fairly well interconnected by dirt roads and trails, it makes little sense to walk it, or to walk part of it, or, more generally, to walk on the plateau. Like the mountainous area S of the 108 Mae Sariang/Hot road and SE of Mae Sariang, which is peopled by the Pwo Karen (Treks 18 & 19), Lawa country, sometimes referred to as the Ob Luang plateau, lends itself especially to exploration on two wheels (or in a jeep). It is just conceivable that Trek 21, in keeping with Treks 20 and 22-23, could be managed on a bicycle, but the machine would have to be a very sturdy mountain bike, riders would have to push their bikes in places, and they would need to be exceptionally tough, intrepid and persistent (no liability assumed, and no comeback, please).

As La Ang lies in the heart of Lawa country, far from anywhere, the trek does not end there. From it you must escape either by proceeding via Mae La Oop and Mae La Noi back to Mae Sariang, or by continuing via Ho Gao in the direction of Mae Chaem and ultimately Chiang Mai, or by going back the same way, a return journey to Mae Sariang that you could vary by riding from Chang Mor not via Pa Pae, but via Lao Li and Kong Loi. These three escape routes from pivotal La Ang on the one hand clearly add considerable distances to the overall journey, and on the other cross over to the other three treks in Lawa country, respectively Treks 22, 23 and 20 (see Map 35). Combining Trek 21 with Trek 22 (via Mae La Oop and Mae La Noi back to Mae Sariang) would add 72 kms to the 88-km distance already travelled, making an overall round trip from Mae Sariang to Mae Sariang of 160 kms. Combining it with Trek 23 (via Ho Gao and Mae Chaem) would add 52 kms to the 88 kms already travelled to make an overall trip of 140 kms as far as Mae Chaem, or add 170 kms to the 88 already travelled to make an overall trip of 258 kms as far as Chiang Mai. Combining it with the first part of Trek 20 (first back to Chang Mor and then via Lao Li and Kong Loi) would add 118 kms to the 88 kms already travelled, making an overall round trip from Mae Sariang to Mae Sariang of 206 kms. On a small bike, such as a Honda Dream, which is what can be typically hired in the tourist centres of Chiang Mai and Mae Hong Son, these are ambitious distances to be covering in one day on problematic mountain 'roads', and so it makes sense to spread the combined overall treks over two or more days, spending a night or nights at places en route (more below).

To make a more general observation, Trek 21 like Treks 20 and 22-23 can, of course, be permuted at will. Thus you can combine any one with any, other, and you can ride them in any direction, 'backwards' as well as forwards. Accordingly, the way in which I have ordered Treks 21 and 20 as well as 22-23 within their respective chapters (e.g. in Trek 21 to start in Mae Sariang, proceed via Pa Pae, Chang Mor and La Ang, and perhaps to exit via Mae La Oop and Mae La Noi) is only nominal, and could be rearranged by you to suit your inclinations. However, you would then correspondingly have to pick and choose among the four chapters, sometimes having to read the maps and text backwards. Clearly I cannot detail all the possible permutations in separate chapters. But back to the trek in hand.

With Trek 21 my suggestion is, as said, to proceed from Mae Sariang 15 kms E to the junction, go offroad 46 kms to Chang Mor (officially renamed as Santi Tam, I think), and then continue 27 kms to La Ang. From here I suggest you go down via the big Lawa village of Mae La Oop to Mae La Noi in the Yuam river valley, and from there return S down the H108 road to Mae Sariang. The 160-km-long anticlockwise loop crosses over from Trek 21 to 20 at Chang Mor, and from 20/21 to 22 at La Ang. From the junction on the H108 just E of Mae Sariang to Mae La Noi, a distance of some 115 kms, is nearly all dirt (in 1999). Needless to say, you could do the loop in reverse (clockwise), reading my maps and route detail backwards. I did this loop in January 1999 with Nittaya Tananchai and Doug Boynton. We rode on two little 100-cc Honda Dreams and took 2 days, breaking the journey and spending a night at Ho Gao (near La Ang). I suggest that you likewise spread the trip over 2 days (or longer). On stony dirt, the further you go in one day, and the more tired and careless you get, the greater is the chance that you will crash. But apart from this, taking 2 or more days over the trek allows you to stop and look at things on the way, experience the Lawa and some of their villages, do a spot of camping, unhurriedly enjoy the marvellous scenery, do some bird-watching à la Doug, and generally take it easy and have a good time. Stay at Chang Mor, or, as said, in the attractive traditional Lawa village of Ho Gao (16 kms E of La Ang, near the start of Trek 23, see Maps 35 & 40), in Mae La Oop, or in any village or place. Central pivotal La Ang is the obvious place to break the journey and stay overnight, but I have never found it very congenial.

You can modify the expedition, as already indicated, by crossing over at La Ang not to Trek 22 (continuing to Mae La Oop), but to Trek 23 (proceeding to Ho Gao and Mae Chaem). But another way of modifying it would be to involve the first part of Trek 20, which goes via Lao Li and Kong Loi (see Maps 35 & 36). You could do this in two ways. Either, as said earlier, you could return from La Ang to Chang Mor and then return to Mae Sariang via Lao Li and Kong Loi, tacking the first part of Trek 20 (backwards) onto Trek 21. Or, having arrived at Chang Mor after coming up via Pa Pae, you could simply ignore the Chang Mor/La Ang stretch and go straightaway down via Lao Li to Kong Loi, finishing by returning to Mae Sariang. This would combine the first part of Trek 21 with the first part of Trek 20 only, would eliminate onward Treks 22 or 23, and would shorten Trek 21 as part of an overall journey. The result would be not the long anticlockwise loop via La Ang and Mae La Oop, but would be a new clockwise shorter loop. Proceeding from Mae Sariang via Pa Pae to Chang Mor, and then via Lao Li and Kong Loi back to Mae Sariang, you could complete this 152-km-long circuit in one day, as I have done, perhaps spending a night at Chang Mor if you wanted. The first part of Trek 21, the feeder route to Chang Mor via Pa Pae, is more difficult, spectacular and slower than the feeder route to Chang Mor via Kong Loi (first part of Trek 20), and so, if you are planning to try this new combination, it is advisable to tackle the Pa Pae stretch first, i.e. indeed do the new loop clockwise, rather than the other way round, anticlockwise. It is always wiser to tackle the more problematic part of a trek first, while you are still fresh and have the whole day before you. Further, it is always easier to ride up a problematic stretch, such as that via Pa Pae, than to ride down it. Ride down the easier Lao Li way.

On the subject of difficulty, the first part of Trek 21, from the 108 road via Pa Pae up to Chang Mor, is in my estimation difficult for average to experienced riders. You must ford rivers, proceed along remote lonely trails, and negotiate steep uphill sections (in 1999) in a poor state and partially covered with bulldust. Skilled offroad dirt riders with enduro machines will enjoy the adventure. The rest of the journey, no matter whether you continue to La Ang and then to Mae La Oop and Mae La Noi, or to Lao Li and Kong Loi, is moderately difficult for average to experienced riders on, say, little Honda Dream bikes or their equivalent. In the former case, any problems will arise on the long, lonely, very isolated stretch from Chang Mor to La Ang (one of the remotest trails in Thailand, used by almost no traffic) (Map 37), and the (in 1999) poor connecting trail between La Ang and Du Lo Boe (see Map 39). In the latter case, the dirt road from Chang Mor to Kong Loi is a long gradual descent of gravel and stone (now paved in places), used by a fair amount of traffic (especially between Lao Li and Kong Loi), which should present few problems, but watch out for some sudden patches of sand and bulldust below Om Pai.

With the above considerations in mind, and because of the length and remoteness of the trails, neither Trek 21 nor related Treks 20 and 22-23 are suitable for inexperienced bikers or for novice riders who have casually hired a stepthrough Dream townbike in Mae Hong Son or wherever. Heaven help you if you crash or break down in the back of beyond on the way up to Pa Pae or between Chang Mor and La Ang. By the same token, it would be foolhardy to undertake Trek 21 or any of the three other treks as a solo biker unless you know what you are doing. Go with a friend and preferably with two or more bikes/bikers. Carry water and some food (and even a tent) with you on this trek, as you should on any such expedition, in case you break down, get a flat tyre, or crash, and have to spend a long time waiting for or going to get help. Obviously other bikers and bikes can be invaluable when such mishaps occur.

TREK IT YOURSELF IN NORTHERN THAILAND

About Mae Sariang and accommodation + food there

Trek 21 is launched from Mae Sariang, with its guest houses, shops, restaurants and other facilities. For information on the town, on staying in guest houses there, and on eating out, see Trek 18 under 'Accessing the trek'.

Brief notes on the Lawa

During Trek 21 and in related Treks 20, 22 and 23, you encounter Lawa people at Pa Pae and Chang Mor, as well as at variously La Ang, Mae La Oop and Ho Gao. For some outline information on this ancient and very interesting ethnic minority group, see Trek 23.

*

Trekking route detail

Mae Sariang – H108/junction at km 13 – Rai Lor – Pa Guai – Pa Pae – Goh Mai Lu – Huai Haak Mai Tai – Chang Mor

From the centre of Mae Sariang, ride a couple of kms up the town's long W/E-running Wiang Mai Road, past *Intira Restaurant* (right), the post office (right) and *Lotus Guest House* (right), to the complicated 'crossroads' at the far south-eastern end. Left goes N up the 108 highway 30 kms to Mae La Noi, 98 kms to Khun Yuam and 168 kms to Mae Hong Son. Just a few hundred metres up here is a big fuel station, a good place to tank up. Right goes a great distance down the Thai-Burmese border to Mae Salid and Mae Sot. Straight (eastish) is our route along the 108 road in the direction of Hot and ultimately Chiang Mai. From the 'crossroads' proceed E along the H108 road another 13 kms (ca 15 kms from the centre of Mae Sariang) to a junction with a turning left (N) (see Map 29). The junction, which is not in any village but isolated in the countryside, is marked by a *sala* or waiting hut, many signs indicating some of the villages on and off our route, and km-stone 90 (measured from Hot). Turn left into the side road. Now see Map 38. My distance readings on the map and in the route detail below start at km 0.0 at the junction.

For 9 kms you ride breezily along a purposeful new asphalted road, which is already growing over on either side and which, as you discover, goes nowhere really. At km 2.6 you pass a turning to the village of Pa Maak, 1 km offroad right. The road twists and turns through lovely scenery, passing a turning left to the Salween reforestation station (1.5 kms offroad), before it reaches a river and a ford (km 9.2). Here the new paved road ends at the water, which is the Huai Mae Sariang or Sariang stream (actually more of a small river). Cross the river, riding through the sand, mud and one-foot-deep water, to pick up a poor dirt trail on the other side. Almost immediately you come to the same river twice more, and you must ford it a second and third time. It is the same Sariang river, and now you follow the Huai Mae Sariang upstream and along the valley through wild and beautiful country.

At km 12.9 you come to the first village actually on the trail, **Rai Lor**, a Karen place just to your right. Further along you see the first part of the Karen village of **Pa Guai** across the valley on your right, and at km 17.4 you come to the second part close to the trail, also right. Less than a km beyond this settlement, you reach a

290

bridge (km 18.2), which is followed by a steep climb up a ridge in part through bulldust. You will know when you hit this problematic upgrade! We grew alarmed at it, wondering what lay ahead. But persist. Soon you are on top, with magnificent views in both directions off the ridge. Three kms after the bridge, you come to a *sala* standing on a junction (km 21.2). The way right goes 2.3 kms off-trail to Om Pok, a Karen place, I think. Continue a further km to a second *sala*, which marks another junction (km 22.3). The way left goes 4 kms off-route to Mae Om Long, also Karen, I believe. Has anyone been to these two villages, which could be written as 'Oom' or 'Um' Pok/Long? I never have. Perhaps they are Lawa, after all, or mixed Lawa and Karen. If you have time, go in and take a look at them. You may well the first or one of the first *farang* to do so.

Some 2.8 kms further, you come to a third *sala* and junction (km 25.1). With no one around, we puzzled for some time about which way to go. A sign said only, frighteningly, 'Huai Dua 22 kms'. The junction is an important one. As we finally discovered, left (straight) goes to Pa Pae, while right is the onward route to Chang Mor (i.e. your way). You could continue in that direction without visiting Pa Pae, which from the junction constitutes a small detour of 2.6 kms there and back (2 x 1.3 kms). If you do so, you will have to subtract 2.6 kms from the remaining distance readings, because we did indeed go to Pa Pae. Following our itinerary, therefore, you continue 1.3 kms, passing a turning left for a Royal Project, to arrive at **Pa Pae** (km 26.4). It is a big compact Lawa village, attractive with Christmas plants. It is also a strange place because it is very isolated and quite high up, and yet is developed, with large well-established wooden houses and even streets. I can tell you little else about Pa Pae because we were short of time and stopped only to ask directions. Stop at least for some lunch here, and consider spending a night, perhaps at the health centre. You are certain to have an unforgettable experience. Beyond Pa Pae a way goes reportedly ca 7 kms to Huai Haak Mai Nuea, the northern part of New Huai Haak village (*mai* = new, *nuea* = north).

Now return to the junction (new km reading: 27.7) and turn left for Chang Mor. Here, as anywhere along this trail, follow the power lines if you are in doubt as to which way to go. You proceed 3.6 kms to **Goh Mai Lu** (km 31.3), an attractive elevated friendly place, strung out along the trail. As you approach it, you can see on your left, across the valley, a settlement, which must be Huai Haak Mai Nuea. In the vicinity of Goh Mai Lu you pick up a much better (compared to the trail hitherto) gravel 'highway', which must have been engineered recently. I fancy that the people of Pae Pae, Go Mai Lu and the two parts of Huai Haak Mai use this new dirt road when going to and from their villages, i.e. their access is via Chang Mor and not via Pa Guai and Rai Lor. From Goh Mai Lu to Chang Mor, a distance of 15 kms, you sweep along the new 'skyway', plunging and rising as if on a roller-coaster, snaking around the mountainsides, and passing through superb upland scenery. If ever you were on the Ob Luang plateau of the Lawa, it is here.

Just 1.1 kms out from Goh Mai Lu, you hit a T-junction (km 32.4). Go right for Chang Mor. Left proceeds to **Huai Haak Mai Tai**, which, if you get off your bike at the T-junction, you can see below you in the valley. Incidentally, the foot trek that I mentioned in Trek 20, which proceeds cross-country from Mae Aeb to Mae La Oop, passes through Huai Haak Mai Tai and then Huai Haak Mai Nuea. Going right at the T-junction, therefore, you pass two cement tanks and a settlement (left), soon to reach the turning right (km 34.4) for Huai Dua, which evidently lies 7 kms offroad (and which cannot, therefore, be 22 kms from the Pa Pae junction). Now you bowl along the new elevated gravel road in earnest. You pass on your right side a bald, rounded, twin-topped mountain (ca km 37), then an old shed (also right), followed by a turning left for the village of Toen or Toon somewhere offroad, before hitting a T-junction (km 45.9, let us say 46). You have reached the key junction close to the Lawa village of **Chang Mor**. Right goes down to Om Pai, Lao Li (Mae To) and Kong Loi, while left continues to La Ang. Now you must decide how to proceed. Whatever you do, you now cross over to Trek 20 (see Map 35).

Continuing from Chang Mor
(1) Via Kong Loi (see Maps 36 & 29)
Go right (approximately S) if you want to return to Mae Sariang via Kong Loi, doing the first part of Trek 20 backwards and making the shorter, from now on easier, clockwise loop trip Mae Sariang to Mae Sariang. You have completed about 60 kms so far since starting in Mae Sariang. From the Chang Mor junction, it is a further 6.7 kms to Om Pai, 24.8 kms to Lao Li (also known as Mae To), 41 kms to Kong Loi, and 91 kms back to Mae Sariang, the last 50 of them, from Kong Loi, being on the 108 highway. Your overall round trip would amount to 152 kms. For information about Chang Mor and about the possibilities of staying overnight there, see Trek 20. For details about the onward journey from Chang Mor to Lao Li and Kong Loi, likewise see Trek 20, although in the text of that trek you will have to read the data backwards.

(2) Via La Ang (see Maps 37 & 39, or 37 & 40-42)
(2a) Go left (approximately N) if you want to return to Mae Sariang via La Ang and Ma La Oop, doing the second part of Trek 20 as far as La Ang, and then crossing over to Trek 22 for the stretch La Ang to Mae La Oop and Mae La Noi. If you take this option, you will be embarking on the longer, from now on more difficult, anticlockwise loop trip Mae Sariang to Mae Sariang. You have completed about 60 kms so far since starting in Mae Sariang. From the Chang Mor junction, it is a further 27 kms to La Ang, 44 kms to Mae La Oop, 69 kms to Mae La Noi, and 100 kms to Mae Sariang. Your overall round trip would amount to some 160 kms. For details about the onward journey from Chang Mor to La Ang, see the second part of Trek 20. For information about Chang Mor, where you are now, and about the possibilities of staying overnight there, also see Trek 20.

(2b) Also go left at the Chang Mor junction if you plan to continue to La Ang and then cross over to Trek 23, proceeding to Ho Gao, Pang Hin Fon, Mae Chaem and ultimately Chiang Mai. You have completed about 60 kms so far since starting in Mae Sariang. From the Chang Mor junction it is a further 27 kms to La Ang, 43 kms to Ho Gao, 54 kms to Pang Hin Fon, and 79 kms to Mae Chaem. Chiang Mai is a long way off (some 120 kms from Mae Chaem), but you can reach it on a bike in one day from Ho Gao. For details about the onward journey from Chang Mor to La Ang, see the second part of Trek 20. For details about the onward journey from La Ang to Ho Gao and Mae Chaem, see Trek 23. For information about Chang Mor, where you are now, and about the possibilities of staying overnight there, see Trek 20.

Whichever way you go, you still have a long way to go, so, unless you break your journey in Chang Mor, you had better get on your way. Have a good ride!

Trek 22

La Ang – Du Lo Boe – Mae La Oop – Mae La Noi – Mae Sariang

Parameters

trekking mode: by motorcycle

trek time: variable as trip must be combined with another trek, being preceded by either Trek 20 or 21 or 23 (the latter in reverse). Combined with 20 or 21, could be done in one long day as a loop excursion from Mae Sariang, although interpolating a night stop is recommended; combined with Trek 23, allow at least 2 days/1 night

trek distance: La Ang to Mae La Oop 16.5 kms, plus Mae La Oop to Mae La Noi 25 kms, plus Mae La Noi to Mae Sariang 30 kms (total 71.5 kms), to which can be added the distances of preceding Treks 20, 21 or 23, whichever you choose. Reckon on long overall distances.

degree of difficulty: moderately difficult for average to experienced riders; no problem for skilled offroad bikers or for dirt freaks with enduro machines; the problem with all these treks is not so much with their difficulty, but more with their combined length

tent: not strictly necessary, but advisable, not least as a fall-back

map(s):   see 35 & 39

Overview & strategy

This trek is the third of four substantial motorcycle expeditions (Treks 20-23 inclusive) NE of Mae Sariang in Lawa country. At the same time it is the fifth of altogether six outings made in the mountains to the E of this westerly town (Treks 18-23), and the fourth of five biking excursions (Treks 19-23) in the same plateau area. Trek 22 rides roughly SW 16.5 kms from the small far-flung mountaintop Lawa village of La Ang to the large well-established Lawa village of Mae La Oop (see Map 39), then continues approximately W 25 kms from Mae La Oop down to the main 108 Mae Sariang/Mae Hong Son road in the valley of the River Yuam, hitting that road just S of Mae La Noi, and finally heads S down the 108 highway 30 kms to Mae Sariang, although of course it would be possible from Mae La Noi also to strike N in the direction of Mae La Luang, Khun Yuam and Mae Hong Son. The total distance from La Ang to the H108 at Mae La Noi is 41.5 kms and to Mae Sariang 71.5 kms. As with the other three trips into Lawa territory (Treks 20, 21 and 23), the expedition involves some great offroad biking in splendid scenic terrain.

If you have come to this trek without first doing or reading about Treks 20, 21 and 23, you will be wondering how a trek could possibly start in the middle of nowhere at the remote outpost of La Ang. It is because, in the order that I have presented Treks 20-23 in this book, Trek 22 presupposes that before you get to it you have already completed either Trek 20 or 21 or (in reverse) 23, i.e. that before you ride from La Ang down to Mae La Oop and beyond you have already come up to La Ang either from Mae Sariang via Kong Loi and Chang Mor (Trek 20), or from Mae Sariang via Pa Pae and Chang Mor (Trek 21), or from Mae Chaem via Pang Hin Fon and Ho Gao (Trek 23, but the other way round) (see Map 35 for an overview of all this). Thus, according to my scheme of Treks 20-23, this trek is a continuation of Treks 20, 21 and possibly 23, and those other three trips cross over to this trek. But things do not have to be like this. My order or scheme of the four Lawa motorcycle treks is only nominal, and they could be configured otherwise. Notably, you could undertake Trek 22 the other way round, starting in Mae Sariang, proceeding to Mae La Noi, and climbing to Mae La Oop and La Ang. This would convert the trek from being an exit route to being now the third of four feeder routes to La Ang. In Trek 20 we accessed La Ang via Kong Loi and Chang Mor. In Trek 21 we accessed La Ang via Pa Pae and Chang Mor. Now you would access La Ang via Mae La Noi and Mae La Oop. And a fourth access to La Ang would be via Mae Chaem and Ho Gao. You can see how unassuming La Ang is pivotal to the four Lawa biking expeditions. It is where they all cross over. In this trek, therefore, I shall simply start things off from La Ang, making the presupposition that you have already arrived there by one of the other feeder routes (Treks 20, 21, or perhaps 23). If you come up to La Ang via Mae La Noi and Mae La Oop, you will have to read Map 39 and the route detail below backwards, although at the end I give some km readings as if you were doing the trip this other way round.

Trek 22 comprises, as said, about 72 kms if you wind up in Mae Sariang. As part of an overall journey that includes one of the preceding feeder trips to La Ang, it will, however, have a considerably greater total distance. Thus if you reckon in prior Trek 20 (accessing La Ang from Mae Sariang via Kong Loi and Chang Mor), you will add 118 kms to 72-km-long onward Trek 22, making an overall round trip from Mae Sariang to Mae Sariang of 190 kms. If you reckon in prior Trek 21 (accessing La Ang from Mae Sariang via Pa Pae and Chang Mor), you will add 88 kms to 72-km-long onward Trek 22, making an overall round trip from Mae Sariang to Mae Sariang of 160 kms. And if you reckon in prior Trek 23 (accessing La

TREK 22: LA ANG – MAE LA OOP – MAE LA NOI

Ang from Mae Chaem via Pang Hin Fon and Ho Gao), you will add 52 kms to 72-km-long onward Trek 22, making an overall trip from Mae Chaem to Mae Sariang via Mae La Oop of 124 kms (if you further reckon in the distance from Chiang Mai to Mae Chaem, you can add another 118 kms to that figure, making a total trip from Chiang Mai to Mae Sariang via Mae Chaem, La Ang and Mae La Oop of some 242 kms). On a small bike, such as a 100-cc Honda Dream, which is what can typically be hired in the tourist centres of Chiang Mai or Mae Hong Son, these are ambitious distances to be covering in one day on problematic mountain 'roads', and so it makes sense to spread the combined overall treks over two or more days, spending a night or nights at places en route (more below).

The outing is a motorbike hike only. Because the distances involved are relatively great, and because the villages of the plateau of the Lawa are fairly well interconnected by dirt roads and trails, it makes little sense to walk it, or to walk part of it, or, more generally, to walk on the plateau. Like the mountainous area S of the 108 Mae Sariang/Hot road and SE of Mae Sariang, which is peopled by the Pwo Karen (Treks 18 & 19), Lawa country, sometimes referred to as the Ob Luang plateau, lends itself especially to exploration on two wheels (or in a jeep). It is just conceivable that Trek 22, in keeping with Treks 20-21 and 23, could be managed on a bicycle, but the bicycle would have to be a very sturdy mountain bike, and riders would need to be exceptionally tough, intrepid and persistent (no liability assumed, and no comeback, please).

With Trek 22 my nominal suggestion is, as outlined at the beginning, to proceed 72 kms from La Ang to Mae Sariang via Mae La Oop and Mae La Noi, anteceding the trip with either Trek 20 or – for skilled offroad dirt riders only – Trek 21. This embeds Trek 22 in a satisfying anticlockwise loop ride, launched from Mae Sariang, of respectively 190 and 160 kms, of which the dirt-biking component is (in 1999) in each case some 100 kms! Needless to say, you could do the loop in reverse (clockwise), reading my maps and route detail backwards. I first did the longer version of this loop, combining Trek 22 with preceding Trek 20, in February 1998 with 'Mr Pan' of *Pan House* in Mae Waen (see Trek 18). On small bikes, we completed the circuit in one long tiring day. In January 1999, I redid it with Nittaya Tananchai and Doug Boynton. We rode on two little 100-cc Honda Dreams and took a very leisurely 3 days, breaking the journey and spending 2 nights at Ho Gao and Mae La Oop, although the loop could comfortably be done in 2 days/1 night, staying perhaps at Ho Gao (near La Ang). The slightly shorter version of the loop, combining Trek 22 with preceding Trek 21, could be accomplished in a similar time frame. You could complete it in one long tiring day (experienced dirt bikers only), or more comfortably in two days or more, breaking the journey and spending a night in Ho Gao, or earlier at Chang Mor, or even earlier at Pa Pae, or later at Mae La Oop, or at any two of these places. I suggest that you likewise spread the loop over 2 days (or longer). On stony dirt, the further you go in one day, and the more tired and careless you get, the greater is the chance that you will crash. But apart from this, taking 2 or more days over the combined trip allows you to stop and look at things on the way, experience the Lawa and some of their villages, do a spot of camping, unhurriedly enjoy the marvellous scenery, do some bird-watching à la Doug, and generally take it easy and have a good time. Trek 22 on its own, the stretch from La Ang to Mae Sariang, should take about half a day. For tips about overnighting in Chang Mor, see Trek 20. For details about staying at the attractive traditional Lawa village of Ho Gao (16 kms E of La Ang, near the start of Trek 23, see Maps 35 & 40), refer to Trek 23. For details about stopping at Mae La Oop, see below. Pivotal midpoint La Ang is, of course, the obvious place to break the loop journey and stay overnight, but I have never found it very congenial. For information about accessing La Ang by the various feeder routes, see, of course, their respective chapters (Treks 20, 21 and 23). For a thumbnail sketch of La Ang, refer to Trek 20.

On the subject of difficulty, Trek 22 is in my estimation moderately difficult for average to experienced riders. The further you progress, the easier things get. It is mostly downhill all the way. For gradings of feeder Treks 20, 21 and 23, refer to the relevant chapters. In 1999, the most problematic part of Trek 22 was near the beginning, between Mae Pi Ki and Du Lo Boe, where, taking care, you must go down a skinny little woodland trail with tons of bulldust. The open elevated section between Du Lo Boe and Huai Ha is less problematic, but remains tricky in the sense that the way is poor and awash with stones. For some reason, in 1999 Doug and I both crashed our bikes on it at exactly the same spot just above Huai Ha. Perhaps we were exulting in the stunning views and not paying attention to our riding, but on a curve our front tyres hit a fist-sized stone, and over we went, taking a tumble. I wrecked my gear pedal and had to ride my Honda stuck in first gear a couple of kms to Huai Ha, where some Karen boys bent the pedal out. From Mae La Oop to the H108, the way is a regular dirt road, used by a fair amount of traffic, and the last few kms are paved. I recall most of the route from La Ang to Mae La Noi being very rocky, stony and bumpy, threatening to rattle one's bike to pieces. Skilled offroad dirt riders with enduro machines will relish the adventure. Bearing in mind these considerations, and because of the length and remoteness of the trails in Trek 22 combined with prior Treks 20, 21 or 23, there is nothing on the Lawa plateau for inexperienced bikers or for novice riders who have casually hired a stepthrough Dream townbike in Mae Hong Son or Chiang Mai.

About Mae Sariang and accommodation + food there
Trek 22 is ultimately launched, in the sense that it succeeds either Trek 20 or 21, from Mae Sariang, with its guest houses, shops, restaurants and other facilities. It also, as I outline things in this chapter, ends up there. For information about Mae Sariang, on staying in guest houses in the town, and on eating out, see Trek 18 under 'Accessing the trek'.

Brief notes on the Lawa

During Trek 22 and in feeder Treks 20, 21 and 23, you encounter Lawa people at La Ang and Mae La Oop, as well as at variously Chang Mor, Pa Pae and Ho Gao. For some outline information on this ancient and very interesting ethnic minority group, see Trek 23.

*

Trekking route detail
La Ang – Du Lo Boe – Huai Ha – Mae La Oop (see Map 39)

Leave La Ang by exiting the village's main street (km 0) at its north-western end and passing two cylindrical water tanks. You proceed along a flattish elevated open track that skirts the hillsides almost at ridgetop level, and offers fine views. With the trail veering more W, you soon come to the friendly Karen settlement of **Mae Pi Ki** on your right side (km 3.9). Lower down you reach a small junction in some trees (km 5.4). The junction is marked by a *sala* or waiting hut, and near it there is a green sign saying 'Du Lo Boe forest conservation area'. From the junction a skinny motorcycle trail goes off right to the village of Mae Sa Meng, after which it continues to Pae, Kok Luang, Nong Muan, Kok Noi and Ho Gao, forming a big side loop to the combined routes of Trek 22 and 23 (see Map 40). I have not explored this side route, so these details are unchecked. All the locals speak of it as a 'regular' trail, but it should only be attempted by experienced and skilled bikers. You go straight (left) off the junction, carefully making your way down the trickiest passage of this trek, which is a steep rutted downgrade in a parlous state with bulldust aplenty, set ironically in pleasant elevated woodland. You emerge at a 'crossroads', from which a couple of cement-section streets lead directly into the Karen village of **Du Lo Boe** (km 6.7). There is a grand view W from Du Lo Boe across the valley of the River Yuam, over intervening mountains, deep into Burma with its receding ridges.

Now you follow a mediocre 'road' all the way to Mae La Oop. Rough and stony, it passes through bleak open denuded upland terrain. At a triple junction (km 8.6), where two side trails go off left (S), continue straight, following the biggest way. As you rattle your bike to pieces, concentrate on your riding so that you do not crash, as both Doug and I did a couple of kms short of Huai Ha. You gently descend to a kind of crossroads (km 11.8). The way right (N) goes 1.5 kms to the village of Huai Horm, while left proceeds on a path to Huai Ha, which is visible. Go straight to arrive just 600 m further at a turning left/S (km 12.4), which is the main way to the Karen village of **Huai Ha**, which lies close to the 'main' road. The junction is marked by an incongruous phone box. Huai Ha is where I got my bike repaired for 20 baht. Apply likewise to the nearest village if you have a mishap. From Huai Ha a motorcycle trail reportedly goes across country via Huai Ha Mai to the La Ang/Chang Mor road, hitting it near Saam (see Map 37). I have not investigated this way, so cannot vouch for it. Do not attempt it unless you know what you are doing.

Continue straight from the Huai Ha turning and proceed 4 kms down to Mae La Oop. Just short of La Oop, a way left/N (km 16.1) goes to the village of Dong or Doong Gao (Old Dong) and then Dong Mai (New Dong), beyond which it evidently proceeds as a cross-country motorcycle trail to Por Mae Chu (Pak Pai) and, likewise, the La Ang/Chang Mor road (Map 37). Again, I have not investigated this trail, so cannot vouch for it. Do not attempt it unless you are a skilled offroad dirt rider and know what you are doing. The junction for Dong Gao is marked by a curious pink Chinese-looking house and a pagoda. A few hundred metres further, you come to another junction (km 16.5), marked by a *sala*. Right takes you on down to Mae La Noi, while left or straight brings you into the main street of **Mae La Oop**.

Mae La Oop

This is a large well-established Lawa village, built on the top of a ridge. Its protracted main street runs along the crest of the ridge, and many of the settlement's houses as well as a handful of simple shops flank it. From this eyrie position at nearly 4000 ft, many of the Lawa of Mae La Oop enjoy spectacular views especially N and S. At the beginning of the central drag (actually still outside the village, by the entrance/junction and *sala*), there is a motorbike repair shop. As you go W down the main street, you pass a store or two and, more than half way along, two shops on a bend by a telephone box (right side of road). One of them, the left-hand one, is a possible place to stay. Further along, you come to a fork. Left at the fork brings you to a compound and a small *wat* at the end of the street. If you look roughly ESE from the elevated compound, you can see the village of Dong Gao down in the valley. Right at the fork brings you via a twisting road down to fair-sized Mae La Oop school and ultimately a big new health centre. Consider the centre as another place to stay (more below). The village headman and his house are also to be found in this north-westerly corner. In my adventure travelogue *Three Pagodas* I provided an anecdotal account of Mae La Oop, based on what I found in February 1994, when I first visited it. The reader is referred to that book (Chapter 8) for a more rounded narrative description of the village. Here I will confine myself to a few factual details and to noting some changes that have occurred in the five years since then, up to 1999, when Nittaya, Doug and I stopped by.

In early 1994 there were 160 houses in 'town', mostly simple primitive affairs, high on stilts and with grass roofs, but nevertheless solidly built of wood with spacious front platforms. By 1999 the number must have grown, and certainly everything, and particularly the houses, were more developed. We were told that the Lawa of La Oop had prospered from a couple of years of good cabbage crops, and had invested their earnings in their dwellings. Where the main street used to have a surface of dirt and worn rock, now it was paved. It had had electricity back in 1994, so no change there. Now you can buy petrol in La Oop from a little fuel booth, and there is a *silor* or public-transport pick-up service between the village and Mae La Noi. But in other ways things remained in 1999 unchanged, and Mae La Oop was still a traditional Lawa village. They still had a big water supply problem, which is only to be expected if you build your village on the top of a hill. When the rainwater collected in tanks during the wet season has run out, there is no water, and for drinking water or a wash you have to go halfway down the mountain to a spring. Beyond that, black pot-bellied pigs rooted around everywhere, along with dogs, chickens, buffaloes and cows. There are even sheep at Mae La Oop. As at Chang Mor (see Trek 20), and in keeping with the Lawa, the villagers have dark copper-coloured careworn faces, angular Wa-like features, and a hairiness of face and limb (the men) untypical of smooth-skinned Mongoloid Orientals, such as the Thai. Many of the women are diminutive, and men and women of all ages smoke short pipes. All the children had the same hacking coughs we had heard in Chang Mor. Like Lawa people throughout the Ob Luang plateau, the inhabitants of Mae La Oop are relatively downtrodden people, but friendly.

As you explore around the village, you see many women weaving on the balconies of their houses at simple backstrap looms. Sitting on the floor, they lean back to tauten the warp strings and weave across their laps. They mostly weave material for skirts and shoulderbags. Traditional costumes are still in evidence in Mae La Oop, but – on a day to day basis – only with the women. As in Chang Mor, they wear a black or indigo tube skirt with horizontal banding of dark red or pink, but also sometimes of azure or white. They have a white or beige smock, which as everyday wear is often very grubby, and wear indigo leggings, above which, just below the knee, you can see black bangles made from the lac tree. Sometimes they wear 'leggings' on their arms. Unmistakable are the multiple strings of small beads worn around the neck. The beads are usually coloured coral, but you can also see red, yellow and azure necklaces. Also favoured are silver cup-shaped earrings. Unless it is a special day, perhaps the day of a wedding or important ceremonial sacrifice, you do not normally see the men's costume, which comprises baggy, off-white, heavy cotton trousers and an open jacket of the same colour and material, the ensemble resembling a judo outfit. Many men are tattooed, often from the waist to the thighs, making it look as if they are wearing black culottes. The tattoos often include cat figures.

The Lawa are not just notable weavers, but also fine silversmiths and traditionally, as we saw in Trek 20, workers of iron. There used to be a silversmithery in a house near the entrance to Mae La Oop, where I once observed two young men transforming small stamped bullets of silver into bracelets, fine chains and exquisite round repousséd boxes. The finished products went for sale in Chiang Mai's Night Bazaar. Perhaps the workshop is still there.

On Trek 22, or as you make the loop from Mae Sariang via Chang Mor and La Ang back to Mae Sariang (or the other way round), consider staying a night in Mae La Oop. Consider stopping here as an alternative to overnighting in Ho Gao. The two places are equidistant (16 kms) from La Ang. Or look upon La Oop as somewhere to spend a second night after you have spent a first night in Chang Mor or Ho Gao. One accommodation possibility is with La Oop's headman or *po luang* (*po luang* is a dialect word for the more usual *pu yai*). His name is Boonyeuan Promsermsook, and he is about 45 years old. In 1994 I lodged with Nittaya Tananchai in his large tin-roofed house, onto which he had just built a new extension. A pleasant fellow, he and his womenfolk proved exceptionally hospitable. In those days he owned two elephants. Actually, prior to 1994, he had had four tuskers, but had sold two in order to pay for his extension!

Another place where you could try to lodge is the house and shop mentioned earlier, which is located on the main street right next to the phone box. A young man here, with whose family Nittaya, Doug and I spent a pleasant evening in 1999, volunteered that he would put up passers by (i.e. you) on the floor of his house, providing blankets. He said that from time to time *farang* came to stay with him when taking part locally in organized trekking. His name is Yoon Sen, nickname Yanae. He is a clued-up *farang*-friendly chap, who has even been to Sweden on a student exchange, one of only two people from Mae Hong Son province to have done so.

In 1999, after Nittaya, Doug and I crashed our bikes above Huai Ha, we made our way to Mae La Oop health centre, where a nurse tended our injuries, swabbing our cuts and grazes with liberal amounts of alcohol and iodine – ouch! Although the boss was away for the moment, she said we were welcome to stay at the centre, sleeping either inside the building on the floor or outside in our tents in the centre grounds. We opted for the latter and had a quiet pleasant night, although the compound was a tad scruffy and the washing facilities not up to much, at least not until the doctor returned. Consider staying likewise in this secluded corner at the very edge of the village. From the very health centre compound itself, Doug spied with his scope an Asian emerald cuckoo, some kind of hawk, a golden-fronted leafbird, a verditer flycatcher and a bar-winged flycatcher-shrike.

Mae La Oop – H108/Mae La Noi – Mae Sariang (see Map 39)

Back at the junction and entrance to Mae La Oop's main street, we continue our journey (distance readings resume from km 16.5, as if we had not gone into the drawn-out village). Now you gradually descend a regular dirt road (the H1266) 25 kms to Mae La Noi and the H108 highway. Although it is fairly well used by traffic – there are even, as said, *songtaew* or public-transport pick-ups plying the Mae La Noi/Mae La Oop route – the way remains in places a stony bone-shaker. On the way, you pass first a turning right for some kind of herb-growing place and, I think, the village of Mae Nga. On this initial stretch, if you look back, there are some splendid views of Mae La Oop perched on its ridgetop in a way modestly reminiscent of some eyrie Tibetan settlement. The turning is followed by a second turning also right/N (km 19.6) for the village of Mae Sa Ping Tai (could also be Mae Sa Poen Tai), which lies some 9.5 kms offroad.

At km 24.9 you pass a turning left (S) for a waterfall, and then you come to two ways right/N (ca km 25.5) to the Karen village of **Mae Sa Kua**, visible about a km offroad. I have always been struck by the incomparable setting and beauty of this little place. Its compact hilltop cluster of roofs stands like an island in a sea of surrounding forest. Glints of Karen cerise – from washing hung out to dry in the sun – can be seen amid the brown of the leaf roofs, which together punctuate an endless canopy of green stretching back to the N and merging into bluish mountain ridges in the far background. From the next junction (km 29.9), two ways go off left/S to the Karen village of **Huai Mak Noon**, which is close to the road, and to the more distant villages of Mae Kwang and Huai Poeng, not visible. Now you pass a temporary forestry office left (km 30.2), which might be somewhere to stay the night if you wanted or needed.

The remaining 10 or so kms need not detain us. The road finishes its descent to the valley floor, changes from stony dirt into a paved surface, and passes the regular rural villages of **Huai Rin** and **Pa Maak**, before hitting the main 108 highway at a T-junction (km 41.5), just south of **Mae La Noi**. Right (N) proceeds a short distance over a bridge to Mae La Noi, which is a small assimilated Lawa town with shops and eating places, beyond which you head further N 20 kms to Mae La Luang, 68 kms to Khun Yuam and 138 kms to distant Mae Hong Son, while left (S) brings you 30 kms along a speed road to **Mae Sariang** (km 71.5, measured from La Ang). It is easy to overshoot Mae Sariang, which lies to the right (W) of the highway. Look for side roads right at about the latitude of the big fuel station (left). Just a few hundred metres beyond or S of the fuel station, a way sharp right at a kind of crossroads leads you into the town's long main street.

*

Doing Trek 22 in reverse
In case you are doing Trek 22 and then Trek 20 in reverse, undertaking the Mae Sariang – Kong Loi – Chang Mor – La Ang – Mae La Oop – Mae La Noi – Mae Sariang loop the other way round, clockwise rather than anticlockwise, here are some distance indications, starting 30 kms N of Mae Sariang at the junction of the H108 and H1266 roads just S of Mae La Noi (see Map 39):

Trek 22

Junction H108/H1266:	km 0.0
Forestry (right):	km 11.3
Huai Maak Noon turning (right):	km 11.6
Mae Sa Kua turning (left):	km 13.8
Waterfall (right):	km 16.6
Mae Sa Ping Tai turning (left):	km 21.9
Mae La Oop entrance (right):	km 25.0
Huai Ha turning (right):	km 29.1
Huai Horm turning (left):	km 29.7
Du Lo Boe crossroads:	km 34.8
Woodland *sala*/junction:	km 36.1
Mae Pi Ki (left):	km 37.6
La Ang centre:	km 41.5

Trek 20 (distances continue from La Ang)

La Ang junction (by *wat*):	km 42.0
Mae Lae turning (right):	km 43.1
Saam turning (left):	km 45.7
Huai Ha Mai turning (right):	km 45.8
Por Mae Cho turning (right):	km 55.3
First Om Raed turning (left):	km 60.3
Second Om Raed turning (left):	km 62.2
Chang Mor Luang turn (left) by *sala*:	km 66.0
Chang Mor school turning (right):	km 67.0

Chang Mor Noi turning (left):   km 67.7
Chang Mor junction: km 68.2

Om Pai (left):   km 74.9
Lao Li (= Mae To):   km 93.0
Kong Loi & junction H1270/H108   km 109.2
Mae Sariang centre   km 160.0

Trek 23

La Ang – Sae To Sa – Mae Hae Tai – Ho Gao – Pang Hin Fon – Mae Chaem – Doi Intanon/National Park – Chom Tong – Chiang Mai

Parameters

trekking mode: by motorcycle

trek time: variable as trip must be combined with another trek, being preceded by either Trek 20 or 21 or 22 (the latter in reverse). Trek 23 on its own should be manageable in one long day, although interpolating a night stop is recommended, perhaps at Mae Chaem. Combined with either Trek 20 or 21 or (backwards) 22, allow at least 2 days/1 night.

trek distance: La Ang to Ho Gao 16 kms, plus 36 kms Ho Gao to Mae Chaem (total 52 kms), plus 118 kms Mae Chaem to Chiang Mai (total 170 kms), to which can be added the distances of preceding Treks 20, 21 or 22, whichever you choose. Reckon on long overall distances from Mae Sariang to Chiang Mai of between 250 and 300 kms, much of the journey on poor dirt.

degree of difficulty: moderately difficult for average to experienced riders; no problem for skilled offroad bikers or for dirt freaks with enduro machines; the problem with all these treks is not so much with their difficulty, but more with their combined length

tent: not strictly necessary, but advisable, not least as a fall-back

map(s):   see 35, 40, 41 & 42

Overview & strategy

This trek is the last of four substantial motorcycle expeditions (Treks 20-23 inclusive) NE of Mae Sariang in Lawa country. At the same time it is the last of altogether six outings made in the mountains to the E of this westerly town (Treks 18-23), and the last of five biking excursions (Treks 19-23) in the same plateau area. Thus it wraps up our trekking business with Mae

Sariang and environs. Trek 22 rides roughly NE 16 kms from the small far-flung mountaintop Lawa village of La Ang to the even remoter, traditional Lawa village of Ho Gao (see Map 40), then continues roughly N some 14 kms to Pang Hin Fon junction, before descending approximately E some 22 kms to the district town of Mae Chaem (see Map 41). From Mae Chaem trekkers have the option, finally, of proceeding 118 kms via Doi Intanon National Park (via the summit of Mount Intanon itself, if they wish) and Chom Tong to Chiang Mai. The total distance from La Ang to Mae Chaem is 52 kms and to Chiang Mai around 170 kms. As with the other three expeditions into Lawa territory (Treks 20, 21 and 22), the trip involves some magnificent offroad biking in fabulous scenic terrain. If Trek 23 is combined with either Trek 20 or 21 or (backwards) 22 to form one long west-to-east journey from Mae Sariang right across the mountains to Mae Chaem, Doi Intanon and Chiang Mai (or vice versa), it constitutes one of the finest motorcycling expeditions not only in this book but in all Thailand, comparable to the monster biking hike along the old elephant trail from Mae Hong Son via Wat Chan to Samoeng and Chiang Mai or vice versa (Treks 24 & 25).

If you have come to this trek without first doing or reading about Treks 20, 21 and 22, you will be wondering how a trek could possibly start in the middle of nowhere at the remote outpost of La Ang. It is because, in the order that I have presented Treks 20-23 in this book, Trek 23 presupposes that before you get to it you have already completed either Trek 20 or 21 or (in reverse) 22, i.e. that before you ride from La Ang to Ho Gao and down to Mae Chaem and beyond you have already come up to La Ang either from Mae Sariang via Kong Loi and Chang Mor (Trek 20), or from Mae Sariang via Pa Pae and Chang Mor (Trek 21), or from Mae Sariang via Mae La Noi and Mae La Oop (Trek 22, but the other way round) (see Map 35 for an overview of all this). Thus, according to my scheme of Treks 20-23, this hike is a continuation of Treks 20 and 21 and possibly 22, and those other three trips cross over to this trek.

But things do not have to be like this. My order or scheme of the four Lawa motorcycle treks is only nominal, and they could be configured otherwise. Notably, you could undertake this expedition (Trek 23) the other way round, starting in Chiang Mai, proceeding via Chom Tong and through Doi Intanon National Park to Mae Chaem, and climbing up to Ho Gao and La Ang. I can well imagine that many trekkers, based in Chiang Mai, would want to do this. It would convert the trek from being an exit route to being now the fourth of four feeder routes to La Ang. In Trek 20 we accessed La Ang via Kong Loi and Chang Mor. In Trek 21 we accessed La Ang via Pa Pae and Chang Mor. In Trek 22 I outlined how you could access La Ang via Mae La Noi and Mae La Oop, reading and doing that trip backwards. And the fourth access to La Ang would be via Mae Chaem and Ho Gao, the route of Trek 23 in reverse. You can see how unassuming La Ang is pivotal to the four 'Lawa' biking expeditions. It is where they all cross over. In this trek, therefore, I shall simply start things off from La Ang, making the presupposition that you have already arrived there by one of the other feeder routes (Treks 20, 21 or perhaps 22). If you come up to La Ang via Mae Chaem and Ho Gao, you will have to read Maps 40, 41 and 42 as well as the route detail below backwards, although at the end of this chapter I give some km readings as if you were doing the trip this other way round.

Trek 23 comprises, as said, 52 kms if Mae Chaem is your goal and some 170 kms if you wind up in Chiang Mai. As part of an overall journey that includes one of the preceding feeder trips to La Ang, it will, however, have a considerably greater total distance. Thus if you reckon in prior Trek 20 (accessing La Ang from Mae Sariang via Kong Loi and Chang Mor), you will add 118 kms to the 52-km-long onward journey to Mae Chaem, making an overall trip from Mae Sariang to Mae Chaem of 170 kms, and you will add the same distance to the 170-km-long onward journey from La Ang to Chiang Mai, making a mighty overall trip of nearly 300 kms. If you reckon in prior Trek 21 (accessing La Ang from Mae Sariang via Pa Pae and Chang Mor), you will add 88 kms to the 52-km-long onward journey to Mae Chaem, making an overall trip from Mae Sariang to Mae Chaem of 140 kms, and you will add the same distance to the 170-km-long onward journey from La Ang to Chiang Mai, making a lengthy overall trip of some 260 kms. And if you reckon in prior Trek 22 (accessing La Ang from Mae Sariang via Mae La Noi and Mae La Oop), you will add 72 kms to the 52-km-long onward journey to Mae Chaem, making an overall trip from Mae Sariang to Mae Chaem of 124 kms, and you will add the same distance to the 170-km-long onward journey from La Ang to Chiang Mai, making a sizeable overall trip of almost 250 kms (the shortest of the three overall journeys). On a small bike, such as a 100-cc Honda Dream, which is what can typically be hired in the tourist centres of Chiang Mai or Mae Hong Son, these are (over)ambitious distances to be covering in one day on problematic mountain 'roads', especially all the way to Chiang Mai, and so it makes sense to spread the combined overall treks over two or more days, spending a night or nights at places en route (more below).

Trek 23 is a motorbike hike only. Because the distances involved are great, and because the villages of the plateau of the Lawa are fairly well interconnected by dirt roads and trails, it makes no sense to walk it, or to walk part of it, or, more generally, to walk on the plateau. Like the mountainous area S of the 108 Mae Sariang/Hot road and SE of Mae Sariang, which is peopled by the Pwo Karen (Treks 18 & 19), Lawa country, sometimes referred to as the Ob Luang plateau, lends itself especially to exploration on two wheels (or in a jeep). It is just conceivable that Trek 23, in company with Treks 20-22, could be managed on a bicycle, but the bicycle would have to be a very sturdy mountain bike, and riders would need to be exceptionally tough, intrepid and persistent (no liability assumed, and no comeback, please).

With Trek 23 my nominal suggestion is, as outlined at the beginning, to proceed 52 kms from La Ang via Ho Gao to Mae Chaem or 170 kms to Chiang Mai, anteceding the trip with either Trek 20 or (in reverse) Trek 22.

TREK IT YOURSELF IN NORTHERN THAILAND

Preceding the Ho Gao/Mae Chaem trip with Trek 21 (via Pa Pae) should only be attempted by skilled offroad dirt riders, owing to the difficulty of the route near Pa Pae. This embeds Trek 23, if you push on to Chiang Mai, in an overall ride, launched from Mae Sariang, that goes halfway across Lan-Na or northern Thailand, of which the dirt-biking component is (in 1999) up to 100 kms long! Needless to say, you could do the ride in reverse in any of its permutations, proceeding from Chiang Mai to La Ang via Mae Chaem and Ho Gao and tacking on any of Treks 20-22. You would then have to read most of the relevant maps and route detail backwards (except Trek 22).

I first did Trek 23, running out from Chiang Mai to Ho Gao and La Ang and then back, in February 1997 with Nittaya Tananchai and US couple Pete Alcorn and Kelly Martin. We rode on two Honda Dream townbikes, stayed in Ho Gao, and spent several days over the expedition, exploring the area around Ho Gao. That was the time I discovered and first biked along the short track, hand-cut by local people, crucially linking up La Ang and Sae To Sa, interconnecting the network of routes W of La Ang with the network of routes E of La Ang, and enabling one to travel all the way from Mae Sariang to Mae Chaem or vice versa. To be honest, I have never done this overall journey from Mae Sariang to Mae Chaem or Chiang Mai, combining Trek 23 with one of Treks 20-22, as I am suggesting you do. I have only ever undertaken component parts of the through W-E or E-W journey. Thus in February 1996 I made a round trip by bike from Chiang Mai only to Ho Gao with Nittaya Tananchai. This was the first time I visited Ho Gao, and was the first of three visits to and stays at that attractive Lawa outpost. In February 1997, as said, I made a round trip by bike with Nittaya, Kelly and Pete from Chiang Mai via Ho Gao to La Ang, likewise staying at traditional Ho Gao. Starting from Chiang Mai at 9.15am, we reached Ho Gao at 3.30pm, a ride time of 6¼ hrs, which included a lunch and shopping stop in Mae Chaem. To this 6-hr journey time you could add about another hour for the stretch from Ho Gao to La Ang, meaning that Trek 23, from La Ang to Chiang Mai, is an all-day trip. And in January 1999 I rode in the company of Nittaya Tananchai and Doug Boynton from Mae Sariang via Mae La Oop and La Ang to Ho Gao, doing just the first part of Trek 23 and preceding it with Trek 22 in reverse. Then we went from Ho Gao back to La Ang and on to Chang Mor, Kong Loi and Mae Sariang, essentially doing Trek 20 backwards, and completing the long Mae Sariang to Mae Sariang loop clockwise. We stayed at Mae La Oop and Ho Gao, my third visit to and stay at the latter village.

The upshot of all this is threefold. (1) I have not ridden the stretch from Ho Gao to Mae Chaem since early 1996 and 1997, which means that my route detail and Map 41 may now be slightly out of date and inaccurate. It is possible that meanwhile more of the route has been paved and new buildings have sprung up alongside it. (2) You can implement Trek 23 to Chiang Mai comfortably in one day from Ho Gao and less comfortably in a long day from La Ang. Combined with either Trek 20 or 22 (backwards) or possibly 21, this trek (23) will take you at least 2 days/1 night. Why not do the combined journey in a leisurely 3 days/2 nights? It is safer to proceed more slowly, and you will have more time to stop and look at things on the way, experience the Lawa and some of their villages, do a spot of camping, unhurriedly enjoy the marvellous scenery, do some bird-watching à la Doug, and generally take it easy and have a good time. If you take 2 days, I recommend you break the journey and spend a night at Ho Gao. If ideally you take 3 days, many stopping options are open to you, and they will vary according to which feeder route you ride on your way to La Ang. Coming via Chang Mor (Treks 20 & 21), consider spending a first night at Chang Mor or at Ho Gao, and the second night at Ho Gao or Mae Chaem. Coming via Mae La Oop (Trek 22), consider spending a first night at Mae La Oop or Ho Gao, and the second night at Ho Gao or Mae Chaem. For tips about overnighting in Chang Mor, see Trek 20. For details about staying at Ho Gao and Mae Chaem, see below. For details about stopping at Mae La Oop, refer to Trek 22. Pivotal midpoint La Ang is, of course, the obvious place to break the journey and stay overnight, but I have never found it so congenial. For information about accessing La Ang by the various feeder routes, see, of course, their respective chapters (Treks 20, 21 and 22). For a thumbnail sketch of La Ang, refer to Trek 20. (3) Ho Gao is the nicest place out of the four overnighting options (Chang Mor, Mae La Oop, Ho Gao, Mae Chaem). Because, accompanied by different friends, I have stayed three times now at the village, spending in all many days there, the way has been paved for you to stop especially at Ho Gao. The headman and villagers are used to *farang* motorcycle trekkers such as the likes of you and me stopping by and will welcome you, even be expecting you to stay.

On the subject of difficulty, Trek 23 is in my estimation moderately difficult for average to experienced riders. For evaluations of the severity of feeder Treks 20, 21 and 22, refer to the relevant chapters. Concerning Trek 23, the 3-km-long contouring link between La Ang junction and Sae To Sa is (in 1999) still a narrow motorcycle trail, cut with mattocks out of the hillside. Although flattish, it has some steep kinked little dips down and up. Between Sae To Sa and Ho Gao, there are some long, fairly steep, in places rutted down- and upgrades. From Ho Gao to Mae Chaem, the way is mostly downhill. In 1996 and 1997, the worst part of this stretch was between Ho Mai and Din Kao, where you had to negotiate a succession of four awful downgrades, deep in white bulldust (*din kao* = white earth). Perhaps by now they have bricked or paved the section. Skilled offroad dirt riders with enduro machines will relish the whole long adventure from Mae Sariang across the mountains to Mae Chaem or vice versa. With the foregoing considerations in mind, and because of the length and remoteness of the trails in Trek 23 combined with prior Treks 20, 21 or 22, there is nothing up here on the Lawa plateau for inexperienced bikers or for novice riders who have casually hired a stepthrough Dream townbike in Chiang Mai or Mae Hong Son. You have been warned!

About Mae Sariang and accommodation + food there
Trek 23 is ultimately launched, in the sense that it succeeds either Trek 20 or 21 or 22, from Mae Sariang, with its guest houses, shops, restaurants and other facilities. For information about the town, on staying in guest houses there, and on eating out, see Trek 18 under 'Accessing the trek'.

Brief notes on the Lawa
During Trek 23 and in feeder Treks 20-22, you encounter Lawa people in many villages, including La Ang, Ho Gao, Ho Mai, Pa Pae, Chang Mor and Mae La Oop. For some outline information on this ancient and very interesting ethnic minority group, see below under Ho Gao and also an account in my adventure-travel book *Three Pagodas* (Chapter 8).

*

Trekking route detail
La Ang – Sae To Sa – Mae Hae Tai – Ho Gao (see Map 40)
Leave La Ang by the south-eastern end of its main street (La Ang centre = km 0) and proceed to the junction by Wat Santikiri a few hundred metres outside the village. At the junction (km 0.5) right is the way 27 kms to Chang Mor, while left is your way to Ho Gao and Mae Chaem. Going left, you come onto a narrow track which leads 3 kms to the next village, Sae To Sa. As said earlier, it is (in 1999) a crucial 6-ft-wide motorcycle trail (I'm doubtful about whether you could get a jeep along here), hand-cut by local people, whose importance is quite out of proportion to its size, because it links the road from Mae Chaem to Sae To Sa with the ways from Mae La Noi to La Ang and from Kong Loi to La Ang. It thus enables people to cross from Mae Chaem district and the network of roads E of La Ang to Mae Sariang district with its network of roads W of La Ang, sealing a small but vital gap (actually, there is another obscurer way of crossing the watershed: via Ho Gao, Kok Noi, Pae, Mae Sa Meng and Du Lo Boe – see Maps 40 and 39). Undoubtedly, this link trail will be upgraded sooner or later, and probably the only reason that by 1999 it had not been is that the Mae Sariang/Mae Chaem district boundary and the Mae Hong Son/Chiang Mai provincial boundary pass through it midway, with the authorities unable to agree about who should finance the work.

The trail essentially contours round the mountainside, dipping steeply up and down in a few places. Offering some grand plateau views E, it passes some huts (left) about midpoint, before arriving at **Sae To Sa** (km 3.4). You know you have reached this backward Karen settlement because you come to an especially steep little escarpment, located directly next to a kindergarten, that you must plunge down watched by the nursery infants.

Now the way proceeds straight through the houses and middle of Sae To Sa, which rather resembles a farmyard. People will look up in astonishment as you pick your way through on two wheels. Beyond the village there is a junction (km 3.7). Right apparently goes ca 4 kms (or is that 13 kms?) to the villages of Mae Por or Mae Pok (= Por Mae Cho/Pak Pai?) and possibly Ulae (Mae Lae?) – I have not been up here, so the details are vague and unchecked, but the way may connect with the La Ang/Chang Mor road. Left continues towards Ho Gao, passing on elevated open ground a kind of education centre (right) and a football field in the sky (left), before reaching after just a short distance a junction (km 5.7) near Mae Hae Tai. Left goes a couple of hundred metres to the Karen village of **Mae Hae Tai**, which is an attractive place with some 60 houses, a school and minimal facilities (might be a nice place to stay), while right continues from the junction, marked by a *sala* or waiting hut, through high open terrain, past a big new health centre (left, also a possible place to stay), past a forest fire lookout (right), and then down a long gravelly and rutted descent to a large bridge. Just before the bridge is a turning right (S) for the Lawa village of Moed Long (Moot Long), which lies 4.8 kms offtrail, and just after it is a *sala*.

Not far beyond the big bridge lies a turning left/N (km 11.5) for Kok Noi (2.5 kms offtrail), Nong Muan, Kok Luang and the Lawa village of Pae (12.5 kms offtrail). Beyond Pae comes Mae Sa Meng and then Du Lo Boe. The side route, which forms a loop (see Maps 40 and 39) deviating from the route of Treks 23 and 22, is the other way across the mountains from Mae Chaem to Mae La Noi or vice versa. Do not venture up this way and around the side loop to Du Lo Boe unless you are an experienced offroad dirt biker and know what you are doing. The turning is marked by a waiting hut. Just beyond it there is a second turning left, which is the old way down to the beginning of the Pae trail. Now you cross a second concrete bridge, after which you climb up to the turning right/S, marked by a *sala* (km 15.6), which leads to Ho Gao. Left (straight) at the junction continues to Ho Mai, Pang Hin Fon and Mae Chaem, while right takes you 400 m along a cement-section road to the centre of **Ho Gao** (km 16). As you proceed down this access to Ho Gao, you will find a Christian church high up left, a way right on a bend past some teachers' houses down to the village school, and the headman's house further along the main street on the right, below an earth bank and almost opposite a shop (up left).

Ho Gao

Ho Gao is the old part of the double village of Ban Ho, a new part – Ho Mai – lying a couple of kms further up our route in the direction of Pang Hin Fon (*gao* = old, *mai* = new). In Lawa, Ho (pronounced 'Hoh' or 'Hor') is known as Ying Goh. Said to be 300 years old, Ho Gao is a traditional Lawa village, where many of the women, especially the older ones, still wear tribal costume, even when going about their everyday business, and where men used to wear their traditional attire until about 10-15 years ago (nowadays they wear it only on special occasions). The village is attractively set, tumbling down an elevated hillside, with a fine view SE across a valley to a wooded mountainside. Basically the upper half of the village is Christian, and the lower animist. The place has a nice relaxed feel about it, and the people have always proved unusually friendly and hospitable. In 1997 there were 383 inhabitants in Ho Gao, divided up into 80 families living in 63 houses, of which 36 had 'toilets' (simple huts behind the houses with a squatting footpad-and-hole lavatory and a water pot and dipper). At any one time, around a third of the villagers are absent, labouring in Chiang Mai.

Like Mae La Oop and other Lawa mountaintop villages, Ho Gao has a water problem, or at least had one in January 1999. The stream supplying it with water was drying up, and the villagers would catch the remaining trickle all day in tanks, only turning the taps on for washing and getting kitchen water in the evening. The place is typical of many remote hill-tribe villages in that on the one hand it is being squeezed by the authorities, and on the other is being modernized by them. Thus, as the headman said recently: "We are under pressure. Official growing restrictions come ever closer to the village, and basically the authorities want to move us out to reforest the area." At the same time, however, a solar array has been set up in Ho Gao, costing 750,000 baht and funded by a King's Project, and an expensive telephone exchange system, with a satellite link and powered by the solar plant, is being installed by the headman's house. The solar array has 40 panels, and the villagers use it to recharge car batteries, from which they then run strip lights and whatnot in their houses. Asked what use the Lawa had for telecommunications and space-age technology when none of them had telephones and there were no lines in the village, the headman said that it was so that the people of Ho Gao could keep in touch with their relatives labouring in Chiang Mai, letting them know of any weddings or house-warming ceremonies, so that these workers could then come back home.

Of more practical direct benefit to the villagers, a government scheme is being implemented at Ho Gao which, so to speak, pump-primes its inhabitants commercially. They have been 'given' about 10,000 baht each with which to start a business. The money is invested in seeds, tools, sprinklers and so on, and the people then start growing cash crops such as cabbages, kidney beans and carrots, or raise livestock, subsequently paying back the loan out of their profits. In 1999 the headman and other villagers approached Nittaya, Doug and I and confessed in low serious voices that they and the other Lawa of Ho Gao and neighbouring villages had heard that the world would end soon, destroyed in a nuclear holocaust. They were afraid. Would it happen, and what did we, as informed *farang* from the West, recommend that they should do? All this gives you an insight into the reality of life for relatively undeveloped people such as the Lawa in developing Thailand at the turn of the millennium. It also shows how you, as a foreign visitor, can be put on the spot and made to be an oracle!

As you explore Ho Gao, notice the *galae* decorating the roofs of some houses, a wooden V-shaped gable-end traditional to the Lawa and taken over from them by the Thai. You will find a neglected health centre not far from the solar array and near the eastern end of the village (middle to bottom level). There are a couple of shops in 'town'. One is in someone's house below the headman, and another is attached to the school in a building by the village entrance. In the latter you can sometimes buy vegetables. The 'main' shop is halfway along the village street, above left and overlooking the headman's house below right. It sells soft drinks, eggs, condensed milk, packets of 'Ma-maa' instant noodles, and big fat conical jointlike cigarettes for 2 baht each. You can buy petrol in Ho Gao, both super and ordinary, at 13 baht per bottleful either in this shop or elsewhere.

If you stay overnight in the village, which I hope you will, you will either have to eat whatever food you have brought with you, or buy basics from the shops and cook them up yourself. You will have to fend for yourself, so don't wait for the Lawa to feed you, although any house will be happy to give you some cooked rice. In places like Ho Gao, I often boil up instant noodles bought locally or sachets of macaroni soup brought along, supplementing the brew with stock cubes and vegetables – greens, shallots, spring onions – bought or begged from villagers.

You have a number of accommodation options in Ho Gao, none of them very salubrious. You can stay in the house of headman Moen Sericharoon, the dilapidated health centre, the school, the Catholic church or its grounds, the main shop, or in any house. The low wooden church building, situated at the top end of the village just E of the entrance road, or its level grounds, on which you could erect a tent, are secluded, private and quiet, but a disadvantage is that they have a service there every day between 5 and 6pm. You would have to hunt out the 'priest' to seek permission. On three separate occasions and with various different friends, I have stayed in first the school, then the headman's house, and then the health centre. In early 1996 we stayed in a school classroom, but it was hardly satisfactory because you have to be up and moved out an hour or so before classes, when the school is opened up (quite early). You can also fall into the clutches of the teachers, who may overorganize you, particularly a rather bossy lady, who seems to live in Ho Gao. In early 1999 we put up in the dusty, virtually unused health centre in its two upstairs rooms, which we had to clean up first. We simply erected our tents on the floor, and had a satisfactory night.

In early 1997 we spent several days staying in a back room beyond the kitchen/living room of the headman's house. Moen and his wife are friendly obliging folk, who have repeatedly expressed a willingness, even eagerness, to welcome *farang* visitors, put them up, provide blankets, allow them to wash in the outside 'bathroom' or from the cement water tanks. More accurately, with the headman out for the day, we simply took over his abode, installing ourselves, at the suggestion of a neighbour. A stream of people freely wandered in and out, helping themselves to firewood and tea. They do this all the time, not just in Moen's house, but in each other's houses throughout the village. The great advantage of lodging with the headman or a villager is that you can observe the Lawa at close quarters, watch them cooking and eating, see them sleep round the kitchen hearth, watch the lady of the house chop up banana palm stem or boil up swill for the pigs and then feed the porkers, see her pound rice under the house, listen to the headman make announcements over the tannoy, observe villagers distilling rice whisky, and a thousand other things. The people are very flexible, curious vis-à-vis you, but also quite oblivious to your need for quiet or privacy at night and in the early morning. Also everything gets or is permanently covered in dust; dogs, chickens and pigs run everywhere; and there is constant noise from children, cocks crowing and people coughing and hawking. But it is all part of the fun or experience. Moen and his family turned up towards evening. Before entering his house, he made a ritual offering to the spirits on his veranda, as he always does when he comes home. He put out *lao kao* (rice whisky) and food, which was promptly scoffed by his dog.

During that visit we witnessed an all-day and all-night housewarming party, being given upon the completion of a new house. The whole village was involved, and Lawa came from far and wide from other villages. Everyone brought a present of clothes, money, *lao kao* or whatever, partly as an offering and partly to recompense the new householder, who had to foot the sizeable bill for the shindig. Half a dozen pigs were hacked up and then stewed bones and all in large pans on open fires on the ground. The entrails were washed in a stream far below the village, chopped up and cooked with herbs and spices. At 7pm all the presents were moved into the new house, and most of the merrymakers followed. There was a huge crush inside, and I remember how the festive throng easily and naturally separated along sexual lines into two groups: men and boys on the one hand, and women and girls on the other. We were guests of honour, but I have to admit to feeling uneasy because there were so many youths in the house in various stages of drunkenness. In a Western country this would be a recipe for trouble. But the whole night there was not the slightest aggression. With no policemen nearer than Mae Chaem or Mae La Noi, and no authority figure other than mild headman Moen, it demonstrated how intact the moral fibre still is in this and other Lawa villages. Far from being an occasion for aggravation, the party was – as all such parties are – an opportunity on the part of the girls and boys for prospecting for a partner and for flirting, and all the girls were in their finest costumes. The drinking, fun and games, and singing went on all night, the nearby valleys and mountainsides reverberating with the sound.

From Ho Gao you can make an interesting, if rather arduous, side trip by bike to the Lawa village of **Pae**. It lies NW of Ho Gao, 12.5 kms off the La Ang/Ho Gao route and some 16 kms from Ho Gao (see Map 40). I went there in 1997 with my companions of the time, and it took us all day to do the round trip from Ho Gao, spending quite some time in Pae. Apparently you can walk 3 hrs from Ho Gao to Pae on an old disused path. Pae has some 400 inhabitants and 65 houses, is impoverished, and according to the people of Ho Gao is the most traditional and authentic of the four Lawa villages in Mae Chaem district. At that time only the headman had a vehicle, a motorcycle. We saw men there with striking waist-to-knee tattoos, and, as we found out, they illegally grew a fair amount of opium and also cannabis a few kms away on two little plateaus hidden from view above the village. However, I must warn you from going to Pae for the time being for reasons connected with the following unfortunate incident and story.

With a rather reluctant guide, we walked an hour to the poppy fields, examined them and took photos. A Lawa lass was scoring pods and collecting opium resin, a Chinese man was in evidence, apparently supervising things, while later on our way back to Ho Gao we passed two suspicious pick-ups with Bangkok number plates, whose only business in going to remote Pae must have been to pick up drugs. A week or two after our visit to Pae, the police and anti-narcotics agents raided the village, destroyed the poppy fields, arrested one or more people, throwing them in prison, and deprived the impecunious denizens of Pae not only of their opium, but of revenue from the cash crop. Their suspicion as to the cause of all this misfortune immediately fell on us. We had documented the poppy fields and then gone to the police, which of course we had not done at all. They had it in for us the next time we happened to show up. A year later a *farang* biking friend of mine strayed into Pae, unaware of events, as we were until he learned of them and relayed the story to us. He was mistaken for me, immediately surrounded by a mob of angry local youths, and intimidated. He was probably saved from a worse fate because he speaks fluent Thai and was able to explain himself and things. But the upshot of the misunderstanding on the part of the Pae people is that I and we cannot return to the village for the moment and you are probably unwise to go there until the sorry story has died down. You too might be mistaken for me, or for an anti-drugs agent, or might be 'heavied up', unable to explain yourself, or to your surprise just receive a cool reception. I have twice asked Ho Gao headman Moen to set the record straight, which he claims to have done.

*

Some notes on the Lawa people, their history and culture
The Lawa are one of South-East Asia's many splintered, fragmented and in some cases entropic Mon-Khmer peoples, who also include the Wa, the Lua (or Htin) of Thailand's Nan province and Laos' Sayaburi province (see Trek 5), the Khmu, the Mon and Khmer themselves, and the Mrabri (see Trek 17). They are related to these other groups ethnologically, linguistically and physically, being most closely related to the Wa, who live in north-east Burma (above the Shan State and close to the Chinese border) and also in pockets along northern Thailand's border with the Shan State, Burma. The Lawa language is classified as belonging to the Mon-Khmer branch of the Austro-Asiatic or Austronesian linguistic family. The Lawa are of a racial stock quite other than that of the Thai. Like the other Mon-Khmer tribes, they are short stocky mountain peasant people with the strikingly dark skin pigmentation which is characteristic of Wa-related groups and the angular or 'craggy' facial features and hairiness which is uncharacteristic of smooth-skinned Mongoloid, Sinitic or Siamese peoples such as the the Tai, Chinese, Hmong, Yao and Akha.

Although separated by considerable a distance, with a swathe of northern Thailand and its Lannathai people as well as the Shan State and its Shan people acting as a buffer between them, the Lawa and the Wa can, remarkably, understand each other quite well. Many words in their respective tongues are virtually the same, for example the words for tree, house and dog (*khao, nyie, soh*). I once put this mutual intelligibility to the test in Mae La Oop, reading out to some Lawa elders Wa sentences from a Wa classroom textbook (written in the Roman alphabet), which they had little trouble understanding. The reason for this is that the Lawa and the Wa were once the same people, an original folk or *Urvolk* that arguably also included the Lua. You can hear their oneness or relatedness in their similar names (La-wa, Wa and Lua or 'Lu-wa'), although it must be said that Lua is not the name that the Lua people call themselves – they have no ethnonym – but is a name that has been applied to them by the Thai for convenience's sake. In fact, interestingly, the Thai refer to all three groups – the Lawa, Wa and Lua – as Lua, making no distinction between them. This may be unthinking, but it is also revealing, as if they seem to know that historically the three groups are one and the same. The Lawa do not call themselves Lawa, nor Lua, nor the L'wa of old Thai chronicles, but La-wua (in Mae La Oop) and La-voe (in Ho Gao).

The Lawa, therefore, may not be much to look at today, but they are an ancient, important and very interesting people, or, rather, a vestige of such an *Urvolk*. This folk, and by implication the Lawa, are indigenous to northern Thailand. Once, before the arrival of the Tai peoples from China, they lived all over the area known now as northern Thailand, and even further afield, and had a flourishing civilization perhaps one or two thousand years ago. It seems that they had 'cities' at places like Chiang Saen, Chiang Khong, Chiang Mai, Lampang, Prao and Mae Sariang, which gave rise to these towns, and the Lawa claim with some justification to have founded Chiang Mai, a claim that the Wa also make independently, based on their lore. Lawa artefacts such as clay pipes keep being dug up all over the place, and everything remains to be done in terms of researching this people archaeologically. The aboriginal La/Wa people was disturbed in its heyday first by the Mon, then by the Khmer, and finally, some 900 to 800 years ago, by the southward-migrating Tai, who all established their own separate or joint hegemonies, progressively squeezing the *Urvolk*. Ousted from the fertile lowlands to the hills, this was sundered, with one part being pushed north to become the Wa, another part arguably being squeezed to the north-east to become the Lua, and a third part being relegated to the plateau between Chiang Mai and Mae Sariang to become the Lawa. Here the Lawa declined in inhospitable terrain to become the ethnic minority we now know.

The Lawa might be the indigenous inhabitants of northern Thailand in an even more fundamental way. The English explorer Holt Hallett, who in 1876 encountered Lawa at places like Kong Loi and Bo Luang during his journey from Moulmein via Mae Sariang and Chiang Mai to Chiang Saen, and who recorded his observations in *A Thousand Miles on an Elephant in the Shan States*, reports that the Lawa bury their dead in hollowed-out logs. This practice might link them to the prehistoric people who buried their dead in mysterious wooden coffins, thought to be at least 2000 years old, in caves in many parts of north Thailand, notably near Soppong. Conversely, the Lawa might be these people, having themselves put the coffins in the caves.

These days the Lawa are really only to be found on the plateau NE of Mae Sariang. Here they live in some two dozen villages, eking out an existence. I say 'really only' because actually Lawa live all over Thailand, but over the centuries they have been assimilated either completely or largely into mainstream Thai society. Most Lawa have long since been thus submerged. Examples of places that are Lawa but largely integrated, such that in them you would not know that they were Lawa, but would mistake them for regular Thai villages, are Mae La Noi, Kong Loi, Bo Luang, Bo Sali (near Mae Waen, see Treks 18 & 19) and Hua Lin (W of San Pa Tong). Thus, authentic, unassimilated, identifiably Lawa villages, where some people even still wear tribal costume, exist only around the Chang Mor – Ho Gao – Mae La Oop triangle, although there are reportedly relatively unassimilated Lawa villages elsewhere in Thailand, notably in parts of Kanchanaburi province. It is estimated that the population of unassimilated Lawa in Thailand is 10,000, accounting for 1.5% of the country's hill-tribe populace.

Lawa villages vary in size from relatively large, like Mae La Oop, with some 160 houses to quite small, with perhaps 20 houses. These villages are typically built at an altitude of 3000-4000 ft, many on ridge tops or crests. As we have seen, this gives the inhabitants a good view and traditionally an element of safety, but it leads to problems with the supply of water. Village houses are primitive dwellings, solidly constructed of wood, raised high on stilts, with grass roofs (increasingly the tendency is to use galvanized metal sheeting) and spacious front platforms or balconies. To enter a house, you climb up a wooden ladder onto the balcony. The balcony is used for preparing food, for washing up (the bits fall through to the chickens and pigs underneath), and for drying washing. Ladies weave on the balcony, or make roofing panels, and visitors can sleep there too. Inside the house there is basically one big room, which has areas partitioned off to form sleeping cubicles for family members. There is little or no furniture. The central feature is the hearth, which is a shallow wooden box on the floor containing sand and smouldering logs. The family cook here, sit around it, eat, relax, smoke their pipes, keep warm in winter, chat to friends, and frequently sleep. Hanging above the hearth is a bamboo tray, used for smoking bits of meat. A feature of Lawa houses, as you will find out if you stay in one, is that people have little privacy. In a village, everybody freely wanders in and out of everybody else's house all the time, even if the owner is not there.

The Lawa have a near-subsistence agricultural economy. They grow rice, maize, livestock, marrows, Chinese mustard, aubergines, chillis, and so on. Very recently, encouraged by the authorities, they have started growing cash crops such as cabbages, carrots and kidney beans. The occasional Lawa village grows opium for its own use and as an illegal cash crop, but the Lawa are not traditionally associated with opium. They have become clever at constructing terraced paddy fields in steep awkward terrain. Traditionally, many Lawa men have worked – and still do work – as itinerant labourers in other towns and villages and, for example, in mines.

The Lawa diet is very simple and monotonous. Almost every day, three times a day, they eat sticky rice, marrow soup, chilli dip, a dried fish and sometimes some stewed or smoked meat from a sacrificed animal or from the hunt. They do not have regular cups of tea or coffee as we do, but instead drink water drawn from a spring and kept in old plastic engine-oil containers. The Lawa are big drinkers of rice whisky, which they distil themselves from rice husks, water, yeast and palm sugar. Of an evening, sitting on the floor with friends around the hearth, they will drink this home-made hooch with a kettleful of China tea brewed on the fire.

If you were a Lawa woman, your typical day would be as follows: you would get up at first light, get the fire going in the hearth, and cook breakfast – fresh sticky rice and squash soup. Then you would either do the washing and look after your many children, or, more probably, go to your field, in which case the grandparents would look after the children. Your field is on a mountainside often far away, involving a long trudge in the hot sun. On your way back from hoeing, weeding, harvesting or whatever, every day you gather a heavy load of firewood, which you lug back uphill on your back to the village. You fetch fresh spring water – down in the valley, of course – or cajole your children into getting it. You pound rice in the rice stamper under your house. At regular intervals you distil rice whisky under or in your house. It takes about 3 hours to make 2½ bottles. You won't drink this yourself, but your husband, the headman and friends will polish it off in an evening. From time to time you weave smocks and skirts for yourself and your daughters. You rarely wash, or so it seems to *farang* visitors, you smoke your pipe all day long, and to the Western outsider your pots and pans look filthy, greasy and soot-encrusted. You are quiet, uncomplaining, and accept your hard lot. If you are young, you probably dream of marrying a Western boy and fleeing to live like a princess in England or Germany or Switzerland.

Lawa men build houses, saw up timber, carry it to the village, also work in the fields, go hunting and fishing, slaughter and butcher wild and domestic animals, make gunpowder, go away to labour, otherwise gamble and have a lazy time smoking and drinking. Some men are engaged in silversmithery, for which the Lawa are famous. They produce objects on their own account (e.g. the decoration for Lawa pipes), but mainly to order for outsiders. Dealers from Chiang Mai come by with bulletts and ingots of silver, leave their requirements, and later call to pick up the finished products. Lawa smiths make fine silver chains, bracelets, necklaces, earrings, and exquisitely repousséd boxes. If as a tourist you buy silverware in Chiang Mai in the Night Bazaar or in one of the handicraft factories, there is a good chance that it was made by a Lawa man in a Lawa village. Other men work as blacksmiths, forging machetes, chains and suchlike.

316

Metal working has traditionally been a celebrated and distinguishing feature of the Lawa. In 1876 Hallett observed them manufacturing metal articles in Bo Luang village, and reports that they mined and smelted red iron oxide near Chang Mor, transporting the ingots by elephant to their villages. Evidently there was a ready demand for the resulting wrought iron products all over Siam. This Lawa metal work was carried out not just NE of Mae Sariang, but elsewhere in northern Thailand. Thus Hallett finds Lawa mining and working iron, for example, in the Wiang Pa Pao area (halfway between Chiang Mai and Chiang Rai on Route 118), around Mae Suai (N of Wiang Pa Pao), and in the Mae Lao valley (S of Chiang Rai in the direction of Pan and Payao).

The Lawa are not Buddhists, but animists, i.e. they believe in spirits, which reside in things. If they are Buddhist at all, they are animists who have acquired a veneer of Buddhism. In this respect an element of controversy attaches to the religion of the Lawa, for there is a school of thought which believes that, far from being basically animists who have overlaid their animism with Buddhism, they are actually fundamentally Buddhists who fell into animism after their displacement into the hills by the Mon and Tai. Whatever the case, it cannot be denied that in Lawa villages you can often see traces of Buddhism in people's houses – little shrines and Buddha figures and amulets on shelves. Some Lawa, like a number of their Wa cousins, are Christians, having been converted by missionaries. There are Christian Lawa and churches, for example, at Ho Gao, Ho Mai and Mae La Oop.

Animist Lawa believe in a pantheon of spirits, including the spirits of the sky, the mountain, forest, village, village entrance, house, field, people, the human body, and of many natural phenomena, such as the virgin jungle, trees, fallen trees, streams, landslips, spiders, ants, and so on. The Lawa also worship their ancestors. Signs of animism in a Lawa village are, besides the sacrificing of chickens and other animals, so-called Solomon's seals (star-shaped bamboo objects) above the lintels of houses, mirrors beside house doors, and cotton strings around people's wrists, ankles and necks. These are all devices for warding off evil spirits. Spirits can be bad as well as good. While the good ones need humouring or propitiating, the bad ones require appeasing. This is done by offering food to the spirits or, as indicated, by sacrificing animals to them. In Mae La Oop, two ceremonies, held annually, are especially important. One is to honour the ancestors, and every July the villagers offer one buffalo to the spirits of their forebears. The other is an offering to the spirit of the village. Made every 10 November by the two oldest inhabitants of La Oop, it involves the sacrifice of eight pigs or cows or whatever – the type of animal is rotated, while in other Lawa villages the number of animals offered differs. It is entertaining watching the Lawa put out food as offerings for the spirits. Within seconds a passing dog has bolted the food. The sacrificing of animals and proffering of food has another amusing aspect, though not for the poor animals. As the headman at Ho Gao said: the spirits don't have very big appetites, nor do they like chillies, so when we make an offering, we take a pig or a cow if we can and add chillies, and then we have a jolly good feast!

Illness is also a spiritual matter: it is a sign of some disharmony between the ill person and the spirit world. When a person is ill, either some spirits are missing from the afflicted person's body, which have to be coaxed back into the body, or some evil spirit has entered the person's body, which has to be exorcized. Another Lawa belief pertaining to the body and spirits is that certain people are inhabited by the spirits of tigers. This enables them to carry out amazing feats of strength or endurance. They can, for example, cover great distances very fast, and are held actually to be tigers. The Lawa further believe that the entrails of animals can be read to see if the omens are good or bad, e.g. for ploughing or starting the harvest.

The Lawa are monogamous, and divorce is unusual. Upon marriage, a girl goes to live with her husband's family – residence is patrilocal. Girls marry young, soon after puberty, when school is finished, i.e. when the girls are 13 or 14. The suitor's family pays the bride's family a bride price. This involves a certain amount of silver in the form of old coins and family heirlooms. The giving of the bride price is largely symbolic and ritualistic. The silver heirlooms come back again to the man's family, remaining in the family and being handed down through the generations. An interesting thing about the coins is that many of them are old silver Indian rupees bearing the heads of "Queen and Empress" Victoria and Kings Edward V11 and George V. The coins have come overland from the former British colonies of India and Burma. Another interesting detail concerning marriage is that some of the older Lawa villagers, for example in Mae La Oop, are married to Khmu and Khmer people. The latter sometimes come across from Thailand's Nan province, from Laos or from Cambodia to marry Lawa or at least to trade with them, subsequently intermarrying with them. This might seem surprising until one remembers that all three minority groups are from the same Mon-Khmer stable, and are ethnically, linguistically and historically related. Ancient channels of communication and trading connections still remain open between them, however tenuous.

When a member of their community dies, the Lawa do not burn the body Buddhist-style, but bury it. It seems, as said, that in the past they interred corpses, together with items belonging to the deceased, in wooden coffins made out of hollowed-out logs. After the death there is a wake, animals are sacrificed, and people eat and drink. The corpse is kept in the house of the deceased for a day or two, and the village youngsters process around it singing. This processing is an eagerly anticipated opportunity for girls and boys to flirt together and touch each other accidentally on purpose. Lawa funerals are not very solemn affairs.

Some Lawa villages have special clannish hereditary chiefs (akin to the *maha* of the Wa and the *sawbwa* or *chao fa* of the Shan), with power and status being passed down through certain 'noble' families. The Thai authorities are currently trying to stamp out this feudal practice by democratizing the way such chiefs and also conventional headmen are chosen. Peter Kunstadter reports that these special families enjoy a *samang* (= *khun, chao*) lineage, some claiming to be able to trace their pedigree back to the last Lawa king, Khun Luang Wilanka, or at least to one of his princes, although in reality they can probably trace their descent back only ten generations. Some villagers owe allegiance to these chiefs, the *samang* receiving payments of meat and money. With their ritual knowledge, the *samang* are also held to be the local guardians of Lawa culture. Another person important in Lawa society is the *lam*, a spiritual leader or shaman who is often the oldest man in a village. The *lam* and to a lesser extent the *samang* are able to summon up the spirits.

Lawa women, we said, like to weave on their balconies and, like Karen women, are champion weavers. They work at simple backstrap looms, one end of which is attached to a house wall or a block of wood, while the other forms a backrest. A woman sits on the floor of her veranda, leans back against the rest, tautens the warp strings, and weaves across her lap. The women mostly weave material for their traditional skirts and shoulder bags. Nowadays Lawa tribal costume is not worn every day in all Lawa villages. It is still worn every day in the remoter, more conservative villages, such as Ho Gao. It is worn mostly by the women, especially the housewives and older women. Lawa men mostly do not wear their traditional costume any more every day, wearing it only on special occasions. The women who still wear costume every day have a workaday version and a kind of Sunday best version for celebrations. They typically wear a black tube skirt with horizontal pink or wine-red banding; a shiftlike smock coloured white or fawn (white for unmarried girls, fawn for married women); indigo leggings, held in place by black bands; and above these, just below the knee, bangles made from the lac tree (the bangles look like elephant hairs). Sometimes they also wear, so to speak, 'leggings' for the arms, held in place by a silver band. The most distinctive thing about Lawa women are their orange or red strings of beads, worn around the neck in thick layers. In large holes in their ear lobes they wear big cup-shaped silver earrings. The costume is completed with a white or pink shoulder bag and mandatory little pipe.

The men (on ceremonial occasions) wear simple, baggy, off-white, heavy cotton trousers and an open jacket – the whole reminiscent of a judo outfit. Some Lawa men still wear another kind of 'clothing', tattoos. Traditionally they bear two tigers on their backs to fend off evil spirits, and down their thighs – from waist to knee – they have densely tattooed emblems (such as cat figures), which make it look as if the men are wearing black lycra cyclists' shorts!

*

Ho Gao – Ho Mai – Pang Hin Fon – Mae Chaem (see Map 41)
From Ho Gao to Mae Chaem is 36 kms, mostly downhill. Readings resume at Ho Gao centre at km 16, as if continuing from km 0 in La Ang. From Ho Gao to the

junction at Pang Hin Fon, you proceed roughly N, after which you head broadly E. Ride out of Ho Gao, back along the cement access road, to the junction and *sala* (km 16.4). Left (S) goes back to La Ang, while right brings you after a couple of kms up to the Lawa village of **Ho Mai** or New Ho (*mai* = new) (km 18.4), which is a recent offshoot of Old Ho or Ho Gao. It lies mostly to the left of the road, and on the right there is, I seem to remember, a Christian church.

Now, swinging right or eastish, you continue ca 4 kms to the junction for Din Kao, encountering on the way the (in 1996 and 1997) worst section of the route from La Ang to Mae Chaem. As it steeply descends, the 'road' is, or was at that time, punctuated by four passages of deep bulldust, which always caused us difficulty. The worst one is the last, near the bottom, by the junction, where there always seemed to be people waiting, who could watch you as you floundered down or up the sea of powder and underlying stones, having a free laugh. Perhaps this problematic section of the road has meanwhile been improved or bricked over. At the junction (ca km 22.5), a paved way goes right to the Karen village of **Din Kao**, while left continues to Pang Hin Fon. 'Din Kao' means 'white earth', which is the colour of the ground hereabouts, including the bulldust.

In beautiful scenery and shadowing a fine mountain ridge or long outcrop on your right, you pass a settlement (right), a watershed development office (also right), and a health centre (left), to arrive via a steep down-and-up road of dirt, stones and dust at the village of **Pang Hin Fon** (km 26.8). Look upon the watershed development office and health centre as possible places to stay overnight if you want or need, perhaps because you have had some mishap or have got caught out by nightfall. Pang Hin Fon has shops and even an incongruous telephone box (run off solar power and using a satellite link), and is, as far as I can make out, Hmong and Karen. After the main part of the village, you climb up 3 kms past a secondary part of Pang Hin Fon, possibly known as Ton Ya, also Hmong (km 29.2), to arrive at a junction (km 29.7).

At the junction, which always used to have a real wild-west feeling about it, there are a couple of makeshift buildings selling provisions, noodle soup and fuel. You get the impression that they are the beginnings of a junction village. From near the staging-post junction, there are some superb views N of mountains and a valley, in which settlements lie dotted, and ENE of Doi Intanon, Thailand's highest mountain. The way left from the junction proceeds reportedly to the villages of Huai Hia, Mae Toom and Mae Ngan Luang (the latter 24 kms away). I have not yet been up this trail, but there is certainly some great motorcycle exploring to be done up here, and you may even be able to find a new way through to Mae La Noi. At the junction you pick up (in 1997) a piece of new asphalt highway. As the years roll by, this will no doubt be extended, making a fine metalled road perhaps from Mae Chaem to Pang Hin Fon or even to Ho Gao and Mae Hae Tai. Go right at the junction for Mae Chaem.

Heading broadly E now for Mae Chaem, you ride for a bit on the new mountain highway, passing a Hmong settlement on your left, possibly known as Pang Ma-O (km 30.2), before hitting dirt again. After 8 kms you reach a turning right/S for the villages of Tuan and Tab (km 37.7, or 14 kms from Mae Chaem), not far offroad and probably Karen. And at km 40 you pass Kiu Ton forestry office (right). In the vicinity of this office, there are some great views across Mae Chaem town and the Chaem river valley towards Doi Intanon. Then begins a terrific descent into the valley of the River Chaem on a surface that in 1997 was a mixture of bumpy dirt and brickwork. Now bid farewell to the plateau of the Lawa. Finally you pick up an asphalt surface again and wind your way through outlying villages to a T-junction (km 51). Left goes to villages, including Kong Khan, Sob Chok, Na Hong Tai and Na Hong. From somewhere up here, people raft down the Chaem river to Mae Chaem town. Go right and follow the River Chaem, which flows on your left, for about 1 km until the road reaches a junction. Straight on continues a further km to the weaving village of Tong Fai, while left crosses a bridge and the Chaem river to arrive at a staggered crossroads and the centre of **Mae Chaem** (km 52).

Mae Chaem
Mae Chaem (470 m or 1542 ft above sea level) is a small district town which, like its associated district, takes its name from the Chaem river running through it. It used to be called Muang Chaem, said to mean 'arid town/district'. Whether that is true or not, both town and district are, indeed, rather arid. The district, which along with Um Pang and Mae Sariang is one of the largest in Thailand (remember how it extends W almost to La Ang), consists mainly of mountains and forest, has only some 7% of foothills and flatland suitable for agriculture and rice paddies, and can be very hot, in fact is subject to extremes of temperature. An account I once read put out by the district office in 1990 reported that in January 1986 a minimum temperature of 4°C had been recorded, and that in April 1987 the thermometer had risen to a blood-boiling maximum of 45°C. The town too, as I remember it from many visits in the early 1990s, is a hot dusty dry place. With a population of some 3000-4000 inhabitants (in 1990 the whole district numbered ca 55,500 people), it is set in a bowl on the Chaem valley floor on which the sun beats down mercilessly, heating it up. The sides of the bowl are low hills, which to the NE run all the way up to the summit of Doi Intanon, Thailand's highest mountain. From the town, particularly from its W side, across the river, there are magnificent views of the domed peak and of a prominent pagoda to the right of the summit.

Located around a central staggered crossroads, Mae Chaem is essentially a one-street town, and I remember it as something of a cowboy place, although these days it is no doubt more developed and tamer. The police used to drink whisky in the noodle shops opposite their station; dozens of wild-looking tribals would come into town from the surrounding mountains and congregate around the market, especially Karen, Lawa and Hmong; the eating and staying places were makeshift, mediocre and here-today-gone-tomorrow; in the night you could see ribbons of fire advancing down the surrounding hillsides as a result of slash-and-burn ground clearance; and, curiously for such a macho place, an excessive number of *kateuy* or ladyboys wilted in this little nest, some 30-40 of them. I must confess to always having had a soft spot for Mae Chaem.

Time for an orientation. If you stand at the central crossroads with the river and bridge behind you (see Map 42), Mae Chaem market lies immediately to your right. The road running left to right (N-S) in front of you is the town's main street. If you go left (N) up the long main drag, you will find the police station on your left, some noodle soup and fried rice shops on your right, and some fine old wooden houses (especially left).

These large traditional dwellings, built of dark-coloured teak and raised high on stilts, give an impression of what Mae Chaem and any Thai town must have looked like in the old days. Beyond the edge of Mae Chaem, this road turns into the H1263 dirt road, which goes a very long distance via Mae Na Chon and Pang Ung all the way to Khun Yuam, some 104 kms away – a great motorcycle trek in its own right. If you go right, you proceed along the main drag to its other southern end, where in years gone by there was an open-air 'singing girl' restaurant called *Chai Tung*, meaning 'end of the field'. Perhaps it is still there.

If you go straight across (E) at the central intersection, you pass a small supermarket (right) and a fuel station (left), before heading out of town to arrive at a junction. Left (E) at the junction takes you on the H1192 road up to near the summit of Doi Intanon, through the National Park on the 1009 road and down to Chom Tong, and on to Chiang Mai up Highway 108. Straight or right at the junction takes you on the 1008 road 45 kms to the main 108 Hot/Mae Sariang highway. A couple of hundred metres beyond the 1192/1008 junction, you can find **Wat Pa Daet** on your right side. It is interesting and worth a visit because there are old murals on the walls of the monastery-temple, showing life and clothing in Mae Chaem a century or more ago, and because the *wat* complex houses a kind of weaving centre – at least it did in 1992 – run by two clued-up ex-Thammasat University students, who are interested in promoting local culture, in encouraging Mae Chaem weaving, and in re-introducing the use of natural dyes. Further along the H1008, some 36 kms from Mae Chaem, you can find **Taep Panom hot spring** just beyond the village of Om Khud.

If at Mae Chaem's central crossroads you turn around and go back over the bridge, you come to a T-junction. Left takes you about 1.5 kms to the celebrated riverside weaving village of **Tong Fai**, where many households are engaged in producing especially *tin chok* or hem pieces for skirts in the Mae Chaem style, and where there is a weaving centre. I believe these people are local Tai Yuan or Lannatai, not Tai Lue such as we met in Trek 13. Right (N) from the T-Junction takes you, as we know, up the west bank of the Chaem river out of Mae Chaem, past the turning (left) for Pang Hin Fon, Ho Gao and La Ang, to the villages of Kong Khan, Sob Chok, Na Hong Tai and Na Hong. In the past people used to raft down the River Chaem from about Sob Chok to Mae Chaem, although this might have been curtailed because in the early 1990s a *farang* was killed during such rafting, drowning in a current that was too strong. From Mae Chaem you could make a little half-day motorcycle circuit by going N up this riverside trail to Na Hong, hitting the 1263 Khun Yuam/Mae Chaem dirt road, turning right, and coming back S down to Mae Chaem via Mae Na Chon and Sob Wak (total distance ca 70 kms). Between the T-junction by the central bridge and the turning for Ho Gao and La Ang, there used in the early 90s to be a guest house in a peanut field, called, I think, *Mae Chaem GH*. It mushroomed only to disappear, but perhaps someone has now resurrected it.

TREK 23: LA ANG – HO GAO – MAE CHAEM – CHIANG MAI

Mae Chaem, both the town and the wider district, used to be inhabited only by Lawa and Karen people until Thai from Chom Tong and San Pa Tong moved there. According to the official report mentioned earlier, in 1990 the district population comprised 53% Thai, 40% Karen, 2.8% Lawa, 2.5% Hmong and 0.3% Lisu. Some 46% of these people were Buddhists, 32% animists, and a surprising 22% Christian. There were 31 churches in the district. In 1991 the *ampoe* also boasted 76 elephants. Mae Chaem has always been one of the poorest districts in Thailand. In 1990, 75% of its population earned less than the minimum annual income prescribed by the IMF/World Bank for Thailand, which was 1800 baht! This impoverishment probably accounts for the fact that during the communist insurgency in Thailand during the 60s, 70s and early 80s Mae Chaem district used to be strongly communist. It no doubt also explains the high rate of opium addiction in the district. In the Mae Chaem area, people cultivate principally wet rice, mountain rice, peanuts, yellow beans, shallots, garlic, cabbages, fruits, sesame, potatoes, carrots and other vegetables. They produce yellow bean sauce, weaving, bamboo artefacts, and tobacco. In 1990 there were seven mines in Mae Chaem, producing lignite (at Na Hong), fluorspar, tin and manganese.

I have included all this information because it is illustrative of a portion of Lawa country, the venue of the last four treks, because Mae Chaem is quite an intriguing place, and because you might consider interrupting Trek 23 at the town, spending one or more nights there, which I recommend you do. This would make Trek 23 less rushed, but would also mean that you could spend a whole day exiting the trek to Chiang Mai, starting from Mae Chaem in the early morning and having enough time to take in the summit of Doi Intanon and pass through Doi Intanon National Park at your leisure. If you have come all the way over the mountains to Mae Chaem from Mae Sariang, you probably thought that Trek 23 was virtually at an end, but there is mileage in it yet. Thus consider a night in Mae Chaem. The restaurants and guest houses in town come and go, but you will always find somewhere to eat and sleep. For accommodation, try looking up the northern part of the main street. Beyond the police station there always used to be a gloomy if adequate place called *Hotel Mae Chaem* on the right or E side of the road. Otherwise try the area on the other side of the river (NW corner of town), where *Mae Chaem GH* used to be. Hunt around town – there is sure to be some lodging somewhere.

Also in the northern part of the main street, near *Mae Chaem Hotel*, there used for many years to be a garden 'restaurant' called *Ing Doi*, which means 'leaning into the mountain' or 'in the lee of the mountain' – it lies quasi at the foot of Doi Intanon. They served fair chow here, although the drinks were always overpriced. Otherwise there are always a variety of eating places in the main street, near the central crossroads and opposite the police station. *Ing Doi* was the place where I once got caught up with a party of teachers who were giving a farewell meal for a lady teacher who was leaving to join her husband in Samoeng. A hired pop group began to

323

play, so badly that they inadvertently sounded like the Velvet Underground. The teachers got more and more drunk, danced in front of the band, stamped their feet, raised the dust, and drew quite a few onlookers from the town. Seeing me, the only *farang* in Mae Chaem, a jovial thickset man came over from the merrymakers and invited me to dance – with him. He was the *kru yai* or headteacher, and so there I was in Mae Chaem dancing with a headmaster!

Mae Chaem – Doi Intanon/National Park – Chom Tong – San Pa Tong – Hang Dong – Chiang Mai (see Map 42)

At Mae Chaem you might think that you are nearly home if you are heading for Chiang Mai, but there is still a long way to go (some 120 kms), and a fine journey at that, enough to fill up a whole day, so I recommend that on Trek 23 you spend a night at Mae Chaem and set off the following morning with the whole day ahead of you. You have the little matter of crossing Doi Intanon National Park, which involves biking almost to the summit of Intanon mountain itself. Before you set off, I suggest you tank up your bike and have some warm clothing handy – it is nearly always downright cold riding through the National Park.

With the big bridge over the River Chaem behind you and Mae Chaem market to your right, go straight over the staggered crossroads eastish, past the minimart (right) and fuel station (left), and proceed a couple of kms up the street, swinging right (S), until you come to a junction (see Map 42). Right continues, as outlined above, 45 kms down the H1008 to the 108 Hot/Mae Sariang road. But we go left up the 1192 country road for the National Park and Chom Tong. This road, with a patchy surface, is closed to lorries, and you soon see why. Narrow and steep, it winds relentlessly 24 kms up a shoulder of Doi Intanon to the 1009 summit road. It is a breathtaking road, with some extreme upgrades and numerous hairpin bends – an exhilirating ride, most of it in first and second gear. You rise up largely through hot dry open countryside of mile upon mile of young teak trees with outsize green-gold leaves and also conifers. Through the trees you get some superb views of mountain scenery and especially of Doi Intanon. Ways go off left and right to villages, mostly Karen and Hmong. Then, at the top, you pass through some splendid cloud forest with very tall trees shooting up directly from the side of the road. Beyond this cool gloomy woodland, you hit a T-junction, marked by a checkpoint. You have reached the 1009 summit road. Left goes 9 kms N to the top of Doi Intanon, while right goes 37 kms down to Chom Tong.

Seeing that you are so close to the summit of Thailand's highest mountain, why not make a small 18-km round-trip detour to go and view it? You climb up at high altitude through more excellent cloud forest to the summit. Almost halfway, you pass on your left-hand side a huge new pagoda with the long name of **Pra Mahataat Napametanidon**. The *chedi*, which dominates the scene and is clearly visible from Mae Chaem, offers great views and has a series of large terracotta reliefs arranged in a circle around its octagonal base. The **summit of Mount Intanon** (2565 m or 8415 ft) itself is rather disappointing. A highway, used by droves of Thai and also *farang* trippers in their stinking pick-ups, minibuses and jeeps, goes all the way to the top, meaning that there is little thrill of achieving the summit and that it is overrun, especially at weekends and during Thai public holidays. The top is rounded and flat, and gives no impression of being on a mountaintop. And the military have reserved the summit for themselves, fencing it off, installing radar and communications equipment there, and posting the sign 'Photography Forbidden'. But in the cloud forest before the summit there is said to be some outstanding birdwatching to be done, some of the best in Thailand. The last time I was on top, on the last day of one January, the temperature was 9°C at midday.

Back at the junction of the 1009 and 1192 roads, by the checkpoint, you now descend 37 kms to Chom Tong. This used to be a dream road, on which bikers could swoop down a series of curves through stunning mountain scenery devoid of traffic. But these days, and especially at weekends and during Thai public holidays (forget it at New Year), the 'skyway' is unfortunately something of an ant trail of vehicles with maladjusted engines shockingly spewing out diesel fumes into the pristine forest and jungle environment. You pass through a succession of terrains: cloud forest; bald grassy upland fell country, where the air is distinctly cooler and fresher than lower down, and where the sky is noticeably bluer and the light more intense; dark green jungle and forest; and at the bottom a landscape reminiscent of the South of France, with bushes and low trees, and cactuses growing at the side of the road. Mainly Karen villages lie on and off the route, and you pass a number of waterfalls, two prominent ones being the double **Siripoom Fall** on your left about 7 kms down from the junction, and the **Wachiratan Waterfall** 400 m offroad left, lower down. There is a third and popular fall, **Mae Klang Waterfall**, near the entrance (or in our case exit) to the National Park, which lies some 7 kms out from Chom Tong.

At the bottom of the 1009 National Park/summit road, you hit a T-junction and the 108 highway. Right (S) goes 1 km to the town of **Chom Tong**, beyond which lie the towns of Hot and, far away, Mae Sariang. Left (N), your route, continues up the H108 some 54 kms to the superhighway outside Chiang Mai, and about 57 to the centre of Chiang Mai. I find that this final stretch, like the way from Mae Chaem to Chiang Mai as a whole, is always further than I think. On a very heavily used and dangerous road, with chaotic speeding cars, lorries and buses, you pass through equally congested and chaotic **San Pa Tong** and **Hang Dong**, before reaching the stretch of dual carriageway that winds up at the superhighway, major crossroads and traffic lights near Chiang Mai airport. Go straight across for **Chiang Mai** centre, branching left or right at a fork depending on whether you are aiming respectively for the western and northern part of town, or for the eastern part.

*

Doing Trek 23 in reverse (see Maps 42, 41, 40 & 35)
In case you are doing Trek 23 in reverse, following it with either Trek 20 or 22 or 21 with a view to striking W across the mountains all the way from Chiang Mai via La Ang to Mae Sariang, here are some distance indications, starting at Chiang Mai:

Chiang Mai centre:	km 0.0
Chiang Mai superhighway:	km 3.0
Junction H108/H1009 & turning right just N of Chom Tong for Doi Intanon National Park & Mae Chaem:	km 57.0
Junction H1009/H1192 & turning left (9 kms before summit) for Mae Chaem:	km 94.0
Mae Chaem central crossroads:	km 118.0

Turning left for Pang Hin Fon etc.:	km 119.0
Junction before Pang Hin Fon (go left):	km 140.3
Pang Hin Fon:	km 143.2
Ho Mai:	km 151.6
Ho Gao centre:	km 154.0
Junction before Mae Hae Tai (go left):	km 164.3
Sae To Sa	km 166.6
Junction just before La Ang (go right):	km 169.5
La Ang centre:	km 170.0

Now see the route detail in Trek 22 for distances and km readings from La Ang via Mae La Oop to Mae La Noi and Mae Sariang (refer also to Map 39). Add 16.5 kms to go from La Ang to Mae La Oop, then 25 kms from Mae La Oop to the 108 main road just S of Mae La Noi, and then 30 kms from there to Mae Sariang. In other words add 72 kms from La Ang via Mae La Oop to Mae Sariang, making a total distance from Chiang Mai via La Ang and Mae La Oop to Mae Sariang of ca 242 kms.

For distances and km readings from La Ang via Chang Mor, Lao Li and Kong Loi to Mae Sariang, see the end of Trek 20 (refer also to Maps 37, 36 & 29). Add 27 kms to go from La Ang to Chang Mor, then 41 kms from Chang Mor to Kong Loi, and then 50 kms from Kong Loi to Mae Sariang. In other words add 118 kms from La Ang via Chang Mor and Kong Loi to Mae Sariang, making a total distance from Chiang Mai via these places to Mae Sariang of ca 288 kms.

For distances and km readings from La Ang via Chang Mor and Pa Pae to Mae Sariang, likewise see the end of Trek 20 (refer also to Maps 37, 38 & 29). Add 27 kms to go from La Ang to Chang Mor, then 46 kms from Chang Mor via Pa Pae to the 108 road, and then 15 kms on to Mae Sariang centre. In other words add 88 kms from La Ang via Chang Mor and Pa Pae to Mae Sariang, making a total distance from Chiang Mai via these places to Mae Sariang of ca 258 kms kms.

Part 4

**Treks 24-25: trekking the 'Old Elephant Trail'
between Mae Hong Son and Chiang Mai
south-east of Mae Hong Son town
in Mae Hong Son & Chiang Mai provinces
launched from Mae Hong Son town**

Trek 24

Trekking the 'Old Elephant Trail' (1)

Mae Hong Son – Mae Sa Koet – Nam Hu – Huai Hi – Nong Kao Glang – Huai Mai Dam – Huai Pu Loei – Huai Tong – Wat Chan

Parameters

trekking mode: on foot or by motorcycle

core trek distance: from Mae Sa Koet to Wat Chan ca 85 kms (53 miles)

total trek distance: add 7 kms accessing Mae Sa Koet from Mae Hong Son. Trek must be exited from Wat Chan. Now also add either 55 kms to Pai (can be done by public transport), or, combining Trek 25 with 24, 140 kms to Chiang Mai via Samoeng (for motorcycle trekkers only). Total trek distance from Mae Hong Son via Wat Chan to Pai ca 145 kms and to Chiang Mai ca 230 kms

core trek time: from Mae Sa Koet to Wat Chan: on foot about 4 days/ 4 nights walking whole way (less if you avail yourself of lifts en route); by motorbike 1 day

accessing time: Mae Hong Son to Mae Sa Koet: by public transport allow 1 hr, by own hire bike 20 mins

total trek time: (1) from Mae Hong Son to Wat Chan exiting by vehicle to Pai: on foot allow 5 days/ 4 nights (reckon on a week for this great adventure if you include time spent getting to Mae Hong Son and setting up the trek); by bike 1 very long day or 2 days/1 night (recommended). (2) From Mae Hong Son to Wat Chan exiting to Samoeng and Chiang Mai: by bike only minimum 2 days/1 night

degree of difficulty: as a walking trek: not difficult, but very long and exhausting; fitness and perseverance presupposed. as a biking trek: difficult, for expert riders with dirt skills only

guide(s): not necessary as guides, but very useful as porters

guide name(s): Loe Po Mo, Cha Tu, Lor Sor, Sae Ri, Surasak (see photos)

tent: necessary

map(s): see 43, 44, 45, 46 & 47

TREK 24: MAE HONG SON – NONG KAO – WAT CHAN

Overview & strategy

This is the big one, whichever way you look at it, whether in terms of length, terrain, beauty or trekking exhiliration. No other expedition has given me a greater feeling of accomplishment upon concluding it. The trek takes you from Mae Hong Son town, tucked up in Thailand's extreme north-western corner, some 90 kms SE to the remote staging-post village of Wat Chan, situated in the middle of the extensive mountainous hinterland stretching from Chiang Mai WNW to Mae Hong Son. In doing so, it covers roughly one half of the old way from Mae Hong Son to Chiang Mai (or, more accurately, from central Chiang Mai to outlying Mae Hong Son), which some people, myself included, like to refer to as the 'Old Elephant Trail' because in bygone times, before other ways and roads were pushed through to Mae Hong Son, people used to plod along this route on elephants, when they were not walking it. After the trek, because Ban Wat Chan lies in the middle of nowhere, you must then proceed elsewhere, either exiting 55 kms N to Pai or continuing ESE a swingeing 140 kms via Samoeng to Chiang Mai. If the latter option is taken, you would combine the next expedition, Trek 25, with Trek 24, and you would, broadly speaking, do the other larger half of the Old Elephant Trail, completing the whole 230-km-long route. The trek can be done on foot or – by expert riders only – on a motorcycle. I have not yet done Trek 24 as a biking expedition, but have 'only' walked it. Below I shall describe the trek as a walking trek, as I did it. On the basis of the route detail and maps, experienced motorcycle trekkers will be able to look after themselves.

Now that far-flung Mae Hong Son can be accessed by two fine, if long, mountain roads (the H108 via Mae Sariang and the H1095 via Pai), and is even served several times a day by passenger jet aircraft, it is difficult to conceive of the town being reached by a path through the mountains trodden by elephants and walkers, although as recently as the early 1990s both the above-mentioned roads consisted for long stretches of dirt, making for a gruelling all-day bus journey or an arduous two-day bike trip, as I well recall. The H1095 via Pai was pushed through to Mae Hong Son as a regular road, as said, in the early 90s, before which most traffic for the westerly town went circuitously via Hot and Mae Sariang on the H108, which itself was pushed through to Mae Hong Son as a regular route as recently as 1968. The way to Mae Hong Son via Pai, now followed by the H1095, was by all accounts first laid out during the Second World War by the Japanese, who needed supply lines to support their war effort in Burma. Before this, and before the route via Mae Sariang was opened up, the main and only sensible way from Chiang Mai to Mae Hong Son and vice versa was the Old Elephant Trail via Wat Chan. It is not clear to me exactly when this trail was supplanted by the H108 Mae Sariang route, but probably the switchover was gradual.

Over the years various people in villages broadly along the trail, both old and not so old, have spoken to me of the trail, about the villages along it, and about their using it. Thus in 1992 a Karen teacher woman in and from Wat Chan said that when she was at school in the 4th grade (age about 12), she had to go to school in Chiang Mai. There was no road in those days from Wat Chan to Samoeng and she had had to walk the distance on the elephant trail. She used to walk in a group of 8 people, they carried a whole lot of food to eat on the way, and it took them 5 days of hard hiking to reach Chiang Mai. This would have been in the late 1960s or around 1970. She also talked of having walked from Wat Chan on an old trail to Mae Hong Son. The journey went via Huai Pon and took 2 days, which I do not really believe – perhaps she meant 2 days to Huai Pon and a further day to Mae Hong Son town, which might be feasible. What all this means is that it would have taken her 7 or 8 days to walk the whole elephant trail from Mae Hong Son to Chiang Mai.

Now a little history lesson. Mae Hong Son was put on the map in 1831, before which nobody would have bothered to walk there from Chiang Mai. In that year, as records show, the then ruler of Chiang Mai (which was the most important of the city states making up Lan-Na or northern Thailand) sent an expedition to the region of Mae Hong Son to survey Lan-Na's ill-defined western border. The surveyor-explorers found the land around present-day Mae Hong Son (apparently non-existent as a village or town at that time) rich in elephants. In conjunction with the local Shan, corralling began, and out of the elephant corralling station a village grew up that eventually became Mae Hong Son, which also burgeoned from teak exploitation. The village expanded so rapidly that in 1884 the Chiang Mai authorities declared it a town. In 1893 the area achieved provincial status, being incorporated in 1900 into the northern Siamese *monton* or 'circle' of Payap. Now renamed Mae Hong Son after a local river, the town became the provincial capital.

I give this little potted history of Mae Hong Son and its relation to Chiang Mai because it explains the origins of the elephant trail. The trail must have started around 1831 and been used at first for bringing corralled elephants back to Chiang Mai. As the town grew in importance, more people would have wanted to go there for business reasons or whatever, further using the trail. As Mae Hong Son became important as an administrative centre, various officials would have needed to go there, also using the trail. They went for administrative and political reasons, and to collect taxes. Some might have travelled by elephant, and elephants would have been used to transport goods to and from Mae Hong Son. And so the route became a well-worn trail, and until relatively recently there were dozens of transport elephants and 'pens' in the outpost town, just as there were also in Chiang Mai. Many older people in Mae Hong Son speak of elephants in the yards of almost every second house in town, and of the beasts trundling the trail to Chiang Mai and other local routes until the 1950s.

If I am honest, the precise route of the Old Elephant Trail is unclear, and parts of Treks 24 and 25, purporting to follow the trail, may not exactly do so. However, parts of these treks do seem to follow the old trail, and the treks basically follow the direction of the trail. Starting at Mae Hong Son, the trail might have begun not by going S and then proceeding SE via Nam Hu and Huai Hi to Nong Kao (as in Trek 24), but by climbing up E directly out of the town (behind where the airport runway now is) to either Ban Hua Nam Mae Hong Son or Huai Pon. This would seem to be confirmed by what my informant in Wat Chan said about walking from Wat Chan via Huai Pon to Mae Hong Son. The settlements of Hua Nam Mae Hong Son and Huai Pon lie to the NW of Nong Kao Glang. In Nong Kao Glang, on the route of Trek 24, people said that the Old Elephant Trail definitely passed through their village, and officials used to pass through collecting taxes from Mae Hong Son, taking 7 days to do the whole trail in each direction. I feel sure that from Nong Kao to Wat Chan the trail was the same or nearly the same as that taken in the rest of Trek 24, via Huai Mai Dam, Huai Pu Loei, Huai Tong and Nong Chet Nuai. In Huai Mai Dam a very old man, aged perhaps 80 or 90, said that he used to walk from there to Chiang Mai along the Old Elephant Trail in 5 days. He went via Wat Chan, but after that passed through a string of villages that do not exactly lie on the route of Trek 25. He passed through 'Mae Mu Noi' (Mae Muang Noi), 'Yamoeng' (Yang Moen) and 'Mae Tu Ti' (Mae Tung Ting), issuing at Mae Rim.

If you look at a map, this makes perfect sense. The route he described, which incidentally does not go through Samoeng, efficiently forms virtually a straight line between Wat Chan and Mae Rim. If this is indeed the onward route of the elephant trail from Wat Chan, then it does not follow the more southerly and circuitous route via Mae Daet Noi, Mae Ta La and Samoeng, as described in Trek 25. But this perhaps ties in with what my Karen informant lady in Wat Chan said, namely that in the old days there was no 'road' going that way. Actually, I believe that some or all of the way of Trek 25 via Samoeng was used in the old days, and there is no contradiction here. Undoubtedly there was more than one way from Chiang Mai to Wat Chan and from Wat Chan to Mae Hong Son. The Old Elephant Trail was fragmented, with the ways overlapping in places, branching and interconnecting. Nevertheless, if you were a purist and wanted to travel the 'realest' of all the 'real' routes of the elephant trail, you would have to walk and investigate the way via Mae Muang Noi, Yang Moen and Mae Tung Ting, something I have yet to do.

I have discussed all this at some length because I know that many people are interested in the celebrated Old Elephant Trail. What I have said should be taken as tentative notes on the way towards establishing the definitive route(s), notes that are based on what I have learned when walking and biking. As anyone knows who has tried to gather information 'on the road' in Thailand and especially in hill-tribe country, querying routes and old ways leads to much confusion and a big headache all round. Ask a question a thousand times, and you get a thousand different answers. But enough of the history. Now back to the trek.

Route & time schedule

More specifically, the route and time schedule of Trek 24 is as follows. On Day 1, you go from Mae Hong Son town 7 kms S down the 108 road to a side road striking E (see Map 43). You proceed up this road to the village of Hua Nam Mae Sa Koet (henceforth shortened to Mae Sa Koet), to a checkpoint and the entrance to Mae Surin Waterfall National Park, where you pick up your guides (Karen boys) if you want them, and to the Karen settlement of Nam Hu, which lies some 14 kms from the H108/Mae Sa Koet junction. Beyond the checkpoint the route is a dirt trail all the way to Wat Chan, which is some 85 kms distant from the H108. The first 28 kms, to the far side of Huai Hi, are (in 1999) a fair dirt road, newly constructed 5 or 6 yrs ago. Beyond that, from km 28 to ca km 75 at Huai Tong, the way is poor. On Trek 24 you pass more than half a dozen villages, which are all Karen. Between Mae Sa Koet and Nam Hu, you climb spectacularly up and then along Saam Fa (Three Skies) mountain ridge, and begin to skirt impressive Doi Pui mountain on your left. You spend Night 1 either at Nam Hu settlement or at a primitive forestry office there.

On Day 2, in the morning, you hike 10 kms to Huai Hi (see Map 44), making a long ascent, a drawn-out descent and then a killer protracted ascent to the village, which lies close to Doi Pui and where you have lunch. In the afternoon you continue 2½ hrs to Nong Kao Glang, climbing over two more ridges and passing through woodland country and along valley floors. You spend Night 2 in the pleasant Karen village of Nong Kao Glang. In the morning of Day 3, you walk 2 hrs mostly uphill to the village of Huai Mai Dam (see Map 45), where you have an early lunch. In the afternoon, you hike more than 5 hrs to Huai Pu Loei. This latter is easily the biggest single leg of the whole trek (people said it was around 20 kms long!) and also the most spectacular, as you climb clean over Doi Yao with its two passes through sensational scenery. The whole marathon trek is worth doing for this section alone, which is *possibly the best walk in this book*. After an extended descent, you arrive at Huai Pu Loei, where you spend Night 3.

On Day 4, you walk 2 hrs in the morning on a flattish trail to the big Karen place of Huai Tong (see Map 46), where you snatch an early lunch, and in the afternoon you walk out 2 hrs downhill on a well-made, rather boring dirt road, past the villages of Nong Chet Nuai and Daen, to Wat Chan, some 85 kms from the H108 and the junction near Mae Sa Koet. In pivotal Ban Wat Chan, a 'wild-west' Karen place and the nominal midpoint of the Old Elephant Trail, you have reached comparative civilization (there are shops and food there), but you must still exit the trek. As a foot trekker, you must exit N 55 kms either by hitch-hiking or by public transport to Pai or even to Mae Hong Son. If you still have guides with you, they will want to get back to Mae Sa Koet, taking the bus from Pai to Mae Hong Son. If you are lucky, you might still get a ride out from Wat Chan to Pai during the afternoon of Day 4. Otherwise you will have to spend Night 4 in Wat Chan, taking an early-morning lift and exiting to Pai on Day 5. As a motorcycle trekker, you can either exit to Pai as above, or cross over to Trek 25, continuing 140 kms via Samoeng to Chiang Mai. Some 60 kms of the latter onward route are dirt, and if you add to this distance the 80 kms of dirt travelled in Trek 24, you end up with a dirt ride of ca 140 kms, which is, I believe, *the longest dirt trail in Thailand!*

As said, I have not yet undertaken Trek 24 by motorbike, having so far only walked it, which means that I am not really in a position to give you precise details about ride distances and ride times between the villages, or about the difficulty of individual passages. When you are on foot, you tend to ignore or underestimate the problems you would face on a bike. But the route is ridden by a trickle of bikers. During the 4 days my party was walking, we were passed by a couple of groups of them (all going E-W from Pai to Wat Chan to Mae Sa Koet and Mae Hong Son). You should be able to ride Trek 24 in whichever direction in one day, including the extension to or from Pai. However, on a small hire bike and considering the length and mediocrity of the route, this is in my opinion ambitious timing, and for reasons of comfort and safety I recommend that you take 2 days, breaking the journey and staying a night at a village somewhere in the middle, perhaps at Nong Kao or Huai Mai Dam or Huai Pu Loei. If you plan to tack Trek 25 onto Trek 24, you should allow at least 2 days for the overall ride Mae Hong Son to Wat Chan to Chiang Mai or vice versa, and preferably three. If you do not want to 'camp wild' at Wat Chan or in some other hill-tribe village en route, you will have to cop out midway and go down to and then back up from touristy Pai with all its guest houses and restaurants.

I walked the trek in January 1999 with Nittaya Tananchai and Doug Boynton, and with relays of Karen guides, 5 different boys in all and 3 with us at any one time (one guide each to carry each of our 3 backpacks). We walked the whole distance with the exception of the initial access stretch of some 7 kms from Mae Hong Son town to the beginning of the side road near Mae Sa Koet. That makes some 85 kms from the 108 road/Mae Sa Koet junction to Wat Chan (ca 90 kms for the total journey minus ca 7) – the longest single trek I have ever made. To get the full glory of this magnificent hike, you should hoof the full distance too! The sheer length of an undertaking can add to the attraction already inherently in it. It took us 4 days to complete the core part of the trek, the actual walking, from Mae Sa Koet to Wat Chan. We spent a fifth day setting the trek up (discovering the start, negotiating with and engaging guides, and buying provisions), and a sixth exiting to Pai and then on by bus with the guides to Mae Hong Son (you do not need to do this latter, of course). To this you can add a day reaching Mae Hong Son (e.g. from Chiang Mai) and another day exiting from Pai (say, to Chiang Mai). So, to walk the elephant trail (half of it, the best half) as in Trek 24, you must set aside overall about a week!

However, I fully understand if you do not feel up to trekking the whole 85 kms or 4 days and prefer to shorten the marathon by hitch-hiking some of the way or taking lifts wherever they offer themselves, which is possible.

And if I were to walk Trek 24 again, I would do just this. How you shorten the expedition by taking lifts is connected with the relative beauty or excitement of the various stages. The best part of the trek is the central section, the long haul between Huai Mai Dam and Huai Pu Loei over Doi Yao. Another gem is the climb up right at the beginning, between Mae Sa Koet and Nam Hu, from about kms 5 to 11, where in a series of corkscrew bends you gain some magnificent views down onto Mae Hong Son and its hilltop *wat* of Kong Mu. Perhaps a rather futile stretch is after Nam Hu, where for 3 or 4 kms before Huai Hi you drag up what seems like a hot desolate dirt highway, a stretch we found dispiriting. The least satisfactory section is the last, the 10 kms from Huai Tong to Wat Chan, which we only walked for the sake of being able to say that we hoofed the entire route. It is a regular, new, featureless, hot dirt road, used by some traffic.

Modifying the trek

Thus, if you want to shorten or speed up the trek, consider hitch-hiking perhaps the first 25 kms as far as Huai Hi, or at least the stretch between Nam Hu and Huai Hi, and the last 10 kms from Huai Tong to Wat Chan. This will knock out up to 35 kms or 2 days from the trek, leaving you with some 50 kms or 2 full days, and you will end up with the heart or meat of the expedition. You will probably have to walk anyway the central section from Huai Hi to Huai Tong and almost certainly the centremost section over Doi Yao from Huai Mai Dam to Huai Pu Loei because few, if any, 4-wheel vehicles drive these ways. However, if you are considering incorporating an element of hitch-hiking, a few vehicles do drive in from each end every day, from the H108 to Huai Hi, and from Wat Chan to Huai Tong or further. Our guides said that such vehicles, perhaps used by doctors or teachers, usually pass Nam Hu between 4 and 6pm.

Other ways of modifying the trek include continuing from Wat Chan, as indicated, not to Pai but to Samoeng and then Chiang Mai (Trek 25). This can only really be done by motorbike. It is too far to walk, especially on top of the walk in Trek 24. You could try to hitch-hike through here, but I think you would be unwise to do so unless you had a guarantee that the driver was going right through or at least as far as Mae Hang Ya or Ban Mai, from where you could pick up another lift or a *silor*. Otherwise you might spend many hrs or even a whole day waiting for a lift or lifts. It is more than 90 kms from Wat Chan to Samoeng (140 to Chiang Mai), the villages are spaced out, and the way, although a fairly regular dirt trail, proceeds through the mountains, over ridges, through jungle, and along some deteriorated sections. The trek could be further modified by doing it, of course, in reverse. You could get the daily *silor* from Pai up to Wat Chan (fare about 50 baht) and then walk out to Mae Sa Koet and Mae Hong Son. Further, you could bike from Wat Chan to Mae Hong Son after first riding from Chiang Mai via Samoeng to Wat Chan. In each case you would have to read the route detail and maps relating to this trek backwards, and in the latter case those relating to Trek 25. I can well imagine that this magnificent extended trip, comparable to that from Chiang Mai via La Ang to Mae Sariang or vice versa (see Treks 20-23), would appeal to experienced dirt bikers finding themselves in Chiang Mai. A wacky modification of Trek 24, the kind of thing I would consider another time, would be to ride on a hire bike from Mae Hong Son to Huai Hi, leave your machine there, walk the brilliant central section to Huai Pu Loei, then walk back, even possibly camping near the top of Doi Yao, retrieving your bike at Huai Hi, and riding back out to Mae Hong Son. You could even include an ascent of Doi Pui from Huai Hi (see below). All this would give you the best of both walking and riding worlds. Go for it.

Difficulty & guides
Concerning difficulty, Trek 24, as a walking expedition, is *not* difficult in the sense that you might lose your way, have to scramble, or have to bust through jungle, as in earlier treks in this book. The way is clear, especially (I hope) with my maps, and you simply follow a road and track. However, it is taxing in the sense that the distances are long, both the overall distance and the distances of some sections, notably the 20-km-long stretch between Huai Mai Dam and Huai Pu Loei, which is really enough for one day. Thus, although you should not get lost, you will get exhausted, marching for 4 days in succession in the hot sun. We were tired even without having to carry our backpacks. You would be doubly whacked if you had to do that, including tents, cameras, food and water. As a biking expedition, the trek is in my estimation difficult for average to experienced riders. For enduro riders, riding one to a bike on a decent machine (250 cc or more), and with plenty of dirt skills, you will hardly find a better trip out in Thailand. There are some markedly steep up- and downgrades, some passages where the surface is in a very poor condition, some fording of streams etc., and some distinctly remote and lonely stretches. You could get through here riding one-up on a Honda Dream, but forget it if you are riding two-up. Absolutely forget Trek 24 as a biking trip if you are an inexperienced biker or a novice rider who has casually hired a stepthrough Dream townbike in Chiang Mai or Mae Hong Son. You are bound to come to grief. You have been warned!

On the subject of guides, I would say that you could dispense with guides in the sense that you do not really need anyone to show you the way. You could also dispense with them if you can carry your own stuff. However, hiring (Karen) guides to act as porters makes the walking much more pleasant. Guides also make good company, point out features along the route, can facilitate things for you when you stay overnight at villages, offer an element of security, and can read any one situation better than you. The guides come from the area you are walking through. The downside of hiring guides is that you are then encumbered with them, communication is difficult, and they can cause problems.

The three of us hired a total of 5 guides, 3 accompanying us at any one time. Thus we started out with 3 Karen forestry boys hired at the checkpoint near Mae Sa Koet at the entrance to Mae Surin Waterfall National Park.

These were Loe Mo Po, Cha Tu and Lor Sor. We negotiated the hiring and trekking plan with nice sensible Loe Mo Po, who has expressed a willingness to repeat the trek with other future trekkers or at least help set it up. Also called Pongsak and aged (in 1999) 21, we dubbed him 'Chief Guide' and 'Mr Nice Guy'. He has been with the *pamai* or forestry department for 2 yrs and comes from Huai Ka Min (near Huai Tong). He is a nice guy and was the only one of our total of 5 guides who came the whole way. For at Huai Hi the other two original guides dropped out, and we had to replace them on the spot over lunch.

Thus we lost Cha Tu, aged 19, also known as Surapan and nicknamed by us 'Pretty Boy', and we lost Lor Sor, aged 23, from Huai Mae Ngu, also known as Ti Lo Wit and nicknamed by us 'Hat Boy' (see photo section). As replacements, we took on at Huai Hi: Sae Ri (meaning 'freedom'), a thin silent 17-yr-old with a cap, and Surasak, a boy who carried our heaviest and biggest backback and who turned out to be only 14 yrs old! These latter two, together with Chief Guide, did all of the rest of the trek with us, even as far as Mae Hong Son. However, that was not the duo's intention or, rather, updated intention. Originally they had declared themselves willing to accompany us to Wat Chan or even Pai and Mae Hong Son, but in Huai Mai Dam they refused to go any further, leaving us in the lurch. This is what I mean about guides possibly becoming troublesome. You rely on them, but they are apt to change their minds. In Huai Mai Dam we had to start scratching about for new guides. But no one wanted to join our party, and we lost 2 hrs searching the village. In the end the refractory duo were shamed into going the rest of the way with us, but they were not entirely happy. They said they were getting too far from their homes and families. A further problem with all potential guides in this area is that they are backwoods Karen boys who not only speak no English, but speak poor Thai as well. We paid all these guides between 150 and 200 baht per day, paid for their time walking or riding back to where they started out from, paid for incidental meals and drinks taken by them along the way (e.g. at Wat Chan and Pai), tipped them a bit extra to keep them sweet, and especially rewarded Mr Nice Guy with extra pay for his fidelity. For accompanying us the whole way, I thing he earned 800-1000 baht.

Preparing for the trek
If you implement this trek as I outline it and we did it, you will launch it from Mae Hong Son town. As this is a regular tourist place, you will have no problems with getting there, finding accommodation, and eating. There are dozens of guest houses and restaurants. A number of traveller GHs of various prices and qualities can be found around the lake. Readers wanting do some or all of the trek by motorcycle can hire bikes in Mae Hong Son. Make a thorough inspection of your bike before hiring it, and test-ride it. Stock up with food in the town's market and supermarkets. The day before the trek, ride out on a hire bike to Mae Sa Koet and the checkpoint to organize guides, assuming you want them. In approaching the trek, we

somewhat mismanaged things, a mistake you can profit from. After setting up the trek and guides, we went out the following day late afternoon to stay at the *pamai* office by the checkpoint with a view to starting off early the next morning with the guides. But the office proved unsuitable for staying at. It was a gloomy slummy place used as a camp by the checkpoint boys and not geared up to accommodating *farang*. Further, starting from the checkpoint early in the morning proved unnecessary, and we did not save any time, rather wasted it. You can easily get to Nam Hu, the first stop, in one day not just from the Mae Sa Koet checkpoint, but also from Mae Hong Son town itself. So do not go to stay at Mae Sa Koet, but – after sorting out guides (if applicable) the previous day – start out early on Day 1 of the trek from Mae Hong Son, proceed to Mae Sa Koet, pick up your guides (if appropriate), and set off for Nam Hu.

*

Trekking route detail
Day 1: Mae Hong Son – Mae Sa Koet – Nam Hu (Map 43)
Before you can start walking, you must first get from Mae Hong Son town to Mae Sa Koet and the forestry checkpoint/entrance to Mae Surin Waterfall National Park. Proceed by bus, *silor, tuk-tuk* or hitch-hiking out of the bottom end of Mae Hong Son town some 7 kms (about 6 kms from the Shell petrol station) down the H108 road to the turning for Mae Sa Koet. Mae Sariang-bound buses leave from time to time from the bus station, and if you are planning to spend a night, as we did, at the forestry office by the checkpoint, a private company bus for Bangkok leaves from near the Shell station daily at 3pm (fare to Mae Sa Koet turning 13 baht in 1999). *Silor* (public-transport pick-ups) will leave from the market, and the motorized three-wheeler *tuk-tuks* roam around town. But why not hitch-hike the short distance. The best place to start would be down by the Shell station or beyond. Then you pass the *Imperial Tara Hotel* (right) and other fancy lodgings, a highways department office (left), a turning for a dam project (left), and some woodland, before reaching the Mae Sa Koet turning (left). The junction is marked by a waiting hut or *sala* and signs for *Fern Resort*, and just before the turning there is a little restaurant on the right side. If you cross a bridge and arrive at Pa Pong village with its new bypass, you have gone too far.

Now walk or hitch-hike 3 kms E up the side road (junction = km 0), which is tarred as far as a bridge beyond the checkpoint. You pass a turning for a *wat* (right), a turning (right) for **Mae Sa Koet** village, which lies just offroad, a *sala* (left) opposite the way in to the village, a turning (right) for *Fern Resort*, and a bridge, before coming at a gloomy corner to the checkpoint (right), which marks the entrance to Mae Surin Waterfall National Park. Its associated office is located just offroad (left) in trees. In January 1999, finding that no lifts came, we walked up this pleasant little side road in between bursts of a vicious thunderstorm and squally winds. Fully laden, it took us 35 mins to reach the checkpoint. On and off, some 10 youths live at the *pamai* office, manning the checkpoints in shifts and doing whatever. No one is really in charge, the 'boss' is just one of them, and we found him in a room behind the main office building in bed with a girl! It is all pretty free and easy at this little station, there are zero facilities, the boys come and go on their bikes, we put our tents up (when we inadvisedly stayed there) on the bare cement floor of one of the rooms in the big empty forestry building, and washed at a tap in front of it. Unable to cook in the damp, slummy little compound, and not wanting to broach our trekking provisions, we went to eat and drink at nearby *Fern Resort* – another mistake. The service was slow, we were savaged by mosquitoes in poorly lit surroundings, and the food and drinks were overpriced – 90 baht for a bottle of beer (40 at a shop in Mae Sa Koet) and 65 baht for a small portion of smashed-up chicken with cold rice. And this is supposed to be an upmarket 'resort', where rooms cost 900-1500 baht per night.

At the *pamai* office/checkpoint, pick up your guides, assuming you want some and have already organized them. It took us, unladen, about 3½ hrs to walk from the checkpoint to Nam Hu – allow 4 hrs. We started at 8.45am, arriving between 12.15 and 12.30pm. The distance is about 11 kms from the checkpoint and ca 15 from the H108. You walk broadly SE. Of course, if you start Day 1 from Mae Hong Son, you will hardly equal this. If you arrive in Nam Hu in good time and with puff to spare, consider walking on from there to Huai Hi. On this first leg and all the way to Huai Hi, avail yourself of any rare passing lifts if you feel so inclined and want to get on.

Time log

0 hrs	Set off from checkpoint/entrance to National Park. At first we walked in mist and almost total humidity. You make a long ascent, winding up Saam Fa (Three Skies) ridge.
35 mins	Guides told us of fine views NNE of Mae Hong Son, which we were unable to see because of the mist. Here Doug heard and identified the sound of a great hornbill.
1 hr 10 mins	Pass km 7 'milestone' and continue on up through mixed forest. Along here we broke through the mist into brilliant sunshine to enjoy a magical view of the local mountaintops sticking up through the milky cover.
1 hr 25 mins	View 320/330° down onto Mae Hong Son and Wat Doi Kong Mu with its hilltop pagoda and aerials, which we were at last able to enjoy through a hole in the lifting mist.
1¾ hrs	In the midst of the corkscrew bends, a *sala* and viewpoint (km 9), where we took a 15-min rest. Now Doug heard the sound of a gibbon nearby and marvelled that there were hornbills and gibbons, as well as such great forest and mountains, so close to civilization in the form of Mae Hong Son town.
2 hrs 5 mins	Pass the high-up gash, made by the road on the wooded hillside, that is visible from Mae Hong Son and especially from Wat Doi Kong Mu. Continue up, down, and then up again.
2½ hrs	Spirit house (right). New views. Dirt road levels out, contouring broadly E.
2¾ hrs	Near km-stone 11, a deserted homestead (left), a maize field (right), and a track (left), which according to a blue sign is part of a trekking path project, and which takes you 2 hrs to Khun Nam Mae Hong Son village and then back down to Mae Hong Son town (unverified). Rested a further 15 mins by the homestead.
3 hrs	Just 1 min beyond the homestead/junction: a bridge and a spring (left) in the trees.

3 hrs 10 mins Steep mountain (right), and great forest all round.

3¼ hrs   Magnificent views (ca km 13, left side of road) of cliffs and of a very high mountain ridge, the stepped end of which is Doi Pui (accessible from Huai Hi).

Now downhill all the way to Nam Hu.

3¾ hrs   Cave (left) and almost immediately **Nam Hu forestry office** (right, ca km 14), beyond which you come to a bridge, a second bridge with a little waterfall (left), and then – 200 m beyond the forestry place – a turning left for the Karen hamlet of **Nam Hu** (ca km 15, offroad, left).

Nam Hu, which is dialect for Nam Ru (meaning 'hole spring') and a shortened version of the full Nam Ru Hai Jai, is as far as we got on Day 1, even though it was only lunchtime when we arrived. Consider pushing on a further 3 hard hrs to Huai Hi if you have the energy, where there is more civilization, or a long hour to Loe Po Ki, a quiet spot where you could camp wild. But we liked the look of attractive laid-back Nam Hu, put up our tents by a volleyball/takraw pitch beside the shambolic roadside forestry outpost, got a fire going with wood lying around, cooked lunch and supper (begging rice from the *pamai* boys), showered in the mini waterfall by the second bridge, washed through our clothes and dried them on the first bridge, looked at the cave, investigated the Karen hamlet, and had a good time. When we arrived, we found just one Karen forestry youth at Nam Hu, but by nightfall the number had swelled to 10, including our 3 guides. These boys live and sleep in fair squalor, and Loe Mo Po, Cha Tu and Lor Sor joined them in it. During our stay, we noticed that a steady trickle of trucks and motorcycles pass in each direction (potential lifts). In front of the little cave, there are some air roots on which you can swing like Tarzan.

A couple of hundred metres beyond the forestry camp, lies, as said, the way left to Nam Hu village. Walk in a bit and you find just half a dozen houses to your right and left, a couple of which have some grapefruit trees and, at the time of our visit, lots of delicious juicy grapefruits! The biggest house is on your left. When we called by, we interrupted a Christian service (it was Sunday afternoon), with some of the participants wearing their best Karen costume. Nevertheless, we were warmly welcomed, sat out the rest of the service, were offered huge slices of papaya, and were supplied with boiling water and bowls with which we made instant noodle soup. This wooden house with its huge main room inside would be a good place to stay overnight if you fancied, although you would need a mosquito net. At Nam Hu, in the late afternoon and early morning, Doug did some good birdwatching, and even I noticed an abundance of colourful birds. He spotted grey-headed parakeets (green with a long tail), black-crested bulbuls (olive and yellow), sunbirds, and racket-tailed drongos (very long tails).

Day 2: Nam Hu – Huai Hi – Nong Kao Glang (Map 44)

It is about 3 hrs of walking to Huai Hi, and then a further 2½ hrs to Nong Kao Glang. You trek first SE, followed by N, to Huai Hi, and then N, followed by E, to Nong Kao. We started from Nam Hu at 9am, spent 1¼ hrs lunching in Huai Hi, and arrived in Nong Kao at 3.30pm.

Time log

0 hrs	Leave Nam Hu forestry camp, cross the two bridges, passing the little waterfall and way into Nam Hu hamlet, and proceed uphill, crossing two further bridges, the last near km 16, I think.
	Long climb up.
¾ hr	Reach brow of hill.
	Long descent.
1 hr	Km-stone 19. Road deteriorates somewhat.
1 hr 10 mins	Arrive at **Loe Po Ki**, an apparently deserted forestry outpost with a checkpoint and stream. It would make a nice place to camp wild.
	A flattish road heads approximately E.
	Uphill.
1 hr 40 mins	Km-stone 22 (the marker stone says 53 kms to Huai Tong or 63 to Wat Chan!).
	Long drag up.
	Roadside pond (left).
	In the midst of this wilderness, trudging up this desolate dispiriting dirt highway, we were passed by a boy who was run-walking his bike in first gear. Presently, a man, his former pillion passenger, also overtook us. This is what happens if on a motorbike you get a flat tyre in the middle of nowhere. The man could speak some English.
2½ hrs	Reach a kind of pass (km 25.5) and gain a new view.
	Go round a corner to gain a view of Huai Hi village, with the rear side of Doi Pui towering over it.
2¾ hrs	Arrive at **Huai Hi** (km 25.5).

Huai Hi was another place with grapefruit trees, whose fruit we greedily feasted on, with the permission of the local inhabitants, who also presented us with a bunch of small sweet bananas. Indeed, they are friendly hospitable people here, which is an attractive village of some 20 houses at the foot of the peak of Doi Pui. The Karen of Huai Hi are stoutly Christian, which perhaps accounts for their hospitality to strangers, and I seem to recall seeing a church. You can hire a guide in the village for 200 baht for the round trip and climb up "two hours" to the summit of Pui mountain, camping high up, where there is apparently water. I have not yet done this climb, but it looks promising, and the view from the top must be fantastic. You should be able to see Mae Hong Son town because I think the mountain and the town are intervisible. Someone said that there was a Karen man in Huai Hi who spoke some English, and he may well be the man who walked past us. There must be a forestry office nearby, which would be a potential place to stay if you wanted, although I am sure almost any house in the village would be happy to put *farang* up. We found a rudimentary shop with 5-baht packets of 'Ma-maa' instant noodles, which we cooked up in the house of an old lady, supplementing the soup with tuna sandwiches and fruit. Our party stayed 75 mins in Huai Hi (from 11.45am to 1pm), causing quite a commotion. This was where two of our original three guides gave up on us, but we were soon able to replace them with two new boys. Thus we said goodbye to Pretty Boy Cha Tu and Hat Boy Lor Sor, and said hello to taciturn Sae Ri and kid Surasak, who joined Mr Nice Guy Loe Mo Po, making up a new threesome. The departing duo we paid 300 baht each for their 1½ days of portering plus their journey back to Mae Sa Koet, which they probably had to hoof.

4 hrs	Set off from Huai Hi (times resume from Nam Hu, lunch stop included). Just 100 m beyond the village: a path (left), signed 'To Doi Pui 1-2 hrs'. There is an alternative, less steep route to the summit further along the dirt road.
	Up briefly to a col, passing km-stone 26. Views of steep-sided mountains near and far. The pointed peak at 70° is Doi Ma Prik.
4 hrs 20 mins	100 m down from the col, on a bend in the road, we fork right and down, taking a short cut on a path. But you do not gain much, as it only cuts off a bend in the road – stick to the road. Soon rejoin road.
	Our guides tell us that two ridges have to be climbed over before Nong Kao. Pass km-stone 28.
	Between kms 28 and 29, the engineered road gives out, the way deteriorating by a stream. You follow a 4WD track now all the way to Huai Tong, some 47 kms away.
	Climb very steeply up (problematic for motorcyclists coming down from the other direction!).
5 hrs	Reach top of the first of the two ridges mentioned by the guides. At the top, a path goes off left 1 hr to the summit of Doi Pui (the second and allegedly gentler way up).
	Down through jungle tunnel.
5¼ hrs	Stream and muddy ford.
	Some fine shaded walking down a closed-in valley, across several log bridges, past giant umbrella ferns, and into conifer country.
	Second stream and ford.
	Cross a small intervening ridge. View down onto more open terrain, with paddies on valley floor. Descend.
6 hrs	Reach valley floor, cross stream and log bridge, and pass a couple of field huts left and right.
	Climb up.
6 hrs 25 mins	Reach top of second ridge and descend to village.
6½ hrs	Arrive at Karen village of **Nong Kao**, more precisely Nong Kao Glang and Nong Kao Bon, two parts of the same place rolled into one (*glang* = middle, *bon* = upper). There is a third part, Nong Kao Nuea, not far away.

We reached Nong Kao Glang, which is what I shall call it to simplify things, at 3.30pm, a good moment to hit a village for the night, leaving you adequate time to orient yourself, find accommodation, and wash before dark. As you arrive, you find the village school on your right, together with the headteacher's house, and before you a junction. The way left is the onward route to Huai Mai Dam, while straight on goes into the village. Ahead of you, in the junction, is a blue building, which is the health centre, where we stayed, putting up our tents in its compound. We were able to wash in the bathroom of the health chief's house (raised high on stilts) and also cooked up in his kitchen, eating a 7-baht pack of Muslim noodles (like egg spaghetti) with a tin of Japanese bolognaise sauce that we had nursed all the way from Chiang Mai. The guides as usual melted away, putting themselves up and eating at friends' houses around the village.

In 1999 there were 38 houses in Nong Kao Glang. One of them (down from the health centre on the same left side), where a lady lived who was busy weaving, was well-stocked with bottles and cans of Chang beer, which we greedily tucked into, even though it was warm. The headman's house, identifiable by its telecoms equipment and satellite dish, also had provisions. The village is an attractive place, almost surrounded by mountains, except to the E, where the view is open and the mountains are more distant. We liked this place and had a good time there. Later we tracked down our guides in a house where a party was getting going – they were already spending on the strength of their anticipated guiding pay! The headman, called Da Bu Po, the headteacher, some other teachers and various villagers joined in. Soon a party was in full swing, fuelled partly by *lao kao* and *lao-u* we paid for (rice whisky in different stages of fermentation and distillation). People confirmed that the Old Elephant Trail passed through their village, said that there were 'tigers' or at least cat animals around Nong Kao, and reported the presence of wild elephants near Huai Pu Ling, a village not so far away. When they talked, we found that many of these isolated Karen speak only poor Thai, making any kind of communication difficult. We also discovered that Nong Kao was somewhat tainted by tourism, as a few villagers produced textiles which they tried to sell to us and which they had woven for that purpose – a sure sign of tourism. Apparently foreigners from Pai are occasionally trucked through. Presently 17-yr-old Sae Ri and 14-yr-old boy Surasak went out to vomit up the strong *lao kao* and weak milky *lao-u* pot 'whisky' that they had been mixing up. It was their first outing from home and their first drinking session, people murmured. The next morning they were subdued. Before school, we were invited to breakfast with the headmaster.

Day 3: Nong Kao Glang – Huai Mai Dam – Doi Yao – Huai Pu Loei (Map 45)
It is about 2¼ hrs of walking to Huai Mai Dam, and then a further 5 hrs or more to Huai Pu Loei. You trek SE and S to Huai Mai Dam, and then S, N and SE to Huai Pu Loei, tracing a kink in the route. Day 3 represents easily the longest and most ambitious leg of this trek. Between Huai Mai Dam and Huai Pu Loei, you must climb right over Doi Yao, a journey that even local people speak of in awe, and which they reckon to be 20+ kms long. We started from Nong Kao Glang at 9.15am, spent nearly 2 hrs lunching and sorting out our guides in Huai Mai Dam,

TREK 24: MAE HONG SON – NONG KAO – WAT CHAN

and arrived in Huai Pu Loei at 6.30pm, as darkness fell. In retrospect I can see that we mistimed Day 3. We should have started earlier from Nong Kao, say at 8am, and spent less time in Huai Mai Dam. Then we would have had more time for Doi Yao and would have arrived comfortably at Huai Pu Loei late afternoon. As things happened for us, we found ourselves making a desperate forced march over Doi Yao, with little time to enjoy the spectacular scenery. The latter stretch over Doi Yao from Huai Mai Dam to Huai Pu Loei is really sufficient for one day. If you can engineer the schedule such that you spend a night at Huai Mai Dam, perhaps pushing on to reach it the previous day and staying there in preference to Nong Kao, things would be perfect.

Time log

0 hrs	Leave Nong Kao Glang from the junction by the health centre. Go down to stream and log bridge, then up to more houses, which are:
¼ hr	a second part of Nong Kao. Continue down to:
20 mins	bottom and a second stream. Now up to a kind of:
35 mins	'crossroads' on a mini ridge. At the junction, which is marked by a *sala* or waiting hut, a way goes left to 3 Karen villages – Huai Pom Faad (9 kms, maybe also called Huai Chom Faad), Pa Ka (12 kms) and Huai Gluai (14 kms) – and possibly further to Huai Pon and Hua Nam Mae Hong Son. We go straight. Proceed gently down to a stream and log bridge. 4WD track twists around the valley, rising and falling slightly.
1 hr	Reach a second junction. Straight (left) goes to Nong Kao Nuea (northern Nong Kao), reportedly 30 mins' walk away. Our way curves round right to a hut and paddy fields, immediately fording two streams, and then ascending. Heading roughly SE towards a pointed mountain, you climb very steeply up (problematic for bikers coming down the other way!).
1 hr 40 mins	Ridge top. Down and then a long way up on a stony surface.
2 hrs	Huai Mai Dam school (left), a potential place to stay or camp.
2¼ hrs	Arrive at **Huai Mai Dam**.

We reached this small Karen village of some 20 houses at 11.30am, feeling tired perhaps from the final steep climb up to it or perhaps from the cumulative effect of 2½ days' trekking. If we had fully appreciated what still lay ahead, we might well have given up for the day. I think guides Sae Ri and Surasak knew of the imminent climb over Doi Yao, lasting many hrs, for in Huai Mai Dam their hearts went out of our undertaking, they bridled, and, despite their promises to accompany us all the way to Wat Chan, they would go no further. I think Doi Yao was for them a symbolic threshold, beyond it being another world. The village is another attractive enclosed place, with flowering bushes and some pretty girls. Up left, on the hillside, there is a quaint church. We found a couple of shops in people's houses selling soft drinks, instant noodles and tins of sardines. Above one of them we brewed up our usual noodle soup and ate sardines with rice presented by the household. This was where we met the very old man who

343

talked about the route of the Old Elephant Trail, which, he confirmed, passed through Huai Mai Dam. After lunch we wasted a lot of time combing the village for two replacement guides. The guides themselves did little to help us in this, which peeved us, especially because we knew what lay ahead and that we should be getting on. Potential new guides materialized, only to lose interest again. Nobody could be bothered to climb over Doi Yao. It looked as if we would have to spend the night in Huai Mai Dam, or carry our backpacks over Doi Yao ourselves. But finally, after 2 hrs, refractory Sae Ri and boy Surasak relented, or were shamed into continuing, or were persuaded by Chief Guide Mr Nice Guy, and we set off again, at the tardy hour of 1.20pm. If you find yourself quitting the village after 1pm, you are starting for Huai Pu Loei too late. Do not leave Huai Mai Dam without full water bottles and as many soft drinks as you can carry. Because we mismanaged the timing of Day 3, and because you might do the Doi Yao leg as a day's journey in its own right, I shall start the time log again from Huai Mai Dam, not running the clock cumulatively for the day from Nong Kao.

Time log

0 hrs	Leave Huai Mai Dam from far top end of village, climbing steeply up and over in airy woodland.
½ hr	At a fork marked by a *sala*, go left (straight) for Doi Yao and Huai Pu Loei. The way right apparently proceeds some 6 kms to Huai Pu Ling and to a waterfall, although the way to this much-talked-about village might also start from Huai Pu Loei, or perhaps it can be accessed by both routes. The way right goes also 15 kms to Huai Sai and accesses many other villages offroute.
	Pass a couple of houses (left and right).
	Paddy fields (right) on valley floor.
50 mins	Cement tank (right).
	Heading almost N, enter dark forest with tall trees – real elephant trail stuff!
1 hr 20 mins	Field hut (right) opposite a rocky promontory (left).
	Pass beneath the outcrop and slowly climb up the end of the valley through countryside with an alpine feel and bracken to a:
1 hr 40 mins	low pass on a bend in the trail. From the pass and bend a way, perhaps to fields, goes off left/N. Time for a rest and to admire the view. You can see the onward path climbing spectacularly up the flank of Doi Yao. It looks shattering, but when you come to grind up it, things are not so bad.
	Just a few metres beyond the low pass, a turning left goes a couple of kms to the hidden Lisu village of **Gae Hom**, which grows opium poppies and, so everyone told us, apparently does not welcome visits by outsiders. There is a hut near the start of the side way.
	Stunning views NE towards Pai of distant mountain ridges.
	Toil steeply up to:
2½ hrs	the first of two passes on Doi Yao. Fantastic views all round.

Describing a curve, walk along a saddle of land or the crest of the summit of Doi Yao connecting the first pass with the second. It is a superb high-altitude track, and offers a:

3 hrs 10 mins view left or NNE (40°) to the secluded Lisu village far below.
Climb up to second pass, just before it passing a burnt-down hut.

3 hrs 25 mins Reach second pass on Mount Yao. Huge panoramic views S over ridge after ridge of mountains.
Track skirts round mountainside, then winds steeply down, with some (if you are on a motorbike) very poor, difficult sections.
You proceed round and back up to a:

4 hrs 10 mins mini pass, with views in two directions. Looking left, you can see a gashed mountainside in the (late) afternoon sun.

4 hrs 20 mins Come back round to N side of mountain. The Lisu village is again visible far below, and even Huai Mai Dam, our most recent port of call.
Now you walk roughly S along the spine of the ridge, with – in our case – the sun setting right/W. The trekking is as if through a Mediterranean olive grove, although the trees are in fact pine.
Views in every direction of nothing but forest and mountains for mile after mile. When you see this, you realize that, despite much environmental devastation in Thailand, there is still a lot of cover.
Protracted contour walk along ridge, slightly descending.

5 hrs 5 mins First glimpses of our destination village ahead left.
Steep down to:

5 hrs 10 mins **Huai Pu Loei**.

If you have reached this big Karen village, sited either side of the trail and spilling downhill, before nightfall, congratulations. In fact, congratulations if you have reached Huai Pu Loei at all. Walking fast, and largely unencumbered by backbacks, we arrived here at 6.30pm, in virtual darkness. Because it was already night, and because we did not stop to look around the following morning, I can tell you little about this village. On arrival, we were completely bushed, and it was all we could do to find somewhere to sleep, wash and eat. Many friendly Karen gathered round, and a room in a house was offered to us, but in the end we slept on the floor of a weaving centre. We paid 30 baht for this dusty pleasure – give the same or perhaps 40 baht to whoever puts you up. Halfway down the sloping main street, there is a relatively well-stocked shop on the right side, with beer and soft drinks. The weaving centre is on the same side, but lower down. The house with the room we were offered is just up from the shop, again on the right side. Huai Pu Loei is an elevated village, surrounded by hillsides of conifers, and it was cold in the night. Just before you reach it, at the top end, there is a turning W for Huai Hi Noi and other Karen villages offroute.

Day 4: Huai Pu Loei – Huai Tong – Nong Chet Nuai – Daen – Wat Chan (see Maps 46 & 47)
It is less than 2 hrs of walking to Huai Tong, and then a further 2 hrs to Wat Chan. If you reckon on an hour for lunch in Huai Tong, that makes just 5 more hrs to the

end of the core part of the trek. You proceed about 9 kms S, E and S to Huai Tong, and then 10 kms broadly SE to Ban Wat Chan. On this last day of hiking, there are no big ridges to climb over – it is flattish to Huai Tong and then basically all downhill to Wat Chan. We set off at 9.20am and were ordering noodle soup and cold beers in Wat Chan at 2pm!

Time log

0 hrs	Go down main street of Huai Pu Loei and leave it at bottom end.
	A way goes off left to paddy fields.
	You cross a bridge and stream.
	Passing two more ways off left and then right, you climb up a bit to walk pleasantly through shady mixed woodland.
40 mins	On a flat piece of road, a track, signed, goes off right (W) to Huai Hi Noi and other Karen villages. It joins up with the other way to Huai Hi Noi that heads W just before Huai Pu Loei.
	You walk on the level, then gently down.
1 hr 25 mins	On a bend curving right, two ways go off left on orange dirt to huts and fields.
1½ hrs	Cross a wooden bridge, then descend past a way to rice fields (down right) to:
1¾ hrs	**Huai Tong**.

This big Karen place, some 75 kms from the H108/Mae Sa Koet junction, is a well-established, almost regular, rural village, with electricity, a little grid of streets, a large low wooden church, a health centre, and several little shops. Arriving here at just after 11am, we eagerly bought some iced Cokes at a shop and snatched an early snack lunch. From Huai Tong, a way strikes SW to Nam Som, Kiu Ka Min (Mr Nice Guy's home village) and other Karen places. The time log below resumes from earlier and includes an hour's lunch stop in Huai Tong. Consider hitch-hiking the rest of the way to Wat Chan – you would not miss out on anything.

2 hrs 40 mins	Set off from Huai Tong, proceeding past the health centre (left) and out of the eastern end of the village.
	5 mins out, there is a short cut (left), which you can take if you want. It rejoins the main way later. Somewhere beyond Huai Tong, you cross the provincial boundary separating Mae Hong Son province, which you leave, and Chiang Mai province, which you now enter.
	You pass two cement tanks (left) and at about km-stone 10 pick up a well-engineered dirt road, which coasts ESE down through tall mixed woods and low hills. Fine for driving along, this hot dusty road makes for rather boring walking. Avail yourself of any passing lift.
	You pass a way off right, and then another, which goes to a reforestation area.
	At km-stone 6, there is a view of Wat Chan and other nearby villages.
4 hrs 10 mins	After 1½ hrs of brisk walking from Huai Tong, you pass two ways off right to the village of **Nong Chet Nuai**, which lies away from the road (now see Map 47).

Left side of road: 'Wat Chan Development Centre', which is connected with a local Royal Project.

Lake (left).

Right side of road: a shop and way to **Daen** village, which lies both on and off the road.

Continue straight, ignoring side turnings.

Paddy fields left and right.

Bridge.

Motorbike repair shop and turning (right) for Samoeng (the start of the route of Trek 25). You are now in the main street of Wat Chan.

4 hrs 40 mins Reach centre of **Wat Chan**, with some 4 noodle soup shops (left) and Wat Chan monastery-temple and pagoda in grounds (right). You have reached the end of Trek 24 (the core part) and have covered the first half of the Old Elephant Trail, gaining the midpoint of that trail. Congratulations! Time to celebrate with a cold beer – and a mediocre noodle soup!

Wat Chan

This scrappy dusty village lies miles from anywhere on a key junction. Situated in the middle of the mountainous hinterland that extends W from Chiang Mai and Samoeng all the way to Mae Hong Son town, it is where three dirt trails from Pai, Samoeng and Mae Hong Son (our route via Huai Tong) meet up, and is, as we know, a kind of midpoint on the Old Elephant Trail from Chiang Mai to Mae Hong Son. It is a White or S'gaw Karen place and for me has always had a rough-and-ready, wild-west feel about it. In February 1992, when I first visited Wat Chan by bike from Samoeng, exiting to Pai, it had no electricity, and in early 1999, during two visits that Nittaya, Doug and I made, it had power, but always seemed to be blacked out, making it impenetrably dark at night. A mixture of housing styles can be seen around 'town', indicating different stages of modernization, and in the early 1990s Wat Chan still had a few elephants, in keeping with a Karen staging post. It is a poor place, too big for the surrounding agricultural land on which it relies. Traditionally, people have eaten what they have grown, leaving little surplus to sell. In 1992 most families earned just 3000-5000 baht a year, shopkeepers 8000. At that time there were 65 families or 380 inhabitants in the village, and 121 children attended Wat Chan school. These figures will have risen somewhat meanwhile. The various aid projects that you can see around Wat Chan are a sign of the poverty. Perhaps another symptom of it is the fact that during each of my three visits I have run into grasping people here, although this might also have to do with the fact that quite a few *farang* pass through Wat Chan, especially from Pai. Thus you are likely to be charged rip-off prices for noodle soups and beers as well as lifts to Pai. Spurn them wherever you can. Particularly hard-nosed is the moneybags woman with the store and 'restaurant' opposite the *sala* and entrance to the *wat*. But when you walk in from Huai Tong after a 4-day route march, it is difficult to resist her ice-cold beers and indifferent noodle soups.

According to village documents, Wat Chan used to be called Ko Kor Ti, which is a Karen name, apparently meaning 'base of pagoda'. It became known as Ban Wat Chan (*ban* = village) some 70 yrs ago, taking its name from Wat Chan or Chan monastery-temple, based on the celebrated pagoda in the *wat* grounds. The same documents say that the village and pagoda were built together, about 200 yrs ago, although not too much credence should be given to this. Certainly, a 38-yr-old Karen teacher said in 1992 that her grandparents had lived in the village, while other locals maintain that the pagoda and possibly also the temple predate the village. The documents claim that the pagoda and village were founded by a Karen monk called Po Mae and other people. Initially 6 families and 30 villagers lived there. The names of the temple and village probably mean Moon Temple and Moon Village (*chan* = moon), although they might also derive from a builder of the pagoda called Chan. Evidently the pagoda was renovated some 60 yrs ago by the same monk who built the road up to Wat Doi Sutep, near Chiang Mai. Actually, there is more than one pagoda in Wat Chan. A second can be seen just outside the village on a hilltop to the SE, and there is a third in the NW corner of the village. Together with the central pagoda in the grounds of the *wat*, the two form an almost straight line bisecting the village NW-SE. Locals speak of many deserted temples around Wat Chan, although nobody knows why they are there. About 30 yrs ago, a missionary came to the area, making some converts. There is a church in Daen village and a Christian primary and secondary school in Nong Chet Nuai.

As a result of royal visits during the 1980s, a relatively big Royal Project was started in Wat Chan to try to alleviate the poverty and give local people a supplementary occupation. It was a multiple venture, still operative, and the regally funded buildings relating to its different parts can be seen around 'town'. As you come into Wat Chan from the Huai Tong direction, you pass Wat Chan Development Centre on the left side of the road by a lake. It is probably connected with agriculture. As you leave Wat Chan, going just a short distance down the way for Samoeng, you pass a big Project building set splendidly up right on a hill. I think it is concerned with forestry, and a forestry office lies roughly opposite it, on the left side of the road. In the middle of the village, located in the *wat* grounds (on your right as you enter from the main street), are a series of brown wooden buildings, which constitute a handicraft centre, established in 1987. Here, as another part of the project, people have been encouraged to weave, do wood carving and cultivate silk worms. Initially, people from Isaan came over to prime the silk weaving component. Wat Chan Karen and also project officials admitted that the project had not been entirely successful owing to lack of interest on the part of local people, and for lack of spare parts.

Orientation (see Map 47): coming to the start of Wat Chan's main street from the Huai Tong direction, you pass a bike repair place and a helpful little shop (right), before coming to a junction and the turning (right) for Chaem Noi and Samoeng. Not far down the beginning of the Samoeng dirt road, the Royal Project forestry building just mentioned perches up right, and forestry buildings lie left. Above these latter buildings, on a hilltop, is one of Wat Chan's three pagodas. There must be a path up to it somewhere. On the junction, there are a couple of petrol booths. Now you come to the centre of the village and pass several noodle soup places and shops. A couple of side alleys left off the main street take you to a little grid of roads and the main residential part of Wat Chan. On your right is a waiting *sala* and, on a corner, the *wat* compound. In the compound, which has two fine peepul (pípal) or bo trees, the Royal Project handicraft centre lies on your right, while the temple-monastery and white pagoda are set back left. Then you come to a crossroads, on which there is a school opposite you. Left goes to more of Wat Chan and the third pagoda, straight goes to villages, including Nong Daeng (8 kms) and Pong Kao (9 kms) (unverified), and right is the start of the 55-km-long way to Pai.

If you do Trek 24, either exiting to Pai or crossing over to Trek 25, or if you do Trek 25 in reverse, proceeding from Chiang Mai to Wat Chan and then either continuing to Huai Tong and Mae Hong Son or exiting to Pai, it is likely that you will have to stay in Wat Chan. As I know from experience, this is not easy. But there are accommodation possibilities, and I have overnighted in 'Moon Temple Village' three times. Of course, as a biker, if you cannot be bothered with sorting out accommodation in the village, and assuming you have time, you could go down to Pai, which would make a round trip to Pai and back of a mere 110 extra kms! In Wat Chan you could camp free in the grounds of the *wat*, as we did twice in 1999. But tread carefully here. The abbott and monks did not seem to us exactly welcoming, and made difficulties, although it is almost their duty to allow people to stay. However, when they had got used to us, they relented. Their hands may have been tied by the presence of paramilitary guards of the Royal Project buildings in the *wat* grounds. These officious zealots told us we could not camp anywhere near the buildings (because of their royal connection), heavied it up with us, asked too many questions, demanded to look at passports, although their job is only to oversee the handicraft centre, pretended the same difficulties as had come from the monks, but then similarly relented, and even helped us erect our tents and later insisted we party with them around their evening fire. You get the picture. The washing facilities in the *wat* compound leave a lot to be desired. It is cold in the night at Wat Chan, and in the morning we found our tents covered in dew.

Or you could try the forestry office, which is located, as said, a short way down the road to Samoeng on the left side. Put a tent up here, or perhaps there is a room to sleep in. I have not stayed at these *pamai* buildings, so cannot comment on the option. (There is another forestry place further down the Samoeng road, about 2½ kms out from Wat Chan, offroad left, which might also be a place to put up.) A third possibility is to stay in the house of a Karen teacher lady, who speaks good English. She has a room, apparently nice, where *farang* are welcome to stay for a modest sum. Her Karen name is Tamoo and her Thai nickname is Oot. She is divorced and in 1992 confided that she would like nothing more than to meet a sympathetic Westerner! You can track her down in the school in termtime, although that is hardly necessary, because she floats around Wat Chan, latching onto passing foreigners 'to practise my English'. I am afraid I find her a trifle tedious after a while, but, never mind, she is a good source of information and can sort you out better than the monks or the self-important paramilitary guards.

Exiting the trek
Once you have arrived at Wat Chan from Huai Tong, there are only two ways you can exit the village and the trek, either to Pai, or to Samoeng and Chiang Mai. The latter option crosses over from Trek 24 to 25. If you have walked and/or hitch-hiked Trek 24, you will probably exit to Pai. If you have guides with you and they do not want to return to Huai Tong and beyond, they will have to exit to Pai and then continue to Mae Hong Son. You should pay for their travel time, fares and meals during exiting. Starting early in the morning, you or they can get from Wat Chan via Pai to Mae Hong Son by public transport in one day. On Day 4, we arrived in Wat Chan at 2pm, and you may do so too. This leaves plenty of time to reach Pai during the afternoon of Day 4. Whether you can immediately exit to Pai is a matter of luck. A lift might come or may not. Vehicles mostly go down to Pai in the early morning (conversely, regular *silor* come up to Wat Chan from Pai daily, and may even go to Huai Tong). If you can directly exit, you save yourself a night in Wat Chan. But, if you have guides in tow, you will have to pay to put them up in Pai in a guest house. If you do not fancy this, or if you fail to get a lift, stay overnight in Wat Chan and continue to Pai early next morning. At least one public-transport pick-up goes early (ca 7 or 8am) every day to Pai (fare in 1999: 50 baht per person). When waiting for this ride or if trying to hitch-hike, position yourself by the *sala* in front of the *wat* and opposite moneybags' noodle stall-cum-store. Do not attempt to walk to Pai. The way is too far, the villages en route are too spaced out, and it is a tedious hot stony journey. Do not allow yourself, either, to be ripped off. Wat Chan's *kamnaan* ('mayor') or some other individual with an eye for business may offer to take you for 800 baht or more, as they did us. Turn the offer down. A cheaper lift might still come. However, it would make sense to charter a vehicle if you are a large group, or if you team up with other trekkers stranded in Wat Chan.

Thus at the latest in the early morning of Day 5, you ride for 50 baht per person the 55 kms down to Pai. The *silor* will drop you at Pai bus station or wherever you choose to get out. From there you and/or your guides (if applicable) can journey on by bus to Mae Hong Son. We did this in 1999, catching an air-con bus at 11.30am. The ride is very slow and cramped, and we paid 67 baht each for the privilege. In general, I do not recommend trying to exit Wat Chan to Samoeng, crossing over to Trek 25, without your own transport. The distances are great, the way in places poor, and the area remote. However, it would be fun to exit this way if you could be assured of a lift to Samoeng. Vehicles do go that route, and you might be fortunate to intercept one at Wat Chan. Check just how far the driver is going. In the past people have told me that there is a *silor* going from Chiang Mai via Samoeng to Wat Chan, setting out one day and returning the next. I do not know if this is true, so the information is unverified. If you ride or hitch-hike from Wat Chan to Samoeng, see Trek 25 for route details.

If you have biked Trek 24, you have the option of exiting either to Pai or to Samoeng and Chiang Mai, in the latter case crossing over to Trek 25. It is a further 55 kms from Wat Chan to Pai. Much of the way is stony bumpy dirt, involving several long steep rutted downgrades. Be wary of embarking on this exit leg too late in the day or if you are already tired or flustered. There are no villages en route during the long arid central section. Leave Wat Chan by turning right at the crossroads by the school and swinging round the corner of the *wat* compound (see Map 47). You are on the H1265 road. After 4 kms you pass, I think, Huai Or and yet another part of Wat Chan Royal Project, a forestry station. Now you descend a long way to a mine site, passing turnings left for Muang Paeng and Sob Sa. At a fork, both ways go to the main 1095 road and Pai, but branching left over a bridge is the quicker. Immediately beyond the bridge, left proceeds to Sob Sa and, again, Muang Paeng, while right, our route, brings you round the houses and through Sob Paem to a T-junction and the main 1095 road. Go left for Pai, which is a further dozen kms distant.

The way from Wat Chan to Samoeng is 92 kms, after which it is a further 48 to Chiang Mai, making a total of 140 kms (see Maps 48-50). The first 60 kms are a lonely dirt trail, poor in places, over the mountains. Do not embark on this route unless you are an experienced rider with dirt skills and you know what you are doing. If you have biked Trek 24, you will be adequate to the Wat Chan-Samoeng route, in fact will find it easier than the way over Doi Yao. In setting off for Samoeng and adding another 60 kms of dirt to the 80 already travelled in Trek 24, you will be completing what is, I believe, the longest dirt trail in Thailand. If you are planning to exit Wat Chan to Samoeng, cross over now from Trek 24 to 25.

Trek 25

Trekking the 'Old Elephant Trail' (2)

Wat Chan – Chaem Noi – Dong Sam Moen – Mae Daet Noi – Mae Ta La – Mae Chae – Mae Yang Ha – Sob Huai Fan Hin – Ban Mai – Mae La Ek – Mae Khan – Mae Sap – Samoeng – Mae Rim – Chiang Mai

Parameters

trekking mode:	by motorcycle
core trek distance:	140 kms Wat Chan to Chiang Mai
core trek time:	1 day; allow at least 4 hrs Wat Chan to Samoeng (or vice versa), excluding stops, plus 1½-2 hrs Samoeng to Chiang Mai
total trek distance:	must combine either with 90-km-long Trek 24, making an overall trek distance from Mae Hong Son via Wat Chan to Chiang Mai of 230 kms; or with 55-km-long access journey from Pai to Wat Chan, making an overall trek distance from Pai via Wat Chan to Chiang Mai of 195 kms
total trek time:	combined with Trek 24 at least 2 days; combined with stretch Pai to Wat Chan, for which you should allow some 3 hrs, either 1 long day or 1½ days
degree of difficulty:	fairly difficult, for experienced riders with dirt skills only; no problem for dirt freaks with enduro machines
tent:	take one anyway
map(s):	see 48, 49 & 50

Overview & strategy

This magnificent trek, which is for motorcyclists only, proceeds from the isolated Karen staging-post village of Wat Chan to Samoeng and then on to Chiang Mai. The route, the first 60 kms of which is (in 1999) fairly mediocre dirt, very stony and bumpy in places, strikes first broadly SE to Samoeng, and then E and S to Chiang Mai. Between Wat Chan and Samoeng, it passes though several Karen and Hmong hill-tribe villages, at the same time traversing some marvellous remote mountain country. Especially on the stretch between Mae Daet Noi and Mae Chae (see Map

48), the trail skips scenically along the ridgetops, at the highest points broaching cloud forest. In making its way across the mountains, the route negotiates some lonely stretches. The leg from Wat Chan to Samoeng is 92 kms long, and from Samoeng via Mae Rim to Chiang Mai (to the superhighway) is 48 kms, making a trek distance of 140 kms, which can be done in a day. Allow at least 4 hrs, excluding stops, for the taxing stretch from Wat Chan to Samoeng, and some 1½ to 2 hrs for the stretch Samoeng to Chiang Mai.

In proceeding from Wat Chan to Samoeng and Chiang Mai, Trek 25 ostensibly follows the second and larger half of the so-called 'Old Elephant Trail' from Mae Hong Son town via Wat Chan to Chiang Mai or vice versa. I say 'ostensibly' because the route may or may not precisely trace all or part of the Wat Chan to Chiang Mai leg of the trail. I think it follows the trail at the beginning, perhaps as far as Dong Sam Moen, and it at least broadly shadows the route and direction of the elephant trail either for the rest of the way or for the whole way. For more information on the Old Elephant Trail and on these questions of its exact itinerary, see Trek 24.

Starting as it does in Wat Chan, which is situated in the middle of nowhere or, more charitably, in the middle of the extensive mountainous hinterland stretching between Mae Hong Son and Chiang Mai, the trek clearly presupposes another trek or access journey. Either it presupposes and is a continuation of Trek 24 (from Mae Hong Son SE across the mountains to Wat Chan, which is the first half of the Old Elephant Trail), or it assumes that you access Wat Chan from Pai. Added to preceding Trek 24 (as a motorcycle trek), which is 90 kms long, Trek 25 results in a mammoth combined biking expedition from Mae Hong Son via Wat Chan to Chiang Mai of 230 kms. And adding the 85 kms of dirt in Trek 24 to the 60+ kms of dirt in Trek 25, you end up with a combined total of some 145+ kms of dirt, which is, I believe, *the longest dirt trail and ride in Thailand*. To do Trek 25 on top of 24 would be to do the whole of the Old Elephant Trail. If, on the other hand, you antecede Trek 25 with the access stretch from Pai to Wat Chan, which is 55 kms long, you end up with a combined trip of almost 200 kms, likewise with a substantial dirt component of some 100 kms.

For the combined expedition Mae Hong Son via Wat Chan and Samoeng to Chiang Mai (Treks 24 & 25) or vice versa, you should allow at least 2 full days, breaking your journey at Wat Chan, or at some other village in the middle, or possibly at Pai (the detour down to and back up from Pai would add a further 110 kms to the overall trek distance). For the combined trip Pai via Wat Chan and Samoeng to Chiang Mai (access + Trek 25) or vice versa, you should allow 1 long day or 1½ days. Reckon in some 3 hrs for the Pai/Wat Chan access stretch, which can be added to the minimum of 4 hrs for the Wat Chan to Samoeng leg and to the 1½ to 2 hrs for the Samoeng to Chiang Mai end section. You end up with 8+ hrs of pure riding time, which excludes stops to rest, eat, refuel, take photos, admire the scenery, and explore.

TREK IT YOURSELF IN NORTHERN THAILAND

I have ridden the Wat Chan to Chiang Mai trail three times, first in February 1992 with Nittaya Tananchai on an old 125-cc Honda Wing, then on my own in February 1999 on a 100-cc Honda Dream, and finally also in February 1999 with Doug Boynton, when on two Dreams we came 'backwards', from Chiang Mai to Wat Chan. Incidentally, for you birding folk, Doug spotted two green magpies and a black baza as he was riding along. I can well imagine that some readers might want to do Trek 25 backwards, starting in the big tourist and trekker centre of Chiang Mai with all its hire bikes. If you do, you will have to read the route detail below and also Maps 48-50 backwards. However, to help you, I give the distance readings in reverse order at the end of this chapter. Once you have arrived at Wat Chan, you will have to either exit to Pai or continue to Mae Hong Son, crossing over to Trek 24, and doing that backwards too. If you are doing Trek 25 the other way round, launching it from Chiang Mai, do not allow the fine new asphalt road that you find in places after Samoeng to deceive you into thinking that it is an easy highway all the way to Wat Chan. In 1999 it was mediocre dirt with some brick sections after Mae Yang Ha school for about 60 kms. On the other hand, do not be put off by some lamentable broken-up brick sections after Samoeng, especially between Mae Sap and Mae La Ek (see Map 49).

In my estimation, Trek 25 is fairly difficult for riders of more-than-average biking ability, and should be tackled by experienced riders with some dirt skills only. Dirt freaks with enduro machines will be on cloud nine up here, especially if combining Trek 25 with 24. There is nothing up here, between Wat Chan and Samoeng, and quite particularly between Wat Chan and Mae Hong Son as in Trek 24, for inexperienced bikers or for novice riders who have casually hired a stepthrough Dream townbike in Chiang Mai or Pai or Mae Hong Son. Such riders are bound to come to grief. You have been warned!

Accessing the trek
You can access Trek 25 either from Mae Hong Son, coming over the mountains as in Trek 24 (not via Pai), or from Pai. To access it from Mae Hong Son (expert riders only), see Trek 24 and Maps 43-47 inclusive. To access it from Pai, allowing 2-3 hrs for the 55 kms, which includes plenty of rough stony dirt road and long rutted upgrades, proceed SE out of Pai town on the 1095 road in the direction of Mae Ma Lai and Chiang Mai. After 10 or 12 kms, turn off right (SW) onto the 1265 side road (see Map 47). (If you come to Ta Pai village, you have gone too far, although beyond it there is a second turning right for Wat Chan, which will also do.) You pass through drawn-out Sob Paem village, going round the houses, and after a fair distance, heading broadly S, come to a confusing double junction by a bridge. Go left, cross the bridge and river, and immediately turn right. If I remember correctly, there is a mine site or at least the mine HQ and vehicle compound on the far side of the river, near the second part of the junction. If in doubt, ask for Ban Wat Chan. Now, striking broadly SW, you continue

along a valley floor, past fields, before climbing a long way up to Wat Chan. You pass turnings right (W) for Sob Sa and Muang Paeng, and negotiate at least three protracted stony rutted upgrades, which threaten to shake your bike to pieces. After this arid lonely central section, you come to the village of Huai Or and a forestry station which is part of Wat Chan Royal Project. Now you proceed the last 4 kms to Wat Chan. As you hit the centre of the village, you come to a little crossroads and find a school on your right and the compound containing Wat Chan's temple-monastery and pagoda on your left. Go left at the crossroads, swinging round the *wat* compound, to come to a *sala* or waiting hut (left) and a noodle soup place and store opposite (right). You are in the middle of Wat Chan and its main street. The turning for Samoeng lies a couple of hundred metres further up the main street on the left (S) side. Straight on at that junction proceeds to Daen, Nong Chet Nuai, Huai Tong and the way across the mountains to Mae Hong Son.

Information on Wat Chan and on staying overnight there
For some information about the village of Wat Chan (Ban Wat Chan), about its pagoda and temple, and about staying overnight in the village, which is not so easy, see Trek 24 and also Map 47. Before you leave Wat Chan for Samoeng, don't forget to tank up, although some petrol is available in the villages on the way. Take a bottle of water too, as you always should, in case you break down or get a flat tyre.

*

Trekking route detail (see Maps 48, 49 & 50)
Wat Chan – Chaem Noi – Dong Sam Moen – Mae Daet Noi – Mae Ta La – Mae Chae – Mae Yang Ha – Sob Huai Fan Hin – Ban Mai – Mae La Ek – Mae Khan – Mae Sap – Samoeng

Distance readings
km 0.0   Junction and road for Chaem Noi and Samoeng 200 m west of Wat Chan village centre and *wat* compound with pagoda. Now see Map 48.
          Cross bridge and pass forestry buildings (left) and building (up right), which is part of Wat Chan Royal Project.
km 2.4   Turning left for another forestry place.
          Climb up rutted road, in places through a bizarre 'lunar' landscape, where the earth and rocks have been shifted around and water has eroded them. Descend hill to:
km 9.6   **Chaem Noi**, a big Karen village, mostly right of road, with electricity.
          Describing a zigzag, road crosses valley bottom to climb up into elevated conifer country. In 1999 the surface of the upgrade just beyond Chaem Noi was in a poor condition. Continue 8.6 kms to:
km 18.2   **Dong Sam Moen** (Dong Sam Mun), a Blue Hmong village with a school. Pass a settlement (right).

km 19.6   Turning right to some forestry or watershed conservation place, possibly connected with Royal Project. Roadside km-stone reads '73', which is distance to/from Samoeng.
Turning left for village of Khun Khan Laang, located 3 kms offroad.

km 27.9   **Mae Daet Noi,** a Karen village with a new health centre (right). Especially during the central section of the route between Mae Daet Noi and Mae Chae, the trail skips along the ridgetops amid marvellous scenery. There are stunning views of Doi Intanon, also some lonely stretches. In 1992 we found a military base at Mae Daet Noi, part of whose brief was to destroy opium fields in the vicinity.

km 31.9   Track (right) to??

km 36.0   Mae Ta La forestry office (left) – possible place to camp?

km 38.1   **Mae Ta La,** Hmong village mostly offroad (right), but with new houses and 'shops' springing up by roadside. The place seems to be half in Samoeng district and half in Mae Chaem district. In 1992 we found a Thai-Norway Highland Farm Development project here, and another base charged with destroying opium poppy fields locally.

km 38.7   Turning (left) to forestry/watershed conservation place.

km 41.1   *Sala* (right) and turning (left) to village of Huai Dao, 6 kms offroad.
Turning (right) for Sob Pa Luang.
Another turning (right) for Mae Chae forestry.

km 52.7   **Mae Chae,** Hmong village.
After another 9 kms, dirt road ends (in 1999) near Mae Yang Ha school (right). Henceforth, all the way to Samoeng, road is now largely paved, either with asphalt (some in good condition, some in poor) or with a brick surface (often in poor condition). You come now to a series of settlements, which run into one another and are difficult to distinguish. It is a strange burgeoning 'conurbation' at altitude and far from anywhere.

km 61.6   Mae Yang Ha school (right).

km 62.6   **Mae Yang Ha,** Karen village with church.

km 64.4   **Sob Huai Fan Hin,** Karen village with turning (right).
Cross an open area with lakes left and right. There seems to be some kind of resort or restaurant on the left side – a place to stay?

km 64.7   Arrive at junction at a place called, as far as I can make out, **Ban Mai** (New Village) or possibly Ro Pa So or even Huai Ma Na. There is fuel hereabouts. Right goes 3 kms to Bo Kaew village, which has an opencast tin mine. From Bo Kaew (Kaeo) it is possible to continue S through Doi Intanon National Park to Mae Chaem. Left at Ban Mai continues to Samoeng. Now see Map 49.

Turning (right) to Kha Bu (?).
Wat, police box and *sala* (left).
New stretch of road.

km 70.3   **Mae La Ek** (Mae La Ae) with *sala* (right) and right turn to Mae To (2 kms offroad).

km 73.2   Khun Khan National Park/forestry office (left) – possible place to stay?

km 75.5   *Sala* (left) and turning for numerous villages, including Om Long (+8 kms), Yang Moen or Yang Muang (+ 23 kms), Mae Muang Noi, and Huai Sai Kao (+28 kms). This side road goes a very long way.

km 76.4   **Mae Khan** village, offroad (left).
Bridge.

Alternating brick and new asphalt.

km 82.9   *Sala* (left) and turning (right).

Very badly deteriorated brick surface and downgrade.

Turning (left).

Wat (left).

Turning (left).

km 86.3   **Mae Sap** village and 'crossroads'. Go right, following 'main' road. It is now 5.3 kms to Samoeng centre. In 1992 we observed old ladies weaving in Mae Sap.

Bridge.

Bricked road.

Crossroads and *Samoeng Resort* on corner (right).

Turn right.

Go past *Samoeng Villa* (left), some kind of guest house (right), and a *wat* (left) on a corner, around which the road swings E to cross a bridge over the River Samoeng, pass a post office (right) and a market (far right), and arrive at a T-junction, **Samoeng** town centre, and its main street running N-S. See Map 50 for an overview of Samoeng.

Go left to reach almost immediately a second junction.

km 91.6   Second junction.

Samoeng – Mae Rim – Chiang Mai (see Map 50)

Distance readings (continue as before)

km 91.6   At the second junction, turn right (E) into the H1269 road. From now to Chiang Mai the route is on regular roads (see Map 50). It is 34 kms to Mae Rim and 47 to Chiang Mai superhighway (ca 50 to Chiang Mai centre).

Just a short distance from the junction, you pass a restaurant and a fuel booth (both left).

Climb up 5.4 kms to a junction.

km 97   At the junction, right continues on the H1269 to Hang Dong (and ultimately Chiang Mai, approaching from the S, an alternative but less attractive way to the city). Go left and on the scenic H1096 road continue climbing to a pass.

Descend the back side of the ridge, passing villages, tracking down the Mae Sa valley, and traversing an exceedingly touristy region with a succession of 'resorts', restaurants, waterfalls, orchid centres, snake and butterfly farms, elephant 'training' camps, botanical gardens, handicraft workshops, and 'antique' shops.

km 125.7   T-junction and main 107 highway. Left goes N to Mae Ma Lai, Mae Taeng and Chiang Dao. Go right (S) to reach almost immediately:

km 126.5   **Mae Rim**, a busy, chaotic and traffic-ridden market town. Ride attentively through it and remain alert all the way back to Chiang Mai (plenty of speeding chaotic traffic).

km 139   **Chiang Mai superhighway**. Go straight across for city centre.

Proceed down Chotana and Chang Puak Roads to arrive at:

km 141   inner ring road with moats and **Chiang Mai centre**.

*

Doing Trek 25 in reverse (see Maps 50, 49 & 48)
In case you are doing Trek 25 in reverse, proceeding from Chiang Mai to Mae Rim, to Samoeng and on to Wat Chan, here are some distance indications, starting a couple of kms N of Chiang Mai centre at the crossroads where the superhighway intersects the Chotana Road/Highway 107:

km 0.0   Chiang Mai superhighway
km 12.5   Mae Rim
km 13.3   junction H107/H1096 (go left)
km 42.0   junction H1096/H1269 (go right)
km 47.7   Samoeng T-junction/main street (go left & immediately right)
km 52.7   Mae Sap
km 62.6   Mae Khan
km 65.8   Khun Khan National Park/forestry office
km 68.7   Mae La Ek
km 74.3   Ban Mai (Ro Pa So)/junction for Bo Kaew (go right)
km 76.4   Mae Yang Ha
km 77.4   Mae Yang Ha school
km 86.3   Mae Chae
km 100.9 Mae Ta La
km 111.1 Mae Daet Noi
km 120.8 Dong Sam Moen
km 129.4 Chaem Noi
km 139.0 junction by Wat Chan (go right)
km 139.2 Wat Chan centre/monastery-temple compound with pagoda

Now see end of Trek 24 and Map 47 for information about exiting to Pai or read backwards details given earlier in this chapter. For data about continuing from Wat Chan to Mae Hong Son, via Huai Tong but not via Pai, see Trek 24 and Maps 47, 46, 45, 44 & 43.

THE MAPS

MAP 1

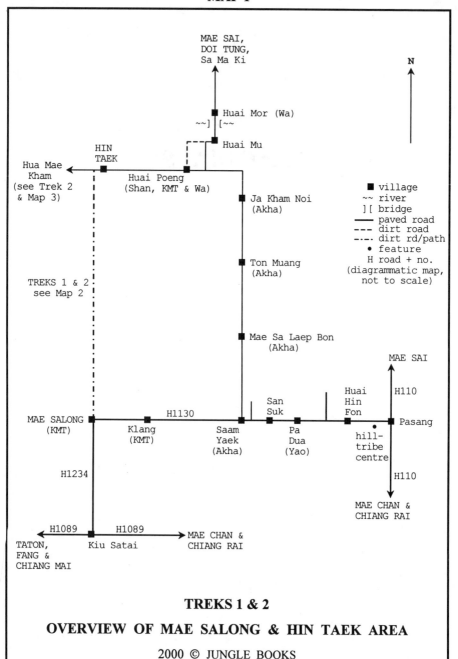

MAE SAI,
DOI TUNG,
Sa Ma Ki

N

■ Huai Mor (Wa)
~~] [~~
■ Huai Mu

HIN
TAEK

Hua Mae
Kham
(see Trek 2
& Map 3)

■ Huai Poeng
(Shan, KMT & Wa)

■ Ja Kham Noi
(Akha)

■ village
~~ river
] [bridge
—— paved road
--- dirt road
-·-· dirt rd/path
• feature
H road + no.
(diagrammatic map,
not to scale)

■ Ton Muang
(Akha)

TREKS 1 & 2
see Map 2

■ Mae Sa Laep Bon
(Akha)

MAE SAI

Huai
Hin
Fon

H110

MAE SALONG
(KMT)

■ H1130

■ Klang
(KMT)

■ Saam
Yaek
(Akha)

San
Suk

■ Pa
Dua
(Yao)

■ Pasang

hill-
tribe
centre

H110

MAE CHAN &
CHIANG RAI

H1234

H1089
TATON,
FANG &
CHIANG MAI

■ Kiu Satai

H1089

MAE CHAN &
CHIANG RAI

TREKS 1 & 2

OVERVIEW OF MAE SALONG & HIN TAEK AREA

2000 © JUNGLE BOOKS

MAP 2

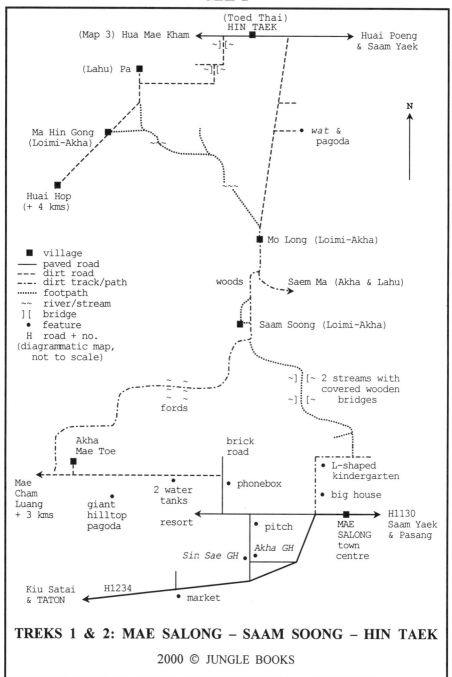

(Toed Thai)
HIN TAEK

(Map 3) Hua Mae Kham

Huai Poeng
& Saam Yaek

(Lahu) Pa

N

wat &
pagoda

Ma Hin Gong
(Loimi-Akha)

Huai Hop
(+ 4 kms)

Mo Long (Loimi-Akha)

■ village
── paved road
--- dirt road
-..- dirt track/path
⋯⋯ footpath
~~ river/stream
][bridge
• feature
H road + no.
(diagrammatic map,
not to scale)

woods

Saem Ma (Akha & Lahu)

Saam Soong (Loimi-Akha)

~][~ 2 streams with
covered wooden
~][~ bridges

fords

Akha
Mae Toe

brick
road

• L-shaped
kindergarten

Mae
Cham
Luang
+ 3 kms

giant
hilltop
pagoda

2 water
tanks

resort

• phonebox

• big house

• pitch

MAE
SALONG
town
centre

H1130
Saam Yaek
& Pasang

Akha GH

Sin Sae GH •

Kiu Satai
& TATON

H1234

• market

TREKS 1 & 2: MAE SALONG – SAAM SOONG – HIN TAEK

2000 © JUNGLE BOOKS

MAP 3

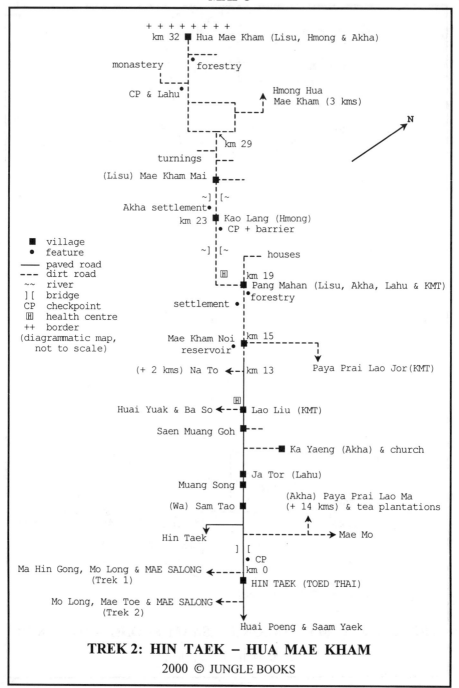

+ + + + + + +
km 32 ■ Hua Mae Kham (Lisu, Hmong & Akha)

monastery ●
forestry

CP & Lahu ●

↑ Hmong Hua
Mae Kham (3 kms)

N

km 29

turnings

(Lisu) Mae Kham Mai ■

~][~

Akha settlement ●
km 23 ■ Kao Lang (Hmong)
● CP + barrier

~][~
--- houses

Ⓗ km 19
■ Pang Mahan (Lisu, Akha, Lahu & KMT)
● forestry

settlement ●

Mae Kham Noi km 15
reservoir ● ■

(+ 2 kms) Na To ← km 13

Paya Prai Lao Jor (KMT)

Ⓗ

Huai Yuak & Ba So ← ■ Lao Liu (KMT)

Saen Muang Goh ■

■ Ka Yaeng (Akha) & church

■ Ja Tor (Lahu)

Muang Song ■

(Wa) Sam Tao ■

(Akha) Paya Prai Lao Ma
(+ 14 kms) & tea plantations

Hin Taek

→ Mae Mo

][
● CP

Ma Hin Gong, Mo Long & MAE SALONG ← km 0
(Trek 1)
■ HIN TAEK (TOED THAI)

Mo Long, Mae Toe & MAE SALONG ←
(Trek 2)

↓ Huai Poeng & Saam Yaek

- ■ village
- ● feature
- —— paved road
- --- dirt road
- ~~ river
-][bridge
- CP checkpoint
- Ⓗ health centre
- ++ border

(diagrammatic map,
not to scale)

TREK 2: HIN TAEK – HUA MAE KHAM

2000 © JUNGLE BOOKS

MAP 4

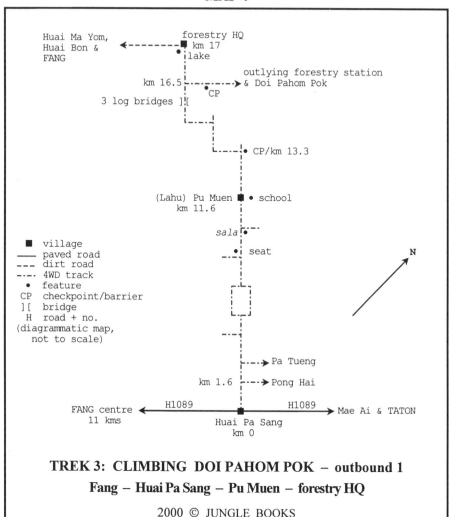

Huai Ma Yom,
Huai Bon &
FANG

forestry HQ
■ km 17
• lake

km 16.5

outlying forestry station
& Doi Pahom Pok

3 log bridges] [

CP

• CP/km 13.3

(Lahu) Pu Muen ■ • school
km 11.6

sala

• seat

N

■ village
── paved road
--- dirt road
-·-· 4WD track
• feature
CP checkpoint/barrier
] [bridge
H road + no.
(diagrammatic map,
not to scale)

→ Pa Tueng

km 1.6

→ Pong Hai

FANG centre ← H1089
11 kms

H1089 → Mae Ai & TATON

Huai Pa Sang
km 0

TREK 3: CLIMBING DOI PAHOM POK – outbound 1
Fang – Huai Pa Sang – Pu Muen – forestry HQ

2000 © JUNGLE BOOKS

MAP 5

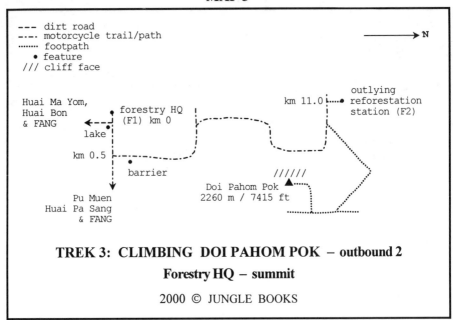

--- dirt road
-·-· motorcycle trail/path
······· footpath
• feature
/// cliff face

→ N

Huai Ma Yom,
Huai Bon
& FANG

forestry HQ
(F1) km 0

lake

km 11.0

outlying
reforestation
station (F2)

km 0.5

barrier

Pu Muen
Huai Pa Sang
& FANG

//////

Doi Pahom Pok
2260 m / 7415 ft

TREK 3: CLIMBING DOI PAHOM POK – outbound 2

Forestry HQ – summit

2000 © JUNGLE BOOKS

MAP 6

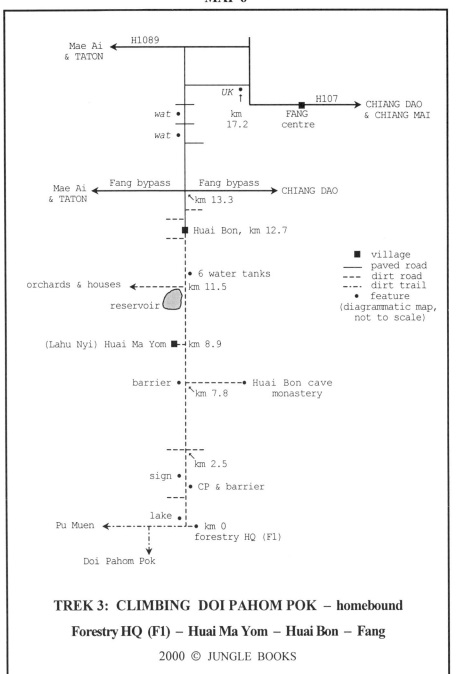

TREK 3: CLIMBING DOI PAHOM POK – homebound

Forestry HQ (F1) – Huai Ma Yom – Huai Bon – Fang

2000 © JUNGLE BOOKS

MAP 7

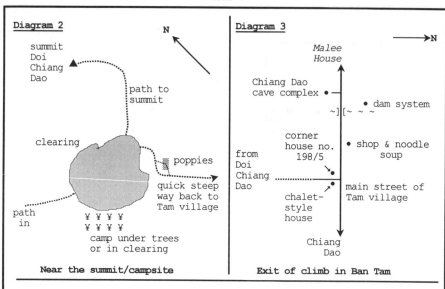

Diagram 2

summit
Doi
Chiang
Dao

N

path to
summit

clearing

poppies

quick steep
way back to
Tam village

path
in

¥ ¥ ¥ ¥
¥ ¥ ¥ ¥
camp under trees
or in clearing

Near the summit/campsite

Diagram 3

Malee House

N

Chiang Dao
cave complex •

• dam system

~][~ ~ ~

corner
house no.
198/5

• shop & noodle
soup

from
Doi
Chiang
Dao

main street of
Tam village

chalet-
style
house

Chiang
Dao

Exit of climb in Ban Tam

Diagram 1

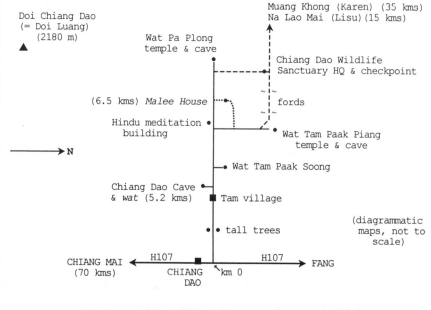

Doi Chiang Dao
(= Doi Luang)
(2180 m)
▲

Muang Khong (Karen) (35 kms)
Na Lao Mai (Lisu)(15 kms)

Wat Pa Plong
temple & cave

Chiang Dao Wildlife
Sanctuary HQ & checkpoint

(6.5 kms) *Malee House*

~|~
fords
~|~

Hindu meditation
building

Wat Tam Paak Piang
temple & cave

N

Wat Tam Paak Soong

Chiang Dao Cave •
& *wat* (5.2 kms)

■ Tam village

(diagrammatic
maps, not to
scale)

• tall trees

CHIANG MAI ← H107
(70 kms)   CHIANG
DAO

km 0

H107
→ FANG

TREK 4: CLIMBING DOI CHIANG DAO

2000 © JUNGLE BOOKS

366

MAP 8

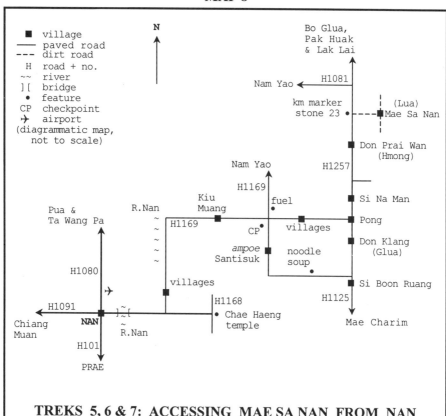

■ village
—— paved road
--- dirt road
H road + no.
~~ river
][bridge
• feature
CP checkpoint
✈ airport
(diagrammatic map,
 not to scale)

N

Bo Glua,
Pak Huak
& Lak Lai

H1081

Nam Yao ←

km marker
stone 23 •

(Lua)
■ Mae Sa Nan

■ Don Prai Wan
(Hmong)

H1257

Nam Yao

H1169

fuel
•

■ Si Na Man

Pua &
Ta Wang Pa

R.Nan

Kiu
Muang

~
H1169
~
~
~
~

■

CP •

villages

■ Pong

■ Don Klang
(Glua)

H1080

ampoe
Santisuk

noodle
soup
•

✈

villages

■

Si Boon Ruang
■

H1091 ←

~
][
~

H1168

• Chae Haeng
temple

H1125

Mae Charim

Chiang
Muan

NAN ■

R.Nan

H101

PRAE

TREKS 5, 6 & 7: ACCESSING MAE SA NAN FROM NAN

TREKS 5 & 6: EXITING MAE SA NAN TO NAN

2000 © JUNGLE BOOKS

MAP 9

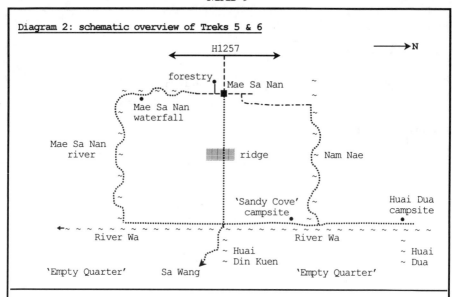

H1257

→N

forestry ● │ ■ Mae Sa Nan

Mae Sa Nan
waterfall

Mae Sa Nan
river

ridge — Nam Nae

'Sandy Cove'
campsite

Huai Dua
campsite

River Wa ~~~~~~~~~~~~~~~~~~~~~~~~~~~~~~~~~~~~

River Wa

~ Huai
~ Din Kuen

~ Huai
~ Dua

'Empty Quarter'   Sa Wang   'Empty Quarter'

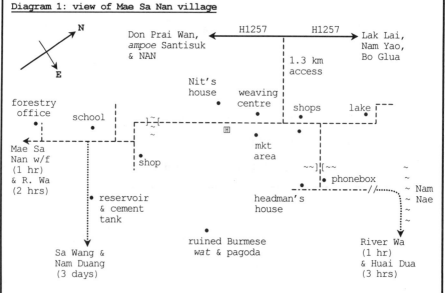

Diagram 1: view of Mae Sa Nan village

N

E

Don Prai Wan,
ampoe Santisuk
& NAN

H1257   H1257

Lak Lai,
Nam Yao,
Bo Glua

1.3 km
access

Nit's
house

weaving
centre

shops   lake

forestry
office

school

mkt
area

shop

Mae Sa
Nan w/f
(1 hr)
& R. Wa
(2 hrs)

phonebox

~ Nam
~ Nae

reservoir
& cement
tank

headman's
house

ruined Burmese
wat & pagoda

River Wa
(1 hr)
& Huai Dua
(3 hrs)

Sa Wang &
Nam Duang
(3 days)

TREK 5: MAE SA NAN – RIVER WA – NAM NAE – MAE SA NAN
&
TREK 6: MAE SA NAN – NAM NAE – R. WA – HUAI DUA & back

2000 © JUNGLE BOOKS

MAP 10

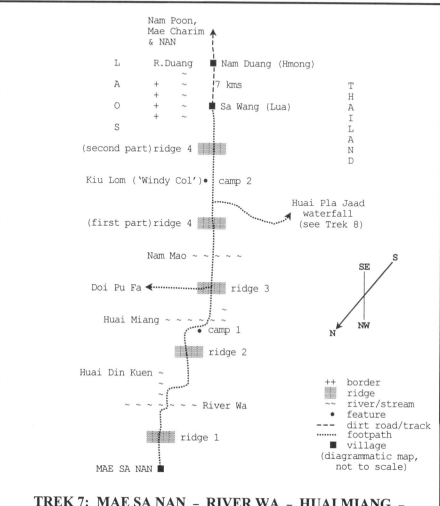

```
                    Nam Poon,
                    Mae Charim
                    & NAN        ▲
                                 ┊
          L         R.Duang      ■ Nam Duang (Hmong)
                      ~
          A         +  ~         ┊7 kms                    T
                    +  ~                                   H
          O         +  ~         ■ Sa Wang (Lua)           A
                    +  ~                                   I
          S                                                L
                                                           A
          (second part)ridge 4 ▨▨▨                         N
                                                           D

         Kiu Lom ('Windy Col')● ┊ camp 2
                                 ┊
                                  ┊.....,         Huai Pla Jaad
                                       `···,      waterfall
         (first part)ridge 4 ▨▨▨          ◄······ (see Trek 8)

              Nam Mao ~ ~┊~ ~ ~                      S
                                              SE      ╲
         Doi Pu Fa ◄············▨▨▨▨ ridge 3    │      ╲
                                 ┊                   ╲
              Huai Miang ~ ~ ~ ~┊~ ~          │      ╲
                              ● ┊ camp 1            NW
                            ▨▨▨▨ ridge 2        N
        Huai Din Kuen ~     ┊
                      ~     ┊                ++  border
                      ~    ┊                 ▨  ridge
            ~ ~ ~ ~┊~ ~ ~ River Wa           ~~  river/stream
                                             ●   feature
                                             --- dirt road/track
            ▨▨▨▨ ridge 1                     ···· footpath
             ┊                               ■   village
       MAE SA NAN ■                          (diagrammatic map,
                                              not to scale)
```

TREK 7: MAE SA NAN – RIVER WA – HUAI MIANG – NAM MAO – KIU LOM ('WINDY COL') – SA WANG

2000 © JUNGLE BOOKS

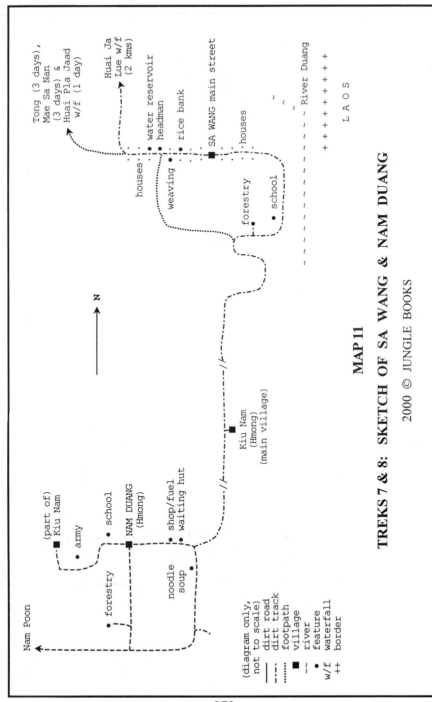

MAP 11

TREKS 7 & 8: SKETCH OF SA WANG & NAM DUANG

2000 © JUNGLE BOOKS

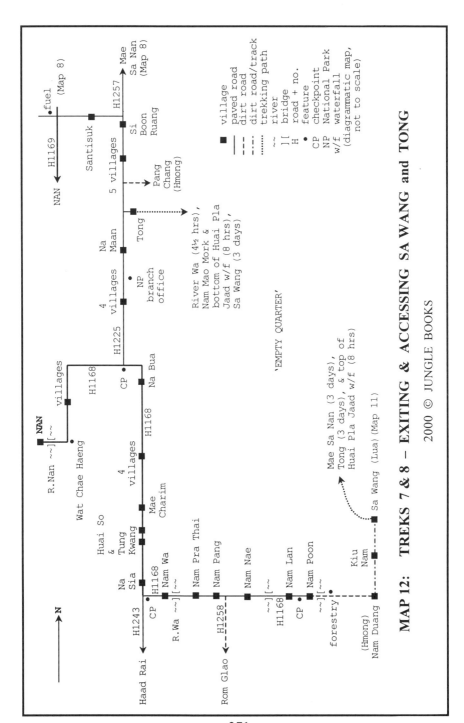

MAP 12: TREKS 7 & 8 – EXITING & ACCESSING SA WANG and TONG

2000 © JUNGLE BOOKS

■ village
—— paved road
--- dirt road
··· dirt road/track
······ trekking path
~ river
][bridge
H road + no.
● feature
CP checkpoint
NP National Park
w/f waterfall
(diagrammatic map,
not to scale)

'EMPTY QUARTER'

River Wa (4½ hrs),
Nam Mao Mork &
bottom of Huai Pla
Jaad w/f (8 hrs),
Sa Wang (3 days)

Mae Sa Nan (3 days),
Tong (3 days), & top of
Huai Pla Jaad w/f (8 hrs)

371

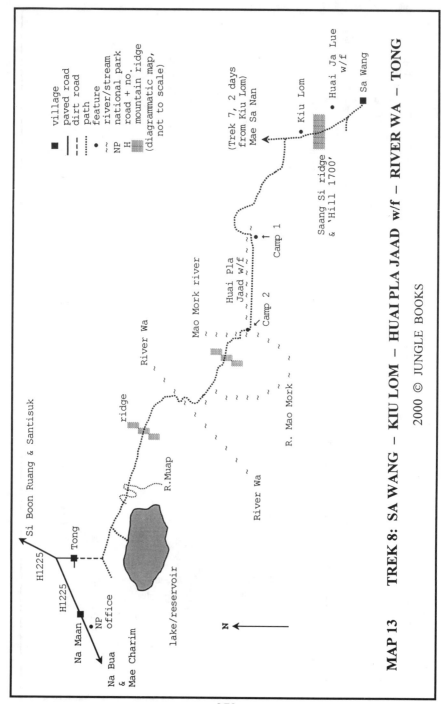

MAP 13   TREK 8: SA WANG – KIU LOM – HUAI PLA JAAD w/f – RIVER WA – TONG

2000 © JUNGLE BOOKS

MAP 14

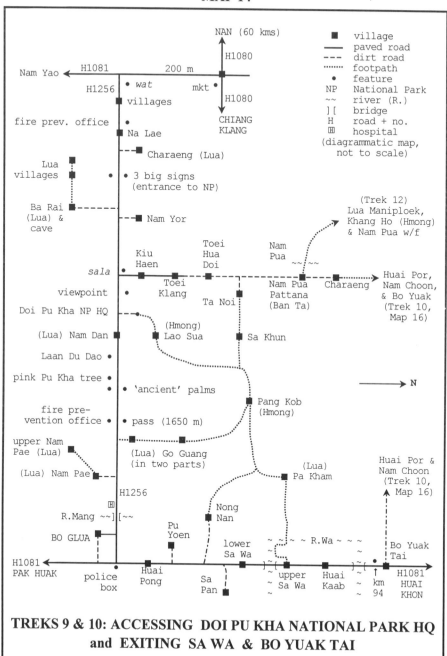

NAN (60 kms)

H1080

H1081

200 m

Nam Yao ←

H1256

wat   mkt •

villages

H1080

fire prev. office

CHIANG
KLANG

Na Lae

■ Charaeng (Lua)

Lua
villages

• • 3 big signs
      (entrance to NP)

Ba Rai
(Lua) &
cave

■ Nam Yor

(Trek 12)
Lua Maniploek,
Khang Ho (Hmong)
& Nam Pua w/f

sala

Kiu
Haen

Toei
Hua
Doi

Nam
Pua

~~~~

Huai Por,
Nam Choon,
& Bo Yuak
(Trek 10,
Map 16)

viewpoint

Toei
Klang

Nam Pua
Pattana
(Ban Ta)

Charaeng

Ta Noi

Doi Pu Kha NP HQ

(Lua) Nam Dan

(Hmong)
Lao Sua

Sa Khun

Laan Du Dao •

pink Pu Kha tree •

→ N

• • 'ancient' palms

Pang Kob
(Hmong)

fire pre-
vention office •

• • pass (1650 m)

upper Nam
Pae (Lua)

(Lua) Go Guang
(in two parts)

(Lua)
Pa Kham

Huai Por &
Nam Choon
(Trek 10,
Map 16)

(Lua) Nam Pae

H1256

Nong
Nan

Ⓗ
R.Mang ~~][~~

Pu
Yoen

BO GLUA

lower
Sa Wa

~ ~~ ~ ~ R.Wa ~ ~ ~
~

Bo Yuak
Tai

H1081
PAK HUAK ←

police
box

Huai
Pong

Sa
Pan

~ upper
~ Sa Wa
~

Huai
Kaab

~
~
~

↑
km
94

H1081
HUAI
KHON

Legend

■ village
— paved road
--- dirt road
.... footpath
• feature
NP National Park
~~ river (R.)
][bridge
H road + no.
Ⓗ hospital
(diagrammatic map,
not to scale)

TREKS 9 & 10: ACCESSING DOI PU KHA NATIONAL PARK HQ
and EXITING SA WA & BO YUAK TAI

2000 © JUNGLE BOOKS

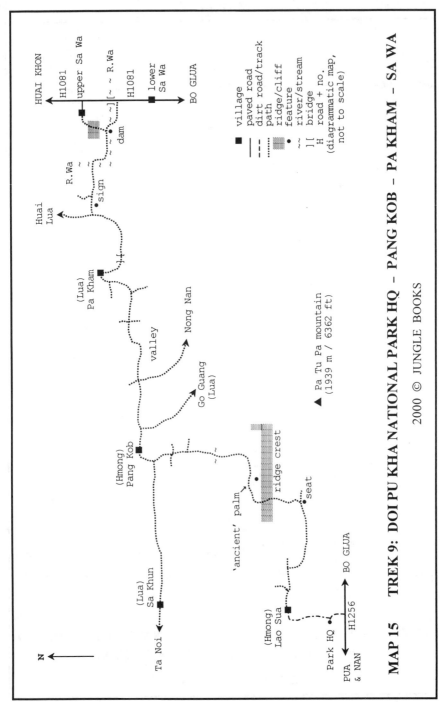

MAP 15   TREK 9: DOI PU KHA NATIONAL PARK HQ – PANG KOB – PA KHAM – SA WA

2000 © JUNGLE BOOKS

N ←

HUAI KHON

H1081
upper Sa Wa

][~ R.Wa

~]

H1081
lower Sa Wa

BO GLUA

dam

R.Wa

sign

Huai
Lua

(Lua)
Pa Kham

Nong Nan

valley

Go Guang
(Lua)

▲ Pa Tu Pa mountain
(1939 m / 6362 ft)

(Hmong)
Pang Kob

'ancient' palm

ridge crest

seat

(Lua)
Sa Khun

Ta Noi

(Hmong)
Lao Sua

Park HQ

PUA
& NAN

H1256

BO GLUA

village
paved road
dirt road/track
path
ridge/cliff
feature
river/stream
bridge
road + no.
(diagrammatic map,
not to scale)

■
|

····
▒
●
~
][
H

374

MAP 16

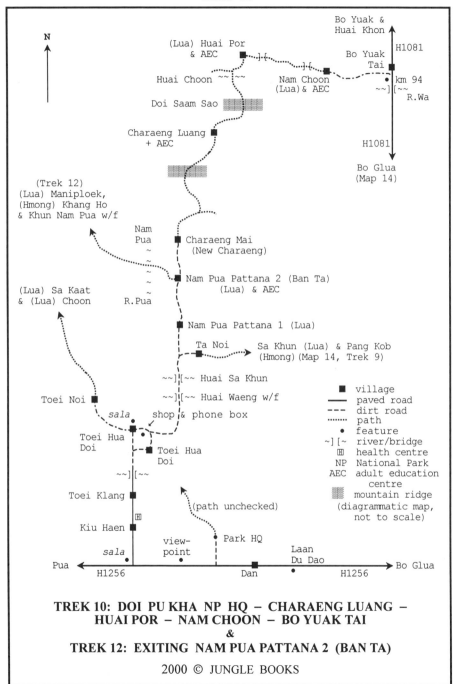

**TREK 10: DOI PU KHA NP HQ – CHARAENG LUANG –
HUAI POR – NAM CHOON – BO YUAK TAI
&
TREK 12: EXITING NAM PUA PATTANA 2 (BAN TA)**

2000 © JUNGLE BOOKS

375

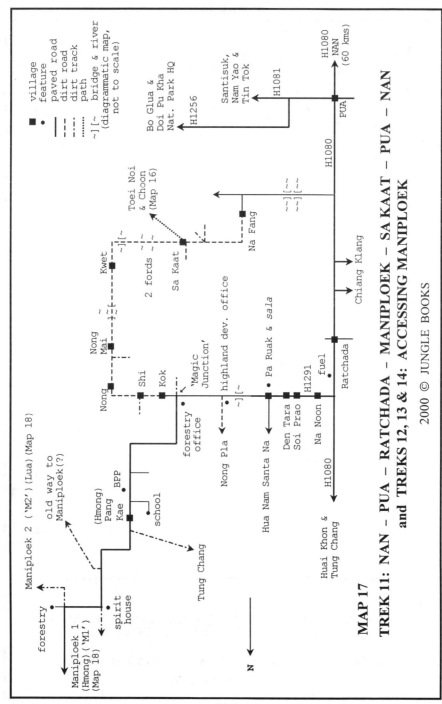

MAP 17
TREK 11: NAN – PUA – RATCHADA – MANIPLOEK – SA KAAT – PUA – NAN
and TREKS 12, 13 & 14: ACCESSING MANIPLOEK

2000 © JUNGLE BOOKS

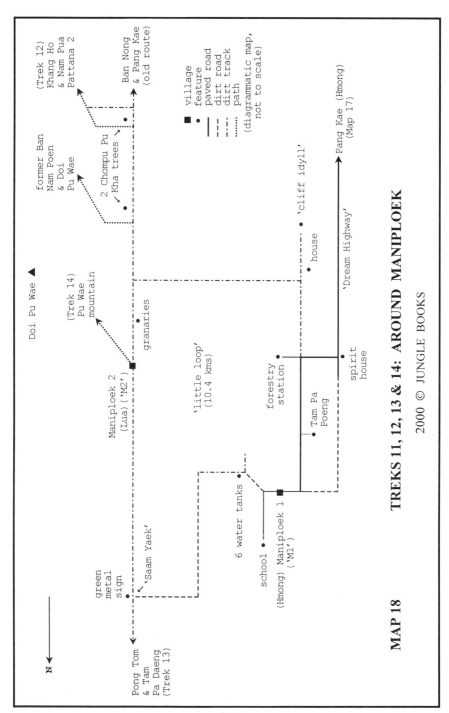

TREKS 11, 12, 13 & 14: AROUND MANIPLOEK

2000 © JUNGLE BOOKS

MAP 18

377

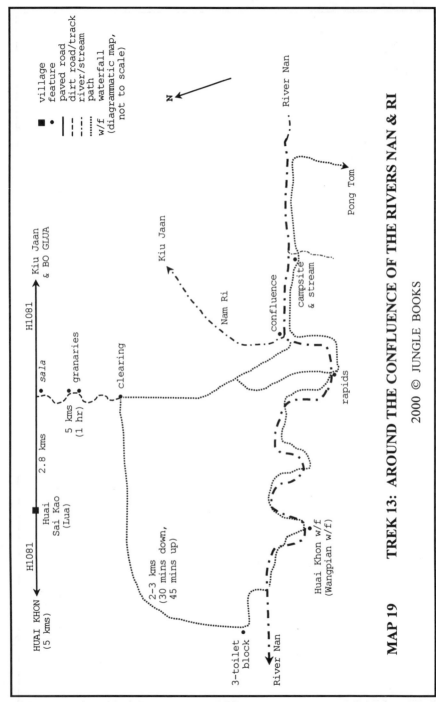

MAP 19   TREK 13:   AROUND THE CONFLUENCE OF THE RIVERS NAN & RI

2000 © JUNGLE BOOKS

MAP 20

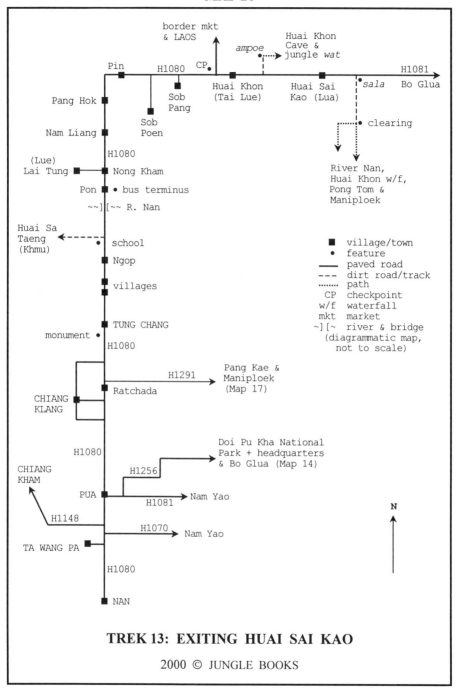

TREK 13: EXITING HUAI SAI KAO

2000 © JUNGLE BOOKS

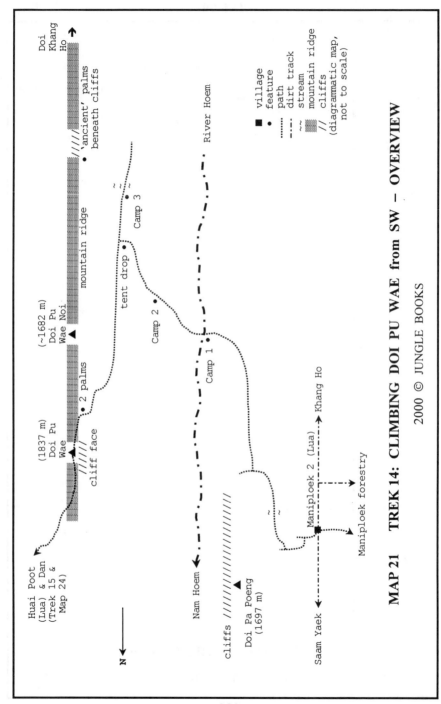

N

Huai Poot
(Lua) & Dan
(Trek 15 &
Map 24)

(1837 m)
Doi Pu
Wae
/////
cliff face

• 2 palms

(~1682 m)
Doi Pu
Wae Noi
▲

mountain ridge

tent drop •

• 'ancient' palms
beneath cliffs

Doi
Khang
Ho
↑

• Camp 3

Camp 2 •

Camp 1 •

River Hoem

Nam Hoem

cliffs ////////////////////
Doi Pa Poeng ▲
(1697 m)

Maniploek 2 (Lua) → Khang Ho

Maniploek forestry

Saam Yaek

■ village
• feature
⋯ path
–·– dirt track
∼ stream
▒ mountain ridge
// cliffs
(diagrammatic map,
not to scale)

MAP 21   TREK 14: CLIMBING DOI PU WAE from SW – OVERVIEW

2000 © JUNGLE BOOKS

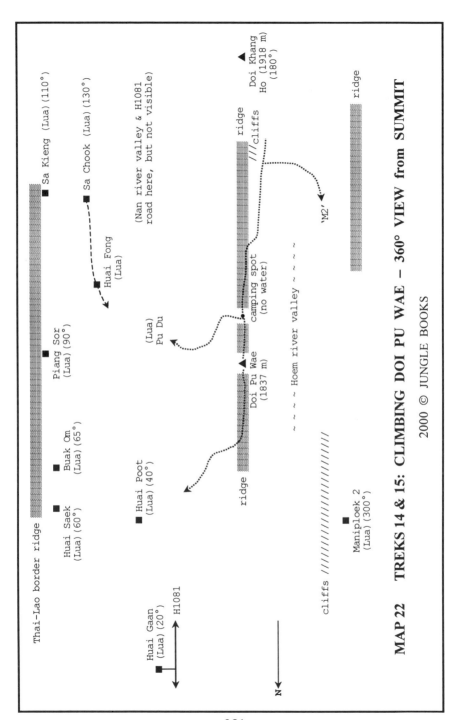

Thai-Lao border ridge

Huai Gaan (Lua) (20°)

H1081

Huai Saek (Lua) (60°)

Sa Kieng (Lua) (110°)

Buak Om (Lua) (65°)

Piang Sor (Lua) (90°)

Sa Chook (Lua) (130°)

Huai Poot (Lua) (40°)

Huai Fong (Lua)

(Nan river valley & H1081 road here, but not visible)

(Lua) Pu Du

ridge

ridge

///cliffs

Doi Khang Ho (1918 m) (180°)

camping spot (no water)

Doi Pu Wae (1837 m)

~ ~ ~ Hoem river valley ~ ~ ~

'M2'

ridge

cliffs //////////////////////

Maniploek 2 (Lua) (300°)

N

MAP 22   TREKS 14 & 15: CLIMBING DOI PU WAE – 360° VIEW from SUMMIT

2000 © JUNGLE BOOKS

381

MAP 23

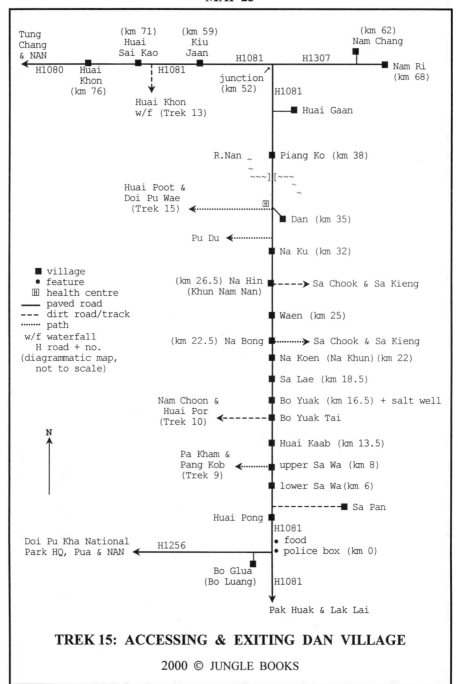

Tung Chang & NAN

(km 71) Huai Sai Kao

(km 59) Kiu Jaan

H1081

H1307

(km 62) Nam Chang

← H1080   Huai Khon (km 76)

H1081

junction (km 52)

Nam Ri (km 68)

Huai Khon w/f (Trek 13)

H1081

■ Huai Gaan

R.Nan ~   ■ Piang Ko (km 38)

~
~~~][~~~
~
~

Huai Poot & Doi Pu Wae (Trek 15) ◄············ Ⓗ

■ Dan (km 35)

Pu Du ◄·············

■ Na Ku (km 32)

■ village
• feature
Ⓗ health centre
── paved road
--- dirt road/track
········ path
w/f waterfall
H road + no.
(diagrammatic map, not to scale)

(km 26.5) Na Hin (Khun Nam Nan) ■---► Sa Chook & Sa Kieng

■ Waen (km 25)

(km 22.5) Na Bong ■········► Sa Chook & Sa Kieng

■ Na Koen (Na Khun)(km 22)

■ Sa Lae (km 18.5)

Nam Choon & Huai Por (Trek 10) ◄------- ■

■ Bo Yuak (km 16.5) + salt well

Bo Yuak Tai

N
↑

■ Huai Kaab (km 13.5)

Pa Kham & Pang Kob (Trek 9) ◄··········

■ upper Sa Wa (km 8)

■ lower Sa Wa(km 6)

--------- ■ Sa Pan

Huai Pong ■

H1081
• food
• police box (km 0)

Doi Pu Kha National Park HQ, Pua & NAN ◄─── H1256

Bo Glua (Bo Luang)

H1081

↓

Pak Huak & Lak Lai

TREK 15: ACCESSING & EXITING DAN VILLAGE

2000 © JUNGLE BOOKS

MAP 24

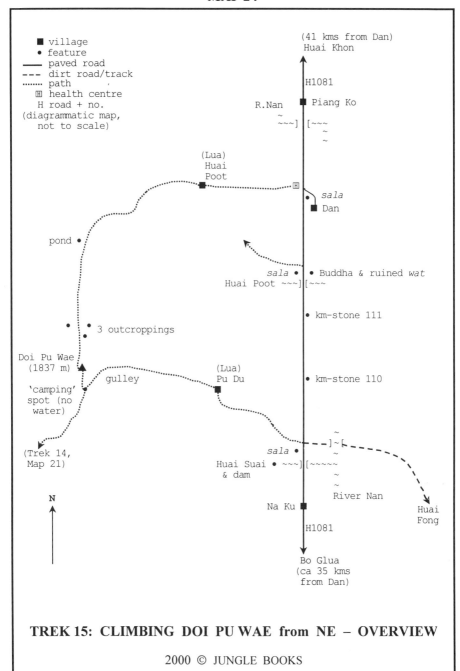

- ■ village
- • feature
- —— paved road
- --- dirt road/track
- ...... path
- ⊞ health centre
- H road + no.
- (diagrammatic map, not to scale)

(41 kms from Dan)
Huai Khon

H1081

R.Nan ■ Piang Ko

(Lua)
Huai
Poot

⊞ *sala*
■ Dan

pond •

sala • • Buddha & ruined *wat*
Huai Poot ~~~][~~~

• km-stone 111

•
• 3 outcroppings

Doi Pu Wae
(1837 m)

(Lua)
Pu Du

• km-stone 110

gulley

'camping'
spot (no
water)

sala •
]~[

(Trek 14,
Map 21)

Huai Suai • ~~~][~~~~~
& dam

River Nan

N

Na Ku ■

Huai
Fong

H1081

Bo Glua
(ca 35 kms
from Dan)

TREK 15: CLIMBING DOI PU WAE from NE – OVERVIEW

2000 © JUNGLE BOOKS

MAP 25

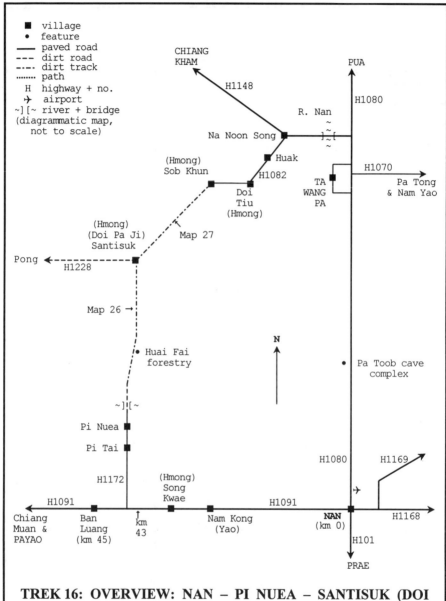

TREK 16: OVERVIEW: NAN – PI NUEA – SANTISUK (DOI PA JI) – SOB KHUN – H1148 & H1080 – NAN

2000 © JUNGLE BOOKS

MAP 26

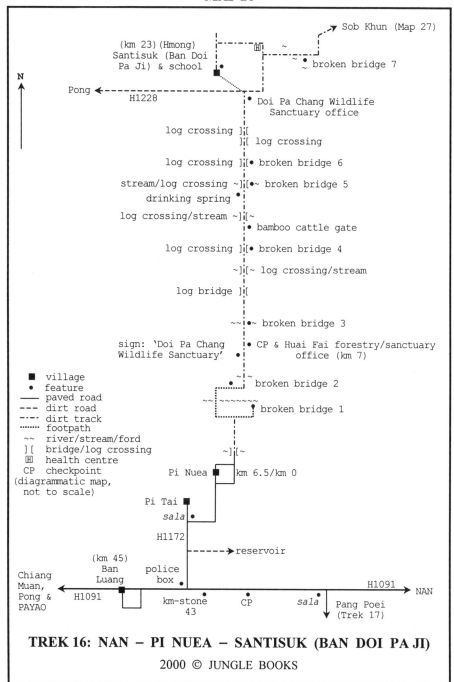

Sob Khun (Map 27)

(km 23)(Hmong)
Santisuk (Ban Doi
Pa Ji) & school

broken bridge 7

N

Pong ← - - - - - - - - - -
H1228

Doi Pa Chang Wildlife
Sanctuary office

log crossing]¦[
]¦[log crossing

log crossing]¦[• broken bridge 6

stream/log crossing ~]¦[•~ broken bridge 5
drinking spring •

log crossing/stream ~]¦[~
• bamboo cattle gate

log crossing]¦[• broken bridge 4

~]¦[~ log crossing/stream

log bridge]¦[

~~¦•~ broken bridge 3

sign: 'Doi Pa Chang   •CP & Huai Fai forestry/sanctuary
Wildlife Sanctuary' •   office (km 7)

■ village
• feature   ~¦~
—— paved road   •¦ ~ broken bridge 2
- - - dirt road   ~~¦~~~~~~~
-·- dirt track   ¦• broken bridge 1
······· footpath
~~ river/stream/ford
][bridge/log crossing   ~]¦[~
Ⓗ health centre
CP checkpoint   Pi Nuea ■   km 6.5/km 0
(diagrammatic map,
not to scale)

Pi Tai ■
sala •

H1172

- - - →reservoir

(km 45)   police
Ban   box •
Chiang   Luang
Muan,   H1091
Pong & ←- - - - - - - - -   → NAN
PAYAO   H1091   km-stone   CP   sala ¦ Pang Poei
                  43   ↓ (Trek 17)

TREK 16: NAN – PI NUEA – SANTISUK (BAN DOI PA JI)

2000 © JUNGLE BOOKS

385

MAP 27

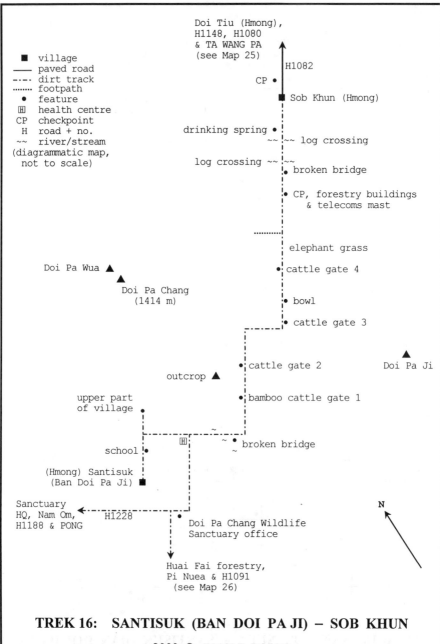

Doi Tiu (Hmong),
H1148, H1080
& TA WANG PA
(see Map 25)

■ village
— paved road
-·-· dirt track
······· footpath
• feature
ℍ health centre
CP checkpoint
H road + no.
~~ river/stream
(diagrammatic map,
not to scale)

H1082

CP •

■ Sob Khun (Hmong)

drinking spring •

~~ ~~ log crossing

log crossing ~~ ¦ ~~

• broken bridge

• CP, forestry buildings
& telecoms mast

elephant grass

Doi Pa Wua ▲

▲
Doi Pa Chang
(1414 m)

• ¦ cattle gate 4

• bowl

• cattle gate 3

• ¦ cattle gate 2

▲
Doi Pa Ji

outcrop ▲

• ¦ bamboo cattle gate 1

upper part
of village •

~

school •

ℍ

~ • broken bridge
~

(Hmong) Santisuk
(Ban Doi Pa Ji) ■

Sanctuary
HQ, Nam Om, ← -·-·-·- H1228
H1188 & PONG

N

• Doi Pa Chang Wildlife
Sanctuary office

↓

Huai Fai forestry,
Pi Nuea & H1091
(see Map 26)

TREK 16: SANTISUK (BAN DOI PA JI) – SOB KHUN

2000 © JUNGLE BOOKS

MAP 28

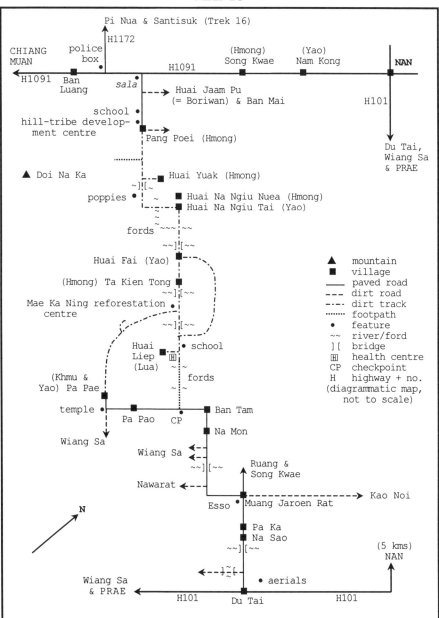

Pi Nua & Santisuk (Trek 16)

H1172

CHIANG MUAN   police box

(Hmong) Song Kwae   (Yao) Nam Kong   NAN

H1091   Ban Luang   sala   H1091

Huai Jaam Pu (= Boriwan) & Ban Mai   H101

school •
hill-tribe develop-
ment centre •

Pang Poei (Hmong)

Du Tai, Wiang Sa & PRAE

▲ Doi Na Ka   Huai Yuak (Hmong)

~]![~

poppies •   ~   ■ Huai Na Ngiu Nuea (Hmong)
!-----.   Huai Na Ngiu Tai (Yao)

~
~
fords ~~~ ¦ ~~

~~]![~~

Huai Fai (Yao)

(Hmong) Ta Kien Tong

~~]![~~

Mae Ka Ning reforestation
centre •

~~]![~~

Huai   • school
Liep   ⊞
(Lua)   ~¦~

(Khmu &   fords
Yao) Pa Pae •   ~¦~

temple •   ■   ■ Ban Tam
Pa Pao   CP

Wiang Sa   ■ Na Mon

Wiang Sa ◄--

~~]![~~

Nawarat ◄--   Ruang & Song Kwae

Esso • Muang Jaroen Rat   Kao Noi ►

N

■ Pa Ka
■ Na Sao

~~]![~~   (5 kms) NAN

◄--]~[--   • aerials

Wiang Sa & PRAE   H101   Du Tai   H101

▲ mountain
■ village
── paved road
--- dirt road
-·- dirt track
······ footpath
• feature
~~ river/ford
][bridge
⊞ health centre
CP checkpoint
H highway + no.
(diagrammatic map, not to scale)

TREK 17: NAN – DU TAI – HUAI LIEP – HUAI YUAK – NAN

2000 © JUNGLE BOOKS

387

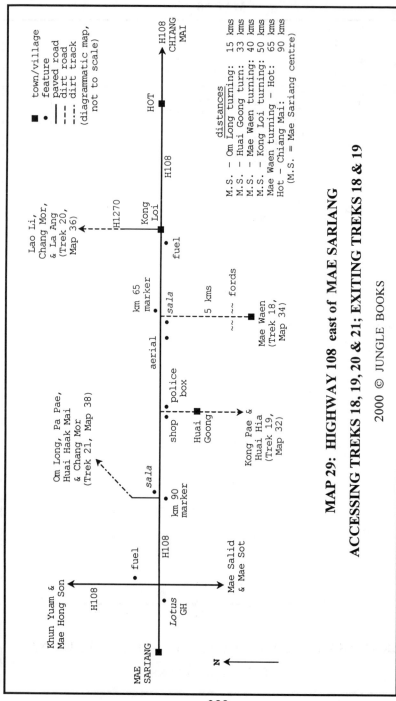

MAP 29: HIGHWAY 108 east of MAE SARIANG

ACCESSING TREKS 18, 19, 20 & 21; EXITING TREKS 18 & 19

2000 © JUNGLE BOOKS

The legend and content of the map:

■ town/village
feature
——— paved road
- - - dirt road
······ dirt track
(diagrammatic map,
not to scale)

H108
CHIANG
MAI

HOT

H108

Lao Li,
Chang Mor,
& La Ang
(Trek 20,
Map 36)

H1270

Kong
Loi

fuel

km 65
marker

sala

aerial

5 kms

~ fords

Mae Waen
(Trek 18,
Map 34)

police
box

shop

Huai
Goong

Kong Pae &
Huai Hia
(Trek 19,
Map 32)

Om Long, Pa Pae,
Huai Haak Mai
& Chang Mor
(Trek 21, Map 38)

sala

km 90
marker

H108

fuel

Khun Yuam &
Mae Hong Son

H108

Mae Salid
& Mae Sot

Lotus
GH

MAE
SARIANG

N

distances

M.S. – Om Long turning: 15 kms
M.S. – Huai Goong turn: 33 kms
M.S. – Mae Waen turning: 40 kms
M.S. – Kong Loi turning: 50 kms
Mae Waen turning – Hot: 65 kms
Hot – Chiang Mai: 90 kms
(M.S. = Mae Sariang centre)

MAP 30

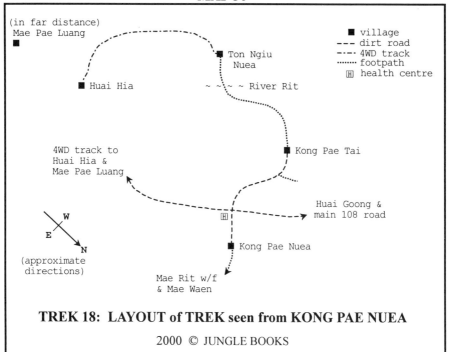

(in far distance)
Mae Pae Luang

■ village
--- dirt road
-·-· 4WD track
········· footpath
Ⓗ health centre

Ton Ngiu
Nuea

■ Huai Hia ~ ~ ~ ~ River Rit

4WD track to
Huai Hia &
Mae Pae Luang

■ Kong Pae Tai

W

E

N

(approximate
directions)

Ⓗ

Huai Goong &
main 108 road

■ Kong Pae Nuea

Mae Rit w/f
& Mae Waen

TREK 18: LAYOUT of TREK seen from KONG PAE NUEA

2000 © JUNGLE BOOKS

MAP 31

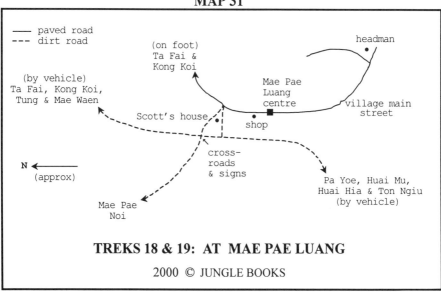

—— paved road
--- dirt road

(on foot)
Ta Fai &
Kong Koi

headman

(by vehicle)
Ta Fai, Kong Koi,
Tung & Mae Waen

Mae Pae
Luang
centre

Scott's house

village main
street

shop

N

(approx)

cross-
roads
& signs

Pa Yoe, Huai Mu,
Huai Hia & Ton Ngiu
(by vehicle)

Mae Pae
Noi

TREKS 18 & 19: AT MAE PAE LUANG

2000 © JUNGLE BOOKS

389

MAP 32

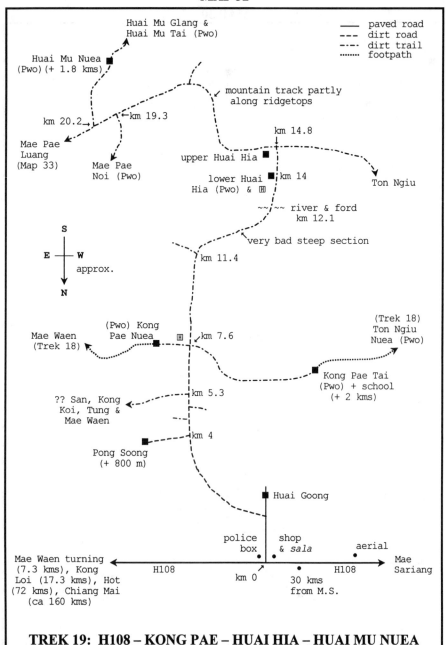

Huai Mu Glang &
Huai Mu Tai (Pwo)

——— paved road
--- dirt road
-·-·- dirt trail
········ footpath

Huai Mu Nuea ■
(Pwo)(+ 1.8 kms)

mountain track partly
along ridgetops

km 20.2   ←km 19.3

km 14.8

Mae Pae
Luang
(Map 33)

upper Huai Hia ■

Mae Pae
Noi (Pwo)

lower Huai ■ km 14
Hia (Pwo) & ⊞

Ton Ngiu

~~/~~ river & ford
km 12.1

very bad steep section

S

E ——— W
approx.

N

km 11.4

(Pwo) Kong
Pae Nuea

(Trek 18)
Ton Ngiu
Nuea (Pwo)

Mae Waen
(Trek 18)

⊞ /km 7.6

Kong Pae Tai
(Pwo) + school
(+ 2 kms)

?? San, Kong
Koi, Tung &
Mae Waen

km 5.3

km 4

Pong Soong
(+ 800 m)

Huai Goong ■

police
box

shop
& sala

aerial

Mae Waen turning
(7.3 kms), Kong
Loi (17.3 kms), Hot
(72 kms), Chiang Mai
(ca 160 kms)

H108

km 0

30 kms
from M.S.

H108

Mae
Sariang

TREK 19: H108 – KONG PAE – HUAI HIA – HUAI MU NUEA

2000 © JUNGLE BOOKS

390

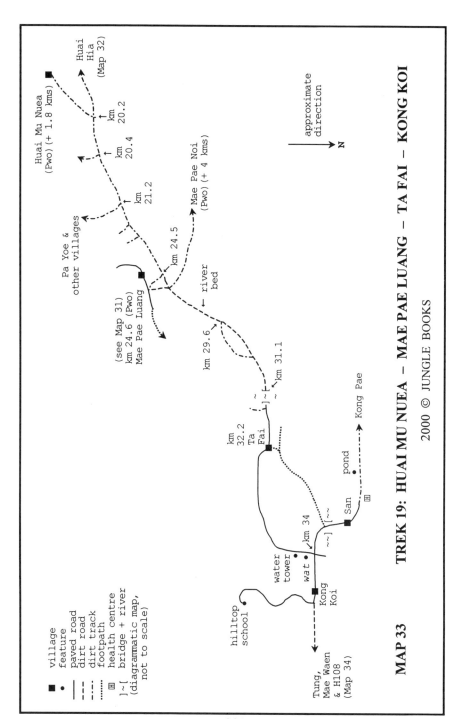

MAP 33

TREK 19: HUAI MU NUEA – MAE PAE LUANG – TA FAI – KONG KOI

2000 © JUNGLE BOOKS

MAP 34

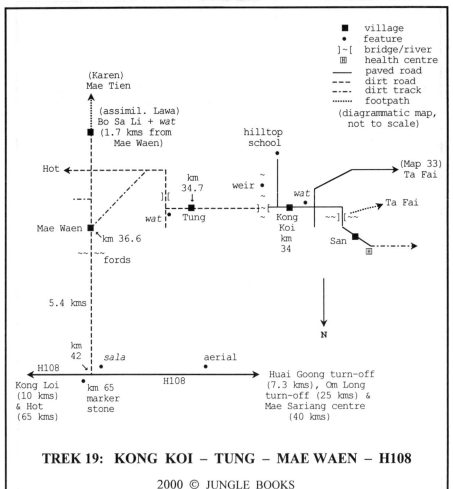

TREK 19: KONG KOI – TUNG – MAE WAEN – H108

2000 © JUNGLE BOOKS

392

MAP 35

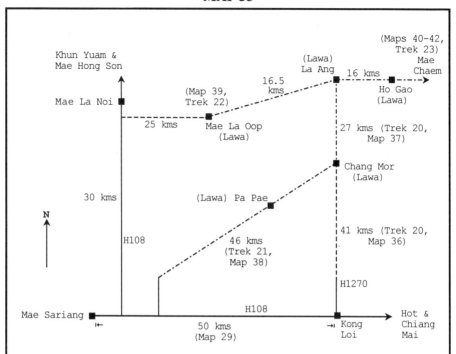

(Maps 40-42, Trek 23)

Khun Yuam & Mae Hong Son

(Lawa) La Ang

Mae Chaem

16 kms

16.5 kms

Ho Gao (Lawa)

Mae La Noi

(Map 39, Trek 22)

25 kms

Mae La Oop (Lawa)

27 kms (Trek 20, Map 37)

Chang Mor (Lawa)

30 kms

(Lawa) Pa Pae

N

H108

46 kms (Trek 21, Map 38)

41 kms (Trek 20, Map 36)

H1270

H108

Mae Sariang

50 kms (Map 29)

Kong Loi

Hot & Chiang Mai

Trek permutations & distances:

```
MS - Kong Loi - Chang Mor - La Ang - La Oop - Mae La Noi - MS:   190 kms
MS - Pa Pae - Chang Mor - La Ang - La Oop - Mae La Noi - MS:     160 kms
MS - Pa Pae - Chang Mor - Kong Loi - MS:                         152 kms
MS - Kong Loi - Chang Mor - La Ang - Ho Gao - Mae Chaem:         170 kms
MS - Pa Pae - Chang Mor - La Ang - Ho Gao - Mae Chaem:           140 kms
MS - Mae La Noi - La Oop - La Ang - Ho Gao - Mae Chaem:          125 kms
```

(MS = Mae Sariang. Same distances if treks done other way round!
Distance Mae Chaem - Chiang Mai: ca 120 kms)

OVERVIEW OF TREKS 20, 21, 22 & 23

2000 © JUNGLE BOOKS

MAP 36

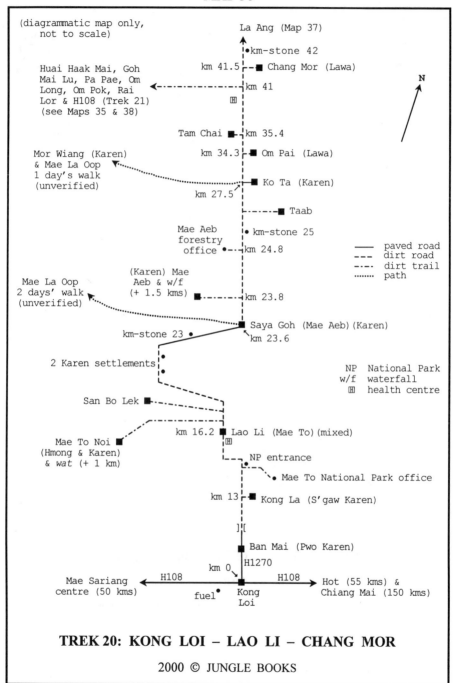

(diagrammatic map only,
   not to scale)

La Ang (Map 37)

• km-stone 42

km 41.5 ┏■ Chang Mor (Lawa)

Huai Haak Mai, Goh
Mai Lu, Pa Pae, Om
Long, Om Pok, Rai
Lor & H108 (Trek 21)
(see Maps 35 & 38)

◄------------ km 41

Ⓗ

N

Tam Chai ■┐km 35.4

km 34.3 ┏■ Om Pai (Lawa)

Mor Wiang (Karen)
& Mae La Oop
1 day's walk
(unverified)

◄········ ■ Ko Ta (Karen)

km 27.5

┌-----■ Taab

Mae Aeb
forestry
office ●--┐

• km-stone 25

km 24.8

(Karen) Mae
Aeb & w/f
(+ 1.5 kms)

──── paved road
---- dirt road
-·-· dirt trail
······ path

Mae La Oop
2 days' walk
(unverified)

◄········ ■········┐km 23.8

■ Saya Goh (Mae Aeb)(Karen)

km-stone 23 ●

km 23.6

2 Karen settlements

NP National Park
w/f waterfall
Ⓗ health centre

San Bo Lek ■

Mae To Noi ■
(Hmong & Karen)
& *wat* (+ 1 km)

km 16.2 ■ Lao Li (Mae To)(mixed)

Ⓗ

NP entrance

●

• Mae To National Park office

km 13 ┏■ Kong La (S'gaw Karen)

]'[

■ Ban Mai (Pwo Karen)

km 0

H1270

Mae Sariang ◄── H108 ───
centre (50 kms)

H108 ──► Hot (55 kms) &
Chiang Mai (150 kms)

fuel ● Kong
      Loi

TREK 20: KONG LOI – LAO LI – CHANG MOR

MAP 37

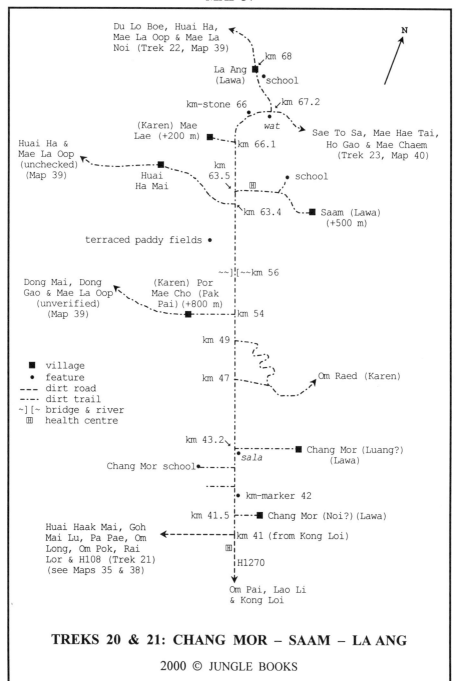

Du Lo Boe, Huai Ha, Mae La Oop & Mae La Noi (Trek 22, Map 39)

N

km 68

La Ang (Lawa)
school

km-stone 66
km 67.2

(Karen) Mae Lae (+200 m)
wat

Huai Ha & Mae La Oop (unchecked) (Map 39)

km 66.1

Sae To Sa, Mae Hae Tai, Ho Gao & Mae Chaem (Trek 23, Map 40)

km 63.5

Huai Ha Mai

school

km 63.4

Saam (Lawa) (+500 m)

terraced paddy fields •

~~]![~~km 56

Dong Mai, Dong Gao & Mae La Oop (unverified) (Map 39)

(Karen) Por Mae Cho (Pak Pai)(+800 m)

km 54

km 49

■ village
• feature
--- dirt road
-·-· dirt trail
~]![~ bridge & river
⊞ health centre

km 47

Om Raed (Karen)

km 43.2

sala

Chang Mor (Luang?) (Lawa)

Chang Mor school•

• km-marker 42

km 41.5

Chang Mor (Noi?)(Lawa)

Huai Haak Mai, Goh Mai Lu, Pa Pae, Om Long, Om Pok, Rai Lor & H108 (Trek 21) (see Maps 35 & 38)

km 41 (from Kong Loi)

⊞

H1270

Om Pai, Lao Li & Kong Loi

TREKS 20 & 21: CHANG MOR – SAAM – LA ANG

2000 © JUNGLE BOOKS

MAP 38

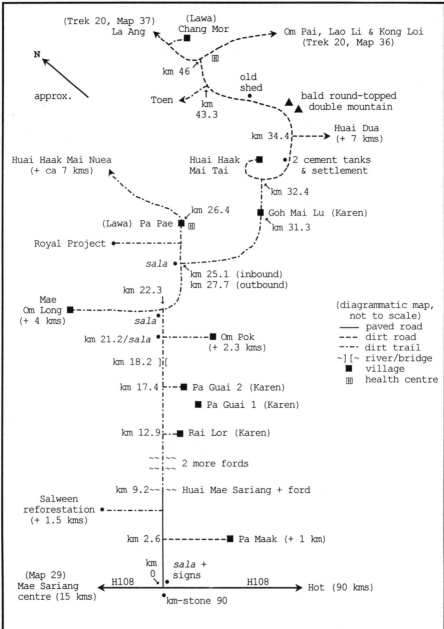

(Trek 20, Map 37) (Lawa)
La Ang Chang Mor ⟶ Om Pai, Lao Li & Kong Loi
(Trek 20, Map 36)

N

approx.

km 46

ℍ

old
shed
•

Toen ⟵ ↑
km
43.3

▲ bald round-topped
▲ double mountain

km 34.4 ----⟶ Huai Dua
(+ 7 kms)

Huai Haak Mai Nuea
(+ ca 7 kms)

Huai Haak
Mai Tai ■
•⟶ 2 cement tanks
& settlement

km 32.4

km 26.4
■ Goh Mai Lu (Karen)
km 31.3

(Lawa) Pa Pae ■ ℍ

Royal Project •-----•

sala •
km 25.1 (inbound)
km 27.7 (outbound)

km 22.3

Mae
Om Long ■
(+ 4 kms)

sala •

km 21.2/sala •----■ Om Pok
(+ 2.3 kms)

km 18.2][

km 17.4 ---■ Pa Guai 2 (Karen)

■ Pa Guai 1 (Karen)

km 12.9 •-■ Rai Lor (Karen)

~~ ~~ 2 more fords
~~ ~~

km 9.2~~ ~~ Huai Mae Sariang + ford

Salween
reforestation •-----
(+ 1.5 kms)

km 2.6 -------■ Pa Maak (+ 1 km)

km
0
sala +
signs

(Map 29)
Mae Sariang ⟵ H108
centre (15 kms)
H108 ⟶ Hot (90 kms)

•km-stone 90

(diagrammatic map,
not to scale)
⟶ paved road
--- dirt road
-·- dirt trail
~][~ river/bridge
■ village
ℍ health centre

TREK 21: H108 – PA PAE – HUAI HAAK MAI – CHANG MOR

2000 © JUNGLE BOOKS

396

MAP 39

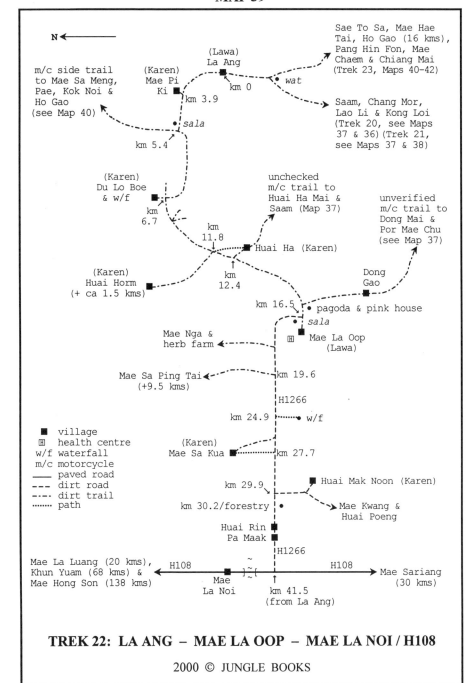

N ◄——————

Sae To Sa, Mae Hae
Tai, Ho Gao (16 kms),
Pang Hin Fon, Mae
Chaem & Chiang Mai
(Trek 23, Maps 40-42)

(Lawa)
La Ang

m/c side trail   (Karen)
to Mae Sa Meng,   Mae Pi   *wat*
Pae, Kok Noi &   Ki
Ho Gao   km 3.9   km 0
(see Map 40)

Saam, Chang Mor,
Lao Li & Kong Loi
(Trek 20, see Maps
37 & 36)(Trek 21,
see Maps 37 & 38)

sala

km 5.4

(Karen)   unchecked
Du Lo Boe   m/c trail to
& w/f   Huai Ha Mai &   unverified
                        Saam (Map 37)   m/c trail to
km   Dong Mai &
6.7   km   Por Mae Chu
             11.8   (see Map 37)
                    Huai Ha (Karen)

(Karen)   km   Dong
Huai Horm   12.4   Gao
(+ ca 1.5 kms)

km 16.5
• pagoda & pink house
sala

Mae Nga &   Ⓗ Mae La Oop
herb farm ◄-·-·-   (Lawa)

Mae Sa Ping Tai◄-·-·   km 19.6
(+9.5 kms)

H1266

km 24.9 ·······• w/f

■ village
Ⓗ health centre   (Karen)
w/f waterfall   Mae Sa Kua ■·········km 27.7
m/c motorcycle
___ paved road
--- dirt road   ■ Huai Mak Noon (Karen)
-··- dirt trail   km 29.9
······· path
                      km 30.2/forestry •   ➤ Mae Kwang &
                                              Huai Poeng
                      Huai Rin
                      Pa Maak

                      H1266

Mae La Luang (20 kms),   H108   ~   H108
Khun Yuam (68 kms) & ◄————— }~{ —————➤ Mae Sariang
Mae Hong Son (138 kms)   Mae   ↑   (30 kms)
                         La Noi km 41.5
                                 (from La Ang)

TREK 22: LA ANG – MAE LA OOP – MAE LA NOI / H108

MAP 40

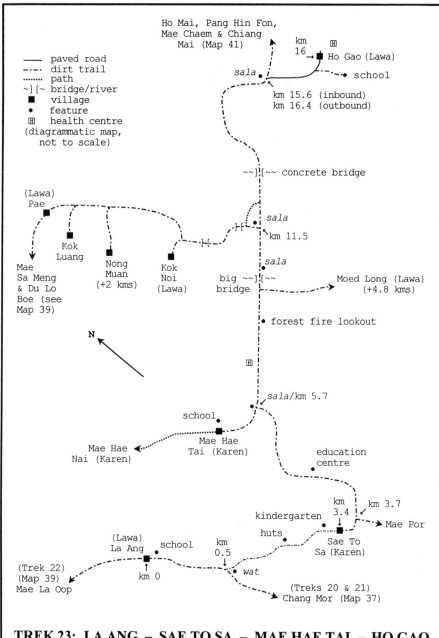

TREK 23: LA ANG – SAE TO SA – MAE HAE TAI – HO GAO

2000 © JUNGLE BOOKS

MAP 41

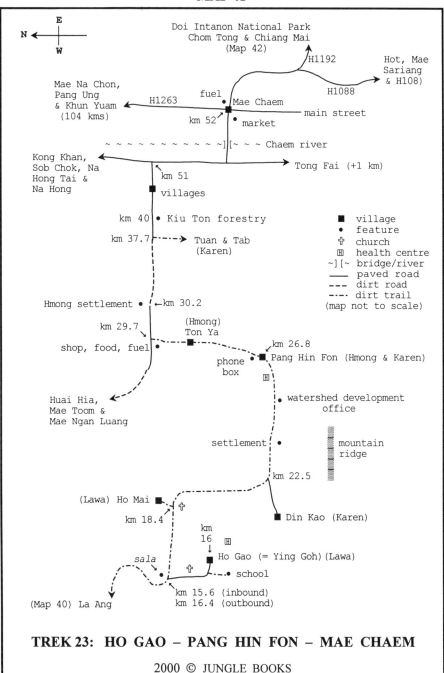

TREK 23: HO GAO – PANG HIN FON – MAE CHAEM

2000 © JUNGLE BOOKS

MAP 42

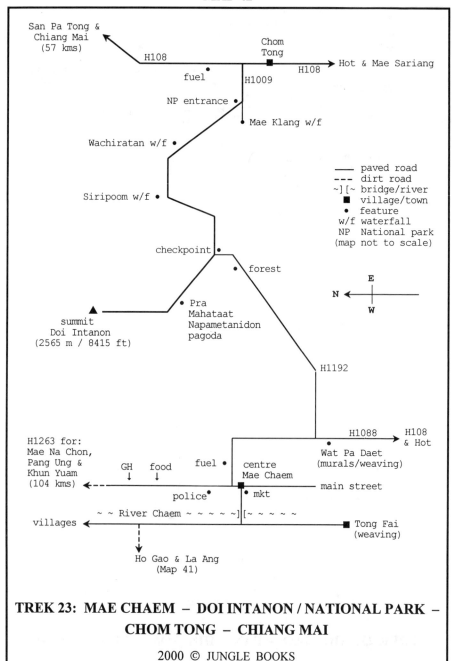

TREK 23: MAE CHAEM – DOI INTANON / NATIONAL PARK – CHOM TONG – CHIANG MAI

2000 © JUNGLE BOOKS

MAP 43

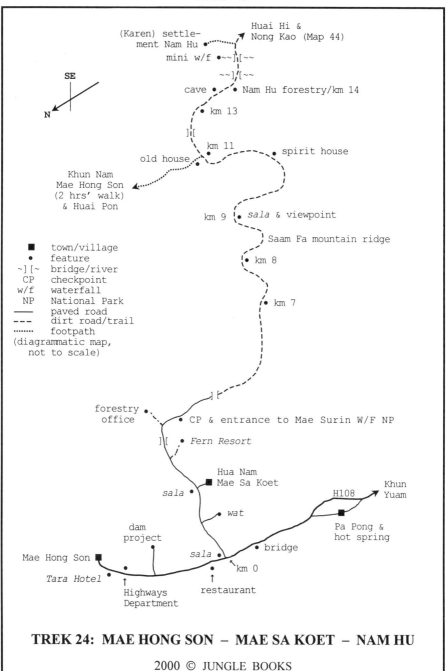

TREK 24: MAE HONG SON – MAE SA KOET – NAM HU

2000 © JUNGLE BOOKS

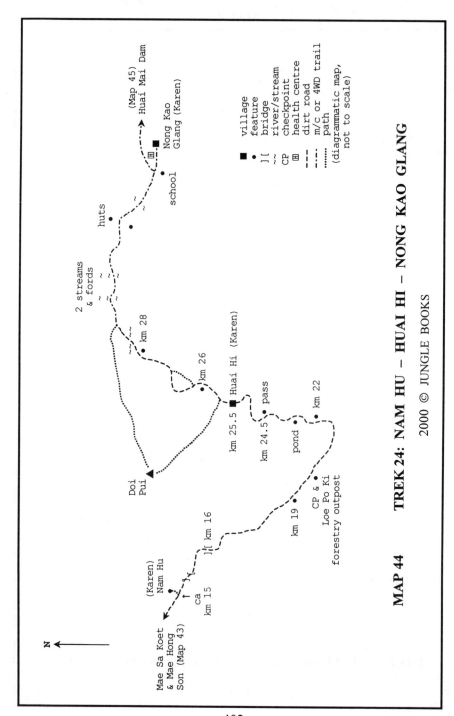

Mae Sa Koet
& Mae Hong
Son (Map 43)

(Karen)
Nam Hu

ca
km 15

km 16

km 19

km 22

CP &
Loe Po Ki
forestry outpost

pond

km 24.5

pass

km 25.5   Huai Hi (Karen)

km 26

km 28

Doi
Pui

2 streams
& fords

huts

school

Nong Kao
Glang (Karen)

(Map 45)
Huai Mai Dam

N

■   village
•   feature
][bridge
~   river/stream
CP checkpoint
⊞   health centre
--- dirt road
-·- m/c or 4WD trail
··· path
(diagrammatic map,
not to scale)

MAP 44   TREK 24: NAM HU – HUAI HI – NONG KAO GLANG

2000 © JUNGLE BOOKS

402

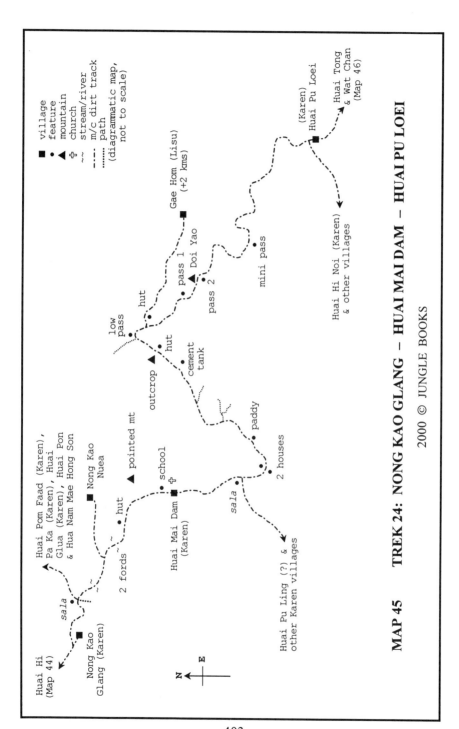

MAP 45   TREK 24: NONG KAO GLANG – HUAI MAI DAM – HUAI PU LOEI

2000 © JUNGLE BOOKS

Legend:
- ■ village
- • feature
- ▲ mountain
- ✚ church
- ~ stream/river
- ─·─ m/c dirt track
- ········ path
- (diagrammatic map, not to scale)

Huai Hi (Map 44)

Nong Kao Glang (Karen)

sala

Huai Pom Faad (Karen), Pa Ka (Karen), Huai Glua (Karen), Huai Pon & Hua Nam Mae Hong Son

2 fords

Nong Kao Nuea

hut

▲ pointed mt

school ✚

Huai Mai Dam (Karen)

sala

2 houses

Huai Pu Ling (?) & other Karen villages

paddy

cement tank

outcrop ▲

hut

low pass

hut

pass 1

▲ Doi Yao

pass 2

mini pass

Gae Hom (Lisu) (+2 kms)

Huai Hi Noi (Karen) & other villages

(Karen) Huai Pu Loei

Huai Tong & Wat Chan (Map 46)

N
E

403

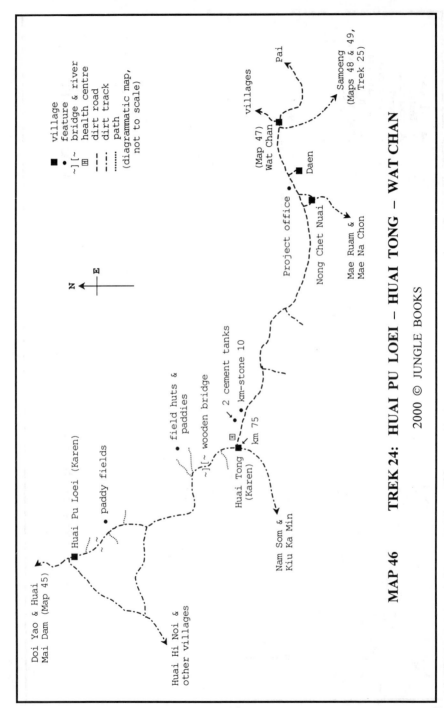

MAP 46   TREK 24: HUAI PU LOEI – HUAI TONG – WAT CHAN

2000 © JUNGLE BOOKS

Legend:
- ■ village
- • feature
- ~][~ bridge & river
- ⊞ health centre
- – · – dirt road
- – · · – dirt track
- ········ path
- (diagrammatic map, not to scale)

Doi Yao & Huai Mai Dam (Map 45)

Huai Pu Loei (Karen)

paddy fields

Huai Hi Noi & other villages

field huts & paddies

~][~ wooden bridge

2 cement tanks

km-stone 10

km 75

⊞ Huai Tong (Karen)

Nam Som & Kiu Ka Min

Project office

Nong Chet Nuai

Mae Ruam & Mae Na Chon

Daen

(Map 47) Wat Chan

villages

Pai

Samoeng (Maps 48 & 49, Trek 25)

404

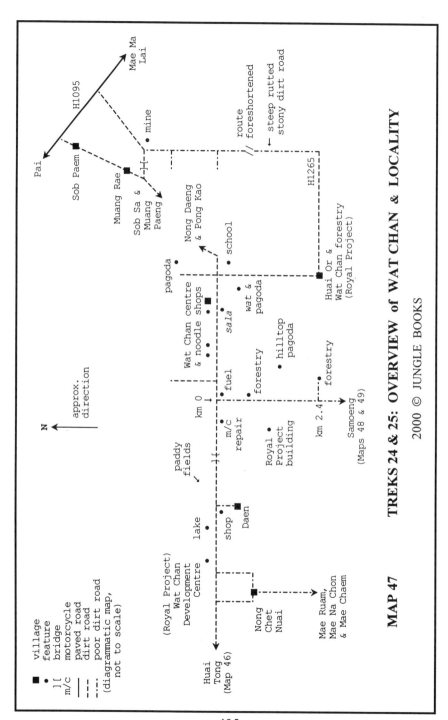

MAP 47 **TREKS 24 & 25: OVERVIEW of WAT CHAN & LOCALITY**

2000 © JUNGLE BOOKS

Legend:
- ■ village
- • feature
-][bridge
- m/c motorcycle
- —— paved road
- – – – dirt road
- ·–·– poor dirt road
- (diagrammatic map, not to scale)

N ←
approx. direction

Pai
H1095
Sob Paem
Muang Rae
Sob Sa & Muang Paeng
• mine
Mae Ma Lai

Nong Daeng & Pong Kao
• school
route foreshortened
← steep rutted stony dirt road
H1265
Huai Or & Wat Chan forestry (Royal Project)

• pagoda
Wat Chan centre & noodle shops ■
sala
wat & pagoda
• hilltop pagoda
forestry
forestry

km 0
fuel
m/c repair
Royal • Project building
km 2.4
Samoeng (Maps 48 & 49)

paddy fields
(Royal Project) Wat Chan Development Centre
lake •
shop •
■ Daen
Nong Chet Nuai ■
Mae Ruam, Mae Na Chon & Mae Chaem

Huai Tong (Map 46)

405

MAP 48

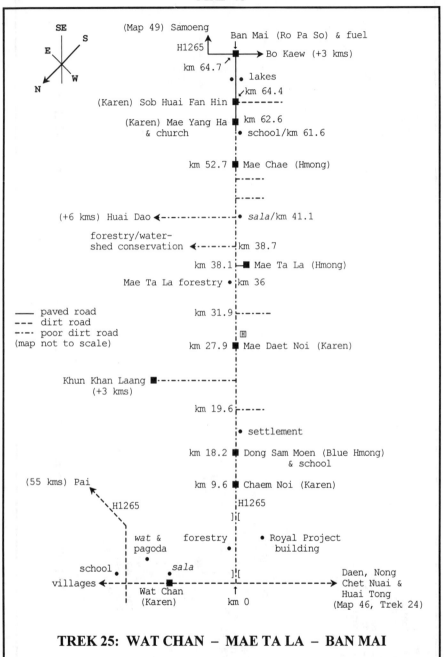

SE
S
E
W
N

(Map 49) Samoeng

Ban Mai (Ro Pa So) & fuel

H1265

Bo Kaew (+3 kms)

km 64.7

lakes

km 64.4

(Karen) Sob Huai Fan Hin

(Karen) Mae Yang Ha   km 62.6
& church   school/km 61.6

km 52.7 Mae Chae (Hmong)

(+6 kms) Huai Dao   sala/km 41.1

forestry/water-
shed conservation   km 38.7

km 38.1 Mae Ta La (Hmong)

Mae Ta La forestry   km 36

paved road   km 31.9
dirt road
poor dirt road
(map not to scale)
                           km 27.9 Mae Daet Noi (Karen)

Khun Khan Laang
(+3 kms)

km 19.6

settlement

km 18.2 Dong Sam Moen (Blue Hmong)
& school

(55 kms) Pai   km 9.6 Chaem Noi (Karen)

H1265   H1265

wat &   forestry   Royal Project
pagoda   building

school   sala
villages   Daen, Nong
Wat Chan   ↑   Chet Nuai &
(Karen)   km 0   Huai Tong
(Map 46, Trek 24)

TREK 25: WAT CHAN – MAE TA LA – BAN MAI

2000 © JUNGLE BOOKS

MAP 49

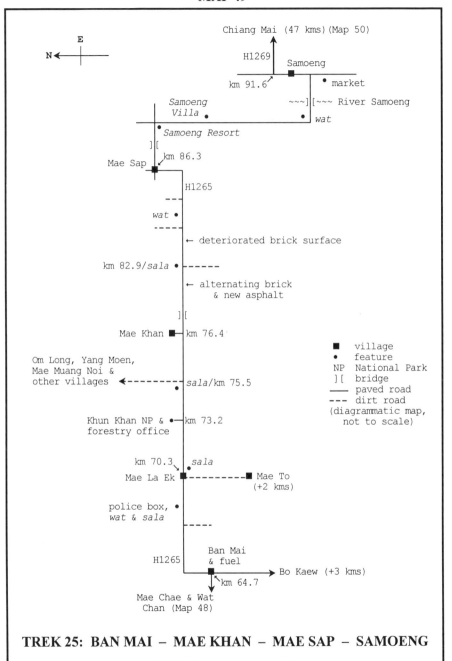

Chiang Mai (47 kms)(Map 50)

H1269   Samoeng

km 91.6   • market

~~~][~~~ River Samoeng

Samoeng
Villa •

• wat

• Samoeng Resort

][

km 86.3

Mae Sap

H1265

---

wat •

← deteriorated brick surface

km 82.9/sala • ------

← alternating brick
   & new asphalt

][

Mae Khan ■ km 76.4

■ village
• feature
NP National Park
][bridge
── paved road
--- dirt road
(diagrammatic map,
not to scale)

Om Long, Yang Moen,
Mae Muang Noi &
other villages ← - - - - - - - sala/km 75.5
                            •

Khun Khan NP & • km 73.2
forestry office

km 70.3   sala
Mae La Ek ■ - - - - - - - - ■ Mae To
                              (+2 kms)

police box, •
wat & sala

H1265

Ban Mai
& fuel
              → Bo Kaew (+3 kms)
■
  km 64.7

Mae Chae & Wat
Chan (Map 48)

TREK 25: BAN MAI – MAE KHAN – MAE SAP – SAMOENG

2000 © JUNGLE BOOKS

MAP 50

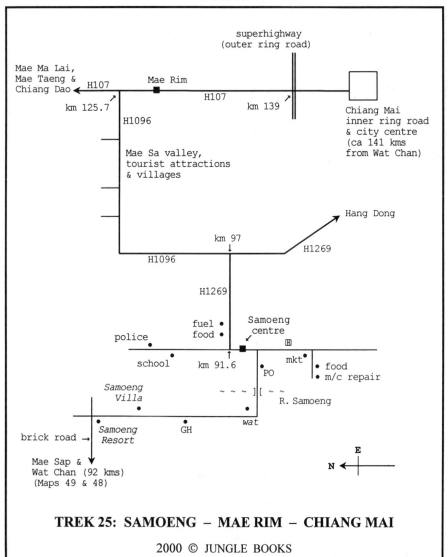

superhighway
(outer ring road)

Mae Ma Lai,
Mae Taeng &
Chiang Dao

H107 Mae Rim

H107

km 125.7 km 139

Chiang Mai
inner ring road
& city centre
(ca 141 kms
from Wat Chan)

H1096

Mae Sa valley,
tourist attractions
& villages

Hang Dong

km 97

H1269

H1096

H1269

fuel
food

Samoeng
centre

police

Ⓗ

school km 91.6

mkt

food
m/c repair

PO

Samoeng
Villa

~ ~ ~][~ ~

R. Samoeng

brick road →

Samoeng
Resort

GH

wat

Mae Sap &
Wat Chan (92 kms)
(Maps 49 & 48)

E

N ←

TREK 25: SAMOENG – MAE RIM – CHIANG MAI

2000 © JUNGLE BOOKS

408

GLOSSARY

This is a glossary of Thai and other non-English words as well as acronyms and abbreviations used in this book.

4WD: four-wheel drive
ampoe (amphoer, ampher, amphur): district, district office
anuraak: forestry protection authority/officials
ban (= muban) (pronounced 'barn'): village
BPP (= Border Patrol Police): paramilitary force operating in the border areas, popularly known in Thai as *dorchodor*
changwat: province
chedi: pagoda or *pratat* or stupa, a monument with a thin pointed spire, containing a relic of the Buddha (allegedly) or the ashes of some prominent person
chiang: city, formerly a *wiang* inhabited by senior royalty
cho fa: the projecting sculpted piece of wood at the top of a gable, often reminiscent of the head and part of the body of a large bird; not to be confused with *galae*
CPT: Communist Party of Thailand
doi: mountain, Mount
dorchodor: Border Patrol Police (BPP)
farang: foreigner, Caucasian, especially European, American or Australian (from 'farangset', which is a Thai attempt at 'français')
galae (galare): an ornamented V-shaped wooden decorative gable-end, mounted like 'horns' on the peak of the roof of a building and being a typical feature of a Lan-Na house
hongnam: typical Thai ablution cubicle combining washing and toilet facilities, the water coming from a big earthenware pot or cement tank to be scooped up with a plastic dipper
Htin (H'tin, 'Htin, T'in): Thai name for the Lua highland people of Nan province
huai: stream
Isaan (Esarn, Isan): large area in NE Thailand, marked by Lao influence
jataka: mythological life story of the Buddha (there are hundreds of such stories)
Job's tear seeds: inedible small white seeds grown locally in northern Thailand, easily strung and used in hill-tribe costume decoration
kamnaan: village 'mayor'
kao soi: tasty dish of noodles served in curry soup, accompanied by a side salad of pickled cabbage and shallots
kateuy: ladyboy
khon muang: local Thai or northern Thai people, local lowlanders, Tai Yuan
king ampoe: sub-district
KMT = Kuomintang: Chinese Nationalist refugees loyal to Chiang Kai-shek, ousted by Mao Tse-tung's communist revolutionaries in 1949 and forced to flee to Taiwan (Formosa) and also south to Burma, Laos and Thailand
kru (yai): (head)teacher
kwan: circle, administrative region (same as *mon ton*)
lai: pattern
lai nam lai: tapestry weave pattern in the form of flowing water or river wavelets used in Tai Lue textiles and associated especially with Nan

409

Lan-Na: area associated with northern Thailand. Once an autonomous Tai kingdom (founded 1296), it was assimilated into Siam in the late 19th century. The kingdom (actually a conglomerate of component semi-autonomous mini-kingdoms or principalities) used to include Chiang Mai, Chiang Rai, Chiang Saen, Lampoon and Lampang, was allied with Payao, and during Lan-Na's 'golden age' (second half of 15th century AD) expanded to incorporate Nan and Prae. At times it spilled out to incorporate territories in modern Laos and Burma. Comparable kingdoms surrounding Lan-Na have been Ayuttaya, Sukotai, Lan Chang, Nan Chao and Sipsong Pan-Na.

Lao: adjectival form of Laos (in preference to 'Laotian', which is derived from French), pertaining to Laos or to a person from Laos, e.g. the Thai-*Lao* border, the *Lao* Army etc.

lao: spirit or 'whisky'

lao kao (= white spirit): schnapps, rice whisky, made from rice and palm sugar

lao-u (lao-oo): pot whisky

longyi (soft 'g'): Burmese wrap-around skirt (not joined into a tube) worn by men and women; like a sarong

Lua: an ancient Mon-Khmer people of Austro-Asiatic stock, called by Thais 'Htin'. In Thailand resident in Nan province near Lao border. Related to Lawa people in north-west Thailand.

mae (short for maenam): river

miang: tree perhaps related to the coca tree, with leaves producing a species of wild tealeaf, chewed by peasants often in small balls rather as sailors chew quids of tobacco; wild tea or the tea-leaf mixture made from these leaves

Mrabri (or Mlabri): nomadic 'Stone Age' forest people living near Nan, called by Thais *pi tong luang* (= spirits of the yellow leaves)

MTA: Mong Tai Army, private army of former warlord and opium baron Khun Sa

muang (meuang): Lao-Thai city state, principality, district, fiefdom; several villages with a *wiang* or *chiang*, bordered by hills and beyond which is another *muang*

Muang Ngoen: area in Laos opposite Huai Khon and between Nan town and Luang Prabang (as the crow flies) which used to belong to Nan, but which was separated off in 1903 by the French in Indo-China and given to Laos. Former home of the Tai Lue of Huai Khon and Lai Tung.

nakrong ying: restaurant singing girl, quasi-prostitute (*nakrong chai*: male singer)

nam: river

nam tok: waterfall

Pali: the ancient sacred language of Theravada Buddhism, understood today mostly only by monks

pamai: forestry

pat thai: meal/snack of rice noodle fried with beansprouts, egg, diced tofu, preserved shredded turnip, dried shrimps, crumbled peanuts etc., and served with raw green side salad

pi tong luang (= spirits of the yellow leaves): Thai name for the rare nomadic 'Stone Age' Mrabri people of Nan province

PLAT: People's Liberation Army of Thailand, military arm of communist CPT

po luang: dialect word for *pu yai*, headman

prasat: monument

pratat (phrathat): grand pagoda or *chedi*

pu yai (baan): (village) headman

sala: open-sided waiting shelter at roadside

samlor (= three wheels): a three-wheeler or tricycle, either pedal-powered (pedicab or trishaw) or motorized (*tuk-tuk*)

sawbwa (*chao fa*): traditional feudal lord or princeling in former Shan States

silor (= four wheels): four-wheeled, open-sided, public-transport pick-up; share-taxi

Sipsong Pan-Na (= twelve thousand paddy fields): former Tai kingdom and stronghold of the Tai Lue at the source of the Mae Khong river in southern China, Yunnan province

sob (sop): (= meet, come upon) confluence (in context of rivers)

soi: side road, alleyway

songkraan: religious festival to mark the Thai new year, held in the hot season and now associated with a lot of gratuitous water-throwing

songtaew (= two benches): a small popular local public means of transport consisting of a pick-up truck with two rows of seats in the back, share-taxi; also called *silor*

SUA: Shan United Army, former name of warlord Khun Sa's MTA

tahaan praan: crack Thai military force, the rangers who wear the black uniform

tai/Tai: pertaining to/someone belonging to one of the many sub-groups of the ethnic Tai family of peoples. Today the Tai linguistic group can be found spread throughout the South-East Asian mainland from as far west as Assam in India to as far south as the Malay peninsula. The group is marked by a strong overall cultural identity, shown e.g. in its house-building style or in its textiles, and includes among other sub-groups: the Tai Siam, Tai Yuan, Tai Yai, Tai Lao, Tai Lue, Tai Daeng, Tai Dam, Tai Nuea, Tai Puan, Tai Kao, Tai Chuang, Tai Toh, Tai Nung, Tai Muai, Tai Muong and Pu Tai.

Tai Lue: ethnic sub-group living primarily in Sipsong Pan-Na, but also found along China's Red River, in Vietnam, Laos and Thailand

Tai Siam: Siamese Tai or Tai of central Thailand, sometimes also referred to as 'Tai Noi' or 'little Tai' in contrast to the Tai Yai (Shan) or 'big Tai'

Tai Yai (= big Tai): Shan, also known as Tai Ngieo

Tai Yuan: ethnic Tai sub-group and principal Tai group living in Lan-Na or northern Thailand, *khon muang*

tam (tham): cave

tambon: sub-division below *ampoe*, precinct

tanon (thanon): road, street

Thai: citizen of modern Thailand

tom yam: hot and spicy Thai soup with mushrooms, lemongrass and variously prawns or meat

tuk-tuk: motorized *samlor* or tricycle, half-car half-motorcycle, so called because of the sound of its engine

UWSA: United Wa State Army, 'Red Wa'

wai: traditional Buddhist greeting, palms of hands pressed together below the chin

wat: temple-monastery

wat pratat: temple-monastery with a grand pagoda or *chedi*

wiang (wieng): 'town' or important village once fortified with ramparts and a moat

wiharn (viharn, wihaan): the building in a temple complex where the Buddha figures are housed, used as main meeting hall

yaam (tung yam): shoulder bag, used by many people in northern Thailand, especially the hill tribes and Tai groups

Yellow Leaves: Mrabri people or *pi tong luang*

USEFUL VOCABULARY & PHRASES

See also glossary above. For politeness, add to the end of every question *kap* (if you are a male) or *ka* (if you are a female).

Organizing a trek:
walk *doen (dern)* เดิน
trek *bai doen* ไปเดิน
path *tang* ทาง
footpath *tang doen* ทางเดิน
guide *khon nam tang* คนนำทาง
backpack *pae* เป้
carry backpack *bag pae* แบกเป้
heavy (backpack) *nak* หนัก
mountain *doi* ดอย
climb (mountain) *khun doi* ขึ้นดอย
two/three/four people *song/saam/si khon* สอง/สาม/สี่คน
alone/one person *khon diao* คนเดียว
today *wan ni* วันนี้
tomorrow *prung (proong) ni* พรุ่งนี้
day after tomorrow *ma reun ni* มะรืนนี้
yesterday *muea wan* เมื่อวาน
three days *saam waan* สามวัน
two nights *song kuen* สองคืน
Is (Nit) here/at home? *(Nit) yuu mai?* (......) อยู่ไหม?
yuu Yes, (he) is here/at home อยู่
mai yuu No, (he) isn't here/at home; doesn't live here ไม่อยู่
I/we want to trek to (Huai Dua) *yaak doen bai (Huai Dua)* อยากเดินไป (.........)
Can you find a guide for us? Is it possible to hire a guide here? *ha khon nam tang hai, dai mai?* หาคนนำทางให้ได้ไหม?
I give 200 baht a day per guide *hai khon nam tang wan la song roi baht dor khon* ให้คนนำทางวันละสองร้อยบาทต่อคน
return/come back *glap ma, (pik* = northern dialect) กลับมา (ปิ๊ก)
maybe, perhaps *bang ti* บางที
Can we leave our motorbike(s)/jeep here? *fak lot wai ti ni, dai mai?* ฝากรถไว้ที่นี่ได้ไหม?
Can I/we have a lift with you in your car/truck? *kor bai duai khon, dai mai?* ขอไปด้วยคนได้ไหม?

During a trek:
ask, go and ask *bai tam* ไปถาม
like to have a rest *pak nuai* พักเหนื่อย
stop for ten minutes *yoot pak sip nahti* หยุดพักสิบนาที
smoke cigarette *soob bulli (booli)* สูบบุหรี่
Come here *ma ni* มานี่
Come and help me/ I need some help *chuai noi, dai mai?* ช่วยหน่อยได้ไหม?

412

I'm/we're lost *lorng tang* หลงทาง
Which is the way to (Ton Ngiu)? *tang nai bai (Ton Ngiu)?* ทางไหนไป (........) ?
How far to (Sob Khun)? *bai (Son Khun) ki kilo?* ไป (........) กี่กิโล?
How much longer now to (Khang Ho)? *ik naan mai ja toeng (Khang Ho)?*
อีกนานไหมจะถึง (........)?

Arriving at a village:
school *long-lien* โรงเรียน
(head)teacher *kru (yai)* ครู (ใหญ่)
headman *pu yai baan* ผู้ใหญ่บ้าน
shop *raan kai kong* ร้านขายของ
I'm/we're hungry *hiu kao* หิวข้าว
I'm/we're thirsty *hiu nam* หิวน้ำ
boil water *tom nam* ต้มน้ำ
boiled water *nam tom* น้ำต้ม
blanket(s) *pahom* ผ้าห่ม
mattress *ti-norn* ที่นอน
firewood *foen (fuen)* ฟืน
candle *tian kai* เทียนไข
oil lamp *takiang* ตะเกียง
electricity *fai fa* ไฟฟ้า

How much? How much does it cost? *taorai?* เท่าไหร่?
Where is the school/teacher? *long-lien/kru yuu ti nai?* โรงเรียน / ครูอยู่ที่ไหน?
Where is the headman's house? *baan pu yai yuu ti nai?* บ้านผู้ใหญ่อยู่ที่ไหน?
Can you get me/us some water? *ao nam hai noi?* เอาน้ำให้หน่อย?
Can I/we boil some water? *kor tom nam, dai mai?* ขอต้มน้ำได้ไหม?
Can I/we stay/sleep here? *pak ti ni, dai mai?* พักที่นี่ได้ไหม?
dai Yes, you can; ได้   *mai dai* No, you can't ไม่ได้
Can we stay in the school (tonight)? *kor pak ti long-lien, dai mai (koen ni)?*
ขอพักที่โรงเรียนได้ไหม (คืนนี้)
Can I put my tent up here? *gang ten(t) dong ni, dai mai?* กางเต็นท์ตรงนี้ได้ไหม?
Where is the toilet/washroom? *hongnaam yuu nai?* ห้องน้ำอยู่ไหน?
Where can I/we wash? *abnahm ti nai?* อาบน้ำที่ไหน?
Do you have some blankets? *mi pahom mai?* มีผ้าห่มไหม?
I/we have sleeping bags *mi tung norn* มีถุงนอน
Is there a shop in the village? *mi raan kai kong nai mubaan mai?*
มีร้านขายของในหมู่บ้านไหม?
Going to buy some sweet snacks *bai ser kanom* ไปซื้อขนม
Like to have some firewood *ao fuen (foen) ma gor fai* เอาฟืนมาก่อไฟ
Like to cook Ma-maa (instant noodles) *kor tom Ma-maa, dai mai?*
ขอต้มมาม่าได้ไหม?
Like to have some rice *kor kao noi, dai mai?* ขอข้าวหน่อยได้ไหม?
find, get hold of *bai ao/bai ha* ไปเอา/ไปหา
I/we need... *yaak dai...* อยากได้......
I'm/we're travelling around *maa tiao (bai aeao = north. dialect)* มาเที่ยว (ไปแอ่ว)

413

Other/general:
vehicle *lot* รถ
motorcycle *lot motosai* รถมอเตอร์ไซด์
petrol (super) *nam man (super [soo-per])* น้ำมัน (ซุปเปอร์)
fill the tank up *taem tang* เต็มถัง
camera *gong tai ruup* กล้องถ่ายรูป
look into the camera *du gong* ดูกล้อง
tobacco *yasoob* ยาสูบ
book *nang soe* หนังสือ
lao kao schnapps, home-brewed whisky เหล้าขาว
strong (whisky) *raeng* แรง
field *tung* ทุ่ง
border *chai daen* ชายแดน
go to sleep now *bai norn* ไปนอน
sit *nang* นั่ง
eat *kin* กิน
buy *ser (soe)* ซื้อ
New Year *pi mai* ปีใหม่
wife *mia* เมีย
husband *sami (pua* = northern dialect) สามี (ผัว)
girlfriend/boyfriend *faen* แฟน
married *taengnaan laeo* แต่งงานแล้ว
single/unmarried *mai mi faen* ไม่มีแฟน
divorced *yaa* หย่า
Where do you live/come from? *yuu nai?* อยู่ไหน?

ordinary rice *kao suai (kao chao* = northern dialect) ข้าวสวย (ข้าวเจ้า)
sticky rice *kao nio* ข้าวเหนียว
(chicken) fried rice *kao paat (gai)* ข้าวผัด (ไก่)
(fried) noodles *(paat) guai tiao/kwitiaow* (ผัด) ก๋วยเตี๋ยว
noodle soup *guai tiao (kwitiaow) nam* ก๋วยเตี๋ยวน้ำ
snacks, cake, sweet things *kanom* ขนม
bread *kanom pang* ขนมปัง
stir-fried chicken and ginger *paat king gai* ผัดขิงไก่
sweet and sour prawns *prio-waan goong* เปรี้ยวหวานกุ้ง
greens, meat and noodles in 'gravy' *raat naa* ราดหน้า

dai Yes, you/I/we can, it is possible ได้
mai dai Can't, not possible ไม่ได้
mi yes, I/we have มี
mai mi Don't have ไม่มี
ru Yes, I/we know รู้
mai ru Don't know ไม่รู้

414

AROUND LAN-NA

A GUIDE TO THAILAND'S NORTHERN BORDER REGION FROM CHIANG MAI TO NAN

Around Lan-Na is a narrative and cultural guide describing an arc around Thailand's north-western and north-eastern borders with Burma and Laos. Ten years in the making, the book masterfully presents the same blend of adventure travel, anecdote, personally researched route detail, and cultural-historical information that the author deployed in his acclaimed *Three Pagodas – A Journey down the Thai-Burmese Border*. Aimed at travellers graduating from the conventional guidebooks, *Around Lan-Na* maps out an exciting off-the-beaten-track border journey by public transport, by motorcycle and on foot from Chiang Mai to Nan, taking in the KMT Chinese outposts of Nong Ook and Mae Salong, the recently vacated opium warlord territories of Hin Taek and Doi Larng, Mae Sai and the "Golden Triangle", the ancient Mekong riverfront towns of Chiang Saen and Chiang Khong, the Tai Lue weaving village of Huai Khon, and a swathe of remote mountainous jungle extending down the Lao border as far as Bo Bia.

The book includes details of treks in unfrequented areas that travellers can make themselves: climbing poppy-covered Doi Chiang Dao (Thailand's third-highest mountain), in Doi Pu Kha National Park, and east of Nan town in the jungles of the Lao frontier. It contains practical tips on how to get by in difficult situations in isolated places. The second half of the book provides the first thoroughgoing exploration of the Kingdom's least-known province and best-kept secret: Nan.

In this guide the culturally-minded reader can learn about the exquisite weaving of the Tai Lue people, Nan's temple murals, and the salt wells of Bo Glua. The armchair traveller can join a trailblazing jungle trek through the "Empty Quarter" guided by ex-communist guerrillas. And the student of northern Thailand can read about the history of Lan-Na, of Chiang Mai, of Chiang Saen, of the KMT and of the CPT insurgency. There are separate accounts of several minority peoples, including the KMT, Wa, Akha, Hmong, Yao, Khmu, Tai Lue, Palaung, the entropic Lua (Htin) and the vanishing "Stone Age" Mrabri ("Spirits of the Yellow Leaves"). Four hundred pages of text are complemented by 36 pages of arresting photographs and 32 maps. Together with *Three Pagodas*, *Around Lan-Na* provides the independent traveller with the most comprehensive account available of Thailand's entire northern border region from the Three Pagodas Pass to Nan.

JUNGLE BOOKS

ISBN 0-9527383-1-7

UK price £14.95

BY THE SAME AUTHOR

THREE PAGODAS

A JOURNEY DOWN THE THAI-BURMESE BORDER

Based on the travels of the author and his Thai wife in northern Thailand over 6 years, *Three Pagodas* is an account of a remarkable 700-km journey through the mountainous jungle of the Thai-Burmese border from Chiang Dao to the Three Pagodas Pass. Starting where the guidebooks leave off, the book describes what it is like to make one's way through this remote troubled terrain, inhabited by insurgent guerrilla groups, warlords, heroin traffickers, migrant hilltribes, and rare minority peoples.

With an eye for the telling minutiae of travel and the poetry of the moment, the author provides a snapshot of the way of life of these peoples, recording the impact on them of the far-reaching changes sweeping the Kingdom in the 1990s. Here the reader rubs shoulders with Chinese KMT refugees, bizarre "long-neck" women, the vanishing Lawa tribe, a jungle demigod, and the last Wa king, or visits mysterious "Spirit Well", Karen rebel HQ in Burma, and "Death Highway"....

Three Pagodas culminates in a 2-week trailblazing adventure through 200 kms of unmapped jungle from Um Pang to the celebrated Three Pagodas. Written in an evocative anecdotal style and enlivened by the - often absurd - humour of the situation, the text is backed up by personally researched maps, background cultural and historical detail, and stunning photos. For armchair traveller and traveller on the ground alike, this unique book is likely to remain the definitive account of a complex and fascinating region for years to come.

JUNGLE BOOKS

"BY TRAVELLERS FOR TRAVELLERS"

ISBN 0-9527383-0-9   UK price £12.95

416